CAN YOU FEEL
THE SILENCE?

CAN YOU FEEL
THE SILENCE?

VAN MORRISON
A NEW BIOGRAPHY

CLINTON HEYLIN

CHICAGO
REVIEW
PRESS

An A Cappella Book

PICTURE CREDITS
The publisher is grateful for permission to use the following photographs:

Section headers
1: Courtesy of Simon Gee
2: © Tony Gale/Pictorial Press
3: © Popsie Randolph/Village Music Archives
4: Courtesy of Northern Sky Archives
5: © Sunshine/Hanekroot/Retna
6, 7: © Colin Moore

Photo Insert
pp. 1, 2 (top): © Three Js
p. 2 (bottom): Courtesy of Northern Sky Archives
pp. 3 (both), 4 (top): © Popsie Randolph/Village Music Archives
p. 4 (bottom): Courtesy of Lewis Merenstein
p. 5: Courtesy of Simon Gee
pp. 6 (both), 7, 8 (bottom): © Colin Moore
p. 8 (top): © B. P. Fallon

Every effort has been made to conctact copyright holders.
Any errors or omissions will be amended in subsequent editions.

Cover design: Rattray Design
Cover photograph: © Roger Ressmeyer/CORBIS

To Jackie Leven,
who continues to steal the highlights

Contents

Preface: The Art of New Biography

The beauty of your thoughts does not reflect the condition of your soul.

—*Arthur Guirdham*

I have never been able to understand the contention that a poet's life is irrelevant to his work.

—*Robert Graves*

The fact that I may be successful at what I do does not mean that I accept that anyone can come along and publish details of my private life, for other people to read, purely for their own personal enjoyment.

—*Van Morrison, 1993*

I never, ever said that I was a nice guy.

—*Van Morrison, 1994*

It's not like I wasn't warned. To steer clear or to stir it up, that is always the biographer's conundrum. But researching and writing a biography of George Ivan Morrison cannot help but be an over-the-shoulder experience. Barely had I enlisted a research assistant to start making calls, when a solicitor was calling her up, professing to represent Mr Morrison and uttering the immortal phrase 'This is not a threatening phone call, but . . .'

No ifs, no buts, here is a man who has fired off more than enough verbal volleys for his feelings to be known. So thanks for the information, but I already gave. Even if Morrison believes he holds the copyright in his own life, the question of whether his wishes should be respected remains. That said, the aura of intimidation Morrison has built around himself has dissuaded a number of potential biographers, suggesting that, on a superficial level at least, the tactic has served its purpose.

And though I had few illusions taking on my task, I can honestly say I never expected quite the level of active interest in my progress Morrison and/or his office displayed. As a result, a number of people who had actually agreed to be interviewed for the book cancelled at the last minute, or simply invited me up to Woodstock and then refused to answer my calls. Of course, it was easy to tell who had been sideswiped, simply because they would begin to recite the party line, 'It would be disrespectful to the artist . . .', 'After due consideration . . .' etc., etc., etc. Whether their non-cooperation has impacted greatly on the book, or on my own perspective, I leave the reader to decide, but I sincerely hope that this volume does not come across as the petulant riposte of a spurned writer (as, sorry to say, the one previous biography of the man does).

The one thing I can guarantee is that Van Morrison will not like the results. Indeed, if I have done my job properly, he will blow a major fuse. But then, what does he seriously expect? As a self-confessed curmudgeon and part-time misanthrope, I could hardly in all good conscience rail at the man for displaying the same traits, but the line between 'Nice Van' and 'Nasty Van' seems to be absolute – not so much a partition as a crossing-over into another dimension, or perhaps a descending beneath the false fog he usually exudes to hide a realer self from the world.

The nineteenth-century French philosopher Charles Fourier once wrote that man has four faces: the one he shows to the world; the one he shows to his friends; the one he shows to those he truly holds dear; and the real one. At certain points, I wondered if Morrison ever showed that fourth and final face in his art, where it should surely be discernible – though the faces he has shown the world certainly give the man good grounds for fearing anyone who seriously documents his progress, or regress, through that world. His has been a voyage of discovery that he has illuminated with breathtaking insight and banal inexactitude, a sometimes searing rage or an apparently transcendental charm, but at no point is there any sense that he has found peace:

Keith Altham: I think he's been fairly consistently difficult. The most disturbing thing about Van is that he's disturbed, and it's unsettling to deal with someone like that. I think he's a man who's gonna be searching all his life for something that he'll never find, [as] he hops from one spiritual idea to another with alarming dexterity. But it [sure] makes for interesting listening.

Unfortunately for Morrison, the net result of this 'consistently difficult' attitude has been a public image that distils down to 'a difficult man with something to hide'. That he can at times be one of the most awkward men on earth, not one of the hundred or so souls I contacted sought to dispute. As Harvey Goldsmith told me, 'When he's on a bad day he's just beyond awful, that's how he is.' And yet, too many close friends spoke of the man's gentleness, his deep reservoir of humanity and (most surprisingly) his outrageous sense of humour for these aspects to be mere glamour.

So wherein doth the real Van Morrison lie, and – more pertinently – why does he hide his finer side from the world? Rest assured, dear reader, the contradictions do not diminish the more one digs in (which will doubtless lead some reviewer crassly to complain that I, a professional biographer, sometimes deal in *equivocations*). These contradictions compound into a greater complexity than perhaps the latter-day work itself suggests – as if what he is ultimately hiding *from* remains too painful for such a thin-skinned soul to confront, and thus be able to move onward and upward. For feel things he clearly does:

Jonn Savannah: He doesn't have a good social interaction with people. I don't think he ever has had. And it could be because of this thin-skinned nature, that he sensates everything and it all affects him, it all hits him hard, that he's developed a way of dealing with the world that comes across as incredibly aggressive and blustering and boorish. Most of those situations must be a cover-up . . . He *must* be a deep thinker – [or] he couldn't do what he does; he couldn't get in those areas – but [once] you've got that flap open to allow creativity out, then everything's gonna come in that same port.

So here stands George Ivan Morrison, a singularly private man who has, of his own free will and with a great deal of tenacity and determination, chosen to work in the most public of arenas, as a singer-songwriter and performing artist (or to put it another way, courtesy of *Rolling Stone*'s Jim Miller, 'His vision is hermetic, his energy implosive; yet his vocation is public'). As a singer-songwriter, he has penned lyrics that have been analysed, advertised, categorized; as a performing artist he has been exposed to the demands of a paying public and a prying media. And still he resents these choices, and the life they have brought:

Clive Culbertson: We [were] talk[ing] about what we were doing and why we were doing it . . . and I said, 'You gotta be happy. You've got everything.' He said, 'Let me put it like this. When we got our break with Them [*sic*], I bought a house, a car and a studio. Then I went to America and I got a big record deal and I bought a bigger car, and a bigger house and a bigger studio, and then [*Moondance*] came out and it went [gold], and I got a lot of money and I bought a bigger house and a bigger car and a bigger studio. You know something, in twenty years I've only ever owned a house, a car and a studio.' He really didn't see it as a step upwards. So I said, 'Van, if it's not outside, then you're gonna have to start looking inside.'

Morrison has had more opportunities than other contemporaries to opt out of the cauldron of public expectation – his fame being far more rarefied than that of the Dylans, Lennons and Jaggers of this world – but entirely surrendering to anonymity, again, is not part of the man's make-up. Though he has often considered the prospect of giving up his hard-won position near the top of the contemporary songwriters' tree, only once – in 1975 – did that decision harden into a resolve, one that lasted almost two years, after which he returned, a changed man in a changed world.

The struggle to find a place for himself in an unfamiliar world had already resulted in a series of highly acclaimed albums that have achieved that musty epithet, 'a classic'. Equally inevitably, the albums that came after the man's re-immersion in the popular stream have struggled to replicate the impact of *Moondance*, *Saint Dominic's Preview* or *Veedon Fleece*, let alone that ever-renewed jewel *Astral Weeks*.

Since his return the critics have sometimes been less than kind, and the public not always engaged – at least not until that remarkable return to commerciality at the end of the eighties. Ironically, the years preceding 1988's *Irish Heartbeat* and 1989's *Avalon Sunset* proved to be in many ways as creative as the years leading up to *Moondance*. The albums *Into the Music*, *Beautiful Vision*, *No Guru, No Method, No Teacher* and *Poetic Champions* each contain work as fine as anything sandwiched between the twin beacons of *Astral Weeks* and *Veedon Fleece*, while the 1980 album *Common One* contains what may well be, all things considered, Morrison's single greatest achievement, 'Summertime in England'.

But even when Morrison has delivered something as wildly ambitious as 'Summertime in England', as consistently inventive as *No Guru, No Method, No Teacher,* or as engagingly commercial as *Avalon Sunset,* past achievements have diminished them before the edifice of a hardening critical perspective. The man's response, veering between some kind of caricature curmudgeon offstage and reborn troubadour on, has failed to give him relief from the ill glare of public curiosity. Indeed, what has been viewed as an increasing eccentricity, as well as his choice of paramour, has in recent years excited a mini-frenzy in the tabloids.

Inevitably, his attempts to suppress information, to dissuade chroniclers of his life and work, and to ridicule the interview process itself have, if anything, merely heightened a general curiosity about what makes this man tick, even among those for whom any interest in his actual art palled some time back. Catch-22. What makes it particularly difficult to subscribe to the Morrison line of argument is that his own attempts at depicting his personal history have been laced with so many evasions, inaccuracies, distortions and examples of selective memory that little he says about his past can be taken at face value (plentiful examples lie within these pages).

If Morrison can't resist applying – as we all do – his own refracted vision, he simultaneously wishes to deny anyone else a point of view. In that lamentable *Back on Top* cut, 'New Biography', he asked, 'Where did they get the info from/Same as before, some so-called friends/Who claim to have known me then' – as if this were some kind of disreputable approach (as opposed to those who cut and paste received wisdom about, say, *Astral Weeks* and recycle it as a *Mojo* article). Apparently this approach fails because they are unable to feel the pain. In fact, it is precisely because these other eyewitnesses don't see events through the blur of pain that seems permanently to surround Morrison that they can recall them with a certain clarity when, by his own admission, 'I can't even remember last week'.

'New Biography' was actually prompted by something as historically valid as a series of articles in Morrison fanzine *Wavelength* about the band Them, based around a series of original interviews conducted by Them authority Trevor Hodgett (Morrison actually said the song was about 'this *Wavelength* fanzine' at a concert in Torquay in 1999). As I was reminded every time I interviewed another member of Them's many incarnations; or the Three Js, who discovered Them; or Peter Lloyd, his brother Martin and Stuart Cromie, who recorded their first demo;

Morrison's memory of events from that time is usually the least reliable and unquestionably the most self-aggrandizing. Given that he alone made something of himself subsequently on a commercial level, this might strike the reader as, well, rather ungracious.

When Steve Turner published an extended essay on the man in a 1993 Bloomsbury coffee-table book, *Too Late to Stop Now*, he actually managed to interview double the number of people Johnny Rogan had previously interviewed for his 'fully-fledged' biography of Morrison ten years earlier. He also maintained a thoroughly respectful tone throughout, having drawn on his own personal experiences with the man culled from their arm's-length friendship in the mid-eighties. Rather than simply accept the book in the spirit intended – and as Turner states at the outset, he was 'not attempting . . . the full-scale biography that Van now deserves' – or even simply ignore it, Morrison ranted about the tome at length at a gig at the King's Hotel, Newport, and wrote a long letter to the publisher listing forty so-called inaccuracies that the book made or perpetuated.

The list said a lot more about Morrison than it did about Turner. In many cases his protests were thinly-veiled attempts to rewrite history The Morrison Way. So when Morrison said that his father wasn't unsociable; that his mother didn't indulge in doorstep evangelism; that he didn't get kicked down the stairs at the Solomon Agency in 1965; that his daughter's name was not Shana; that he stopped writing songs in 1973 because his ex-wife would get half of the income; he seemed to be attempting to alter the past by sheer force of will. Needless to say, on all of these points Turner was the more accurate (save that it was Tommy Scott, not Phil Solomon, who flung him down the stairs), and Morrison's rebuffs served only to highlight a faint grasp on his own history.

Morrison has always threatened to put the record straight. He just never has – and it is doubtful if he could. He has burnt too many bridges, and when interviewed displays too foggy a notion of his own past. And yet this legendary Morrison autobiography, first mentioned in 1974, cropped up again in 1979, 1983, 1990 and the mid-nineties, culminating in an attempt by a literary agent to excite interest at the 1997 Frankfurt Book Fair on the basis of a two-page outline. The interest generated brought Morrison no closer to taking on the task. But then, as he admitted in 1990, 'I'm sort of grappling with a book. It's too early to say whether it's on the way or not. I'm just grappling with remembering.' One suspects that the grappling continued a good while longer. To judge by excerpts from his own 'notebooks' included in the 1974 press kit *Reliable Sources*, Morrison may well have intended to tell his entire life in a single chapter:

The Maritime Hotel was very alive on Friday nights when Them played. A customer at the Bitter End, a girl from Belfast, asked when I'd play there again, if ever. I said I did not know. Charlie Brown was on guitar with us then. I often think of Charlie smiling, playing, funky bitch player . . . With Danny Armstrong on bass . . . The Bloomsbury Café or restaurant was right across the street from the Aaland Hotel. We used to go there for sandwiches when we had the bread, which wasn't very often . . . Boston. Come in Peter Wolf. Roger over and out. Ya gotta look back to see where you're going. That's what Father Francis said.

Hemingway it ain't. Sentence one relates to spring 1964, then it's 1967, then back to the autumn of 1964 at the Aaland. Oh, and then 1968 – Boston. I now know what he's talking about, but to whom is the above meant to be directed? It seems that Morrison the autobiographer would seek to communicate with his readers on the same level as his songs – evoking disparate images in the hope that they might coalesce. Except that they rarely do on the page. There are exceptions but, as with almost every contemporary singer-songwriter, they are few. And still he reserves for himself the right to interpret a very public life and some densely autobiographical songs. As he put it in an early song, 'nobody [else] really knows'.

Van Morrison: When it's time for me to do that, I'll do it myself. I'll sit down and I'll write a book and I'll backtrack and I'll go through everything. I'll say, this song was about *this*. But it'll belong to me and I'll have control of it. If I do that, it won't be somebody else's opinion or theory about what I'm about. [1979]

This element of control remains central to Morrison's psychology and his work. In part, this may be a perfectly natural response to the fact that he did not have control of his work in the sixties – and would never have produced an album like *Astral Weeks* if he had. But it goes a lot deeper. He constantly expresses annoyance at what he views as others' exploitation of 'his' work, even though by his own admission it comes only through him, not from him.

But then within the Morrison mindscape, the songs can somehow be detached from him and his experiences, and yet remain entirely his, their fate to be decided by the choices he may make. He has said that if he had his own way, he would burn the Berns tapes. Those tapes include 'Brown Eyed Girl', the song – like it or not – for which he will be most remembered. Likewise, no matter how much he might portray 'Gloria' as the work of an immature artist, it has stood the test of time and 'New Biography' will not. For Morrison, the criticisms of others – perhaps better educated, more widely read, more musically diverse – are rendered invalid because they are divorced from the white light of creation. But then posterity has always shown a blithe disregard for the legal rights and preferences of the artist. As his ex-wife Janet Planet duly notes, 'It's always been a prickly passage, because his music is for the world – it's out there, all over the airwaves.'

In all of this, Morrison is fighting a losing battle. When he finally stops shuffling his coils, few will remember him for *Days Like This* or *Too Long in Exile*, though one hopes that a long-overdue recognition for the likes of *Veedon Fleece*, 'Summertime in England' and *No Guru, No Method, No Teacher* is just around the corner. All save the last paragraph of his obituary is already written and in those newspaper files. It is time the real story was told. May it send you back into the music.

Clinton Heylin, November 2001

AGE ONE

When the Child Was A Child

1

1945–60: On Hyndford Street

I think [the Irish] are curiously self-made creatures, carrying our personal worlds around with us like snails and their shells, and at the same time adapting to wherever we are . . . cagey, recalcitrant, on the run, bristling with reservations and arrogances.

—*Elizabeth Bowen*

It's got nothing to do with the English scene . . . it doesn't have much to do with the Irish scene either. It's just Belfast. It's got its own identity, it's got its own people . . . it's just a different race, a different breed of people.

—*Van Morrison, 1970*

I come from a working-class background . . . If you're like me, there's nothing to battle against . . . Just be yourself. It's not going to change and you're not going to fit into it. You can't fit into it, stalemate, just relax and be yourself. That's all you can do, just be yourself. Get off that cross!

—*Van Morrison, 1993*

It was on Hyndford Street, in East Belfast, in a small terraced house that had belonged to his mother's family since she was nine, that George Ivan Morrison was brought into the world – to quote a phrase – shortly after midnight on 31 August 1945, at the end of the second global conflict in a generation. His father George and his mother Violet (née Stitt) had been married on Christmas Day 1941, so by contemporary standards their first child had been a long time coming.

As it is, George Junior would be an only child, something that would cause him a certain degree of wonderment and pain as he grew older. His parents, though, seemed contented enough with their three-tier unit, if not their lot.

George Senior, originally of Scottish stock but brought up on Lord Street, part of the same terraced maze as Hyndford Street, was described on young Ivan's birth certificate as an electrician. Being a 'sparkie' was a valuable trade at the time, making him essential personnel at the nearby docks – not that he would have been conscripted into military service anyway. Conscription was considered on a number of occasions but never introduced in Northern Ireland because of fierce antipathy from the Catholics. According to Cardinal MacRory, 'conscription would compel those who writhe under [British rule] to fight on the side of the perpetrators' of partition'. Quite.

The Belfast docks themselves were hugely important to the Allied cause, producing 140 warships and repairing and converting some 3,000 other ships, as well as diversifying into necessary tank and aircraft production. They were equally important for the munitions they could provide, the Short and Harland aircraft factories completing around 1,200 Stirling bombers. George Morrison would continue working at one of their factories after the war. As it is, he would probably have made a fine fighting soldier. Though he was short and stocky, his local reputation was as a hard man, short on words, not because he had naught to say but because he did not like to bluster. He was of classic Scottish Presbyterian stock, even if he 'wasn't religious in any shape or form', as his son would later put it, never having a great deal of time for the religious schisms that continued to fracture Ulster society. It was a view he tried hard to inculcate in his son.

Violet Morrison was a local lass, from the extended family of Stitts. The complete opposite of her husband in so many ways, Violet has been generally portrayed as 'the life and soul of the party'. Described variously as an amateur singer and a tap-dancer, she would never need prompting to do one of her 'wee turns' at the perennial family get-togethers. Though she never seems to have had a vocation as such, save raising her son and maintaining neighbourly relations, Van's childhood chum Gil Irvine believes that her dancing skills extended to teaching tap-dance on a part-time basis.

To live in the terraced streets of East Belfast in the late forties was to know the meaning of living on top of one another. The enclosed environment brought a real sense of community, which was fostered by the female half of the Morrison family. The various strata within a seemingly immutable class structure were reinforced by the very layout of the streets, even the sloping lie of the land conspiring to emphasize the spatial distance between Hyndford Street and 'that mansion on the hill'. As a child, Morrison probably felt that he belonged where he was. As he subsequently observed, 'We lived in a pretty funky neighbourhood. I mean, it wasn't a white-collar district, let me put it that way.' This sense of belonging, of common roots, bound together many of those who would later seek escape through music. All the members of Morrison's first professional band shared the same geographic under-pinning.

Roy Kane: Geordie [Jones] came from one side of the [Beersbridge] Road, Van came from the other. Billy [McAllen] came from down the road a bit. I came from two or three roads over. But I was the snob because I lived in a parlour terrace house. You started off at the bottom of the road with all like terrace houses, which was near the docks. So the labourers lived with a kitchen house, which was just like one room [downstairs] and two bedrooms; and then if you were a tradesman, or a foreman, then you lived in a terrace house with two rooms at the bottom, a parlour *and* a sitting room.

'Wild Children', composed when Morrison was twenty-eight, is the song he would write 'for all the kids born around that time. Because . . . I think there was a heavier trip to conform.' This would be the last generation to grow up with such universal austerity. For their parents, proximity was just one of the forces that inbred conformity. As Gerald Dawe reiterates, 'To know where someone lived was tantamount to knowing their religion. Received wisdom could then take over . . . To know one's place was both a source of strength but also a terrible inhibition . . . Yet within the intimate, even claustrophobic closeness of the working-class districts there were the random open spaces of builders' yards, fugitive rivers and streams, old warehouses, industrial networks and vast walls.' It was to these open spaces that the young Ivan would escape when opportunity allowed.

Gil Irvine: There's a cycle track up at Orangefield. We used to go up there, near the pylon you hear in all the records. It was a special place. It was across a river – it was only eight feet wide, but it was 'across the water'. It was a totally different place. It was like a whole other country because there was water between you and where your mother was.

Orangefield itself, immortalized in its own song four decades later, may have been little more than a municipal park separating the working classes from more aspirational folk further up the Castlereagh Road, but to Morrison, his street friends and family cousins it was a vast open space of possibilities. And from an early age, Ivan was often somewhere else in his mind, even when physical release was out of the question. Projecting a brook into a river, a terraced house into a Spanish castle, the shops at Ballyhackamore into a foggy mountain top became a highly effective way of transcending what was an oppressively mundane existence.

Even as a child Ivan was set to develop a very real capacity for seeing beyond temporal reality. As he would later write, in 'The Street Only Knew Your Name', it was a childhood in which he spent long hours gazing out on his street, all the while envisaging 'all those castles in Spain'. This was a boy for whom the layers that kept the seen world from the unseen were gossamer-thin, where even the odd astral projection was not out of the question.

Van Morrison: I don't see myself as a mystical-type person. But then every now and then these weird experiences happen . . . I'll be lying down on the bed with my eyes closed and all of a sudden I get the feeling that I'm floating near the ceiling looking down. [1972]

Such experiences must have been quite terrifying to a young, only child. Indeed he learned to deny the reality of these experiences. Even the above slip, made to a *Rolling Stone* interviewer when Morrison was twenty-seven, was later depicted as a joke he had 'once told someone . . . that I fly around the room, and again it was made into *something*'. Whether he even shared his initial visionary experience(s) with his parents is open to doubt. He said not, when talking about early feelings of rapture to writer Steve Turner for Turner's book about rock & roll and the search for redemption in the mid-eighties⋆, at a time when Morrison was self-consciously analysing those early experiences:

⋆ Turner's book was published in 1988, under the title of *Hungry for Heaven*, by Virgin Books. It was published in revised form in 1995 by InterVarsity Press.

Van Morrison: I can never remember talking about it with *anyone* when I was a child. It was something I kept to myself because I didn't feel there was even the possibility of talking to anyone about this. I also didn't really feel the need . . . All I was interested in was somewhere to put my experiences – to find out what they were. [1985]

By 1985, Morrison had begun to read of others with similar experiences, which enabled him to begin the process of locating 'somewhere to put my [own] experiences'. In particular, he found that the poet and artist William Blake had experienced visions as a child, and had quickly learned to rue sharing them with those near and dear. As his first biographer Alexander Gilchrist relates, the occasion of Blake's first vision was 'on Peckham Rye (by Dulwich Hill) . . . Sauntering along, the boy looks up and sees a tree filled with angels, bright angelic wings bespangling every bough like stars. Returned home he relates the incident, and only through his mother's intercession escapes a thrashing from his honest father, for telling a lie.' References to Blake would begin to creep into Morrison's work in his late twenties but it would be some time before a friend, probably Chieftain Derek Bell, would provide the biographical similarities.

Not that Morrison was alone among his musical contemporaries in translating childhood visions into the work of a lifetime. The man who made it possible for Morrison to explore such themes in popular song, Bob Dylan, told Ron Rosenbaum in a 1977 interview of how he 'had some amazing projections when I was a kid . . . And those visions have been strong enough to keep me going through today. They were a feeling of wonder . . . You can have some amazing hallucinogenic experiences doing nothing but looking out your window.' Evidently it didn't matter whether it was a terraced two-up, two-down in the bowels of East Belfast, or the corner house on a forgotten street in the frozen Midwest. Or even the dilapidated nether regions of New Jersey, where a young Patti Lee Smith inhabited her own astral plane after a bout of scarlet fever at the age of seven left her in a semi-hallucinatory state for a number of months.

Patti Smith: I always had these rhythms, but I didn't know what to do with them . . . I always felt there was something good [trying] to get out of my body . . . I [always] had this feeling that I was going to go beyond my body physical. [1975]

Though barely a year in age separates Smith from Morrison – and only a further four come between Morrison and Dylan – the chain of popular culture would section each of them arbitrarily. Ten years may separate Morrison's first American hit single, 'Gloria', from Patti Smith's 45 reworking of that Them original, but the records signalled two very different paths from the same confluence. At the time, neither could have known about an unlikely connection at the very core of each of their quests for redemption. Replicating each other's almost schizophrenic artistry from opposite angles (one focusing on words, the other on music, both binding the two forms for a while), each felt driven to search for 'the answer', rejecting every option in turn, never satisfied by any approach to the eternal verities. Both had the profound trauma of an atheist father and a Jehovah's Witness for a mother, sharing the same space in which they would grow up (Lester Bangs, perhaps the most perceptive critic of Morrison's work, came from a similarly unlikely background).

The combination of non-believer and Jehovah's Witness remains a particularly discordant one because every Witness is required to subscribe to a dogma that all non-believers shall be eternally damned. The Jehovah's Witness creed also demands a proactive evangelism, something bound to become irksome to relatives and neighbours alike. In the case of Grant and Beverly Smith, the dilemma turned their daughter away from the Church as she entered adolescence, prompting her memorable declaration of independence, 'Jesus died for somebody's sins but not mine.' Though Morrison would wait until his fifties to make his own statement of apostasy (if that is what 'High Summer' is), a number of latter-day lyrics allude to a childish faith that faded with time. In 1973's 'Street Theory', he expressed a willingness to 'go to church on Sunday, just like my mama did'.* A couple of decades further down the line, he would write an entire song, 'Take Me Back', that expressed a need to get back to a time 'when I understood the light', as if he could still recapture the simple faith of a child when he no longer thought as one.

When that simple faith fell away has not been documented. No obvious trauma, like the one that shattered a nine-year-old C. S. Lewis's secure world, suggests itself, though the 1979 song 'And the Healing Has

---

* The released version of 'Street Theory' – on *The Philosopher's Stone* – dates from the 1980 *Common One* sessions. However, it was originally recorded at the *Veedon Fleece* sessions in the autumn of 1973.

Begun' alludes to a quite definable breach. The young Ivan had followed the familiar path of East Belfast kids, attending Sunday school at the Brethren Gospel Hall (where, if 'Sweet Jannie' is to be believed, he first fell in love) at the end of the street, then graduating to the more socially-mixed St Donard's, which was Church of Ireland. Possibly he began to question his beliefs at the self-same time his mother did – prior to her joining the Jehovah's Witness programme.

Steve Turner in his 1993 account suggests that Ivan's mother's conversion was a bolt from the blue; 'No one seems sure exactly how her conversion began or how long it lasted, but what is certain is that she became an ardent member of the local Kingdom Hall *sometime during the 1950s* [my italics]. Some of the older members can still remember Van attending morning services with her, but George Morrison never made an appearance.' The non-appearance of George Senior may suggest a certain antagonism. On the other hand, it may have coincided with his attempts to find employment in the USA. Indeed, this may explain why Violet turned to the family of Witnesses in the first place, and why she was permitted to persist whilst George remained an implacable atheist.

Morrison would subsequently attempt to dissuade anyone from assigning the slightest significance to this period under his mother's tutelage, when he 'shared' her new-found faith. He would insist to one journalist in 1985 that 'My mother was [a Witness] for a while – a brief encounter, that was all . . . I was taken to a couple of meetings. I found them quite pleasant.' This does not tally with what he had told Turner the previous year, that his mother 'went for a few years'. Clearly this was no mere dalliance. And yet he would still feel compelled to question Turner's version of events some six years later. Writing in response to Turner's *Too Late to Stop Now*, he refuted the suggestion that Violet had indulged in doorstep evangelism. Turner checked back with Belfast believers and they assured him that she did (after all, it was obligatory for all members).

The one reference in Morrison's lyrics to such doorstep evangelism, in 1973's 'Contemplation Rose', suggests that it was something he remembered with a certain distaste: 'Got *Watchtowers* and *Awakes* for free . . . but you can't take me down that way/as I'm not sinking'. In later life, he preferred to depict his mother's 'flirtation' with the Jehovah's Witness movement as part of a quest similar to his own.

Van Morrison: I wouldn't describe my mother as religious. I think that would annoy her. She's a free-thinker. My father was an atheist. My religious sense doesn't come from the Church, it comes from music . . . gospel music. It's a much more universal spirituality . . . I did some research on religion by myself. If my family had been very religious, I doubt whether it would have interested me. I'm more likely to reject things which people try to impose on me. When I was young in Belfast, I saw so many Catholics and Protestants for whom religion was a burden. There was enormous pressure and you had to belong to one or the other community. Thank God [*sic*] my parents were strong enough not to give in to this pressure. [1997]

Evidently Morrison's mother was one of those independent-minded souls who defined Protestantism along the same lines as George Bernard Shaw, as 'a great historic movement of Reformation, Aspiration, and Self-assertion against spiritual tyranny, rather than that organization of false gentility which so often takes its name in vain in Ireland'. The rest of East Belfast, where faith often wore a fierce face, may not have seen it in quite the same way. As Morrison later said, with characteristic understatement, 'We didn't go to church all the time, but it was a very churchy atmosphere . . . that's the way it is in Northern Ireland.'

The way that Gerald Dawe portrays the area in which he and Morrison grew up, in his *The Rest Is History* monograph, suggests that the pressure 'to belong', alluded to in the above quote, was unrelenting. Dawe describes 'a staunchly protestant and loyalist area [full of] Orange halls . . . In the grand St Donard's Church of Ireland at the Bloomfield intersection, barely ten minutes' walk from the leafy Cyprus Avenue and suburban North Road . . . Morrison would have heard an austere lesson in Christian faith, duty and reserve . . . From the Union Jack flying above the Orange halls, to billboards proclaiming proverbial wisdom from the Bible, assemblies and religious instruction at school, it was impossible not to absorb the teaching and cultural values of the protestant church . . . Protestantism was after all not solely "a religion", but a way of life.'

Dawe may be overstating the case, but not being Protestant or Catholic, instead opting to subscribe to one of the evangelical creeds now making their way from America, was to set oneself apart, and thereby to alienate oneself from *both* sides of the divide. Fellow East Belfast muso Roy Kane, in a single anecdote, graphically conveys how fiercely Protestant East Belfast was in the fifties:

Roy Kane: On a Sunday in Northern Ireland you could have starved to death 'cause nothing was open – that Protestant ethic. The Catholics had a different attitude. Their Sunday finished at twelve o'clock, and everything opened. If you were lying starving in a Prot area, you had to wait until the shops opened in the Catholic area.

And yet, Morrison and his contemporaries can still make light of the religious divide that existed. In 1986, at the height of the Troubles, he would insist that, though 'East Belfast was totally Protestant, there was a couple of Catholics. But . . . there wasn't any problems, there wasn't any friction or anything like that.' He was more circumspect some years earlier, merely saying that 'If there was tension, I didn't see it.' Hyndford Street neighbour Gil Irvine recalls there being Catholics living on the street, but 'nobody bothered. They were just good neighbours . . . [Religion] would never come up in conversation – you know, "Hold on, I'll be out tomorrow afternoon, 'cause I'm going to church."'

Maybe not, but Morrison's own lyrics allude to at least a couple of occasions when he did go to his family's new church of choice – 'just like my mama did'. There are those who not only remember the young Ivan attending Saturday services 'down at the Kingdom hall', but insist that it was a regular occurrence for a while. These Jehovah's Witness meetings did contain a musical element, which he celebrated self-consciously on 1978's 'Kingdom Hall', where he conjured up a scene of these believers 'having a ball/ . . . and the choir was singing'. But then an only child, separated from his father by a deep, wide ocean, was bound to see much of the world through his mother's eyes. He was still not old enough, nor aware enough, 'to reject things which people [might] try to impose on' him.

He may have been less open by the time his mother took him 'to a faith-healing thing once . . . that just turned me off'. Evidently, his mother was open to this type of experience long before her son. Yet he may have hoped for an explanation of that mysterious sense of rapture that occasionally stole over him. Such was his concern that he seems even to have feared for his very existence.

Van Morrison: I did have delusions. At one time I thought I wasn't going to live very long. That was when I was young . . . I was a complete recluse. [1979]

Yet again, though, when Steve Turner compiled a catalogue of neighbours to support his assertion that Morrison was a lonely child, he would insist he was no such thing. Rather, he was shy. Not lonely. It took until very recently, in informal conversations with singing partner Linda Gail Lewis, for him to admit to someone that he *had* been very lonely as a child, often required to fend for himself as his mother involved herself in social activities, in or out of church, and with a father away from home or at work. Boyhood chum George Jones confirms that he was 'left to his own devices at home a lot'. Shy by nature, he may not have realized the level to which he internalized everything, nor that avoiding any eye contact with the neighbourly faces on Hyndford Street might be deemed peculiar.

Ethel Blakely: If Van had come home from school and found me out the back speaking to his mum, he would have just walked past with his head down. He wouldn't have looked at his mum and he wouldn't have spoken to me. You could tell by his face that it was an effort for him even to come in. [ST]

His playmates shrugged it off when he proved a less than willing cohort in their games, but marked him down as Different. Neighbour Rod Demick insists he was 'never a great communicator, even when he was relaxed, talking to friends'. Gil Irvine, who lived just two doors down, took his friend as he found him but confirms that he was quite introverted. Interestingly, in the light of subsequent behaviour patterns, Irvine also depicts Morrison as someone for whom, even as a child, 'there had to be a reason for doing things – otherwise he wouldn't do it. He would play games until he got bored and then that would be it, he didn't want to know.' The low boredom threshold would carry over into adult life, as would his lack of interest in replicating something he had done earlier. However, given the opportunity to share a new enthusiasm – a song, a comic, a TV show, a film – the young boy could come over all sociable.

Gil Irvine: Van was one of the first people in the street that had a television. You used to [have to] vie for his favour. Van would maybe invite you in to watch 'Children's Hour' – *The Range Rider, Cisco Kid* . . . [And] we used to go to the cinema on Saturday mornings, what was called the ABC Minors. [It'd be] a comedy movie. *The Three Stooges* or something like that. Then you got maybe a serial, like *Flash Gordon*, and a main movie. It was usually a western. And this would get you out of the house on a Saturday morning.

Most of the time, though, Irvine found young Ivan to be someone who found his own way of keeping himself occupied: 'Nine times out of ten, if you went down to get him to come out to play – when you were eight, nine, ten, eleven – you'd find he'd be in the house reading something, whether it'd be American comics or books.' There was nothing remarkable about the pre-pubescent Ivan's fascination with American comics, nor his avid collecting of mags and paperbacks depicting adventures of the Wild West. This genre of pulp fiction sold by the hundred thousand in the years after the war. At a conference in Swansea in 1995, when asked about literary influences in his youth, he took a certain delight in detailing such an anti-intellectual obsession. It was probably the novels of Zane Grey and his ilk that first lodged a mythological America in the Morrison psyche. He soon came to idealize the land and its people in terms previously reserved for those castles in Spain.

America was a place of dreams and aspirations not only for Van, but for his parents too. Many years later, when their son's success had allowed the pair to share some of those dreams, his mother Violet would admit to a local Belfast journalist that the pull of America remained strong: 'When I'm here I want to be there, and when I'm there, I want to be here.' In a single sentence, she articulated the strange yin-yang attraction that Ireland continued to exert on the souls of emigrants as it had ever since the Irish famine drove so many from their native soil.

The pull of the promised land on George Senior was such that, in the early fifties, he went to the US hoping to hold down a job long enough to bring his family there. Though Gil Irvine thinks he went to Seattle, a song débuted by Morrison in 2001, 'Choppin' Wood', confirms it was Detroit. 'Choppin' Wood' also affirms how his father felt obliged to go overseas 'just trying to make a living', and that he actually 'sent for us once, but everything fell through'.

Gil Irvine: He had brothers over there. He used to get records sent across [by them]. I think George went over to try and get a job, and he brought me back a leather holster for my cowboy guns.

George Senior was thoroughly taken with the sounds of American music some time before he experienced them first-hand. For now, though, Gil and Ivan's first love remained cowboy lore and all that entailed. Hence the leather holster. Nevertheless, Ivan couldn't help but grow up 'listening to American music' – the popular music that his father liked to collect and play. It was doubtless a gradual process, but at some point he made the connection between the America he liked to read about and the one these singers sang about. Indeed, one might suggest that he latched on to his early American singing idols, like Lead Belly and Sonny Terry, precisely because they came closest to the frontier sensibility he found in the pulp fiction of the day.

That these tales of adventure directly fired his own imagination is something Morrison alludes to in 1973's 'Fair Play', where he leaps across fields, turning to his erstwhile companion, and says, 'Geronimo/ A paperback book . . . fill[s] my mind with tales of mystery, mystery . . . and imagination'. Poe's gothic tales, anthologized in numerous pulp paperbacks, added another piece to his Americana quilt – though not at the expense of the Wild West figures that first tripped his thought processes, rekindled in the opening image of 'Beside You' (as realized within *Astral Weeks*), in which one particular figure of the imagination took on the aspect of blood brother. As Jack Lynch wrote in his 1983 career overview of Morrison, 'The opening image of Little Jimmy shows a child sneaking out of his home, escaping to adventure and a childlike ritual rendezvous. Broken Arrow, possibly his fantasy figure, beckons – innocence led by imagination on the road to experience.'

Morrison's rare capacity to pass from the real world into an imaginary one in the twinkling of an eye enabled him to see the slightly grubby world in which he lived as a truly magical place. Once, when asked whether he felt he'd acquired an early innocence from growing up in Belfast and wandering the hills and countryside around the city, he replied that it wasn't innocence – 'more like magic. Magic is always there, but a lot of times you don't see it . . . If you want to pay attention to something that is uncomplicated, you will develop that.'

And so, in 'Beside You', he passes in double-quick time from the reality of a quiet Sunday in East Belfast, with only barking dogs to split the silence, to a 'diamond-studded highway' where he could happily 'roam from your retreat and view'. Likewise, in the majestic 'And It Stoned Me', a trip to the county fair becomes a magical experience when he is caught in the rain and finds himself getting 'stoned off nature' itself. He would describe that song in 1974 as simply 'remembering how it was when you were a kid', seemingly unaware that such experiences were as uncommon as his perception of them.

'And It Stoned Me' was written at a time when he was still looking for 'somewhere to put my experiences'. As were 'Beside You', 'Cyprus

Avenue', 'Joe Harper Saturday Morning' and 'Country Fair'. But of all the songs from the period when his childhood remained a vital source of inspiration, the one that conveys with the most immediacy the way his inner and outer worlds could interface is a song he refrained from releasing, 'Hey, Where Are You?'. Demoed in the months that separate *Astral Weeks* and *Moondance*, it was perhaps rendered redundant in his mind by 'And It Stoned Me'. Or perhaps he considered the transition in the song too surreal: sharing one of those 'days of blooming wonder' with his childhood sweetheart, talking of roaming in the forest and dancing in the sea, he is interrupted in his reverie by a grey man at the bus station asking, 'Have you got your ticket?' Dragged back into the real world by this pecuniary demand, he can't help but ask, 'Hey, where are you?'

Seemingly unable to share such experiences with his parents (or bus conductors), he longed to share them with someone – and when he would, the inspiration would linger long enough for it to come out in *Astral Weeks*. For much of his childhood, though, he was obliged to enjoy his imaginary adventures alone.

As he later put it in 'Madame Joy', he was required to tell himself, 'Let your midnight and your daytime turn into love of life/It's a very fine line/But you've got the mind, child'. His belief that he had what it took to carry on was largely self-instilled. And yet, if something he said in his early thirties is to be believed, he did get to meet 'someone who knew who I was – I was a kid and he taught me who I was. He said, "I know who you are," and in a very subtle way laid a thing on me. And I believed what he said.' A similar figure would crop up in 'Joe Harper Saturday Morning', though still without his identity being revealed. He may or may not have enjoyed a more corporeal existence than Morrison's Broken Arrow. However, he seems to have encouraged this young kid to start writing things down.

Van Morrison: I started writing poetry when I was really young, before I knew what poetry was and what lyrics were. [1978]

How much the thoughts he scribbled down as a callow child reflected the same 'sense of rapture' as later lyrics Morrison alone knows, though he has admitted that '*some* of my songs are . . . definitely . . . influenced by my childhood in Belfast'. It has been his early adolescence that he has mostly chosen to idealize, as if locked in that time period in his dreams.

The majority of songs that capture that glow find our hero with a constant companion, and a female one at that. That sense of companionship would come only after years of isolation.

The childhood that preceded such revelation has prompted less reflection from an adult Morrison, perhaps because he spent much of it trying to come to terms with a perspective so singular and social skills so poor. It was only when music began to impinge on his furtive imagination that his world would change for the better, and he would feel born again. The young Ivan, though, was no musical prodigy, despite the musicality that existed on both sides of the family. The moment when it began to make sense came considerably later than certain statements suggest. One suspects it may have been when his father returned from America with a suitcase full of records acquired on his travels. One name in particular stuck out. It could hardly fail to. After all, what kinda name is Lead Belly?

2

1947–60: His Father's Footsteps

It all started way back when I was two and a half years old. Ringo, my
father's friend, would bring over some Hank Williams records and sit on
the stairs and listen to 'Kawliga'. My grandfather would keep an eye on
me while my mother and father were at the movies, and I would make
him play records over and over again . . . I'd always ask him to play Big
Bill Campbell at the Grand Ole Opry . . . and one about a little red
patch on the seat of some guy's pants; 'Cattle Call' and 'Texarkana
Baby' by Eddy Arnold; and Tex Morton, the yodelling cowboy, singing
'Big Rock Candy Mountain' and 'My Sweetheart's in Love with a Swiss
Mountaineer'. What a record! Jimmie Rodgers singing 'Mother the
Queen of My Heart' and whippin' that old TB.

—*Van Morrison, 1974*

I knew I was gonna do music, way back, way back. There was never
any doubt. When I was three, I knew.

—*Van Morrison, 1989*

In some part of his memory bank, Morrison may well believe that such
was his instinctive love of music that he could enjoy Hank Williams
singing about a tobacco-store Indian cigar-holder in love with an antique
statue of an Indian maid when barely a bairn. But then, a serious collector
like him must also know that he was eight years old when 'Kawliga' was
released, on the death-ridden heels of that last, fateful ride. At least when
the myth of Morrison the musical prodigy was reinforced in song –
1973's 'Foggy Mountain Top' depicting him 'listening to this music/

Ever since the age of three' – the musical references were more plausible: Jimmie Rodgers's 1927 recording of 'T For Texas' a.k.a. 'Blues Yodel No. 1'. Hank Williams came later, but stayed longer.

Much has been constructed, on the back of ubiquitous plugs from his son, regarding George Morrison's musical tastes and their impact upon young Ivan. But in his formative years, it was probably his mother's musical tastes that held sway, especially when his father was away. His mother was no music collector, but she was by all accounts a very fine singer, with a good ear and populist tastes. According to her son, she didn't sing professionally, though 'she did [do] some local sorts of shows . . . the dance-band era, that sort of thing'. Jim Day confirms that she used to sing with his band at the Jubilee Ballroom, as well as at weekly family get-togethers.

Billy McAllen: His mother, she was a bit of a singer. They used to have parties at home, just the relatives in, [a] few drinks. I used to sit and play the guitar for them and say the aunt or the uncle or the mother would've sung a song. The stuff they were singing was old to me.

These informal singalongs left an abiding impression on Morrison. He described them to an interviewer in 1998 in still glowing terms: 'My mother sang and relatives would come around on a Saturday evening. They'd go to the club first and then come back and have a few drinks and sing songs. "I'll Take You Home Again, Kathleen", "Danny Boy". My uncle used to sing that one, "I'm a Rambler, I'm a Gambler" . . . People were just into music and it didn't matter what it was called.' On an earlier occasion he depicted these get-togethers as an opportunity for 'people [to] sit around and sing old Irish songs, and start crying'.

The relationship between ostentatious displays of emotion, singing and drinking was established early on in Morrison's mind. It was reinforced by his mother's choice of songs, which ran the full gamut from sentimental to maudlin. Of the generation for whom the obviously trained singing of Irish tenor John McCormack represented the epitome of style, Violet would invariably be the first to suggest 'I'll Take You Home Again, Kathleen', 'Danny Boy', 'She Moved through the Fair' or 'The Star of the County Down' – all recorded by McCormack – at one of these Saturday-night serenades. She could also impose her dulcet tones on the likes of 'Goodnight Irene', the first Lead Belly song her son probably ever heard, or 'Sweet Sixteen' – or just 'whatever was on the radio'.

Van Morrison: My mother was a great singer – and still is. She could sing anything from Al Jolson to 'Ave Maria'. [1978]

It was surely from this side of the family that Morrison also developed a penchant for the kind of MOR fare that has featured in many of the latter-day sets, where songs like 'That's Life', 'Buenas Días Señorita' or 'Send in the Clowns' remain a more likely occurrence than any offering from *Astral Weeks* or *Veedon Fleece*. Neighbour Gil Irvine even thinks 'it was his mother who taught him how to play harmonica', the first instrument the young Ivan took up when deciding to play music too. She also bought her son his first records, at a time when it was the idea behind the song that appealed more than any actual musical chops.

Van Morrison: My mother used to get these records out of Woolworth's. Things like 'Turkey in the Straw', 'She'll Be Coming round the Mountain' and cowboy songs. They were low-budget records on red vinyl . . . 'On Top of Old Smokey' was another one. [1998]

The sentiments of this kind of cowboy song were likely to overlap with those found in comic-book accounts of the West. These were also the type of songs first seriously anthologized by Texan academic John Lomax in his 1910 collection, *Cowboy Songs and Other Frontier Ballads*, which proved to be just the beginning of his prodigious collecting activities. As he set about compiling a second collection, *American Ballads and Folk Songs*, he convinced the Library of Congress that they should fund the documenting of American folk-song on a crude portable electronic recording machine, before it passed from the national consciousness. So it was that he set out in 1933, with his son Alan in tow, hoping to find examples of 'the old styles "dammed up" in America's more isolated areas'.

One of John Lomax's more inspired brainwaves was to record a number of black convicts, hoping to document 'the [sort of] Negro who [has] had the least contact with jazz, the radio and with the white man'. They stumbled across just such a man in Angola Prison, Louisiana, serving a second term for assault with intent to murder. Huddie Ledbetter or, as he would henceforth be known, Lead Belly, was a truly remarkable untutored repository of ethnic song.

How remarkable, that first visit to Angola Prison barely revealed.* On his release from Angola the following year – an event for which Alan Lomax subsequently acquired much of the credit – Lead Belly was signed to an exclusive contract with father John that netted him two whole cents per record. Over the next fifteen years he would draw enough media attention to feature in a *March of Time* newsreel and in *Life* magazine – whose headline to their feature read 'Bad Nigger Makes Good Minstrel' – but when he died, aged sixty-four, on 6 December 1949, he was living on welfare in New York City. The following year, mainstream folk combo the Weavers recorded 'Goodnight Irene', which proceeded to sell over a million copies. They followed it up with Lead Belly's arrangement of 'Cotton Fields'. Now that Lead Belly was dead, he could finally making a living. Though young Ivan would have heard the Weavers' sanitized renditions on the radio, and his mother's at get-togethers, he probably had to wait for his father to return with one of Moe Asch's Folkways albums to hear the authentic article. Its effect, though, was immediate.

Van Morrison: [My] major influence was Lead Belly . . . If it wasn't for him I may never have been here . . . I didn't really hear a lot of things that were going down when I was [in Belfast]. I heard some of them, and wanted to hear more, but I couldn't, because it was happening over here [in America] . . . So I just grabbed as many Lead Belly and [Woody] Guthrie and Hank Williams records as I could grab, and tried to learn something. [1970]

Morrison, who would later describe hearing Lead Belly for the first time as 'the greatest thing since Swiss cheese', dated his epiphany to when he was ten or eleven, i.e. the mid-fifties, after both Lead Belly and Hank Williams had sung their last, and long after Jimmie Rodgers got whipped by that ol' TB. How exactly a ten-year-old Ulster lad related to songs about Mississippi floods, the voracious appetite of crop-eating beetles or the freight train out of Mullaine (*sic*) is as great a conundrum as the fact that someone like Lead Belly found a place in his father's collection.

That collection, according to the son, already included the gospel singing of Mahalia Jackson, Sister Rosetta Tharpe and the Clara Ward

---

* John and Alan Lomax returned a number of times to Angola to record Lead Belly's repertoire, ultimately cataloguing over a hundred songs from the man.

Singers. Young Ivan was also exposed to 'the early Armstrong stuff, which was different from the later stuff. It was before he went commercial . . . [And my dad] had all the swing-band stuff – Tommy Dorsey, Artie Shaw, Harry James. He [also] had Charlie Parker's first-ever record.'

But what really interested the young lad was his father's 'collection of blues records . . . people like Muddy Waters, and Sonny Terry and Brownie McGhee. I was hearing [this stuff] constantly.' It was probably through the likes of Sonny Terry, who played harmonica on Lead Belly's original Folkways recording of 'Goodnight Irene', that father and son first alighted on Lead Belly. Indeed, Morrison would later recall that 'the very first record I ever bought was "Hootin' Blues" by Sonny Terry . . . it cost one and sixpence in Smithfield [market],' and it was presumably the hope of emulating Terry's trademark riffs that originally prompted Morrison to take up the mouth-harp.

Sonny Terry would become almost as important an influence as Lead Belly. His seminal recordings with Brownie McGhee on Prestige include a number of songs later covered by Morrison, such as 'Midnight Special', 'Take This Hammer' and 'I Got a Woman'. He would also provide Morrison's first opportunity to hear the blues played by an electric band: 'It was [an album] called *Back Country Blues* . . . in fact it was urban blues . . . The first thing I ever rehearsed with Them was one of their songs, called "Custard Pie".'

The tastes of father and son did not always converge so precisely. Lead Belly seems to have been of passing interest to George Senior but, as the son was to say some time later, 'I connected with the gospel and Lead Belly – heavily connected with Lead Belly.' Possibly his initial interest in gospel was the afterglow of a failing faith, kindled by early memories of the Kingdom Hall. But, however much Morrison subsequently portrayed his father as one of only a handful of serious record collectors in East Belfast, George Senior was not the only music collector on Hyndford Street, nor the sole influence on his son's tastes.

Gil Irvine: Obviously we [kids] didn't have the money to go out and buy records, so you'd maybe try and coax your parents into buying something a bit more popular – which [of course] nine times out of ten they didn't do. John McCullough had a radiogram in his house, but all he had was like country and western, Hank Williams [etc.]. [At the Morrisons'] you were listening to Van's father's records, which was blues and jazz.

There was no shortage of exposure to the late Hank in Hyndford Street. Not only would family friend Ringo sometimes bring a bunch of 78s over and have a Hank Williams night but, according to Morrison, he could usually hear McCullough's gramophone 'from five or six doors down – they used to leave the doors open'. Though his father and friend liked their Hank unsullied by Irish harmonies, Morrison claims he would sometimes get together with McCullough: 'I'd play with him or he'd just be singing in the back or something. There was a lot of music going on in the street.' Lead Belly, though, would remain private music for a little while yet, awaiting the second wave of popularizers, led by the rambunctious Lonnie Donegan, before he truly passed into the public domain – at the expense of much of the music that was coming out of Ireland.

Van Morrison: When I was growing up in Belfast, [all] I was listening to [was] American music. Irish music was going on all around me, but that was nowhere. I was looking for something different. [1982]

And yet he did have access to that rich homegrown tradition, through his mother's records and the songs she liked to sing, even if there is some truth to later assertions 'that folk music was not something that was readily available . . . you couldn't just walk in and hear it, as you [could] walk in and hear rock & roll later on'. According to Morrison, 'the only local traditional folk group that I [ever] heard were the McPeakes', best known for their original arrangement of the traditional Scottish lament 'Wild Mountain Thyme'. What he has not publicly acknowledged is the opportunities he had to hear the McPeakes first-hand. According to guitarist Mick Cox, the whole family knew the McPeakes, as evidenced by an occasion some years later when a twenty-one-year-old Van returned from a little three-piece tour round Ireland to find his parents getting ready to head off for one of their get-togethers.

Mick Cox: We came back from one [gig] and he said, 'I've got to go home now.' It's about [midnight]. We arrive back at Hyndford Street, walk up to the door, door opens and both [parents] are dressed up. [So] we went back out to the car, we all got in and off he drove down these side-streets. Stop at this tiny little terraced house. Knock on the door. Walk in. His mum took her coat off, and just started dancing with all these Irish musicians. They were the McPeake family. I didn't even know who they were! They all took turns in singing. [It] finished at five o'clock. That's how his folks influenced him. [His mother] had an incredible knowledge of Irish music.

Family get-togethers and friendly singalongs were not young Ivan's only exposure to live music. The first experience of music in a public place to impress itself upon him came when his father took him into town one day, 'and there was this jazz band playing on the back of a truck. I was, like, five.' As he grew older, and his father's collecting continued apace, he would be allowed to tag along when George went record-hunting. This would involve trips to Smithfield market, in which there were a number of record stalls and where, as Morrison depicts it, 'you'd go for a certain R&B side and they'd already have it out for you. They knew what you were coming for.'

The incongruous pair would then head for Atlantic Records, a shop on Belfast's High Street opened by Solly Lipsitz and Tom Cusack in 1953. Solly Lipsitz describes how he and Cusack 'started out with collectors' records – both jazz and operatic, and at that time there were a lot of embryonic jazz collectors. Van's father used to come *every* Saturday. He was more interested in the blues side of things – Howlin' Wolf and Little Brother Montgomery – but . . . I remember Van very well in a grey school cap.' Morrison says he 'just connected with it right away', the record-collecting bug having been genetically transferred from father to son. Unlike his father, though, young Ivan wasn't content just to listen to these unearthly sounds, he was determined to find some way of replicating them – heavy Ulster burr notwithstanding.

Recently Morrison confirmed an early interest in performing, speaking of an audition 'for the BBC when I was fourteen. There was an ad for a television programme and they were looking for talent. I wrote a letter and they asked me to audition. I sang a folk-song, and because I didn't know all the words I rewrote it . . . The BBC never wrote back!' If he did indeed make his recording début as a folk-singer, it was not as a traditional Irish folk-singer but as the bastard son of Lead Belly and Sara Carter.

Van Morrison: I had this book, it was called *The Alan Lomax Folk Guitar Book*, and it was mainly based on the Carter Family style, which was a picking style, and that's fundamentally the folk style as we know it today. So that's what I was learning. I listened to records as well, of the Carter Family and Lead Belly, while I was practising. [2000]

His father had already asked Solly Lipsitz's advice as to what kind of guitar he should buy his thirteen-year-old son. Morrison believes 'it must have been in Joe Kavanagh's place [in Smithfield market] – it was called I Buy Anything'. He presumably also sold anything – including the kind of acoustic guitar on which a self-taught lad might acquire some musical 'shapes'. Morrison had already been given the usual opportunities at school to learn an 'acceptable' musical instrument, to accompany the kind of state school-approved music played at daily assembly or in the weekly music lesson. However, he never felt the slightest desire to become involved with a curriculum so imposed.

Van Morrison: When we had music classes, we'd sit and blow recorders or something. If that was a musical education, then I just wasn't impressed. I just wasn't impressed at all. That's what I couldn't figure out about that period of time – in music class they'd give you these dopey little things to play instead of just getting a record player and saying, 'This is good and hope you dig this,' or 'Here's another guy.' They had a lot of facilities that I thought they weren't using. But at home I just lapped it up. [1974]

And yet, at Orangefield School for Boys, to which he had graduated in 1956, after six years at Elm Grove Primary School, there resided one of Ireland's most noteworthy young folk-singers, Davey Hammond. Though he was ostensibly an English teacher, pupils contemporary with Van recall how Hammond took little persuading to bring out his guitar and play something folky. He insists that he made no real impression on Morrison – not that Morrison made much impression on Orangefield – admitting that 'If he'd listened to people like me he would never have written a line. He believed in nobody but himself.' Morrison says he *does* remember Hammond singing the traditional American ballad 'Casey Jones' in one of the classes he taught, though this was presumably meant as a lesson in lyrical content, not a music lesson *per se*.

The adolescent Morrison was simply not willing to learn conventional wisdoms in a rote way. Just as he preferred to envisage a music teacher whose communication skills extended to 'This is good – dig this!', so he struggled to come to terms with the education process itself, believing that he was one of those to whom, in the words of teacher-turned-terrorist Padraic Pearse, 'all such dangerous knowledge was hidden'.

Van Morrison: The scenes I went through at school didn't really teach me much. I learned a little that I had to expand on myself, but most of it didn't really help me to learn to cope with *anything*. [1970]

Of course, the young Ivan wasn't about to meet his teachers half-way, or leave that large chip on his shoulder at home. He made it clear how he viewed himself at this time when talking to his first chronicler some years later: 'I mean, we were freaks in the full sense of the word, because either we didn't have the bread to go to the sort of school where we could sit down and do our own thing, or that type of school didn't exist.' By his own admission, he ended up 'skip[ping] school quite a bit'.

Van Morrison: I wasn't brought up in this sort of driven thing when I was a kid. I mean, that sort of thing was around . . . things like, 'You can't miss going to school' . . . but not really in my house. [1994]

This can only have compounded his personal isolation, laying him open to verbal, and possibly physical, attacks by that breed of bully seeking to turn on anyone they deemed 'freaks in the full sense of the word'. Though no concrete evidence exists depicting Morrison as someone bullied at secondary school, his later pugnacity and reflexive mode of verbal counter-attack bear all the marks of the bullied boy-turned-man (several ex-friends suspect it may account for the pre-emptive way he has been known to rebuff 'friends'). He was certainly ill-equipped to defend himself at Orangefield, being neither tall nor broad. Only when his love of music meant he could join a gang/band was he able to experience again the sense of camaraderie he may have known at Elm Grove but mislaid at Orangefield.

His own intellectual curiosity would in later years lead Morrison to re-evaluate the importance of education. When, in 1994, he tabled a list of ways to avoid music-industry pitfalls entitled 'How Not to Get Screwed', point five was: 'Go to school. If you're in a position to, try to get a proper education first.' Some twenty-one years earlier, he recorded one of his great lost jewels, 'Madame Joy', in which he portrays his muse-teacher with something close to awe: 'Got a taste of all religion, comes on with the new/In her hair a yellow ribbon, and she's decked out all in blue'. Depicted as someone who steps lightly in the university of life, 'Madame Joy' is there '[to] help them understand'. The one question he asks of Madame Joy he would later answer for himself in

'Fair Play': 'Can I learn the language?' Her reply would be the same as his: 'Have you got the mind?'

It was a question he would ask himself only after leaving school with no qualifications save a meaningless school leaving certificate – merely confirmation that he had endured the system and could now enter the real world at the still tender age of fifteen. Morrison would later insist to Steve Turner that this *was* a qualification, such was the deep sense of academic failure he felt as an adolescent. His subsequent willing acceptance of honorary doctorates from two local universities vividly illustrates this autodidact's psychological need to compensate for earlier educational disappointments.

His extra-curricular education had, however, continued apace. If the subtext of a number of his early compositions can be taken at something like face value, this included a deepening friendship with a girl he had known since they were children. As it is, the taboo nature of young love crops up in a number of early songs, notably 'Little Girl', in which he would insist that 'I don't care what they say . . . I've got you in my soul / fourteen years old'.

References to this fourteen-year-old girl, 'so young and bold', would never entirely disappear from the songs of George Ivan Morrison, though after the catharsis of 'Cyprus Avenue' her ghost seems to have been summoned only occasionally, on the likes of 'Country Fair' and 'Orange-field'. This relationship doubtless vied for attention with the most important thing in the young boy's life. Not surprisingly, the pair shared a common bond through music – something they shared in their souls as well as in their homes.

The music in question, though, was not the blues and jazz of his father's collection (and generation), it was the beefed-up form of rhythm & blues and rockabilly now being played by rock & roll bands. Another of those songs from the months after *Astral Weeks*'s completion that would fall by the wayside, called simply 'Rock & Roll Band', describes two star-crossed lovers living every day 'never ever thinkin' we'd get much older',★ nor wondering about the wherefores and whys as they dance to a rock & roll band. With what will become a familiar nostalgia infecting his lyrics, the singer asks rhetorically, 'Wasn't that a time? Wasn't that a soul time?'

★ This is an allusion to a line in 'Bob Dylan's Dream': 'We never thought we could ever get old'.

Of course, Morrison was not the only one for whom the bloom of first love coincided with the transatlantic aftershocks of popular music's explosive new sound. Nor was he the only one to whom rock & roll was some kind of answer to nightly prayers. But he was far better equipped than most of his contemporaries to recognize the roots of this revolution in the music he had spent much of his adolescence assimilating – even if he still remained too young and unsure of himself to seize the moment, however much his female friend tried to get him to believe in himself. Initially, he simply received the new sounds with the same openness with which he embraced the various strands of his father's (soon to be outmoded) listening.

Van Morrison: When I started listening to music the *Melody Maker* was a jazz mag . . . So I heard blues, country music, pop music in those days, all of it with an open mind . . . I grew up in a household where I heard all the real music, so when I heard 'pop' I didn't have to rush out. I loved Little Richard and Fats Domino, but I had the background of hearing this other music since I was three [*sic*]. So it wasn't such a big injection, like with [other] rebellious teenagers when they heard rock & roll. [1997]

He didn't feel the need to participate in the wanton destruction sparked by the presence of an authentic American rock & roller in February 1957, but he would still recall the effect the slightly balding, middle-aged Bill Haley, of 'Rock Around the Clock' fame, had when he came to Belfast: 'They just ripped out all the seats in the theatre, they ripped the place apart.' For young Ivan, this music was simply something he had been waiting for.

3

1957–62: Riding on the Side

When [Lonnie] Donegan came along, I thought everybody knew about it . . . I thought everybody was hearing the same things I was, but they weren't . . . I think I was really lucky to grow up at that time and hear what I heard then.

—Van Morrison, 1994

In January 1956, a 1954 recording of a 1942 Lead Belly version of a traditional railroad song, by a Glaswegian ex-banjo player by the name of Lonnie Donegan (real name Anthony, the 'Lonnie' was a tribute to American singer Lonnie Johnson), entered the UK singles chart, sparking a localized revival of traditional folk music in an idiom that also drew on jazz and blues. The name it was given, taken from an obscure late-twenties American musical antecedent, was skiffle.

Donegan had recorded 'Rock Island Line' eighteen months earlier with the Chris Barber Band, of which he had been a founding member back in 1953. But it was only when Decca lifted the two Donegan vocals – 'Rock Island Line' and 'John Henry' – from that Chris Barber album, in response to 'public demand', and issued them as a single by Lonnie Donegan and His Skiffle Group, that the phenomenon found its feet.

And how. 'Rock Island Line' entered the UK charts on three separate occasions in 1956, and in May of that year even breached the previously impregnable US Top Ten. And yet the appeal of Donegan's fifties recordings – and we're talking about a man who had a couple of dozen hit records, and three number ones, in the years before the Beatles advanced on his rudimentary template – may not be obvious to a modern audience. Certainly his recordings, if not the songs themselves, have not dated well. The appeal of skiffle – like punk rock twenty years later, another British reinvention of American musical forms – was its simplicity of style. As Charlie Gillett puts it, in his seminal *The Sound of the City*:

The simple instrumental accompaniment of the skiffle group – guitar, bass and washboard (or, in sophisticated groups, drums) – attracted countless young people who lacked the musical ability to be jazz musicians or even effective popular musicians, but who could easily learn three or four chords, and strum and sing the skiffle repertoire, which Donegan, now on his own, quickly developed.

In other words, Donegan unwittingly returned folk music to the folk, in an era when radio was considered the primary medium of entertainment other than cinema, and where Donegan's way of performing these songs, 'with a quick dance beat, in a high, nasal, fake American voice', was best suited. If the novelty value of his sound wore off in under a year in the States, he was able to trade on the songwriting skills of Lead Belly, Woody Guthrie and A. P. Carter till the end of the decade in Britain, where homegrown talent seemed as wafer-thin as pastrami. That is, until all the kids who had learnt to play bad skiffle developed into the kind of guys who could play good pop, thus doing away with the likes of Donegan himself, whose last hit, Lead Belly's 'Pick a Bale of Cotton', left the UK charts the week 'Love Me Do' entered them.

George Ivan Morrison was another of those kids, even though he had already attended his father's prep school for folk, blues and jazz. Ascending into uncharacteristic eloquence, Morrison would later write, in the notes to the *Skiffle Sessions* CD, of how 'given the geographical distance between me and my heroes, skiffle arrived where and when I needed it. It was too good to be true. What had once been an eccentric taste in American folk-blues was now a popular hit. Music was the common denominator and skiffle provided a bridge between what I had always been listening to and what everyone else was suddenly discovering. Although he doesn't get credit for it, Donegan was a major motivator, not just for me, but for many kids with musical ambitions . . . When I formed my first band with my friends, we called ourselves the Sputniks.'

The Sputniks, one of a number of such 'bands' to have sprouted up in the working-class areas of Belfast (and indeed that other ferry port, Liverpool), centred entirely on Hyndford Street. Gil Irvine came up with 'a type of kazoo called the Zobo', whilst Hank fan John McCullough tied some string to an old tea-chest and next-door-neighbour Walter Blakely scratched at his mother's washboard with her stray thimbles. This left Van and Billy Ruth, the only two boys in the environs possessed of the arcane mysteries of A, D, and E, to play whatever resembled a tune. Reflecting its moment, the boys' set was, as Irvine recalls, 'all Lonnie Donegan, Johnny Duncan, Nancy Whiskey, people like that'. Formed in 1957, at the height of skiffle (and coinciding with Russia's ascent into space), the Sputniks played their share of youth clubs and Women's Institute meetings for the sheer fun of it.

The adolescent Morrison, though, perhaps sensed that there might be more to this music-making lark, and shortly before the band outlived its usefulness, in the winter of 1959, he drafted in a guitarist-singer he knew from a school across the way, Bill Dunn, and débuted a slightly different sound at a school concert, much to the consternation of a number of his peers.

Bill Dunn: He was at Orangefield Secondary at Christmas 1959 and I was at Ashfield. He had to get permission from the headmaster for me to join a band at Orangefield that was supposed to be exclusive to pupils there. I did a good Elvis act and, besides, I owned the only guitar in our street. The band never had a name, but it was a success that Christmas.

According to Morrison, this modified skiffle band – and as he subsequently observed, 'it didn't matter what you played, *everybody* called you a skiffle group' – *did* have a name. It was called Midnight Special, after the song that was the centrepiece of their highly compact set, Sonny Terry and Brownie McGhee's plea to the governor to let that metaphorical midnight special 'shine its ever-loving light on me'. He would claim that he played this school concert 'because one of the teachers asked me to do it'. One presumes that teacher was Davey Hammond.

Morrison doubtless felt great just getting up there, showing his fellow pupils that he had found something he loved to do, and that he was going to carry on regardless. Midnight Special, though, quickly ran out of steam, and Morrison was obliged to find another set of willing cohorts who had (mis)spent their youth clustered around a crystal set, trying to tune in to Radio Luxembourg late at night – though probably not after listening to 'jazz and blues records during the day/And Debussy on the third programme', as Morrison portrays his homelife in 1991's 'On Hyndford Street'.

Gil Irvine: Nearly everybody had what you call a crystal set. You got maybe one radio in the house, and you went and bought a crystal set which you could wire to the frame of your bed as an aerial, and you could pick up stations like Luxembourg, rather than having to listen to what the BBC was churning out at the time. In that era you very seldom got popular music on the radio . . . [and] very few people had record players . . . that's why people used to tune in to Luxembourg.

As a result, finding a set of musically-attuned misfits in the confines of East Belfast in the late fifties proved nowhere near as problematic as might now be the case. The secret ciphers used by teenagers at this time were bound by the language of the radio. Humour was defined by Sunday mornings listening to the BBC, especially the anarchic insanity of Spike Milligan, Harry Secombe and Peter Sellers, known collectively as the Goons.

Van Morrison: Sunday mornings, if I remember, was the Goons, then *Round the Horne*, Jimmy Clitheroe, they seemed to be all on a Sunday. The Goons were huge in Ireland: kids I grew up with talked like that all the time. [1989]

During the hours (and days) that might lie between the BBC reverting to its mainstream mundanity and Luxembourg beaming its signal out into the late-night air, there was always forces radio, as it was generally known. Set up for the homesick GIs stuck in Germany, awaiting the completion of their obligations under the Marshall Plan, forces radio must at times have seemed like it was beamed from Mars. Only when the records it played arrived, from whatever exotic location they might be acquired, did the music begin to seem real.

Arty McGlynn: The most important [radio] programme I heard was an American network station from Hamburg or Frankfurt. I used to tune in to that. It was Little Richard, it was Gene Vincent. I was hearing stuff that I couldn't hear on BBC or Irish radio. That was my source. All I could hear on BBC when I was twelve was Ruby Murray or Big Ben's Banjo Band or the Billy Cotton Band. It wasn't really what I wanted to hear . . . [But] I'd hear a number from an American airforce thing, and I'd go down to my local record shop. I'd walk in at fourteen [and] this guy would order it, and it would take like a month to get it. And then it'd finally come, and then I'd devour the record . . . It was also a bicycle shop, that sold batteries for radios. You didn't have record shops in those days in Northern Ireland, you had multi-shops. You had grocery shops that sold bicycles, bacon, lamps . . . You could have a drink in a grocery shop – it was a bar also.

Arty McGlynn would have to wait a further two decades before playing with Van the man, but their teenage experience was a shared one, as members of a secret society defined by record matrix numbers. For the fifteen-year-old Morrison, who had already exhausted the musical possibilities his street offered, it was time to expand his frontiers.

How Morrison originally met up with the quartet who called them-selves the Thunderbolts nobody seems very sure.★ Guitarist Billy McAllen suspects that singer George Jones may have first introduced the others to 'wee Van', who shared McAllen's chord-strumming ambitions. On the other hand, he wonders, 'Van would have lived nearer to [keyboardist] Wesley Black, and I'm wondering if it was Wesley who brought him round one night. But there were so many of us all messing about together. Roy [Kane] says he told him to clear off and get a saxophone.' Though Kane remembers Morrison as a thoroughly distinc-tive player, a guitarist remained surplus to their requirements.

Roy Kane: He was playing with the Sputniks, they broke up and he came round to join us. As I remember it, we didn't need or want another guitar player, and then he took up the sax and came round [again] . . . Whenever Van came round and wanted to play guitar, he always played what I always thought was a very funny style of guitar but which I now know to be a blues style. He just had a style that didn't tie in with the sort of stuff that we were doing.

The Thunderbolts had evolved out of the same skiffle scene as the Sputniks, having been formed in much the same way. In Billy McAllen's words, 'We all went to school together, in the same class and everything – George Jones, Roy and myself . . . I was the first one to get a guitar. I used to go to my father's cousin to learn guitar three nights a week, and then I used to bring my guitar down to George Jones's house and teach him things.' Through 'Geordie' Jones, McAllen met up with another

★ The band's name has sometimes been mistakenly recalled as the Thunderbirds.

guitarist, one Bill Dunn, of the Midnight Special experiment. As McAllen remembers those times, 'We all messed about together, play[ing] in the skiffle groups . . . It was all skiffle in those days and then we got electric guitars. Everybody was into the Shadows. I thought I was a young Hank B. Marvin. We played every Shadows tune that came on the charts.' If Morrison remained stuck down his own musical side-street, the Thunderbolts had 'progressed' to the hospital circuit.

Roy Kane: We played at hospital stage productions, which was a variety show. We were the group. There was a girl singer; there was a [guy] singer; there was two guys playing the accordion; there was a magician.

Billy Harrison, frontman for the Gamblers before Morrison made them into Them, remembers how everyone 'used to meet at the City Hall, get on to the bus and head off to whatever hospital, [and give] free shows. There'd be a couple of comedians; a girl I knew and her two friends did a harmony thing, she asked me to play with them – and Van had done that stint as well.'

The boys from Belfast Tech knew that they lacked not only a real singer but a proper PA. As a result, though they acquired a regular gig at the Brookborough Hall, McAllen suggests that 'we used to play instrumentals all night'. What they really needed, aside from a workable sound system, was a sax player who could sing a bit, to share vocals with George Jones as required. Morrison was neither, but willing to show that he could be.

Gil Irvine: He told me he'd conned his way into a showband. He told them he was a saxophone player. His father bought him a saxophone, and he wouldn't come out to play. All you could hear was Van practising the scales. He'd told them that he had to hand [his previous band] a month's notice, which gave him a month to learn how to play saxophone. Saxophone players who played rock & roll music were very rare at that time.

If legend has it that Morrison went away and learned how to play the saxophone after his initial rejection by the Thunderbolts as 'potential second guitarist', Kane is not so convinced it was a question of cause and effect. However, he *is* sure that 'somewhere along the line Van went and learned how to play the saxophone, and it was a different sound [we were playing]. We'd gone from guitar bands like the Shadows into the rockier, American-type bands, where you had saxophone coming in.'

Morrison himself did not connect his learning the saxophone with any specific attempt to join a band when discussing these days with the editor of *Now Dig This* thirty years later. In his mind, it came 'at the time when I got into rock & roll . . . I started studying tenor with a guy called George Cassidy in Belfast, learning to read music . . . I decided I wanted a sax when I heard Giuffre doing "The Train and the River". I couldn't get enough of it after that . . . He's my main influence on saxophone . . . When I joined my first rock & roll band, I was still listening to blues and progressive R&B and jazz. I never saw rock & roll as the whole picture.'

George Jones remembers how Morrison made a difference. The band, pre-Van, derived its repertoire from the likes of Cliff Richard and the Shadows, and Mark Wynter – which dates it to 1960 at the earliest★ – when Morrison came along 'raving about Jerry Lee Lewis, Ray Charles, Chuck Berry. So he turned us towards the great American originals.' Having forced his way into the Thunderbolts, young Ivan was now 'bugged' by the fact that there was certain material his new band felt obliged to perform, no matter what kind of record collection their new sax player brought to the party.

Roy Kane is probably speaking for the others when he says, 'We lived in a different world from Van, or at least I did. I lived in a "what's happening in the music charts [and] movies" world. I don't think [his father's blues collection] meant anything to Geordie or Bill either. 'Cause it wasn't mainstream.' Morrison has admitted to all too real constraints when talking of this period:

Van Morrison: [It was] Johnny Kidd and the Pirates material. Shadows, Cliff Richard, Jerry Lee Lewis – mainly Jerry Lee . . . [but] you couldn't really play the blues then . . . it was very esoteric to do blues at that point. [1986]

But then virtually no one played 'gigs' in the early sixties in Northern Ireland, they played dances, and these dances were strangely orchestrated affairs. Arty McGlynn conveys a flavour of the times:

Arty McGlynn: The church didn't like you playing rock & roll in the parochial hall. Jitterbugging was banned in parochial halls in the late fifties. If you jived, then you had to leave the hall. There were no dances during Lent, so you went

★ Mark Wynter's first hit single, 'Image of a Girl', did not chart until 27 August 1960.

to England. [Or for] six weeks you're on the dole . . . It was [still] a church-ridden place in the fifties.

Phil Coulter, another of Morrison's later musical collaborators, confirms the fact that jiving was 'seen to be in some way . . . decadent', though in some ballrooms, which were less rigid, they 'allowed one jiving session per night: three tunes were played and that was a good session. If you dared to jive any other time, a bouncer tapped you on the shoulder.' There was also no drinking in most dance halls, which remained unlicensed premises, making dancing, flirting and listening to the music your only real options as a paying punter. Such dances were the only gigs going for any serious musician.

In the case of the Thunderbolts, who at various stages went through a full pack in stage names before reverting to their original *nom de plume*, their three regular gigs were at the Brookborough Hall on a Saturday night, at the Harrier's Hall on Port Street and at a place called simply the Hut, on Chamberlain Street – 'all within throwing distance of our homes', to quote Kane. Billy McAllen believes that once 'Van got the saxophone . . . we started to do all local stuff here: parochial halls, Orange halls, church halls, some of the ballrooms in town, [we'd even] travel down the country. We used to do a lot of playing about. In those days you could play anywhere. Funnily enough, all our band were Protestants but we used to go to Catholic places. Nobody really cared in those days.' The only time the boys got to play anything left-field was when they entertained local lads and lasses underneath the arches.

Roy Kane: Where Geordie lived, at the back of his terrace house was a[n old] piggery, and there was an archway. Geordie's bedroom was over that arch, and in that archway it was like a natural cave, where you got the reverberation and echo, and we used to sit in there and play. Geordie's dad had a flatbed lorry, and we used to stand at the back. That was the stage. And all the wee fellows and wee girls from the area used to come round and watch you play. All very innocent. But there was no official playing, we were just playing on [the] back of the van . . . Our whole world lived around Geordie's house, 'cause that's where the music was.

How long the boys remained content to trundle along in this unchallenging way is unclear. There is close to two years between young Ivan leaving school and establishing the Monarchs, the showband that would finally take Morrison and the lads across the water. In the meantime, Morrison was given some grief from his stolidly working-class parents, for whom music was an interest-cum-obsession, but never a career option. One learned a trade if one's (lack of) education precluded acquiring a profession. In Van's case, this meant joining his quietly desperate father at the shipyard or serving an apprenticeship as an engineer at one of the local engineering firms, such as Musgrave & Co. Morrison Junior, though, was already determined to avoid a life spent 'going to the shipyard in the morning light', as those at Musgrave & Co. quickly discovered.

George McDowell: He'd come to us against his will. He was only there because his mother wanted him to be. He never developed any relationship with the boys in the shop because he was like a conscript. He was there on sufferance. [ST]

After equally fleeting employment as a meat cleaner and a chemist's assistant, Morrison ended up sharing a window-cleaning round with a brick shithouse-sized Teddy boy by the name of Sam Woodburn. Dressed in his knee-length drape coat and brothel creepers, and with 'a wild turn in his eye', Woodburn was another extreme character for young Ivan to latch on to, though again the job remained secondary to music – the listening *and* the playing – and, if we are to believe Morrison's memorable account in 1982's 'Cleaning Windows', to reading Jack Kerouac's *On the Road* and *The Dharma Bums* and other esoteric works that evoked a world still some way out of reach.

Meanwhile, the Thunderbolts had begun to do a bit of freelancing, setting up their own dance and pocketing the proceeds. Perhaps this first taste of taking the cash convinced them that a living could be made making music; perhaps it was simply the need to evolve or die that now led the Thunderbolts to reinvent themselves as yet another Irish showband.

Roy Kane: There was [now] Geordie, Billy, Van, myself and Blackie [Wesley Black] on keyboards. We used to hire out the Willoughby Unionist Hall, which was at the bottom of the Woodstock Road . . . and we played at it and took the money. We had a couple of speakers that were screwed on to a piece of flatboard, with a couple of hinges and legs on them. They weren't even speaker boxes . . . Then all of a sudden we turned into this nine-piece showband, and we were rehearsing up at Dougie Knight's [cycle shop].

It was mutually agreed that they would become the Monarchs. If acquiring a three-piece horn section was a statement of intent unto itself, such a large band would now have to pay its way – no more playing under the arches. This move meant a degree of financial freedom – enough to kick the window-cleaning sideline into touch – but it also meant tighter constraints on the repertoire they could play. As Morrison characterized it some years later, 'We used to play in those places where if you didn't play what they wanted to hear, you were lucky to get out alive.'

Though Morrison likes to depict the Monarchs as 'like a pop group with blues infiltration, which nobody was really hip to at that stage of the game', the rest of the guys knew that they were no pop group. Like it or not, they were a showband, a genre seemingly unique to Ireland. Vincent Power is doubtless correct when he states in his authoritative history of showbands, *Send 'Em Home Sweatin'*, that the showband format was originally devised around 1955:

The showband phenomenon in Northern Ireland was invented by the Clipper Carlton. The Strabane band lit the fuse that led to the showband explosion of the sixties by literally putting a show into their stage routine. It was known as Juke Box Saturday Night. While other orchestras merely provided the musical accompaniment for those on the dance floor, the Clippers became the centre of attention. They metamorphosed from musicians to entertainers, wore colourful suits, got rid of the music stands and moved around the stage. The Clippers transformed the dancing ritual simply by being themselves.

Dave Glover, another bandleader, would take credit for the first use of the name 'showband', but whatever its antecedents, by the early sixties the showband scene so totally dominated the Irish music scene that non-showband gigs were few and far between. The big ballrooms would book bands like the Royal, the Dixies, and 'the Clippers' (as the Clipper Carlton were universally known). Even the social clubs looked to book local showbands.

Roy Kane: It was always showband-oriented. The big places to play were the tennis clubs – that's where all the totty was. You had Belmont Tennis Club [nearby]. We [also] used to play the recognized ballrooms. The only places that would have been open on a Sunday would have been Catholic-oriented establishments . . . the Astor Ballroom . . . all the parochial halls . . . [whereas] you used to play the Orange halls on a Friday and Saturday night.

The repertoires of showbands went beyond the eclectic. A recording from 1963 illustrates one well-known showband segueing between Johnny Mercer's 'Fools Rush In', Johnny Cash's 'I Walk the Line' and the Beatles' 'I Wanna Hold Your Hand'. As Brian Hogg suggests, they 'were peculiarly Irish, a tumble of pop tunes and sentimentality, a frantic dance music playing the hits, but in its own honed style of racket mixed in [with] rural sweetness'. They were also a phenomenon, in the true sense of the word – the frontmen of popular showbands were not only extremely well paid but were treated much like pop stars, even though they were rarely encumbered by hit records of their own. The night any popular showband hit town, there would be a line around the lucky ballroom a couple of hours before opening, and a pervasive air of expectancy. As Father Brian D'Arcy told Vincent Powers, 'It's impossible to explain to people today the kind of hysteria generated by the showbands. You see, nothing can compare to it now. Today's generation doesn't know what it was like to live in an era of no communications.'

For Morrison, it was the kind of apprenticeship with which no engineering firm could compete. He learned how to keep rotating songs, as sets changed on an almost weekly basis to take account of new routines, new chart sounds. As he says, the most important lesson he learned was 'never do the same thing twice'. But there was a downside to the showband phenomenon – it was a business run by and for the benefit of businessmen, not the bands. As such, it provided Morrison with his first introduction to the ways of the world, prompting him to later dub a certain kind of shakedown the Drumshanbo Hustle (apparently after an unspecified incident playing with the Monarchs in the town of Drumshanbo).

Arty McGlynn: It was awful music that you had to play. It was a singer- and management-controlled situation, and the musicians had no say whatsoever in anything that was going on. You couldn't ask what you were getting for the night. You were paid a wage, that was it, and if you were a troublemaker you were out – just gone, buried – and the other bands wouldn't touch you 'cause the manager [would say], 'This guy's trouble.' You were isolated. So you just had to shut your mouth [and] work.

Another requirement for membership of the clan was displays of showmanship (hence the derivation), not just from vocalist(s) but from every member of the ensemble. The recalcitrant Morrison was obliged to come out of his shell and give those maternal performing genes rein, something that apparently had to be forced upon him.

George Jones: Van was reluctant to do the showband steps. He did it . . . He would have preferred to leap in the air, do a Jerry Lee Lewis or Chuck Berry's famous guitar walk. Jumping and diving off stage in rock & roll frenzies was Van's kick. He wasn't really one for standing in a uniform symmetrical line, doing steps and singing 'Send Me the Pillow That You Dream on'. I mean, he did it. There was no other outlet. He had to conform and play in the band to earn money to live. He could certainly never be called a classic showband man. He knew from the start that it wasn't what he wanted.

Others, though, relate tales that suggest Morrison took to the odd show-stopping antic like a proverbial duck to the wet stuff. Herbie Armstrong, an aspiring musician at the time, says he caught Morrison and the Monarchs some time in 1961 (more likely 1962), and that Van 'was sitting on the singer's shoulders playing the saxophone . . . He wasn't supposed to be the focus of the group but he's the one I really remembered.' Local musician Harry Baird also remembers an occasion when Morrison sat in with his own showband, the Regents, at a young farmers' dance in Randalstown. The scene Baird paints reminds one not so much of someone ahead of his time as a performer already oblivious of his audience:

Harry Baird: This audience were all farmers, six feet two and built like elephants, with the shit still on their boots. We were booked for a five-hour dance and we were struggling . . . Someone asked Van if he could sing a bit and he said, 'Oh yeah' . . . He was out in front of us, and when he started to sing the whole hall just stopped dancing . . . We were all behind Van wondering what the hell was going on. So I edged round to look at him and his face had gone purple! . . . He was freaking out, going crazy, and the crowd just watched in amazement.

In the Monarchs, extrovert displays tended to be rather more choreographed. In particular, Billy McAllen describes their rendition of 'Daddy Cool' as one where 'we all used to jump on the dance floor. Van jumped on the dance floor with us, and we stood with the guitars behind our heads and our legs open, and Van crawled underneath our legs. He wasn't shy on stage. And Wesley Black would lie on top of the piano, playing upside down.' 'I Go Ape' also provided Morrison with some kind of a cue. Though such a demonstrative performer would still feature in the early Them, he would be quickly discarded when Morrison began to realize some of his commercial dreams, rarely to be resuscitated save for the odd balletic kick on a seventies encore.

Van Morrison: It was a completely different scene then. Things weren't so personal. We had a kind of showband where egos weren't involved, and people weren't getting uptight over small things. I played the guitar, sax, drums: we all swapped instruments and had a good time. But in no way was it my scene up front. I was riding on the side. [1972]

In the years before the Beatles, any commercial concerns extended to keeping punters happy and playing enough gigs to avoid the onset of responsibility. Morrison put it succinctly enough in a 1991 interview: 'I was too young to know whether it was saying something, or not saying something. It was enough to do it.' And again, in 1993: 'The original idea . . . was just to get out of your working-class environment and make a living out of playing music . . . that simple.' And yet, it would be fair to say that during 1962 and the winter of 1963 the Monarchs slowly upped the ante, encroaching on the locals' affections, whilst also venturing as far as Carrickfergus Town Hall or the Calypso in Lurgan. Their favourite watering-hole, though, was Thompson's Restaurant on Belfast's Arthur Street, where they were allowed to display some real R&B roots. But 'making it', actually 'making it', was never an option, at least not without risking the odd fatality. Forty years further down the line, at a concert in Swindon, Morrison attempted to encapsulate those days:

There was Lead Belly. There was skiffle. There was show bands. There was rock & roll. There was rhythm & blues. There was soul. There was jazz – trad, mainstream, modern. And there was funk. There was folk. There was funny. And there was ha-ha. And then if you almost killed yourself, you might [just] make it.

Things, though, were beginning to happen across the Irish Sea. By the spring of 1963, bands who had formed in Liverpool with no greater ambition than the Monarchs – and less of a musical education – were riding high in the charts, writing their own songs and reinventing the efforts of Willie Alexander, Chuck Berry, Carl Perkins, Lead Belly, Willie Dixon and Leiber–Stoller. For these Belfast boys, though, the water was wide, and there seemed no obvious way to cross over.

4

1963–64: Leaving Ireland

When I started out playing in groups, I had Bo Diddley records when nobody knew who Bo Diddley was. That was around 1960. I used to play these records to people and they just couldn't figure them out. I used to play musicians records by Bo Diddley and Muddy Waters and they just didn't know how to react to them. And then three years later, some English group would record one of the songs and these same people would come along and say to me, 'Wow, did you hear that?'

—*Van Morrison, 1974*

The fact that George Ivan Morrison was fully acquainted with the kind of music the Beatles and the Stones were about to transmogrify long before these English boys could spell rhythm – let alone play with it – may not be a great bone of contention. On the other hand, Morrison and his fellow Monarch George Jones have through the years reinvented the Monarchs as some kind of pioneers of R&B, in the face of a mountain of evidence to the contrary.

Van Morrison: People didn't really know what rhythm & blues was until . . . groups like the Beatles did 'Twist and Shout' . . . Then all of a sudden everybody started to cop on. But we were playing [it] long before that and everybody was saying 'What is it? We can't relate to that kind of music.' [1972]

In truth, the Monarchs took few chances during the time they spent playing in and around Belfast. Only when they made the crucial decision to move to the mainland and 'get serious' did they attempt to reinvent themselves in a more R&B guise. And that reinvention came in response to circumstance, not as a precursor to opportunity. By the spring of 1963, the first waves of Beatlemania were crashing against the shores of Ireland, and for the first time the showbands' monopoly seemed under threat.

The Monarchs may not have been natural risk-takers, but by 1963 they were certainly looking for a way to transcend the Irish music scene, which remained deeply parochial. As George Jones puts it, 'our main aim was to get away from the Irish showband scene'. For him, it was simply a case of the guys in the band 'suddenly realiz[ing] Van was [equipped] with a great wealth of knowledge, after listening to his father's records day after day after day. We [also] decided that the Irish pop scene wasn't for us. We'd trimmed down, got rid of a lot of members.' Billy McAllen disputes the suddenness of the change:

Billy McAllen: Even in the Monarchs, I used to go round to Van's house practically every day [and] we sat and listened to records and got the guitars out and messed about. He'd say to me, 'Listen to this here.' That's where I first heard it all, in Van's house. All we really heard [elsewhere] was the pop stuff. [But] most of the groups in those days, you had to play the popular music. If you were to go to some of those gigs in town in those days and play a lot of blues stuff, they'd have booed you off. They wanted to hear whatever was popular at the time.

For most of the Monarchs it was getting off this rock, rather than some high-minded desire to play R&B, that first enticed them to cross the high sea to bonny Scotland. The way McAllen remembers it, the Monarchs were playing one night in Portadown 'and these two Scottish guys, who were members of a Scottish band, had this guy with them who was supposed to be their manager, and they thought our band was great, and this manager guy said to us, "Would you ever fancy coming over to Scotland? I could get you plenty of work over there."'

Simple enough. Jones still applies an R&B spin, suggesting that the 'two Glasgow guys . . . were very much under the influence of Alex Harvey's soul band . . . portraying what we loved, which was [that] Ray Charles[-style] soul music. We just went [there] on this premiss that these two Scottish guys were gonna lead us into a different world.' Scotland was certainly that, and the vagueness of the offer failed to dissuade the Monarchs from forsaking their long-time drummer, their Irish roots and the security of familiar roofs and indulgent parents on the word of a strange Scotsman. But then, there was doubtless a realization that it was now or never.

George Jones: [Our parents] were hesitant, but they knew how dedicated we were. They watched us night after night out the backyard, [rehearsing] in the furniture van. They'd seen us go through the transitions of showbands, big bands, different names, till we finally said, 'This is what we want to do.' In the end, we won them over . . . Van was sixteen and a half, and I was seventeen.* We found a guy called Harry ['Mac' Megahey], who was not a singer of sorts but was a good baritone [sax] player, who knitted in well with Van. Roy [Kane] didn't actually go to Scotland. He stuck by his job. Hence we had the two Glasgow lads – one of whom was a drummer, Laurie McQueen, the other guy was a straight soul singer. Van primarily played sax. But Scotland seemed the closest landmass to get off Ireland – to us it was international. To travel even to Scotland was a real big deal. But this guy, Frank Cunningham, convinced us. [He] said, 'I've got you eight or nine weeks' work. Get over here. Get settled in.' So we all packed our jobs in on this guy's word. We arrived in Pollok in Glasgow and he had a weekend['s worth of work].

Only a refusal to admit their folly to parents stopped the Ulster lads from taking the first ferry out of Stranraer. The situation in Pollok was verging on third-world. Jones recalls how they were living 'in [t]his council house in Pollok, five of us. Plus [Cunningham and] his four or five kids, his wife and his mother-in-law. It was horrendous. We played out in the garden.' A contemporary piece in a local Glasgow paper, entitled 'Pollok's garden jam session', confirms the fact that 'several of the septet . . . have been staying with their manager, Mr Frank Cunningham . . . before starting a tour of Scotland on Thursday. And his large corner garden . . . make[s] the open air a natural rehearsal spot.' The article presciently suggests that 'after touring Scotland, the boys move to England, and sometime in August they hope to tour Germany'. This was precisely the way things panned out, save that they promptly ditched manager Frank.

George Jones: We started making our own way, menial gigs, just eating money, [but] worked our way right round the top of Scotland. It [became] a

---

* Jones is a year out. Morrison celebrated his eighteenth birthday whilst the Monarchs were in Germany.

hilarious adventure. It could have been two months, three months or four months . . . We were battling against the cultural elements – we stuck faithfully to our stuff, and some places we did click, but if we got a church hall somewhere it was disastrous. They were shouting out for Jimmy Shand tunes . . . [So] one night in the Beach Ballroom in Aberdeen, we said, 'Look, we're going round in circles here. We gotta go to London. If we go to London, we'll make it.' That was our naïvety . . . So we pooled all our money together and . . . we headed for London. We hadn't a clue.

The weeks of scuffling around London have subsequently taken on a life of their own, each event acquiring new dramatic resonances with every passing year. The night they accidentally parked in the House of Lords car-park has come to conclude with Morrison, who had been sleeping under the van in his socks and shorts, having to scrabble after their minibus as it receded into the early morning fog. Likewise, by the time Morrison got to tell *Rolling Stone* about the audition that would finally spirit the (now International) Monarchs across the Channel, the boys had apparently turned into a gang of Cockney 'tea leaves': 'We played about six numbers, and the cat comes up and says, "You're really fantastic, one of the best things that I've ever seen or heard in my whole career managing this club, but there's just one thing wrong. You're a scruffy pack of bastards, and if you get some suits you get the job." So we went off and ripped off about seven suits.' In fact, all the boys' suits needed was a quick dry-clean to remove a thin layer of dust from the low road, a procedure financed by an old friend from Scotland, who bailed them out and steered them right.

George Jones: We're just wandering around the West End aimlessly. We're now down to starving level, living on tins of drinking chocolate. [But] we were really hesitant about declaring defeat and ringing home for money, and out of the blue we passed a guy and I said, 'I know that guy.' It was [someone] that we had backed in Scotland, a one-hit wonder called Don Charles, and he said, 'What are you guys doing here?' I just said, 'Well, we're starving.' Told him the story. He said, 'I'll help you out. No problem.' He took us round [to] the Wimpy [hamburger] Bar [and fed us] . . . took all our suits out of the wagon, took [them] into a one-hour cleaner, got them all cleaned and then we went to Hyde Park and hung from trees, while [a photographer] did publicity shots. He took them round to his agent [Ruby Bard], who turned out to be the agent of the Temperance Seven, Kenny Ball's Jazzmen and Georgie Fame, who was playing the Flamingo Jazz Club in Wardour Street. She liked the [band] and said, 'Would you do an audition?' It was in the Flamingo Club – that was Van's first encounter with Georgie Fame – and she signed us up. She got us two or three gigs at US airbases. We gradually got some spending money and then she asked us to go to an audition for [some] German clubs . . . there was about three thousand bands – but we finished up getting a gig.

It was August 1963, and they were indeed going to Germany – along with just about every aspiring British beat combo. As Morrison recently observed, 'Now you have to go to America. In those days you had to go to Germany. That's the way everybody was doing it. They had these auditions where they just ran bands through, twenty bands in one day, and decided ten of them are going and ten aren't.' The German adventure began well.

Billy McAllen: We were supposed to be signed up for one month in Heidelberg, one month Frankfurt and one month Cologne. The first month we played in Heidelberg we went down a storm. So the guy that owned the club asked us if we'd stay on for another month.

After a little schedule-shuffling by their agent, Ruby Bard, the Monarchs ended up staying a second month in Heidelberg, which meant that they only got a fortnight in Frankfurt and a fortnight in Cologne. It was to prove an important part of the learning curve. Bard concurs: 'It was good experience for any young group to play Germany at that time. They had to develop their set in order to survive.' And develop their set they did, whilst learning about life, the universe and everything.

George Jones: It was the first English-speaking band ever to go into the German clubs in Heidelberg . . . most of the British bands were going up north . . . We did our thing. It was lucky that we *did* go to the south, because we wouldn't have been ready for the north . . . But it was hard work. It was eight at night till three in the morning, seven nights a week, and a Sunday matinée, which was primarily for the young Germans. The rest of the time was for American GIs and prostitutes and drunken Germans. The fights we witnessed at our age – knives and everything! It [became] the background music to these brawls. And we became men very rapidly . . . The Americans were stationed in Mannheim, but they all drifted into Heidelberg. So the American influence wasn't very evident during the day, apart from the stores, but at night all the

GIs walked about. This was heaven, especially for Van. He'd never seen coloured guys in Northern Ireland.

Morrison wrote his own snapshot account of these days in his journal, later incorporating a snippet into the *Reliable Sources* press kit, which helps convey a flavour of the times: 'Heidelberg. Tram lines. The Odeon Keller, lots of good beer. My one and only movie scene. The Bahnhof. Mark Twain Village. The hotel brawl. Bratwurst. American cigarettes. Soldiers. And the music fills the room as I'm writing. Miles Davis music. Big Ricky. Cognac. My surprise birthday party. Seven sets a night. Seven nights a week. Matinées Saturday and Sunday. The eagle flies on Friday. An apprenticeship they call it, paying dues. That's what it's called.' It was the GIs who held the greatest fascination for Morrison. Indeed he soon learned that if he went up to the actual army base, there were not only all these great records to hear, but other perks as well.

Billy McAllen: In those days the GIs would come into the club[s] looking for all the German girls. Well, all the German guys hated the Yanks because of this, and [so] fights used to start [all the time]. Next thing, all the American MPs [would be] running in with their batons. We just kept playing away! . . . We were earning money but you kind of just blew the lot, enjoying yourself . . . We used to go up to the [American] camps, and they used to let us hear all these records. Van was always into that stuff . . . We used to love going up to the camps, because you got great grub and you got free drink and you used to get cartons of cigarettes dead cheap.

According to Morrison, there was one specific soldier who helped open the door for him. Talking in 1998, he spoke of a GI named Lee 'play[ing] guitar and singing with us one night. He did "Stormy Monday". And he had this record player in the hotel and he played all this Bobby Bland stuff. I don't like talking in biblical terms but it was like a real eye-opener. I really wanted to do songs like these.' The implication here is that, despite those home courses in American sounds, he wasn't doing this kind of material until the moment he was shown how to do it right. George Jones told biographer Johnny Rogan that Germany 'was where Van became the basis of what he is today. For the first time in his life he met American coloured GIs who dug soul, blues and all the music that he was weaned on. Van drifted away every day to get near coloured guys . . . [and] he suddenly became a big influence on the Monarchs.'

Again, this sudden transformation. Again, not the way his fellow Monarchs remember it. Not even Morrison:

Van Morrison: We had this piano player [Wesley Black], who was into Jerry Lee. So he used to come and listen to my Jerry Lee singles, and we'd gradually try to introduce them, and then Ray Charles. Bit by bit it was becoming more of an R&B band. [1994]

If Morrison, Jones and Black saw Heidelberg as a haven of R&B, somewhere they could learn their trade and wail, the other members of the Monarchs were more concerned with booze and birds. The Scottish duo who had first led them astray that spring had always been one step removed from the Irish contingent in the band, but in hedonistic Heidelberg they began to become seriously disruptive. As McAllen remembers it, 'The two Scottish guys started to hit the drink so hard that we had no control over them. The big drummer fella, he started fighting with people. [And] he was like a six-foot-two docker from Glasgow.' The Belfast boys decided to summon Roy Kane from his safe Belfast home, thus restoring the original Monarchs line-up (augmented by Harry Mac). Not only was Kane a solid, dependable drummer, he was also a big lad who knew how to handle himself – not that Jones pointed out the possible need for additional muscle when phoning Kane to tell him about life in the palace of sin.

Roy Kane: I was happy enough working away in the Co-op in York Street until I got this phone call, telling me how wonderful it was [in Germany]. And then to go out there and find they wanted me out there 'cause they needed a drummer/singer . . . [But there was no] time to rehearse . . . I just packed the job in and went out [there]. That was about September 1963* . . . You're talking about an eighteen-year-old fellow who had lived in a pretty straight [part of] Belfast, and I'm walking down the steps into this cellar club and here's this bar with a shelf built in behind it, and these birds in bikinis serving drinks to these guys. We more or less walked straight on the stage and started playing . . . It was [mostly] trying to keep the band sober enough to go on stage. There was an awful lot of tension in the band because of the two Scottish guys – they had left the band but they hadn't left the immediate area, [and] they had caused a lot of fights.

* Roy Kane's passport is stamped 25 September 1963, providing a definite date for when he left Britain.

Kane was not greatly impressed by the reality that lay behind Jones's hard sell. Not only had the band already worked their way through most of their wages, but they had been required to move out of the club accommodation and were having to fend for themselves.

Roy Kane: I don't know what debt or danger they'd got themselves into, but I know there was hardly ever any money going about. There was no such thing as pay-day. Harry Mac, the baritone sax player, was the paymaster, and he used to dole you out so much if you needed something to eat . . . The people that owned [the club] owned flats, and all the staff that worked in these places all stayed in the flats. The boys, when they first went out, used to stay there but they were thrown out because they got friendly with too many of the girls.

Such hardships failed to faze the others, who had become acclimatized to life on the road by their months in Scotland and London, but Kane sensed he had made a big mistake. Having arrived with less than a month left of their Heidelberg residency, he was doubtless hoping that money and accommodation might be more forthcoming at the next place they were scheduled to lay their hats.

Billy McAllen: We had to pack all the gear up, carry it up the stairs, set it out on the footpath, all the speakers, amplifiers, guitars, everything, then [we'd] call for two or three taxis to take us down to the train station. We went from Heidelberg straight to Cologne. We got all the gear off the train, ordered more taxis, went down to the club. There was nobody about. We got all the gear on the stage, we got it all set up and started to rehearse, and this guy comes in, the manager: 'What you do here?' We say, 'We're the Monarchs. We're playing here.' The guy says, 'No, no, no. You don't play here. You are in Frankfurt.' Same club, the Storyville Club, but we should have gone to Frankfurt. So we had to pack all the gear, down to the train, same thing again.

Kane's mood hardly improved when 'all of a sudden [the landlord] starts discovering broken things and burns in the carpet when [we] were leaving the digs we were staying in . . . and then the money [we] were going to get at the end of the month for playing was halved to pay for all these fictitious "damages" . . . We were totally ripped off, tired, played out, fed up, [and we] wanted to get home.' The mood of the other guys also began to slide, as they found their Heidelberg set was not going

down quite so well in Frankfurt. Or Cologne, where the Mersey Sound
had become all-pervasive.

Morrison had already encountered the first aftershock of the Britpop
explosion in Heidelberg, 'just as we started to kick off on the R&B
thing'. As he was about to launch into the fourth number of their set
one night, he was approached by an American GI, who wondered aloud,
'You guys ever heard of Dave Clark?'

As it happens, the couple of months when the Monarchs had been
playing Heidelberg coincided with that brief moment when Britpop was
an entirely European phenomenon. The Americans had yet to experience
Beatlemania and, as Roy Kane recalls, the Americans 'had been letting
[us] hear all the American records, which the likes of the Beatles were
all doing copies of. So our guys were tending to do these American
versions of [the] records. And then when we moved up to Cologne,
which was the British section, everybody was wanting to hear the Mersey
Sound – which was the songs we were doing, but with a different feel
to them.' The set-list required another overhaul, just as the band had
acquired something of a licence to experiment.

George Jones: We went up to Frankfurt, which was still German, but very
much touched by the British element. It was mainly young Germans that were
going to the nightclub we [played at], the Storyville Jazz Club, and they were
being influenced by the Beatles, and we had to change our complete programme.
We had to play the Fourmost, the Beatles and Johnny Kidd and the Pirates.
They were playing the stuff that we were doing from the originals. We had to
adapt ours to make it sound British, 'cause it was all pop stuff. Kids were coming
up and saying, 'You must play zis. Zis is very good, zis is the Beatles.' 'Yes, we
play that tune.' 'No, but you must do it the Beatles way.' Instead of the Isley
Brothers. So it was a complete trauma, and then we moved on up into Cologne,
which was even worse. It was right smack bang in the British sector, so we had
no escape at all. The Cavern bands all headed to Hamburg, but we were sort of
cutting our way through Germany. By the time we got to Cologne we were
just playing for money. We had suddenly come complete circle, back to the
[British] pop scene.

The relentless nature of the gigging was also beginning to wear the
boys down. Inevitably some of them began to pop pills, just to keep
going. These were readily available in the bars of Cologne, and it was
either that or slump down, worn out and wasted, half-way through a set.

Billy McAllen recalls the endless grind: 'We were playing from eight at night to three in the morning – you got a ten-minute break every hour – but then you had to do a matinée on Saturday and Sunday, four to six or three to five, and then you started at eight again. When we went to Cologne, these RAF guys used to give us Bennies. But some of the places out there, the boys were on real hard drugs.' Occasionally the grind would become too much, and the Monarchs would metamorphose into a precursor of both the Velvet Underground and the Grateful Dead:

George Jones: We did a lot of things to pass the time, the boredom of playing every night. We gagged about, leapt all over the place. We'd start an instrumental that might last for fifteen minutes and maybe call it 'The Green Head', and the guitar player'd take his guitar off and leave it on the floor and let it feedback on its own, [then] pull the guitar towards him. [What with] the fatigue, the boredom, you really find out if you love your music.

The extent to which the Monarchs had to put their principles on hold was demonstrated one night when they were offered the opportunity to make a record. A gay German producer named Ron Kovacs had taken a shine to one of the guys – George Jones – and wished to make him a star, a process apparently achievable by recording an appalling single he had written. As Morrison later put it, 'We needed the session money; you do when you're drinking your pay every night.' The quality of the songs in question is betrayed by their titles, 'Twingy Baby' and 'Boozoo Hully Gully'. As Roy Kane ventures to suggest, 'There was nothing there at all, but we put a real right-up-your-arse track down behind it, [a] good beat-boogie instrumental.' The boys did the best that they could in the circumstances (they must have done something right because the damn thing actually charted in Germany).

George Jones: The two songs were absolute crap . . . we tried to jizz up what there was, we tried to boogie-woogie it. If you notice, [the A-side] is very 'What'd I Say' – that's all we could put to it. So we [were] laugh[ing] at [the whole thing], but he paid the guys all £50 each, which was an amazing amount for the session.

The £50-per-head session fee was just what the band needed – to get out of Germany and re-evaluate the whole basis of the band. George Jones now admits, 'We were all fairly demoralized. We hadn't been home for ages. The last thing you're thinking about is Northern Ireland. But we'd grown up. We told Ruby Bard we were taking some time out. We came home by train, and picked up the minibus where we'd left it at Dover, and then we drove up to Liverpool and caught the boat back to Belfast. I got a bit fed up with starving, so I joined an Irish showband.'

Roy Kane also decided enough was enough, and called in at the Co-op to see if his old job was still going. George Jones remembers that 'Van and Billy and Harry Mac and Blackie went back to London, and goofed around for a while.' In fact, for a couple of months they were operating as a four-piece, playing around Britain, awaiting a time when the pop world might really open up. Eventually, though, they too felt the call of home.

Billy McAllen: We were based for a while in Shepherd's Bush. It was like a big hostel place this couple owned, but they used to have a big basement and we used to rehearse there. [We] just treated it like a job – maybe start rehearsing at ten o'clock in the morning. Come one o'clock, switched everything off, round the corner to one of the local cafés, had our lunch, back round again, rehearse for another couple of hours. And then we used to do some of the American airbases up and down England. [It was] Van, myself, George Jones [*sic*], Harry Mac, Wesley Black. We actually travelled from London, Glasgow, playing round Glasgow, down to London, back to Glasgow, inside a fortnight, up and down, up and down, up and down . . . We stayed there for a good while, and I think we were all getting a bit cheesed off. I decided I was going to come home, and then we all ended up [back] home.

The Monarchs had finally run its course. Given that they had crammed a number of years' experience into the nine months they'd been away, it is not surprising that the various band members now remember these experiences in a montage of desperate-then, hilarious-now flashbacks. The whole adventure had proved both salutary and life-enhancing, serving in the years to come as a reminder of some real roots, and keeping one member grounded when all around were trying to elevate him.

Van Morrison: Put yourself through working the clubs in Germany, on up to when the R&B movement thing was happening in the sixties; put yourself through being in a situation where you're supposed to be a somebody. The thing that has carried me through is the time I put in when I was a nobody. [1978]

The bond that the boys formed was one destined to last a lifetime. Sporadic as Morrison's contact with the other Monarchs was destined to become, clearly a part of him longs for that time when, in George Jones's words, 'you were giving your life for music. We were dirty together. We shared a sink down in the municipal toilets. It was like soul mates. And through it all, the music reigned supreme. I will always see in Van now, what there was then . . . We broadened our outlook in Germany. We were educated in a form . . . that we were able to bring back to Northern Ireland. The only religion we had was music. [Even] eating was a sideline.' In the first flush of later successes, Jones would get a call every now and then from a homesick Morrison in California, longing to talk about the old times, and he would hear Van saying, 'That was the real music. That was the real time. When it was raw, and we were learning it.'

Asking today for a profile of the eighteen-year-old Van Morrison from his fellow Monarchs prompts a series of subtly distinct portraits of an observer of others' scrapes. Billy McAllen insists that he 'always felt [Van] was a bit different. He always had that bit extra in his music, the feel he had for it,' whilst the Morrison that Jones prefers to describe 'was deep – most of us didn't know what he was talking about . . . [But] we accepted him the way he was . . . He learned comradeship and how to fit in with a band. This was important. Van was known as a loner: a quiet, retiring guy who kept to himself . . . [but] he was accepted as one of the guys in the Javelins and Thunderbolts. He fitted in. Other people hadn't given him the chance to fit in.' Roy Kane is less sure. It was not just that the other guys in the band had all gone to school together, grown up together, chased girls together – though that was certainly part of it. For him, there always remained something of the outsider in his erstwhile buddy.

For Morrison, it was a time and place when he could believe that he belonged to some common cause, implicit in everything they did. Though the Monarchs fulfilled a role his family no longer could, they too had to be discarded as it became clear that the others' ambitions failed to match his own. The fact that Morrison, McAllen and Co. returned to an Irish music scene that remained in a form of cryogenic storage must have been doubly depressing. The contrast with a London bursting at the seams with possibilities only fed the compulsion to get back there.

Billy McAllen, for one, did not waste any time securing another showband gig in Belfast. The Manhattan Showband may not have been the Monarchs, but they seemed open to suggestions. When they said they were seeking to augment their sound with a brass section, McAllen offered to introduce them to a great sax player. If Morrison was grateful for the gig, he wasn't about to admit it. It was presumably he who then suggested his old friend, Geordie Sproule; whilst McAllen brought in another old buddy, Herbie Armstrong, from the fast-fading Twilights. Armstrong found himself one of those invited over to Hyndford Street to hear the kind of music you didn't hear showbands play: 'He would stick on all these records that I had never heard before. The first time I ever heard Bo Diddley . . . was at his house.'

Billy McAllen: That was the start of the Manhattan Showband. We used to go over to London once a month with the Manhattan . . . it was [always] the same Irish club we used to go to, in Camden Town, and they had digs above the club for the bands, and a big kitchen, and they used to fill the fridge every day. Irish clubs, [though,] you couldn't play a lot of the blues. It was just the popular music of that day. They were wanting all this stuff like the hucklebuck – dance music that the showbands were playing here. So they were expecting us, being a showband from here, to play all that crap when we went over there. We didn't particularly like it, but you got a few pounds by playing it. If it was popular, we played it.

At least they got to return to London, and there were nights off, grub in the larder, and places to go and hear 'real' music. Camden Town itself had a number of clubs – but it was in Great Newport Street that Morrison's next epiphany occurred, in the company of Herbie Armstrong and a not-so-impressed Geordie Sproule.

Geordie Sproule: Me and Van were with a band in Hatton [Garden] in London . . . we were in the Regency Rooms, playing with the Manhattan Showband . . . and we went to [Studio 51] . . . We went in, and Van was watching the group but I didn't think they were worth tuppence . . . I think it was the format, and what they were doing. [They] sounded to me like a poor man's Rolling Stones.

The band in question was the Downliners Sect. What really impressed Morrison about the Sect was the simple fact that 'they were doing it then; really *doing* it . . . There were suddenly lots of R&B groups around that came out of the woodwork, that just got into that [sound] when they discovered it could be done. Nobody thought it could be done before that.' Sproule's assessment of the Sect as 'a poor man's Rolling Stones' may more accurately mirror history's view, but the third man there shared the man's excitement, if not the epiphany:

Herbie Armstrong: I think Van had had the idea of forming an R&B group before that night, but when he saw the Downliners Sect he said, 'That's it, that's the sort of group I want to have.' . . . We were both drinking cider and leaping up and down on these army-style beds, when he told me he'd written a song. It was called 'Could You Would You'. [ST]

This is the first independent reference to Morrison writing his own songs. Sproule thinks it still sounds a little early. He insists, 'I never saw Van writing at all.' In fact, he remembers one occasion when he was writing 'a wee song' himself and Morrison asked him, 'What are you doing?' However, Morrison himself dates the first time he performed one of his songs to his time with the Monarchs in Germany; when Harry Mac said, 'Let's do one of your songs.' Only then did it apparently '[for] the first time . . . enter my brain'.

The significance to Morrison of that evening at Studio '51, though, did not stem from any notion of performing original material. The Sect at this stage were strictly a covers band. Rather, after 'visiting this club a couple of times', he felt that he 'want[ed] to open an R&B club. That was . . . the extent of [my] ambition.' In order to fulfil this ambition, though, he would have to give up making ends meet in the Manhattan Showband and, more crucially, persuade other musicians likewise to surrender the security of the showband circuit. Mr Morrison himself would provide, at no extra charge, a wing and a prayer.

AGE TWO

The Story Of Them

5

1964: Good Times

Practice and opportunity very soon teach the language of art . . . Spirit and poetry, centred in the imagination alone, can never be taught; and these make the artist.

—*William Blake*

[The Maritime] was incredible. Sometimes, when it worked, something would happen, and the audience and the musicians would be as one.

—*Van Morrison, 1970*

We were nutters on stage. We did whatever we felt like doing. There was no routine . . . When it came to the end of the night you didn't really want to stop. It was an unbelievable period.

—*Billy Harrison*

Print the legend. The truth is one curdled mess of memories. At least it is when it comes to events in the spring of 1964 in Belfast city centre, a band called simply Them, a trio of young promoters known as the Three Js, and an ex-seamen's mission by the name of the Maritime Hotel. The speed with which everything happened – from rehearsal room to record contract inside three months – may account for much of the blur, but let us not discount self-aggrandizement, much of it from a man who seems to begrudge anyone else a significant role in his rise, George Ivan Morrison.

The Van Morrison version of events has undergone its own meta-morphosis since that spring afternoon in 1965 when he penned the elegiac 'The Story of Them'. A seven-minute depiction of 'good times', conjuring up a world barely tasted before it was snatched away, the song relays how 'with the help of the Three Js/[we] started playing the Maritime'. By the early nineties, though, Morrison was telling interviewers, 'After Germany I went back to Belfast and opened an R&B club at the Maritime Hotel.' This from someone who, by his own admission, 'can't even remember last week', successfully removes a number of characters from those 'good times'.

After Germany, as we know, Morrison returned first to London, where he discovered that all the music he had been listening to at home, but could barely get any fellow musos to play, was now filling the clubs and pubs. He had been beaten to the punch by a bunch of Richmond renegades, tacking a Bo Diddley beat on to that Buddy Holly bop. 'Not Fade Away' – no way. That the Rolling Stones had cracked it, in a way that fellow progenitors like the Pretty Things and the Downliners Sect never would, was a turn of events Morrison would continue to resent on their behalf.

Van Morrison: I was doing what I was doing when the Rolling Stones were still in school . . . maybe three years before they got together . . . I was doing that years before it became popular, but nobody saw it. They just saw it when they wanted to see it – and when somebody told them to dig it. [1973]

Violet Morrison would later tell a San José DJ that Jagger actually 'spent an inordinate amount of time listening to Them in the early English pub days and . . . [then] usurped Van's style'. In fact, the one person worried about the competition at this point was her only son, whose formative attempts to pen R&B-fuelled diatribes on occasions mimicked those of Jagger–Richards. Thus, on the first Them album, 'You Just Can't Win' danced around the Stones' own 'Play with Fire'. (The world that Morrison's imaginary princess attains in this song – 'You're up in Park Lane now/And I'm somewhere around Tottenham Court Road' – so close at hand, yet out of reach, perhaps unconsciously mirrored the equally compact geography of East Belfast, with Park Lane as its Cyprus Avenue.)

The key difference between the Stones' 'Play with Fire' and Morrison's 'You Just Can't Win', as Brian Hogg astutely observes, is that 'where[as] Jagger warns, asserting his still-felt superiority and daring her condescension, Van is bitter, scornful, spitting out the early low-life, sneering at the changes'. Here was a man unimpressed by the wonders of West End life, who couldn't wait to get back home.

Back in Belfast, Morrison's main problem was that he had no one on whom, by sheer force of personality, he could impose his vision. Returning to the familiar streets of East Belfast, he initially tried to enlist his fellow Monarchs. According to George Jones, 'Van reappeared in Belfast, saying we had to grow our hair long like the Rolling Stones, the Yardbirds, all the London bands. He reckoned you had to walk around looking way out. We said we weren't interested, we had a living to earn.' When he struck out with his cohorts from Germany, he turned to Herbie Armstrong, who had shared that experience at Studio '51. Unfortunately Armstrong was as reluctant as Jones and Co. to live on a wing and a prayer in the land of showbands. It seemed as if Morrison's grand scheme was fatally impaired at the outset.

Van Morrison: It started out that we were trying to establish an R&B club in Belfast . . . [but] by the time I decided to do it . . . the original people changed, because they were working in other bands and all of a sudden they didn't think it was such a good idea . . . By the time the thing got off the ground, it was sort of half of what it was supposed to be. [1986]

Actually, Morrison was surprisingly easily persuaded to abandon his plan. Rather than turning on Armstrong for rejecting his overtures, he found himself jammed in a phone box, whispering to Herbie, who was trying to set up an audition as guitarist for the Brian Rossi Orchestra, instructing him to 'Tell him I play saxophone.' So much for his expressed determination to break out of that showband straitjacket! Morrison duly auditioned for Brian Rossi and returned to the fold. At least he was now getting to play some harmonica and sing a couple of numbers – 'I was doing R&B numbers like Ray Charles – "Sticks and Stones" or "What'd I Say" or some slow R&B songs; and I was sticking some tenor [sax] solos in as well' – and earning a wage. All the while, though, he continued to nag his friends to share in his dream.

It was mostly with Geordie Sproule, an older, wilder Belfast cowboy, that he spent his downtime. And down is what he was. Sproule remembers, 'He was [always] knocking about at Crymbles [Music Shop] . . . He was trying to get his feet in the music business . . . He was very quiet. He just liked my company. People say that I influenced him, but I can't really see it. [But maybe] the way I used to get [it] on to get noticed,

Van picked up from me . . . I [also] used to make the songs up as I went along. I could stand on stage and make a song up.' Morrison, though, still needed a stage on which he could 'get it on'. The bridge to that stage was Crymbles, the music shop at which every would-be and wannabe muso hung out on a Saturday, messing with the equipment until they could raise a deposit for the next never-never purchase.

At this stage Morrison was no exception, his later claim that he 'ended up [forming a band] with other people that I didn't actually know' belied by the whole *raison d'être* of a place like Crymbles. There were no musicians in the cloistered confines of Belfast who didn't know every other semi-pro muso. The scene at Crymbles was such that everyone got to check out and be checked out; and the band he eventually *joined* was an already established entity. Indeed, according to those with good reason to remember, it was the members of this band who approached him, *with a view to making the band more R&B-oriented.*

All the time the Monarchs had spent cutting their teeth in Germany, the Gamblers had remained a semi-pro, sub-showband substitute for the real thing. Fronted by Billy Harrison on guitar and vocals, augmented by an occasional second rhythm guitarist, but with Ronnie Millings and Alan Henderson always occupying the drum and bass slots, the Gamblers remained mere chancers until the Britpop explosion, when Harrison realized that they might be setting their sights a tad low.

Billy Harrison: Ronnie and I knew each other from working in the dairies. I had played in and out of different bands and showbands, [some] Irish music, the whole bit. Ronnie had a wee group, Three Stars or something, [with] another guy on guitar and Alan [Henderson]; and Ronnie asked me to come and hear them and tell him what I thought of them . . . It was the British Legion Club, next to Dobson's dairies. Afterwards Ronnie asked, 'What do you think?' . . . I said, 'Give your guitarist the push and I'll play with you.' We all lived five minutes' walk from each other, and I used to get Alan down to my house and teach him what I could with the bass. This was all fifties rock & roll and some popular gear, a lot of Chuck Berry, but we had no definition of ourselves . . . Showbands were the big thing in Ireland – north and south. They had it sewn up for the bread. There were very few groups about – [maybe] the Stratotones – but I always liked the American rock & roll thing, Chuck Berry, Eddie Cochran . . . We were doing gigs, but we weren't getting big money. [Then] I remember playing Portadown Town Hall one night and it was that Dave Clark Five thing out at the time – 'Glad All Over' – and 'Twist and Shout' as well.

You could have played the one number all night. That's what they wanted to hear.

Offered a chance to change, Harrison was anxious not to let this opportunity slide. He decided 'to model the group on Johnny and the Hurricanes. [We] didn't want two guitars in the group any more, we wanted keyboards. That's where Eric Wrixon came in.' Wrixon, a cousin of the Monarchs' Billy McAllen, was another regular at Crymbles.

Eric Wrixon: A guy called Denver, [who was] a rhythm guitarist and singer, had just left [the Gamblers]. They were doing all [this] Carl Perkins, Chuck Berry, some Bo Diddley. I was [only] there two or three weeks before Van joined. They had decided to give up this other thing of backing mainstream artists and form an R&B/rockin' type of band. Everything happened in Crymbles Music Shop. I met Billy [there]. It was a big social club on Saturday mornings. We were rehearsing in Dougie Knight's [bicycle shop] and then, a couple of weeks after, Van appeared . . . [But] all the rehearsals without Van were as an R&B band – one of the reasons they had me in the band was [because] I could play harmonica as well as piano.

As to what the Gamblers had been dealing themselves in their first few weeks as a quartet, Harrison recalls, 'We were playing more rhythm & blues, the Chuck Berry idiom [but still] leaning towards rock & roll – the original "Hippy Hippy Shake", before the Swinging Blue Jeans got their hands on it, Little Willie John's "Fever", that sort of thing. And we were heav[il]y into early Presley. [But] we [still] weren't playing anywhere, just rehearsing.' As such, it would be fair to say that the Gamblers' repertoire lacked any real sense of danger, something Morrison could assuredly introduce, courtesy of his father's stupendous record collection.

As it is, nobody seems too sure how or when Van Morrison got asked to augment the ever-evolving Gamblers. Wrixon told Them historian Trevor Hodgett that he and Billy went along to see the Manhattan Showband at the Orchid Ballroom, and 'they actually did a rhythm & blues set as a showband . . . We were speaking to Van afterwards, and Van said, "Well, I like the rhythm & blues sets, but the rest of it I can do without," and Billy [just] said, "We have a rhythm & blues band. Why don't you come along?"' Harrison, though, thinks that he already knew Morrison wanted to pack in the showbands, having perhaps heard of his attempt to form his own band. Harrison had known Morrison for some time, and actually stood in with the Monarchs on a couple of occasions. To his mind, though, Morrison remained a saxophone player who played a bit of harmonica. What he did not, could not, know was that the sax/harmonica player on whom he was prepared to gamble was a white R&B singer to curl the blackest toes ever dipped in the Delta.

Billy Harrison: We had both done the hospitals entertainment bit – [we] used to meet at the City Hall, get on to the bus and head off to whatever hospital [and give] free shows . . . and Van had done that stint as well . . . But then Van was first and foremost a saxophone player, and that's all he was. He was actually brought into the group to make up the saxophone, to make the Johnny and the Hurricanes/Booker T and the MGs line-up. He wasn't brought in as a singer at all. Nobody knew he could bloody sing!

Morrison knew, and he quickly determined he would mould *his* new band into the combo he'd left London hoping to create. He alone knew that he could breathe life into these songs vocally. Though Harrison hung in there with the odd vocal staple through the days of the Maritime (indeed he sings lead on one of the demos Them recorded in early June), Morrison became the frontman in the Gamblers soon enough.

Ronnie Millings: We were playing popular stuff but then we moved right down into R&B. Billy and Van worked them all out [together]. Once you were into that music, then you started listening to that music, so you got into it. We never played any hits [again] . . . Billy was the lead vocalist, then he started sharing, and then [Van] gradually took over . . . which [certainly] worked out for the best.

Their would-be saviour has chosen to depict the band's early days as fraught with disagreement. In 1998 he recalled that it was a question of 'trying to sneak [R&B songs] into the set with Them . . . they just wanted to jam it. I don't think they wanted a singer . . . there were never any rehearsals – just jams. And they turned up the amps when I sang.' Harrison's description provides a clarity altogether lacking in Morrison's account:

Billy Harrison: We used to practise at Dougie Knight's, and that's where it all came out about the blues thing . . . suddenly people were calling it rhythm &

blues. Van didn't have the restriction of the showband so suddenly out came a harmonica, and a bit of singing. His father probably had the best blues collection in Ireland. In fact I had the loan of the records, to learn stuff. See, Van would come up with something he knew from his father's collection . . . which you hadn't heard. Then he'd end up [borrowing] the record from his father's collection – I don't know whether his father ever approved – [so] you had an idea [of] what it was he was getting at.

Few of the tensions alluded to by Morrison feature in the others' accounts, though the process whereby Harrison went from singing most songs, to sharing vocals, to having the occasional slot was rather rapid. By his own admission, 'Van [simply] knew a hell of a lot more blues songs than I did . . . When I was chanting, Van was blowing the harp or saxophone . . . [but] then Van was doing more and more [of] the numbers, because he already knew them . . . [which] allowed me to concentrate more on the guitar.' Bassist Alan Henderson also believes the combination to have been a happy accident: 'We were into the rhythm & blues scene with the Gamblers, but we didn't have the information that we needed. That [only] came when we met up with Van, because he had such a fantastic knowledge of the music.'

At the time, Morrison seems to have kept his reservations to himself. He didn't even tell the other guys about an audition he attended for another band. His reasons for attending it he also kept to himself. Presumably even in those early days, when something genuinely radical was being shaped in the dank space above Dougie Knight's bicycle shop, Morrison was unconvinced that the Gamblers were what he really had in mind. Possibly he felt that Harrison exercised too much say as to the band's direction. Perhaps they failed to swing like the Monarchs. Whatever the case, he was looking for an alternative when an ad in the local evening paper, the *Belfast Evening Telegraph*, caught his eye. The ad, which ran from Monday 6 April 1964 to the following Thursday, read:

R&B CLUB opening city centre – Groups apply immediately. Also wanted, Bass Guitarist and Harmonica player for resident Group. Phone 649508.

Many years later Morrison owned up to responding to this advert, telling the editor of *Now Dig This* how it 'blew me away when I read it.

It said, "Musicians wanted to start R&B club." I went and met these guys . . . and they said they wanted to start this R&B club, and they were looking for people [to play] . . . Only two people showed up from the ad.' His unvarnished memory can't stay the course, though, and soon enough the self-aggrandizer is back on top: 'So I went out and found this club . . . called the Maritime Hotel . . . I had to just get musicians in at short notice, so the people that I really wanted, I couldn't get.'

The first part of Morrison's account accords reasonably well with other participants'. Very few people *did* turn up in response to the ad, placed by 'the Three Js' – Gerry McKervey, Jerry McKenna and Jimmy Conlan – and when Morrison turned up for the audition he was accompanied by Geordie Sproule. The fact that there is not a single Gambler who remembers the ad, let alone considered responding to it, suggests that Morrison intended to audition for the vacancy as 'harmonica player for resident group', not to put himself and his 'mates' forward as an alternative. The Gamblers would not enter the picture until it became clear that without them the audition was going to be one big bust.

Gerry McKervey: My music interest was in promotion. We were trying to find places like [the Cavern] to open. We had a few pounds, which we made from the folk concerts [we'd arranged], and we decided we'd open a rhythm & blues club. There was a band about at the time called the College Boys, run by Sammy Smith. He said, 'We can play rhythm & blues.' But it was just another Beatles group . . . So then we decided we'd put an ad in the paper to form a rhythm & blues group. We put an ad in the [*Belfast Evening*] *Telegraph* for people to turn up at a pub on the Old Park Road. What we had was the three of us [and] Paddy McAuley, who worked for me and played the drums, [who] brought his drum kit along. He also had a Philips amp and a Shure microphone. You should have seen the people that turned up! Towards the end of it, in came Van. He had another character with him, a ginger-haired guy. This guy had a bottle of wine in his pocket . . . [he] looked like a wino . . . Van came up, and we asked about [the other guy]. Van said, 'Oh no, he's only with me.' We told him what we wanted to do. He said, 'Right, OK,' and he just went up to the mike and he busked. He didn't sing anything that meant anything, he just busked. We just closed everything else down and said, 'Right, Van, that's exactly what we're looking for.' This wailing harmonica and the voice! So then we asked him about forming a group . . . As far as I can remember, Van [told me he] wasn't playing with anyone. He was doing sessions at the Plaza Ballroom for Brian Rossi, but he wasn't employed as a member of the band . . . [However,] he said, 'I have four friends and they're [already] playing. They're calling themselves the Gamblers. They are rehearsing above Dougie Knight's record shop. Look, come down, and we'll see what we can work out.'

The audition in question must have taken place on Saturday 11 April, two days after the final ad ran and a day after the R&B club opened. And McKervey is quite correct when he says that the College Boys opened the R&B club at the Maritime, on the 10th, even though their unsuitability had become obvious prior to their Maritime début. Hence the ads. McKervey and his fellow promoters may have hoped that the addition of a harmonica player and a bassist might transform the College Boys into a credible R&B band. It was not to be.

McKervey and Conlan believe it was their introduction to Morrison that led to his joining the Gamblers, something that Van's own comment about 'just get[ting] musicians in at short notice' appears to confirm. However, this simply cannot be the case. The Tuesday after Van's solo audition, the five-piece was making its unbilled live début – on the same day they were advertised in the *Belfast Evening Telegraph* under their new name – and three days later they opened 'the R&B club at the Maritime', never to look back. Events fit the facts only if Morrison returned to Dougie Knight's on 11 April, prepped the band prior to the Three Js' arrival – leaving out details of his attempt to secure a better gig – and that very evening auditioned with them for the position of the Maritime's resident group.

Gerry McKervey: [When we arrived] Van had briefed them as to why we were coming, and we all just sat down together and discussed what we were going to do . . . It was a real dive! One room, up a wee side staircase. And they were a general rock & roll group. They didn't know anything about [our ad].

Billy Harrison can't recall 'how [the Three Js] came into the picture actually', but gigs for 'groups' in Belfast were few and far between. Harrison remembers just three venues: the Gala, Betty Staff's in Arran Street and Sammy Houston's in Victoria Street, all of which were for 'a tenner a night, take it or leave it – but you'd have played for nothing, just to get playing'. What the Three Js were attempting to do was certainly far-sighted. When they presented themselves to the band that Saturday night, they must have seemed something of a godsend.

Billy Harrison: They came along to us [with] the idea of starting a blues club, to take the place of this jazz club . . . [which] used to be at the Maritime Hotel on Tuesday and Friday night . . . [and] which was stopping.

Once it was agreed that this quintet met the R&B club's requirements, the Three Js sat down with the musicians and set about thinking up a name that held a little more resonance than the Gamblers. It was Eric Wrixon who came up with the single word by which they would pass into pop-lore. As the band only gradually came to realize, it was perhaps 'the first time anyone had given themselves a name that was a single word. We were going to be known simply as Them.' The Three Js quickly devised a set of snappy ads to catch everyone's attention. Running on consecutive nights in the *Evening Telegraph*, starting on the following Tuesday, were the following cryptic messages:

WHO ARE? WHAT ARE? THEM? [14 April]

WHEN? AND WHERE? WILL YOU SEE THEM? [15 April]

RHYTHM and BLUES and THEM – WHEN? [16 April]

Finally, on Friday 17 April, an ad in the Entertainment section announced, 'Rhythm & Blues Club, To-night, 8.30: Introducing THEM – Ireland's Specialists in Rhythm and Blues. Maritime Hotel, College Square North'. In fact, this was not Them's Maritime début, which occurred the day the first ad ran.

Billy Harrison: The first time we played there, we actually went and did a spot on the last night of the jazz club. We did three or four numbers to a trad jazz crowd – which didn't go down awfully well.

The local jazz club had changed its name some months back to the Belfast Jazz-Beat Club, and began booking more contemporary bands. An ad in a February 1964 *Evening Telegraph* presented the trad jazz of the Apex Jazzmen on the same bill as the Emeralds, who apparently offered the 'Latest Beat Sound'. It was an experiment that ended with Them's début. The Maritime's association with jazz was definitively consigned to the past on the Friday Them made their official début to a small but appreciative crowd, largely comprising students from Queen's University and the College of Technology, in whose shadow the Maritime stood.

At a time when word of mouth was all there was, it took only a matter of weeks for these Friday-night sessions to become weekly infernos of fevered rhythm & blues, to crowds whose size exceeded not only expectations but also every safety law in town.

Billy Harrison: The first week it was about thirty or forty people, the next week there was maybe eighty or ninety, the third week there were queues past the Tech, and that was at six o'clock for a gig that started at half-seven. It was just unbelievable. It just exploded. You just couldn't get in. The place was licensed fire-wise for 120 people, and we had three hundred people.

Eric Wrixon: After the second week, there was a fight outside and queues. It needed an outrageous band, and Them in the beginning were totally outrageous. There certainly wasn't a band in town walking around with colourful clothes and long hair. It was just one of those bands that worked. The sum was greater than the parts.

Inevitably what had started as a very loose arrangement, where McKervey 'hired the room from the manager, every Friday night . . . [but] we didn't actually draw up a contract or anything', soon required a certain professionalism simply to control the crowds that began to overrun the place within three weeks of Them's opening. McKervey's solution was straightforward enough: 'We went and got membership cards printed – we wanted to be able to stop people at the door.'

Three J Enterprises also sought to formalize its relationship with Them. McKervey drew up a simple contract of employment wherein 'Them got paid wages per night for every gig they did. The balance we put into clothes, the minibus, promotion, advertising.' However, the contract placed no time-limit on Them's employment, reflecting the way that Gerry, Jerry and Jimmy shared the band's idealism (and inexperience). Meanwhile the youngest of the Three Js, Jimmy Conlan, began trying to secure the band some grander bookings, until word of mouth from the Maritime served to knock down the last few remaining doors.

Jimmy Conlan: I remember trudging round the bigger dance-hall operators in the city and pushing Them, or trying to get bookings for Them, and meeting a certain resistance because they didn't fully know what we were talking about. Once we had combined the group with the Maritime, the kids certainly locked on to it very quickly, and they very quickly understood what was happening.

Even as other gigs began to fill Them's dance-card, the Maritime continued to be that special place, and with a very special audience. This was in part because of its location, with its back turned to the Royal Belfast Academical Institution and the College of Technology. But equally significantly, its central setting marked a step apart and yet a world away from the parochial halls and ballrooms that had too long dominated the roster of Belfast venues. Its slightly scuzzy appearance only served to endear it to those, like Gerald Dawe, who found not only Them but themselves:

The [Maritime] in 1964 was the focus for Queen's University students and the outward-going and confident working-class young. In this most work-orientated of cities, where status and prestige were intrinsically linked to one's 'steady' job and prospects, the students had an identity of their own . . . They had a fool's pardon when they ventured through the city centre and would have been treated with short shrift during the mid-sixties had they made their presence felt at the ballrooms and larger dance halls whose audiences were, to a man and woman, working hard for the rest of the week . . . It's hardly surprising, therefore, that the students would find their own venues such as the Maritime . . . [which] became synonymous with R&B, the music which symbolized a breaking away from, and loosening of, custom. On the ground floor a café faced up to a flight of stairs, and along the narrow institutional-like painted passageway, there was a small dance hall. It had a low stage and bands would often walk through the audience to reach the stage, or, having finished their set, simply jump down from the stage and mill about with the audience.

Them's association with the Maritime may have barely lasted out the spring, but they were destined to remain inextricably linked. It was because of Them that the Maritime (and, as it became, Club Rado) would always be viewed as the home of R&B in Belfast; and it was because of the Maritime that other local musicians continued to name-check Them. Eric Bell – who, after playing guitar in Morrison's first post-Them incarnation, co-founded Thin Lizzy with Phil Lynott – remembers seeing 'the original Them at the Maritime about six weeks after they'd taken up the residency. It was really raw and very rhythmic, and they seemed very advanced musically. There was lots of good little groups around, but this was the first raw rhythm & blues thing I think anyone had seen.' Arty McGlynn, another guitarist who would later play with Morrison, felt that there was 'a totally different energy than you had in a parochial hall or an Orange hall or a civic centre. It was a social revolution – a different mentality – people that wanted out of the system.'

In later years Morrison would champion the memory of the Maritime, suggesting that only at the mission were Them ever truly in their element. In conversation with Ritchie Yorke ten years later he still rhapsodized about 'the way we did the numbers at the Maritime; [it] was more spontaneous, more energy, more everything, because we were feeding off the crowd. And it was never really captured on tape.' Whatever its energy source, at the centre of this maelstrom was a truly transformed frontman. With all constraints removed, and suffused by his performing muse, Van Morrison became a man possessed.

Peter Lloyd: I was very impressed by Them at the Maritime. Van was a bundle of energy . . . on sax, harmonica and vocals. He was the dynamo . . . He was *so* into it. Whether he was aware of the audience or not, I don't know. He'd have his eyes shut. He'd be diving from left to right on stage. He'd be rushing from side to side, doing splits. He was definitely the thing that hit you. He gripped the crowds . . . [and] he certainly turned on the girls.

In those early days, Morrison did not restrict himself to vocals and the odd burst of harmonica. The sax slung round his neck was still a part of his act, as he threw in the odd trick picked up in the German nightclubs. His childhood chum Gil Irvine recalls Van mimicking 'the usual things from saxophone players, through watching . . . movies like *Rock around the Clock* and *Blackboard Jungle*, where you'd see saxophone players land on their back, playing the saxophone. Van used to do that, get on tables, do whatever had to be done to attract attention. He [was] a different person on stage.'

Should the memory of another contemporary Irish guitarist be reliable, Morrison's antics in Them were not confined to such stage-managed gestures. In a lather after a fifteen-minute slow burn through 'Turn on Your Lovelight', he would often jump off the stage and just start spinning round, a sort of whirling-dervish type of dance using a cape that he had. Billy Harrison, Them's erstwhile bandleader, was never sure how much control Morrison actually had over his onstage persona: 'He used to go spare. He used to stalk up and down the stage – all aggro. Backwards and forwards. Maracas, tambourines, everything would get lost in the crowd.' But noticed he most certainly was.

All of this was a quite unexpected transformation, mystifying to anyone privy to the offstage Morrison. Gerry McKervey still doesn't know where it came from: 'Maybe he devised all this in his own head. He was able to project onstage what he couldn't project in social company. He would sing things that maybe he thought, but he couldn't have sat and said the [same] things.' Everyone agrees that this onstage dervish would just as quickly withdraw behind his own eyelids as soon as he came offstage, returning to some horizon in the distance only he could see. McKervey remembers the nineteen-year-old Morrison as a 'very hard man to communicate with. If we sat round here, everybody else would talk and [Van] would just be sitting there . . . If you talked to him about a piece of music, yes, out it comes, but if you were talking generally, he'd have nothing to say.' Music remained Morrison's sole *raison d'être*, offstage and on, night and day, even as local notoriety beckoned.

Jimmy Conlan: I remember spending an afternoon with him once. He took me around his old haunts, drinking with his companions . . . [But] you needed to have an in-depth knowledge of his subject – music. When he was in company with his friends, they would talk about all the old blues hits, the big names in R&B, but at that time it was a bit over my head. I loved the idea of the whole thing, but you never got round to relating to him in any deep, meaningful way. He didn't relate on ordinary, everyday subjects. He was completely focused on something else.

When Gerry McKervey had first booked Them into the Maritime, he had set himself six weeks for the venture to break even. Needless to say, after six weeks they could barely keep up with the demand. Organist Eric Wrixon recalls, 'We would, on the average Friday night, play three or four gigs in Belfast *before* we went to the Maritime. In those days a gig was forty minutes.' This might be a slight exaggeration, but they *were* playing to two or three entirely different crowds in a night and, as drummer Ronnie Millings observes, 'After the third week everybody knew who Them was . . . There wasn't a place in this town [we couldn't play], all we had to say was, "We want to play here." . . . We were treated as the Stones or the Beatles as regards the fans we had. It was unbelievable.' And oh so fleeting.

6

1964: Gotta Walk Away

Before the boom started, you played maybe once a week and you
rehearsed about three nights – for sheer fun. [It] was more jamming and
busking and seeing what came out of it than somebody formally coming
in and saying, 'Scuse me, I've written three songs.' You had people
sitting around . . . with bottles of cheap South African wine, strumming
and playing and doing things, just waiting to see what happened. It was
a lot of fun, but it wasn't very commercial-oriented.

—*Eric Wrixon*

With hindsight, it may seem inevitable that the kind of hysteria Them
generated at the Maritime would lead very quickly to the land of record
contracts and a less localized form of fame, but this does not take account
of how genuinely isolated the youth of Ulster felt from the mainstream
of British pop culture. Certainly the circumstances that led to Them's
recording the demo tape that would result in an approach from a record
company (or two), and the band being spirited away to Albion, hardly
smacked of a grand design. It would appear that even the idea of cutting
a demo was something that had to be introduced to the band.

Stuart Cromie: I sold amplifiers in the evening, went round the dance halls.
One particular night I went into the Maritime to try and sell a bass amp and,
realizing that this group of lads had absolutely no money, persuaded them that
maybe a demo disc would be an idea. After a couple of weeks, they made a date
for it. They came round to the recording studios, made the recording, and then
informed us they hadn't enough money to pay for the demo disc[s].

Peter Lloyd, Cromie's business partner of sorts, was the man who ran the studio in question, situated in Cromac Square. He also remembers some problem over payment for the session, though the way he remembers it, 'We were charging three guineas an hour at the time, and [Them] only had a fiver. But they were so good we let them run on.' Not that the studio – conveniently located in the city centre – was exactly state-of-the-art: 'We couldn't record during the day. We were above a solicitor's office, so we had to wait until he'd gone home. We had a Revox. [It was] very simple. Five mikes, no EQ, no compression.'

However, it was the one and only studio in Northern Ireland, and Them had somehow stumbled upon it. As the only studio they were used to recording showbands, not R&B bands. All three members of Peter Lloyd Sound were in attendance that day, and thought Morrison and Them sounded like something out of the ordinary.

Martin Lloyd: They got set up and they were all mucking about and then, more or less straight away, they went into 'Stormy Monday' and Bo Vance, a soundman who used to work with my brother, turns to me and says, 'Ooh, this fellow could go far.' Van really stood out, especially the voice.

'Stormy Monday' *was* indeed the first song cut that day. It was also one of those songs introduced to the band via Morrison Senior's record collection. A T-Bone Walker original, like showstopper 'Turn on Your Lovelight' it could take on a number of permutations, lyrical and/or instrumental, at the Maritime. Though within the confines of a converted ex-dental technician's shop it took on a more muted shape, the rich blue tone of the vocalist would never sound quite so young again. Slim Harpo's 'Don't Start Crying Now', which barely three months later would become the A-side of their first 45,★ was also taken at a far more sedate clip, one more suited to Van's busking style of delivery – although it lacked much of the sheer animal energy later found in its Decca guise. These two songs – along with Billy Harrison stomping his way through 'Got My Mojo Working' – were pressed on to a three-song demo disc (of which forty-nine copies were made, collected and paid for by the Three Js – contrary to Cromie's recollection).†

★ 'Don't Start Crying Now' c/w 'One, Two Brown Eyes' would be released by Decca on 4 September 1964.
† Producing only forty-nine copies was a way to avoid duty, which became due if fifty copies were pressed.

Gerry McKervey: The demo tape was all part of promoting Them . . . We made the demo tape, and we got the little, thin demo discs and I think we sent them out to the various record companies – not to get them gigs, more to get the record companies interested.

The only time Morrison ever talked about these demos, to *Rolling Stone* in 1970, he imbued them with some Maritime magic, describing them as 'closer to our music than anything we ever recorded. I'd like to hear them now, to play them for people and let them hear how we were.' What he was probably remembering was not so much the two covers he sang that day, but the two Morrison-penned originals they also ran down (when he finally got to hear these recordings again, at a friend's house in the early nineties, an animated Morrison was transported back by the unique spirit captured). The master tape of these two originals – 'Gloria' and 'One, Two Brown Eyes' – was deposited in a bank across the street from the studio by the Three Js,★ where it languished in a vault for nigh on three decades. Only when Gerry McKervey was reminded of its existence, in 1992, was the tape exhumed. On it he found the earliest extant recording of Van Morrison's most famous anthem. And her name was . . .

The fact that Them were doing their own material in the spring of 1964, pre-Kinks, pre-Who, was unusual enough. The Beatles excepted, almost every British powerpop combo relied on the same staple diet of R&B/soul standards from which to cull their basic repertoire (and even the Fab Four were still playing half a set of covers). If Morrison would tell *Record Mirror* the following year, 'I don't write in a particular style,' the early Morrison compositions – with the exception of Them's first B-side, 'Philosophy' – adhered to that familiar 'boy–girl thing', self-consciously modelled on whatever blues riff came to hand. And though every 'original' in the Them repertoire would come to be copyrighted by their London management to Morrison – and Morrison alone – the songs at this point were not so much 'composed' as wrought out of the ether, the product as much of daily jamming sessions at Dougie Knight's or somebody's house as of Morrison's tortured psyche.

Indeed Harrison believes that 'Gloria' 'was "written" in my mother's front room', and that it was a result of 'trying to put songs together, playing riffs and different chord sequences. "Gloria" seemed to pop up

★ The tape was deposited on 12 July 1964, presumably a day (or two) after the session.

out of it. So did "Philosophy".' Wrixon is even more unequivocal in his attribution, insisting to Steve Turner that 'if I were a hard-nosed barrister, I would argue that some of the royalties from that song should be shared with Billy Harrison. It was [he] who came up with the riff.' Morrison says not. Though he might admit that the riff in question owes more than a bar-chord or two to Bo Diddley, he once told an audience in Copenhagen in 1994 that he copped it and/or crafted it 'about a fucking year before I met anybody in Them . . . I was sitting in my room one day, and I picked up my guitar . . . and I played these chords exactly like this.'

Whoever conceived that simple riff, the words were certainly all Morrison's, and it was an enticing enough tale for people soon to begin to wonder about the muse responsible for such unprecedented inspiration. Neighbours in East Belfast were certainly non-plussed. They knew Gloria was the name of Morrison's favourite cousin, who had died of cancer whilst the Monarchs were in Germany, i.e. precisely the time when Morrison says he wrote 'Gloria'. If neighbour Walter Blakely remembered the two as being 'very close, almost like brother and sister', she was still on his mind thirty-six years later, when he would tell Linda Gail Lewis, 'about his cousin Gloria. He told me she died [young] . . . he said that I reminded him of her. I['d] asked him if he'd ever [known] a woman who really, really loved him for him . . . and he said she did.'

On the other hand, Eric Wrixon thinks there was a girl at the Maritime, and her name was G-L-O-R-I-A. As Gerald Dawe has surmised, 'whatever the speculations as to who "Gloria" actually was (a fate which pursues many of Morrison's lyrics . . .), the focus is on the man and not the woman. That is what the shouting is all about.' And that night-prowling riff, the strutting vocals and the repressed tension of the performance combined to convey a sexual menace it took the Stones another four years to approach.

The manifestation of a real sexual charge from Morrison took everyone by surprise. Despite their time in the red-light districts of Germany, no one in the Monarchs seems able to confirm just how sexually experienced the young Morrison then was. Neither does anyone remember Morrison having a 'steady' in the days leading up to Them. And even in Them, when his sexual presence spumed off the Maritime stage every Friday night, girlfriends were few and far between.

Billy Harrison: There was a couple of girls he knocked about with the odd few weeks over here, but he never really had a steady. There was a blonde-haired girl called Rose. She ended up one night on the stage in the Maritime. She was pissed out of her lid. We all nearly were . . . Anyway, she got buried under all our gear, and she was just left there.

Presumably Morrison was saving his energies for those moments when he could turn on a couple of hundred lovelights (or, perhaps, the death of his cousin turned him further inward, the songs becoming his only real outlet for such passion). 'Gloria' was not the only example of Morrison fixating on some object of desire in song. 'One, Two Brown Eyes', also now demoed, was another Maritime favourite, which according to Harrison 'was written at a practice session at Romano's Ballroom, in Queen Street in Belfast. We were practising in it, and Van had an idea for something he'd been shouting. We were playing it and he was singing something different every time, and [my girlfriend] Vivien [finally] stood and wrote down in shorthand what she thought he shouted.'

If it was 'Stormy Monday' and 'Don't Start Crying Now' that vied for attention on those scratchy demo discs, the originality of Morrison's own songs was a secret worth holding on to. Whilst the Three Js distributed their forty-nine demo discs to interested parties, Them's trio of overseers continued to reinvest Maritime monies, as well as part of the sums now rolling in from activities away from the seamen's mission:

Gerry McKervey: Other promoters were beginning to ask us about them. But the first thing we did was take them down to Duke's and arranged credit: 'Go in there and get whatever you want.' The Beatles wore uniforms, but they were taking the odd gear: leather trousers, button-down shirts. The next thing we got was a photographer. We got 'em all dressed up in all this new stuff, and it was all to be moody. We took them down to the City Hall here, and we put them in amongst the columns. We took the photos and we had them made into postcards . . . We['d] bought a van for them by then, a minibus . . . We then decided, 'Let's get a few more nights for them.' We got them into the Inst., which is a school that ran music nights; we got them into Sammy Houston's; we got them into the Fiesta Ballroom.

The spring of 1964 was a heady time in Belfast. Barriers, religious and social, seemed to be tumbling down. Though the so-called religious divide remained omnipresent, there had always been an unspoken exemption for local musicians. As Harrison observes, 'When you get into music and you're playing, the guy's a musician. There's no mention of what religion he is. He's only what he is, as regards the music. [But] there was always the Catholic area and the Protestant area, which you couldn't always walk through safely if you were of the wrong persuasion.' On a Sunday night, though, there were only two gigs in town, both left of Belfast. As it was, Them were always welcome at St Theresa's Hall, even before the McAuley brothers, both Catholics, joined the band.

Such was the demand for the band that they even secured a regular lunchtime gig at the Plaza in Belfast's city centre. Happy to use as a rehearsal space a Mecca ballroom, which doubled as a coffee shop/ sandwich bar for itinerant office workers, Them would take the opportunity to begin gearing up for a night of relentless gigging.

Ronnie Millings: They used to let us in at lunchtimes to [play for] office staff, who'd come in for a coffee, [but] it was a big dance hall. We used it as a practice [for] any new numbers. We'd play for about an hour, and the [manager] guy was giving me seventeen quid just for coming in . . . [We were getting] paid to rehearse. All the office staff went in there. All the young girls [would be] dancing.

The regular Friday ritual involved wrapping up at the Plaza around two in the afternoon, and then making 'the scene at the Spanish Rooms', immortalized in 'The Story of Them'. The Spanish Rooms, though, was no music venue. It was where the band bonded over a few pints of scrumpy – a flat, murky moonshine cider. According to Harrison, the band acquired enough of a taste for this fermented apple juice to desire their own supply on tap: 'Two pints of this stuff, you fell down the stairs, you didn't even feel it. We used to buy a keg of this, hang it in the back of the van. It hung on the roof and if you wanted a jar you went over.' Inevitably, occasions arose when prising them away from the Spanish Rooms became an art unto itself.

Jimmy Conlan: Van was very much himself – a bit uncontrollable. I do remember having to go looking for them up in the Spanish Rooms more than once. They were supposed to be on, and I had to go up and say, 'C'mon, lads.' They were all sitting . . . drinking cider.

Of course, a generous dose of alcoholic apple juice helped brace the band for any unfavourable reaction – not at the Maritime but on those occasions when the Three Js' booking policy took them further afield.

One night it also spurred them on to directly challenge one of the most popular showbands in town to a musical duel, a showdown doubtless fuelled in Morrison's case by four years of kowtowing to the *status quo*. The battleground was the Academical Institution, a stone's throw from the Maritime and already home turf to Them.

Ronnie Millings: We were doing a show at the Inst., and there was this popular showband, Dave Glover['s] . . . on first, and his last number before we came on was 'Walking the Dog'. So we all decided, 'Right, we'll [open with] it.' . . . The showbands used to run the place. [But] we just blew them out of sight that night. This guy had been going for years. Then the boys came on and tore the place apart. Van was doing 'Love Light', throwing the maracas down [on] the floor, it would build up and then – chop – drop it down, then build it up again . . . And they just stormed the stage that night. We were on fire. It was like a wave coming right over the stage.

However much the overthrow of an established order seemed imminent in Belfast, there were plenty of places outside the city where 'She Moved through the Fair' was still considered a contemporary ballad. The Top Hat in Lisburn, the Flamingo in Ballymena, the Queen's Hall in Holywood and the Queen's Court in Bangor still represented the outer limits of urban culture. When the Three Js booked Them to play at the Imperial Hotel in Brae it required a night in the hotel – an adventure in itself. Unfortunately the band ran up a drink bill that took care of that night's takings and then some, perhaps because they were still suffering from culture shock.

Eric Wrixon: In the early sixties there was an incredibly huge gulf between Belfast and every other city in Northern Ireland. We got average receptions, the occasional good reception, quite a few receptions where people just stood with their mouths open . . . [but] we got bottles thrown in one or two places. [TH]

The Three Js may have been interested in increasing the band's profile outside Belfast, but 'in town' they were already local celebrities. News of their musical chops also disseminated widely. While the Three Js had been busy circulating those demo discs, Peter Lloyd was playing the source tape to interested parties on behalf of the band. As a result, when it came time to move on, the Three Js would be left high and dry. Instead it would be local-lad-done-good Philip Solomon – who ran a successful publishing/production company in London and had a booking agency through his wife – who would bring home some Irish bacon, and brother Mervyn Solomon who, after a sustained campaign, would take credit for 'discovering' Them.

Mervyn Solomon had established links with the Cromac Square studio at which Them had recorded their demo tape. It was Mervyn who had bought the main recording machine, a BTR-2, for Peter Lloyd and brother Martin Lloyd confirms that 'he would have been in and out of the studio quite a lot'. And yet Solomon has long claimed that his first exposure to Them was as a live band, informing Steve Turner that he heard 'a lot of jazz in [Morrison's] voice'. If he did, he was in a minority of one. There are precious few jazz inflections in the four Lloyd demos. This was an out-and-out blues singer offering to meet you in the bottom.

Mervyn Solomon: My first recollection was coming through those [Maritime] doors and seeing Van sliding across the stage, singing 'Turn on Your Lovelight'. He got himself all worked up, he opens his legs and he slides right across to the other side. And the kids really ate out of his hands in those days . . . I called them over after the show and said, 'I'd like to see you boys [again]. What are you doing Sunday morning?' They all said, 'Lying in bed.' Van came up here with another two [from] Them, and we started to talk. [OM/CH]

Solomon apparently instructed the band to present themselves every Sunday, and they would prepare an album's worth of material, 'and when I'm happy that you've done it properly, then we'll go across to London and we'll record it'. Solomon depicts Morrison as someone who 'used to tell all the rest of them to keep quiet. We used to sit and discuss what he would want done, and the boys didn't say very much. He was keen as mustard. But he didn't think he was ever gonna make the charts in the UK.' Surely not then, and not with Them! The idea of Van Morrison telling Billy Harrison to shut up without rueing his words is simply not credible. Harrison's considerably more reliable memory paints Mervyn Solomon almost entirely out of the picture:

Billy Harrison: Peter Lloyd was the sound engineer. He had been with Decca, and he knew everybody in Decca. He was also building his own amplifiers. That's how we knew Peter. He had his own little demo studio in Cromac Square. [We did] a three-chord version of 'Stormy Monday' – everything was a three-chord version in those days! Peter took the demo to Decca. He knew [A&R head] Dick Rowe. And Decca's main agents here were Solomon and Peres, and that's how the Solomons got involved. They didn't find the group.

Peter Lloyd also remembers 'getting quite friendly with Them – going up to Billy's house [where] we'd discuss how they were going to go [make it] . . . I can remember sitting with Billy and the rest of the band, discussing how we should go about it.' This sounds a lot more like the early Them, even though these discussions occupied only a matter of weeks. Within three weeks of cutting the demos, Them were being courted by a quite insistent Phil Solomon, Mervyn's older brother, who had arrived in Belfast in the company of Dick Rowe.

Phil Solomon: I first heard about the band from my brother Mervyn, who was the Decca distributor for Northern Ireland. He rang me up and said he'd heard a band and would I come over and have a look. I didn't want to go over on my own, and I was very friendly with Dick Rowe of Decca, who was head of the A&R department, and I asked Dick to accompany me to Belfast.

Though Lloyd no longer remembers how that all-important initial contact was made, according to an interview in 1965, he took the tape to a top London press agent – presumably brother Philip – who sent a telegram the next day saying, 'Very interested. Please send details.' Perhaps it was Mervyn who passed on Lloyd's recommendation to brother Phil. He certainly now joined the fray, as Eric Wrixon recalls Mervyn boasting, 'I have this big brother who manages all these inter-national artists. We can get you a recording contract.' Both Lloyd and Mervyn Solomon seemed to be working towards a common goal that would benefit them naught – signing Them to Phil Solomon's company.

Later in 1965, Lloyd told *Ulsterweek* that he personally took the tape to Dublin, not London, 'and when agent Phil Solomon, who handles the Bachelors, heard it, he sent recording engineer Peter Sullivan to Belfast. Later, at a Sunday recording session, handled by Decca recording chief Dick Rowe, and attended by one of the Bachelors, Them signed a recording contract with the Solomon Agency.' Though no one seems to know what happened to Peter Sullivan, there was indeed a meeting at the Cromac Square studio involving Them, Phil Solomon, Dick Rowe, and one or more of the Bachelors. Mervyn was also in attendance – although, according to Stuart Cromie, he displayed little knowledge of or regard for the band. However, the meeting in question was not on a Sunday, but on a Saturday morning. It came after a Friday-evening discussion that had extended into the wee small hours, after the Solomons and Rowe had caught Them in their element, wowing the locals at the Maritime. Nor was it a recording session. For Phil Solomon and Dick Rowe, hearing the Lloyd demos sufficed.

Phil Solomon bringing along Dick Rowe was indicative of two things: a tight relationship with Decca; and an A&R man champing at the bit. As Phil Solomon notes, 'Our relationship with Decca went back many, many years. My father had been friendly with Sir Edward Lewis, and at that time Dorothy, my wife, represented the Bachelors, who were one of the biggest [acts] on Decca. So if we had something we'd asked them to look at, they would come along and if it [looked] right, we would work out a deal.' Rowe was still smarting from turning down the Beatles – though only someone with tin ears would have signed them on the basis of *that* Decca Audition Tape. Despite the success of the Rolling Stones, he was ever hungry to reinforce his credentials for recognizing talent, or at least raw 'potential'.

Andrew Loog Oldham: Dick Rowe was not the man who turned down the Beatles but . . . the man who signed the Stones . . . Dick Rowe was good at his job for a very long time; anybody can have a hit, but can they have another, and another? . . . Dick Rowe enjoyed a remarkable run and held an exemplary track record, starting in the early fifties with David Whitfield, the Beverley Sisters, Winifred Atwell, Jimmy Young and Dickie Valentine, all huge long-term sellers. When rock & pop showed up, he still came to the table, signing Tommy Steele and Billy Fury . . . He also signed Tom Jones, Engelbert Humperdinck, Jet Harris and Tony Meehan, and, of course, the Stones. That is some track record.

The simple fact that Rowe accompanied the elder Solomon to a place like the Maritime signified the kind of clout Phil could call on. Though he remained a bit-player in the unfolding drama, Mervyn Solomon likes to suggest that *he* was the one in control of events, and that Rowe was there for the taking, as if he'd just emerged from A&R school – minus the ears that made him the best in the British end of the business.

Mervyn Solomon: The Maritime club was made in such a way that you didn't know when you walked through the club downstairs what was going on upstairs, 'cause it was really two separate rooms. So we thought when we'd get a signal that Philip [Solomon] and Dick [Rowe] were arriving in the car, we would signal people to start carrying girls down in faints and screaming. Maybe we overdid it a little bit. Dick came through the front door, walked up the passage, past the café, and was just up the first flight of stairs and the girls were coming past him yelling, and we reached the second level and he turned round and said, 'Look, I really don't need to hear them. I want them.' [OM]

Rowe probably *was* as much beguiled by the reaction to the band as by the actual music, but then his job was to find popular acts, not classical composers. Certainly Billy Harrison, who still remembers Rowe coming 'over with Mervyn and Phil Solomon one Friday night, to check out the reaction', believes that 'they were[n't] very interested in the music at all, but they were obviously aware that the Beatles had opened the doors to this sort of music'. Phil Solomon's reaction to seeing Them that night probably reflects Rowe's own: 'I thought they were a very scruffy-looking bunch, and Van used to turn his back on the audience. [But] he impressed everybody. He had good songs, a very good voice but no presentation whatsoever.' Both Rowe and Solomon still took a few doubts with them to the studio at Cromac Square, where they had some business to attend to, and some tapes to hear.

Stuart Cromie: Our studio was four storeys up, which happened to be an old dental laboratory. It was knocked together with six-inch nails, and one night – I'm pretty certain it was a Friday night – the phone rang. There was a pay-phone box directly below the door, and you dialed 28338 and we would answer the phone [and hear the tell-tale beeps]. We went to the window, looked out and threw down the keys, and you let yourself in. That was our door entry system. This particular night, Phil, Mervyn, [Dek and Con] out of the Bachelors, and a fourth man, [presumably] Dick Rowe, came up. What we very often did was play recorded things we thought they'd be interested in. On that particular night they bought [some] music written by Dave Glover, and played by [his] showband – bought it outright for a couple of hundred quid.

These men from the mission presumably already knew that there were other demos to be heard. Lloyd and Cromie agree that during this evening Phil Solomon decided to sign Them to his production company, whilst Rowe agreed to put out their records. According to Cromie, though, the demo tape was played only after much resistance from Mervyn.

Stuart Cromie: I [suggested], 'Stick Them on.' . . . Mervyn had already heard the [demo] recording of Them and hadn't liked it . . . and said, 'Ah, they're bloody rubbish. Don't bother putting them on.' [So] I shut up, and went on with what I was working at. Then later on, I said something again about sticking it on, and [one] of the Bachelors said, 'Stick it on.' They'd finished their commercial end, and we stuck it on. And the next thing, Phil turns round and says, 'That's commercial.' And Mervyn says, 'Oh, is it?' [And Phil says,] 'Have them here at half-past nine tomorrow morning.' I went out in my car, and I went to Van's house and Billy Harrison's house. Pete went out to the other boys' houses . . . They were there about half-nine . . . and I was there out of pure curiosity . . . One of them handed me a contract and said, 'Have a look at that.' And I looked at it and said, 'I wouldn't sign that. I think you could negotiate a better deal.' . . . It was 50 per cent to Phil, 50 per cent to the group – and they paid all expenses. It was . . . a three-year contract . . . But it was like, 'Oh it's a chance to get into showbusiness etc., etc.' They, needless to say, signed it. [But] the organist wasn't able to sign it, 'cause he was underage.

Perhaps it *was* the playing of the demos, at whoever's behest, that finally persuaded Phil Solomon to sign the band, but he cannot have been entirely unprepared, coming along in the morning with a contract all ready for Them to sign. Harrison seems to think that, even when speaking to the Solomons after the Friday show, 'Phil was all contracts, contracts, the whole bit.' Solomon views the contract offered to Them as a standard one for the times.

Phil Solomon: I had a one-page contract or a two-page contract. We didn't use lawyers in those days, we didn't have accountants to look at things. If an artist wanted to record, we put out a very, very simple contract and if they accepted it, they accepted it; if they didn't, they could take it away and get their own advice on it, but we were never interested in sixty-four-page documents. We presented Them with a contract, they wanted to record, and they signed.

One would certainly be hard-pressed to prove that Them were treated any worse than the likes of the Stones, the Kinks or the Who, all of whom would have cause to rue the haste with which they signed initial production and management deals, even if all three ended up with far more sympathetic producers. In Them's case, though, they allowed themselves to be bound to the Solomons on every front. As Phil Solomon readily admits, 'We signed a deal with Them [for] music publishing, everything – and then we signed a deal with Decca for Them.' Under the umbrella of Solomon's publishing company, Hyde Park Music, the band surrendered not only half of their recording royalties but half of their song publishing – after the deductions Cromie remembers so well. The band were also signed to the Dorothy Solomon Agency, who would represent and manage all performances. Unfortunately, Dorothy's experience of the Irish music scene had failed to include a bunch of scruffy East Belfast lads with chips on their shoulders and attitude to spare. The Bachelors they were not.

Eric Wrixon, Them's underage organist, was the only one unable to sign the next three years away, his father having the necessary worldly wisdom to see the contract for what it was – feudal. If the argument he presented to his son was that he shouldn't sacrifice his education, at a subsequent meeting with Mervyn Solomon he apparently simply informed him, 'I'm not signing that crap.' Wrixon was not the only member of Them to require his father's signature. So apparently did George Ivan. However, his father *did* sign the contract, presumably at his son's insistence, possibly at a later meeting at a local solicitor's.

According to Dick Rowe, the contracts were not signed on the spot. Rather, 'Philip had given the group [the] contract[s] and told them, "... meet us at the airport by 7.30 [the following day] and have it signed". When they arrived they hadn't signed it because they wanted to ask him a few questions. He casually said, "Well, you'd better be quick – the plane leaves in thirty minutes."' Though this sounds a tad melodramatic, it also sounds like Phil Solomon. The contracts were duly signed, though not by Eric Wrixon (he still flew to London with the rest of the guys to record for Decca. He would be paid a session-fee for his work, which would earn him a few quid more than the others).

Even in hindsight there is a surprising lack of bitterness from the other members of Them at the way things worked out (though Harrison's enmity towards the Solomons shows little sign of abating). Drummer Ronnie Millings admits, 'We signed too early. But then when you're in the sticks and somebody comes in with a piece of chocolate cake, you jump at it.' Harrison insists that their options were limited, and that there was a lot of hot air floating over Belfast in those days: 'Lots of people were interested, but the Solomons were the only ones that actually came up with anything. There were lots of people suddenly [saying], "Oh well, I can do this for you," all trying to jump in . . . [But] the Solomons had the whip hand, 'cause they were already [in bed] with Decca.'

In fact, some of these other options were more real than the guys might now like to admit. The members of the band seem to have collectively shut out any recollection of the expressed interest coming from Philips Records, though appraised of an offer they certainly were. The legal owners of the demo tapes – the Three Js – who had been so imprudent as to leave a copy for the engineer to play to whomever he pleased, were not yet out of the picture.

Gerry McKervey: We were approached by Philips. [Someone] had come over and had seen them on the Friday night in the Maritime, and they asked to meet us in Romano's Ballroom the next evening. This wee man from Philips started talking: 'What's the chances of [Them] coming over to London and signing up [with us]?' . . . There wasn't any figures talked about, he was just talking about the opportunity . . . When we met the band on the [following] Thursday, we told them about the Philips thing. [Then] Van said to me, 'Mervyn Solomon has been to see me and they want us to sign up with Decca.' Mervyn was able to dangle facts and figures. We said to them, 'Right then, [I guess] the Philips deal's off.' He said, 'Well, we said to Mervyn that we would meet him tomorrow, Friday, at [the] solicitor's.' We realized that was it, but we were invited to go as well . . . All we could do was [say], 'What about us?' The solicitors [said], 'Well, we're going to draw you into the contract as a sixth member of the group' . . . and we'd be paid accordingly. Then they were whisked off away to London. The rhythm & blues club ran one more night. We turned up the next night and there were two policemen on the door and the manager of the hotel, who said, 'I'm sorry. I've got a booking.' . . . That was us out of the Maritime as well.

From being the most exciting thing happening in Belfast, the Maritime reverted to being just another club, fronted by another tin-eared manager hoping to make a shekel or two. Jimmy Conlan understandably feels that the caretaker Joe Turner 'did the dirty on us, no question about it. And we were dealing with him in a fairly straight manner . . . He ran the whole shooting gallery for quite a while. He knew we didn't have anything in writing, [and] stepped in. He was an opportunist.' Though the Maritime would spawn a number of bands like the Mad Lads and the Wheels who are fondly remembered by locals, no contemporary Belfast band would replicate the impact of Them. When the Maritime changed its name to Club Rado it signalled the end of an important association.

For the Three Js, the end of their promotional dreams came early, with the reinforced realization that it always pays to have something in writing. By the time Morrison came to write 'The Story of Them', less than a year later, he would have been given his own reminder of the importance of getting good legal advice. It was a lesson he would continue to ignore. Returning from the band's brief spell in London that July, Morrison found that all the heady optimism of spring had vanished in the summer breeze. In the last few lines of 'The Story of Them' he would paint a picture of this solitary young man, 'look[ing] up at the Maritime Hotel/Just a little bit sad/Gotta walk away . . .' And walk away he did.

7

1964–65: Angry Young Them

My first impression of Van Morrison was that he was a terrific singer. No, I take that back. I thought he was a really dirty singer. Everything he did had a real big pair of balls to it.

—*Jimmy Page*

It was the first weekend in July 1964 when Them arrived in London, centre of the pop universe and a whole new testing-pad for their aspirations. Four of the five band members were rookies in the political and social capital of Great Britain, and if their frontman already knew what it was to starve in this city of nine million uncaring souls, Morrison was just as unaware of the musical chops required to make it in this metropolis. Thus it was that Them found themselves encamped outside one of the West End's proverbial dives, Beat City, a beat-up basement off Oxford Street, looking up at a handmade poster advertising Sounds Incorporated – Britain's MORish answer to Booker T and the MGs – plus, er, support.

For all their cockiness, the Belfast band were genuinely nervous about their London début, with Morrison the worst of the lot. He was struck down with a real case of the jitters – *mal de scène*, big-time – which required Peter Lloyd, previously enlisted by the Solomons to chaperone the band around London for the weekend, to 'obtain a quarter-bottle of whiskey, and we got that in him and he went on . . . Van [simply] wouldn't go on. He was scared . . . [But] he didn't go down at all well. They were giving him a slot.' The account of Stuart Cromie, who was on a buying mission to London, suggests that the whiskey was in fact a necessary acquisition to get the band *back* on stage, after a quite disastrous first set.

Stuart Cromie: Pete and I used to go to London to buy electrical stuff . . . [and] Pete was asked would he do [some] roadie[ing] for Them, who were coming over to be viewed by members of Decca. I [believe] it was [at a place] called Beat City . . . Sounds Incorporated were the main act. Them went on prior to Sounds Incorporated and were total rubbish. I think it was mainly nerves. Phil [Solomon] actually said to Pete, 'Get them back on the plane tomorrow,' and he left . . . After they got off the stage, we took the boys into the manager's office. All they wanted to do was go out and play with the wee girls. [But] we rammed them into this office and we gave them one hell of a lecture. [Then] we asked the manager, 'Can they go back on again?' He said, 'The last tube's at twenty past eleven. The kids won't be staying anyway, and I'll be burning electricity.' I think it was Pete's suggestion, 'Would a bottle of whiskey help to pay for the electricity?' [So] Pete went out and bought two bottles of whiskey, one [of which] was given to the manager, and the other one the boys drank . . . Pete phoned the London Palladium, 'cause the Bachelors were on, and managed to get hold of Phil, and persuaded Phil to come back to see them a second time. We had the boys really hyped up . . . standing at the side of the stage as Sounds Incorporated were playing their last number. Before they could even get their equipment off the stage, the boys had started to play. The majority of kids had [already] rushed out to get their coats but the next minute I felt the pressure of people behind me and there were about five rows of kids. I think it was [during] the third number Pete pushed his way through the crowd, hits me on the shoulder [and says], 'Decca. Half-nine tomorrow.'

Decca Three Studios in West Hampstead had been booked for the whole of 5 July 1964. According to Cromie, the morning was spent rehearsing, with the session only beginning in earnest at 1.30 in the afternoon. Tapes rolled until half-past six, at which point the band found themselves surplus to requirements, returning to their Soho B&B. Not that they had spent the afternoon twiddling their thumbs, having cut three Morrison originals – 'One, Two Brown Eyes', 'Philosophy' and the ubiquitous 'Gloria' – as well as a usable A-side, 'Don't Start Crying Now', and subsequently-discarded versions of something called 'Groovin'' (presumably one of Them's instrumental vamps), 'You Can't Judge a Book by Its Cover', and their stage *tour de force*, 'Turn on Your Lovelight'.

Prior to the session, though, they had been obliged to run their 'arrangements' past Arthur Greenslade, brought in by Phil Solomon to help shape the band's raw sound. It was common practice for record companies in the sixties to augment groups with session musicians, not necessarily because band members were incompetent but simply to save on session time. Thus the Byrds' 'Mr Tambourine Man' features exactly one Byrd, vocalist Jim 'Roger' McGuinn. The Decca regime rarely went quite so far, and the bands usually welcomed an experienced hand to help steer things in the right direction. Indeed, Them were more than happy to accommodate most of Greenslade's suggestions.

Eric Wrixon: It was a five-track session. It was supposed to be enough for a single and an EP . . . Arthur Greenslade was the guy who was in the studio with us, sorting things out. We had no studio experience. We weren't talking to our producer, we were talking to Arthur Greenslade, who walked around the studio going, 'Try this! Can you just set this like that?' They wanted a couple of originals, they wanted a fast song, they wanted a slow song, that sort of format . . . The big record companies, they just told you what to do. You weren't asked for an opinion.

However, producer Dick Rowe wasn't happy with the sound, despite Greenslade's input, and sought to introduce a session drummer – much as Alan White had replaced Ringo Starr on the first Beatles EMI session. Mervyn Solomon remembers 'the boys [getting] needled when they saw these session men . . . [but] they just weren't proficient enough at that point'.

The threatened mutiny caused by the introduction of session drummer Bobby Graham required a compromise if the session was going to proceed at all. Martin Lloyd shares Solomon's belief that 'a session drummer was drumming away in some booth, and Ronnie was drumming away in his booth, but I don't think they had him on'. The members of Them, though, continue to subscribe to the view that Ronnie Millings remained in the mix, and that 'Gloria' was actually propelled by two drummers. Martin Lloyd also remembers Phil Solomon arriving at some point: 'He came in, looked around, listened to a bit and went. [But] I don't think he got a very warm reception.' Perhaps the band was already beginning to suspect just how uninterested their new manager was in their personal welfare.

If Rowe sought to minimize the input of certain band members, they have subsequently returned the favour. Harrison dismisses Rowe as someone who 'claimed A&R on [the session], and didn't arrange fuck all'; whilst Morrison has caustically described Rowe as someone who 'was hanging around in the control booth when we did "Gloria"'. For once Mervyn Solomon is in full agreement with Morrison:

Mervyn Solomon: Van had his own ideas on arrangements. But Arthur [Greenslade] . . . really did help to put the thing together . . . Dick [Rowe] was sat there, but it was Arthur – and myself. Van worked very hard on those sessions.

Though Mervyn Solomon remained unaware of Morrison's attack of stage fright the previous evening, he was witness to its after-effects in the studio, '[When] we did the rehearsing in the studio [Van] was not too bad, [but] by the time they came in for the [actual] session, all he kept doing was shaking. He was [really] nervous.' Morrison had been made to feel that this might be his only shot at the prize, and was reacting accordingly. Rowe was therefore required to make one contribution to the process, and it was an important one. He convinced Morrison that he needed to inject a lot more vocal presence into 'Gloria' than the demo possessed, berating him to 'really shout – make it aggressive', until he was satisfied.

Despite the injection of menace, 'Gloria' was disregarded as a potential single. Instead, Solomon decided to make 'Don't Start Crying Now' the public's introduction to Them. It was not a good choice, lacking the kind of hook that would send the likes of 'You Really Got Me', 'The Last Time' and 'I Can't Explain' into the charts in the next six months. Indeed Solomon seemed to have very little faith in the band one way or another, dismissing them at the end of the session, then sending them back to Ireland on a boat, to await the release of whichever two songs he elected to release on a single (in fact Morrison's own 'One, Two Brown Eyes' would occupy the B-side of Decca F11973).

Eric Wrixon: The Solomons were [saying]: 'We'll be doing this record deal for you [to] release this record. We'll send for you when we need you. Until then, look after yourselves.'

Ironically, the two-month hiatus between recording and record proved something of a godsend for the band. With nothing to do but wait, and with the kudos of a record deal, they bided their time in Ireland; in Wrixon's words: 'We came back and played the circuit [and] . . . we were creaming money. We were doing maybe twelve, thirteen gigs a week, every week.'

As the band's reputation extended beyond Belfast's boundaries, though, they found themselves playing some unfamiliar dance halls, and when a sudden outbreak of penny-throwing occurred at a dance in Donegal, they were unsure of the cause – though Morrison was quoted at the time as saying he thought 'the trouble stemmed from our long hair' – but when the ritual recurred in Lifford, they cut short their set. Their roadie Pete Docherty suggested that the real cause was 'when the girls screamed, their boyfriends became jealous and decided to take it out on us'.

The following week, the band found itself booked at Cookstown Town Hall, and again the pennies came. A budding local journalist, Paul Charles, remembers the scene: 'It seemed to me that a few of the lads were a bit put out by the fact that their girlfriends were screaming at Van and his cohorts, and started to throw their loose change on stage, and then there was a wee bit of [verbal] exchange between the group and the audience.' That exchange was not so much friendly banter, more like verbal crossfire. Indeed, this most legendary of out-of-town Them gigs duly ended in a full-scale riot – prompted, if the other band members remember rightly, by a stunningly tactless streak in their previously taciturn frontman.

Billy Harrison: Once you get out into the country, forget it – it's like long-hairs playing in redneck Texas . . . We were OK in places like Lisburn and Newtownards, but you got to remember the country in Ireland is *still* the country . . . [When] we played Brae [we were] billed as the Them Showband . . . [But] it was Cookstown [that really] started [the penny-throwing]. That was Van. The biggest industry in Cookstown is bacon, sausages, pig-farming. We played the town hall. They were used to showbands. They were not ready for an R&B group. They weren't ready for [any] group, let alone Them. 'Cause we just did our own thing on stage. Groups to [these] people meant the Shadows, clean-cut guys doing steps and all this. And there were these five blokes who looked like they'd each come off a different building site. We just walked out, didn't chat the crowd up, didn't have a set repertoire, didn't play for the crowd, [but] played for ourselves. Van very rarely ever spoke to the crowd at all. Van just played harmonica, blew saxophone and sang. 'Cause at that stage Van would blow the harp or saxophone while I was singing. We were [still] sharing it between us. But we were not going down well – didn't bother us, we kept playing. Next thing, the pennies started coming on to the stage, big brown pennies. [Well,] we stopped and picked them all up. That really got up their noses. It started getting a bit hairy and the curtains came over but, prior to the curtains coming over, the worst thing [that] you can do, Van did. He said, 'Goodnight, pigs.' There was a virtual riot. We ended up in the mayor's office locked in, police arrived [and] escorted us out in a Land Rover. They would have killed us if they'd got their hands on us – they really would. But that's when you start to learn [that] there's no such thing as bad publicity. That hit the papers, and then it became the norm to throw pennies at us if we played outside Belfast – which we [then] collected.

The Cookstown incident seems to have left Morrison wholly unfazed, even though he managed to put not just himself but the whole band in danger of becoming the following day's bacon sandwiches. Press reports of the incident refer specifically to 'dancers alleg[ing] that a member of the group made a derogatory remark about them at the end of the dance'. The scale of the mayhem was something else. Even the support band, the Stratotones, found themselves caught up in it, as the crowd stoned their van until they saw their name and let them through. Billy Harrison in no way exaggerates the danger, which a report in a local paper graphically conveys:

A crowd of about 300, some armed with bottles and stones, gathered at the entrance to the [town] hall after the dance on Saturday night, at which the group received a poor reception. The group were locked in the building for about thirty minutes until police, under District Inspector James Faulkner, succeeded in getting the crowd to leave the vicinity of the hall. Them were then escorted out of the building to their van by police who accompanied them to the outskirts of the town. Using side roads, they returned to Belfast through Portadown as a large crowd, armed with bottles and stones, had gathered at the north end of the town, expecting the group to return home via Antrim.

If the actual lobbing of said pennies represented an unwelcome expansion of the parameters of legitimate criticism, even for Ireland, Cookstown proved to be the first of many such occasions in Morrison's career to date when he has felt compelled to inform one or more members of an audience exactly what he thinks of them. Not that any subsequent outburst has had quite the pithy economy of his fond farewell to Cookstown. The boys were probably looking forward to returning to the mainland, where the crowds tended to voice their dissatisfaction in a less life-threatening way.

Unfortunately it wasn't at all clear whether there would be another opportunity afforded Them. Despite signing a three-year deal with Solomon, they knew that was strictly a one-way option, and they still might find themselves back on the College Square scrapheap. Mervyn Solomon, their one point of contact with the family firm in these months, recalls how their lead singer, having seemingly yielded up his only three originals at the Decca session, 'occasionally used to come down here and say, "Oh, I've got a great new song." And I would say, "Well, Van, [let's] wait and see what's going to happen." There was no use promising him anything, 'cause we didn't know.'

Perhaps Morrison still expected everything to happen with the immediacy of those heady few months in the spring. The release of 'Don't Start Crying Now' on 4 September 1964, two months almost to the day after Them recorded it, finally resulted in the band being summoned back to London. But if they thought that this was the beginning of better days ahead, they were sadly mistaken. Though Wrixon had continued to play with the band back in Ireland, his failure to sign on the dotted line made expulsion inevitable. What Solomon had in mind was no weekend trip, but a sustained two-month assault on mainland Meccas and the mass media. Patrick McAuley, the same man who had played drums at that Three Js audition five months earlier, was drafted in as Wrixon's replacement.

It soon became apparent that the Solomons had no real idea what they had taken on. When Phil Solomon advanced Them the money to buy some fashionable gear (and an advance was always just that) he expected the boys to return in matching suits, Beatle-style – which they duly did but with hidden cargo also stashed away. About to make their television début, Them were expected to conform to the anodyne format of prime-time sixties 'pop' shows. However, when it came time to perform for the camera, the individual elements reasserted themselves.

Billy Harrison: We were scruffy fuckers but that was our image. We were individuals, not five typecast guys in the same suits, the same haircuts. But Tommy Scott, who had something to do with the Solomons, was dispatched with a handful of money by Phil Solomon, to take us to Carnaby Street to get us smartened up. The boys got the gear that they fancied [for us] . . . [but] we'd [also] scarpered along to the ex-army surplus store and bought these combat jackets and forage caps. And that's when we did *Thank Your Lucky Stars* for 'Don't Start Crying Now'. So up we went to do [the show], and the revolt set in: 'Fuck this! I'm not going on dressed like this.' The boys appeared, and Alan was the only one who kept the Carnaby gear on. Phil went buck-mad when we went back down to London [but] was told, 'That's the way we are.' I was the spokesman. He'd expected us to come back looking like the Shadows. It was just, 'Fuck it, we're not going to be told. We'll be ourselves.'

Such notional acts of independence were hardly the extent of the Solomons' problems. As Phil candidly admits, 'It was difficult for Dorothy to book Them. She hadn't got a string of clubs she could book [the band] into. People had to ring her . . . We booked a lot of showbands.' Initially, Dorothy even tried to book Them on to the lucrative London-Irish circuit, but that idea lasted one gig only.

Billy Harrison: Phil Solomon hadn't a clue how to manage a group like Them . . . We had a gig in Shepherd's Bush and we stopped outside, and it was the Shamrock Club. And we all looked at each other – 'We're not a showband. We don't do this' – and we drove away. We never even went in.

Uncompromising. Counterproductive. The net result may not have been the Solomons' washing their hands of Them, but it was close enough for R&B. If Them didn't want to play the Irish circuit, Them didn't play. When they did find a place to play, like the Pontiac in Putney, they were just as likely to start trouble as to start playing. Harrison remembers one night there when Van was doing 'his usual back-to-Cookstown-pigs thing with [some] guys in the toilet. I throw him out the door, and I end up fighting two guys for him . . . ['cause] Van couldn't have fought his way out of a paper bag . . . We'd gone to see . . . someone. Van got to [making] his usual caustic comment, and someone took it the wrong way.'

Meanwhile, the only money coming to Them was what the Solomon Agency deigned to advance. It was not a lot, and it was hard work getting it. The Aaland Hotel, where the band had been deposited, at least provided its own in-built entertainment, as well as a traditional English breakfast to keep body and soul together.

Ronnie Millings: During the week we were buying a loaf of bread and cutting it up between us. We were doing one show a week, but some of these bands in London were fantastic, and you're going on playing after them [thinking], 'They're better than us.' . . . We stayed in Holborn. [DJ] Jimmy Savile used to stay in the same digs as us . . . It used to say outside, 'Girls beware! Jimmy Savile lives here.' Girl reporters wouldn't go in on their own. Little Walter, he stayed there. His breakfast was a half-bottle of rum in the morning. We're all tucking into these fries, [putting] toast [and] sandwiches in the pocket, [knowing that] this is our last meal of the day.

The few individuals from the Emerald Isle they occasionally ran across were invariably stunned to learn of the hardships they were suffering, even as they were seen miming to their latest single on national TV. Geordie Sproule is one of those who remember running into Morrison in London: 'I was [there] with a showband and I was getting thirty quid a night, and Van had signed up with the Solomons and was starving. I think I gave him five shillings and something to eat.' Peter Lloyd tells a similar story, of 'meeting them somewhere around Russell Square. They had come back from [overseas] . . . and Philip had picked [up] all the equipment and not given them any money. I think they were staying in the YMCA, and we took 'em out for fish and chips . . . Talking [with us at] that time, they were very anti-Phil.'

A couple of months' living on a daily fry-up and slices of Mother's Pride might not have qualified these Belfast boys to swap stories with some of the blues veterans also holed up in the Aaland, riding on name-checks from the likes of the Stones and the Yardbirds, but they did manage to bond with a couple of living legends. In Morrison's case, he began a real friendship with one of the blues greats.

No matter how prickly Morrison could be when confronted by reporters, when it came to music, especially if it involved learning from someone like Chess harp-player Little Walter, it was a case of 'How'd you do this? How'd you do that?' As Morrison wrote in a journal he kept at the time, 'Little Walter was very reluctant to show me some harmonica things but . . . he made it sound like a sax and a trumpet. Sometimes I would run errands and then he would show me something, like playing a harp in several keys.' According to Harrison, Alan Henderson, Van and he were invited by Little Walter on stage at the Manor House one night, and Morrison got to sing with the great one. Unfortunately the little musical community at the Aaland became a bit too friendly for the management's liking:

Billy Harrison: We ended up having sessions in the flippin' lounge with Little Walter and John Lee Hooker. It was Little Walter we got [really] friendly with. We were jamming in the lounge – we started off with just a guitar, [but then] drums ended up coming in, and then everything else. Didn't go down awfully well. Hooker was there as well. I [also] remember meeting Sonny Boy Williamson and Muddy Waters . . . Little Walter took us round to meet them.

Perhaps exposure to the authentic article rubbed off on Them for they were soon back in the studio, recording a follow-up to 'Don't Start Crying Now', and this time they had a riff as memorable as anything the opposition could muster, even if no one seems too sure who conceived it. Most folk have given Jimmy Page – then one of London's best-known session guitarists – credit for not only playing the 'Baby Please Don't Go' riff at the session, but also coming up with it. Harrison, though, is adamant that, though Page 'played rhythm guitar' on the session, the riff was devised by him (Eric Wrixon states that 'the world is full of witnesses who can testify that Billy Harrison had been playing "Baby Please Don't Go" live exactly the way it turned out on record'). In fact, the riff in question was an inventive reworking of an earlier Paul Burlison riff, from 'Train Kept a-Rollin' ', a song later part of the Yardbirds' repertoire.

'Baby Please Don't Go' was recorded shortly after Them's return to London, as Solomon decided none of the cuts from July did the deed, having already scheduled a second 45 for November 1964. Their two-month sojourn also gave Them the opportunity to work on some songs for a début LP. Before work could begin, though, Solomon needed to find a producer who could both whip Them into shape and at the same time deal with any problems that might arise from his troublesome charges. Solomon already had an American producer in mind, someone with a proven pedigree and a commercial ear. As co-author of 'Twist and Shout', 'Under the Boardwalk' and 'Everybody Needs Somebody to Love', Bert Berns was more than just a producer of hits. Equally importantly, Berns shared Solomon's approach to the business side of things – as Morrison later discovered to his cost.

Phil Solomon: I loved the type of work that Bert did in America. I'd been over on a number of occasions and I'd met Bert through the publisher Bobby Mellon. On [my] second visit over there, he was recording the Drifters . . . I thought that Bert knew the American market from beginning to end. I was a newcomer and Dick Rowe hadn't had very many big smashes in the States. I thought the answer was to bring Bert over to record Them. He suggested ['Here Comes the Night'], we liked the song and went ahead [and recorded] it.

Much bad press has come Phil Solomon's way for his treatment of Them – and indeed fellow Irish exports Taste and the Mad Lads. At no point, though, do the members of Them, Morrison included, seem to have given Solomon due credit for the two deeds that gave Them the commercial breakthrough they sought, but ultimately squandered. His first good deed was undoubtedly the recruitment of Berns, which led directly to Them recording 'Here Comes the Night'. And though Solomon was smart enough to put Morrison's 'All for Myself' on the B-side, thus retaining half of the single's publishing – 'so as to get a [free] ride' – he also realized that 'if you're looking after an artist's best interests, you [always] go with the best song'.

Not only did Berns offer the band 'Here Comes the Night' – itself little more than a rewrite of 'There She Comes', a song he had previously cut with the Exciters – he also put his production expertise at the band's disposal. And they found his whole approach something new and exciting.★

Billy Harrison: Bert was a breath of fresh air. In those days everyone had a BBC mentality: 'You stand on this X and you don't fucking move!' Recording studios were exactly the same. Dick Rowe and everybody else, that's the way they were! Every note pristine. Bert Berns walks into the studio, lifts a drumstick in the middle of the recording, starts beating a cymbal and says, 'Let's get this cooking, lads.' There wasn't a man in Britain [who] would have done that. But he was running the session. And that's where the life came from. He also did overdubs . . .'cause he bounced things down, having left a free track.

Berns may well have made the process come alive but he also made the band work, and work, until they had an arrangement that met with his approval (he would later do the same with 'Brown Eyed Girl'). The recording of 'Here Comes the Night' came only after a laborious set of rehearsals. Millings, for whom this was his last session, believes 'it took us four days. We worked on it and worked on it, and then we got it. We were rehearsing it, [but] the only place we could rehearse was the studio.' Only at the end of four days was there a song for Them to record.

★ The songs that appear to have been recorded by Bert Berns were 'Baby Please Don't Go', 'Here Comes the Night', 'All for Myself ', '(It Won't Hurt) Half as Much', 'I Gave My Love a Diamond', 'Go on Home Baby' and 'My Little Baby'.

Billy Harrison: I remember sitting in Decca when Bert said he had this song, and he came out with 'Here Comes the Night'. He had a riff and that's all he had, and we sat and we worked at it, and we came up with what you hear. We worked it out sitting in the studio – but no engineers or anything.

Phil Coulter, who was then working for Phil Solomon as a songwriter, 'distinctly remember[s] walking into the Decca Studios in West Hampstead, for a session Bert had with Them . . . he was doing a run-through of 'Here Comes the Night' . . . [and] I knew this was a hit!'. At the time, though, it was simply one of a handful of songs Berns was recording for Them's first album. It was more important to establish the band's R&B credentials than to make such an overt grab for the pop audience. That was where 'Baby Please Don't Go' came in, and where Solomon would do his second good deed, albeit after losing one more band member to his penny-pinching ways.

The belt-tightening reached such a nadir by November that a second member of the original quintet decided he'd had enough and quit. Ronnie Millings turned up one Friday for his weekly 'salary' and was told that there was no money left. With a wife and kids to feed and clothe, he swapped his drumsticks for a driving licence and by the following day 'was driving the Bobby Patrick Six about. It was the first thing that came along.' With management unwilling to incur any 'unnecessary' expense, the band was advised to make do with its four remaining members, McAuley reverting to drums, leaving the organ to temporarily gather dust.

Should it have been Solomon's intent to divide and rule, the strategy was working out just fine. As Harrison observes, 'If it had been the original group when things started to happen, I think we'd have stuck together. 'Cause we'd all come up together . . . [but] you're hanging on in for your dreams, even if you're starving. You're young, you're bulletproof!' Solomon seemed determined to push his bulletproof Belfast boys to the limit. When the November release of 'Baby Please Don't Go' failed to set the pop world alight, an(other) appearance on *Thank Your Lucky Stars* looked like being the last roll of this particular die.★ The barely-solvent quartet now found out just how draining it can be to hang on to dreams.

★ Harrison appears to be referring to an undocumented appearance on *Thank Your Lucky Stars*, which was recorded at the Alpha TV Studios in Birmingham. Them's original appearance on the show was on 20 September, but it is unlikely he has confused dates. The band did perform 'Baby Please Don't Go' on *Ready Steady Go!* in December, so a return trip to Aston at this point seems likely.

Billy Harrison: The Sunday we had done *Thank Your Lucky Stars* [in] Birmingham, I hadn't slept for three days – I'd been driving and we had no money to go to hotels or anything – and we got in the studio. The Beach Boys were over on their first visit. We hadn't had the chance to wash or change clothes. We had shadows, eyes sunk in our heads, the whole bit. I remember trudging around the corridors – two of the Beach Boys came up and they [just] stopped dead. They must have thought we were on make-up for some [horror skit]. We came out of there and I drove back to London and we were in the [café] on the Monday morning and I fell asleep in my breakfast. I just went donk!! . . . [McAuley] was asthmatic [and] after pushing the van in the fog, I thought he was gonna croak. There was a quick rustle 'round [and] we had enough money to put Pat and Van in a YMCA, and Alan Henderson and I slept in the van from the Monday to the Friday. We stole milk off the doorsteps. We lived off milk and a packet of biscuits for four days – the two of us – and then we got the money off Solomon and came home on the boat on Friday. On the Saturday night we played the Inst. for a tenner, and we were bloody glad of it. But everybody was pointing [their] finger. There was no 'Well done, lads. You've opened the door for the rest of us.' [They were] jealous as hell . . . The ordinary punters, they loved us because we were their own people and had made it, but the musos resented it greatly . . . Then, [on] New Year's Eve, 'Baby Please Don't Go' went into the Top Forty, [and on] 6 January we went back over and played Birmingham Town Hall, and Tom Jones was sixth on the bill.

The initial failure of 'Baby Please Don't Go' had been a lot less expected than that of 'Don't Start Crying Now', at least in Decca quarters. That trigger-happy intro alone should have ensured chartdom, even if the decision to squander perhaps the definitive Them track, 'Gloria', on its B-side relinquished Them's only realistic chance at a number-one single.* Initial sales, though, proved disappointing.

It was Solomon's connections and business acumen that now turned things around. He was on good terms with Vicki Wickham, who produced *Ready Steady Go!* for the ITV network, and over lunch one day Solomon persuaded her to make 'Baby Please Don't Go' the weekly *Ready Steady Go!* signature tune for the forthcoming series. Solomon chooses to downplay the stakes, but admits that he 'needed some help and [so] I went to Vicki Wickham and she played ball. She was a nice

---

* According to Phil Solomon, it was Pat Campbell, who was in charge of promotion for him, who chose 'Baby Please Don't Go' as the A-side.

woman, [and] she liked the record.' Wickham's gesture returned 'Baby Please Don't Go' to regular airplay status, and within two weeks of its appearance as *RSG*'s signature, it entered the charts at twenty-six, eventually nestling in the Top Ten.

Thanks to Bert Berns, Them also had the perfect follow-up. Solomon wasted no time in preparing the ground for 'Baby Please Don't Go''s successor, 'Here Comes the Night'. He was just as determined as the band to ensure that this opportunity did not go to waste. The third Them single was released on 5 March 1965. Despite Lulu's version of the song – also produced by Berns – having already flopped, the Them performance went straight into the charts, buoyed by appearances on all three national TV pop shows – *Thank Your Lucky Stars*, *Ready Steady Go!* and *Top of the Pops*. With that insistent, toe-tapping beat, courtesy of Ronnie Millings, a quintessential hook and rasping vocal, 'Here Comes the Night' climbed to number two in the UK charts, beaten off the top slot by the Stones' first all-original 45, 'The Last Time'.

However, the success of 'Here Comes the Night' might also be seen as a renunciation of the band's roots. Morrison has certainly considered its release a turning point: 'When we recorded that . . . song . . . which was a poppy sort of song . . . that's when everything went wrong.' At the time, though, everyone in Them was enthused about working with Berns, and their goal remained the same as Solomon's – to keep making hit records.

Morrison's 1997 statement, to an interviewer, that he didn't 'really know why I became famous, because I wasn't one of those people that wanted it' is denied by his own words, voiced in an *NME* 'Lifeline' questionnaire back in April 1965, at the height of Them's success. Asked to express his personal and professional ambitions, he gave the same answer to both questions: 'To make it in the pop business.'

Mervyn Solomon: At that point the [whole] group would do anything. They were determined to get on. Van always knew what he wanted and he sulked if the others didn't do it the way he liked. But he wasn't a prima donna – not at that point.

In the self-same 1997 interview, Morrison took a more credible position when depicting fame as 'something that happened to me, and I couldn't get back to where I was before that'. Two years earlier, when writing a little edict entitled 'How Not to Get Screwed', he advised any potential pop star to 'test the lifestyle. Find out if your personality fits show business, because if it doesn't, don't bother in the first place.' So speaks the voice of experience. Like many a pop star who had spent their youth aspiring to 'make it', when success finally beat a path to his door, Morrison found it did nothing to assuage the void at the centre of his being. Perhaps it was this shock to the system that turned him from shy to sullen, from personable to petulant.

Unfortunately, no one had briefed him as to when to turn off these traits. When it came time for him to give his first interview to the national pop press, he was ill-prepared for a spot of glad-handing.

Keith Altham: My first interview with Them I chose to do largely on the basis of something Eric Burdon had told me . . . [It was] a story about Van Morrison in the early days . . . He managed to get harassed by a bunch of Teds in the audience, who were giving him a bad time, and went to the microphone and started to read them poetry, ending up with 'To wank or not to wank, that is the question.' . . . The formula for the *NME* at that time was interview anything that comes into the Top Thirty . . . I went to a rehearsal room to see them, and Morrison was in conversation with Bert Berns, who I really didn't know from Adam. I waited for a little while, [but] their conversation didn't seem to be about to break up and I'd been there for about half an hour, so I said, 'Will you be able to do the interview now, Van?' to which Van responded in his usual charming manner, 'Can't you see I'm busy. Fuck off! . . . I don't have the time. I'm talking to Bert. You should be interviewing Bert Berns – he's the genius.' Anyway, he sent me over to talk to Billy Harrison, who proceeded to clean his fingernails with a jack-knife . . . So I duly wrote it up as rather tongue-in-cheek, so that anybody who actually had half a brain could see that the whole thing was a send-up. I got called in by the executive editor two days later, when the thing was printed. He apparently had quite a close relationship with Phil Solomon. So I stood there . . . and he said, 'Keith, this article on Them – had a call from Phil Solomon, close friend. He didn't like it. Don't do it again.' . . . [Back then] it was slightly unusual to be rebuffed. [But] I don't think I was the only one. I seem to recall Richard Greene on *Record Mirror* getting pretty much the same response.

Nor was this the only time that Morrison's use of the f-word created ructions for Them. When various unwary souls listened to the Them track, 'Little Girl', on a charity album issued by Decca for the Lord's Taverners Fund, they found not only an unabashed paean to a fourteen-year-old schoolgirl, but also, audible to the more bat-like as the song entered the fade-out, an unmistakable Belfast accent shouting, 'I wanna fuck you!' On a pop record in 1965!! The first pressing was unceremoniously yanked, and reissued minus the extended fade,★ but this was clearly a bandleader tearing at his leash. Needless to say, Solomon was not used to such, well, ingratitude.

Phil Solomon: I found that they had an image which was very, very difficult to understand. I had the same problem with two groups from Ireland, and everybody else was so easy to work with: if you wanted to do an interview, it was arranged, they'd be there on time, they'd be very respectful to the interviewer, they answered questions and that was it. But Them had an attitude problem the whole time.

Thankfully Solomon's close relationship with elements of the media allowed much that he would rather leave unsaid out of the papers. The Lord's Taverners album story never ran. Nor did a story in a Belfast paper about the royalties the ex-drummer of Them never saw. In Them's case, Phil Solomon knew he was fighting a losing battle, something he recognized and tried to turn to his advantage. Coming up with the Angry Young Them moniker was his highly original way of promoting these unmarketable colts.

Morrison would later dismiss the new 'image' as 'a publicity gimmick by Phil Solomon's publicity department', belittling it as something 'that was promoted by Decca Records . . . they wanted it to be more outrageous than any of the other groups – more moody, more difficult, more everything than anyone else'. If Morrison preferred to think of Them as 'five young lads from Belfast who liked their parents', he wasn't about to let any poor unfortunate interviewer in on the secret. Back in Belfast, local journalist Chris Ryder tried to downplay their reputation – 'their image is one of moody, dirty, long-haired boys . . . nothing could be further from the truth' – but could only offer as evidence the fact that they 'all wash regularly'.

An opportunity for the entire nation to see the real Them and bathe in their moody magnificence came that Easter, when they somehow snuck

---

★ Only the first pressing of the scarce *14* album contains the full take. Even after correcting a number of errors on the original UK edition of *The Story of Them* CD-set, the US version still failed to restore the full version of 'Little Girl'.

on to the bill for the *NME* Pollwinners Concert at Wembley's Empire Pool echo chamber. This annual jamboree was usually confined to the acts that had figured in that year's readers' poll, something Them's all too recent success precluded. But there they were, sandwiched between Donovan and the Searchers – possibly at the instigation of MC for the evening Jimmy Savile, an early champion of the band. This particular Pollwinners Concert was – indeed remains – probably the finest ever gathering of British pop acts under a single roof, with the Beatles and the Stones sharing a bill for the one and only time, ably supported by the likes of the Kinks, the Animals, the Moody Blues, Dusty Springfield – and Them.

Determined to take this opportunity to show the real roots of the band, Them segued from their current hit into a seven-minute slice of 'Turn on Your Lovelight'. It was certainly an audacious move at an event where even the Beatles and the Stones confined themselves to familiar hits. Unfortunately, the limitations of 1965 PA systems and the lack of atmosphere in this aircraft hangar of a venue made Them's attempt at infusing some danger into the occasion a qualified success at best. Morrison, though, hung on to the song like a terrier, wailing over the blunderbuss pounding of Pat McAuley's drums (his brother Jackie having assumed the organist's role earlier in the year). Perhaps this Pollwinners performance proves Morrison's later assertion that 'Them wasn't the right vehicle for that kinda music, for any kinda extended songs. In that context, it wasn't a workable thing.' In Them's defence, the band's abrasive style had rarely gone over well with the London audiences, going right back to their début at Beat City.

Billy Harrison: I never, ever liked playing in London. Hated it. Never went down well in London . . . I remember standing on stage with Van on gigs in inner and outer London, both of us pissed off, and starting to do a Lenny Bruce routine between the two of us on the microphone – 'Wasn't born here.' 'No, I know, but sure am dying here.' . . . He was a big Lenny Bruce fan. We were slagging the crowd off, but they didn't realize . . . The 100 Club would have the same half a dozen groups turning round, with guests in there, but if you were to go in . . . when Alexis Korner was there – you could have been Jesus, [but] you weren't Alexis Korner! We were [mostly sent] out around the Midlands, the north, Scotland and the west country, which suited us fine.

Harrison believes that the band's slightly threatening image was a boon. To him, there were 'so many groups of the day [that] were typecast

– and Them weren't. Nobody got any interviews. There was a group running all over Britain playing, that had two hit records, and nobody knew a thing about Them. There was a great curiosity level because of that, and that actually helped the group.' Morrison would prefer us to believe that he willingly returned the mantle of success to its shelf:

Van Morrison: When I was in Them, it was anti-climactic. 'All right, so I'm a star, but I don't want it.' So I gave it back: 'There it is. I don't have to be on *Top of the Pops* every week, I don't want to be a star.' [1978]

In fact, Them's descent from the heights of two Top Ten hits was precipitous, and quite unplanned. Harrison emphasizes how much of a live draw the band remained on certain parts of the mainland, but without further hits even this local notoriety would eventually run its course. As it was, the choice of singles didn't reside with the band but with the management.

Phil Solomon: Dick Rowe in many cases worked for me. We gave the records to Decca but we owned them . . . To be perfectly honest, I don't think the band were in a position to make decisions in those days. It was either Tommy Scott, my head of A&R, or Dick Rowe who would make the decision [about the choice of studio, while] I think the [choice of] single was Dick Rowe and myself.

The follow-up to 'Here Comes the Night' chosen by Solomon was a Morrison original, 'One More Time'. Van, though, had very little idea how to write a pop song. 'One More Time' lacked both the raw rasp of 'Gloria' and the snappy drive of 'Here Comes the Night'. Coming as it did on the back of two big hits, its release in June 1965 was accompanied by a certain fanfare but, as Harrison archly observes, 'it was never single material . . . Phil Solomon made these decisions. He put out "One More Time" because it was Van's number, and he had the publishing . . . I remember arguing to get "Half as Much" out instead. The single bombed.'*

With their momentum lost, the band was in danger of imploding again, just as the release of Them's first LP hinted at depths still untapped.

---

* Harrison would eventually get his way, but by the time Solomon released 'Half as Much', in August, he had already left the band.

The eponymous album actually opened with the kind of clarion call that could have taken the singles chart by storm – if only 'Mystic Eyes' had been released as a 45 at the time of optimum impact. Instead, it would follow 'Half as Much' into singular oblivion five months later, backed by another cut from the uncharted album. In the States, though, where singles invariably came from albums and 'Mystic Eyes' was promoted as the follow-up to 'Gloria', it followed its predecessor into the lower regions of the Hot Hundred.

Indeed the impact of 'Mystic Eyes' on the other side of the pond seems to have helped define Morrison as an original voice (in Britain, both Them hits were covers, whereas in the US they were both Morrison originals). Greil Marcus certainly remembers the first time he heard 'Mystic Eyes' on the radio: 'I'd never heard anything like that. A piece of music that was supposedly made for airplay, [with] this long instrumental introduction that was really the whole song.' 'Mystic Eyes' was a real dose of Them, not some Bernsian pop confection. Its sheer originality may even have been enough to buck the trend and make the UK charts. After all, it had been Them's ability to ad-lib that had originally set them apart.

Billy Harrison: Van didn't write songs – he wrote ideas and then the song came as he was performing. He never had a song written down – maybe words here and there on cigarette packets – but you'd start to diddle around between numbers with some riff and he'd put something on top of it and gradually it would evolve . . . [and] Them were probably the best group at ad-libbing of anyone. Many's the time on stage I'd just start to play a riff, the boys just fell in and then Van just threw words on it. A lot of [the songs] started life like that – over the course of time it got refined. But never deliberately. It just happened.

Morrison agrees. At least he did back in 1965, when he described to a Belfast reporter how '"Mystic Eyes" just happened. We didn't plan a note. It was during the first recording session for the LP, and we were just busking around. Someone started playing a fast riff and we all just joined in. The lyrics I sing at the end were just words from a song I had been writing at the time.' The song in question, he later told an American journalist, was inspired by an occasion in Nottingham Park when he was walking alongside a graveyard wall and saw some children playing next to it.

Van Morrison: You know, man, there was life and death beside one [an]other . . . so close . . . yet so different . . . And then I thought of the bright lights in the children's eyes . . . and the cloudy lights in the eyes of the dead. [1966]

This type of self-conscious exposition would be quickly consigned to the past, but the working methodology Harrison and Morrison describe would not. Sadly, in the case of 'Mystic Eyes', the refining process was apparently effected by the pause button on the recording machine. Tommy Scott, who became *de facto* producer of Them sessions after Berns's return to the States, has described how 'Mystic Eyes' was 'pieced together . . . from a ten-minute track, originally conceived as an instrumental . . . [but] after blowing his harmonica for about seven minutes, [Van] suddenly burst into this spontaneous lyric'. As was often the case, the tape was not rolling on this original performance. The released take condenses that ten-minute take to single length, snipping out the beginning and end. As Brian Hogg notes, 'there's a point, just at the final fade, where the organ screams uncontrollably into white noise, [telegraphing] the imminent collapse'.

'Mystic Eyes' was one of the products of a new-found recording freedom, away from the clinical confines of Decca. Having discovered a more central studio – in Denmark Street – which they preferred, Them felt inclined to experiment with the structural limitations of the pop music Solomon thought they should be making. What their new studio, Regent Sound, was not was deluxe. Even by the standards of mid-sixties London studios, it was, to quote Kinks/Who producer Shel Talmy, 'a shit-hole . . . an awful place with egg-boxes up on the ceiling for sound baffling . . . there were stains on the stains. It was no more than a demo studio.' This was a large part of its charm. Andrew Loog Oldham had stumbled on the studio in the early months of 1963 and had been using it ever since to cut some of the Stones' raunchier recordings – a fact surely not lost on Ireland's premier R&B exponents.

Andrew Loog Oldham: It was a mono studio and . . . everyone agreed that recording in mono would be better. Mono had the element we needed; what you hear is what you get . . . Regent Sound was magnificent . . . [It] was no larger than an average good-sized hotel room. The control room was the size of a hotel bathroom, but for us it was magic. The sound leaked, instrument to instrument, the right way. You'd hear the bottom end of Charlie's drums

bleeding through Keith's acoustic, and vice versa . . . Put them both together
and you had a wall of noise.

Them, too, realized that this was a great place to record R&B. It was
also cheap enough for Solomon not to balk at the band spending spare
afternoons in there, working out ideas for songs. It was here that Harrison
came up with the idea of wiring the piano microphone through the
tremolo unit on the guitar amplifier, which is how he gets that surreal
phasing effect on John Lee Hooker's 'Don't Look Back', perhaps the
best band arrangement on Them's début LP. It was also here that they
recorded the likes of 'Just a Little Bit', 'You Just Can't Win' and 'I'm
Gonna Dress in Black'. However, the most ambitious statement from
those spring sessions would not be released until the autumn of 1967,
when Solomon was looking for a way to exhume Them's remains one
more time.

Billy Harrison: 'The Story of Them' was recorded in Denmark Street . . .
That [song] again came out of sitting idle and starting to play riffs. It was just a
jam and Van shouting words off the top of his head, and then sitting down and
things getting talked about . . . The Maritime was over, Northern Ireland was
over, and that's what that's all about. See, the guys he's talking about, like Big
Kid Boppin', those were mates of mine that came down and were bouncers at
the Maritime . . . Even [after] we went back without Ronnie, when the group
was a big hit, the old days were still better. That's why 'The Story of Them'
sounds like something that's all over. It is.

Its belated release, the lack of recording information and the sense that
this is an epitaph-in-song has led many to assume that 'The Story of
Them' was a product of the band's last sessions in 1966. The fact that the
song was recorded when 'Here Comes the Night' was still hovering
around the charts suggests just how quickly disillusionment set in. There
is no real disagreement as to the prime source of that disillusionment.
With two hit singles and concerts galore, the band was still living a
breadline existence that sat in stark contrast to the plush West End offices
of the Solomon Agency.

The next person to bale out was scarcely expected. Peter Bardens had
replaced Jackie McAuley on organ shortly after the Pollwinners Concert,
only to find that he was being taken into Phil Solomon's confidence, a
process that duly accelerated his departure. As he told *Trouser Press* some

years later, 'What happened was that the manager . . . thought that my English accent meant I was more intelligent than the others, who were Irish. Of course I wasn't, but he would always ring me up and get me involved in all sorts of intrigue. In the end I'd had enough of all the back-stabbing, and I surprised everyone by telling them that I was going . . . There was too much intrigue.' The bandleader and general organizer was not far behind:

Billy Harrison: We paid our own expenses for *Top of the Pops* [in Manchester], and we didn't know we were getting paid for it. In those days the TV people themselves put it across very strongly that they were doing you a favour . . . Plus I was already chivvying about 'Where's such-and-such money gone? . . . What the fuck's going on?' . . . The promoters used to pay me a lot of times. I'd come back to London with two or three grand in a money belt . . . [And] the first we knew about 'One More Time' was when we heard it was released. That was part of the whole scenario of me leaving. That, and then the boys grumbling about getting ripped off . . . [So we go] into the office, [the] five of us sitting there, and I [confront Solomon]. In front of my face, he went round them one at a time and they all shut up, none of 'em said a word. Left me sitting on my own. Phil knew I was the one that was going to make trouble for him, so he worked on the old basis of divide and conquer. He alienated the rest of them from me . . . This created a rift between me and the rest of the band . . . After this confrontation with Solomon I just left. No sour grapes, just left . . . Once I was gone, they had no spearhead. He could push them about whatever way he liked.

What Solomon did not seem to realize, and Morrison would only recognize when the band was on its last legs, was that the dynamic that made Them unique was greater than the sum of its parts. Though he was hardly Jimmy Page, Harrison's departure finished the Them that was. Solomon had got his way, but in the process the cash cow's milk began to dry up.

Eric Wrixon: Solomon's attitude was short-term, with no investment. So he was a crucial part of . . . why the band fell apart . . . You got to remember [that] in those early days, the driver, the boss, the energy came from Billy Harrison. He was the guy who went out and got things done, and everybody fell in behind him . . . He was very much the bandleader . . . [ ] . . . Van was the very artistic, laid-back, 'Ach, it doesn't matter, man' sort of person. Billy Harrison was 'No. He owes us another 20p, let's have it!' . . . When people offered not to pay us, Billy changed their thinking very quickly . . . [ ] . . . Billy was the guy that said, ' 'Scuse me, we haven't been paid for four days. Can I see some books?' Which is why Billy had to go. [But] I don't think Van realized, in certain situations, Billy was fighting everybody's corner. [CH/TH/CH]

As with many subsequent dealings involving 'the industry', Morrison would only learn about solidarity the hard way, and after the fact. Though it would take him a while to extract himself from the Them situation, as he said in 1986, 'By that point I'd left . . . in my head.'

Harrison was the lucky one. He left a band at the top of its tree. However, it would not be his last association with Them. When his replacement, Jim Armstrong, baled out in similar circumstances, Harrison agreed to complete a brief European tour as a for-hire guitarist in Van Morrison's Them. One night in a hotel bar in Stockholm, Van finally turned to Billy and admitted, 'You were right, pal. What you said about the Solomons – I see it now.' Forced to take 'a wee bit more interest in the contracts and things', Morrison now knew the extent to which Harrison had kept the whole venture afloat.

Deep down, though, Morrison had always wanted to cast Them in his image alone. His nemesis, Phil Solomon, was now prepared to let that happen – as long as he allowed himself to become a complicit leader of a sham Them. And, initially at least, he was willing. However, when Pat McAuley also decided he'd had enough within days of Harrison's departure, the new captain was in danger of going down with the ship. Harrison and McAuley returned to Belfast and duly announced that they were re-forming Them – minus Van Morrison. With more original members outside the band than in, Morrison and Henderson were dispatched back to Belfast to put together a new band around this nucleus. The first guitarist Morrison thought of calling was his old Monarch buddy, Billy McAllen. The offer he made, though, was less than tempting.

Billy McAllen: They were actually on *Top of the Pops* that Thursday night, [when] Van rang me to come over and join Them. I was playing in a band here, earning pretty good money. So I says, 'Van, as a matter of interest, what's the money?' 'Ten pounds a week.' I says, 'You're joking.' I was earning more money here.

Around the same time, Morrison and Henderson ran into the Three Js, out for a coffee one night in Belfast centre. Any rancour left from the end of their association had long since dissipated, and Gerry McKervey asked how it was going. Morrison found himself admitting that they had sold themselves short: 'We're getting seven pounds a week. It's nothing very good, Gerry. D'ya see [us on] *Top of the Pops*? We still only got seven pounds a week wages.' Ronnie Millings also remembers a time when 'Morrison was hankering to come back here and form the group over again, to get back the sound he had originally'. In order to do that he would have had to tell Solomon to shove his contract where the sun don't shine, and that still wasn't something he was prepared to do. After everything that had gone down in the months since he'd last enjoyed Mom's cooking, his personal and professional ambitions remained the same: 'To make it in the pop business.'

8

1966: Getting Twisted

There was no motive behind anything you did [back then]. You just did it because you wanted to do it and you enjoyed doing it. That's the way the thing started, but it got twisted somewhere along the way and everybody involved in it got twisted as well, including me.

—*Van Morrison, 1967*

You can't take something like that, put it in a box and place a neat little name on it, then try to sell it. That's what they tried to do. That's what killed Them.

—*Van Morrison, 1973*

How complicit Morrison was in the removal of Billy Harrison is not entirely clear. Perhaps his contribution was simply to do nothing. Manager Phil Solomon claims that the leadership of the band was never an issue to him, that he 'was only really interested in Van Morrison . . . The musicians behind [him] meant nothing to me. The song publishing was always with Van. If Van co-wrote something with A, B or C, that was their business to sort out.' However, to the singer himself it had always been something of a bugbear. The recently-departed Peter Bardens remembers how the nineteen-year-old Morrison 'had trouble communicating his ideas to the others . . . [but] there was always conflict and tension over who was leader . . . and sometimes Van's eyes got all glassy – you knew he was about to erupt!'.

Harrison, though, was more than a match for Morrison. He commanded a loyalty from the other 'original' members with which Morrison could not compete. As the only band member who stood up to Solomon, though, he became an easy target. After his departure, Harrison 'got word from a couple of people that Van had been auditioning musos in the 100 Club before I left. I think this was a whole move. The Solomons wanted to break him away from the group.' It seems Morrison was getting caught up in the management machinations.

Morrison returned to Belfast at the beginning of September 1965 as the unquestioned leader of Them. Unfortunately, there was no Them left to lead. Starting almost from scratch, Morrison and bassist Alan Henderson initially began rehearsing with a local band, the Misfits, until Mervyn Solomon – concerned about Billy Harrison and Pat McAuley's threat to form an alternative Them – pointed out that the new band would contain more Misfits than members of Them.

It was back to the Maritime, this time for a series of auditions. Caretaker Joe Harper suggested a number of possible recruits, including guitarist Eric Bell, but it was Mervyn Solomon who came up with the most suitable replacement guitarist, Jim Armstrong. Armstrong believes he was approached even before Morrison came home, Solomon turning up at his father's house in a Rolls-Royce.

Ray Elliott, a local sax player who dabbled in other wind instruments, was also probably suggested by Mervyn Solomon. Elliott's recruitment indicates that Morrison was already planning to take a more soul-infused direction. Initially, the new line-up rehearsed with a drummer named Michael Duff. Morrison, though, said he wanted someone 'more drivey' and, returning to the Misfits, asked drummer John Wilson if he would be interested. Thus ended two months of inactivity, as a new five-piece Them was born. Perhaps surprisingly, this proved to be the most stable outfit since Them Mk 1.

After a couple of weeks of rehearsals, on 24 September 1965 they returned to Lisburn, where they unveiled a new forty-minute set at the Top Hat Club. The following night Them were in Ballymena, blowing away a few more cobwebs before they went back to England for a relaunch. Arriving in London, they were summoned to Phil Solomon's office the following Monday.

Solomon had spent an anxious few weeks, promoting a single and an album by a band that no longer existed. The experience does not seem to have mellowed him. Jim Armstrong, who had given up his job as a bank teller for the opportunity to play guitar full-time, remembers how Solomon's 'first greeting to me was, "You're the young man who worked in a bank. You should have stayed there." He took us to a little café down from Oxford Street – Cat Stevens's father owned it – and bought us coffee and sandwiches. First week's wages, deduction for sandwiches.' John Wilson confirms both incidents, along with Solomon's relish when telling the new recruits that they 'should have stayed in Ireland. He laughed [at the fact] that we'd actually come over to join the band.' Wilson relates a familiar litany of the way band members continued to be treated by management:

John Wilson: Basically . . . we were just told what to do. You arrived Monday morning and got your wages . . . To sit for hours waiting to get your pittance was very degrading . . . It wasn't very pleasant . . . The whole situation was not very comfortable . . . Even I could see that they were strangling the goose that laid the golden egg. Nobody cared about Van, and he certainly didn't get any preferential treatment. Nobody was interested. They treated him just the same way as they treated the rest of the band, like we were idiots from Ireland. There was always talk in the band about the fact that Van wasn't really getting the money he should be getting.

If the financial veil remained as impenetrable as ever, this new line-up at least offered Morrison the chance to pursue a new musical direction, evident from their very first public performance, for which Morrison has given much of the credit to Ray Elliott, who 'was a jazzer from way back . . . I wanted to get a lot more jazz-oriented people in the group.' The Belfast *City Week* review of their Lisburn début, with its slightly reproachful tone, suggested that acceptance of their new sound might yet be hard won:

There was an emphasis on soul jazz that would have raised an eyebrow if played by any other local group. The sight of Van Morrison and new boy Ray Elliott chase-chorusing their way through a two-tenor version of 'The Train and the River' would even have stimulated a Royal Showband fan who had arrived a night early.

With the new boys scarcely bedded in, they found themselves put to work on a second Them album barely three months after the release of the début collection. This was the era of two albums a year, whoever you were and whatever your label. Unfortunately, Phil Solomon still held the view that 'Van [simply] wasn't capable of writing enough songs

for two LPs at that stage.' From his own point of view it was important
to retain the same mix of covers and originals published by or licensed
to Hyde Park Music. That début platter achieved an acceptable balance,
with six Morrison originals augmented by three of Bert Berns's cast-offs,
of which 'I Gave My Love a Diamond' was comfortably the best. For
this second instalment, Solomon chose to persevere with Tommy Scott,
who had produced the few remaining tracks on *Them*.

Morrison has certainly given the impression over the years that he
never had much time for Scott's production values. Indeed, when a
friend of his in the early eighties accidentally let slip on the phone that
he was working with Tommy Scott, he was met by an excoriating volley
of verbal abuse from the other end of the line. When he asked who this
Scott guy might be, he was met by a second such volley, as if Morrison's
animosity towards Scott was a matter of record. Morrison has consistently
suggested that only Berns 'had any conception of what we were trying
to do'.

Van Morrison: All those other people had some weird conception of what
we were about. I never quite found out what it was . . . Between 'em they
didn't have a solitary idea as to what we were doin' . . . We'd go into the studio
and make a track, and then get it back with about ten ton of echo on it. They
were all trying to make it sound like something else . . . Once you get a tape,
you can do just about anything and everything with it. That's exactly what they
did. They mixed it, they remixed it, then took things out, then put things in
. . . There were so many times it was happening in the studio, but it was
distorted on disc. [1973]

Tommy Scott was Them's third and last producer, Dick Rowe having
produced just that first afternoon in a Decca studio. But Scott also had
some aspirations as a pop songwriter, and as a Solomon employee each
of his contributions earned as much for the management as a Morrison
original.

John Wilson: I personally didn't understand what Tommy [Scott] was all
about, from a producer's point of view. He was not really suggesting [the type
of] things that the band would have been about. He was more concerned
[with] the band recording material he had written . . . [ ] . . . If my memory
serves me well, there were a few tunes that I was sure I'd heard before by people
like Nina Simone, and I suddenly found out, no, this was one of Tommy's

tunes! [Solomon] realized the power of copyright and the money to be made through publishing. [CH/TH]

Though no Scott originals found their way on to the first Them album, three of his offerings appear on the second. According to Scott, this was simply because 'Van had lost interest at one stage. I think he was looking to get out of the set-up . . . Van went dry for a while . . . I think I recorded everything that Van wrote during that period. We used to do as much of Van's material as possible.'

Others involved in the sessions view the inclusion of Scott songs as a matter of policy. Jim Armstrong sarcastically portrays Scott as someone who would come in and say, ' "Here's a wee song I wrote on the Tube on the way in this morning." Whatever was number one last week, he wrote [again].' Phil Coulter, another fledgling songsmith in the grip of the Solomons, told Johnny Rogan that he didn't think 'anyone with half an ear could say that it was strong material. That was a great bone of contention . . . Van had plenty of songs. [But] Scott was an aspiring producer-songwriter and his priority was to get his songs on there.' (Coming from the man responsible for atrocities like 'Puppet on a String' and 'Congratulations', this might strike the reader as, well, rather rich.)

As it is, not only was one of the three songs Scott contributed to *Them Again* co-written with Phil Coulter, but the song in question, 'I Can Only Give You Everything', became a garage-band staple. Of Scott's other two contributions, 'Don't You Know', indebted as it may be to Oscar Brown's version of the traditional 'Work Song', was the kind of jazzier torch ballad Morrison had as yet failed to write himself; while 'Call My Name' was the kind of pop fare even Beatles albums were expected to contain at this point. The album evidence tends to support Scott's contention that 'Van went dry for a while.' Of the five Morrison originals on *Them Again*, 'Could You Would You' appears to have been an old song, while 'Bad or Good' and 'Bring 'Em on in' were strictly album-fillers.

However, the other two Morrison compositions on *Them Again* both led to greater things. 'My Lonely Sad Eyes' suggests the first poetic touches from Morrison's pen, with an opening couplet that works almost as well on the page as on the ears: 'Fill me my cup, and I'll drink your sparkling wine/Pretend that everything is fine, 'til I see your sad eyes.' The title is itself all wordplay, the possessive pronoun implying that the lonely sad eyes are his when the lyrics make it clear that they are hers, and she may or may not be his (à la Dylan's 'She Belongs to Me', doubtless an influence). Nor does the recording try to mask the hurt. As Charlie Gillett later wrote, ' "My Lonely Sad Eyes" has [a] warmth . . . [that] makes you realize how rarely Van allows anybody to come close to him, how he hates to open up.'

'Hey Girl' was even more startling. Armstrong believes that 'the G6–C6 feel – very pastoral, with flutes . . . was [a sign of] Things to Come,' and it is hard to argue with his assessment. Brian Hinton, who calls the song 'a kind of mutant take on "Good Morning Little Schoolgirl" ', feels tempted to depict 'Hey Girl' as 'a dry run for "Cyprus Avenue" ' in the very passivity of its observer, 'noting everything, but unable to act or even move'. The song certainly taps directly into an almost pastoral nostalgia, destined to become a primary theme in years to come, notably on *Astral Weeks*.

Sadly these two remarkable originals – as well as the radical arrangements Them found for Screaming Jay Hawkins's 'I Put a Spell on You' and Dylan's 'It's All Over Now, Baby Blue' – were lost among the sixteen-track cornucopia of *Them Again*. This album was a product of the haphazard way it came together, with Scott and Morrison trading off their contrasting approaches one song at a time. Scott got his way on the likes of 'Hello Josephine' and an ersatz 'Turn on Your Lovelight', whilst Morrison retained his own, more distinctive approach on offerings like 'Baby Blue' – that genuine rarity, a Dylan cover to match the original.

According to Armstrong, there was also a version of 'Stormy Monday' recorded at these sessions (presumably the one later issued on a Dutch EP) that was originally fourteen to fifteen minutes, but 'it came out . . . with three guitar solos [and] flute solos cut out. Just the vocals and that was it.' Indeed the whole way the album was cobbled together suggested an ill-directed haste, born of a misguided thirst for 'product'.

John Wilson: I had been told that Van [had already done] quite a lot of recording with session people . . . My memory of [the sessions] was we'd meet upstairs in a pub somewhere down Soho and we'd run over a few bits and bobs, and then we were down to a studio [for] a day and a half. The guys in the band were all good players. Phil Coulter [also] played piano and vibes on that *Them Again* album. But to have someone as creative and talented as Van Morrison and, for the first time, have a group of musicians around him who were actually musicians . . . and just leave it to its own ends . . . was so stupid.

Morrison would later complain about being 'forced to perform under those circumstances', but at the time he had very little choice. He certainly seems to have had almost no say as to what went on the final album, with the likes of Jimmy Witherspoon's 'Times Getting Tougher than Tough' and T-Bone Walker's 'Stormy Monday' being passed over in favour of more obvious pop fare, despite being more representative of Them's new sound. *Them Again* was rushed out in January 1966, along with a single from the pen of Tommy Scott, 'Call My Name'; the failure of both releases suggested that Them had about run its course, at least in the UK.

Though the original band never consolidated their initial success, their stage show had always been a fiery act to follow; and, whatever its failings, the release of Them's début album merely reaffirmed their strengths. However, the band that was touring as Them in the winter of 1965–6 barely resembled the one represented on either record. As Morrison himself observed twenty years later, 'the records we made had nothing to do with what we were playing live. They were purely manufactured, produced items . . . The most obscure pieces of music we could find on blues albums, that's what we were playing.' Needless to say, such a contrast drove Phil Solomon absolutely nuts.

Phil Solomon: They always had an attitude problem, and it was mostly Van. The actual problem was he couldn't care less if it was a success or a failure. He would get on stage and do what he wanted to do. He never wanted to be [coached]. We [coached] other artists but never Van Morrison . . . He would never take direction.

The Them of *Them Again* were not about to do Tommy Scott numbers (they also proved awfully reluctant to perform either hit). The result was often an impasse between audience and artist, one that would only widen with the years as Morrison grew ever more determined to assert his right to play what he wanted. But he could also be a frustratingly inconsistent performer, someone who when he came up against apathy would, in Eric Wrixon's words, 'not really confront an audience head on. [He'd] sulk. His general reaction to an audience he doesn't like is to turn his back on them . . . offer them nothing and walk off. He just punishes them by contributing nothing.'

Phil Coulter: I remember . . . when Them were in the charts they did a gig at the Lyceum and they were booed off the stage . . . [Van] improvised to a great extent while he was singing, even in the studio. And if he was in an inspired mood you got some terrific things, as we did, recording with him way back then. But if he was in an ordinary mood or a dull mood, you got some rubbish. That was the price you paid for going for the spontaneity.

But then Morrison's attitude on stage, where the Solomons were powerless to intervene, had always been uncompromising. Jackie McAuley remembers how he tended to deal with hecklers: 'People used to ask Van, "Do you know any Cliff Richard numbers?" and he just wouldn't answer them. Just give them a look: this is it and fuck you . . . He really stood his ground and never went into covers when you were under pressure to do it.'

Sometimes, though, the audiences would simply not pay attention to unfamiliar fare. As Armstrong recalls, 'Some of the universities were great, but other gigs were awful, like the Top Rank ballrooms, where they were wanting to hear "Here Comes the Night". We were doing "Stormy Monday" . . . You have to tell people what to expect . . . [But] there were times Van came off raving 'cause we were doing Jimmy Witherspoon's "Times Getting Tougher than Tough" and he liked the jazzy feel to it, with vibes and sax.' Armstrong recalls a particularly memorable show at St Mary's College in London, which began with a decidedly unsuccessful attempt to revive Van the showman:

Jim Armstrong: We used to start with 'I'll Go Crazy', and Van appeared at the back of the stage with a glass in hand, and a joint. He drank the wine, took a run and jumped over the speaker, slid down the stage [and] hit the mike stand. The roadie [had to] pick him up . . . [But] it finished up, we did a version of 'The Train and the River', and they [actually] pulled the plug, 'cause we were going on and on.

In fact, instances of Morrison on the verge of losing it were becoming disturbingly common, as the conflict between his 'art' and audience expectations began to tear him apart. To have walked on stage in 1965 with a glass of wine and a joint was certainly not the smartest of acts. A large part of the blame was being directed by the other members of Them at a new lady on the scene, a London lass by the name of Dee.

No girl in Belfast, it seems, had been able to hold on to Morrison's affections. Indeed, on one occasion when he was on a ferry to Liverpool with Peter Lloyd's brother, Martin, and was seen waving goodbye to some girl, Lloyd asked him if he was sorry to leave and he replied, 'Oh, it's just good to be on the road.' Despite his writing a number of songs fixating on (the same?) childlike girl, Morrison's first adult affair seems to have been with a mother figure. The mysterious Dee has even been accused of being a Solomon plant. If so, it was hardly an inspired strategy.★ Not only was she encouraging Morrison to experiment with drugs, but Armstrong (and others) believe he was no longer 'in an environment where he could write'.

Jim Armstrong: We actually arrived for him one day and he wasn't going to go [with us]. He was staying with this girl Dee, and the radio came through the window. He was fighting with her. The roadie went in and just threw him in the van . . . [But] when I went to London, he was [already] living with Dee, who was [some] sort of mother image. She used to say, 'Put your scarf on, Van. There's [money] to get twenty cigarettes and a bottle of wine.'

Billy Harrison, who was still apprised of band secrets by bassist Alan Henderson, believes that Dee was probably responsible for Morrison's 'getting a star-complex . . . Dee [was] well older than Van . . . She was a very bad influence. What she was putting down his ear I don't know. [But] wee Van was a hard "smoker". She was the only one he took up with over there . . . She was the one I think that made Van think he was God. 'Cause there was a sudden [shift]. Van and I were about as close as Van could be with anybody, and she came on the scene and he just sort of drifted away from the group totally.' The kind of drugs he had begun taking only widened the growing gulf between him and the rest of the band. Until now, he had confined himself to the ubiquitous pills. And ubiquitous they were. As he told an audience in Sheffield some thirty years later:

In the sixties, when you had a couple of hit records, and you were part of a group, they used to send you on the road. And you never came home. You used to go up the M1 in a Ford Transit – you were just out there – and you could be out there for a year, and never even wind your watch. When you'd been out there for about eighteen months, suffering from serious exhaustion, then the management sent you to a doctor – that's what they called them – 'quacks' as we know them at this point. All these so-called rock stars going to

★ Solomon has no recollection of such a woman, and it hardly sounds like his style.

see the quack to keep them going – because it's a big money-making machine for the management. Anyway, to cut a long story short, this German doctor I went to in Belfast said, 'Take this little bottle of pills – I call them railway carriages.'

One day in Phil Solomon's offices, though, Morrison was discovered smoking his 'funny fags' in the toilets – presumably an intentional gesture of rebellion – only to find himself being thrown down forty-three steps. Mervyn Solomon would tell Steve Turner that it was his brother Phil who 'booted Van down the stairs . . . From that day on it was very much a manager and his act. He didn't like him after that.' (They were hardly bosom buddies to date!) Both Morrison and Phil Solomon deny the story, though Philip says he instructed Tommy Scott to tell them to do it elsewhere, and that Tommy Scott took it upon himself to throw Morrison down the stairs, 'Tommy's about the same size as Van, but Tommy was a tough little fella from Glasgow and would take no nonsense from anybody.' This might help to explain the subsequent antipathy felt by Morrison.

The net result was an increasing iciness in the two crucial business relationships Morrison still had, and a perhaps deliberate attempt to deliver a 'drug' song – though it was not one Solomon ever countenanced for release. 'Mighty Like a Rose' was littered with references to the kind of teacher who'll 'teach ya how to roll a joint', as the subject learns about 'turnin' on in the classroom'; and even 'gettin' sugar cubes for breakfast/ Ya know what I mean'. Perhaps Morrison later grew embarrassed by such an adolescent celebration of drug-taking, as he insisted on 'Mighty Like a Rose''s removal from the 'complete' 2-CD collection *The Story of Them*, on the specious grounds that it was a demo and never meant for release.⋆

If Morrison was determined to alienate his audience, his management *and* fellow band members, all in pursuit of his muse, he had also begun to acquire a contempt for promoters that was not merely counter-productive, but verged on commercial suicide. Phil Solomon recalls one occasion when 'my wife nearly lost her licence through them. She gave them a date somewhere and they turned up at the wrong venue. And

⋆ Originally appearing in the UK on a mid-seventies Them rarities collection in the Rock Roots series, 'Mighty Like a Rose' seems to date from the same session as 'Friday's Child'.

agents were licensed by the LCC in those days and if we did anything wrong, you lost your licence.' Never one to respond well to confrontation, Morrison became ever more surly as he and the band became increasingly unreliable.

Billy Harrison: They played a gig somewhere between Brum and Manchester. They turned up at this gig late – and I'm talking about the roadie carting the gear through the punters to get it on the stage – so the promoter's not a happy chappy. Van arrives about three-quarters of an hour after that. The promoter 'bones' him. He's the singer, he's fronting the band, and [Van turned round and said,] 'Do you fuckin' know who I am?' Last time they worked on any of [this promoter's] gigs . . . I [was] playing the Oasis Club [in Manchester] . . . after I left the band, and [the promoter] said, 'They'll never be back here.' They'd let him down. They hadn't turned up for a gig. And he proceeded then to tell me about other promoters. They'd let a few guys down. The word went round. No hit record. Shittin' promoters. End of work.

It may well be that Morrison was looking for a way out. If, as he later claimed, he had already left in his head, then his attitude does not sound so surprising. What alternatives there were he had yet to figure out. Perhaps, as Brian Hogg wrote, 'Them was always Van Morrison, struggling against a bizarre environment, uncompromising and bitter, each seeming contradiction an addition to his anger.' That he felt totally isolated he has made crystal clear, admitting that 'when I was with the group I was still kind of on my own . . . I was always on my own.' The band certainly shared few illusions about their frontman. When fan Chris Murray approached Them for autographs prior to a show in May 1966, he was surprised to find Morrison missing. He asked Alan Henderson where the singer might be, whereupon the bassist nodded towards the bar 'and cautioned me to "go easy" because Van was in a bad mood. I looked over and sure enough Van was stood at the bar on his own, looking mean and moody.'

John Wilson: Van had an agenda of his own . . . I always got the impression that Van certainly wasn't comfortable with the band. He just seemed like someone who was in torment, trying to find some way out . . . where he could do what he really wanted to do . . . I can remember the band messing round with stuff that sounded just like *Astral Weeks*. That's the way I felt he was going at that time . . . When Ray Elliott was in the band, we had the opportunity to play a different type of music [but] it never really happened due to bad management, too much drink, not enough discipline . . . Everything was a total shambles . . . Even though I was young, I realized that [Van] was having problems with who he was, and what he was supposed to be doing with himself. So that would . . . come across in his performance[s].

It must have seemed at times that everything in Morrison's life was unravelling, and he with it. According to Armstrong, even Dee was no longer around: 'She did a runner one time and that was it. We arrived back to London and she'd gone, and all the belongings out of the flat had gone.' So much for home life. At least Morrison had begun writing again. 'Friday's Child', in particular, was something of which he could be proud – and the fact that it survived in the live set until 1974 suggests that he was. Yet another idealized portrait of a life-affirming lass, 'Friday's Child' sounds like the continuing adventures of Miss 'Mighty Like a Rose'. This time she seems quite prepared to use sex as a means to attain her dreams: 'There ya go, rainbows hangin' 'round your feet/And you're makin' out with everyone that you meet'.

Recorded shortly after the release of *Them Again*,★ 'Friday's Child' would have made an ideal single. Phil Solomon and Tommy Scott had other ideas, having seemingly lost faith in Morrison's songwriting abilities. Their choice for the eighth and last Them single was a Paul Simon composition. Up until a couple of months earlier Simon had been wandering the streets of London himself, playing folk clubs and dingy cellars – until, that is, his producer Tom Wilson dubbed some rock musicians on to one of his acoustic dirges and turned 'The Sound of Silence' into an American number one. Eric Wrixon suggests a possible motive for Solomon's directive:

Eric Wrixon: The minute Phil's music company did a deal with the music company in America that Simon and Garfunkel were part of, every artist in the stable recorded a [Paul] Simon song the next week.

Them dutifully learned the song in question, but even a valiant attempt to do an arrangement of their own was scuppered by Scott:

★ *Them Again* was released on 2 January 1966.

Jim Armstrong: Tommy Scott says, 'We're gonna do this song ["Richard Cory"].' We took a demo away and . . . Van and I sat and worked [out] this guitar/harmonica thing, and we sat in the studio and recorded this [arrangement]. And I never heard it again . . . Then the next day Tommy Scott says, 'We're going back in the studio. We're recording it like Paul Simon.' I said, 'That's fucking Mickey Mouse.' He says, 'Do you want to play on the session or not?' and hung up on me. The guys went to do the session, and there's two other guitar players sitting [in].

Armstrong would not hear that original version of 'Richard Cory' until it was accessed for *The Story of Them*. Though Morrison told him that he walked out of the rescheduled session, he obviously stayed long enough to record a usable take, for it became their next single, backed by Tommy Scott's 'Don't You Know'. When Armstrong attempted to re-enact Harrison's previous confrontation with management, Morrison again opted out, leaving Harrison's replacement replaying the same no-win scenario.

Jim Armstrong: I said, 'Look, we're getting fucked about here.' 'Cause there were a lot of other things [wrong], money-wise. We were playing in Newcastle and they were paying seven hundred and we were told we were going for three hundred – minus 35 per cent. We all got together and said, [Enough]. So I went down to meet Phil Solomon and Van didn't weigh in . . . the four guys in the band walk in, and Van wasn't there. It just fizzled out . . . When[ever] we confronted the Solomons with stuff, Van opted out. We'd go down and have a meeting with them, and Van [wouldn't] turn up . . . They'd say, 'You're due some royalties, Van' . . . [and] he'd get a couple of hundred quid to buy a new [three-piece] suite . . . That's when I left the band and I went home to Ireland.

Ironically, Armstrong's temporary replacement on a series of European dates was Harrison himself, now merely a hired hand. The band Harrison had formed, though, was now coming apart at the seams. If Armstrong had already baled out, John Wilson wasn't far behind.

John Wilson: I just couldn't take any more . . . We'd had an accident coming [back] from Scotland, the van got sort of bashed up a bit. We went home to Ireland, and I remember being at a meeting with [the Solomons'] agent at the time, Maurice King, and there was talk of America, [but] I knew enough was enough . . . There was a general consensus [that] everybody wanted to [quit], but I think the rest of the guys were looking forward to maybe going to America.

The lure of America persuaded Armstrong to return to the fold, while a youngster named David Harvey took over on the drums. Phil Solomon had been trying for some time to set up an American tour on the back of two entirely different hits Stateside. 'Gloria', having become *the* garage-band anthem, particularly on the coasts, had just been covered by the Shadows of Knight, who had taken it sailing up the American charts – alongside Them's very own 'Mystic Eyes'. The distrust between Solomon and Them, though, had reached such a pitch that they refused to accept on trust any promise of a percentage of receipts.

Phil Solomon: Somebody arrived from America because 'Gloria' had been a hit on the west coast. He wanted to take them over to do some dates, and I got the boys together. I said, 'Look, this is a promotional tour. I don't know how it'll go . . .' [They said,] 'How do we know what we're gonna get?' I said, 'I'll send Tommy Scott with you, and Tommy will do all the dates, and you'll get a percentage of the gate.' 'Ahh, but what happens if nobody comes in?' 'Well, what do you want me to do?' 'Well, it's your records . . . give us a guarantee and pay all our expenses?'

Solomon agreed to their terms, intending to take the percentage of the gate himself. America, though, was an awfully long way even for Solomon's extended reach, and the band quickly learned to disregard the concerns of his chosen emissary, Tommy Scott, ostensibly along to record a live album at shows in LA. They showed a similar disregard for Solomon's American tour representative, who made them stand in New York airport's VIP lounge whilst he delivered a five-minute litany of 'things they had better not do'. After assorted press interviews, they flew on to San Francisco, where the following morning the rep. was found in bed with a fifteen-year-old girl.

Their next stop was Los Angeles, where they were scheduled to make their US TV début on *American Bandstand*, before beginning an eighteen-night residency – plus six matinées – at the legendary Whiskey-A-Go-Go in West Hollywood. Run by Elmer Valentine, the 300-capacity club was jammed to the rafters most nights, to see Them headline over Captain Beefheart the first week, and over the Doors the second. When the boys in the band found out that beer was a non-deductible freebie, the elder Morrison set about tutoring his American namesake in the ways of the world.

Jim Armstrong: Our drink tab in the Whiskey – beer was free and spirits half-price – was $2,600 in two weeks. The guys introduced [Jim Morrison] to alcohol, and he couldn't handle it. He wrecked rooms and stuff like that. He and Van were thrown out of the Whiskey one night for shouting, 'Johnny Rivers is a wanker.' . . . Van didn't particularly like what he was doing. He didn't want to go and play to a crowd of screaming kids. But he couldn't communicate that to anyone else . . . He was not doing his job . . . a lot of the time. [TH]

Armstrong is not the only one who remembers an increasingly bellicose, potentially violent Morrison working his way along the west coast. Doors drummer John Densmore, in his autobiography, writes of the way that Them 'slammed through several songs one right after another, making them indistinguishable. Van was drunk and very uptight and violent with the mike stand, crashing it down on the stage . . . I didn't understand why a guy with so much talent had to drink to get up on stage, or why he was so self-conscious up there.' Journalist Danny Holloway recollects another show that summer, at a club in Long Beach, where Morrison actually declined into incoherence:

The band was pretty wrecked that night, but they played the songs we knew and loved. And they were so strange in appearance that even the cruisers bothered to look, which they rarely did. Throughout the night, Morrison would pull the mike to his lips and incoherently mumble the words. Most of the time, he sang with his eyes closed and a couple of times he'd reach to his pocket for a harmonica and then cram it into the microphone, a move which resulted in a form of audio-agitation rather than any musical contribution.

Them's Bacchanalian bender continued throughout the tour, culminating during a series of shows in Hawaii in early July. According to Armstrong, the first night 'the band played well, and the guy accused us of being drunk. The next night we got absolutely smashed and Van fell into the drums, and the guy said, "That's what I wanted. That was brilliant."' A certain latent fury in Morrison now rose to the surface, as at San Luis where, Armstrong recalls, during 'Gloria' – a song Morrison presumably did not want to play – he 'picked up a mike stand and tried to hit Ray Elliott with the mike stand . . . He wasn't really communicating to the band at this stage.'

And this was a man in love! One can only imagine how he might have behaved had he not just met the woman whom he was destined to marry, and who would inspire many of his greatest love songs. It was at a show in San Leandro that they first met, barely forty-eight hours into his first trip to the States. According to the lady in question, Janet Rigsbee – later dubbed Janet Planet by her poet husband – 'I looked at him, he looked at me and it was alchemical whammo.'

Though she was absent from the eighteen-day beer festival at the Whiskey, Janet came and stayed with Morrison throughout a two-week residency at the oddly-named Losers North club in San José. An angelic-looking girl, Janet was born in Corpus Christi, Texas, to a mother who, according to one writer, was 'a dedicated elementary-school teacher with a secret drinking problem'. When Janet was a child they moved to the Bay area, where she soon became a successful model. However, like her new beau, when the pair chanced to meet Janet was already looking for a way out of the life she had found for herself:

Janet Planet: I got involved in San Francisco with an agency which was a casting agency, but they also cast TV commercials and modelling. And so what I ended up doing was a lot of modelling and TV commercials, which I absolutely hated. It really kind of screwed with my head . . . That's when I met Van. So it was easy to just dump that and go. I met Van the first night he was in America. It was at a roller rink in San Leandro. I had never been to a rock concert before . . . We really connected in a very spiritual way, so we tried to spend as much time together as we could while he was touring up and down California. [JS]

One immediate result of a new love entering Morrison's life was a song quite unlike anything he had written to date, and a starting point for an album it would take him two years to complete – and a lifetime to live up to. Morrison would later claim that 'Ballerina' was inspired by 'a flash about an actress in an opera house appearing in a ballet', but there is little doubt that it is Janet he is imploring to 'fly awhile/straight to my arms/little angel child'. Armstrong remembers working on the song between gigs: 'He had all these words. We sort of formalized it, 'cause there was no structure to it.' They even attempted the song one night in Hawaii, unaware that it was some kind of signpost to a future that would not involve Them. For now the general feeling was, as the man in the song said, 'The show must go on.'

For the first time since the Maritime the band were calling the shots and pocketing the proceeds. Half-way through their residency at the Whiskey, they found out just how much of a premium their management applied for their risk-taking. Solomon's guarantee to the band turned out to be a fifth of what the club-owner was paying. Feeling that Them was already on the edge of destruction, the band decided to take the money themselves and shove the consequences.

Jim Armstrong: Elmer Valentine owned the Whiskey . . . and second week Ronnie Higham, his secretary, said, 'I have a cheque. We've already sent one off to Phil Solomon. Would you like to take this, or shall I forward it?' I said, 'I'll take it.' The cheque was for $10,000 . . . Van was there. I said, 'Look at this.' I took the cheque. It was lodged . . . Solomon [then] sent two guys, like road managers. He was sending them to gigs to try to collect the money. We then turned round, as a band, and said, 'We're not playing till we get the money up front.' We had to hire a heavy. He had a gun. His job [had been], 'Here's a photograph of this guy, he hasn't paid his money . . . break both his arms and legs.' Mother John – he was our joint bodyguard. We had to pay him, and [from then on] we got the money before we went on. We walked out [of] the Fillmore [saying], 'We [want] the money before we go on.' Phil Baine said, 'I've never done this.' 'Well, fuck, you're doing it now or we're not playing.' We walked out, and he followed us out. And we're standing outside, and he [finally] goes . . . back inside and count[s] out the money. But that was because these other guys were coming up to try and get the money. We played Santa Monica Civic Auditorium and I get handed a subpoena, and this Mother John chased him . . . took [the subpoena] off my hands and went after him. I never appeared in court.

Knowing that he had been outmanoeuvred, and had precious little chance of seeing either the band or the money again, Phil Solomon called Tommy Scott home. However, behind the scenes events continued in a way that the band seemed quite unable to control. Armstrong believes that 'Richard Cory' was withdrawn. 'It [had] just [been] released, and [was] getting lots of airplay. We applied to get extensions to our visas. That was fought.' As the endgame was played out, the band found themselves sitting with a certain well-known club-owner after a show, lamenting their lot. Ever practical, the club-owner finally said, 'Seems to me there's only one way to solve this. First-class return air-fare to London. Two thousand. Shoot the motherfucker.' The owner had grown to like the boys and said he could arrange this if they wanted. None of the boys, though, would agree. If they had known what Solomon still had in store for Them, perhaps some might have cast their votes differently (Harrison insists that if he'd still been in the band, Solomon would have been a dead man).

Phil Solomon later told Johnny Rogan that 'a court case eventually came, and it was settled out of court . . . [but] by the time the lawyer's expenses were paid, we'd lost very heavily on it'. This isn't quite the full story. Solomon did indeed contact his attorney in New York, one Walter Hofer, even though he 'was sick of it at the time. I couldn't have cared less about them. I had other fish to fry.' The band meanwhile retained an American lawyer of their own, not only to do battle with Solomon but also to help them get an extension to their work permits.

Jim Armstrong: There was $30,000 left, and there was an out-of-court settlement. Solomon got $10,000, [the lawyers] got $10,000, and the band got $10,000.

However, according to Solomon, the settlement made also 'severed our contract. Any money that was due for records up until that date, and thereafter, came to me and they got nothing – but they kept the money from the tour. So they received no [future] royalties whatsoever on the records. Decca didn't have a direct contract with Van Morrison, they had a contract with Hyde Park Music. [So] when I severed my relationship with [Them] they could have entered the market, [but I presume] Dick Rowe didn't want to get involved.'

If Solomon's memory is sound – and there is a very substantial sum riding on it – it seems incredible that the members of Them ever signed such an agreement. The fact that Them gave up all of their 'mechanicals'* in perpetuity for the sake of $10,000 suggests that no one in the band had any idea of the potential value their intellectual rights might have in the ensuing years. It does, however, help to explain the very real poverty in which Morrison would be required to live for quite a while, and the burning animosity each and every band member still feels towards their

---

* 'Mechanicals' is the shorthand term for the royalties paid on mechanically reproduced music carriers, i.e. records.

ex-manager. With Solomon's many contacts in the music business, a re-formed Them was a non-starter back in mainland Britain. Once again, Morrison found himself high and dry, back in Belfast, without a band and with precious few prospects. Janet was obliged to remain in California, awaiting word of when her new love might 'fly awhile'.

AGE THREE
An East Coast Point Of View

9

1966–67: Can't Stop Now

The best autobiographies are confessions, but if a man is a deep writer all his works are confessions.

—*George Bernard Shaw*

[Van] lived in a world of his own. His dreams were sweet but reality was bitter. He was a cryptic person. Gentle and quiet at the best of times, but given to sudden fits of anger . . . Everybody kept telling him how big a star he was, but nobody could tell him how to make a living out of it.

—*Donall Corvin*

The year that separates the end of Them's west-coast adventure from the beginning of Van Morrison's east-coast redeployment, coinciding with the release of 'Brown Eyed Girl', saw the man disappear from most people's radar. Bouncing between London, Dublin and Belfast for much of the time, he was obliged by financial constraints to impose on friends and family. Phil Coulter, another ex-employee of Hyde Park Music, remains in little doubt as to the cause of many of his problems: 'He was abandoned in Belfast *because* [my italics] he'd broken with Phil Solomon.' Coulter was one of those friends Morrison now turned to.

Phil Coulter: Those were dark days for Van . . . I remember Van, in my house in London, after a particularly disastrous American tour. He said he was having nothing more to do with Them. [So] he went back to Belfast and did very little.

Coulter wasn't the only person in London to witness an increasingly morose Morrison. Lemmy Kilminster, of Motorhead fame, has referred to Morrison sitting in 'a shabby two-shillings-a-week hotel room', looking up at a cracked ceiling and muttering, 'Times are bad.' The Morrison he remembers was still 'drinking heavily and given to fitful temperamental outbursts'. 'He Ain't Give You None', which seemingly refers to the period immediately preceding its 1967 composition, has Morrison owning up to leaving digs in Notting Hill Gate when still 'in such a state'.

If London provided no answers, nor did Dublin, whither Morrison eventually departed for a few days. While there he ran into photographer/writer B. P. Fallon in the Coffee Kitchen, a late-night coffee bar off Molesworth Street, who remembers that 'he was very down, depressed. The band he'd formed to play the kind of music he loved was breaking up and it looked like his dream was going down the toilet.' Nevertheless Morrison welcomed the opportunity to jam with two aspirant Irish outfits, the End and Eire Apparent, though End guitarist Henry McCullough believes it amounted to no more than whipping out 'his harmonica and play[ing] a few blues'.

A return to London failed to yield similar outlets. Gigging opportunities for any solo artist – for that is what he had become – were largely confined to the folk clubs around Soho. Al Stewart, who was MCing at the legendary Cousins on Greek Street – haven to every folkie for fifty miles around – recalls Morrison coming down to perform on a couple of occasions, seemingly intent on emulating the folk-blues fusion of guitarist Bert Jansch. The one thing Morrison actually shared with Jansch was a profound admiration for Dylan. Both recognized what he had done to the pop music scene in the eighteen months since he had given that folk sensibility an R&B infusion, having been introduced to that nasal twang in its acoustic phase. Morrison well remembers hearing Dylan's second album, an all-acoustic affair, in the days when Belfast felt like home.

Van Morrison: I think I heard [*Freewheelin' Bob Dylan*] in a record shop in Smith Street. And I just thought it was incredible that this guy's not singing about 'moon in June' and he's getting away with it. That's what I thought at the time. The subject matter wasn't pop songs, ya know, and I thought this kind of opens the whole thing up. You don't have to write about 'I found my thrill on Blueberry Hill.' . . . Dylan put it into the mainstream that this could be done. [2000]

Morrison instinctively sensed the validity of Dylan's transition to 'folk-rock', and paid homage to the success of his fusion with a delicately understated rendition of 'It's All Over Now, Baby Blue' on *Them Again*. A respecter of lyrics, Morrison nevertheless made his own subtle change to Dylan's farewell to the folkies, telling his listeners to 'forget the debts you've left', not 'the dead you've left'. Even in the autumn of 1965 Morrison was looking to clear decks and move on. If only he could figure out 'how to make a living out of it'. How long Morrison remained in London that summer nobody seems too sure. It was probably just long enough to find out that he was *persona non grata* at the various recording companies based in and around Manchester Square.

Back in Belfast, other musicians were now carrying the R&B beacon. Rory Gallagher, Ireland's second great blues export, whose band Taste included ex-Them drummer John Wilson, came up from Cork largely because of the association. He later told a radio reporter, 'We really felt, because Van and Them had taken off in Belfast, [that] it was a lot more rhythm & blues-oriented, whereas Dublin was more pop and soul bands. The scene in Cork wasn't too bad, but we were attracted to Belfast.' But that legend only hindered its instigator, who found little tolerance for his attempts to assert a degree of artistic independence – not that an increasingly brusque manner helped matters.

Eric Bell: I had a feeling that Van was doing all this himself. He had nobody at all helping him. [But] he wasn't the type of guy that you could sit and talk with. He was very wrapped up in himself, very intense. He was probably thinking what he was going to do with himself. Ireland is that type of place, where you come back and you're Elvis for a week and then you're just another bloke.

As late as 1974 Morrison would still be bemoaning the situation he returned to eight years earlier: 'For Belfast my ideas were too far out. In England, I don't know whether they were too far out, or I [just] wasn't in . . . Perhaps I was ahead of my time.' And yet, despite insisting to Coulter that 'he was having nothing more to do with Them', he refused to be the one who drove the final nail into the band's coffin. Instead a makeshift Them, minus drummer David Harvey, re-formed on Morrison's return. Those few weeks in London had probably brought home just how little had changed. The reconstituted Them lasted just one gig, at Derry Embassy Ballroom, with Morrison's cousin Sammy Stitt, a well-known harmonica player in town, sitting in on drums.

Jim Armstrong: The band was awful. There was still the bad feeling from the American tour, and the drummer was all over the place. I said, 'Forget it, I [can't] hack this.'

Morrison was being pulled under by a tide of keening despair. He certainly didn't want to trade on the Them association, but knew of no other way to keep body and soul together. Geordie Sproule, one of his few close friends, paints a picture of a man on the edge of some very slippery slope: 'He was very down. He had no gigs or nothing. He had to pick up the pieces again . . . When he came back here, it was like he was gonna have to start all over again.' Determined to reinforce a sense of *déjà vu*, or perhaps bereft of alternatives, Morrison asked Billy McAllen and Roy Kane from the Monarchs to play the fills and batten down the beat. When Them bassist Alan Henderson opted out, he enlisted Mike Brown from the Alleykatz, but the new combo's début hardly suggested a new dawn.

Billy McAllen: Roy and myself were playing in a resident band [at] one of the big ballrooms in Belfast. So we played the first hour and a half, then . . . Van came and met us at the place. We all jumped into Roy's Volkswagen Beetle – [the gig] was in Newry Town Hall – with guitars and everything. We had rehearsed a bit with Van, doing [the likes of] 'Here Comes the Night', 'Baby Please Don't Go'. But when . . . we went on and played, some of them started to boo him and throw pennies from the balcony.

Kane thinks that it was Morrison's refusal to play the already-rehearsed Them material that prompted a revival of penny-throwing. Van presumably knew all along that the songs he was now penning were unlikely to go over big in Belfast, but it was now or never, as one of his new songs admitted. 'The Back Room' relates a conversation with a certain Charlie, who tells him, 'Man, you gotta go out there and do somethin' for yourself . . . or else you gonna be sittin' 'round here, like *nothin'*'. Dismissing those who 'go through the motions', perhaps an allusion to his current performing self, the singer spins out his new mantra, 'Gotta do my thing'. Though the song dispels any notion that Morrison was intending to abandon his muse, however tough times might be getting, there was little doubt that Belfast itself had become the back room.

'The Back Room' was one of a number of original songs now recorded on a new reel-to-reel tape recorder at Hyndford Street, where Morrison was again ensconced, playing his guitar into the night, 'improvis[ing] vocals until he hit a rich seam', searching for a connection with his muse *in absentia*. Morrison would later allude to the unique way he worked on his songs with his tape recorder, contrasting the results with those later achieved in the studio:

Van Morrison: In Belfast, all my songs . . . [were] done the way they're supposed to be done. It's good and simple, doesn't come on heavy. [Even] 'TB Sheets' isn't heavy. It's just quiet. [1970]

The process itself was starting to fascinate him as he began to apply himself to the art of songwriting, something he had previously treated largely as a diversion from performing.

Van Morrison: I never really got a chance to write until after Them. I'd written before that . . . but people weren't really into original material when I started. They were into copies of American R&B. [1973]

The first flutterings of a new approach had been felt in America. Even before his ballerina first came to him, Tommy Scott remembers Morrison coming up and asking him to look at something, wondering if it was 'too disrespectful'. The song was called 'The Queen's Garden', and the lyrics featured Van's first transvestite-in-song: 'See the Duke in drag, waving a yellow flag/Walking in the Queen's garden'. This was one of a number of songs he now worked on with his trusty reel-to-reel.

The image of the Queen's garden would crop up again in a song Morrison was to record the following year (though it would not be issued until 1970, on the dubiously named *The Best of Van Morrison*). 'Joe Harper Saturday Morning' ventures into the same twilight world as 'He Ain't Give You None', depicting 'the child [who] held a ball in the garden with the old queen', in a way that left it unclear who might have 'kissed the lips . . . of all the strangers'. The imagery here comes from old-time folk music, 'the child [who] held a ball in the [Queen's] garden' being ultimately derived from 'Sir Hugh of Lincoln', where a regal Jewess cruelly murders young Hugh after he has accidentally thrown a ball into her garden. The role of Joe Harper, caretaker at the Maritime, is never explained, though he may be the figure who advises the singer – much like Charlie in 'The Back Room' – to 'shine my glory all around . . . [to] not disguise what I did, [nor try] to keep it underground'.

Clearly the stuff now flowing out of him no longer came solely from the lexicon of the blues, even if it retained its fair share of Chicago-based inflections. Morrison had begun the juxtaposition of incongruous characters and surreal scenarios – a trick almost certainly picked up from Dylan (think 'Ballad of a Thin Man') – that would lead to 'Madame George' via 'Joe Harper Saturday Morning'.

However, as already indicated, Morrison's fascination with androgynous predatory males, and the sexually precocious youngsters they attract, did not suddenly flare up in this pair of songs. It can be found in an earlier excursion into the seedier back streets of the big city, 'He Ain't Give You None', which finds the singer being warned of the dangers of heading on down to Curzon Street, which is 'where old John flogs his daily meat'. Slipping into spoken prose, our singer admits that he got messed up 'round somewhere called Notting Hill Gate'. Portraying a back-street love affair with another young urchin, Morrison lapses back into blues cliché: 'in the back street I gave you my jelly roll'. As the song enters its final fade on the original released take,* Morrison can't help inserting a further *double entendre*: 'a drag, that's what you call it, the name of the game'. In a matter of months 'the little boys' would abandon old John for the more effete companionship of Madame George.

If 'He Ain't Give You None' was the first Morrison song to depict such precocious boys, the precocious young girl had long been a feature of Morrison's songwriting, ever since the steamy promise of 'Gloria'. Indeed it had become almost the core theme in his work, with songs such as 'Hey Girl', 'Friday's Child' and 'Mighty Like a Rose' leading critic Lester Bangs 'almost [to] come to blows with friends because of my insistence that much of Van Morrison's early work had an obsessively reiterated theme of paedophilia'. On the other hand, it may well have been one particular young girl who appeared repeatedly in Morrison's work.

If so, it should come as no surprise that this idealized figure now crops up in a series of similar situations, each idyllically described. Thus 'she' is pictured alluringly 'in the purple heather, on a hillside, mountain fog will stray', in 'I Love You (The Smile You Smile)'; to then be 'laid upon the grass in summer-time' ('Who Drove the Red Sports Car?'); before

---

* The version of 'He Ain't Give You None' on the *Bang Masters* CD is an inferior alternative take. I am referring here to the take issued on the original *Blowin' Your Mind* album.

walking along the golden sand holding hands, in 'Little Girl', and then again, almost word for word, in the unreleased 'Lorna'.* Perhaps most memorably she could also be found 'down in the hollow/playing a new game . . . in the misty morning fog/With our hearts a-thumpin'', in 'Brown Eyed Girl'.

Seemingly the subject of 'Who Drove the Red Sports Car?', one of the best songs Morrison was writing during these months, she is portrayed as someone who taught Morrison to 'read between the lines'. She also knew how to prick his balloon. Morrison would flit between any number of names, but the Joanne of 'Philosophy' and the Lorna and Sweet Jannie of later songs shared more than the singer's wish to be her fool, and/ or carry her books to school. Here was someone who, by his own admissions-in-song, he had 'been in love with . . . ever since you were in [Sunday] school'.

The clearest internal evidence that we are dealing with the same girl is the way that in each successive song this (first) love remains perpetually fourteen: whether she is 'so young and bold, fourteen years old', in 1968's 'Cyprus Avenue', or 'only fourteen summers/and God knows', in 1966's 'Mighty Like a Rose', or just plain 'fourteen years old', in 1964's 'Little Girl' (which contains none of the coyness of Morrison's maturer ruminations) where the singer admits, 'I love you and I don't care what they say . . . I've got you in my soul/fourteen years old'. On the earlier Lord's Taverners take he doesn't stop there, as a desperate need gets the better of him and he wails into the fade-out, 'Love you, need you, love you, I want to fuck you, oh child'. Having made 'Good Morning Little Schoolgirl' sound almost chivalric, someone unceremoniously pulls the plug.

When our girl returns, on *Them Again*'s 'Hey Girl', our singer has learned to curb his language, but not his need. After asking to hold her hand in the seemingly perennial morning fog, the narrator blurts out, 'Little child, I want to walk your dog' – an obvious allusion to the sexual act, courtesy of bluesman Rufus Thomas. This time, though, he does seem to 'care what they say'. Afraid that she is 'so young/I don't know what to do', he threatens to make a fool of her. Just as the whole song teeters on the brink of 'Little Girl' territory, the music lopes into a long fade, Morrison throwing in as an aside, 'There goes your younger sister',

---

* 'Lorna' being one of a number of songs demoed for Warners Publishing in the months between *Astral Weeks* and *Moondance*.

as if it is only her presence that is keeping this (?unrequited) lust in check. 'Hey Girl', as Brian Hogg has remarked, is 'ostensibly nostalgic, but simultaneously hinting at the illicit love for a younger girl'. The hints only grew more persistent.

Several of the songs he was now writing continued to fixate on this schoolgirl figure, even as the singer passed into young adulthood. On 'Ro-Ro-Rosey', though she has advanced as far as sweet sixteen, she is still 'not yet grown/she never goes out on her own'. Nor is she any longer accessible, living as she does 'way up on the avenue of trees'. The tongue-tied singer has all but clammed up, and when he chances to meet her one night, 'I see her face, her smile, her hair/I cry, "Oh, uh uh uh uh, uh uh uh uh"'. Though this vision reminds him of when she was 'the apple of my eye', she has passed beyond his world. He reverts to the silent voyeurism of 'The Back Room', where he asks the time, anxious that he might fail to catch a glimpse of 'another girl that's comin' home from school/Lookin' so cool'. The girl(s) who enter 'The Back Room' or live up on Cyprus Avenue seem to have become snapshots of past passion that, like a photograph, cannot replicate the experience, only remind the singer of how it once was.

Morrison has always fiercely resisted autobiographical interpretations of his songs, often in the face of indubitable evidence, so it is hardly surprising that he himself has never publicly alluded to such an important relationship. And yet it seems quite inconceivable that such a young, inexperienced writer could construct such an internally consistent universe, and place at its centre a girl perfectly suited to her surroundings, save from personal experience. The relationship in question seems to have coloured his life in such a profound way that it took some years for him to transcend 'her' as a primary thematic preoccupation. One cannot help but wonder whether this young muse was an idealized version of a departed schoolfriend.

Certainly, if his most ambitious work to date drew from real life, then this schoolfriend's death from tuberculosis, when still at secondary school, was almost as traumatic as the later death of his cousin, Gloria. 'TB Sheets', which he was also working on in the last few months of 1966, is a song that continues to seduce the listener into believing that it is something not only *real*, but true. Janet Planet, in the sleeve notes to the 1970 album *His Band and the Street Choir*, tried to put paid to this unshakeable belief, presumably at Morrison's prompting, insisting that 'All that really did happen to Van, make no mistake. Only there wasn't anyone else there with him. To lay that bare once and for all – he was sickeningly alone, afraid and ranting to be neither.' Since we can reasonably assume that Janet Morrison was not in Belfast in the 1950s, she – like us – has only Morrison's word on the matter, and a notoriously unreliable witness he has generally proved to be.

Van Morrison: This thing about songs being about you all the time is absolutely absurd . . . [Something] like 'TB Sheets' . . . is complete and utter fiction. I think someone at some point had written that this song was about me . . . It's nothing to do with me, it's total fiction. [1997]

Indeed, no plausible biographical incident has yet been produced to fit the details in the song. The suggestion, in John Collis's potted biography, that the song is about his ex-landlady/lover Dee seems to be nothing more than unsubstantiated rumour. Perhaps, as Tennessee Williams eloquently expressed it, and in keeping with most of Morrison's work, the song is merely 'emotionally autobiographical, [i.e.] it has no relationship to the actual events of my life, but it reflects the emotional currents of my life'. If so, 'TB Sheets' comes from somewhere truly stormy.

As Bangs observed, 'it sound[s] like the man . . . was in terrible pain, pain most of Van Morrison's previous works had only suggested'. The suffocating nausea of 'open up the window and let me breathe . . . I can almost smell your TB sheets' has a sense of emotional depth found in all Morrison's best work, but the fetid morbidity is embraced just once more, in 'Slim Slow Slider'. By 1969 'TB Sheets' was no longer even part of the live set, as Morrison's silence about the song became another echo he refused to recall. However, he had already discussed its subject matter with the bassist with whom he had been playing the song throughout the year of *Astral Weeks*:

Tom Kielbania: I think the only song he did talk about was 'TB Sheets'. Basically, that was about a girl that he went to high school with, and she was dying of tuberculosis, and I guess he really liked her and he went to see her in the hospital, and she really didn't care about him as much as [wanting to know], 'Did you bring my radio?' That's why I think [the] radio pops up in a lot of his songs.

Morrison's explanation to Kielbania certainly helps explain the song's curious coda, in which the narrator offers to 'turn on the radio for you

. . . if you wanna hear a few tunes', before assuring her that everything will be all right.

Confirmation that 'TB Sheets' was one of a handful of songs with which he was now tinkering comes from a poor-quality home demo tape that later passed into collecting circles. One of the few people who got to hear these abstract recordings back then was guitarist Eric Bell, who found himself invited to jam along with some of the results. It was a surreal enough experience to remain embedded in his memory banks thirty-five years later.

Eric Bell: Crymbles Music Shop. We all used to go there every Saturday afternoon. Nobody ever bought anything, but there were about forty people in the shop so anything that was happening around, you would hear it in there. Van just walked in one day and we all stopped talking. He was [something of] a legend, even at that point . . . Everyone knew when he was back in town. When came into the shop, he went upstairs first. Then he came down about ten minutes later with one of the sales guys that worked upstairs, and the sales guy was pointing over in my direction. So Van walked over towards me and said, 'Can I speak to you for a minute?' He asked me what I was doing, was I free that night, and did I know where Hyndford Street was. And I went up to his house that night. His mum and dad said they were going out, and left me and Van in the sitting room. He had this incredible tape recorder. It was all chrome, looked really professional, a reel-to-reel, and he had a little practice amp. [So] I plugged in my guitar and he said, 'I want you to jam along with these songs, man.' He put on this tape, him and an acoustic guitar. Why he didn't play it in front of me I don't know. He was giving me 100 per cent [of his attention], I suppose. I just jammed over these things, and he just said, 'Yeah, that's nice.' [The material] had that 'TB Sheets'-type feel.

Needless to say, the invitation to Hyndford Street was hardly a whim on Morrison's part. Bell's bluesy leads were just what he needed to complete another experimental quartet. Augmenting the Alleykatz rhythm section, Bell was put to work learning a set still built around the Them canon. Morrison irreverently christened the new band Them Again.

Eric Bell: He gave me the first two Them albums, with the songs marked that he wanted me to learn, and he said, 'We'll have a full rehearsal at this place called Dougie Knight's' – it was a cycle shop and a record shop at the same time

. . . We had [this] rehearsal, Mike Brown on bass and Joe Hanratty on drums. [It was] mostly Them songs. I remember we were doing 'Gloria' and I was doing the backing vocals, and he just stopped the song and he came over and said, 'Shout them, man. You're only whispering.'

Van Morrison and Them Again had been booked to make their début at a new venue in Belfast's city centre, the Square One Club. A story in the *Evening Telegraph* heightened anticipation among the local music fans. That inner conflict, though, between giving paying punters what they doubtless wanted and asserting some ill-defined artistic right to play whatever he felt inspired to perform, again served to alienate what was a staunchly loyal crowd of R&B fans. When it came time to play, Morrison decided to rip up the set-list and scupper any expectations.

Eric Bell: They were all expecting us to walk out and immediately start [playing the intro to 'Here Comes the Night']: a real polished thing, [with] all the songs, one after another. And I thought it was going to be that way – until we did the first gig . . . We opened [the place], and it was packed. Just queues of people the whole way up the stairs. I'd never seen nothing like it before. It was amazing. Anyway, we went on to play, and I had this list of songs on top of my amplifier, numbered, so I was psyching myself for the first song and Van turns round and says, 'Start a blues in E?' I said, 'What about the list?' And he said, 'Fuck the list. Start a blues in E.' So that was the very first moment on stage . . . and he would do that all the time. You just didn't know what the guy was going to do . . . He'd play sax sometimes, just take a solo now and again. [But] he just threw Them to the wind. He was trying to do different stuff.

Despite such an inauspicious first outing, Them Again survived for about three months, playing the likes of the Jazz Club, Clark's, Queen's University, and Carrickfergus Town Hall, though the gigs did not get any easier, or Morrison's stage manner more accommodating. At the band's second or third gig, in the middle of the set, Morrison turned around and told the musicians to stop playing, before walking up to the mike and intoning, 'To wank or not to wank, that is the question.'* When this didn't generate a sufficiently instantaneous response, Morrison requested all the wankers in the hall to put up their hands. As Bell wryly recalls, 'We all went home early that night. Van was obviously out of

---

* See also Keith Altham's Eric Burdon story, page 102.

his head . . . I think he was a bit pissed off at being back in Belfast . . . It was about three hundred years behind the times as far as he was concerned.'

And yet he persevered, bereft of options and short of fuse, until it came to a gig at Queen's University. Despite a happy historical association between Queen's and the original Them, Morrison once again seemed frustrated to be back there. This time he succeeded in alienating not only another perplexed audience but also the one musician who had kept the whole shebang on the rails.

Eric Bell: It was sort of a rag ball. All these students painting everything in sight. When we got on the stage, it was all covered in wet paint. There was [also] drink available, so we all had a few beers. We went on to play, and Van came over to the bass player, who came over to me and said, 'Van says turn down, you're too loud,' so I turned down and then Van, [who] was playing guitar as well, turned up. So I thought fuck this and I turned up as well. And that's what the [whole] gig was like. At the end of the night, [while] waiting on taxis, I said, 'Van, I'm leaving the group tonight.' And he said, 'There's your money, man.' That was all he said.

Morrison may have felt that the band had already served its purpose. Perhaps he could even see a chink of light at the end of this particular tunnel. Bell remembers the band's roadie, with whom Morrison seemed tight, 'telling me I should stick with Van and he might take me to America with him. [He] said there was someone in America he was keeping in touch with, and . . . he was banking a lot of his hopes on this bloke.'

Fortunately, there really was such a person. It was none other than Bert Berns, who had been keeping tabs on the ex-singer of Them while going through the process of setting up his own record label, Bang, under the umbrella of Atlantic Records. This was an association that doubtless struck a chord with Morrison, though it didn't last long enough for him to appear on an Atlantic subsidiary. Morrison remained blithely unaware of all the ructions going on with Bang – which had been launched in spectacular fashion at the end of 1965 with the chart-topping 'Hang On Sloopy' by the McCoys (a song Billy Harrison says Berns had previously offered to Them). Even Berns's erstwhile business partners never found out exactly what the deal was, before it changed.

Jerry Wexler: Bert was eclectic, a tireless go-getter and hit-maker. But then things started to get funny. He insisted on unjustifiable control over the publishing company. There were signs that he was running with some wise guys. Next thing, he sued us for breach of contract and the whole deal blew up. We said goodbye to Bert and Bang – not cost-free: Neil Diamond, Van Morrison and the McCoys remained with him . . . Only later would I learn of his obsession with power. He was intrigued by the wise guys, loved hanging with hoodlums and trading gangster stories.

Morrison viewed Berns as the guy who turned it around for Them, producer of great soul-stirrers and author of beat classics. He later told Ritchie Yorke that the Berns deal 'wasn't really that spectacular, money-wise' – one of the great understatements of all time – 'but it was pretty hard to refuse from the point of view that I really respected Bert as a producer. I'd rather have worked with Bert than [with] some other guy with a bigger record company.' The implication is that he was in a position to be choosy, and *chose* to work with Berns. This impression has been reinforced by later statements indicating that he 'was in the process of getting a solo deal with Philips Records which somehow didn't come to fruition because it was taking so long. Then I got this call from America to do a couple of singles there . . . [and] I got myself involved in that situation, so by the time the Philips deal was ready I couldn't do it because I was already in over my head with this other company.'

Actually the 'process of getting a solo deal with Philips Records' comprised a single meeting with an A&R guy from the Dutch division of Phonogram, at the Marquee club in London, the primary purpose of which was to persuade Morrison to go over to Holland and play some gigs with some kind of pseudo-Them. Though there is no hard date for this meeting, the gigs in question took place two months *after* Morrison signed a recording contract with Berns. Morrison knew all along that any 'offer' from Philips was not based around interest from the UK label, but was a by-product of the somewhat legendary status Them enjoyed in the Netherlands, thanks to almost weekly coverage in Dutch pop magazine *Hitweek*.

Driven by the lack of recording activity to get in touch with Morrison via his mother – who was apparently running her son's 'fan club' at the time – *Hitweek* were informed that he was hiding in a monastery. Unperturbed, writer Willem de Ridder continued to call until he got to speak to the boy himself, and a meeting was arranged in London with

the reporter and Dutch Decca A&R man Anton Witkamp. As a result
of this meeting, Morrison was persuaded to undertake a four-day promotional tour of the Netherlands, promoting a 'third' Them album,
Them One More Time, cobbled together from stray single and EP tracks
and released in January 1967. Once again, Morrison was being asked to
trade on an association he had gone to great pains to deny. Witkamp
later gave a euphemistic account of the Dutch adventure in his sleeve
notes to the 'Friday's Child' EP, released later in 1967 in Holland:

[It] was soon agreed that Van should come to Holland for some concerts. Van
arrived on March 9th (a shy, nervously moving red-haired boy, by no means
the 'big shot' lots of people expected), rehearsed with his backing musicians
(Dutch top group Cuby and the Blizzards) and appeared the following three
days in a radio show, six concerts and top TV pop-show *Fanclub*. Though the
tour was not as well promoted as Van deserved, musically it was one of the
highlights of Dutch pop-history. Every place was packed, everybody seemed
to know the lyrics of 'Gloria', 'Don't Look Back'. 'If You and I Could Be as
Two' and other Them favourites and many concerts gave the fantastic impression of a Harlem negro-church ceremony. Everybody deeply admired Van's
unique voice, perfect timing, wonderful phrasing and biting interpretations,
and everybody wondered why this boy – who didn't seem to care about a
stage-act – wasn't ranked among the world's top singers. Van's disappointment
about the tour-promoters could not hide his gaiety and amazement about the
reception and the treatment he got from the Dutch public.

The tackiness of the whole mini-tour idea was brought home by
Herman Brood, a Dutch musician, who remembers Morrison having to
'just . . . stand there, you know, in these crazy circumstances – there
were more people standing on the stage than in front of it. There he
stood among the audience in [t]his candy-striped suit . . . he had bought
. . . specially for the occasion . . . But that voice, it really brought the
house down.' Witkamp's private view of the visit was also that it had
been less than a roaring success.

Morrison's hopes of a lucrative little earner were dashed. He returned
to the UK with barely £60 – hence his 'disappointment'. Bandleader
Harry 'Cuby' Muskee believes that there was a discussion about the
possibility of Morrison doing some recording with Cuby and the Blizzards at the end of the tour, but the shamelessly shambolic shows shattered
any such scheme. Wherever his future lay, Morrison prayed it would not

be on the nostalgia circuit. In fact he was already committed to Berns's little empire. On 9 January 1967 he had put his name to a six-page recording contract with Bang Records, hoping to finally put his past behind him. One of a handful of amendments Morrison inserted into this standard Bang recording contract read:

Company agrees that Company will not make any reference to the name THEM on phonograph records, or in advertising copy in connection with the recording of Artist.

The record contract Morrison signed that day probably still gives him sleepless nights. It certainly continues to make the man's hackles rise. As late as 1987 he was still insisting that he 'paid for myself to go over to New York. All the books say that Bert Berns paid for me to go over, but Bert Berns never paid for anything – ever.' Amendment six of the contract, another of Morrison's insertions, stipulates, 'Company shall pay Artist's transportation from England to the United States as a non-returnable advance to Artist.'

The contract required Morrison to come up with 'the equivalent of twelve seven-inch 45rpm (single-faced) commercially and technically satisfactory record sides' for each year the contract ran. It also gave Berns's company 'the right in its sole discretion to call upon Artist to record additional master records up to the equivalent of 25 double-faced seven-inch records during each calendar period'. As well as constraining the artist from 'perform[ing] any selections which he has performed hereunder for any other person, firm or corporation for the purpose of making phonograph records for a period of five years from the final expiration date of this agreement', it gave Bang 'four successive options to extend the term of this agreement for four successive one-year periods, upon all of the same terms and conditions hereof'. In other words, Morrison was tying himself to Berns's recording factory for up to five years – during which time he could be called on to record sixty-two songs a year! And all for a desultory advance of $2,500 per annum.

For such a paltry sum, Morrison also made himself liable to 'all costs incurred in or incident to the recording of the Artist's performances hereunder, including but not limited to salaries and fees payable to Artist, if any, musicians', singers' and actors' salaries and fees, fees payable to unions and to union trust funds, cost of arrangements, copying charges, rehearsal costs, Company's necessary travelling expenses, if any, cartage of musical instruments, studio rentals, technicians and tape costs, editing, dubbing and redubbing costs and expenses'. As and when the released recordings earnt out the advance – as of course they would – these deductions would become the subject of some highly creative accounting. Having decided that he could only give Berns everything, Morrison threw in ownership of the masters, as well as surrendering any say as to how the results might be packaged:

All performances recorded hereunder, all recordings released hereunder and all derivatives made therefrom, shall be entirely the property of the Company to be used by Company in any manner it sees fit . . . [as well as] the right to add to, delete from, change, modify or amend the performances of Artist by any and all means, including new or different instrumentalists, vocalists, sound effects, orchestrations &c.

After the education meted out by Phil Solomon, it seems extraordinary that Morrison would willingly accede to such terms. Morrison was clearly not thinking about the possible consequences of signing such a contract, just as he self-evidently put pen to contract without taking legal advice – something that prompted him to put at the top of a list of suggestions on 'How Not to Get Screwed' in a 1995 newspaper article, 'Get a lawyer. Don't sign a contract or any piece of paper relating to gigs, recording or management without first consulting a lawyer. If you can't afford one, then borrow the money. You must have good legal representation.'

In 1967, though, Morrison was fixated on just one thing – grasping his only realistic opportunity to record again. The few additions made by him to the contract were concerned with ensuring that Berns commit himself to releasing what he was given. The second of these amendments required Bang 'to actually record the minimum number of record sides required to be recorded during each period of the Agreement', whilst clause seventeen of the contract's addendum required that 'during each year of the term of this agreement, Company shall cause to be released in the United States at least three "singles" records and at least one long-playing album embodying performances of Artist'.

The months spent back in Belfast – highlighted in 'Hard Nose the Highway' as among the hardest times he had known – had been long enough for Morrison to display a reckless disregard for his own best interests. Rushing headlong into the beckoning arms of a man straight out of the Maurice Levy school of artist management, Morrison tied himself to someone who, in the words of Jerry Wexler, 'was running with some wise guys'. If Berns made Solomon look like a lightweight, he talked a good game. From what Morrison indicated to Janet Planet, during a year's exchange of love letters, he knew all along that he was bargaining from a desperate position. Someone as shrewd as Berns undoubtedly knew it too.

Janet Planet: He really was trying to get something together for himself over there, and Bert was really the only person who stepped up to the plate and said, 'I want to do this.' [JS]

Whatever the premium, Morrison was prepared to pay it just to get the hell out of Belfast. He would escape for the first time in March 1967, but it would be only a temporary reprieve. It would take a major hit record to get him away from this hopeless island for good.

10

1967: He Ain't Give You None

I'm into a completely different thing now. Now there is no limit to
what I can do. I plan to use the type of instrumentation that I like and
be completely free . . . I'm not planning to fall into the background.

—*Van Morrison, 1967*

Barely two weeks after returning from the Them Revue fiasco in the
Netherlands, Morrison found himself at A&R Studios in New York,
recording an album's worth of songs under the watchful eye of
Bert Berns. Berns had assembled a crack team of session musicians,
including at least three components of Dylan's 1965 electric sound:
guitarist Al Giorgioni, bassist Russ Savakus and pianist Paul Griffin.
The Sweet Inspiration were also on hand, to provide backing vocals
should they be required. Berns knew the importance of having the
most responsive musicians, especially with an artist as mercurial as
Morrison.

Berns seems to have had very little indication of the sound Morrison
had in mind when signing him to Bang. Even if he had been given access
to Morrison's home demos as reference material, the strummed tunes
and slurred vocals hardly revealed the potential of even a 'TB Sheets'.
According to Morrison, upon landing in New York he headed straight
up to Berns's office in the Brill Building to play 'the songs for him. They
included tunes I was writing when I was with Them . . . I had all this
material ready to go, and Bert switched on the tape recorder and said,
"Let's start going through some songs for your session." The tape
consisted of myself singing and playing guitar and someone banging a
tambourine. We played through all the songs on the tape machine and

Bert said, "You know something, that really sounds good just by . . . yourself, like that." '★

Morrison apparently interpreted Berns's enthusiasm for his new songs in their raw original form as an indication that he would be content to record them in this folky, acoustic style. Berns had no such intention, and when Morrison arrived at 112 West 48th Street on 28 March 1967, he found himself in 'a whole different scene: there were three guitar players, bass, drums – it was like a big production number and I felt that a lot of it was unnecessary'. He would later parody what he viewed as Berns's tendency to over-produce in one of the 'revenge' songs recorded to get out of the Bang contract in the winter of 1969, mockingly chanting, 'Yeah, we'll get a guitar . . . we'll get three guitars/No!, No!!, we'll get four guitars/and we'll get Herbie Lovelle to play drums/and we'll do the sha-, sha-la-la bit'.

The reference to that 'sha-la-la bit' suggests that one of the songs whose transformation aggrieved Morrison most was a wistful little love ballad written about an old brown-eyed love. Though 'Brown Eyed Girl' presumably addressed the same one, two brown eyes memorialized on the first Them 45, Morrison predictably complained about Bang's putting 'out publicity to the effect that it was written specifically about somebody I knew'. Morrison informed *Rolling Stone* in 1970 that he wrote 'Brown Eyed Girl' as an acoustic song but gave up control of the end product to Berns.

Van Morrison: This fellow Bert, he made it the way *he* wanted it, and I accepted the fact that he was producing it . . . I'd write a song and bring it into the group and we'd sit there and bash it around and that's all it was – they weren't playing the songs, they were just playing whatever it was. They'd say, 'OK, we got drums so let's put drums on it,' and they weren't thinking about the song; all they were thinking about was putting drums on it . . . But it was *my* song, and I had to watch it go down. [1970]

This may partially explain Morrison's later reluctance to perform what is still his best-known song. One of his closest friends during the late sixties, Jon Gershen, remembers how, even at each other's houses, 'he

---

★ What happened to this mouth-watering tape is not known, though a solo demo of 'I Love You (The Smile You Smile)' was found among the Bang tapes when the compilation CD *Bang Masters* was being prepared, and was duly included on that set.

would never do "Brown Eyed Girl", ever – he didn't want to be associated with that . . . [but] I remember when I was out in California [in 1972], and we were just sitting around playing some guitars and out of the middle of nowhere, for some reason, he just started playing it and he said, "You know, this song has never been done right," and he proceeded to play it on the acoustic guitar and it was really very different – it wasn't this beboppin' thing. It was a Van song.' Gershen was one of the chosen few 'fortunate enough on many occasions to hear him play songs alone, on an acoustic guitar, unfiltered'. As a result, he was able to get a handle on 'what the difficulty would be [arranging these tunes], because . . . there would be [so] many different ways that you could approach one of his songs . . . in some cases, too many ways'.

Berns was not so perceptive and, as the late Lester Bangs once noted, all his arrangements seemed determined to head south of the border. 'Brown Eyed Girl', which according to Bill Flanagan's notes to the *Bang Masters* CD, 'was struggled with for hours, evolving over 22 takes from a Latin arrangement to its final form', was no exception. In fact most of those twenty-two so-called takes were false starts and breakdowns. Only four takes were completed and, on the evidence of the first complete version (take six – included on *Bang Masters*), the problem was not the song's sensibility, but simply getting 'this beboppin' thing' sufficiently honed for Van's strident vocals to bebob along on top of that burbling bass.

After his reinvention as an 'album artist', Morrison has tended to ridicule Berns's traditional approach, but at the session itself he seemed just as keen as Berns to turn his own non-arrangement of 'Brown Eyed Girl' into a hit single. Photos from the session show Morrison listening attentively to playbacks, and taking note of specific suggestions from Berns. They also show an exhausted, head-in-hands Morrison at the session's end.

It was the crafting of 'Brown Eyed Girl' that proved so draining. Indeed after 'Brown Eyed Girl' was finally berthed in hitland, a lame cover of 'Midnight Special' and a not-so-special grab at Berns's own 'Goodbye Baby', covered previously by Solomon Burke, were all that Morrison could muster. As Brian Hogg observes, Morrison's 'attempts to liven up ["Goodbye Baby"] stray much too far from the original's deep slowness and into a jerky, slapstick counterpart'. Perhaps Berns thought he should Latinize even soul songs.

On one level that first session suggested there was little in Morrison's locker save one impulsively catchy 45. When Berns tried to involve him in a joint composing session, asking him to help finish a song he had begun penning, he declined, 'Bert wanted me to write a song with him that would be a hit, but I just didn't *feel* that kind of song.' The song in question was 'Piece of My Heart', which thanks to Etta James and Janis Joplin became almost as much of a standard as 'Brown Eyed Girl'. Morrison was allowing his concerns about 'success' to get in the way of making commercial music. Berns, though, was not about to surrender the initiative, as recording engineer Brooks Arthur recalls:

Brooks Arthur: Bert loved and identified with the rebel in Van, but wanted to keep him closer to the centre when making records. Van was obsessed with feel. Bert had great commercial sense . . . Rumour had it Van was pretty explosive, and he was [certainly] intense, but totally focused. [That first session] was a long night, though.

Berns was also required to operate as Morrison's interpreter when his musical instructions became monosyllabic. Morrison's inarticulacy in the studio made it necessary for him to be surrounded by those musicians inclined to be telepathic. He seems to have imagined that what *he* heard in his head was what everyone else must be hearing. The one comment preserved at the outset of 'He Ain't Give You None' (take four) suggests just how hard it could be for the musicians to follow his line of thinking: 'I think it should be freer, you know? We should have a free thing going. At the minute we have a choke thing going. You know what I mean?' Er, not really. In later years listeners would not hear such opaque instructions again, even if that 'obsess[ion] with feel' never coalesced into anything he could communicate with words. Instinct was all.

The following day's session showed just how far his instincts could take him, if the musicians were sufficiently skilled to ride his musical tail-coat. It began with a startling gambit. Unveiling an altogether deeper side, 'TB Sheets' was a song Morrison looked to do in one cathartic take. It actually took two, and even that seemed too much for Morrison to bear. Brooks Arthur remembers the singer breaking down after the released take: 'He was just torn apart. He was sitting on the floor in a heap like a wrung-out dishcloth, completely spent emotionally.' It is perhaps amazing that he ever played the song again.

'TB Sheets' was certainly intense. Indeed Greil Marcus, in his *Rolling Stone* review of *Astral Weeks*, would damn the song for its 'sprawling, sensation-dulling . . . embrace of the grotesque . . . This [is] Van Morrison free from all restrictions, of song, of melody, of verse and chorus, free from all limits but far too early.' Bangs would rightly dismiss Marcus as 'squeamish' (failing to point out that Greil's daughter had contracted the disease in Europe and had to endure painful treatment for a number of months afterwards). Certainly the song shoots right down to the bone, as Julie's panic sinks deep into the pit of the singer's stomach, whence it emerged in one ten-minute technicolor yelp.

Thankfully Berns was not squeamish. Indeed, the fact that he released 'TB Sheets' unexpurgated gives the lie to certain later Morrison pronouncements. This reconstructed version of events has Berns telling him he wants four singles; 'So I went in there and made four singles . . . eight songs.' However, Janet Planet insists that 'he *knew* there was an album', whilst also giving Berns 'a lot of credit for letting it happen, for not filling the album with his [own] songs'. The contract signed back in January proves that both parties knew there would be an album of songs, referring as it does to the release of an album (and three singles) every year that the contract was scheduled to run.

'TB Sheets' was never single material, even as a three-minute edit. This was a blues that only the weight of an album could withstand, and Berns was more than happy to make it the centrepiece of *Blowin' Your Mind!* The other songs recorded on the 29th, 'Spanish Rose' excepted, would have been equally out of place on a 45. 'He Ain't Give You None' and 'Who Drove the Red Sports Car?', clocking in at around the five-minute mark, and dealing with perverse emotions, were hardly obvious candidates for airplay. They announced to anyone listening that the ex-frontman of Them had developed a deeply personal style of confessional songwriting, the imprimatur of a serious singer-songwriter. He had joined the fast-swelling ranks of those with an eye on the crown Dylan had temporarily vacated, courtesy of a dodgy motorcycle.

With songs like these, it was important to have a music publisher – and Berns was not about to offer him an alternative to his own publishing company, Web IV Music. It was presumably made clear to Morrison that his signature on a publishing contract was required if he wanted his new songs out and about. Two days after the second and final session, Morrison put his name to a contract that made his previous recording contract seem like a licence to print money.

Agreeing at the contract's outset 'to give us your exclusive talents as author and/or composer of musical compositions for the period of five years', Morrison was hitching himself to the Berns organization lock, stock and barrel, and for some considerable time to come. The half of his publishing royalties he gave up to Web IV was not an uncommon percentage in those days – though a desultory $500 advance certainly qualified as parsimonious. 'The right to recoup out of monies otherwise becoming payable to you hereunder, 50% of all costs incurred by us for producing demonstration records of compositions hereunder' also allowed for accounting practices that would be largely impossible to dispute. The final clause takes on its own irony in the light of all the lawsuits and countersuits that would ultimately arise from this contract: 'We have advised you to seek professional advice with respect to the signing of this agreement.'

If Berns's investment in Morrison now totalled $3,000, he was not about to let the singer stay in New York at Bang's expense. With every intention of exercising his contractual 'right to add to, delete from, change, modify or amend the performances of Artist by any and all means', Berns shipped him back to Belfast once they wrapped up loose ends on 31 March. As Morrison later informed Janet, 'They said, "We're going to release the album, we're going to release the single. If it's a hit, we'll bring you back."'

It was 'Don't Start Crying Now' all over again – save that 'Brown Eyed Girl' had 'hit' writ large across it, and Morrison's return to Belfast in the spring of 1967 hardly replicated that of the conquering hero he'd been, back in 1964. Still strapped for cash, he was again obliged to fall back on whatever status as a live performer he still had in Ireland. It was time to revive Them (Yet) Again, minus that uppity guitarist. With the ever-dependable Alleykatz rhythm section still willing to wing it, Morrison sought recommendations for a new guitarist. The Alleykatz had been doing a fair bit of gigging with another Irish combo, Just Five, whose guitarist, John Cox, Morrison had heard all about from Just Five lead singer Sam Mahood, an old friend. Cox, though, found Morrison no easier to comprehend than Eric Bell had. When Van took to a spot of auto-destruction Cox took his leave, as brother Mick recalls:

Mick Cox: To say [Van] was wild in those days [would be] a vast understatement. He came on stage [one] night in a fit of drunken rage. He didn't have a guitar so my brother asked a mate, who had a beautiful Gibson 175, 'Can Van borrow your guitar?' 'Yeah, [of] course, man.' And as he's finishing the last number, he starts swinging it about and smashes it to smithereens. Van walks off and the guy's standing there, [crying,] 'Why'd you do that, man?' He said,

'That's art, man.' My brother left after that. He rang me [in London] and said, 'There's this mad guy. I don't know if you wanna try [playing with him].'

The next time Morrison made it to London, he called on brother Mick (in the diary he kept at the time, Cox wrote, 'Met Van. Came up to flat. Didn't say much. Left.'). And yet Cox must have made some kind of connection because Morrison asked him to come to Belfast, offering to let him stay at his parents' place initially: 'and let's see what's going on' – Van-speak for seeing if there was any spontaneous musical chemistry. When Cox arrived at Hyndford Street, Morrison immediately took his sax out and said, 'Follow this.' If Cox was getting the same kind of audition as Bell, his laid-back temperament suited the situation far better. He soon witnessed Morrison stripping back the layers, as he previewed some of the songs he would not record for another year and a half.

Mick Cox: He was keeping it under the surface all the time. It was coming out with people that he trusted. Live, he was just doing 'Gloria' and 'Baby [Please Don't Go]'. [But] he never sat around the fire and played any of those things. It was all the new songs. [SG]

Cox remembers the twenty-one-year-old Morrison as someone who 'was very serious about the music because he knew, even if subconsciously, that something was about to happen'. Like the *Don't Look Back* Dylan, though, Morrison was expected to act out a discarded persona whenever he took the stage. Morrison was now touring under his own name for the first time, though Cox recalls it being mostly 'as a support act . . . on a similar circuit [to] that we had done in the Alleykatz in the North'.

Mick Cox: It was a hanging-out situation . . . doing these gigs to keep the money coming in. Because the promoters would give you cash at the end of the night and that was it. I had flown over [from London] and straight into a gig – I knew all the changes for 'Gloria' and the other material just from listening to it. But he wanted a much more comprehensive approach to music, because he had so many more influences than the blues stuff. [SG]

One day in July 1967 Mick Cox awoke to find Morrison at the door of his flat in Limestone Road, clutching a new seven-inch single. It was the Bang pressing of 'Brown Eyed Girl'. Cox immediately put it on his mono Dansette record player. He remembers that Van 'was really pleased with it', any reservations about its overt commerciality reserved for a later date. Morrison even felt inspired enough to add the song to the band's repertoire, where it sat alongside 'Here Comes the Night' (from which its riff had acquired a few tips). Convinced he had a hit-in-waiting, he wrote to his long-distance girlfriend with the news.

Janet Planet: Van wrote me a letter [that] said, 'The first single's going to be "Brown Eyed Girl". So what you need to do is listen to the radio, and when you hear it on the radio, that will be your signal to know that I'll be coming back to New York, and then I'll fly you out.' . . . I sat there in Marin County . . . turned on my AM radio and listened every day. And then one day there it was. [JS]

By August 1967 the single was picking up strong airplay all over the States, and it was time to bring Morrison back to the US. An album comprising all eight songs recorded in March was also now mixed and ready to roll. And Morrison proved as good as his word, summoning Janet and her young son Peter to the hotel Bang now put him up in, almost opposite Berns's offices. It had been over a year since the lovers last met, but absence really had made their love stronger. In 'Sweet Thing' Morrison would encapsulate both the feeling of loss with which he had been living and the sense of relief that only reunion could bring: 'You shall take me strongly in your arms again/And I will not remember that I even felt the pain'.

For a brief moment, everything seemed to be working out. The single was a major hit, such that Berns organized a (somewhat belated) launch party for him – on a boat cruising down the Hudson. Photos of the party show a slightly glassy-eyed Morrison, in silk shirt, his beautiful flower-child girlfriend on his arm, Berns throwing a fatherly arm around him as his imposing associate Carmine towers over them all. The brief set Morrison delivered that night was one for the time machine:

Janet Planet: It was just a boat full of revellers. In the midst of all this, a heartbreakingly young Van singing his heart out. I think that was one of the reasons he was so great back then. He really had something to prove. He was really trying to get [it] over, whereas . . . I'm not really sure he wants to please people most of the time. Back then he really wanted to get somewhere, and get his music understood. [JS]

The Morrison–Berns relationship, though, was entering rocky waters. After signing a contract back in January that surrendered control of just about every aspect of the material he'd record in March, Morrison was duly appalled by the end product. Later on, he would evade responsibility for the album's content, describing the record released – the crassly named *Blowin' Your Mind!* – as lacking 'anything to do with where I was at'. Quite how an album comprising *all* eight songs recorded in March 1967 didn't represent that particular singer-songwriter is something he has never really addressed. If the album was a failure 'conceptually', it failed at the song-selection stage, and one presumes that it was Morrison who picked the six originals recorded at A&R. In all likelihood the young Morrison misunderstood the increasingly powerful conceptual baggage twelve inches of plastic had begun to acquire post-*Pepper*. As late as 1973 he was still insisting that 'an album is just an album . . . It may reflect where you were at in one given period of time . . . [But] an album is roughly forty minutes of music, that's all.'

Only when Morrison – and/or his producer – came to terms with the fact that an album had to be something *more* than forty randomly sequenced minutes of music would he produce work of sufficient focus to excite critical attention. As it is, side one of *Blowin' Your Mind!* makes for one of the great single-sided albums in rock, immediately seducing listeners with that three-minute, three-second 45, before leading them down the back streets of 'He Ain't Give You None' to the oppressive ward where the singer's object of teenage adoration lies dying. However, the second side, save for a five-minute flicker of intent on 'Who Drove the Red Sports Car?', does rather sound like a bad Latino band auditioning a new singer.

Though Morrison bitched to Janet about the mix, it was the shortage of strong songs that told in the end, not the instrumentation, not the mix, not even the cover, about which he was rightly furious. Its druggy connotations, that strange swirl of sprouting brown vines around a young and sweaty Morrison, and a truly awful title, incensed just about the only non-drug user in town. Here was someone who, in Janet Planet's words, 'never has been, never will be anything approaching a psychedelic user – wants nothing to do with it, wants nothing to do with any drug of any kind' (which doesn't explain certain references in 'Mighty Like a Rose' and 'Joe Harper Saturday Morning', but what the hell . . .).

How much of his discontent Morrison actually vented on Berns neither party is about to say. One legend retold in Michael Ochs's unreliable notes to the *TB Sheets* repackaging project in 1973 portrays Morrison as someone who 'seemed to lose his temper a lot . . . When things didn't go right Van would get furious . . . throwing his guitar against the wall in anger . . . he'd often say, "You don't understand me, but believe me, I know what I'm saying."' Nobody remembers such petulance at the original sessions in March.

The twenty-two-year-old Morrison was more likely to keep his feelings pent up, or vent them on Janet, than actually confront the man he considered responsible. Only after Berns was no longer around would Morrison let his real feelings come out in the 'revenge' songs he recorded in 1969, one of which he dubbed 'Blow in Your Nose', detailing an album being released the following week: 'It's got a psychedelic jacket, and it's called *Blowin' Your Nose*. It's a gorgeous album cover, you should see it. It's groovy.' An unamused man, in an unamusing moment. Another factor that might have dissuaded Morrison from airing his grievances at the time was one of Berns's 'associates', who was always hanging around the office.

Janet Planet: [Bert] was certainly in bed with some scary creatures. Carmine was the kind of the muscle that was always there, and just sort of did 'stuff' – took care of [things]. He was a piece of work. [JS]

In fact it seems to have taken Van some time to realize that Berns was not merely 'a writer and . . . a musician. He was also a businessman too, like a very heavy business cat.' Though he accepted that 'there's no other way you can be in New York – you're either doing business or you're not in business', he belatedly admitted he 'didn't know where that was at. [So] I had to find out.' Janet bore the brunt of a painful acclimatization.

Janet Planet: We were really kinda two people against the world. [But] that was true for our entire relationship . . . There wasn't a whole lot of diversion and social interaction and friends. [JS]

Morrison's idea of 'social interaction' seemed to be confined to catching every blues and jazz legend he could as they passed through the musical hub of the eastern seaboard. Janet well remembers the two of them 'troop[ing] . . . around to see every single one of the classic blues singers: John Lee Hooker, Muddy Waters, Howlin' Wolf, Bobby "Blue" Bland, the Kings – B. B. and Albert – Ike and Tina, Buddy Guy, Jackie

Wilson, the list goes on and on . . . He absolutely couldn't be bothered with any of his contemporaries – OK, maybe . . . Dylan – but he was the most ardent and life-long humble fan of the great blues singers.' His interest in jazz was bound to flower again in the heart of the only eastern city where jazz clubs could scrape a living. He later talked about the time he went down to hear jazz great Roland Kirk, and 'there were only three people in the audience – but he went ahead with the show anyway'.

Part of Morrison's culture shock stemmed from the fact that some of the Afro-American artists he and his British contemporaries considered demigods were viewed Stateside as almost the musical equivalent of panhandlers. One day Morrison found himself in conversation with Berns, discussing Sonny Boy Williamson, and Berns told him, 'He's nothing. In the States, people don't even know who he is.' It was one more step in Morrison's extra-curricular education in the ways of the world. That day he learned that 'Berns, who had produced big soul records, only thought in terms of sales and contracts.'

At least Berns was not foolish enough to skimp on the marketing essentials. With 'Brown Eyed Girl' in the charts, and a second single scheduled, Berns suggested they put together a band to promote Bang's new solo artist. Morrison initially tried to coax Mick Cox into flying over from Ireland. However, Cox had just received an even more enticing offer, the opportunity to tour with Eire Apparent and their new stand-in guitarist, Jimi Hendrix.*

Morrison was thus required to recruit a trio of local musicians – guitarist Charlie Brown, bass player Danny Armstrong and drummer Bob Grenier duly constituting Morrison's sixth combo in just over a year. Morrison seems to have enjoyed the experience of playing with these American musicians, especially his new guitarist, noting in 1974's *Reliable Sources* how he 'often think[s] of Charlie smiling, playing, funky bitch player'.

One suspects Brown cracked a smile or two the night they were booked to play New York's Bitter End. Bert Berns's widow, Ilene, later described how 'the press were invited along, and the only way to describe the way [Morrison] behaved in front of them is . . . unprofessional'. Pianist Jeff Labes, later the mainstay of many a Morrison band, was with the support act at 'the End' the night that Morrison was scheduled to

---

* Their lead guitarist had apparently been busted in Canada and was unable to tour the States with the band, so Hendrix agreed to cover for him.

headline. He was somewhat taken aback when Van 'walked on stage, took a look at the audience and walked straight off the stage and into a taxi'. Such displays of 'artistic temperament' didn't drive just Berns to distraction, they helped establish Morrison in the media's eye as a 'difficult' artist.

Morrison was proving equally troublesome in the studio. Though at some point he dutifully trundled into Century Sound to record a follow-up to 'Brown Eyed Girl', the end results almost suggest a deliberate attempt to sabotage such hard-won success. Recorded in a single session were 'Send Your Mind', 'The Smile You Smile' and 'It's All Right', three songs penned in a hurry. On 'It's All Right' Morrison actually wonders aloud, 'How can I say so many words and so many syllables/In such a short space of time as this?' Profound stuff. Worst of all was a song Berns relegated to the B-side of the next single, with a title silly enough for it to qualify as one of those 'revenge' songs. The lyrics to 'Chick-A-Boom' read little better than those of 'Blow in Your Nose': 'I'm going away, but I'm coming back/With a ginger cat/What d'ya think of that?'

If this was one way of asserting artistic independence, it showed a surprising willingness to sacrifice the clout that commercial success could bring simply to make a point to one's producer. Ultimately, the joke was on him, Berns issuing 'Ro-Ro-Rosey' from *Blowin' Your Mind!*★ as the A-side of a record which, even as a follow-up to 'Brown Eyed Girl', failed to bother *Billboard*. At this point, Morrison finally confronted Berns, demanding back some of the decision-making he had previously signed away.

Janet Planet: Bert was around, paying attention, and actually being very nice, always very gentlemanly. He seemed a little bit bewildered sometimes. A little bit distracted, not 100 per cent there, like he had a lot on his mind. But he was always very nice . . . The problem [Van] had with Bert was that Bert really wanted to completely orchestrate and completely mould what [he] was going to do and what he was going to be, and after a certain point Van just bridled at that . . . So they did have some harsh words, and he did want to have more input into how the music was going to go. [JS]

★ The single version of 'Ro-Ro-Rosey' has girl singers overdubbed but is otherwise the same take as on *Blowin' Your Mind!* This mix, though, remains unavailable on any official CD.

Morrison may at this point have begun to withhold some of his new songs from Berns. A song as important as 'Ballerina' – written a year earlier – was never recorded by Bang. Neither was 'The Queen's Garden'. However, a number of songs he was now preparing to record affirmed much of the promise embedded in side one of *Blowin' Your Mind!* But first he needed to make Bert understand just how unhappy he was with the sound blowin' through Berns's mind.

According to Morrison, the disagreement was resolved by Berns saying, 'Well, you make the second one and you do whatever you want to do.' In fact, he really wasn't about to let Morrison do whatever he wanted to do and, according to Janet, it was Berns who lost his cool when the next session(s) came around.

Janet Planet: It was time to go in and do some more recording and Bert wanted to basically do what he always did, which was hire all the session musicians, have charts written based on how he felt the music should be . . . and this time around Van just said, 'No, it's not how I want to do it.' . . . And I think Bert got really mad: 'What do you know? I'm the guy who knows everything.' . . . I guess we'll never really . . . find out exactly what Bert wanted to do at those sessions that made [Van] so nuts. Because he didn't really harp [on about] that to me, he just sort of said, 'It's not happening, and he wants me to do it his way, and I've got to do it my way. I've got this new material, and he's going to screw it up.' [JS]

Morrison could surely have claimed justifiable homicide if he had strung Berns from the nearest streetlamp for what he perpetrated on the recording they now made of 'Madame George', a song precious to artist and fans alike. Recorded at the same time as 'The Back Room' – itself some kind of coda to the previous evening's goings-on at Ford and Fitzroy – 'Madame George' was Morrison's most personal song to date – that is, until Berns decided to bathe it in a gaggle of girl singers, and then douse it in some lost soundtrack from the last cocktail party in town.

Indeed, all four songs Morrison presented in the last month of their association were songs of and about Belfast – not the Belfast of the present, but rather some ur-Belfast that blended disparate elements of a boy and his town. 'Madame George' and 'Beside You' would both become reborn on *Astral Weeks*. 'Joe Harper Saturday Morning' would have to be content with its status as something of a lost Morrison classic. All were leaps of fancy borne on the wings of imagination, i.e.

self-consciously poetic. When he finally came to talk about the songs from this period, Morrison would stress that 'all the [songs] on [*Astral Weeks*], and a lot of my early albums, were just channelled. They just came through. I mean, I'd get whole lines, whole verses just coming through. It's almost like automatic writing – *not* automatic writing, I want to emphasize that – but similar. I'd just write them down. I got whole songs like that.'

The process was not something over which Morrison ever felt he had full control, but as he told one trusted writer back in 1977, 'if the spirit comes through *in a Madame George-type song* [my italics], that's what the spirit says. You have very little to do with it. You're like an instrument for what's coming through. It's the same thing as a primitive tribe of Africans, Indians, nomads or whatever – when they start getting up and doing their ritual and doing the dance, it's just what's coming through.'

'Madame George' was exceptional. Rather than getting lines and verses coming through, in this instance the whole song 'just came right out'. Received whole, it is a song about which Morrison has been careful to avoid specifics – 'The song is basically about a spiritual feeling.' If so, he found spirituality where angels might have feared to tread, in the boudoir of some drag queen 'sitting on a sofa playing games of chance/With your folded arms in history books you glance', seemingly frozen in the moment when that 'childlike vision [came] leaping into view'.

Normally, this was not the way Morrison worked, in Belfast or in New York (it is pure speculation where the song was actually written down). Lines and verses were normally disentangled from the bric-à-brac of these transmissions. The way Morrison chose to describe this process was appropriately abstract: 'When I get this inspiration coming through me, then I write it down. Or it can come in a musical idea, without words, and then the words are added. Or it can come in a spontaneous poem.' The way that Janet Planet remembers the process, it usually required a tad more crafting:

Janet Planet: Van would sit in front of a two-track reel-to-reel recorder with a guitar in our living room for hours upon hours upon hours. Then I'd go back and meticulously transcribe his roughed-out lyrics. Slowly but surely, those tapes were honed and refined into beautiful songs. [JS]

If 'Madame George' was one of that rare breed of songs that 'just came right out', 'Beside You' seems to have been of the type 'that you think about, and consider where you'll put each bit'. Morrison would later designate 'Beside You' one of those 'kind[s] of song that you'd sing to a kid, or somebody that you love'. What he doesn't say, but the song does, is that it was directed at both.

In the original version of 'Beside You' – which I seem to be alone in preferring to its revered remake – the specifics of the song are unmistakably East Belfast. The 'hillside retreated view' from which our second-person subject wanders is surely Cyprus Avenue, home of Ro-Ro-Rosey. However, it is only 'out on the railroad', or in a familiar pastoral landscape 'where the hillside mountains glide', that the singer can imagine standing beside her. In the 1967 version this is not enough, so he waits outside her window at night, 'crying as ecstasy surrounds you'. This dramatic image – which Morrison subsequently dissolves by making *her* the one who cries in the night – portrays his need as being as great as her own. The advice dispensed in 'Beside You' comes back at the singer in 'Joe Harper Saturday Morning' (or, as originally titled, 'Go See Joe Harper'), as the (same?) two characters 'turn on outside of the bus shelter'. As the singer takes his leave, he feels ready to 'shine my glory all around'.

'Beside You' and 'Joe Harper Saturday Morning' are probably the last recordings made with Berns. They may, as Morrison insists, have 'never [been] intended as anything but demos made to see if I liked Bert's studio'.★ If so, they suggest that Berns had finally begun to cut Morrison a little studio slack. Gone – at long, long last – is that chirping female choir. Indeed 'Joe Harper Saturday Morning', the only one of these songs to bear a recording date on the tape boxes (11 December 1967), is just guitar, bass and drums, the same set-up with which Morrison had been playing live, presumably with the same musicians.

Morrison recently said that, given a choice, he'd 'burn the [Bang] tapes . . .'cause [they're] not representative of me or what I do'. Yet these last two recordings suggest he had at last found his true voice. The issue of whether Berns would allow him to direct these visions the way that he found them became a moot one on 30 December 1967, when Berns was found dead from a heart attack in a New York hotel room.

★ The information on the Bang tape-boxes is generally less than helpful, though it does seem that songs can be grouped by session, if nothing else. For my best guestimates, see the Sessionography at the end of the book.

Janet Planet: We were at the hotel when we heard that Bert had died. We were just mortified, because things had been going really badly, and Van felt really bad, because I guess they'd parted having had some big fight or something . . . Even though he did love Bert, it was a strange relationship. It was really a relationship that lived and died in the studio . . . I remember we didn't go to the funeral, which probably was a mistake . . . I think [Van] had a really bad feeling about what was going to happen. [JS]

Born with a congenital heart condition, Berns knew that his time might not be long. But to those directly within his orbit, his death came as a profound shock. In Morrison's case, he had the added guilt of knowing that their relationship had gone from bad to worse in recent months; whilst Berns's widow, Ilene, couldn't shake off the suspicion that Bert's struggles with Morrison had added a whole new set of stresses. As she sat reading the contracts she now inherited, she perhaps also realized that she had the Irish singer by the contractual short and curlies.

11

1967–68: The Drumshanbo Hustle

I'd signed a contract with Bert Berns for management, production, agency and record company, publishing, the whole lot – which was professional suicide as any lawyer will tell you now . . . Then the whole thing blew up. Bert Berns died and I was left broke.

—*Van Morrison, 1997*

The events in the months immediately after Berns's death would permanently scar Morrison. Whatever his disagreements with Berns, he genuinely respected him. His death, though, left him in the hands of people who had no interest in his career, and no compunction about enforcing the contracts he had signed – down to the last letter. Less than a week after Berns's funeral, the annual option on Morrison's recording contract fell due. If Morrison imagined that he would simply be released from it, he was quickly cured of any such illusion.

The 'meeting' that took place on or around 9 January 1968 subsequently inspired two of Morrison's most caustic songs, and forever coloured his view of the music industry – though the characters he was now dealing with were not so much corporate suits as made men. In 'Drumshanbo Hustle', recorded for *Hard Nose the Highway* (though not released until twenty-five years later, on *Philosopher's Stone*), Morrison comes over all cryptic in most of the verses, as if that knock on the door might still come. However, there is no mistaking its subject matter from the chorus: 'They were trying to muscle in/on the gigs and the recording and the publishing/You were puking up your guts/when you read the standard contract, you just signed'.

Twenty years later, Morrison felt 'inspired' to re-examine the incident in 'Bigtime Operators'. This time there was no ambiguity about its subject matter, nor about the kind of people with whom he had been dealing: 'They tried to have me deported, stop me from getting work, blacklisted me all over . . . Oh, they looked like politicians, but underneath they were thugs'. The song itself, little more than a rant, indicated just how indelible a mark had been left by his dealings with the post-Bert Bang.

Janet Planet: One of the memories I'll take to my grave is Carmine pounding on our hotel-room door at the St George Hotel in Times Square going, 'Van, you're finished in the business. D'you hear me?' . . . It was scary . . . Carmine was said to have broken a guitar over Van's head . . . He was a scary mob guy, and Van has this lifelong ability to forget that he can't act out, and every now and again he runs into somebody he can't act out with, and Carmine was one of those guys. We figured out really quickly that this was a serious, serious situation, and that we were in big trouble . . . And Ilene really did have the power at this point. [JS]

Some of her husband's business methods had perhaps rubbed off on the widow. Though she would later paint herself as the innocent party – 'I had two small babies, one of them born three weeks before Bert's death, and I just wanted to get on with my life' – Ilene played her part in making things as difficult as possible for Morrison:

Janet Planet: The unholy hell that was unleashed upon him when Bert died was really horrible. Ilene was convinced that it was Van's fault, that Van's rancour had finally pushed him over the edge and he had the heart attack. And she vowed to . . . make sure that he'd never work again. [JS]

Carmine may have been working beyond his brief, but the stories with which Morrison regaled other musicians feature doors being shot up; even the contract negotiation memorialized in 'Drumshanbo Hustle' comprising a gun to the head, and an offer he couldn't refuse. Ilene Berns preferred a more legalistic tack. As Morrison states in 'Bigtime Operators', he really was facing the prospect of an enforced trip home.

Janet Planet: The first thing [Ilene] did was go through all the paperwork and ascertain that Bang Records had been ever so slightly remiss in their duties of filing the appropriate work papers for him to be working in New York, which he was doing, promoting the album. And she notified Immigration. And of course we had no money. Every now and again we'd get these statements from Bang, and it was absolutely amazing how the numbers just seemed to add up so there was never any money there . . . So there we were in New York City, and he had been [officially] deported. His passport was stamped. He had a ticket to Canada, because apparently you had to purchase a ticket and present it to Immigration and show that you were leaving . . . We really were two babes in the wood back then. [JS]

There was only one way out. To Janet's credit – and Morrison's eventual chagrin – she agreed to marry George Ivan Morrison, something she subsequently admitted was primarily to help him avoid deportation, deeply in love as they continued to be. If the New York civil ceremony was simple, it saved Morrison from certain expulsion. But the forces massed against the pair were not about to leave it at that. The fact that he was now required to head underground in the face of 'malicious rumours' was something later alluded to in 1993's 'Bigtime Operators'.

Though Morrison insists he 'was really clean', rumours of a drug bust spread far and wide. A journalist who interviewed Morrison in 1971 insists he *was* busted. John Payne, flautist on *Astral Weeks*, says he heard that Morrison 'couldn't go to Europe because he had been caught in possession of marijuana in the United States, and he could leave to go to Europe but then he wouldn't be able to come back'. Though no criminal record has ever been found, something was holding Morrison back from returning home for a visit, even if it was probably something as mundane as his unresolved status as a resident alien.

Meanwhile, his career hung in limbo. Even the songs he had recorded under strained conditions back in the autumn Ilene seemed to have no interest in releasing. Rather than confront Ilene and her associates head on, Van and Janet tried to find some kind of place in New York where they might not easily be found. Morrison was clearly spooked. Where they eventually ended up sounds like a cross between 'Madame George' and 'He Ain't Give You None':

Janet Planet: We stayed at this place that was kind of midway between Times Square and the Village . . . in this industrial section . . . It was like something out of *Barton Fink* . . . I was not good at choosing accommodation back then. [And] of course, *I* had to do all of this kind of shit . . . The next spot I chose after we got out of there was this really kind of cool hotel in the Village, right on Bleecker . . . It had a kitchen and it had two other rooms, and it was really inexpensive. And I thought, this is so cool . . . Well, the first night we were there, we went downstairs to go have something to eat, and there were all these transvestites coming down the stairs . . . At night the hotel became very *active*. So we tried to be out of there most of the time. And from there we moved up to Cambridge. [JS]

The choice of Cambridge, Massachusetts, was an interesting one. Essentially a university town, centred around Harvard University, it lies across the river from that most English of New England cities, Boston. Morrison enjoyed the fact that it had 'a lot of funky clubs, and a lot of bars where you [could] see R&B performers', and it was still no more than four hours from the hubbub of New York City. Morrison rarely revealed his real reason for being in Massachusetts, though his long-standing bassist Tom Kielbania remembers him once alluding to the fact that 'he didn't have a very good relationship with Bang Records. There was a lot of hostilities there, and he [had] got paranoid of the whole situation.' By the time John Payne joined the pair in September, his ostensible reason for skipping New York had become 'wreck[ing] some PA equipment at some club, [so] no one would hire him any more'.★

Living down on Green Street, Morrison could take in the various clubs that served the student population. He was also able to connect with the small music community based in Boston. Almost the first musician to befriend Van was the lead singer in a local rock band, the Hallucinations (shortly to be renamed the J. Geils Band). Peter Wolf remembers how he and Morrison 'would spend hours listening to music and hanging out at clubs. [Back then] there seemed to be a certain hopefulness – a sense that your dreams, if you worked hard enough, could come to fruition.' Hard evidence, though, was thin on the ground.

Wolf helped push Morrison as close to the limelight as he was prepared to go at this time. Having his own show on a local radio station, Wolf would plug Morrison's newer material, and even cajoled him into doing the odd teeth-pulling interview. One night he invited Morrison on stage at the Boston Tea Party, the biggest and best-known club in town, where he joined the Hallucinations on 'Gloria'. According to legend, Morrison

★ This apocryphal story was again wheeled out as fact by Barney Hoskyns in an article on the making of *Astral Weeks* in the December 2001 issue of *Mojo*.

was incoherent with drink and the crowd began to boo, at which point Wolf stepped to the mike and angrily addressed the audience: 'Don't you know who this is? This man *wrote* the song.' Whether this impressed the audience into rapt appreciation has not been documented. They can certainly be forgiven for their ignorance of the strange apparition's true identity.

Unfortunately, all Morrison had left to trade on was this kind of past association. Only gradually did he begin to face up to the fact that as a result of 'this Bang Records situation . . . the only way I could make any money was to go and do live gigs'. And that meant playing the likes of 'Gloria', 'Here Comes the Night' and 'Brown Eyed Girl'! It also meant putting together another band.

Tom Kielbania: I was going to Berklee School of Music in Boston . . . He was just starting a group, all-electric . . . so I went in and I auditioned and he liked the way I played, and that was that. This was in late winter/early spring of '68 . . . We had a real good group. The drummer's name was Joey Beebo; [the] guitar player was only sixteen years old. His father was a history professor at MIT, and we used to practise at his house. This was in Cambridge . . . We were doing the electric stuff, we were doing a lot of blues stuff, the stuff from the *Blowin' Your Mind!* album, and a lot of the Them stuff . . . The first time we played with Van was the First Annual Boston Pops Concert. It was very early spring, [and] we played out in Boston Commons.

If money remained airtight, thankfully the student lifestyle and the whole ethos of the sixties counter-culture enabled Morrison to find a set of musicians willing to rehearse endlessly for the pocket-money an occasional gig would bring. As Janet observes, at least they 'had his performance royalties, and that's what saved us . . . not even his perform-ance royalties in this country, his performance royalties from Britain. His mum sent us a cheque. That's how we got out of the City Squire [in New York] . . . It wasn't very much, but to us a couple of thousand dollars was a fuck of a lot of money back then.' Eventually Morrison and his well-rehearsed cohorts managed to secure a residency at the Tea Party, for which they received a further thousand bucks. Janet believes that they ended up living on that money for the next eight months.

Van Morrison: The fact is, sometimes you do something because you've got no money, OK? Sometimes you're starving, sometimes you do things for *that* reason. It all comes down to survival and you can't intellectualize survival, because either you survive or you don't. [1990]

This period would remain embedded in Morrison's consciousness for a long while. It was finally immortalized – along with the months after Them's dissolution – in 'Hard Nose the Highway', where nothing going down in California was 'half as bad as it was/In Belfast and Boston'. Sheer tenacity now carried him through. As he told a journalist thirty years later, 'I dug in my heels, basically. I just wanted to do music and I wouldn't let them beat me at it. But a lot of people just gave up.'

Morrison's sole psychological crutch was his wife. It would be unwise to underestimate the importance of the role Janet now played. Here was someone who, in Tom Kielbania's words, 'seemed optimistic about everything'. Whenever dark clouds began to form around her husband's head, she would try to blow them away. Morrison came clean in 'If I Ever Needed Someone', a song first demoed in the early months of 1969. For him, only she can 'lead me through the darkness, and on into the light/To stand with me when I'm troubled, and help me through my strife' (a nice little skewing of the Cockney rhyming-slang for wife).

Music provided Morrison with his only other solace in Massachusetts. In the summer of 1968, he was particularly struck by a critically acclaimed début album from a bunch of Canadian misfits who discovered a lost America in the backwoods of upstate New York. The Band's *Music from Big Pink* was expected to be the public unveiling of America's finest bar band, but instead of the volcanic eruptions evident on Dylan's 1966 world tour, they conveyed the sense of peace they'd found in the isolated community to which they'd retired.

One song in particular, Dylan's 'I Shall Be Released', enabled Morrison to confront the future with a degree of optimism. As he later put it, 'I was in Boston and having a hard job getting myself up spiritually. I couldn't relate to anything I heard on the radio . . . Then one day this song came on the FM station and it had this particular feeling and this particular groove . . . It was totally fresh.' Morrison felt inspired enough to attempt to replicate that feeling. 'Brand New Day' became his own anthem of hope. It would not be recorded, though, until he had disgorged a more painful soundtrack of sorrows. To record that soundtrack, he would have to construct a quite different sound from the one with which he had saddled himself since leaving Belfast. As it happened, by the end of the summer his electric band was on its last legs, and sheer economics dictated a more understated approach.

Tom Kielbania: What happened was Joey Beebo's lease ran out and he went back home to New York, and the guitar player had to quit 'cause the summer was over and he had to go back to school. [So] then Van said, 'Let's try going acoustic. I got some ideas. I'd like to try something different.' As soon as we started doing the acoustic stuff, he was coming up with all the[se] new songs. He did a lot of writing at that time. Now whether he had been writing these and he just never played them before [I don't know], but every week there was one or two more songs he was coming up with. 'Moondance' popped out of that era. [It was I who] started playing the jazz-walking bass line for 'Moondance'. That's what kinda started giving it the feeling . . . I was going to school to study jazz, so I gave a jazz influence to the music.

The jazzier influences in Morrison's musical make-up had been afforded little opportunity to shine since the days of Ray Elliott and Them. Though popular perception defined him as a pop singer with a blues background, he had been thinking of something lighter, more free-form, since those last days of Them. In fact, his electric Boston band had performed a jazzier version of 'Brown Eyed Girl' for a local Boston TV station, with a sax teacher from Berklee, Charlie Mariano, introduced especially to play a series of jazz solos.

Playing with just acoustic guitar and bass, though, limited the parameters of improvisation, and Morrison and Kielbania both agreed to scout for a musician who could alternate between sax and flute. Needless to say, it was the Berklee School of Music that again came up trumps. Sitting in one day on a jazz jam session, Kielbania got to hear fledgeling flautist John Payne. Afterwards, he approached Payne and told him, 'I'm playing with this guy Van Morrison. You should really come [and] sit in with us. We're playing at this club called the Catacombs.' Payne's entire musical background was jazz. A Dixieland clarinet player until he heard Thelonious Monk, he was duly inspired to take up the sax; and, after hearing Charlie Lloyd, the flute. He arrived at the club, which was in a cellar on Boylston Place, near to school, with his flute in its case. The initial vibes hardly struck him as auspicious.

John Payne: Tom [Kielbania] came out [and said to Van], 'Oh, this is the flute player I talked to you about.' . . . He looked up . . . and seemed not irritated,

not negative, but just . . . not there − . . . not warm at all . . . So I didn't feel
that good. He didn't say, 'Oh, how are you doing?' or anything . . . So I heard
the first set, and I didn't like it . . . [ ] . . . I thought of leaving but . . . just kind
of hung around . . . And then Van came out just before they went on [for the
next set], and said, 'Do you want to sit in?' And I went, 'Oh, sure.' So I went
up there and he started singing the first number, and I listened for a while and
then came in. Even before I came in, I could tell this was a singer of a calibre
I'd never played with before. But I couldn't feel this from the audience . . .
because this wasn't my thing . . . But once I was up there I could really feel
[that] this was . . . just coming from a much deeper place . . . I started playing
with him and I noticed he would react to what I did. I mean if I played
something, he was listening to it. I'd never played with a singer who was paying
attention to what I did, [such] that I could notice . . . So at the end of the first
number I was like, 'Wow, that was great.' And the second number he does is
'Brown Eyed Girl'. And he starts singing it, and I knew that song. I didn't know
whose it was, but I'd heard it around, you know . . . And I [suddenly] realized
he isn't covering somebody's song. This is *his* song . . . That night he offered to
pay me − and they were making almost nothing. The crowd was thirty people,
maybe . . . [but] he offered to pay me a few bucks out of the take, and I said,
'No, no, I just sat in.' [Then] he said, 'Will you come back tomorrow?' I said
sure. [NC/TP]

The Morrison–Kielbania–Payne trio was to last barely four months,
and their only studio recordings would be a handful of publishing demos
cut in New York that autumn, but in the few weeks that they played
together at the Catacombs★ they formulated the sound that would
constitute the template for the groundbreaking *Astral Weeks*. Morrison
was at last developing a sense of intimacy in his performances that he
would seek to replicate with more ostentatious set-ups in years to come.
As he later put it, 'For the first time I sang for people who were sitting
down.' He was also involving his audience in the act of creation, as a
review by Eric Kraft of one of these shows amply illustrates:

He makes his way to the stage at the Catacombs, joining Bob Kilbania [*sic*],
who plays upright bass, and flutist John Payne, who is trying for a spot in the
tour group. He gets his guitar tuned, carefully adjusts the mike placement,
brows knit, anxious that everything be right. He begins with 'Cyprus Avenue'.

★ The residency may well have lasted only a couple of weeks.

He's so involved with it, so into it, that you have the feeling you're involved in a very intimate communication with him. He winces and strains to bring the song up from far within him, producing at times a strangely distant sound that carries a lyric of loss and disillusionment. He sings with great care, making certain that none of the lyrics, none of the tone and intonation are lost to the audience. He is a performer beautiful to watch in his absorption. He has total control over the number and, by now, over most of the audience as well.

The Catacombs was clearly a special place. Elsewhere, he was not always received so respectfully. On such occasions, Morrison usually chose to refine trademark techniques for dealing with crowds not prepared to listen. Whatever constraints the lack of amplification imposed, this was the same man who used to do mid-song comedy routines with Billy Harrison as a gesture of contempt for a particular type of audience.

John Payne: We were opening for Tim Hardin [one time] . . . It was just a coffee house. So [there were] all these high-school kids with their dates, and Van Morrison was the opening act. And they don't really care. They're waiting for Tim Hardin – so they're talking . . . Van just stops in the middle of a song. So we stop . . . We wait. Finally, he's real quiet. I think they might not have noticed we had stopped. He might have said something to the crowd . . . He leaned over and said something about a certain bass line, 'Do the bass line in this song,' and [he] started singing a song about putting down the audience, making fun of the audience . . . ['cause] he can just make up words . . . [and] improvise a song with lyrics [at will]. [NC]

It perhaps didn't occur to Morrison – who had been brought up in one of the most eclectic environments imaginable – that the music he, Kielbania and Payne were presenting was not only different, but rather obtuse. They were not playing for a jazz audience, after all. The only crossover between jazz and rock to date had been the kind of jet-fuelled free-jazz blasts coming from the Motor City, where the musicianship was questionable and the volume deafening. Most audiences were simply not used to songs whose length was ill-defined, and whose structure was amorphous. It was not as though the three of them didn't rehearse. Payne recalls how 'he wanted to play every day – so you'd go to play with him whether we were working or not'. These sessions were just never used to formulate arrangements. Morrison later developed a way of describing this process, though it is unlikely that he had any real awareness of what he was reaching for at the time. In all likelihood, it was a preternatural desire to capture the moment, rarely given rein in the studio, that drove him to 'break out of this rigidity' long before the process acquired any aesthetic baggage.

Van Morrison: I just wanted to break away from this kind of structured thing at that point . . . The slow stuff that King Pleasure was doing, he stretched the words, everything was extended . . . that's what I was into. I just wanted to get back to playing and singing really, so it was like getting rid of everything and starting again. It was just guitar, voice and singing the songs. So *Astral Weeks* came out of this desire to break out of this rigidity, to extend the lines and chop it up. [2000]

The songs Morrison was now pulling out assumed their shape only in the moment of performance. Payne, who felt particularly inspired by the approach, fondly recalls these early shows:

John Payne: That was probably some of the best playing I ever did with him, because it [was still] that moment of first discovery – which is a trick I've used many times since in a recording studio . . . don't practise it or play it live a bunch of times. Put it together, the first time . . . [Most of the time] I didn't know what tunes he was playing, [or] what keys they were in. He would just start playing. I would wait awhile and come in. [TP]

The lack of any recordings from these shows★ makes it a guessing game how much the bridge to *Astral Weeks* was in place when Morrison began to play with Kielbania and Payne, and how much the three of them erected in those last few weeks in Boston. However, we do know that three of the *Astral Weeks* songs were composed by the end of 1967, and according to Morrison, '*Astral Weeks* was something I lived with. I had the songs around for [quite] a while before I cut it.' If the framework to most of the songs probably pre-dates the trio, Kielbania recalls that 'we worked on the words a lot . . . that summer'.

They doubtless also began to frame a 'concept' in performance. As Morrison told Ritchie Yorke, '*Astral Weeks* was a whole concept from beginning to end. It was all thought out up front. Originally it was

---

★ Apparently Peter Wolf has a recording of one of these shows, but it is unlikely to receive wider circulation.

supposed to be an opera. By opera, I mean multiple visual sketches.' It is a quote Morrison has perhaps lived to regret, as all sorts of commentators have read their own meaning into that phrase 'multiple visual sketches'. But he was clearly already thinking in terms of an album. When Mick Cox, who had been working on an album with Eire Apparent in New York, took the opportunity to head up to Cambridge and spend some time with his friend, he found '[Van] was doing the tracks that were to become *Astral Weeks*. I stayed up for two or three days and recorded some stuff with him – just fantastic music.'

In order for Morrison to get into a studio and start recording these 'multiple visual sketches', though, there were still a couple of loose ends he needed to tie up – like getting out of his current publishing and recording contracts; securing new publishing and recording contracts; oh, and finding someone sympathetic to his thinking who had the requisite purse to finance the necessary recordings whilst keeping Morrison's small combo together during another period of transition. Serendipitously, just such a person found his way to Boston early in September 1968, and rapidly began extracting him from his prior deal whilst arranging a more attractive alternative.

Needless to say, none of the parties responsible for bringing Morrison into the Warners fold agrees on the sequence of events in which Morrison's world turned. According to Joe Smith, who would end up having the most dealings with Morrison, it was English A&R guy Andy Wickham who initially tracked Morrison down with a view to signing him direct to Warners. The central problem, as Joe Smith quickly discovered, was the need 'to negotiate [him] out of his previous deal and straighten out his immigration status'. After meeting with Morrison at the Catacombs, and finding out just how complicated his circumstances were, Joe Smith referred the matter to George Lee. Lee, by his own admission, 'had a unique position at Warner Brothers. I was originally with the record company, as VP of the east coast [operations], and then I became the head of the music publishing. [But] I still retained my position at the record company as well.'

When Lee ventured up to Boston, he found someone who 'was opinionated in his own little way, but . . . was a gentleman'. Lee already knew about the serious contractual difficulties, and he too tap-danced around the idea of signing Morrison. No matter how much Morrison forced himself to play the eager young wannabe, the Berns contracts presented an intractable problem.

Janet Planet: It was really hard for him to get representation. It was really hard for him to get people to want to work with him and get behind him . . . He's not Mr Gladhand, 'Hey, how are you?' . . . It was like pulling teeth to get anybody interested . . . But the [real] reason it took him so long to get to another deal is because in all of the Bang contracts it said that anyone who negotiated with Van who had him leave any of those contracts would be liable for breach of contract and would be sued. And we had every reason to believe that they would do that. [JS]

It is not clear why Warners did not simply pay Bang/Berns off and be done with it. Possibly they suspected that if Ilene Berns caught a sniff of major-label interest she might raise the ante on freedom. In the end they were obliged to muddy their hands – as Joe Smith duly relates – but at this point George Lee went in search of a production/management team that might be willing to take Morrison on, and could be trusted to share their 'good fortune' with the label. Enter Bob Schwaid, who had worked for Warners Publishing before going into artist management, in partnership with record producer Lewis Merenstein.

Lewis Merenstein: I was going to produce artists, and [Schwaid] would manage them. Inherit Productions was the production arm. Schwaid–Merenstein was the partnership name. So we went up to Boston. We were told that eight or nine producers had not been able to comprehend what [Van] was doing, because they went up there thinking they were gonna hear 'Brown Eyed Girl', and it was another person with the same voice! . . . I knew the people who owned [this] studio, Ace Recording Studio, 1 Boylston Place, and he played the beginning of 'Astral Weeks' and I started crying. It just vibrated in my soul, and I knew that I wanted to work with that sound. We had good chemistry right away. It was just Van sitting there by himself . . . Tom Wilson was going up to Boston three days after I went, to think about producing him, [but] there was no hesitation once I'd heard 'Astral Weeks'. He physically came back with us . . . We talked about [King Pleasure's *Mood for Love*]. That was my favourite thing . . . I told him that was my favourite [record] of all time.

While Merenstein was connecting with Morrison on a musical level, talking about all the jazz records he had produced, his great friendship with Tom Wilson – producer of seminal recordings by Sun Ra, Bob Dylan, the Velvet Underground and the Mothers of Invention – and generally sharing aspirations over a few drinks, the Schwaid half of the partnership set about extracting Morrison from the publishing side of his existing contracts. On 12 September 1968, Web IV Music and George Ivan Morrison entered into an agreement of release, in 'which Web IV . . . release[d] Morrison from his obligations under the aforesaid song-writer agreement [dated 31 March 1967], upon condition that he faith-fully comply with the terms and conditions of the release'. The financial aspects of the agreement neither party will deign to discuss, though Janet Morrison believes it involved a settlement of around $75,000. The agreement also carried a number of obligations, which included the following key clauses:

(a) to submit to Web IV for publication three original compositions per month, written by Morrison, for a period of one year, totalling thirty-six original and publishable songs. Web IV reserve the right to accept the musical compositions as submitted.

(b) to assign to Web IV one half of the copyright in any composition written and recorded by him and released on a 45rpm single phonograph record within one year from September 12, 1968.

(c) to include two compositions owned or controlled by Web IV in any 33⅓rpm long-playing phonograph record which was recorded by Morrison with[in] one year from the date of the release and which contained at least two musical compositions written by Morrison.

So much for the conceptual integrity of *Astral Weeks*! The decision to include 'Madame George' and 'Beside You' on that first album for Warners was a commitment made to Bang's publishing arm, both songs having been copyrighted to Web IV. Their appearance on *Astral Weeks* fulfilled the third condition of the agreement of release. The second contractual requirement was easily met – by simply not issuing a single from *Astral Weeks*. The first clause, though, presented more of a problem. Morrison was not about to give Web IV any song he might actually intend to record, and thirty-six songs did seem like an unreasonably demanding obligation. Morrison's solution was an original one, though one fraught with potential legal pitfalls: he would record three dozen nonsense songs in a single session.

Lewis Merenstein: When Van did come to New York, and we started working with him, there was an arrangement made with Bang that if Van gave them a certain amount of tunes, that they would release him from the agreement. I recorded those tunes with Van at Mastertone Studios. That was a very interesting experience. He got all of his grievances out at Bert Berns and Bang during that session.

The few lyrics recorded at Mastertone that do not qualify as spontaneous gibberish come across as a series of raised digits to Ilene Berns. In 'The Big Royalty Check', Morrison sings of 'waiting for my royalty check to come, and it still hasn't come yet. It's about a year overdue. I guess it's coming from the Big Royalty Check in the sky'. Not surprisingly, Berns failed to see the funny side.

Ilene Berns: He then turned over a tape to me that . . . consisted of ten [*sic*] bursts of nonsense music that weren't even really songs. You could never have copyrighted them. There was something about ringworms and then he sang something about 'I gotta go in and cut this stupid song for this stupid lady' . . . [But] I just wanted to get on with my life, and so I didn't bother to take him to court and sue him over the songs I didn't get. [ST]

On the other hand, Berns reserved the right to make this breach of their agreement an issue at a later date. When Morrison went after her for those overdue royalties in 1973, he found himself on the end of a countersuit. Nor did Ilene discard all those songs recorded after *Blowin' Your Mind!* As soon as Morrison had proved his commercial worth with *Moondance*, out came *The Best of Van Morrison* – which was not even the best of the rest. She was not done either, for in 1973 out came *TB Sheets*, which finally unveiled those prototypes of 'Beside You' and 'Madame George'. Bitterness on both sides would outlast the various suits.

Meanwhile, other shadier members of the Bang family continued to hold on to that original recording contract with its one-way option for renewal.★ Warners were anxious to get on with reviving Morrison's career and so, with the Warners music publishing deal signed and sealed, Joe Smith found himself dealing with a couple of guys in Italian suits who were insisting 'that they would have to get "something", since they allegedly had some investment in Bang . . . A friend of mine, the late Joe Scandore, [who] was Don Rickles's manager and had some

---

★ The contract required Bang to release three singles and an album for each year of the contract, so in fact they would have been in breach of their own contract come January 1969, had Morrison bided his time.

connections, arranged the meeting and the price . . . Lew [Merenstein] had the paper on Van, but I didn't want to leave any doors open for future problems.' So it was that Smith ended up in a scene straight out of *The Godfather*, as later relayed to Steve Morse from the *Boston Globe*:

Joe Smith: The word was there was some mob money involved. Van was sitting in Cambridge, Mass., at the time, destitute . . . [but] a friend of mine who knew some people said I could buy the contract for $20,000. I had to meet somebody in a warehouse on the third floor on Ninth Avenue in New York. I walked up there with twenty thousand-dollar bills – and I was terrified. I was terrified I was going to give them the money, get a belt on the head and still not wind up with the contract. And there were two guys in the room. They looked out of central casting – a big wide guy and a tall, thin guy. They were wearing suits and hats and stuff. I said, 'I'm here with the money. You got the contract?' I remember I took that contract and ran out the door and jumped from the third floor to the second floor, and almost broke my leg to get on the street, where I could get a cab and put the contract in a safe place back at Warner Brothers.

For the time being, these twenty unmarked, non-sequential bills remained the extent of the label's investment in Morrison (though, according to Bob Schwaid, 'Joe Smith [also] gave me the wherewithal to free Van from Bang . . . no questions asked'). As a result, Morrison tied himself to another production/management deal, this time for a minimum of three albums. Finally he had enough money to enable him to return to Manhattan, and to bring with him two musical cohorts and a wife. The resolution of all money matters with mobsters also removed something of a weight from his shoulders.

Lewis Merenstein: We had signed . . . a production deal, and Inherit Productions had an agreement with Warner Brothers. He was signed to Inherit Productions . . . And we also had a fifty–fifty publishing deal with Van. We were fifty–fifty with Van; and Warners was fifty–fifty with all of us. That was publishing. And then we signed a production agreement with Warner Records. I think Warners wanted to have everything in place [before signing Van]. [When] we went up there, he [said he] wanted to be with us – because at the time Van had pretty much no finances.

Though he would later eschew the idea of anyone 'managing' his career, save himself, at the time Morrison felt as much in need of management as of production expertise. Even after the Schwaid–Merenstein arrangement came to an end in circumstances again fraught with acrimony, Morrison continued to display, in the words of his friend Jon Gershen, 'a big thing about a manager – that meant something to him. Unfortunately, he attracted some people that were slightly shady, that were [just] looking to get involved in something.' Even though he had again been required to give up high percentages of publishing and 'mechanicals' to his new management team, at least he was now getting something back – psychologically *and* financially.

Lewis Merenstein: We took him back to New York, put him up in a hotel, fed him, gave him money, really supported him, and nurtured that portion of his life while we were seeing what could be done with Bang Records – that [matter] hadn't been cleared up yet.

Initially, it was exciting just being back in New York, the promise of success in the big city enticing Kielbania and Payne into joining him. The pair were allocated a room in the famously crumbling Chelsea Hotel on West 23rd Street. Almost immediately, the trio found themselves playing a residency at the Scene Club. Rather than the cash in hand they had been receiving back in Cambridge, though, they were now obliged to live off handouts from Schwaid–Merenstein.

Photos from the Scene residency capture the likes of Warners' Mo Ostin and Joe Smith taking in the ambience and checking out the repertoire of their new artist. Whilst Payne alternated between sax and flute and Kielbania banged away on his stand-up bass, an impassioned Morrison in a shiny new set of stage clothes played his acoustic Martin and sang his heart out to the fortunate few. Journalist Bob Sarlin's review of a set at the Scene indicates a certain bemusement greeted this strange jazz trio, which already looked set to test the resolve of their new label:

He had been booked on the basis of one nearly forgotten hit record, 'Brown Eyed Girl'. But here he was performing with only [*sic*] a bass player and his own guitar . . . singing long, intricate and mystical songpoems. The audience was not very respectful, and it's true the songs did seem out of place in this rock cellar. The sweetness and sadness of these long songs did dent the audience's resistance, but there was too much to overcome. He had been typed as a singles artist, relegated to the AM bands, and he was not to be allowed to attempt anything else.

Among those at the Scene who were able to lock into the music were rock luminaries Janis Joplin and Jimi Hendrix. Morrison later bitterly observed, 'It seemed the musicians dug it but the general public didn't know what we were into.' It would stay that way for some time to come. And yet, when it came to an album, Lewis Merenstein was planning to push Morrison even further in the direction of King Pleasure. Merenstein would take on much of the responsibility for capturing the aesthetic, as Morrison continued to rely on the serendipity of the moment to be born again.

12

1968–69: Venturing into the Slipstream

[*Astral Weeks* is] still the most adventurous record made in the rock medium, and there hasn't been a record with that amount of daring made since.

—*Elvis Costello*

I think I opened up an area with *Astral Weeks* that hit a lot of people's nerves. But you can't really say that they're my favourite songs.

—*Van Morrison, 1977*

I think *Astral Weeks* was definitely the transitional album . . . [I was] coming from a deeper unconscious level, getting more in touch with the unconscious.

—*Van Morrison, 1990*

For a man who depicts himself as 'starving, literally . . . when *Astral Weeks* came out', the album Warners released in January 1969 was an extraordinarily audacious statement. Even in an era so rich in blatantly uncommercial rock classics – from *The Velvet Underground and Nico* (1967) to Captain Beetheart's *Trout Mask Replica* (1969) – *Astral Weeks* was a non-starter commercially, impenetrable to the casual listener and without any obvious single. Yet at no point does pressure seem to have been put on Morrison to come up with something more mainstream, or even to include a releaseable single.

Nineteen sixty-eight is hardly the starting-point for the rock album. Though Morrison would later claim that 'the album concept didn't really exist' when he came to record *Astral Weeks*, he was lagging some way behind more successful peers in the conceptual stakes. The previous year had been the year of *Sgt Pepper's Lonely Hearts Club Band*, *Something Else*, *Piper at the Gates of Dawn*, *John Wesley Harding* and the aforementioned Velvets' début. Into this marketplace Bang had released *Blowin' Your Mind!*, a self-evident ragbag of songs, lacking an overriding style and uncertain of intent. Its lack of recognition led to a re-evaluation on Morrison's part. The result was an album that amounted to far more than the sum of its eight parts. And yet, Morrison says he perceived *Astral Weeks* as an anti-rock statement.

Van Morrison: I didn't really want to be in the rock & roll scene. So I thought I'd have to do an album that was just singing, and songs that were about something. So I did get out of the rock & roll scene to some extent. Then the critics started saying that [*Astral Weeks*] was a rock album! . . . They were good reviews and all, but they were saying it was a rock album, and the whole point was not to make a rock album. [1986]

Actually, the most prominent and important contemporary review of *Astral Weeks*, by Greil Marcus in *Rolling Stone*, said no such thing. Marcus was adamant that 'the music is not rock and roll in any ordinary or hyphenated sense; rather it is music that is intelligible to us because of rock & roll; intelligible, given the complexities which hide behind the simplicity of intent, because of [the likes of] *John Wesley Harding*'. Indeed *Astral Weeks* was as much of a reaction against the indulgences of *Sgt Pepper* as Dylan's *John Wesley Harding*, being recorded in the same number of sessions, with a similar mix of acoustic and electric instruments. In both cases, the released albums exuded a certain conceptual integrity arrived at only after the fact – though one key difference was that Dylan captured those twelve songs days after their composition, whereas for Morrison, arriving at *Astral Weeks* had been a long, hard road. The two albums also shared a fable-like quality, one quintessentially American, the other more European. As Gerald Dawe has written:

Like Bob Dylan leaving Hibbing, Minnesota, at the turn of the decade, Morrison was willing to use whatever he wanted, to make up his own tradition out of diverse musical influences and literally forge a different kind of music . . . [What] Morrison made in *Astral Weeks* [was] an imaginative repossession of his own past and the language and landscapes associated with it . . . The world of rivers, gardens, railway lines, particular avenues, can be identified with Morrison's youth in east Belfast. [But] the site of that past becomes emblematic, rather than turned into local colour . . . the naming of streets, districts, regions, takes on an incantatory significance . . . Cyprus Avenue is not only a place, it was the idea of another place; the railway, the river: all are conduits through which Morrison's imagination is freed . . . [But] *Astral Weeks* is not the sudden breakthrough it has so often been described [as] . . . the main thrust of the songs remains close in theme and imagery to his earliest recorded work with Them: tracks such as 'Hey Girl', 'Philosophy' and particularly 'Friday's Child' . . . [as well as] his first recordings with Bert Berns for Bang Records, such as 'Joe Harper Saturday Morning' and 'The Back Room' . . .

. . . not that the line between 'The Back Room' and 'Cyprus Avenue' is exactly linear. Morrison arrived at the songs he now planned to record only after rejecting many of those he would demo for Warners Publishing in the next six months. As it is, the likes of 'Hey, Where Are You?', with its narrator turning on at a bus stop which is rapidly transformed into a forest where he can roam, smacks of the same kind of temporal shift used on 'Cyprus Avenue'. On the other hand, 'Rock & Roll Band' takes as its starting-point a line from someone else's dream to reconstruct days when 'they' danced to a rock & roll band.

Just as Dylan rejected every basement-tape song that led him to *John Wesley Harding*, Morrison felt sure enough of his instincts to discount the likes of 'Moondance', 'Brand New Day' and 'Domino', as well as lost love-songs like 'Magic Night', 'I Need Your Kind of Loving' and 'Bayou Girl' before the sessions even began. Indeed, the internal logic of the released album seduces the listener into imagining it must have been planned that way, even though Morrison subsequently denied striving for such an obvious singularity of mood:

Van Morrison: It wasn't meant to be like that . . . it didn't really surface the way it could have . . . I didn't have the same mood in mind for the whole album . . . The way I wrote it [was] as an opera, at the very beginning, and I've still got it like that in poetry form. [1970]

Perhaps the notes that inhabit the album's rear sleeve were part of this original 'opera . . . in poetry form'. They certainly read like part of the same mosaic, lines yearning to be blurred by melody and interplay in the poetry of performance. Morrison, though, reserved the right to move parts from one world to the other, later insisting to Ritchie Yorke that 'it's hard to draw the line between songs and poetry; some of my songs are poems. "Madame George" for example.'

'Astral Weeks' was clearly another. Opening the album with such a self-consciously 'poetic' couplet was surely a statement in itself. With the lines 'If I ventured in the slipstream, between the viaducts of your dream/where immobile steel rims crack, and the ditch in the back roads stop', Morrison took on the same mantle as the *John Wesley Harding* Dylan. Though he would later disavow such a self-conscious style, it would account for certain critics' permitting themselves to treat Morrison seriously as a poet, something Johnny Rogan ridiculed in his 1983 biography:

The reason Morrison's lyrics fail to astonish is that he is far more a singer/ performer than a poet. 'Beside You' sounds a good love song, and Morrison's vocal repetition of lines gives it added power. On the printed page, however, it appears meaninglessly repetitious and indulgent, with deliberately vague allusions ('the pointed idle breeze') and imprecise images ('the diamond studded highway') being thrown in for purely decorative purpose.

Rogan betrays his own 'literary' background here – assigning inappropriate two-dimensional strictures to a three-dimensional art form. Only when one sees poetry as *solely* the preserve of the page – in which case goodbye Shakespeare, *adieu* Homer – do his criticisms hit home. Certainly Morrison succeeds as an oral poet according to the definition applied by Albert B. Lord in the hugely influential *A Singer of Tales*: 'For the oral poet the moment of composition is the performance. In the case of a literary poem there is a gap in time between composition and reading or performance; in the case of the oral poem this gap does not exist, because composition and performance are two aspects of the same moment . . . An oral poem is not composed for but in performance.'

Even the repetitious nature of Morrison's imagery on *Astral Weeks*, using commonplaces in an archetypal way, bespeaks the oral poet. When Morrison told an interviewer in 1985 that 'the oral tradition is the closest to what something actually *is*, because it's the way somebody is saying the thing [but] it's also the way it's being said', he came a lot closer to describing the core of his art than he perhaps realized.

(To cite a single example of Morrison the oral poet: the performance of *Astral Weeks*'s 'Sweet Thing' at the 1990 Montreux Jazz Festival. At the previous show, three days earlier, the recently reintroduced song had taken off down a familiar musical avenue as Morrison interjected a 1978 coda about how 'the more you do it/the more it becomes a beautiful obsession'. At Montreux, though, when the band began trading musical motifs, Morrison transposed the entire eight-line opening from 'Astral Weeks', distending each line until it fitted into the 'Sweet Thing' template. Such an impromptu segue suggests that *Astral Weeks* may indeed have been an opera of 'multiple visual sketches', on occasions interchangeable.)

On *Astral Weeks*, it is the ears that Morrison seeks to seduce.★ It would be nice to think that the subtle lyrical changes from the Bang versions of 'Beside You' and 'Madame George' are of the studio moment, but it matters not – the words fit the context, and the context is oral. Even the poetic title-track 'Astral Weeks' becomes abstract on the page. Its place is on a record, *this* record, a collection of songs released from the undertow of East Belfast conformity. As Morrison later said, 'Astral Weeks' is 'one of those songs where you can see the light at the end of the tunnel . . . I don't think I can elaborate on it any more than that.' Like many of the songs on the album, it is about escape, or the dream of escaping. In this context, it is hard to see how a lot of the songs could have been written anywhere but Belfast. Morrison admitted as much in 1984, excepting just a single – unnamed – song which he says he wrote in New York.

This would suggest that Morrison had been holding back half a dozen of his finest songs for over a year, until he found a musical mass solid enough to withstand their weight. Indeed, a number of witnesses affirm that they saw *Astral Weeks* coming, on the basis not of the official albums but of little things they would hear Morrison play in the back rooms of Belfast and Boston.

My personal candidate for the one song Morrison wrote in New York would have to be 'Cyprus Avenue', the culmination of a strand of his songwriting that he would rarely return to – the sense of physical loss that lost love can bring, wrapped around a vision of innocence personified. 'Cyprus Avenue' is one of those songs that can't help drawing the listener in, inviting interpretations as to its meaning. Morrison even gave an

---

★ It remains one of the handful of Morrison albums to still appear, even in the CD era, minus any lyric sheet. Thankfully, the lyrics are reproduced in Ritchie Yorke's *Into the Music*.

uncharacteristic largesse to such considerations when describing the song to Donall Corvin as 'a sketch about a lot of various feelings, moods', before insisting, 'I don't write with an interpretation; that's up to the listener.' If you say so, Van.

'Cyprus Avenue' is not so much a single sketch as a series of sketches – circular in that they begin and end in the temporal universe, with our singer still 'conquered in a car seat', watching the ubiquitous little girls walking back from school, rooted in the moment. The presence of these little girls is really a trigger, one that the narrator has pulled a number of times before. As the opening line betrays, he is not merely here by chance, he is 'caught one more time' on this grand thoroughfare – the use of 'caught' here, suggestive of taking a chance, contains concomitant danger of being found out. Indeed, there is a real awareness of guilt in the song. As Lester Bangs later wrote:

I've almost come to blows with friends because of my insistence that much of Van Morrison's early work had an obsessively reiterated theme of paedophilia, but [in 'Cyprus Avenue'] it is something that at once may be taken as that and something far beyond it. He loves her. Because of that, he is helpless . . . Nature mocks him. As only nature can mock nature. Or is love natural in the first place? No matter. By the end of the song he has entered a kind of hallucinatory ecstasy; the music aches and yearns as it rolls on out. This is one supreme pain, that of being imprisoned as a spectator.

Actually, the song departs from the avenue of trees after the first verse as Morrison passes through a series of hallucinatory visions, the first of which places him at the centre of some Americanized image of the romantic troubadour, as the singer visualizes walking along the rail tracks clutching a bottle of cherry wine. This is Lead Belly suffused with the spirit of Jimmie Rodgers. The second vision he takes direct from the folk lexicon, romanticizing the return of his lady with 'rainbow ribbons in her hair'. But, almost immediately, the pain of the present begins to intrude as he recalls the one and only fourteen-year-old he ever loved, and suddenly, for two lines and two lines only, the song switches to the past tense and a past love, back on this all-too-familiar avenue of trees, when *she* 'came walkin' down in the wind and the rain, darling/When you came walking down, when the sun shone through the trees'. The singer breaks down in his despair, insisting that 'nobody can stop me from loving you, baby/So young and bold, fourteen years old'. And we're back to 'Little Girl', back in the present, but a present superimposed by the past. *She* is gone. Only the counterfeit Catholic girls remain to taunt the singer.

On the other hand, maybe it's just about 'unobtainable totty':

Roy Kane: [Cyprus Avenue] was the street that we would all aspire to − the other side of the tracks. And [it really was] the other side of the tracks, because the Beersbridge Road had the railway line cut across it; and our side of it was one side of the tracks and Cyprus Avenue was the other . . . and going back to this Sunday thing, there was an Italian shop up in [Ballyhackamore], [with] an ice-cream parlour, and that's where all the young ones used to go of a Sunday. Whenever we had finished playing, we used to walk up to [the Sky Beam] for an ice-cream, or a cup of mushy peas and vinegar . . . We would have been acceptable [at the Beam] because we played in a wee group . . . We used to take a short cut up Cyprus Avenue, 'cause that's where all the expensive houses and all the good-looking totty came from. [And] maybe you'd get a chance to talk to some bird from the other side of the tracks on the way up . . . [Ballyhackamore] was a melting-pot where all the young ones went to, but mostly upper-crusty totty . . . There's a couple of big girls' grammar schools up 'round that direction . . . That would have sunk in[to] my head as [much] as his. I think that's what he was going on about in 'Cyprus Avenue' − the unobtainable totty.

Perhaps. Certainly 'Cyprus Avenue' represents a whole new level of sophistication to Morrison's songwriting, suggestive of a new, mature phase. It can be seen as providing both closure and a starting-point − so it's no surprise that it was the song with which Morrison elected to start the first session for his second solo album, booked for the evening of 25 September 1968, at Century Sound Studios. Walking into the studio that very evening, he met for the first time a set of musicians he had only ever encountered on the credits to albums on Blue Note and Prestige. Producer Lewis Merenstein had decided to make *Astral Weeks* a genuine jazz experience.

Lewis Merenstein: He was not an aficionado of jazz when I met him. R&B and soul, yes; but jazz, no. I only heard Van sitting, playing his acoustic guitar, and when we got in the studio he played exactly what he did in Boston. What changed was the musicians I chose to put underneath him. That gave a jazz feeling that he later carried on into *Moondance*. If you take the music out of

Astral Weeks, you'll hear what Van played in Boston. The musical energy of *Astral Weeks* came from the great players. That was the jazz background that I had, [and] that I brought into it. 'Cause I didn't hear it as rock & roll – or 'Brown Eyed Girl' – I heard somebody being reborn. I knew what 'Astral Weeks' was talking about.

The bad news – from their point of view – was that both of the other musicians in Morrison's band now found themselves sidelined. Payne can't remember how he was told, but he knew before the first session that 'they were going to get someone else to do the flute stuff'. Kielbania remembers being told by Van himself, who gave the impression that he played no part in the decision-making process.

Tom Kielbania: He said, 'Look, I know this is gonna hurt you but they want to do it this way.' But I got to show all the bass lines to Richard Davis. He embellished a lot on them, but I gave him the feeling . . . I think they had this whole thing planned – they were gonna get the best jazz musicians they could find. These were all heavyweight jazz [players].

As Payne's successor, Graham Blackburn, has observed, Morrison 'professed to be a jazz fan, and I think he listened to a fair amount of stuff, but he *really* was from a totally different world'. It was Merenstein's world, and his call (even if Steve Turner attributes the choice of musicians to Bob Schwaid, at the behest of Warners, who 'didn't want to overspend on sessions'). In fact, Schwaid–Merenstein's contract with Warners simply required a delivered, sequenced album. Merenstein's first call was to Richard Davis, who was designated session leader and, in consultation with Merenstein, came up with the likes of guitarist Jay Berliner (who had played with Charlie Mingus), percussionist Warren Smith Jr and Modern Jazz Quartet drummer Connie Kay.

Lewis Merenstein: Richard Davis was the calibre player. When you wanted to have a great session, you hired him because he'd get there early and start practising, and when other musicians walked in the room there was such awe and respect that they came to a different level of playing . . . And if you listen to the album, every tune is led by Richard and everybody followed Richard and Van's voice . . . I knew if I brought Richard in, he would put the bottom on to support what Van wanted to do vocally, or acoustically. Then you get Jay playing those beautiful counter-lines to Van.

Richard Davis: No prep, no meeting, never heard of [the guy]. I was relating to Lew and Bob, not him. They wanted me to gather a particular group together, [guys] that I liked to play with. I picked them for certain reasons, [as] demonstrated in their performances [on the record]. I picked Connie Kay because he made me feel very comfortable to play with. I nicknamed him the Security Officer, 'cause he made you feel very secure, his subtle way of playing and his command of what he was doing. And Jay Berliner has a reputation of being able to play any type of music.

The album's three sessions needed to be booked around Davis's predictably packed schedule, thus spanning a three-week period in late September/early October. If Davis was the key musical component, the one person whom Merenstein made Morrison meet before the sessions was arranger Larry Fallon, even though their initial meeting 'was just to get chord-sheets for the tracks'. This sense of separation from the other musicians carried over to the sessions themselves.

Richard Davis: As far as Van Morrison goes, he was remote from us, 'cause he came in and went into a booth . . . And that's where he stayed, isolated in a booth. I don't think he ever introduced himself to us, nor we to him. He was just somebody who walked into a studio and did something. And he seemed very shy. So that's what it was – just us playing together, and whatever he was doing, in my memory, was beside the point. It wasn't like all of us getting together into a huddle, see what the next play was gonna be. Fortunately for him it all fit the package for him to do what he had to do . . . Some people can envelop you in their performance, and it makes you feel like you're doing what they're doing – I've worked with many artists who had that rapport – [but Van] didn't do a goddamn thing . . . We had what you call a lead sheet, [which is] a skeletal frame of what is to be done, and you have to fill in the flesh. What you fill in [comes] through your own imagination – nobody can tell you what to do. You just play it . . . What I was doing was a kind of lyrical bass line. It was not a typical thing I was doing. And [Lewis] gave me credit for making the whole thing happen.

Davis takes a certain delight in shattering a myth imposed by subsequent listeners: 'Some people are real disillusioned when I tell them about making [*Astral Weeks*]. People say, "He must have talked to you about the record and created the magic feeling that had to be there . . ."

To tell you the truth . . . he didn't make any suggestions about what to play, how to play, how to stylize what we were doing.' If Morrison's detachment from the sound that surrounds him on *Astral Weeks* is in some sense shocking, it is confirmed by the other musicians involved. Connie Kay told *Rolling Stone* that he *did* go and ask Morrison 'what he wanted me to play, and he said to play whatever I felt like playing. We more or less sat there and jammed.' The musicians to a man credit Merenstein with providing the right environment.

Jay Berliner: I think [Lewis] had the idea of using jazz musicians on a rock session. I remember that they had some special ideas about this record. They gave us all this freedom to play whatever we wanted to do, which was [something] that we were[n't] used to. It was pretty much left to us. I was interested to see Connie Kay on a rock date, 'cause he was very well known as a jazz drummer with the Modern Jazz Quartet . . . [But] it was a group effort. Everybody was heavily involved. Just by listening to it, you can hear it – all this energy!

Warren Smith Jr: Bob Schwaid and Lewis Merenstein . . . were expert at selecting the people that could do things, rather than specify[ing] what it was we could do . . . They had what you call lead sheets – in other words the structure of the song was there. [But] in many instances, nothing was exactly specified other than the structure of the song and we would create certain things that would fit in. They had some suggestions, but a lot of it was added according to our own ingenuity. [Morrison] was very young and very shy. He didn't say a lot. If he wanted something particular he might venture out, but for the most part he stayed in the control booth.

Morrison was doubtless a tad intimidated by the calibre of musicians Merenstein had been able to gather together. He later admitted as much: 'The songs came together very well in the studio. Some of the tracks were first takes. [But] the musicians were really together. Those type of guys play what you're gonna do before you do it, that's how good they are.' Their special vibe soon began to rub off on the singer:

Jay Berliner: [On] some of the tunes [Van] got very emotional. He really got worked up to a fever pitch. He came out of the booth a couple of times very excited. Especially that first session – they were very, very happy with what was going on.

Over the years, though, the master revisionist has come to insist that he didn't 'feel comfortable at all, even though [the album] did justice to what I was trying to say. My producer, Lew [Merenstein], must have pulled himself up to scratch to do it, but I had something else in mind . . . I was kind of restricted, because it wasn't really understood what I really wanted on the date.' In fact the only real barrier to communication, Morrison's inarticulacy, was overcome in and by the music.

Lewis Merenstein: [Van] showed up and did what he was doing, and had all the opportunity in the world to say what he wanted, or change what he wanted, and anything he says now is in hindsight . . . He came and he played his tunes, and if he didn't like something or he wanted to do it again, we did it again. It's just that the songs were so much a part of the newness of where he was coming from that they just came out in a wondrous fashion. And the musicians there – because they were so spontaneous – were able to pick up every nuance and filled it, filled it, filled it. You listened back and there it was. Beautiful.

John Payne, an eyewitness throughout, pretty much agrees with Merenstein's version of events. *If* songs were not fully realized, he feels that Morrison's 'communication skills may have been more at fault than anything else. If he'd really let anyone know, "This is what I want, this way," it might have happened that way. It certainly would have been considered. It wasn't like they ramrodded it through or anything. No one was saying, "No, we're doing this."'

The booth out of which Morrison sang was not the only barrier to verbal communication. His demeanour at that first session suggested someone already on the astral plane. As Payne recollects, 'He seemed spaced out. He appeared as though he was in a lot of personal pain.' Berliner gets more specific: 'You could see clouds of smoke inside the vocal booth. I don't know what it was, [but] he called it the Vegetable Weed.' Needless to say, no self-respecting jazzer was going to be fazed by such a sight, and the band played on. John Payne, who was itching to enter the fray, remembers thinking that Berliner in particular 'looked as though he were getting into it . . . I'm not saying that [the others] were all just sitting there, thinking another day, another dollar, but I couldn't say for sure that they weren't.' Berliner certainly enjoyed a rare licence.

Jay Berliner: I played a lot of classical guitar on those sessions and it was very unusual to play classical guitar in that context. What stood out in my mind was the fact that he allowed us to stretch out. We were used to playing to charts, but Van just played us the songs on his guitar and then told us to go ahead and play exactly what we felt.

The first session went exceptionally well: within four hours they had recorded 'Cyprus Avenue', followed by the two songs in which Web IV retained copyright, 'Madame George' and 'Beside You', whose place on the album was thus assured. With these three key songs cut to his satisfaction, Morrison turned his attention to one of those tunes imbued with the presence of a new love: the song destined to become the title track. For Payne, the sight of yet another song he had been playing live about to be recorded with this other flautist proved too much, and he pleaded for the opportunity to show what he could do.

John Payne: They were using [our attendance] as a way to get us paid some money . . . [as] it came out of the recording budget. But occasionally they would ask Tom [Kielbania] questions about how a song [went], because he really knew what was going on with these songs. He [had] played them for so long with Van. And, of course, being a bass player, when they made a chord change, he had to make the change . . . [But] it was fairly simple harmonically . . . I believe 'Astral Weeks' was not particularly one they were going to do . . . It was [right at] the end of the first session. He said, 'Well, let's do one more,' and I'd be yelling, 'Let me play, let me play' – because I was young and foolish and didn't know my place – 'I can play as well as he did – I can do what he's doing.' . . . And [for] the next two sessions they just used me. Just to save money in the budget [probably].

The unknown flautist responsible for those fluttering little fills in 'Beside You' and 'Cyprus Avenue' would not even get a name-check on the sleeve as Payne eased himself on to the stool he felt should have been his from the outset. He remained on hand the following week, when they returned to the studio with slightly different personnel. As Berliner was doing another session, Barry Kornfeld was brought in on lead guitar. Payne remembers that 'they got a string quartet to play the rhythm part on "Young Lovers Do", and then they wanted to do "Madame George" . . . They wanted them to improvise, and [the quartet] didn't know how to improvise, so they got rid of them. They paid them all and did other things.' Merenstein recalls some indefinable tension at this second session, and after three hours everyone took a break that would last a full fortnight.

Only 'As Young Lovers Do' from this session would make the album, as the opening track on side two, where its lounge-jazz sound still sticks out like Spumante at a champagne buffet. If the second session proved quite a comedown after the adrenalin rush of the first, the fortnight's wait must have compounded Morrison's rising sense of frustration. The other musicians' schedules remained chock-full until 15 October, when those who had seen out that original session reassembled.

Whatever else was recorded at the 1 October session still resides in vaultdom. According to Warners' files, there were two out-takes, an early version of 'I've Been Working' and a song listed simply as 'Train'. The latter song, dismissed by Morrison as a basic blues number that didn't fit, was probably the song demoed for Warners Publishing at this time, listed as 'On a Rainy Afternoon'. Retaining a familiar bass and flute-based arrangement, it features that ubiquitous 'barefoot angel child', this time playing down by the railroad track, and at its end the singer thinks he hears a train coming – cue train noises from Morrison on harmonica. A wise omission.

On the 15th, Morrison set the tone for the (final) session by recording two paeans to his wifely muse – 'Sweet Thing' and 'Ballerina' – at the very outset of proceedings. The remainder of the session was spent searching for a way to bring the album to some kind of resolution. The next song recorded was apparently called 'Royalty'. It lacked the necessary nobility. They also messed around with a song called 'Going Around with Jesse James', presumably another evocation of the Wild West by a young Belfast cowboy. Morrison later told Yorke that 'that last song on the album wasn't supposed to be there – two other songs were supposed to be there instead'. This may well suggest that Morrison intended to return to Little Jimmy and Broken Arrow. And yet he elected to record something of a quite different hue, taking the album somewhere altogether darker.

John Payne: He started doing 'Slim Slow Slider', which I don't think we'd ever done live. He had a book full of songs . . . Janet kept track of all the songs Van wrote . . . I don't know why he decided to do it . . . And we were first doing it with the drums, with Richard Davis and Connie Kay and the guitar player and the vibe player and me and Van – all of us were playing. Then I started playing soprano [sax] on the thing, and Lew said, 'OK, I wanna try it again. Start again. And I want just the bass, the soprano sax and Van.' [NC]

Merenstein caught the spirit of the song by stripping things down. Its starkness would be further accentuated by the lack of string overdubs, unlike the remaining songs. The song itself was a first cousin of 'TB Sheets'. As with its kin, the narrator is obliged to watch some young girl die, utterly impotent in the face of her death-like desire: 'Every time I see you, I just don't know what to do'. However, unlike the fated Julie, the heroine in 'Slim Slow Slider' is bent on her personal path to destruction: 'I know you're dying, baby/I know you know it too'. Morrison has not confirmed the obvious inference – that the subject of 'Slim Slow Slider' is a junkie – preferring to depict the lady as someone 'who is caught up in a big city . . . *maybe* [she] is on dope'. Either way, the song's inclusion at the end of the album, in the words of Bob Sarlin, 'complete[s] the passage from childhood to the harshness of adult reality', aided and abetted by a very abrupt splice at song's end.

John Payne: On 'Slim Slow Slider' there's a huge cut. Right before the end they take out minutes of instrumental improvisation of me and Richard Davis, and Van too, single-string improvising on guitar, which you don't hear him do much . . . I would estimate three [to] five minutes of instrumental stuff . . . it [felt] like a long process . . . We went through stages [until] we got to be avant-garde kind of weird, which is what you hear after the splice – all that weird stuff we're playing – but there was a whole progression to that. [TP]

Merenstein, though, was unimpressed by what he heard, and asserted his prerogative as the album's producer, chopping the song so that what one critic described as 'a conga drum frighten[ing] the sax off into the fade' is all that audibly remains of a savage cut.

Lewis Merenstein: The last song was a stretch in the concept that I was hearing – what he was talking about, the [sense of] mystery. Basically, 'Slim Slow Slider' belonged on a different album. It didn't feel right. Whatever Van had in mind – [and] Van objects to anybody having any thought about what he's doing, or any opinion – it felt like [it should go] where I put it, at the end of the album. [But] the [instrumental coda] was a long, long ending that went nowhere, that just carried on from minute to minute to minute . . . If it had [some] relativity to the tune itself, I would have left it there.

At least one critic, *Fusion's* Ken Emerson, was on Merenstein's side: 'It is partly by dint of contrast that "Slim Slow Slider", weighing in at a mere 3.20, is such an arresting song. The essence of Morrison's problem here is that an ending, if it is to be the right ending, implies a structure which his improvisations do not possess.'* Perhaps it was Merenstein's use of his producer's veto here that prompted Morrison to later portray him as 'someone who came around and watched us practise, and called himself a producer' – a shameless slur on one of the man's few genuine collaborators. He has certainly never explained why he offered the song at the session if he didn't want it considered for the album. As it is, this other-worldly coda was just what was needed to complete an over-whelmingly powerful twelve-inch platter.

According to Kielbania, 'Slim Slow Slider' was not the only song that needed a little trimming: 'Most of the songs [were] so long, each one could have been a side of an album. They went in and cut out a lot of the solos. It was one big hairy jam. It was fantastic, but everything was too long.' Some of the fades snatch the songs away just as they seem on the verge of uncharted territory. Such decisions were presumably made at the same time that the strings – magnificently scored by Larry Fallon – were overdubbed at Mastertone Studios. Morrison, who was also privy to the process, now began to come up with his own ideas of how the strings should sound just as the album was being put to bed. Warners were anxious for product, and Merenstein just wanted to wrap it up.

Lewis Merenstein: I know how exhausted I was after that period of time – [after] the three days of doing it, taking the tapes to Mastertone, putting the strings on it, coming back the next day and putting it together, and mixing it and getting the whole thing done . . . There was [also] tension in the studio 'cause this was a new experience for Van, and certainly when we started overdubbing, it was a totally new experience for Van. I remember there were struggles between him and Larry about the strings. Larry had certain arrangements, Van wanted to change things.

---

* Emerson was wholly unaware of the edit made to the song at the sequencing stage.

Though at this point it must have been clear which songs were going to be on the album, the actual sequence was one more part of the process over which Morrison exercised no control. To Merenstein's credit, he seemed instinctively to see the wisdom of intercutting the songs for a new muse with those delving into another Belfast. As Rick McGrath put it in *Georgia Straight*, 'the listener is . . . given eight poetic insights into love: four are entrances, four are exits'. According to Merenstein, the sequence was not something that they actually discussed.

Lewis Merenstein: I sequenced the album – totally. As a producer, one of the elements is [to know how to] package the artist – I get a concept of what the whole thing sounds like . . . I don't think he even saw the album cover before it came out . . . Warners just put the thing out there really quick. I was really disappointed for [engineer] Brooks [Arthur] – he put in all this time and energy [and got no credit] . . . [But] it was basically a concept album – *I* felt it was that. That was why I put 'In the Beginning' [on side one].*

The album as released may have been Merenstein's idea of a concept album, but it was not apparently Morrison's. Between then and now he has come to insist that there was a lot 'more to it than the album. The album's just a piece of [this opera]. There's a whole lot more stuff that I've got . . . There's a definite story, and it all fits together . . . You can't really get into it in thirty-eight minutes. Plus the way the album was done, I didn't get a chance to get into it either . . . My producer told me, "You've got so much time to finish this album," and . . . I only got that time. And I didn't really get into it as much as I thought I would, because of that . . . If I had [had] my way, it would have been a different thing.'

Morrison's view of the album would shift as the critical plaudits grew. However, even in the year of its release, Jon Gershen remembers that it was never something 'he really wanted to talk about . . . There is a recurring theme in a lot of conversations I had with him . . . that [*Astral Weeks*] as it came out, as it was released, was not the album he intended it to be. That was a consistent theme: "They ruined it. They added the strings. I didn't want the strings. And when they sent it to me, it was all changed. That's not *Astral Weeks*."'

---

* The titles for the two sides of the album – 'In the Beginning' and 'Afterwards' – which have excited much debate over the years, appear to have been entirely Merenstein's idea.

Perhaps not, but it is the record as released – an album mixed, sequenced and produced by Lewis Merenstein, having ensured it was recorded with some of the best jazz musicians around – that has come to be viewed as one of the few works in rock to stand comparison with the best of Dylan. Morrison has preferred to belittle the role of his collaborator, reluctant to share any glory whilst happy to highlight disagreements. Despite portraying himself as 'the tool of people anxious to get a product on to the shelves', nothing could be further from the truth. The fact is that the fusion Morrison and Merenstein achieved in tandem was something only someone in love with music could have captured on tape. Nor is it a sensibility Morrison ever fully captured again – despite a number of attempts, suitably disguised.

John Payne: The thing that's interesting about the album is [that] it doesn't remind you of any other album . . . It's a jazz–pop fusion . . . but it's fused the same way. Van doesn't sing any differently [these days] . . . but the backing is different. And the feel and training and the background of the musicians are different. And what they think of doing is different . . . *Astral Weeks* had a jazz flavour, but the musicians weren't just people playing jazz . . . they all had flexibility. All those musicians in there knew how to go with the flow, and [how to] mine it. [TP]

Jon Gershen: [After] *Astral Weeks*, you flip a switch . . . and never look back. Even though he tried to recapture that from time to time, I don't think it ever really happened. To me, it was always a self-conscious attempt to recapture that.

Anyone fortunate enough to have heard this material at the Catacombs or the Scene, or who would later attend one of the dozen or so shows the trio played in the winter of 1969, must have found the contrast with *Astral Weeks* rather striking. Whether an album using the sound of the many demos from this period – featuring Morrison on acoustic, Tom Kielbania on bass and John Payne or Graham Blackburn on flute – would have had anything like the impact of *Astral Weeks* must be seriously open to doubt.

Tom Kielbania: He always had this idea of what he wanted, but then when the album was all done I asked, 'Is this really what you were looking for?' He said, 'Well, not really.' Even though it was good, I don't really think it was what he wanted to do. But he had to – he had no choice. Van's whole thing was 'They're songs.' He doesn't like it when they get overdone. They [can easily] get completely destroyed because people put so much music to 'em, you lose the effect of what the songs are supposed to be . . . I think it lost a little [of] the music. I think it went . . . a little too much on the jazz side, because before it was kinda mixed together. It lost the folky feeling. [And] nobody knows what we sounded like when we played together.

And yet the initial impact of *Astral Weeks* was hardly spectacular. Indeed, when Merenstein delivered the album to Warners, they seemed less than delighted with what they received: 'They said, "Where's 'Brown Eyed Girl'? Where's Van Morrison?" I think they were shocked. Nobody knew – except the critics. Then it became the album to listen to. George Lee had the belief in us . . . [But] no one [else] at Warners knew what it was until somebody at FM radio picked it up, [and] critics started talking about it. Then they [began to] respond properly.'

The lacklustre response at Warners may even have prompted Morrison and/or Merenstein to consider giving them a single. In late December 1968, they returned to Century Sound to cut a single song, apparently called 'The Sky Is Full of Pipers', with Warren Smith and Jay Berliner from the *Astral Weeks* ensemble, Tom Kielbania on bass and Buddy Salzman on drums. No such song ever appeared, and in the end no single accompanied the January 1969 release of *Astral Weeks*.

For the attentive few, the album may have been a life-changer, but as John Collis wrote in the introduction to his wafer-thin book on Morrison, '*Astral Weeks* . . . delighted us in a self-sealed vacuum, barely affecting the sales of upright basses and flutes, let alone sending the river of popular music off on a new course.' Warners would admit as much in full-page ads they ran for its successor the following year, which informed readers, 'It may be a little tough to find 1969's *Astral Weeks* in some record stores. Damn shame. It wasn't adopted by the Pepsi set and ended up as what you might call a critically acclaimed but obscure album . . . If you want it and can't find it, yell at the store's record buyer. Loud, because you're the customer and you're always right. Undo the veils of potential obscurity.'

If reviews were decidedly thin on the ground, they were also largely devoid of insight. Nick Logan in *NME* compared Morrison to flamenco guitarist José Feliciano, one of the more absurd comparisons in the history of pop journalism. *Melody Maker* recognized *Astral Weeks* as 'one of the strongest albums of the year', but accorded Morrison little acreage. It was left to an incisive review from Greil Marcus in *Rolling Stone* to set the critical bandwagon rolling:

Van Morrison . . . has now released a unique and timeless album, called *Astral Weeks*. The limits and restrictions are no more in evidence than on [his] previous record, but the limits of the blues, as they exist for Van Morrison, have been abandoned as well . . . What might seem arty at first proves to be a new place to go, a new kind of music to hear, as conductor Larry Fallon often abandons the structured comforts of conventional melody, rhythm and time in an attempt to create and sustain mood, [providing] a basis for Van's own creations . . . *Astral Weeks* is serious and it is also a profoundly intellectual album. Not in the sense that it requires some grand intelligence to 'understand' it or to dig it . . . Rather, it is 'intellectual' in the same way that Nathaniel Hawthorne's room, filled with moonlight, was a place and a time for the intellect and the emotions to live together.

Marcus's piece, which came with a brief overview of Morrison's career to date, ran at a time when *Rolling Stone* was fast becoming an arbiter of kudos for much of America's young adult readership. The decision not to release a single actually worked in the album's favour, retaining its integrity and ensuring that no one song got singled out for FM airplay.

Marcus also went on to play a crucial role in the album's latter-day rediscovery, commissioning Lester Bangs in 1978 to write about one desert-island disc for a book he was planning to edit (published by Knopf in 1979 as *Stranded: Rock and Roll for a Desert Island*). That essay, again included by Marcus in the posthumous collection of Bangs's best pieces, *Psychotic Reaction & Carburetor Dung*, remains the definitive prose piece on *Astral Weeks*, as Bangs placed the album in a context real enough to include a lot of people who overlooked the album on its release:

It sounded like the man who made *Astral Weeks* was in terrible pain, pain most of Van Morrison's previous work had only suggested; but, like the later albums by the Velvet Underground, there was a redemptive element in the blackness . . . It did come out at a time when a lot of things that a lot of people cared about passionately were beginning to disintegrate, and when the self-destructive undertow that always accompanied the great sixties party had an awful lot of ankles firmly in its maw and was pulling straight down. So, as timeless as it finally is, perhaps *Astral Weeks* was also the product of an era . . . Certainly it is not a young man's record; there are lifetimes behind it . . . It's no wonder that Morrison's protagonist turned away from Madame George, fled to the train station, trying to run as far away from what he'd seen as a lifetime could get him. And no wonder, too, that Van Morrison never came this close to looking life square in the face again, no wonder he turned to *Tupelo Honey* and even *Hard Nose the Highway* with its entire side of songs about falling leaves. In *Astral Weeks* and 'TB Sheets' he confronted enough for any man's lifetime.

This assessment of the album largely accords with the view of its producer. Merenstein believes he stumbled on Morrison when 'he was raw. He was being reborn, he was a child again. He never achieved that again. He searched all over the world of poetry for various ways of expressing himself, but the rawness, the nerve endings weren't there – because he's not *there* any more.'

Doubtless this is not a view that the latter-day Morrison would share. Twenty years on, reflecting on the lifetimes that lay behind *Astral Weeks*, he asserted that 'to sing about innocence you need experience . . . To be totally, completely innocent is absolutely useless and will get you absolutely nowhere. They will cave you in.' And 'they' really had come very close to making him cave in. In the light of such a statement, it should not be surprising that he did not wish to venture into this particular slipstream again.

AGE FOUR
Before The Wind

13

1969–70: Entering the Mainstream

If a child is to keep alive his inborn sense of wonder without any such gift from the fairies, he needs the companionship of at least one adult who can share it, rediscovering with him the joy, the excitement and the mystery of the World we live in.

—*Rachael Carson*

Sometimes I think I may just be an underground thing. I can't mix, you see. That's my problem. You have to be able to mix if you want to be in show business.

—*Van Morrison, 1968*

There wasn't a big marketplace for him. What he was doing musically certainly wasn't what people knew. He wasn't an easy act to book. And he had great needs. We got him advances; spent money on him; put him . . . where he wanted to be.

—*Lewis Merenstein*

As Schwaid–Merenstein continued to subsidize their new artist, awaiting the release of the first album under the new Warners/Inherit imprimatur, they were temporarily relieved of one ongoing expense, flautist John Payne. As Christmas rolled around, and talk of a European tour came to naught, Payne sensed that the continuing torpor, punctuated by too few gigs and even less recording, was not about to dissipate.

John Payne: The big problem [for] a jazzer is those three chords. I mean, I

marvel at how those rock and blues guys can continue . . . [So] it was getting
less exciting to play with him . . . Between that and not going to Europe, [but]
just sitting around in Manhattan and nothing ever coming through; and missing
coming back [to Boston]; and hanging out there just [to] play with Van for an
hour and a half a day – it got to be kind of a drag. [TP]

Payne's last documented involvement would be on a handful of
publishing demos recorded for Warners shortly before the holidays, a
week or two after the trio made its TV début on a local New York
programme (after Morrison point-blank refused to lip-sync to a pre-
recorded track). His departure was perhaps unduly hasty. *Astral Weeks*
was due out at the turn of the year, and a makeshift schedule had
been pencilled in to promote it, starting at the recently revived Avalon
Ballroom in San Francisco on 29 January 1969. With a certain flair for
timing, Morrison only succeeded in filling Payne's shoes the day before
departing for the west coast.

Graham Blackburn: There I was in [Woodstock], with . . . no visible means
of support and . . . some mutual friend knew [Van] was in town, looking for
someone to jam with. And so I went round and played with him, and we got
on. He was leaving for California the next day for a promotional tour for *Astral
Weeks*. It was mid-winter and he asked if I wanted to go along. I was delighted.
It was just him, myself and Tom Kielbania. I started out just playing flute, but
I alternated [with sax]. He was never very clear about what he was about to
play, so it was always difficult standing there waiting for him to start, [trying] to
figure out what instrument I should have to grab.

That opening show was reviewed by Greil Marcus for the now defunct
SF Express-Times. He noted the presence of 'a strange-looking cat with
a stand-up bass and a jazz musician with a saxophone and a flute', but
when 'Morrison walked on to the stage . . . almost nobody noticed . . .
He looked, for a moment, like a kid who'd been given permission to
hold out on stage for a little while.' Breaking into 'Astral Weeks',
Morrison interspersed the trio of songs from side one of *Blowin' Your
Mind!* with a resequenced *Astral Weeks*, to a small but friendly crowd. As
a public début of one of the dozen finest works in rock, it passed most
folks in the Bay area by. This was a low-budget launch. At least Morrison
got to headline (outside California he would be saddled with second
billing). Further evidence of the corner-cutting nature of the tour came

after the show, when Kielbania found he 'had no place to stay. Everybody had somebody to stay with, and they just left me there. This guy I went to high school with, he shows up at the concert, and he was staying at a flophouse. It was a dollar a night. It was terrible.'

Thankfully, the week-long residency that followed at the Whiskey in LA – still run by Elmer Valentine – was sufficiently prestigious for the guys to be housed at the infamous Tropicana Motel. As Kielbania fondly recalls, 'I got to jam with the Doors . . . They were rehearsing down the street. [Van] says, "You wanna meet Jim Morrison and the Doors?"' In the three years since the Doors had taken some tips from a bunch of crazed Ulstermen by the name of Them, they had become one of the biggest rock bands in America (Morrison's namesake was days away from the notorious incident when he flashed at the audience during a show in Miami which was to prove the beginning of the end). The foursome were delighted to see Van again, and Blackburn 'was [greatly] impressed by the fact that [these] musicians knew him, and respected him'.

Despite continuing to command respect from his peers, though, Morrison no longer warranted headline status at the Whiskey. Nor was his belligerence overlooked by paying punters, even if he continued to engage in verbal fisticuffs whenever incomprehension beckoned.

Tom Kielbania: There was some other band at the Whiskey on the same bill, some rock & roll band. [So] there's a lot of teenyboppers there, and we're playing this real serious music and you can hear them talking in the background. He [just] stops playing and says, 'Will you shut the fuck up and listen.' . . . A couple of times we would play to very small audiences, and the people really knew what was going on, and we would play and play and play, and you could see Van was communicating with 'em, [but] it was finding a place to play.

Graham Blackburn was a virtual novice when it came to such shenanigans, but he was greatly impressed by what he calls Morrison's 'quality . . . of intenseness – [which] made it all meaningful. I think that's what grabbed everybody. He had a non-existent stage presence – until he started to sing . . . He would never announce anything, he would never even look at the audience . . . and certainly never cut audiences any slack . . . but it was [all] OK, once he started to sing.'

It is doubtful whether Morrison would have got away with such behaviour at three Midwest dates that followed on from the Whiskey, in Cincinnati, Chicago and Detroit, where he was obliged to play

understudy to the Jeff Beck Group, to far rowdier crowds. And yet, even
in such unsavoury circumstances, he resisted playing the Them originals
the audience might have known. As his material became ever more
introspective, Morrison withdrew into himself both on stage and off, his
lack of showmanship a self-conscious barrier to general acceptance.
Reviewing a show that summer at the Café Au-Go-Go, Danny Goldberg
highlighted the contradictions thrown up by Morrison's onstage persona:

As a performer, Morrison is tantalizing often to the degree of irritation. He is
so wrapped up in the perfection of his work and the feeling of his song that
he hardly recognizes the audience, acknowledging them occasionally with a
bemused smile, surprised, it seems, that anyone can keep up with him . . .
[when] he reluctantly played his smash single of 1967, 'Brown Eyed Girl', the
tune seemed frivolous compared with his new introspective material.

Morrison wasn't the only one frustrated by the lack of recognition his
masterful Warners début album was generating out in the trenches.
Merenstein began to worry that, whatever the artistic achievement, his
and Schwaid's ongoing investment might become a bottomless pit –
especially when their artist indicated an unwillingness to play second
fiddle to any more volume merchants.

Lewis Merenstein: He wouldn't tour; . . . he wasn't doing the old stuff; the
album wasn't successful; [and] there was no great calling for him. That [pop]
world was [seemingly] over for him . . . We tried to get him work, [but]
whatever we got him wasn't enough. He wasn't playing, [and] he had the two
guys [to pay].

So when Morrison expressed a desire to move a hundred miles upstate,
to the still largely unknown hamlet of Woodstock, at the foot of the
Catskills, he went there with Schwaid–Merenstein's blessing. The costs
of living upstate were a fraction of what they were in Manhattan,
and the move meant that daily incursions into the office for help or a
handout would perforce abate. The arrangement also suited Graham
Blackburn, who was already living up in Woodstock, in a house he had
built himself.

Graham Blackburn: After we came back from the first round of touring in
California and the Midwest, he was looking for somewhere to live and I actually

suggested he move to Woodstock, partly out of self-interest. Rehearsals would
be a whole lot easier if I could get him to live here, and he was very excited by
the fact I knew some of the other musicians in Woodstock who he regarded
highly, like . . . the Band.

Whatever relief the Morrisons leaving New York brought to
Schwaid–Merenstein, the move to Woodstock, and the very real sense
of detachment from city life that such an idyllic setting gave, marked the
start of a gradual disconnection from his New York management team
(his next would-be saviour, Mary Martin, would do her best to encourage
the passage from separation to divorce). In fact, when problems arose
upstate, and a more practical hand was required, Morrison would like-as-
not call George Lee at Warners rather than his manager Bob Schwaid,
even though Lee's brief certainly did not extend to A&R duties.

George Lee: He used to call me on [what seemed like] a daily basis. This is
when he lived in an old shack in upstate New York. He would call me up, and
say, 'George, George, there's no water in this building.' 'So why did you move
into it? . . . Why don't you call your managers? Why're you calling me?' He
said, 'Because I know you'll do something for me.' . . . He'd call me up for a
handout, instead of them . . . I only talked to Van when he had problems, and
he had problems every hour. I said, 'Why don't you call the record company?'
He said, 'No, I only like to talk to you.' 'Cause I was in New York . . . he [felt
he] had more of a relationship with me than he did with the record-company
executives in California . . . He was a little shy, but he would come up and sit
in the office, and just sit and not talk – he wanted to say things, but he didn't
say them.

Less than six months away from the festival that would make it
world-famous, Woodstock retained much of the charm that had led the
likes of Dylan, his manager Al Grossman, Peter Yarrow of Peter, Paul
and Mary, and banjo picker Billy Faier to use it as a getaway from the
helter-skelter pace of New York. Sadly for Morrison, Dylan had just
moved to the old Walter Weyl home in Byrdcliffe, and was a matter
of months away from forsaking Woodstock altogether, weary of its
cocoon-like atmosphere. Indeed Morrison would never get to meet
Dylan during his time in Woodstock, even though, in Janet's words,
'Van fully intended to become Dylan's best friend . . . Every time we'd
drive past Dylan's house – Van didn't drive, I did – Van would just stare

wistfully out the window at the gravel road leading to Dylan's place. He thought Dylan was the only contemporary worthy of his attention.'*

In fact, the great man was suffering from a form of songwriter's 'amnesia' brought on by enforced isolation. The backwoods vibe that had inspired Dylan to write some of his greatest songs in the years 1964 to 1967 had assuredly passed from his hand, just as the same vibe began to imbue Morrison. The location that Van and Janet happened upon could hardly fail to inspire, even before the plumbing was fixed. The house, Kielbania remembers, was 'on top of a mountain . . . [It] was beautiful. He had this huge, huge picture window in the living room and that's where we used to practise.' Rented from the concert promoter Sid Bernstein, who had been responsible for booking the Beatles at Shea Stadium, Jon Gershen recalls it as 'a rambling single-storey house that had been built into some rock cliffs overlooking the valley below, with a spectacular view of this beautiful lake'. Finally in Eden, after several seasons in hell, Morrison was at last able to savour the moment, the tensions of his previous subsistence existence draining away. Kielbania recalls how he had been 'having a lot of problems with headaches. He was going to a chiropractor. He was very, very paranoid. He was very uptight. He just couldn't control it.' If so, Woodstock was a (temporary) cure-all.

After the exegesis that was *Astral Weeks*, it seemed as if he was at last beginning to clear away a lot of psychological debris, learning to dissociate himself from past baggage. Jon Gershen remembers being somewhat taken aback when Morrison's parents actually came to visit their long-lost son and his new family. To Gershen, at least, 'the whole juxtaposition of it all was kinda bizarre [even though] he seemed to get along with them OK'.

Morrison also seems to have enjoyed the anonymity of Woodstock, later enthusing about how he was able to travel on the bus to New York and nobody knew him from Adam. And still his well-documented ambivalence regarding fame could occasionally lead him to imagine a greater name-recognition than might be his due.

Jon Gershen: One [time] we got talked into doing a formal senior prom at Saugerties High School, and he happened to call up that day, 'Can I come?' He

---

* The first documented meeting of Morrison and Dylan would not occur until the summer of 1981, when Dylan attended one of the *Beautiful Vision* sessions in Sausalito.

got in the car . . . *Moondance* was already out, and people were starting to figure it out, and he had some very interesting psychological twists about what it meant to be somebody in the music business. That whole [Them] thing had twisted it, and he had wanted to put that all behind him. And yet there was a residue of that on some level, 'cause at this prom he turned up in shades. He felt like he was making the scene – we had to make up a name for him – but *nobody* knew who he was.

The couple who greeted Morrison's parents on their visit were still very much in love. Indeed, everyone who encountered Van and Janet in this period believed that theirs was a unique relationship. Janet herself, looking back at what was 'a gentler, more deferential time', agrees that 'there really did appear to be a rare and beautiful story there, a *Love Story* of immortal proportions'. Many of the songs now coming from Morrison's pen were expressions of an overwhelming gratitude and love. In one of his great lost compositions, 'Bit by Bit' (later covered by Roy Head), Morrison sang of 'learning how to love you in my own special way/Day by day, bit by bit'. Of course, his 'own special way' required a whole set of allowances to be made for that 'artistic temperament'.

John Payne: She was very sweet. She worshipped him artistically, and yet I couldn't figure out how she put up with him. She was very calm. She was totally devoted to Van and his career, and to believing in him. [ST]

Payne had the opportunity to witness what difference the relocation was making when invited up to Woodstock after a return gig in Boston that summer, at which he had guested on soprano sax. As usual, Janet played the perfect hostess, whilst Morrison veered from surly to sociable according to the breeze. As Payne notes, 'She [certainly] made up for Van in terms of [having] very good people skills.'

Others also noticed the way in which Janet operated as Morrison's personal interpreter of the world at large. Elliott Landy, who had recently added Dylan's *Nashville Skyline* to his list of photographic credits, remembers Morrison as someone who 'needed [some] kind of external system. As a private person he was diffident to a point [where] he was hardly able to cope with life. Around the house, as in everyday life in general, he was a complete failure, just able to write songs and sing them. For the rest, his wife took care of [everything].'

Only two people can know how much Morrison gave back to his

loving wife. And yet even the unequivocal love songs that date from this time are largely concerned with *his* needs. 'Crazy Love', one of his most affecting songs, paints its subject in an angelic light but, as Ken Brooks has written, it also displays 'Van's first intimation of possessiveness. Every stanza concerns [itself with] what she gives to him, there is no reciprocation.' At no point does Morrison suggest that he gives as good as he gets, and however much his young wife revelled in the role of muse, that suffocating neediness would ultimately take its toll.

In fact Morrison was increasingly thrown upon the company of his wife, as his two sidemen began to tire of his demanding perfectionism, whilst the locals maintained a stoical distance. Graham Blackburn was the first to bale out, as even rehearsing became sporadic: 'It got to a stage where he needed an even longer period of not playing, [just] to gestate. We kind of got laid off while he needed to think about things, and in the interim I joined another band.' It may well have been Morrison's intent to bring matters to a head. He now began to add building-blocks to the sparse sound used for the past six months. Kielbania found him bringing in another guitar player, John Platania, and a drummer, Bob Mason, who had been playing with the Fugs, though when it came to any new material, 'we would always run down acoustically, and then try it electric'. The paranoia that seemed to envelop Morrison continued unabated, compounded by the perpetual threat of a drugs bust. Kielbania suspected that he saw the writing on the wall.

Tom Kielbania: We moved to Woodstock, and we did a job in Montreal, and Boston, and another one in upstate Massachusetts, and we played at the Felt Forum. But jobs were few and far between, and I was getting kinda antsy because nothing was going on. He didn't seem to want to do anything, he didn't want to play. He was paying me $75 a week just so I wouldn't leave . . . Basically he was paying me just to go up there and practise with him all the time . . . [But] the guy that was his road manager was pushing cocaine, and the narcs were always on our tail. It was a pretty heavy scene in Woodstock. The road manager got busted . . . right after I left.

The departure of Kielbania and Blackburn meant that any plans Morrison had for a more electric sound were put on hold. Instead John Platania recalls that he and Morrison 'wound up doing . . . like a duo sort of thing. Some of it was in bars. And then there was the Newport Folk Festival in 1969, where it was just Van and me on stage . . . [We did] a lot of the *Astral Weeks* stuff . . . We did a bunch of gigs that way.'

However, before the four-piece had its day, they did venture into New York, where they recorded a bunch of demos at the Warners studio, the first hard evidence that Morrison had not been idle during his country retreat. There had been a number of demo sessions before this, during which approximately twenty compositions were recorded, many of which pre-dated *Astral Weeks* in genesis; but they would all be rejected, save 'Come Running', for its successor.

Graham Blackburn: [Though] we did other things too . . . my memory of it is that all we did was record 'Domino' for a year . . . I had no idea of what the master plan was. He wasn't exactly communicative, even if he did have a plan [of] what he was working towards . . . We did a lot of sessions . . . I never realized so much of it was being recorded, but it seemed to go on for month after month after month.

There is indeed a plethora of attempts at a prototypical 'Domino' on the various Warners demo tapes. Though it was tried every which way – acoustic solo, with flute and stand-up bass, with and without harmony vocals, even with handclaps – the song recorded that winter bears little lyrical resemblance to the version that was later a hit single. Indeed its closest kin are 'Joe Harper Saturday Morning' and 'He Ain't Give You None', for here we are back in the Queen's garden, with our singer playing ball outside the wall until he 'threw it inside your garden tall'.

If the man over yonder wall is not Madame George, he is equally strange. Domino, who lives all alone with his dog, evidently gets his kicks from watching others make out. This time the singer does not spare his feelings, as he seems to in 'Madame George'. Domino is unmistakably cast as a figure of fun: 'He let us in and we drank the wine that went to our heads/and we used to lay on a feather bed and laugh at the man called Domino'. On one of these early incarnations, the singer is even joined by 'a girl I used to know . . . I loved her so'. As they 'tried it fast and . . . tried it slow', they would sing about Domino.

The subsequent incarnation of 'Domino' would retain just chorus and melody line, being recast with the lyrics of another song of the period, 'Down in the Maverick'. However, the original version exists in Warners' vaults, being recorded at a pukka recording session in March 1969 with Kielbania, Blackburn, Jay Berliner, drummer Al Rogers and a pianist and trombonist. As Kielbania remembers it, 'they had all kinds of rhythm instruments, congas and stuff. It was almost like a Hugh Masekela-type thing, all acoustic. Then we did an electric version – I think Graham played sax on that – a real rock & roll-type version.' The idea of the session seems to have come from Merenstein, blown away by the song and determined to find a usable single. Morrison was not so sure, and kept Merenstein dangling, even as he continued to cut demo after demo.

Lewis Merenstein: We had a [little] rehearsal studio up at our office. Van could come up there with a guitar and a bass player. [But] these demos were recorded at Warners, [who] had a little demo studio for songwriters . . . Warners had us go back in [to demo songs] because they had put up money for the publishing portion and they wanted more material, even before *Moondance* was ready to go. [It was] probably also to get advances from Warner Brothers for his living and everything else. Warners wanted to feel that they had enough publishing to warrant giving advances. And also for his next album – to see what would [work]. A lot was worked out up there.

On these demo tapes Morrison generally used Kielbania and/or Blackburn, save for a handful of demos recorded at the Record Factory with Platania and Mason in tow. Excepting a solo demo of 'Come Running', none of the songs later featured on *Moondance* seems to have been demoed prior to the Record Factory session.★

Hearing the likes of 'Caravan', 'Everyone', 'Brand New Day' and a semi-acoustic 'Come Running' in this rudimentary form can't help but take the listener back to *Astral Weeks*, throwing into stark relief how much the songs were commercialized by their album arrangements. And yet the strength of these songs shines just as clearly from that single afternoon session – indeed Morrison's singing has a fierce precision that would be sacrificed to the need for a grander sound on the record. What these 'electric' demos cannot resolve is whether this sound reflected Merenstein's idea of what suited Morrison, or how much it signalled Morrison incrementally edging away from *Astral Weeks*.

Merenstein *was* aiming to refine the sound they'd found on *Astral*

★ The following *Moondance* demos include additional musical accompaniment: 'Caravan', 'Brand New Day', 'Everyone', 'You Set My Soul on Fire', and 'Come Running'. Solo demos of 'These Dreams of You', 'And It Stoned Me' and 'Nobody Really Knows' also date from this period.

Weeks, not abandon it altogether. So, when work began in earnest on the second Warners album, on 30 July 1969, Morrison found himself back at Mastertone with the three key components of that previous statement – Warren Smith, Richard Davis and Jay Berliner (Buddy Salzman again substituted for Connie Kay). The only musician there at Morrison's instigation was pianist Jeff Labes. If the session went well enough – with versions of 'Everyone' and 'Caravan' successfully completed – Labes sensed that the battleground for the album's sound was already being staked out.

Jeff Labes: The first session we did on any of that material was with some of the same guys on *Astral Weeks* . . . but it was more of a soft feel. It was more into swing than . . . what Van really wanted. So he was frustrated with it and he told Lew in no uncertain terms, 'This isn't it.' And I think that fortified his view that he had to get younger guys, who were part of something else.

By the following session, when he would attempt 'Moondance' itself, Morrison insisted on bringing along his own guitarist, John Platania. The *Astral Weeks* rhythm section, though, remained. Percussionist Warren Smith was slightly taken aback by the change in direction, although he felt it was 'kinda refreshing to hear somebody with his voice do that type of a song – that intrigued me'. The 'Moondance' session would be the last to feature musical components selected by the producer rather than the artist.

John Platania: Van brought me in. He wanted me on the album. But Merenstein had a lot of the people from *Astral Weeks* [in mind] . . . Van sort of manipulated the situation and . . . got rid of them all. For some reason he didn't want those musicians. [MW]

By July, Morrison was in the process of putting a band of his own together, consigning that semi-acoustic jazz-combo style to the back room. John Platania was retained, becoming a valuable musical collaborator, but the two-piece experiment was abandoned at an open-air festival in Woodstock that summer (no, not *that* one). Sound Out was an annual event organized by a woman who ran a clothing store in the centre of Woodstock, and had a farm half-way between Woodstock and Saugerties. Jon Gershen believes this was probably 'the concept that led to the big festival. She'd been doing it for a number of years, and the local people showed up and put blankets on the ground, and whoever was around would be booked, and people had picnics. It was very benign.' Morrison saw the festival as a way of announcing his musical credentials to the local community, and assembled a selection of local musicians to accompany him on a brief set, somewhere way down the bill.

Jon Gershen: There seems to be quite a bit written about how meticulous he was with arrangements and rehearsing, but it was not like that. He showed up to this outdoor festival without a group, and there were two [other] bands in Woodstock at that time . . . one was called Chrysalis and the other was [the Colwell-Winfield] Blues Band, and essentially what he did was . . . grab a few from each of those two groups and throw this back-up group together. I don't know whether they went off into the woods and he ran through a few things but . . . he got up [with] this pick-up band, and he proceeded to do *Astral Weeks* material. No one was really familiar with this stuff! [But] we were watching him at the peak of his powers, [and] he was on fire. We knew the people that were backing him up, and they were just trying to keep it together. Basically it was just him with the guitar, and he was just wailing . . . I had never seen anything like it. He was able to really project what he was trying to do with the *Astral Weeks* thing . . . That night it had another element to it. It was really in your face, and very pure.

Much as it might appear that the *Moondance* band was born during this performance of a purified *Astral Weeks*, not all of the musicians needed familiarizing with the songs the afternoon of Sound Out. John Platania was already conversant with the material, as was Jeff Labes. Labes had been introduced to Morrison some time earlier by the drummer in the Colwell-Winfield Blues Band, Chuck Purro, who had been playing with Morrison up at his house. He remembers someone who 'was looking for new people to play with up there. He was going out and doing small venues. So we jammed, and got along very well, and I started playing piano with him . . . And Woodstock had a wonderful Sound Out during the summer . . . They just put up a stage in a field. [And] I found myself jamming with Van.' Though Labes believes he had been shown 'The Way Young Lovers Do', 'Cyprus Avenue' and 'Astral Weeks', he also thinks that they had already begun playing the *Moondance* material as well.

Jeff Labes: Right from the beginning it was new songs, [what] would later become the *Moondance* album . . . He had this new material he was very excited about. He was ready to go into a new direction. I think Warners had pretty much told him, 'You have one more chance.'

Sound Out proved to be the death-knell of the Colwell-Winfield Blues Band – as Morrison 'acquired' their pianist and horn players, Jack Schroer and Colin Tilton. However, it took a trip down to the big city for the newly constituted ensemble to find its drummer.

Gary Malabar: At the time I was signed to a band called Raven, and we were signed to CBS Records . . . My roadie came in one night [and said], 'Hey, check this [album] out.' That record happened to be *Astral Weeks*. I listened to *Astral Weeks* and I said, 'There is no one on this planet that is doing this – not even Dylan.' Well, Van . . . was playing that week at the Gaslight on MacDougal Street in New York City, with Jeff Labes. I went down and introduced myself. They were a little quartet, very loose, playing some of the tunes [from the album], more folk[y] stuff, Jeff on piano, an acoustic bass player. I offered to sit in. Soon after that I was invited to come up and rehearse with Van in Woodstock for an up-and-coming record – what became *Moondance*. That was August 1969. I remember us pretty much rehearsing each tune, but I never remember us drilling them into the ground . . . I was [even] living at Van's house for a while. Most of the guys lived up there. I was the nomad, [so] when we rehearsed for a few days in a row, Van would let me stay there.

Having prised these musicians away from their respective bands, Morrison found himself spending a great deal of time with two brothers from another aspiring Woodstock outfit, the Montgomeries. However, neither David nor Jon Gershen was interested in becoming one of his employees, preferring just to hang out and make music. They had their own record deal to make (initially with Atlantic and then with Capitol Records, for whom they would make two albums as Borderline), but were greatly impressed by the performer they had seen at Sound Out – and vice versa.

Jon Gershen: The next day my brother and I were in town, sitting somewhere having a few drinks, and he came in and sat down next to us and he said he was really into what we were doing [and suggested], 'Let's do something.' . . . [I guess] we were a self-contained band, and he couldn't have *the* Band, so he attached himself to us. The other thing I think he liked was that we were busy with our own career, and it was not a big thing for us. He would call and say,

'What are you doing? Why don't we get together and do some playing?' . . .
We had a rehearsal studio in the house that we had built, and he used to come
by at the drop of a hat . . . There were huge numbers of people who had no
idea who Van was in Woodstock. I think that's why he liked us because we had
no idea about anything to do with his past. We just took him at face value . . .
We would get together and we'd just play. He liked to do a lot of different
kinds of music – he would do Hank Williams or blues, anything that came to
his mind. We would be doing stuff of ours, and then [we'd say], 'Well, let's do
some of *your* stuff' . . . To this day I've never heard any other performance of
['Friday's Child'] – all we knew was how he taught [it to] us . . . The thing with
him was he didn't have really good interpersonal skills and he didn't have, like,
friends in the true sense. My brother and I were the closest thing to friends that
he had. He could be doing [his albums, for which] he would enlist musicians –
he knew what he was looking to do – but that was that. And then there was
having some kind of contact with *friends* – people [who] weren't looking to see
what they could get out of him . . . One of the things that set us apart was that
we didn't have a business relationship with him. Because it had nothing to do
with money, we could get together and just have fun, and get down to the
things that he really was about – mining great old music, getting into the essence
of that stuff.

Gershen quickly realized that this was a man who was very much
alone – save when he was making music, his one and only real means of
communication. Even then he remained highly self-conscious. The
confusion generated by his thick Ulster accent only compounded any
latent tendency to shut himself off from the world. Janet recalls various
instances when 'nobody could understand a word he said. It was like
a foreign language. Some of the most hysterical conversations [I'd heard
in] my life were between Van and various telephone operators . . . There
was no communication going on, and of course he would get madder
and madder, and they would hang up on him and he'd have to call back.'
Gershen also depicts him as someone who was 'really out of his
element . . . far away from home and . . . very unsure of himself.
[And] when he starts talking, most people don't know what he's saying
because [of] his accent, so now he's reaching a point where maybe
he should not bother talking because it's too painful. What a lot of
hanging out with us was about was a way for him to connect, being
"one of the guys".'

The Montgomeries were as free of agendas as they came. They also knew the guys in the Band, an association Morrison was especially anxious to reinforce after an initial introduction through Graham Blackburn. Blackburn told Steve Turner that 'he was very impressed by [the Band], and really wanted to meet them; which was funny because they were equally impressed by him'. Gershen thinks not. He suggests that this was hardly a mutual-admiration society. Rather, it comprised a man who had trouble making himself understood, caught in the company of musicians recast by the master of the put-down, Dylan. For these down-home boys, Van Morrison was an interesting, if occasionally tiresome, Anglo-Irish eccentric. No more, no less.

Jon Gershen: He came to Woodstock because Dylan lived there. It was pretty self-evident. For Van, Dylan symbolized [someone who could] light up the road ahead. But because he didn't get [together] with Dylan, he settled for the next best thing, which was the Band. But they represented something else entirely. I think to him they were the authentic article, and he just tried to get in their world, to be with them . . . There weren't too many people that he would focus on and be still, and [just] listen to what they were saying – 'cause usually he had something going on in his own mind that he was involved with. [But] he really was a big fan of the Band . . . It's so ironic, because [when] I was hanging out with Van . . . it would make his week if he could get together with Richard [Manuel], spend a little time at his house. [But] I also would run into people in the Band [separately], and their attitude was that Van was largely a novelty as far as they were concerned. When they were with each other, he was sort of a funny kind of thing to them. They really didn't take him all that seriously. There's a lot of revisionism that goes on – because now Van's music is all over the place, and we know what happened to the Band. Now you have Robbie [saying], 'Well, Van was always our favourite guy.' But I was there. He was like a court-jester figure to them. You could barely understand [him], and he was doing strange things musically [while] obviously trying to ingratiate himself into their fold. Richard, being the sensitive one, was cool with Van. The others would say, 'Van, I'm busy.' . . . My impression was that he was tolerated, that they understood that he was an interesting character, [but only] later on [did] it begin to change a little bit – [as] he became more successful.

As it happens, the Band were at the summit of their success (and influence), with their seminal second album all done and dusted, whereas Morrison was still scrabbling at the foot of his particular mountain. The extent to which he wished to emulate these guys and assume their direction is affirmed by certain instructions he gave to his new key-boardist:

Jeff Labes: When I met him up there, he used to go round, hang out with [the Band] all the time. Matter of fact, he bought an organ at one point and he asked Garth Hudson for a recommendation of what to get. I wanted to get a [Hammond] B3, but Garth suggested the Lowry that he used. Almost nobody in rock & roll used a Lowry! [But] Van had him come round and give me a few lessons on it. He'd [just] sit there and play his old white gospel songs.

Whilst Morrison tried to talk up his relationship with the boys from Big Pink, his wife sometimes felt the need to curb his enthusiasm. On one occasion, when Morrison informed an interviewer for *Jazz & Pop* magazine that he 'and Richard Manuel were thinking of making an album of Ray Charles songs', a surprisingly forthright Janet jumped in straight away: 'Oh no you're not – I heard you two talking about it, and you were very big on it, but he was just kind of scared.' Morrison immediately began to back-pedal, muttering about how 'maybe, if we could just get the studio to come here . . . we could sit around here, and work it out'. It was one of a number of pipe dreams Manuel would encourage in the inebriated state in which he greeted all visitors – not that Morrison wouldn't sometimes arrive at the Manuel residence similarly lubricated. Like Manuel, he used alcohol not so much to loosen inhibitions as to dull those all too raw senses.

Janet Planet: He was absolutely drinking back then. Alcohol is definitely his drug of choice. He doesn't need anything to expand his mind any further . . . He needs the downer – the closer-offer. [JS]

If the booze usually made him mellow, sometimes it allowed a man with a lot of inner anger to reveal himself. Lewis Merenstein remembers the twenty-three-year-old Morrison as 'very quiet, other than when [drinking]. That was the destroyer of all things.' Though Morrison's drinking had yet to become a serious problem, Janet was rightly con-cerned, even though (or perhaps because) most of his drinking took place away from the homestead.

Jon Gershen: The drinking thing was a fixture of his existence at that time. We liked to drink too, and when you're living in Woodstock, between gigs

there isn't a whole lot [else] to do. [And] in between sets you're drinking. But
he went notches above that . . . He would come over with a quart or a fifth of
Johnnie Walker Red [whisky], he'd plump himself down on the floor. He'd
have a bunch of records under his arm. Before the afternoon was done, [the
whisky] was gone. That was largely [him], and it had no effect on him that I
could tell. [But sometimes] it would be like, 'C'mon, let's go, we got to meet
so-and-so', and I'd get up to go and I couldn't walk. I just chalked it up to the
clichéd Irish ability to hold drink . . . Janet was trying to rein him in. I think
she knew that what was going on was very dangerous . . . [but] a few times a
week we would go out for the night and do some serious drinking. A couple
of times I tried to keep up with Van's whisky intake, only to end up having
him literally carry me out of the bar! Driving back to our house on those back
country roads, it's a wonder none of us ended up wrapped around a tree!

The bitterness that sometimes came out when he drank could also
surface when he went into composing mode. Cut off as he was from the
world of business deals, Morrison was still carrying invisible scars from
his recent travails. The after-effects would sometimes creep into songs
of supposed serenity. In the twilight world of 'These Dreams of You' he
couldn't help dishing it out: 'You never really heard my call/when I
cried out that way'; while the seemingly upbeat 'Glad Tidings' spoke of
businessmen who 'shake hands and talk in numbers'. As Brian Hinton
observes, 'the opening and closing line [of the song] – "and they'll lay
you down low and easy" – could be either about murder or an act of
love'. 'Street Choir', the title track of Morrison's third Warners album,
would direct equally pointed questions at another unspecified target:
'Why did you let me down? And now that things seem better off, why
do you come around?' Such songs were spawned by an increasing
awareness of just how badly ripped off he had been. His suspicions were
stoked by a meeting he had with the Montgomeries' New York attorney.

Jon Gershen: He had an incredible mistrust of the business – and for good
reason [as] we found out later . . . We took him into the city to talk to our
lawyer, who was negotiating our deals . . . He said, 'Could you take me in one
day, I've got these problems. They're screwing me.' So our lawyer said, 'What's
the problem?' and he said, 'Well, I've written these songs and they're major hit
records, and I've never seen a penny. And I have no money. Is there anything
you can do?' . . . [Our lawyer was] listening to what he had to say, and he said,
'Well, let me make a few phone calls while you're here,' so within five minutes

he said, 'You know, your stuff is totally screwed up. All your publishing is really a mess.' . . . I can't recall the figure but it was a large [sum] of money that he felt was tied up in badly-distributed royalties. I know he took his card, but I don't know what happened.

Just as it finally dawned on Morrison how much his lackadaisical attitude to the business end of things had cost him, he began to harbour a not necessarily justified sense of grievance against his current management team, illustrating a remarkable capacity for seeing himself as the wronged party in any dispute. By the summer Merenstein began to sense a fierce antipathy whenever he sat down at the studio console.

Lewis Merenstein: It was a struggle because he was pulling away . . . I started with him on [*Moondance*], helped with the selection of material. I was up at the Warners studio with him working on some of the stuff. But even in the rehearsing of it when I went to Woodstock, we weren't as close. I think that's when Mary Martin started sneaking around the scene up there . . . He had a [big] confrontation with Schwaid. [By] that particular time, [Mary] Martin was involved, and that's when he started pulling back . . . At A&R I remember Van [being] enraged at the bass player. It was a bad scene . . . That's when I started to play less of a role. I remember tempo was always a struggle with Van. Van is not a tempo person. When he's singing sometimes, the rhythm goes off . . . [but] by that period, Van certainly had much more sense of himself. He had more confidence.

Symptomatic of a new determination to assert himself were the versions of 'Domino' cut back in March, neither of which he would countenance for release. As Kielbania remembers it, 'He didn't want to release ["Domino"] because he didn't want them to make money off of him. He was playing hardball. He didn't like people taking advantage of him. He felt everybody was screwing him.' Morrison's other sideman at the time was not impressed by his man-management.

Graham Blackburn: [Though] I totally respected what Van was doing as an artist . . . sometimes it seemed he was exhibiting pretty poor business skills, pushing people to the limit . . . His general attitude to everyone was somewhat curmudgeonly, so one took with a grain of salt whatever he might have [said when he] actually complained about people.

Ironically, it was Morrison's desire for a more commercial sound that now clashed with Merenstein's vision. His producer's reluctance to sacrifice entirely the interesting musical avenues *Astral Weeks* had opened up duly became a real source of contention; and after the 'Moondance' session, at which Morrison and Merenstein were again at loggerheads, the latter found himself out of the picture.

Jeff Labes: Lew kinda got pushed off the album as *Moondance* went forward. It was a slow and steady decline. Van would talk about being pushed around by those guys, and [about how] they had no idea what he wanted to do . . . At one point there was a big break . . . He started booking studios on his own.

The famous album take of 'Moondance' would prove to be Merenstein's last contribution as Van Morrison's producer. Shortly afterwards he was caught in the crossfire of what was essentially a dispute about percentages and publishing, which would ultimately result in Schwaid–Merenstein taking the easy way out, and Warners assuming complete control of the artist's contractual obligations.

Lewis Merenstein: [Mary Martin] threatened [that] the album [would] not continue. She was going to pull Van from continuing the album, and we had a commitment to Warner Brothers – they *were* the ones who directed us to Van. So I honoured our responsibility to Warner Brothers and relinquished a title, and relinquished a lot of my involvement with *Moondance*. She was taking over management, and subsequently there was [going to be] a lawsuit, but [then] Warners interceded. They wanted to buy us out of all our publishing and also out of the production, so that anything that went [on] afterwards [would] not [be] ours. Mary wanted to take him off on his own – which eventually happened . . . Van wanted out of his deal . . . We probably did have a choice, and made the wrong choice. We probably could have said no, and let it all slide out . . . [but] we had a big investment with Van.

Mary Martin, who had begun to take an active interest in Morrison's affairs, came from the Albert Grossman school of intimidation-in-negotiation – she had in fact cut her business teeth acting as Grossman's secretary in the days when Dylan ruled the roost. If she had learned from Albert everything she'd ever need to know about brinkmanship, she now overplayed the hand she'd been dealt. Merenstein and Schwaid could have called her (and Van's) bluff. The contract they had with him was 100 per cent waterproof, and the only person likely to suffer from calling a halt to proceedings was Morrison, who was again teetering on the verge of great things, ready to jump – or fall off the face of the earth for good.

However, Morrison had for once picked a winner in Ms Martin, and Schwaid–Merenstein allowed themselves to be bought off for another undisclosed sum. The title that Merenstein relinquished, and warranted, was co-producer of *Moondance*. The ever-gracious Morrison would later depict him as 'a kind of executive producer, who [was] an ex-engineer'; and Merenstein would be listed as 'executive producer' on *Moondance*, which would still be called an Inherit Production (as would *His Band and the Street Choir*, though Schwaid–Merenstein's involvement long ago reached ground zero). Given all her various Woodstock connections, courtesy of Grossman, it should come as no surprise that Martin lighted on Morrison as a target for her management skills. However, she was not the first person to have offered to straighten out his affairs.

Jon Gershen: He had some manager who had managed Richie Havens . . . he was a real sleazy guy. But [Van] didn't seem to have good radar about things like that. If somebody said, 'I can do this,' it was like, 'Really? OK.' So that guy disappeared, and was replaced by some other guy who was also totally incompetent . . . [He was] disoriented about how to get from point A to point B, how to make things happen. He had some ideas about what it was he was trying to accomplish, but he didn't have a clue as to how to make it happen.

Martin, on the other hand, assuredly did. She immediately set about renegotiating the Warners Music contract for Morrison's songs, helping to set up a new publishing arm, Caledonia Soul Music (later Vanjan Music), to administer those songs not already copyrighted under the old deal (she also put an end to any more demo sessions at Warners).

Two-thirds of *Moondance* having been demoed back in spring, the remaining songs were worked up in Woodstock that August; thus the album was again all but conceptualized before Morrison began any serious studio work. As Merenstein faded from the frame, the sessions switched from Mastertone to A&R. Fortunately, Morrison had chanced on someone, in Jeff Labes, who was able to formalize his ideas, enabling other musicians to follow where he led.

Jeff Labes: [Each song] was always . . . a finished product. And he'd know just exactly how it was going to go. Arranging with him was just a question of taking his descriptions, and writing the notes out for the players . . . Often he will come back to something that he tried, but like a lot of creative people he wants to try it different ways to see how it really settles right . . . He's got very sharp ears, and he hears it *his* way, [so] he tries to surround himself with guys that can deliver what he hears.

As Morrison grew increasingly sure of the strength of his ideas, he developed the confidence to go against the musical grain. Some years later, when it was John Altman's task to arrange Morrison's repertoire for a late-seventies return to the live arena, he found himself listening intently to the album version of 'Into the Mystic'.

John Altman: I took the arrangement down off the record. There's a particular point where there's a horrendous clash musically, where the horns are playing a B natural and it's a G minor chord, and I thought Jack Schroer is making a mistake so I corrected it in the part. We were rehearsing and [Van] stopped the band and turned to Peter Bardens and said, 'No, no, no, what you're playing there is wrong. Play it on your own.' We're throwing it around, and I suddenly [said to myself], 'Hang on a minute. This is the spot where there was that clash.' So I said, 'I think I know what the problem is, Van,' turned to Pat, the tenor player, and said, 'Play a constant B natural,' and we ran it again and he said, 'That's fine.'

As with the *Astral Weeks* sessions, Morrison also showed that he was not afraid to let other musicians give rein to their instincts. The important thing was to capture the spirit of live music on that unforgiving magnetic tape. Drummer Gary Malabar, who would end up shaping the album's mix, thinks it was this fearless quality that made *Moondance* such a genuinely musical experience.

Gary Malabar: Van didn't do well with the electronic media – he [couldn't cope] with a poorly-mixed headphone set. That headphone set pretty much had to sound like a record when he put those headphones on. [But] everybody was rebounding and reacting off each other, which is a wonderful way to make a record. Van never seemed to be frightened of the outcome. In other words, we went in there with no premeditation – 'We want it to sound like this jazz record or that rock record' – there was none of that. Van never seemed to be afraid of anyone's interpretation or musical prowess at the time. Whenever somebody went with it, I never saw him rearing back and going, 'Oh no, don't do that.' . . . Once Van started hearing the first playbacks, I remember his guard dropping, [and] it [was] a free-for-all from that point on, knowing something was [always] being achieved . . . After we did the takes, we all agreed on the [best] take. And then whatever enhanced overdubs went on . . . Like, we put the horns through the Leslie speaker, we did some tambourine, we did some background vocals. But basically that lead vocal and that basic [track] was the take . . . [When] I asked [Van] to do some overdubs, he never seemed to be worried about the outcome, 'OK, try it.' All I remember was forward motion.

Morrison's decision to produce *Moondance* himself meant that he cut himself off from the one outside input a sixties rock artist could usually rely upon (it needs to be borne in mind just how unusual it was for a rock artist to produce his own work in 1969). Despite such dangers, from here on Morrison would become the self-styled (co-)producer of all subsequent albums. As he said in 1987, 'I'm a producer. Even if I hire another producer, I'm still the producer.' In the case of *Moondance*, although he admitted that 'some people [i.e. Merenstein] came up here to Woodstock, and we pushed around ideas . . . no one knew what I was looking for except me.'

What he lacked was the temperament of a good producer. Impatient at the best of times with the recording process, he would become frustrated when a session wasn't going the way he hoped it would. With no one else calling the shots and the musicians fixated on their own parts, it became his responsibility to change things around, to refocus the sound until it righted itself.

Graham Blackburn: It seemed as though every other week we were in the studio recording 'Moondance'. Van likes to be spontaneous in the studio, but it's a spontaneity that he has to wait a long time to achieve . . . He would try and get himself in the mood and get a groove going, but then at the end of it he'd say, 'It's not right, it's not right.' No one knew what was going on. We'd all be pulling our hair out and then we'd have to do it all over again. [ST]

The problem with the title track perhaps stemmed from the fact that, as Morrison later put it, 'It started out as a saxophone solo, really. I used to play this sax number over and over, any time I picked up my horn. I didn't put words to it until later.' As a result, he may have been trying to stretch the song out, *à la Astral Weeks*. Drummer Gary Malabar remembers how 'the horn guys [certainly] wanted "Moondance" to be more out there – more abstract jazz. I think at that point we were trying to make the song just be the song, and still let them play on it. We really didn't want it to go into [that] John Coltrane area.'

In the end, it was the one song Morrison had to admit Merenstein got right. As Jeff Labes says, 'We must have recorded that [song] like a dozen times, each time trying some different nuance. [But] he always went back to the original. I think what he actually found out about the song was that it's so strong you almost can't mess with it.' He also found that, when it came to jazz, Merenstein's instincts remained the truer, even if he had become one more influence to be denied.

Van Morrison: If you're talking about influences, sure, [they're] there . . . But I've got to the point where I don't need all those people now . . . I've matured into my own thing. I'm very grateful that they were there, but I don't need them any more. [1970]

On a purely musical level, there is a certain truth in this statement. With *Astral Weeks*, Morrison had begun to transcend his roots until, with the ten songs on *Moondance*, he confidently blended all the styles he had previously self-consciously explored. From the torch-ballad 'Crazy Love' to the gospel-infused 'Brand New Day', from the languorous title track to the R&B-inflected 'These Dreams of You', from the breathless 'Come Running' to that epic opener, 'And It Stoned Me', it was a *tour de force* of almost every style rock music could currently contain. As Gary Malabar rightly recognizes, 'How do you define *Moondance*? In the truest sense of the words, those ten songs can't justifiably [be] put into rock, jazz, R&B, soul, blues. For now, we'll put it into the rock category.' After making a commercially catastrophic 'anti-rock' statement, Morrison was deliberately 'trying to find a way to connect what I was doing with my contemporaries'. *Moondance* was an unashamedly commercial grab at the prize, as Morrison readily admits.

Van Morrison: [*Astral Weeks*] was a success musically, and at the same time I was starving. Practically not eating. So for the next album I realized I was going to have to do something [that sounded] like rock or [continue to] starve . . . So I tried to forget about the artistic thing because it didn't make sense on a practical level. One has to live. [1986]

Having discovered that making 'anti-rock' albums was a sure-fire way of struggling, Morrison still wondered where his Warners advances had gone. This time there was no great sleight of hand. He had been living on them for the past year. *Moondance* was his way of admitting to himself that he had pushed the envelope of innovation a tad far. Designed to be more accessible, it excluded some of the more adventurous songs Morrison and his band were now recording. One of the cast-offs, 'Listen to the Lion', would form the centrepiece of *Saint Dominic's Preview* two years on. However, this ten-minute excursion into the sound of words would have sat uneasily in the midst of the mellifluous *Moondance*.

Once again, though, after all the bitterness resulting from wresting control away from Merenstein, Morrison entrusted the sound of the album to a third party, willingly relinquishing control of the mixing process. It was as if a film director had shot his own script and then handed over the editing to someone else. This would become a common thread in his career: here was someone who insisted on control at every turn in the recording process, only to surrender it at the final stage.

Perhaps in his own mind's eye, he fulfilled any personal need by recording the material as best he could. What happened to his songs afterwards he was content to leave to happenstance. A couple of years later, opining about the difference between recording and mixing, he informed a journalist that 'the truest way you can come to any kind of real recording is doing it live . . . and get[ting] it within the first two or three takes. That's where it's really true to what you're doing. When you do a thing and mix it, then it becomes something else – a production.' That is certainly what they had done with the *Moondance* songs – the title track notwithstanding – before the *auteur* removed himself from the process.

Van Morrison: What I like is playing the songs and the spontaneity of recording [them]. Mixing . . . I can't stand playing with knobs, levels. It's out of my domain. I supervise it but don't have to be there twenty-four hours a day. [1984]

In the case of *Moondance*, he barely supervised. According to engineer Elliot Scheiner – who would end up sharing the task with drummer Gary Malabar – when it came time to mix the album, Morrison announced he was returning to Woodstock for Christmas. He simply asked Scheiner to take care of the job, and to send him a copy when it was done. Malabar was the one musician who retained any input, simply because he wasn't thrilled about spending Christmas in a bitterly cold, snowbound hamlet in upstate New York. As such he asked Scheiner if he could stay and 'be in the mix sessions'. And so Scheiner and Malabar mixed *Moondance* whilst Morrison, ensconced in the snow-cased Catskills, unwrapped his Christmas presents.

The album, as it now came together, defined a whole new concept: FM-friendly. The American airwaves had been undergoing something of a revolution in the previous three years, and *Moondance* was to prove one of its greatest beneficiaries. Though there was a single this time around, the lower-rung chart success of the 'Come Running' 45 hardly accounts for the album's immediate acceptance by a whole new spectrum of young adult listeners. As Lester Bangs recognized, in his *Rolling Stone* review, 'Unlike Van's masterful *Astral Weeks*, this one will be immensely popular; Van's picture already fills the windows of record stores and his new music is getting more airplay on FM stations than anything in recent memory.'

Most people would date the beginning of the 'FM revolution' to the day in April 1967 when Tom Donahue took over the graveyard shift on a local Bay area radio station, KMPX. In fact, Donahue was not its originator, though he would be the ultimate beneficiary of KMPX's decision to broadcast rock music to album-oriented listeners. Greil Marcus recalls the 'absolute shock, to find this radio station, KMPX, that had a couple of hours of free-form [rock] radio in the midst of a foreign-language station. This guy named Larry Miller, who was from Detroit, would be playing all this stuff that you never, ever heard on commercial radio. Tom Donahue . . . [then] took over on KMPX several months later, and it became an all-music station.'

Morrison had always been something of a favourite in the Bay area, since back in the days of Them, but the presence of KMPX meant that, in Marcus's words, 'by the fall of 1967 there was a media outlet in place so that something like "TB Sheets" could get saturation airplay in the Bay area . . . [Van] was a presence, he was someone to reckon with [in the Bay area] from the time that *Blowin' Your Mind!* came out, in a way that he wasn't elsewhere . . . When *Astral Weeks* came out, the dam broke. Everything on that record was being played on the radio all the time. It was like they put it on and never took it off. By now it was KSAN. There had been a strike at KMPX, and everyone had left and started another free-form FM station.' By the time Morrison made his first San Francisco solo appearance, in the winter of 1969, the FM revolution was taking over stations across the country. Graham Blackburn recalls them doing 'a bunch of radio interviews after [the gigs], and they'd always be earnest young people [from] FM stations'.

How aware Morrison was of the extent to which he was becoming a leading FM artist by aural osmosis is undocumented, but he subsequently said he had felt that he 'had to make something that was going to get played on the radio. I was getting screwed by these people. I was getting no record royalties, no publishing royalties, no nothing . . . The only way they couldn't screw me was airplay, because that came direct from BMI.' ★ *Moondance* was just such an album, with at least half of its contents – 'And It Stoned Me', the title track, 'Caravan', 'Come Running' and 'Into the Mystic' – adopted as the FM equivalent of standards.

Shut away in Woodstock, without access to any of the major FM stations, Morrison was presumably unaware of the album's impact, no matter how commercial his intent may have been. The moment of realization seems to have dawned one fine day in April 1970, when Morrison found himself back in San Francisco, for a concert at the Fillmore West which was also scheduled to be broadcast live by KSAN. As he was being driven around town, he found himself half listening to the radio.

Greil Marcus: When he came in the spring of 1970, I did an interview with him, and he was with Janet. I went over to San Francisco and picked him up in my car, and I just had the idea that we would drive around and talk. I had interviewed him before, at the Avalon Ballroom in [January] 1969, and I had done a quite long piece for *Rolling Stone* on *Astral Weeks*. So we're driving around in the car, and I drove him over Marin County, back to Berkeley . . . and ultimately I drove him back to San Francisco. [This took] most of the day, and most of the time we had the radio on. We would be talking, [but] everywhere we went we'd be hearing Van Morrison. So Janet is saying, 'My God, Van. You're really big here.' And you could just see him get the idea that he didn't have to tell anybody who he was in the Bay area. That was really something different for him.

That very day, Morrison also got to meet Ralph Gleason, the *San Francisco Chronicle*'s long-standing jazz critic and co-founder of *Rolling*

★ Broadcast Music Incorporated (BMI) is a performing rights society formed in 1939 as a rival to ASCAP (American Society of Composers, Authors & Publishers).

Stone. Marcus remembers that all 'they talked about [was] jazz. They were talking about obscure recordings and who played on this. They were talking like obsessive, cult-like jazz fans. Van wanted to meet Ralph because he'd been reading Ralph for years. He admired him. And he knew he was a friend of musicians. I think Ralph was a legendary figure to Van.' The whole experience suffused Morrison with a warm feeling about the Bay area. Janet presumably still thought of this as 'home'. If Morrison was already half sold on the idea of moving west, the rapturous reception he got at the Fillmore gave him one more reason to think he might find real recognition here. However, it was soon time to return to Woodstock. Janet was expecting their first child. After all their trials and tribulations, it really must have seemed like (yes, seemed like) a brand new day.

14

1970–71: The Sweet-Tempered Innocent and the Prickly Bear

I remember . . . Mary Martin, Van's miracle worker of a manager at the time . . . once saying to me at about the time of the recording of [*Street Choir*], 'Janet, don't let him get too happy – the music will start to suffer.' I thought at the time that it was a most shocking sentiment, and naturally paid no attention to her point. My one and only obsessive activity during my time with Van was this fool's errand: to MAKE him happy!

—*Janet Planet*

The success of *Moondance* was bound to change everything. For the first time, Morrison stood to benefit from a hit record – even though this was the third time he had achieved a degree of commercial success. As John Platania observes, Mary Martin was beginning to 'straighten his affairs out and really got him secured in the Warner Brothers stable. She was really important in financial terms and in a guiding managerial role at that part of his career. She fixed up his publishing and that's when the money really came in.' Even Martin, though, still failed to gauge Morrison's moods. She began to push Morrison into making another album, both to consolidate the success of *Moondance* and to bring in the publishing revenue.

Jon Gershen: As he began to plan the follow-up to *Moondance*, he [officially] hired Mary Martin . . . Mary knew the music business backwards and forwards, and within a few short months had created a disciplined strategy for Van to follow. She was a real 'taskmaster' and forced him to get serious about getting the new record done, and then going on the road to promote it. Mary wanted this new album [*Street Choir*] released quickly . . . Mary [also] had a plan to put a world tour together, that would give him the 'visibility' she felt he needed to get to the next level.

There seemed to be no shortage of songs Morrison could record. He had half a dozen songs left over from his previous two albums, as well as a number of usable outlines demoed for Warners under the old Schwaid–Merenstein deal. *Moondance* had yielded at least four out-takes: the ambitious 'Listen to the Lion', the contagious 'I Shall Sing', a second stab at 'I've Been Working', and a song that reversed 'Glad Tidings' into a truly cynical take on New York City, 'Nobody Really Knows'.★ Other releaseable songs sketched out in the hiatus between the two Warners albums included 'Wild Night'; a lounge-jazz 'When the Evening Sun Goes Down'; a pair of love-songs to Janet, 'Bit by Bit' and 'If I Ever Needed Someone'; the unfinished 'Sit Down Funny Face'; and a sister song to 'And It Stoned Me', 'Hey, Where Are You?' There was also 'Domino', a song that had already eaten up more tape than all of the above combined.

The decision to record only a smattering of these for the successor to *Moondance* smacked of deliberate policy on Morrison's and/or Martin's part. Perhaps Schwaid–Merenstein had not fully relinquished their share of the publishing on these songs (if so, it meant the same old percentages). A couple of years later, Morrison alluded to instances where he had allowed business decisions to interfere with his music-making instincts, having spent 'a lot of time lately just getting the business end of things straightened out. For a while there I was doing more of that than anything else, and my music suffered.' *Street Choir* seems to fit the bill.

The album that Morrison began to record that spring, with a certain haste, was another radio-friendly collection. Perhaps the airplay already greeting *Moondance* was beginning to go to Morrison's head, for he entirely forgot about 'the artistic thing'. The radical shifts in sound made between each of his three solo albums to date was forsaken. Instead

---

★ According to the Warners files, Morrison recorded a song called 'Nobody Knows When You're . . .' for *Moondance*. This could conceivably be the old blues song 'Nobody Knows You When You're Down and Out', but is more likely to be the Morrison original 'Nobody Really Knows', especially as the song appears on the Warners Publishing demos among *Moondance* material.

Morrison set about making the first of four albums that would rework the musical blend achieved on *Moondance* in permutations a-plenty, but without any intent to advance the template (at least not until 1972's *Saint Dominic's Preview*). At the same time as *His Band and the Street Choir*, together with its three hit singles, consolidated the commercial success of *Moondance*, the album cut the ground away from those critics who had previously championed Morrison as an important new rock artist.

Lewis Merenstein: I don't know what words Mary was putting into his ear about you are the new messiah of music, [but] I came from a background of jazz musicians – we [only] talked about making great music.

On some level, Morrison couldn't resist participating in the game. Everything from the *Moondance* album cover to the press interviews to advertising copy conspired to build up this chronically shy singer into a 'rock star'. The process began with the cover of *Moondance*, shot by Elliott Landy, the man behind the lens on recent Band and Dylan album covers. And yet Landy remembers Morrison as a most reluctant participant in the image-building process: 'The pictures [on the cover] look very personal and intimate – he did everything I asked for. He just didn't radiate all this intimacy actually. He realizes his publishers want to sell a commercial product, not portray him as a person, [and] that was what was depressing him. But he had accepted the rules of the game, so he played along as well as he could.' Of course, he was still some way off achieving the necessary financial security, as he admitted that spring to a *Jazz & Pop* reporter:

Van Morrison: I'm not rich; I probably could be, but I don't really do things that I'm expected to do . . . If I really wanted to make money, it's not hard. You just have to do it – you got to physically go out and do it, be in a certain place at a certain time and play, [and] put on an act. [1970]

The critical acclaim now greeting *Moondance*, and the revisionism that simultaneously accrued to *Astral Weeks*, also brought a whole new level of stress. For the first time since the days of Them, Morrison was pushed to grant interviews and glad-hand the press – even if the folks at Warners had no illusions about the difficulties they were going to have projecting this artist. As Joe Smith told *Rolling Stone* the following year, 'Van doesn't throw off star quality, he's a silent, very private guy . . . I think [if] he has an influence . . . he'll go in the back door. He himself will not be a star . . . [He] detests playing gigs. He [just] wants to sit home and make music.' Not only could the man's shyness curdle into surliness, but he remained an often inarticulate subject. Asked by the man from *Jazz & Pop* for any message he might have for the nine-to-five fraternity, his reply was a cross between hippie patois and gibberish:

Van Morrison: How you gonna tell somebody who's gotta get up in the morning at 8.30 and go out to work, how you gonna tell that person that if he cools it, he can put his mind at rest – how you gonna tell people that? [1970]

The man also displayed a profound distrust of those who sought to interpret his lyrics, which was unfortunate as the words on *Astral Weeks* and in certain key songs on *Moondance* ('And It Stoned Me', 'These Dreams of You', 'Into the Mystic') now prompted a generation inspired to analyse the lyrics of Dylan and his 'children' to speculate upon their import. At the *Moondance* sessions themselves, Morrison had already recorded two songs that suggest an oppression of the spirit, the upbeat 'Glad Tidings' and the decidedly downbeat 'Nobody Really Knows'. Both apply the needle to these interpreters. In the former he asks them 'not to read between the lines'; in the latter he ridicules someone who asks the singer to sing a song one more time because they believe that they know what it means, having been with him the previous night when he wrote it in his dreams. On *Street Choir* he would dramatically compress the number of levels on which the lyrics could operate, denying his audience any real songs open to such literary analysis.

If Morrison hated discussing his songs, he seemed no more anxious to take his new music to the converts who came in the wake of FM saturation play. In fact, he *was* anxious to take the studio band out on the road. He was just unwilling to play the gigs he was being told he should if he wanted to 'further his career'. His contempt for the 'circuit' was vividly expressed to one journalist that summer:

Van Morrison: The way it is now, if you don't do this gig and that gig, you don't work . . . Maybe you're offered this fantastic gig, and it's out in the middle of nowhere and you gotta travel on planes and shit like that, and by the time you get there you're wasted. And [then] you wait around for maybe about eight hours, and by the time you get on stage the audience is wasted. They've seen everything there is to see already, heard everything there is to hear, and they're ready to fall asleep . . . Festivals is a whole other scene. [1970]

After a whole decade of playing to people not usually there to see *him* perform, Morrison was interested in playing only to his kind of audience, in places intimate enough for some visceral connection, and preferably close enough to home for him to be able to play the gig, load up the van and head back. Another reason for the sparsity of gigs in this crucial period was a lack of real organization. As Graham Blackburn puts it, 'When we originally went out, it was like, pick up an itinerary, some plane tickets and wander off into the night.' That only changed when Morrison brought in Tom Reynolds, a friend of Graham Blackburn's, who not only put their gigging on a more professional footing but also, as Blackburn says, 'made a real serious effort to function as Van's father-confessor'. Unfortunately, the *Moondance* band itself got to play barely half a dozen gigs before a key component was obliged to quit.

Gary Malabar: After the record was completed, there was a little period of time when we were working around some of the little clubs around Woodstock with that band, and then we started venturing out. I remember we did some shows in Long Island. We did a show in Boston; we did Springfield, Massachu- setts – we all piled into two cars and we had a van [with] the equipment. Actually we opened up for the Band [one time]. And then [my band] was signed to Columbia Records.

Bob Mason was temporarily drafted back in. As Jeff Labes remembers it, 'We start[ed] to mess with these songs a little bit. Sometimes [Van] would get a little restless with a song, and he'd start to pump his hand behind his back to the rhythm section.' Perhaps he was unconsciously missing the steady hand of Malabar.

Even with the kind of low-key touring Morrison had in mind, His Band still needed a walking, talking drum machine. Again, he found what he was looking for in his own backyard, at the Café Espresso, which served as a focal point for the Woodstock music scene. Dauod Shaw believes he was playing with the guys from the Paul Butterfield Blues Band when 'Van came and sat in. After the set he wanted to know if I was interested in rehearsing with him. Jeff Labes was [still] playing with him at the time. I remember going up there on afternoons and just jamming and playing. I never got asked to join the band. It was like,

"What are you doing this weekend? You wanna go to Canada, do a gig?" Then we started working on material for the *Street Choir* album.'

Woodstock remained the focal point of operations. Trips into the city were usually for the purpose of recording, though not necessarily with an album in mind. One song cut by the *Moondance* band before work began on *Street Choir* was 'Really Don't Know' (on *Philosopher's Stone*). It is another song about being disconnected from reality as Morrison admits to 'feel[ing] like I don't belong'. Its downbeat nature was probably what kept it from consideration for *Street Choir*, though Morrison says he probably just forgot about it.

Jeff Labes: We lived in Woodstock. So any time we did a session, we'd drive down a hundred miles and then we'd drive back . . . Van was in a position of being the boss so . . . you don't want to upset him, you don't want to get him riled up in any way. On the other hand if you could exchange jokes, he's one of the funniest guys you could be with. And I think everybody was aware in those days, he could go either way. He could kinda shut down or he could be very personable . . . Van is the kind of personality that controls the mood, [which means] if you're in the car with them, whatever they want to do, that's what you do.

Morrison still preferred to prep his material in Woodstock. Unfortunately, it had no studio suitable for demoing material, just the state-of-the-art set-up at Albert Grossman's Bearsville Studio. Even so, he was determined to try out the songs he had in mind at some kind of demo studio, preferably a low-budget one, before incurring real studio costs. He turned to the newest recruit in His Band, then in the process of constructing a makeshift studio upstate, and asked him to create the necessary environment.

Dauod Shaw: Initially . . . Van wanted to try some live recordings. I had always been interested in recording, and at that time I was starting to put together a small studio in Woodstock. So I grabbed a Revox two-track, I had a couple of vintage Neumann tube mikes, and I started scouting around for some place to record. I found an old church and we would just load in. I'd set up a pair of mikes and we would just run down some tunes with the tapes running. They became like a working thing for the album. Then we headed into A&R Studios in New York.

If the musicians were used to Morrison's pulling songs out of thin air, few of them were privy to his composing process. An exception was Jeff Labes, perhaps because it devolved to him to shape the final arrangements. Even he was surprised at the way the songs often came in blocks, as if brought on by a tidal wave of psychic energy:

Jeff Labes: He was writing them quickly. He'd turn on a cassette machine and start with a guitar in his hand, and it would kinda come to him. And then he'd sit back, listen to the cassette and write down the words. Very few people can write songs that way. With Van, it's kinda channelled through him . . . In recent years he['s] talked a lot about it. It just comes through him. He has this creative energy that rushes through him at various times. And it can last for two or three weeks, and he's a madman for that period. He can't stop, he's running. And then he's exhausted for a couple of weeks after that. He would get paranoid and feel funny . . . That's why he's so sensitive that his performances be magical. That at least inspires him, and he feels the muse. If he's doing good shows, then [it's] almost as good as writing, [but] when he's writing, it's hard [for him] to do anything else.

The songs they began demoing in this tiny church in Woodstock hardly tapped into the same channels as those on *Moondance*. The best of the bunch, save for the album's title track, could all be found on the Warners demo tapes pre-dating *Moondance* – 'Domino', 'I've Been Working', 'If I Ever Needed Someone' and 'Funny Face' (which would evolve into 'Virgo Clowns'). Aside from a couple of spatial instrumental jams, all Morrison seemed to have in his notebook was lightweight fillers like 'Crazy Face' and 'Give Me a Kiss'. Perhaps his inner focus had been dimmed by the bright lights. The show at the Fillmore that April may have set Morrison thinking about California, but it took a key component in His Band further afield.

Jeff Labes: I left the band. I actually left the country [later that year and] moved to Israel. At that point we had reached the stage of Lear jets and playing the Fillmore, and it just seemed like something I didn't want to be around – [there was] a lot of duplicity, false values, star worship. And what I learned from Van was that it didn't make him very happy. As a matter of fact, it tended to make him [far] less polite . . . When he was out on the road, he would get very short. He could be really curt with [the crew]. He definitely had conflicts with the cult of personality, and he wanted his privacy. That's one of the biggest issues for him.

Seeking to preserve his own momentum, Morrison now felt compelled to record whatever he had to hand, something he touched on years later, talking to Desmond Hogan: 'At certain times I had to do certain things, and that's really the way it was. I didn't have a choice . . . It wasn't a matter of sitting up in an ivory tower at the time and saying, "I wonder whether I want to do A or B or C" . . . There was a lot of compromise [involved] . . . but it got me to a point where I did have a choice.' He also gave Ritchie Yorke the impression that *Street Choir* was the result of some arm-twisting, describing it as 'the sort of thing where someone was on my back to get something cranked out, even though *they* knew it was wrong'.

Before the New York sessions had really begun to flow he was telling the *Jazz & Pop* man, 'I don't think you should throw together an album, go in there and say, "This is gonna be an album we're gonna have to make some money with, and get something commercial and throw it together and put it out" . . . [because] it is something that you're gonna have to listen to in ten years.' And yet that is precisely what he proceeded to do. Except for the title track and Top Ten single, the album's songs would receive very few public airings after their initial promotional half-life.

By the time the band transferred to A&R, Morrison seemed in a real hurry to get in and get out. As usual, he was hoping to cut the whole thing live, which initially helped push things along. Engineer Elliot Scheiner, back at the console after fulfilling post-production duties on *Moondance*, again found himself blown away by the vocals this man could come up with live – such that he invariably 'retained his original live vocals . . . He'd just get out there and sing, and he was *always* in tune.' However, at some point during the first set of sessions, Scheiner and Morrison had an exchange of words and Scheiner found himself out in the cold, with a meaningless 'Production Co-ordinator' credit to his name. Unconcerned by the marked difference between a modern sixteen-track studio like A&R and a derelict church, Morrison turned to drummer Dauod Shaw for technical input (for which Shaw would receive Assistant Producer billing).

Dauod Shaw: [I guess] I was the musical director, which seemed to be a strange role for me. But it was a role that Van kinda put on me. Elliot thought he was going to be the co-producer, but then again I never saw him calling takes or asking people to change parts . . . I didn't consider myself co-producer. Van would ask me questions and I would give him answers, but it was never a defined role.

The other person whose input Morrison valued was his wife, Janet. *Street Choir* provided her with a first hands-on role in the man's recorded output, as a backing vocalist. Beginning to acquire musical ambitions of her own, Janet doubtless hoped that involvement in the process might also provide a way to divine her husband's inner needs. After all, as she duly observed, 'He doesn't do anything else. He doesn't have hobbies. He doesn't do anything else but music. It's his entire existence, his entire life. That's all he does. That's all he knows about. And he knows a lot about it . . . He couldn't boil water, he couldn't drive the car, he couldn't fix the toaster. That's all he did.'

For the moment, at least, Janet continued to define herself on her husband's terms. Jon Gershen phrases it thus: 'I think she really wanted success for him, but she was not an operator in the business. She was his protector.' Her attempt to fulfil 'this fool's errand: to make him happy' had recently yielded its greatest *coup*, a daughter, christened Shana Caledonia Morrison. The hours leading up to the birth had proved fraught enough for the father to call for moral support.

Jon Gershen: One night he calls up and he says, 'You gotta get over here.' 'Well, where are you?' 'I'm at Kingston hospital.' 'Oh my God. What happened?' I figured, [with his driving] he'd been in a car accident. 'No, Janet is in labour and I'm going crazy. I don't know what to do. You better get over here.' So [my brother] Dave and I went over there and we went into this reception area and there he is – alone. It was a *long* labour. And we sat there the entire time, until the doctor came down and said, 'Everything's OK.' 'It is?!' . . . That always stuck in my mind. It speaks volumes to me about how it was for him. There just wasn't anyone [else] around.

If the album Morrison was now recording had an overriding theme, it was of the great personal debt he owed to his muse, especially in those songs he now forced himself to finish to fill out the collection. 'I'll Be Your Lover, Too' finds him offering 'to take good care of you', though he requires *her* to reach out to him first lest he should become 'the one who's always reaching out for you'. The maudlin 'Funny Face', remade into the sprightly 'Virgo Clowns', again required Funny Face to 'light up [her] golden smile' in order to take away *his* misery and gloom. In her role as his interlocutor, Janet almost became the public face to the music, a role she says she was happy to assume.

Janet Planet: I was a sweet-tempered innocent, many beautiful pictures were taken and the people at Warners were always very eager to use them on the covers of albums and such. They also believed that my image, precisely because it was so enigmatic, was the perfect visual to describe what was going on musically. The thing was, everybody knew that I played some part [in] what was going on creatively, but nobody knew exactly how it worked! Van [certainly] wasn't talking, and couldn't be pressed for details.

As part of her new public role, Janet even became his sleeve-note writer. In the blinding glare of hindsight, the notes accompanying *Street Choir* exude the same kind of misguided optimism as its songs. When Janet asserts, 'I have seen Van open those parts of his secret self – his essential core of aloneness I had always feared could never be broken into – and say . . . yes, come in here. Know me,' she betrays a bad case of wishful thinking. Looking back, Janet indicates how close she felt they were at this time to achieving a lasting happiness – chimerical as the illusion proved to be.

Janet Planet: As misguided and ultimately futile as this mission of mine was [to make Van happy], during the time we became the Street Choir and made *Street Choir* I really thought I was winning the battle! I still think that there is much to love about the songs on this album: 'Blue Money', 'Crazy Face', 'Call Me Up in Dreamland', 'Domino' – these are just great songs in any era, but certainly one important thing to remember about this one in particular is that Van was at his most relaxed and contented in his personal life; this was no small accomplishment after the last few years of struggle and travail. We were finally really LIVING in a dreamland – believe it or not – it was that magical a time . . . The photos [for the *Street Choir* sleeve] were taken during a family birthday party of [my son] Peter's. It had been a lovely afternoon, very relaxed, and the band had set up and played in our front yard for the families of Peter's friends and, of course, our own very extended group of band members' families. Shana was a few months old and the apple of her daddy's eye . . . For me, *Street Choir* was a musical manifestation and paean to real happiness, such a fleeting commodity, so hard-won and hung on to about as successfully as a juggler balancing spinning plates on sticks.

Whatever struggle was going on in Morrison's life at this point, it is not always easy to hear it coming through in the music. Stripping 'If I Ever Needed Someone' of the intimacy of previous demos – solo on guitar and then, even more powerfully, at the piano – hardly enhanced it. The *Street Choir* take doesn't speak of duality, just lack of commitment.

And if the choice of 'Domino' as the lead single suggested that he had finally overcome his ambivalent attitude to hit singles, when Janet asked him to play it to a journalist that summer, he said, 'What for? . . . What if somebody says it's terrible?' – still not entirely sure that he wanted to hear the judgement of a third party (Janet informed the scribe, 'He's been liking it during the days and hating it at night'). And yet, when Morrison finally completed the album – after a name change from *Virgo's Fool* to *His Band and the Street Choir*, and a last-minute reworking of the title track and a.n. other 'in order to get them right' – he insisted on exposing it to the person whose musical opinion he valued the most, Richard Manuel. Though Manuel gave 'Domino' the thumbs-up, he delivered – perhaps unconsciously – a most hurtful rebuttal.

Jon Gershen: You'd pick up the phone in the house and it would be Van: 'What are you doing?' 'I dunno. What are you doing?' 'Well, I've got some tapes of *Street Choir*. Why don't we go over to Richard's? I'm *sure* he wants to hear them.' In my mind I'm thinking maybe and maybe not, but in Van's mind it was a projection of what he [wanted]. [So] we did. I picked him up, and Richard was further down towards town. I remember going there . . . and Van had the tapes. It was probably 11.30 in the morning and Richard was already on his second tumbler full of straight vodka – with no effect whatsoever. Van was all excited about the tape: 'Richard, I've got the tape.' 'The tape?? [Oh, the tape.] Well, put it on,' and he put the thing on and Richard walked over to the upright piano and started fiddling on some tune that he was working on – while the tape was [rolling]. I was [inwardly] cringing. You knew that what Van was there to do was share something that he really was proud of, with [someone] that he thought the world of, and to [Richard] it was not really a critical issue. After a while I think he [just] took the tape off.

After 'Domino' became a Top Ten single – his first since 'Brown Eyed Girl' – critic Bob Sarlin speculated about whether it was part of a strategy to 'break back into the singles field and so expand his album audience'. Certainly *His Band and the Street Choir* was incontrovertible evidence that he 'had chosen to abandon the goals of *Astral Weeks* for more commercial intentions'. John Platania, who had replaced Labes as Morrison's arranger, believes that 'he had designs on getting stuff air-play[ed] on radio'.

After the success of 'Domino' and its two less commercial sequels, 'Blue Money' and 'Call Me Up in Dreamland', Morrison previewed his next album with 'Wild Night'. Though they all charted, none replicated the success of 'Domino'. Ultimately Morrison came to dismiss *Street Choir*, all the while abnegating personal responsibility for its failure to achieve critical acceptance (it certainly wasn't a commercial flop, climbing higher than *Moondance* in the *Billboard* charts).

Van Morrison: Somewhere along the line I lost control of that album. Somebody else got control of it, and got the cover and all that shit, while I was out on the west coast. I knew what was happening to it, but it was like I couldn't stop it. I'd given my business thing over to somebody else and although I had final approval on things, they just went ahead and did the wrong thing. [1974]

At the time, though, he seemed very happy with the album, as assistant producer Dauod Shaw affirms: 'He was feeling pretty good at that time, it was really kind of a positive vibe around that whole record. There wasn't really any dissent.' In the light of the fact that he made himself sole producer, that the song selection was entirely his, and that the musicians were a hand-picked crew of Woodstock wonders, it is hard to see where any blame for the tepid nature of the collection can alight, save on *Morrison's* brow.

If Morrison really was 'out on the west coast' when *Street Choir* was put to bed, it was in keeping with his inclination to walk away from an album when it was merely a bunch of unmixed songs. Perhaps Mary Martin was responsible for making *Street Choir* 'an extension of *Moondance*', which was how she described the album to *Rolling Stone* prior to its release. Possibly Morrison was already plotting his escape from the eastern seaboard, at the same time as Martin was planning her departure into A&R. Given that Morrison's relationship with Berns and then Merenstein had lasted barely an album, it is perhaps not surprising that he was already edging away from Martin.

Gary Malabar: The thing I remember the most is the lack of communication with people. There was never any supportive communication. Mary pulled it together for a while, but Van even became disenchanted with Mary. But he had a degree of difficulty sown into him, especially with management.

Just as Martin was becoming one more expendable operative, Morrison announced to those whose livelihood depended on him that he was moving to California. John Platania has laid the blame for the decision squarely at Janet's door, insisting, 'He didn't want to leave but Janet wanted to move out west. He was manipulated into going.' Jon Gershen again refutes the band's party-line:

Jon Gershen: All of a sudden I'm hearing Van is moving to California. I remember having a conversation with him where I said, 'What is this with the California thing?' He says, 'Well, Jon, that's where it's happening.' 'It is?' 'Woodstock is dead now. It's all in California, so that's where I'm going.'

Having at last found an even keel, Morrison seemed to be deliberately destabilizing his situation. He would later claim the lease had run out on their place, and that 'the guy had somebody else he wanted to put into the house at that time. I didn't have another place to go and I was on the west coast . . . so I just looked for a house out there.' Meanwhile Woodstock was apparently 'getting to be such a heavy number. When I first went, people were moving there to get away from the scene. Then Woodstock itself started being the scene . . . and that was the complete opposite of what it was supposed to be.' Neither scenario joins up the dots. He was now in a position to buy an even more beautiful place upstate, whereas California remained an expensive alternative. He was also moving to the one area where he had something verging on celebrity status, hardly an obvious way of escaping 'the scene'. Moving three thousand miles west also scarcely seemed the best way of keeping His Band together. Unless it was some kind of loyalty test?

Dauod Shaw: I had built a studio from the ground up, and then it was like, 'Well, we're moving to San Francisco.' . . . It was all of a sudden. Almost a year went by when I spent half my time in airplanes and living in hotel rooms in Marin County, to make gigs and work at the studio, [before] I sold my interest in the studio and I moved to San Francisco.

By the spring of 1971, the Morrisons had decided to make their home in Fairfax, whence Janet had first come. Returning his wife to a place where she knew people and had roots may have been presented as a selfless gesture, but Morrison was too restless to stay put for another year, and certainly not for another Woodstock winter. As he put it in 'Starting a New Life', 'Girl, we been standing in one place for too long a time/ When I hear that robin song, I know it won't be long . . . we're starting a new life'. Though the place they found retained a backwoods vibe, things would never quite be the same again.

Jeff Labes: They had this beautiful house up in Fairfax. It was a great environment. It was like what Woodstock had been. It was another change. We talked about that. Fairfax is also a timeless place. Very much like Woodstock. Little town, houses up in the hills . . . but [their relationship] started to get rocky right during that time. I'd come for three, four weeks, then I'd go home, then I'd come back. Perhaps within a year of my returning [from Israel] it started to crumble . . .

15

1971–72: Listening to the Lion

By [the time we moved to California], our life was very traumatic and horrible. I couldn't stand any more of his rage as my daily reality. I worried about its impact on the children . . . I couldn't reconcile the fragile dream with the emotional chaos which kept intruding and crashing everything down.

—Janet Planet, 1998

There is precious little evidence of that 'rage as [a] daily reality', or its attendant 'emotional chaos', on Van Morrison's fourth Warners album, *Tupelo Honey*. Morrison would later claim that he intended to make a country & western album, incorporating songs like 'Wild Side of Life', 'Crying Time' and 'Banks of the Ohio'.★ Now that *would* have had the requisite emotional chaos – songs about murdering one's true love, and being lured 'to the places where the wine and liquor flow'. 'Wild Side of Life', in particular, might have struck the requisite chord, with its tale of a marriage on the rocks because of her desire for 'the glamour of the gay nightlife'. He would record the song for his next album, before reviving it for an Irish TV show in September 1973, after everything had indeed come crashing down.

Whether or not Morrison thought a great deal about the subject, it should have been clear that a move to California was a return to a life(style) Janet had impetuously left behind back in 1967, when she moved to New York. John Platania confirms that 'Janet wanted to get

★ Contemporary live performances include renditions of 'Jambalya', 'Let It Be Me' and 'Tennessee Waltz'.

into acting, but Van wanted a traditional woman at home, and I know that bothered her . . . She was a strong person. People used to offer her modelling assignments and acting roles, but Van flatly refused to allow her to do these things. The lack of socializing drove her crazy.'

If the lack of socializing drove *her* crazy, when she did socialize, it drove *him* crazy. One of the few positive comments Morrison chose to make about Steve Turner's book was prompted by an allusion to occasions 'when he came back off the road [and] his wife brought a lot of friends back and that annoyed him'. Morrison wrote two words in the margin: 'True plus'. The cracks came early, and lengthened daily. This notoriously private man couldn't help letting his feelings show in a rare contemporary interview:

Van Morrison: Some people don't seem to understand that you gotta work, y'know . . . Like I can dig hanging out when it's time to hang out. I dig having friends. But if I'm in the middle of working on an idea and I gotta stop because some people have come over to hang out, I may blow it. It's part of that fame trip, but it also has something to do with living in [the Bay area]. [1972]

It hardly takes a marriage counsellor to read between these lines. But then he was doubtless perturbed to find that the doting Janet was a thing of the past. When she was interviewed by a local Boston paper less than a year after the move west, Janet tried to put a positive gloss on their relationship but failed, describing her husband as 'incredibly Irish to live with . . . he comes from that whole thing. And, of course, he has a temper and he is always moving. He has to be doing something. He doesn't like a lot of people around. With more than two people he gets uncomfortable. He doesn't like performing, because he doesn't like the idea of all those people looking at him. Really, he is a recluse. He is quiet. We never go out anywhere. We don't go out to parties, we never go out.' Here was the first public reference his wife had made to Morrison's temper. It was also a declaration of independence – speaking something close to her mind to a media representative. As an artist, Morrison was afforded the opportunity to clear the air, or air his troubles, in song. Her options were more limited.

Initially, Morrison preferred to present the pretence that all was hunky-dory. *Tupelo Honey* became his first album of artifice, something he would later attribute to the 'fact' that 'it consisted of songs that were left over from before and that they'd finally gotten around to using. It wasn't really fresh.' In fact only 'Wild Night' and 'When the Evening Sun Goes Down' on *Tupelo Honey* appear to pre-date *Street Choir*, and they were two of the most successful songs on the album. Jon Landau, in his *Rolling Stone* review, actually recognized 'Wild Night' not just as 'a statement of the past, [but] a song done almost from memory, encompassing the style and form of some of Van's earliest music'.

Morrison recalls 'Wild Night' being 'originally a much slower number, but when we got to fooling around with it in the studio, we ended up doing it in a faster tempo'. The demo bears him out, having none of the song's later drive. The impetus for that jive-reggae intro came from Morrison's new guitarist, Ronnie Montrose, who remembers how 'one afternoon as I was messing around with what is now the intro on the record, [Van] stopped me and matter-of-factly said, "Ronnie . . . that thing you just played . . . that's the intro, don't forget it."' He didn't, and it became one of Morrison's most memorable singles.

'Wild Night' and 'When the Evening Sun Goes Down' were both attempted at sessions at the Wally Heider studio in San Francisco.* However, these initial sessions did not go according to plan, assuming that this plan was to complete an album in three weeks of sustained effort. Only four songs met Morrison's criteria after recording – 'Wild Night', 'Moonshine Whiskey', 'I Wanna Roo You', and '(Straight to Your Heart) Like a Cannonball'. According to the Wally Heider studio engineer, it took a fair dose of moonshine whiskey just to get him into the necessary frame of mind to record these.

Stephen Barncard: That whole three weeks he was too drunk to really do much else except do his tune, [in] one take, and then leave . . . We'd get the band rehearsed, then Ted Templeman would go to the hotel, pick up Van, put him in the studio, we'd set him up standing in front of a mike with his acoustic guitar . . . He can't sing without his guitar. He's got to have that guitar there, he's got to be forming chords and actually going through the changes because it affects his timing. Fortunately, he's a good player. [But] he didn't want to be in a booth. They were all just lined up facing the control-room glass, no baffles . . . We did one or two takes, he'd go back to the hotel and then the band would go on to the next tune . . . He wanted to show up, have the band be

---

* It is my belief that the alternative version of 'When the Evening Sun Goes Down' on the B-side of 'Wild Night' also dates from these sessions; the album version deriving from the later sessions at Columbia.

ready, and perform . . . He didn't like to hang out in the studio at all. I don't
even know if he waited around for playback . . . He would just get annoyed. I
don't think he like[s] recording at all. He just hates the whole process.

It would appear that Morrison was having to work on an album when
he still hadn't settled on a new home – hence the hotel. This was
probably trauma enough, but he also seemed to lack songs. The sessions
reconvened a few weeks later at a new studio, with two of his ex-
drummers, Connie Kay and Gary Malabar, brought together for the first
and last time. By now Morrison's new co-producer, Warners in-house
man Ted Templeman, had been given his baptism of fire-water, and was
receptive to a little coaching from those more conversant with the man's
working methodology.

Gary Malabar: I remember Teddie being a bit intimidated with Van, and me
telling him, 'Look, just be ready. You might not get the sound you want.
Certainly with Van you're not going to wind up taking eight hours just to get
a drum sound. This guy wants to put on headphones, and get in there and do
takes of songs and really not go through the technical end of it.' And he looked
at me, like, 'Oh really.' Van used Connie Kay on drums [when] we cut 'Tupelo
Honey' – I wound up playing vibraphones and percussion – and I remember
Teddie being very miserable 'cause he couldn't tune in what he wanted for that
song. [But] that's what was allowed for the time given – or Van would maybe
get mad and walk out of the studio, and not want to deal with it.

Thankfully Templeman was more impressed by Morrison's 'ability as
a musician, arranger and producer', describing it at the time as 'the
scariest thing I've ever seen. When he's got something together, he wants
to put it down right away with no overdubbing . . . I've had to change
engineers who couldn't keep up with him.' Despite going through three
engineers on *Tupelo Honey*, Templeman himself, to his credit, hung in
there. He was rewarded with a co-production credit, completing those
stages Morrison preferred to disregard:

Van Morrison: I gave [Templeman] co-production credit for doing the things
I didn't want to do – [like] making sure it was mixed. I'd send him the tapes
back and tell him how I wanted it mixed. I could be anywhere, like on holiday,
and I'd ring up and tell him I wanted it mixed like this. He'd go in with the
engineer and mix it. [1990]

A second set of sessions, at the San Francisco Columbia Studios, went more smoothly, as Morrison reverted to rehearsing the material pre-session. Flautist Boots Houston remembers how 'when[ever] we went into the studio, we would just play a whole set straight through without repeating anything.' Overdubs would be confined to backing vocals, horns or other such subtle embellishments. The basic tracks remained intact. Within a matter of days they captured seven songs, including one genuine masterpiece, and one honey-roasted perennial. The genuine masterpiece, though, would not make it on to *Tupelo Honey*, suggesting that Morrison fully intended to release another collection of commercial songs.

If the version of 'Listen to the Lion' already held over from *Moondance* was, in Malabar's words, 'pretty fuzzy', the *Tupelo Honey* take – which would be deferred for one more album – was fully focused and dazzlingly ambitious. Eleven minutes long, with only as many lines, it dated from those idyllic days when his love really did 'come tumbling down'. Pressed to explain its elusive content by Irish journalist Donall Corvin, Morrison prevaricated, 'What can I tell you? The words say it all. It's Leo coming out of the Virgo in my horoscope. That's as much of an answer to it as any.' Not unduly helpful, but then the song is little more – and yet so much more – than a *tour de force* of scat singing (an equally burbling ten-minute scat version of 'Into the Mystic', recorded at the Lion's Share eighteen months later, might almost lead one to think the man could do this to any of his songs). This was precisely where the *Astral Weeks* songs had been threatening to go when the fader went down at Century Sound – to that place 'behind the word[s]'.

Van Morrison: Each word has got a connotation . . . and the thing is finding what's behind the word – what meaning it has and what emotion. I'm really into vocal repetition as a definite art form. [1977]

It may well have been a last-minute decision to save the song for a rainier day. Its place on *Tupelo Honey* seems to have been taken by a wordier expression of possession, 'You're My Woman', recorded a few days after the other Columbia cuts.* 'You're My Woman' may have

---

* 'You're My Woman' has a Warners master number that is not sequential with the other Columbia cuts, which are PCA 511–516. 'You're My Woman' is PCA 548, suggesting a later recording (or at least filing) date.

served a more direct purpose, to reassure his woman that he still loved her, even if Steve Turner believes he can hear 'a tinge of desperation. The words were strong . . . but they sounded more like stiff reminders than celebrations.' Ronnie Montrose says that Van penned the song 'in his inimitable Zen fashion', sitting at the piano, during the sessions themselves.

'You're My Woman' wasn't the only song now recorded that seemed to look back on a brighter day. 'Old, Old Woodstock' is unashamedly nostalgic for a place and a time barely past but gone. Morrison was already bathing time spent upstate in that familiar pastoral glow. Perhaps he realized that he had made a serious mistake, something he threatened to correct whenever he made one of those late-night calls to the Catskills.

Jon Gershen: When he moved there he used to call me – in the middle of the night – and say, 'What's happening? What's going on in Woodstock?' He missed the whole scene . . . There was a time when he actually said to me, 'I really want to buy a house [there].' It was clear to me that part of him had wished he'd never left.

The album as released in October 1971 had more than a whiff of nostalgia, a feeling reinforced by its almost bucolic cover, on which a resplendent Lady Godiva-like (albeit clothed) Janet sits astride her white steed, with her husband walking beside them. The back of the cover only accentuated the sense of country comfort, with Morrison perched on a fence, a homely-looking Janet clutching his thigh, and the horse in its pen. Morrison later blamed the cover for the myth 'that I was living on a ranch and had horses on that ranch. I didn't have a ranch, I didn't have a horse . . . This is all part of the fuckin' mythology.' If Morrison grew to dislike the message seemingly conveyed, it didn't stop him repeating the trick on the sleeve of *Veedon Fleece*, for which he was photographed in the ancestral grounds of some hotel he was visiting, with a pair of Irish wolfhounds he didn't own.

However, the most potent myth surrounding the album – that here was a contented couple – owed less to the cover than to the title track, which would become a landmark song for Morrison (and enough of a trademark for him to re-use the melody on 1992's 'Why Must I Always Explain?'). 'Tupelo Honey' dripped with sugared sincerity. And, as a protestation of unyielding love it remains persuasive – 'the album's motif or intensification through repetition [being] given an ultimate statement on this cut', to quote Jon Landau. Janet, though, was becoming inured to the romantic songsmith inside. She realized that these songs came from some place she would never be able to reach.

Janet Planet: I would have done anything for the man who wrote those songs, who whispered in the night that they were true. I wanted more than anything to make him happy. But I just couldn't do it . . . I was confusing the music with the man. The music was everything you could hope for as a romantic. The man was a prickly bear. [1998]

The carefully crafted image presented on *Tupelo Honey* may have failed to convince the only person who knew the daily reality, but it again did the trick commercially. After another glowing review in *Rolling Stone*, it continued Morrison's assault on the American album charts, even if reviews elsewhere were more mixed, with London-based Charlie Gillett, writing for the Boston-based *Fusion*, nailing the album to his critical mast and crying wolf:

[Morrison] has developed one of the most idiosyncratic vocal styles of our time, and justifies comparison with Buddy Holly, Smokey Robinson, Otis Redding, and Dylan. But what he hasn't got, and maybe never will have, is a hint of vulnerability, which gives listeners a way into the songs, and a role to play in them . . . What I'm aware of is a process of decision-making, of the real Van Morrison deciding where to pitch his singing voice. I'm often impressed with what he does, but not enchanted into forgetting that the voice on the record isn't real.

Only in performance was Morrison sometimes able to forget himself long enough to let that inner voice out, as he did when débuting the title track acoustically at a couple of informal sets at the Lion's Share. Indeed a live album at this juncture might have dissipated many critics' deepening doubts. In September 1971, with *Tupelo Honey* in the stores, he recorded one of his most memorable concerts at Pacific High Studios for both his record label and KSAN-FM, who broadcast the ninety-minute set to an enthused Bay area radio audience.

Presumably Warners were already devising provisional plans for a Van the man live album. If so, Pacific High provided a perfect environment. With room for no more than two hundred souls, the converted plastics plant was a sixteen-track, Dolby-equipped, quadraphonic sound studio, complete with live chamber echo facility. Every Sunday evening since the early summer it had been broadcasting live concerts on KSAN, introduced by self-styled guru of the FM airwaves Tom Donahue.

The set recorded on 5 September 1971 gave a far greater sense of Morrison's dynamic range and breadth of influences than any single album to date. From Woody Guthrie's 'Dead or Alive', which he'd heard as a teenager on a Lonnie Donegan 78, via 'Hound Dog' and 'Just Like a Woman' – which explicates its implicit transvestism by making 'it clear/there's queer in here' – to the mawkish MOR of 'Que Sera Sera' and 'Buenas Días Señorita', Morrison vamped through every strain in his musical make-up. As a career overview, it was equally ambitious, incorporating 'Friday's Child' (much to the mystification of his west-coast audience) and 'Ballerina', as well as the bulk of the latest fab waxing, including a positively frenetic 'Wild Night' and a piano-based, full-on electric 'Tupelo Honey'. A single album of highlights, *Van the Man* would become his first vinyl bootleg.

As stories began to proliferate in the west-coast years of Morrison's erratic live persona – in inverse proportion to the number of memorable shows – the evidence of Pacific High would remain the ultimate counter-argument. It took Morrison just two months to flip the other side of the coin, at a brief residency at the Winterland Ballroom, recently opened by Bill Graham, at which he stormed off the stage barely forty minutes into one of the shows. He would later claim that he had been angry with his band – the very same guys who had played with such joyfulness at Pacific High.

Van Morrison: I did a couple of shows last year that just got blown up out of proportion. I did a show at Winterland and some other place, I forget, that they just took and blew up . . . Then after those shows, all this stuff started to go around about my performances . . . You're not *on* every night. You *can't* be on every night. But I can honestly say that with this group of people, it's mostly on . . . [But] it's not a rock & roll stage show . . . What people expect is not what they should expect from what I do . . . You've got people coming to see an image . . . that they read about in *Rolling Stone*. [1973]

In fact, for much of the period between *Tupelo Honey* and *Hard Nose the Highway*, Morrison would become a disturbingly unpredictable presence on stage, there being some nights, in the words of Yorke, 'when Van was damn near plastered out of his skull on booze, barely able to recall the lyrics to his songs, as he reeled and rocked'. The 'other' show that 'they just took and blew up' came just over a year after the Winterland incident, Morrison displaying a similar contempt for an audience across the bay in Berkeley. Two and a half songs into a badly advertised, ill-attended show at the Community Theater, he was seemingly about to cut loose on Willie Dixon's 'I Just Want to Make Love with You' when, as Greil Marcus reported in *Creem*, 'Van, [who] had been playing in a dim blue light . . . ordered "the spotlight" out. Didn't have his shades, he said. Not in LA, whatever that meant. The stage was [now] completely dark.' After 'a throwaway version of "Listen to the Lion", [followed by] a flat "Caravan"', Van announced his sixth, and as it transpired last, number – 'Misty'. Marcus was not amused:

'As I wander through this garbage world alone,' Van muttered, seemingly vaguely pissed at the audience . . . There was a lot of emotion to the show; Van Morrison is incapable of breathing without emotion. But this time it was gratuitous, bitterness without a target that deserved it, an insult without any context that could make it real . . . [and] it'll be a while before I pay money to see him again.

Presumably Morrison's real target was not the attendees, but the absentees – the result of just two days' notice. The Community Theater is not of insignificant size, and however significant the artist, it required promotion to sell it out. Morrison, though, wanted to gig when the whim took him. As he said at the time, 'Sometimes I feel like gigging at four in the morning, but nobody's around.' He missed the intimacy of a club like the Café Espresso (or the Catacombs or the Maritime).

Indeed, he began to idealize the experience of playing clubs at precisely the point when he had at last transcended the fleapits of America. In 1979 he reminisced about the difference between gigging at a club and 'play[ing] a concert . . . [where] you don't see anybody. You go out there, do your bit and go back to the dressing room, and it could have been anyone out there. After a club gig you may meet some nice people, and they'll take you back to the house, and maybe you'll sing with a guitar and the whole place is singing . . . In a club they're just glad to see you and they don't EXPECT you to do everything that was on the album.' He soon found a club in nearby Mill Valley that went some way towards fulfilling such an unrealistic criterion – the legendary Lion's Share, a shit-hole par excrement.

Ed Fletcher: The Lion's Share . . . sucked. It was a dive. But it was an amazing place. Van used to call up and say, 'I feel like playing. Call and see if we can just show up.' It was always with the understanding that you can't call the media. Just wanna keep it low profile. You'd get there and they were mobbed – it was shoulder to shoulder.

The Lion's Share was nothing if not obliging. Morrison's new manager, Stephen Pillster, remembers how his boss 'would call up his band early in the afternoon to see if they fancied having a blow that night. I would then call the club-owner, who would just cut one of his acts for that night, and let the headliner open for Van.'

Dauod Shaw: Before we would go out on a tour, we would play the Lion's Share because it was totally relaxed, and it was a good place to play in front of an audience the material that we'd been rehearsing, see how it worked [and] sharpen the show.

An example of just such a pre-tour run-through, in February 1973, was broadcast on local radio and circulates in bootleg form. The two sets display a similar eclecticism to Pacific High, offering up Budd Johnson's 'Since I Fell for You', Lenny Welch's 'Misty', Hank Williams's 'Hey Good Lookin'' and Fred Neil's 'Everybody's Talkin'' amid the usual Morrison-composed fare. Duplicating just two tracks across two hour-plus sets, the shows offered definitive interpretations of a pair of songs from his latest album, 'Listen to the Lion' and the title track, 'Saint Dominic's Preview'.

The release of these two songs suggested that the critical subtext underlying many a review of *Tupelo Honey* had hit home as Morrison at last changed direction. The return of an ambition above and beyond mere entertainment ensured that *Saint Dominic's Preview* was declared something of a comeback, largely because the album contained three songs that between them clocked in at around twenty-seven minutes. Abandoning the self-imposed commercial constraints evident in the past three collections, Morrison signalled a return to aspects of the increasingly revered *Astral Weeks*. Needless to say, he denied any such intent:

Van Morrison: Usually the concept [for an album] doesn't come around until you start listening to the playbacks . . . Sometimes it is [a conscious decision], sometimes it isn't. It depends what you're working for, and whether you do it all at once, or in pieces . . . or if you're overdrawn at the bank that day. [1972]

Such were the whims on which the internal integrity of a Morrison album could still hang, even if the financial argument no longer held water. *Saint Dominic's Preview* seems to have been the first album since *Astral Weeks* to have been recorded in a single stint of sessions, although at two studios, Columbia and Pacific High. However, there *was* a change of producer at the half-way stage – actually the removal of co-producer, Ted Templeman. Though at the time Templeman said little about what led to the termination of their association, a decade later he portrayed himself as one in a long line of victims of the man's short fuse, describing his erstwhile boss as 'a marvellous talent, a fantastic singer, but he's fired everyone who's ever worked with him – all his producers, his managers, his attorneys. He's so unpredictable . . . but I'm not the only one who would say that . . . because he would change his mind *all the time*.'

Templeman's disappearance left Morrison without a more objective voice to suggest a sequence, or to separate songs that were fun to record – like 'Almost Independence Day' – from those that might warrant release. In the case of 'Almost Independence Day', it is hard not to surmise that this eleven-minute jam was a filler for when inspiration failed. In the spring of 1972, he had admitted to one journalist that he had 'two more songs I've got to put together, and right now I don't know where they're gonna come from'.

Yet the sessions with Templeman had been quite productive, the title track probably being the last song Morrison recorded with him. 'Saint Dominic's Preview' was certainly a welcome return to more gritty subject matter, with a lyrical core lacking in recent efforts.

Morrison would later insist that he hadn't written the song 'with anything in mind . . . [it] is just a stream of consciousness. It doesn't mean any particular thing. It's a sketch . . . the words, the syllables, just came out of my mouth and I wrote them down.' At the time of its composition, though, he informed a Boston journalist that it was definitely 'influenced by my childhood in Belfast'. He was even more specific to *Rolling Stone* reporter John Morthland, describing it as 'about the scene going down in Belfast . . . The central image seemed to be this church called St Dominic's where people were gathering to pray, or hear a mass, for peace in Northern Ireland'.

It was surprising subject matter simply because of Morrison's long-standing decision not to address this volatile issue. That he had views, though, was never in doubt. After the Troubles again flared up in the aftermath of Bloody Sunday, the deteriorating situation in Northern Ireland continued to prey on his mind, particularly as his parents remained in the heart of East Belfast (they would join their son in California the following year, presumably in part because of the worsening situation). Tom Kielbania, himself a Catholic, remembers Morrison mentioning a few times during their association how he had 'a lot of friends in Belfast who thought he couldn't take the heat, with all the stuff that was going on. And they held that against him. That bothered him, that his friends thought that.' By 1972, though, he was telling American journalists, 'I don't think I want to go back to Belfast. I don't miss it with all that prejudice around.'

The pull of those roots runs through 'Saint Dominic's Preview'. Homesickness could consume him whenever some echo sought to call him home, even whilst trying, in his own words, 'to make this whole [California] thing blend'. Even the reference in the lyrics to Buffalo, New York, is a reference to missing home, in this instance the home town of drummer Gary Malabar.

Gary Malabar: I always used to be at Van's, and then when nothing was going on he'd go, 'Well, where are you going?' and I'd go, 'I'm gonna go jump in the car and go back to my home town, hang out with the guys for the weekend and play.' 'Cause I was always used to playing six nights a week. And he'd go, 'Well, why don't you stay here and hang out?' . . . And [then] he wrote that [line] in 'Saint Dominic's Preview', 'It's a long way to Buffalo/it's a long way to Belfast City too' – that was him crying out, saying, 'Well, you know what, I would like to return to my place too, 'cause I miss it.'

The album as a whole, though, lacks commensurate lyrical ambition. Indeed the songs that dominate each side of the album – 'Listen to the Lion' and 'Almost Independence Day' – have a lyrical content that is all but inconsequential. Even 'Saint Dominic's Preview' wanders from its brief to sideswipe those still 'flying too high to see my point of view'. This was all part of Morrison's guilt-trip at having 'everything in the world [he'd] ever wanted', and wondering why it was he couldn't raise a smile.

With hindsight, *Saint Dominic's Preview* now seems like even more of an escape from content than either of its two immediate predecessors.

As Steve Turner observed, it was 'his first album not to have love as its major theme', save perhaps for the three pop songs that kick off proceedings – assuming that 'Jackie Wilson Said' celebrates the 'kinda love . . . [that can] knock me off my feet' as much as the overpowering effect of hearing Jackie Wilson's 'Reet Petite'. The album then veers into more ambitious fare with the breathtaking 'Listen to the Lion' and, for a side and a half, fully sustains the listener's interest.

Unfortunately, 'Almost Independence Day' is a grand failure, the first of its kind. That it was a 'stream of consciousness trip again' was obvious to all – with those boats returning to the harbour, and the cool night breeze, and . . . er, 'it's almost independence day/way up and down the line' *ad infinitum*. Time to change channels. The stock of imagery was becoming ragged and worn. And yet, when it came time to sequence the album Morrison overlooked a more suitable candidate for inclusion, albeit a relic from the *Astral Weeks* era. Recorded at the same location as 'Almost Independence Day', the resurrected 'Wonderful Remark', at eight engaging minutes, complete with fluttering flute, would have rounded out an album unafraid of comparison with previous work of stature.

Instead, the paying punter got an album that *Rolling Stone* called 'the best-produced, most ambitious Van Morrison [album] yet', but singularly failed to equate with *Moondance* or *Astral Weeks*. Dave Marsh at *Creem* voiced his suspicion that *Saint Dominic's Preview* merely 'seems newly seminal, as though Van were finally capable of a conception that might transcend (though never dwarf) the brilliance of *Astral Weeks*'; whilst British 'zine *Cream* carpingly referred to the way that 'several of the songs are teeming with pleasingly poetic images, [but] they . . . seldom link together to present a concept or philosophy'.

If *Saint Dominic's Preview* was an attempt to blend some of *Astral Weeks*'s ambition with the musical fusion achieved on *Moondance*, it required more than its title track to address real issues in everyman's existence. Unfortunately, this was the last thing Morrison had in mind. A few months after the album's release, he told one journalist that 'a record doesn't detail a person's change[s]'. He phrased it more aggressively to another professional listener: 'What does a person's personal life have to do with music? . . . These journalists are writing about their game – and it doesn't have anything to do with the cat that's living the life.'

Morrison may even have originally intended to dispel some of the unwelcome interest in his songs' lyrical content by inserting a number of covers. At least ten out-takes were recorded for *Saint Dominic's Preview*, almost all of them covers, ranging from John Lee Hooker's 'Boogie Chillun' to the Everlys' 'Let It Be Me' via its country cousins, 'Wild Side of Life' and 'Down by the Riverside'. A soul ballad like 'Drown in My Own Tears' may well have expressed a sentiment he was feeling as his marriage crumbled, but it was one he shut out of his writing. Though he ended up sticking out an album composed entirely of originals, he continued to give the impression of someone who had already 'confronted enough for any man's lifetime'.

Van Morrison: You start writing songs, and it's just like everything else in life – it's just the way it's going. Then you have a couple of albums out and you get these reviews, and these people are saying, 'Well, this means this about that, and he was going through that when he wrote this.' You read these things and you go, 'Who are they talking about?' . . . So you get to the point where you're afraid to write *anything*, because you know somebody's gonna make something [out] of it . . . I'm very unanalytical about what I do . . . People seem to want to get in there and find out . . . [but] these are things I really don't even want to think about. [1985]

Such fearfulness now threatened to come between him and his art. Indeed the next album, recorded whilst his wife was preparing to leave for good, would take self-denial to a new level, though not a new art form. As this self-denial crossed over into his personal life, Janet was already working out her notice as his wife. Though John Platania remembers her making 'subtle complaints about the relationship . . . all that she would say was that he was difficult to live with'.

Morrison chose to keep his private problems from those around him, even those, like Platania and Jeff Labes – now returned from Israel – who had been with him since those halcyon days in Woodstock. Instead, he invited his old friend Jon Gershen to travel out to the coast without letting him know how close to the edge his marriage had become. What he couldn't put in his songs, he seemed equally unable to express to his old friend.

Jon Gershen: He invited me out [to California] to stay for a week. It was right after *Saint Dominic's* [came out]. I got picked up at the airport and I went up to the house, and they had dinner waiting for me and we were catching up on Woodstock news, and everything seemed OK. [But] he had booked me in a hotel, and as we were driving back he says, 'Well, you know, I'm splitting up with Janet,' blah blah blah. It was like, 'Why didn't you tell me this before? What are you talking about? I just got here and you're laying this on me.' It put me in an awkward position. I listened to his side of it and I listened to her side of it, and it was just clear that things had reached [the end]. He was becoming pretty famous in the business, and it had begun to take its toll. I think that was really a big part of it. I realized at that point, even though we had talked a lot on the phone, an era had passed. That trajectory was doing some things that weren't all that positive as far as his psychology was concerned . . . He was getting wealthier, and that was changing some things. Now when he said to some flunkey, 'Get me something,' they would move. And you know what that does to people. It was getting difficult to keep what had been a sensitive relationship together. There was too much going on – there was no way to control it any more. It was bigger than anything she could handle. In Woodstock it was on a scale she could manage . . . but in California, there was no way he was going to be contained. [But] he was not really able to verbalize exactly what was going on . . . When I got there, it was bizarre. I had only known Van and Janet as a couple. And she had a way of always being close by, [being] protective of him. [So] he invites me out there in the middle of this thing that's going on between them – oblivious to the fact that this is not a good time [to hang out] . . . It didn't occur to him that that would not be something I would want to share with him – the dissolution of his marriage . . . But he was not really put together in a way that could conceptualize basic [interactions]. [Instead] it was like, 'Let's have some fun' – missing the days of old.

On 17 November 1972, Janet finally moved out on her increasingly difficult husband, taking their daughter Shana and her son Peter with her. On 26 January 1973, Janet Elizabeth Morrison filed for dissolution of their marriage, citing irreconcilable differences. Not surprisingly, she asked for custody of their daughter, as well as child support and a division of their community property. The community property listed in the petition included a $40,000 savings account, a 1972 Mercedes and interests in a recording studio – which Morrison had just finished having built at the back of their property. It would be completed just in time for Morrison to record a number of new songs – songs of bitterness and need, but precious few lyrics displaying regret or remorse.

16

1972–73: Hard Times and Fine Lines

Van Morrison: If you just put on the tape machine and record six hours' worth – who's going to put out six hours? . . . It's the difference between art and show business.

Danny Holloway: Do you sacrifice your art for show business, or is an album like *Moondance* [just] another side to your musical spectrum?

Van Morrison: . . . I did sacrifice, but I don't think I'm going to sacrifice any more. I feel like I've been sacrificing all along, to a certain extent.

—*NME, 1972*

Not only did Morrison at last have, in his marital breakdown, powerful subject matter to hand, but as of the autumn of 1972, he at last had his own studio on the premises, to catch as catch could each flurry of inspiration. It represented a persuasive aesthetic, especially for someone as quixotic as Morrison. As he said at the time, 'If there's something to put down, you have to go in and take care of it when it's happening.' With the establishment of Caledonia Studio, his regular band of musicians could take turns crafting the disparate images collected whenever he opened himself up to channels of communication.

Gary Malabar: I used to try to talk to Van about his composition[s]. I realized that a lot of Van's composition came from free writing, little streams of consciousness. He had a book [he used to write in], 'The Jazz and Poetry of Van Morrison', and one day it was open and I read some of it, and I realized [that] he took his lines from his thoughts and just reassembled them – just as [if] somebody [was] re-examin[ing] their own work and go[ing], 'I'll take this line and I'll put it with that line and that line, and now I'll read it.'

Morrison's band of musicians was still based around a familiar core of east-coast refugees – ever-present John Platania, drummer Daoud Shaw and the recently repatriated Jeff Labes, whose arrangement ideas were always good and who had been sorely missed. Along with local bassist David Hayes, Platania and Shaw became accustomed to the impromptu calls from Caledonia. Because Labes retained his east-coast base, his transcontinental passage to appear at a session usually signalled a more serious intent.

Jeff Labes: He had this studio. He had an eight-track machine there, which was sort of old technology, but it was a really nice room . . . That was a very hard thing for him, having his own studio. The thing he discovered was when you're not pressured to perform by the clock, there's more of a possibility of wasting time fooling around, going down avenues that you wouldn't ordin-arily, trying [unnecessary] things. He's talked about this a number of times – [it] looks like freedom but in the end it's much better to be pressured, 'cause then you really get right down to the business. When I came in, I was [coming] in from New York so I might have added to the pressure – 'We've got this guy here. We'd better produce.' So I think in a way [my presence] helped him.

Even when Labes was around, the results continued to be variable. Morrison still aspired to capture a certain kind of feeling 'that'll never be on a record', an allusion to the fact that 'there's many things that will never go on my records that are . . . better [than *Astral Weeks*] . . . I sing my best when I'm sitting around with a couple of friends.' In this sense, Caledonia served as a conscious emulation of the days when he rehearsed in his front room in Woodstock. Indeed its attempts at self-contained intimacy sometimes got in the way of sheer practicalities.

Ed Fletcher: They were doing 'Snow in San Anselmo', and I push open the door to the studio, which wasn't a large place, and there was a forty-piece Madrigal choir in there. I almost knocked them all over.

Whatever the problems with Caledonia, the very proximity of the new studio seems to have inspired a rush of material akin to those early Woodstock days. *Saint Dominic's Preview* had been in the shops only a matter of weeks when, on or around 21 August 1972, Morrison began work on a slew of new songs, starting with the title track to his next collection, 'Hard Nose the Highway', and a remarkable new song, 'Madame Joy', which by its very name harked back to *Astral Weeks*.★

In fact he had been working with Joe O'Connell on a film script based on 'Madame George'. According to Morrison, Madame Joy was meant to carry on from 'Madame George', a kind of part two, though any relationship between the songs seemed designed to elude all save Morrison himself. 'Madame Joy' is an idealized teacher of men, someone who bequeaths 'a taste of all religion'. Only when she 'walk[s] past that old street corner . . . looking for her boy' does the listener wonder if we are back on Ford and Fitzroy. The fact that it took Morrison twenty-five years to release a song that breathes such joyous sound suggests an almost wilful perversity.

Steve Turner reflects a common misconception when he asserts, in *Too Late to Stop Now*, that 'the greatest indication that [Van] was headed for a dry period was the fact that [*Hard Nose the Highway*] contained only six Van Morrison songs'. This is misleading. There would actually be around thirty songs recorded at the *Hard Nose* sessions between August and November 1972, three-quarters of which were original compositions. Of these, two would appear (in re-recorded form) on the next album, the seminal *Veedon Fleece*; a further nine on *Philosopher's Stone*; whilst 'Feedback out on Highway 101' would be scheduled for inclusion on a 1977 Warners collection of out-takes which would be nixed; and 'Spare Me a Little (of Your Love)' – one of the most impassioned vocals that autumn – seems to have been earmarked (along with another four originals, recorded at a separate session) for a Jackie DeShannon album that never happened.

Morrison was also co-writing songs with John Platania, though his trusty guitarist would have to wait until 1997 for the likes of 'There There Child' and 'Try for Sleep' to see the light of day. Meanwhile, a regular slot at the 1973 shows would have to suffice for 'Paid the Price'. Despite Morrison's marital problems, the vibe at the sessions remained extremely positive, and he managed a number of first takes, something that, as Jeff Labes says, 'he always loved . . .'cause he wanted that magic. Like Sinatra did.' Dig those first takes indeed.

★ Even Morrison has admitted that he does not sing 'Madame George' on the song of that name, he sings 'Madame Joy', though no reason for the name change has ever been offered.

John Platania: [*Hard Nose*] was a great album to work on . . . It was very loose. He usually gave everybody free rein to play. He would [just] give general ideas of what to play . . . That's what I loved about it. I knew what he wanted. He never wanted screaming guitars – he always mentioned 'no screaming guitars'. He had a sound, he had a vision . . . He always does . . . an incredible amount of stuff . . . 'The Great Deception', he recorded that on his back . . . He improvised. It was done off the top of his head . . . The guide vocals, 60 maybe 70 per cent was stream of consciousness, right off the top of his head. [MW]

With such a wealth of material, and a pleasing diversity of styles, Morrison's mind turned to the possibility of putting out a double album. It seemed the obvious way around the stylistic jumps that had dogged the previous three collections, and it might allow him enough latitude to slip in a few of the covers also worked up at the sessions, including Sonny Terry's 'Take This Hammer', Lead Belly's 'Goodnight Irene', Hank Williams's 'Hey Good Lookin' ', Sam Cooke's 'Bring It on Home to Me', a lush reworking of the McPeakes' arrangement of 'Wild Mountain Thyme' and a song he had learned from watching *Sesame Street* with his daughter Shana, 'Being Green'. His record company, though, were less enchanted by the idea and, after much discussion, it was impressed upon Morrison that a single album would do. Morrison was bound to balk at such control, and a subtext of disillusionment with Warners permeated promotional interviews for the single-album composite they deigned to release.

Van Morrison: What can you say on forty minutes of wax? . . . If I could put out a triple album without being hassled about it, I would put it out. It would be a lot more of an honest representation. I could easily make a triple album of the music that I wanted to put out, but there's so much involved . . . If you want to talk about those [Warners] albums . . . that's just what got out on the records. You don't see what's in the can . . . I've got stuff in the can that's got nothing to do with the mood of those particular albums, but [that] I did . . . at the same time . . . What I'm trying to say is that when I'm doing an album, I'm not just doing an album, I may be doing four albums . . . I mean, I've got stuff in the can from the *Street Choir* album that was totally uncommercial. I've still got it in the can because it's not acceptable unless you look at it as jazz . . . There's all kinds of directions happening in the music. But when it comes time for an album, you have to limit it to one direction. [1973]

The album he permed from this wealth of material, *Hard Nose the Highway*, simply refused to confine itself to a single direction and Morrison found himself quite unable to sequence the best material in a way that hung together. Eventually, he settled for 'just trying to establish how hard it [is] to do just what I do', though even he found it difficult to sustain the title track's bitter tone over two sides. What he ended up with instead was 'one side [that] has a kind of hard feeling, while the other is soft'.

Absent from the finished album are any songs indicating the death of a great romance. Indeed there is no evidence that he *even* cut a version of 'Paid the Price' – his most direct, and personal, song about the break-up with Janet. Though it contains its share of hard feelings couched in a wild accusatory tone – 'your forced superiority, your azure delusions of grandeur/are [not] gonna cut you free . . . you're as cold as ice, you're not Miss Nice/and I paid the price' – such feelings fell on stony ground. Perhaps the closest he came to letting the break-up impact on his recorded work came with the Sam Cooke classic 'Bring It on Home to Me', with its deliciously bitter opening, 'If you ever change your mind, about leaving me behind/Bring your sweet loving, bring it on home to me'. Omitted from the album, it was a nightly showstopper.

On *Hard Nose the Highway*, Morrison preferred another of those richly romantic word pictures. 'Warm Love' is not merely nostalgic in its portrait of a day in the country but, in this context, deeply escapist. It was one of a trio of songs used to dilute the deep core of resentment found on 'Hard Nose' itself, as well as 'The Great Deception'. 'Wild Children' and 'Snow in San Anselmo' are equally nostalgic, but for alternative pasts. The former, which perhaps should have been called 'War Children', was apparently written 'for all the children born around that time – because . . . there was a heavier trip to conform'. 'Snow in San Anselmo', more of a mood piece, is juxtaposed by his resolve to 'Hard Nose the Highway'.

Morrison persevered with the discontinuity of moods on side two, where a nursery rhyme ('Being Green') and a fine traditional Scottish love-song ('Purple Heather'⋆) are separated by another dose of 'Almost Independence Day' – this time with lyrics. Given the numerous alternatives, and the fact that it occupied enough space for three songs, 'Autumn Song' ill suits its prominent position, being unmemorable in melody and

---

⋆ The song is generally known as 'Will Ye Go Lassie' or 'Wild Mountain Thyme'.

metre, and with lyrics to send Keats's cadaver revolving for eternity. It also opened Morrison up to some surprisingly savage reviews, with Charlie Gillett again jumping to the head of the queue:

Hard Nose the Highway is flabby with words. Blushing blues makes purple prose. Looking back, it's clear that Van was rarely a great songwriter, often being content with occasional striking phrases while the rest of the words were embedded deep in the texture of the music. Even more paradoxical, he isn't technically a very good singer either, restricted to two or three keys and tones . . . but rather than try to bluff his way through, Van Morrison chose to invent a new kind of music which would make his singing legitimate . . . The trouble with *Hard Nose* is that although the music is often 'interesting', it doesn't have a convincing emotional basis.

And yet *Hard Nose the Highway* was the first album over which Morrison says he exercised complete artistic control. Perhaps, as Brian Hogg pithily observed, '*Hard Nose the Highway* fumbled on the Morrison mystique [because] Van overreached himself, unable to see his limitations.' Judged harshly by some at the time, when a great deal of hype circulated around the live shows that 'promoted' it, it has been even more brutally dismissed by posterity. In subsequent fan-polls, *Hard Nose* regularly features as a contender for Least Favourite Album.

Of the original songs on the album, perhaps only 'Warm Love' and 'Hard Nose the Highway' could have sat comfortably alongside 'rejects' like 'Madame Joy', 'Bulbs', 'Spare Me a Little', 'Country Fair', 'Contemplation Rose' and 'Drumshanbo Hustle'. The fact that Morrison preferred the merely sour 'Great Deception' to a slice of realism like 'Drumshanbo Hustle', bristling with genuine resentment, certainly gives an impression of someone ill-equipped to assume 'complete artistic control'.

If 'Drumshanbo Hustle' did not itself prompt Morrison to re-examine the Bang situation, this attempt to lyrically reconstruct the months after Berns's death came as a direct result of a new legal contretemps involving Ilene Berns. Morrison later said that it was what he was feeling at the time, suggesting that it *did* inspire renewed legal action against Web IV and Bang. In January 1973, shortly before Janet filed for divorce, Morrison decided to go after all those missing royalties, in the hope that he might box Ilene Berns into enough of a legal corner for her to surrender all the rights to the Bang material. Citing Berns's 'failure to account and pay royalties' as 'wilful and deliberate', Morrison demanded of the courts 'rescission of the Agreement and the Release, and the return to plaintiff of the ownership of all musical compositions written or co-written by plaintiff'.

There were two immediate results of this precipitate action, neither of which was what Morrison had presumably intended. First, Berns set about assembling another Bang compilation from the various tapes (having deleted 1971's shamefully misleading *Best of Van Morrison*). The resultant *TB Sheets* gave the world its first chance to hear Bang versions of 'Madame George' and 'Beside You', as part of a genuine representation of the best of the Bang material. Attractively packaged, with notes by Michael Ochs, the album proved a great success, and indeed a more durable listening experience than current Warners product.

Ilene Berns also took the battle to Morrison on the legal front, issuing on 23 May 1973 a cross-summons on Warners and Morrison 'joining them and others as defendants in the action, together with an answer to the [original] complaint containing counterclaims against the Warner defendants, as well as against the plaintiff and the said other defendants in the action'. Berns smartly brought into play Morrison's quite blatant breach of the original September 1968 agreement:

In purported compliance with [the 1968 agreement of release] plaintiff submitted thirty-two musical compositions to Web IV, all of which are completely unpublishable because they contain vulgar and coarse language, and are entirely devoid of any substance of originality or artistic merit. Web IV has not accepted any of these musical compositions as consideration for the release.

By reason of the foregoing, and plaintiff's bad faith in knowingly submitting wholly unpublishable musical compositions, the release is void for total failure of consideration and failure of the condition precedent contained in paragraph 5 thereof . . .

By reason of the foregoing, Morrison remained obligated under the afore-mentioned exclusive writer's contract during the five-year period stipulated therein, i.e. [from] March 21, 1967 [up] to and including March 21, 1972 . . .

The value of Morrison's music publishing up to and including March 1972 would have been a tidy old sum. It certainly comprised the bulk of Morrison's own net worth. He had no real alternative but to settle, having opened another can of worms not to his taste. The ongoing suit may also have accounted for the ignominious fate of 'Drumshanbo Hustle'. In the end, Morrison achieved neither of his objectives. Berns retained control of all the Bang material, which she would shortly afterwards sell to CBS, whilst benefiting from a repackaging project Morrison's legal action had prompted. The fact that Warners had also been dragged into the dispute – presumably as a result of unpaid royalties due to Web IV from *Astral Weeks* – cannot have sat well with them.

Fortunately for Morrison, despite an unexpected fall from commercial grace, he was flavour of the month at Warners come the summer of 1973, as the shows he was playing in the States and Europe attracted unprecedented coverage and Warners were given the OK to record a number of shows for a possible live album. The resultant release would become the kind of landmark many other live albums could only aspire to. It would also be the double album Warners would not countenance for *Hard Nose the Highway*.

The Too Late to Stop Now tour – as it came to be tagged – was Morrison's most ambitious set of shows to date. It came at a time when he had rediscovered some of his earlier love of performing. According to Morrison, this was unrelated to changing circumstances. Rather, at a Carnegie Hall show in the autumn of 1972, 'something just happened. Click. I was just standing on the stage and I was singing and it just hit me, I was back into performing.'

Janet's spectre, though, remained a nightly presence throughout the tour, a number of covers being introduced that appeared to directly address his 'situation'. Morrison especially couldn't resist inserting a couple of songs that dealt with money-grabbing women. If Sonny Boy Williamson's 'Take Your Hands out of My Pocket' didn't make the point, an extra couplet he inserted into Sam Cooke's 'Bring It on Home to Me' did, changing the whole tenor of the song. The singer was no longer able to offer his love jewels,* having given her 'all the money I had in the bank/At no point did you say thanks'. The bitterness that built up in the months preceding the divorce settlement would never entirely dissipate. A quarter of a century later he told an audience in Oxford, as part of a spoken monologue in 'It's All in the Game', 'By the time solicitors get involved, it doesn't matter whose fault it is.'

Other songs of heartache also regularly featured in the shows, Morrison entering an entirely different space with the handful of covers that punctuated each performance. Some years later Morrison would seek to

---

* Cooke's original recording included the lines 'I'll give you jewellery/And money too'.

suggest that, in order 'to perform, I almost have to assume another identity. I have to almost play a part . . . Otherwise I couldn't do it. So I'm playing a role, and doing the music within that context.' During the 1973 shows Morrison became a singing method actor. The man who sang Bobby Bland's '(When You Got a Heartache) Ain't Nothing You Can Do' was hardly play-acting; nor was the man pleading for someone to 'Help Me'; just as the person singing about how 'love brings such misery and pain/I'll never be the same, since I fell for you' was living inside his material.

For Morrison, it continued to require a supreme act of will just to get up there. As he admitted after the 1973 tour, 'For me, performing requires a tremendous amount of concentration. I'm not someone who just plugs in and gets it on.' He had always suffered from intermittent stage fright, usually staving it off with alcohol, something alluded to in a 1972 interview: 'I get into [playing live] in a different way than a lot of people. Like I dig singing the songs, but there are times when it's pretty agonizing for me to be out there.'

It was precisely this inner conflict between the fear of performing and his fearlessness as a performer that made the nights when Morrison was 'on' so compelling. Lewis Merenstein describes the process thus: 'He explains himself when he performs . . . He's holding on to the microphone and standing there, can't let go. He's fearful, [even] turn[ing] his back to the audience . . . [It was] not something he really relished doing.' But then, as Jeff Labes states, 'whenever he goes on stage, he's always looking for the magic to happen, and so anything that gets in the way of that is an irritant'.

Van Morrison: In order to be a musician in this business, you also have to assume that show-business trip. And that's when the existential thing comes in . . . the illusion begins. I have to become a performer. First of all you're a musician, but once you step on the stage and you're going to give those people what they want, that's when the illusion takes over and you become a performer. [1974]

Having previously complained about audiences who 'expect a certain thing and when they don't get exactly what they expect, it throws them off balance', by 1973 he was willing to meet such audiences half-way. The tour again began with warm-up shows at the Lion's Share before the valuable publicity of an appearance on the prime-time *Don Kirshner's*

Rock Concert in April, and concluded with two nights at London's Rainbow Theatre in late July. It featured not only favourites from previous Warners albums – like 'Cyprus Avenue', 'Into the Mystic', and the title tracks of his last three albums – but early hits like 'Here Comes the Night', 'Gloria' and 'Brown Eyed Girl', rearranged for a brave new world.

The band Morrison had put together was dubbed the Caledonia Soul Orchestra, after a fabled eighteen-minute instrumental out-take from the *Street Choir* album. It provided the most musically sophisticated sound any of his fans had witnessed in a 'rock' context, with the basic rock combo of Jeff Labes, John Platania, David Hayes and Dauod Shaw augmented by sax player Jack Schroer, two violinists, a viola player, a cellist and a trumpeter. The possibilities galvanized Morrison, as Shaw recalls: 'As a frontman, he liked having all that power at [his] command – he has always loved Sinatra, [and] those textures.' Even with such a battery of musical alternatives, though, Morrison insisted on the ability to improvise around any given arrangement.

Jeff Labes: We'd had these string players in to work on [*Hard Nose the Highway*], and he liked it and said, 'Hey, let's get a string quartet for the road.' [But] sometimes Van would do songs in longer or shorter versions, so we had to have signals to get them in – it wasn't always in the same place.

Though the shows evolved out of the Caledonia experience, Morrison integrated the old and the new, whether borrowed or blue, working up something like forty songs on the three-month tour, including a dozen covers; two-thirds of the latest album; and riveting rearrangements of 'Cyprus Avenue', 'The Way Young Lovers Do' and 'Sweet Thing' from *Astral Weeks*.

By the end of the tour, though, he was already describing *Hard Nose* as 'just a record of old songs . . . [that] doesn't have anything to do with my life or the way I live . . . My only present is the gig tomorrow night, and the gig after that.' Though every *Hard Nose* song save 'The Great Deception' and 'Autumn Song' was performed at the shows recorded – at the LA Troubadour, the Santa Monica Civic Auditorium, and at its finishing end, at London's Rainbow Theatre – only 'Warm Love' and 'Wild Children' from the latest collection would feature on the official document of the tour.

The Rainbow shows, in particular, would linger in the memory long after Morrison had moved on to newer challenges: partly because these, his first shows in London since the days of Them delivered on the unnecessary hype; partly because of the half-dozen performances immortalized on the live album; but primarily because of an hour-long TV/radio simulcast transmitted nationally by the BBC. Morrison had hit upon a musical style engaging enough to inspire even those for whom its historical context remained a mystery.

Paul Charles: [The Caledonia Soul Orchestra was] so different from everything else that was going on. [But] if you want to take references . . . Van knows the showband sound, and knows how to use the magic of the showband sound, and he [had] found a way of setting it inside contemporary music.

If the Monarchs in Heidelberg seemed a lifetime away, the CSO concerts were just as demanding, both physically and emotionally. A *Rolling Stone* journalist, reviewing the tour, couldn't help but notice how 'everybody is working overtime . . . at keeping Morrison's spirits up'. However, even the collective resources of an eleven-piece band and long-standing road manager Ed Fletcher couldn't always save Morrison from deep melancholia.

John Platania: He couldn't cope with it at all. He would cancel shows. He would talk about it as much as he possibly could, and then just go into periods of silence. But everybody knew it was killing him. [ST]

Dauod Shaw: Occasionally I'd get a call at two in the morning, [to] go out looking for food . . . [but] it was a very difficult time for Van. I could see what he was going through. It was like the rug was pulled from under him. He was miserable. He was really torn up. I knew a lot of stuff was going on, just [by] looking at him.

The presence of his three-year-old daughter, Shana, on the UK leg of the tour should have acted as a balm for Morrison's troubled spirit. However, Jeff Labes remembers how Shana's presence simply resulted in 'a lot of pressure from Janet. He had his daughter with him, and had a housekeeper taking care of her, [but] Janet would [still] call him all the time, harassing him, telling him to bring her back. At one point he was offered [an] additional concert somewhere in Germany, and it was huge money for those days, [but] he was so tired out, he turned it down.'

Janet doubtless had some very real concerns regarding her ex-husband – most notably, the possible effect his continued drinking might be having on his state of mind. According to Steve Turner, his consumption of endless bottles of whisky had been a major factor in their estrangement, and though 'Janet almost succeeded in making him give up . . . he would then become secretive, and hide bottles in the bathroom'. Morrison later denied hiding bottles in the bathroom. As for the drinking itself, his response to Turner was the classic hard drinker's state of denial: 'Because I'm Van Morrison, I can't do anything that's considered to be ordinary.'

His level of drinking was anything but ordinary, as Morrison well knew. Those around him began to suspect that he was in need of professional help. At the end of the tour, he too began to consider how much his drinking was bound up with his need to perform, and how much it was his way of dulling his daily pain. The one time he ever talked at length on the subject was in conversation with his first chronicler, Ritchie Yorke,* in 1977. Having given Yorke some insights into his songwriting for the author's 1975 book, Morrison perhaps felt he could allow himself the luxury of candour in his company. Certainly he gave Yorke an uncharacteristically convincing analysis of the dangers of addiction:

Van Morrison: The heaviest dope I ever did was alcohol. I've done stuff like hash and grass, which isn't really heavy dope. But alcohol is a different story – it's a real heavy drug, a real motherfucker . . . I was always looking for the bell to ring. I was always waiting for that bell. So you're either too high, and you're drinking because you're so fucking high you want to maintain that high, or you're drinking because you're low and you want to get up there and get high . . . with the result that . . . you go down like a bomb . . . When I first started drinking, it was working for me. It was great. Like when you're doing a gig and you're in a band and you're in the truck and there's nothing to do in the truck, and the gigs are all the same and the hotels are all the same . . . When I first started drinking everybody was doing it. That was before they discovered marijuana . . . The main drink was wine – and even that was a romantic throwback to something . . . One day the switchboard lit up and I saw where it was all going. I saw what alcohol could do to people, and I saw that it wasn't

---

* This fascinating addendum to the conversations that comprised Yorke's 1975 pop bio, *Into the Music*, was published in two parts in the American monthly *Stagelife* in July and August 1977.

Angry Young Them pose on the steps of City Hall, spring 1964.

Them, Mark One, spring 1964.

Them, again, 1966.

Comparing notes with Bert Berns at the 'Brown Eyed Girl' session, 28 March 1967.

Morrison, Kielbania and Payne await their New York début, autumn 1968.

On stage at the Scene, autumn 1968.

Lewis Merenstein and Richard Davis, Morrison's collaborators on *Astral Weeks*, at the time of those 1968 sessions.

Morrison in Montreal, *circa* 1971.

Morrison in Manchester, 1985.

Morrison in Manchester, with Clive Culbertson (far right) and the Chieftains, 1988.

The Man from Del Monte, 1998.

Morrison and Michelle Rocca while away a limo ride, 1996.

A smile for Linda Gail Lewis, 2000.

a good thing any more. Plus I wasn't a teenager any more myself . . . I realized
I was growing up . . . You have responsibilities . . . you've got to think about
getting your act together. I didn't even know what it had been doing to me . . .
[but] in Ireland *everybody* drinks. Nobody gives it a second thought. You're
Irish, number one, and you're a drinker, number two. [1977]

After little more than three months on the road, the cumulative
pressures had built up to such an extent that Morrison faced a stark
choice: he could either embrace that supposed breakdown or take a long
break from everything and everyone he had come to rely upon, avoiding
any kind of environment where he might be inclined to party. Perhaps
what he needed most, though, was the quiet land of Erin coursing
through his blood again. He presumably never expected the immediacy
with which inspiration would come running once he set foot on Irish
soil for the first time in six years. Ostensibly there to record a half-hour
show for national TV station RTE, he was in reality returning to the
only place where the healing could begin.

AGE FIVE
Keeping a Stiff Upper Lip

17

1973–74: A Commercial Cul-de-Sac

Books are not the doors, they are only the windows.

—*Louis-Claude de Saint-Martin*

There's a big part of me that's just strictly involved with the island of Ireland . . . I'm a citizen of Europe and America but I belong to, specifically, Ulster.

—*Van Morrison, 1984*

It really came to me when we were in Ireland that he's really a mad Irish poet. That's his genetic make-up.

—*Stephen Pillster*, Too Late to Stop Now

On 20 October 1973, less than three months after his Rainbow triumph, Van Morrison returned to Ireland in the company of his latest manager, the hapless Stephen Pillster, and a woman he was calling his new fiancée, Carol Guida. The trip was intended as a vacation, pure and simple, and after checking into a Dublin hotel, they took off in a hired car, visiting Cork, Cashel, Killarney and Arklow. However, the trio never ventured across the border on to Morrison's home turf. The Troubles still troubled him, and with his parents now ensconced in Mill Valley, close to his Fairfax home, he passed up the opportunity to rekindle former associations.

Home, though, was never far from his mind, if the songs he now started to write are any kind of indication. The song that would open *Veedon Fleece*, 'Fair Play', came 'from what was running through my head', its elegiac tone set for others to follow as its narrator looks out on the lakes of Killarney, thinking of another time and a love 'forever fair', when a paperback of Edgar Allan Poe filled his mind with tales of mystery and imagination. Morrison also felt prompted to rework an earlier song. 'Country Fair', which concludes what many consider to be his finest post-*Astral Weeks* collection, finds Morrison back in a familiar dream-scape, when 'we were too young to really know . . . [as] we laid out in the long green grass/and never thought that it would pass'. An older, gentler Ireland was assuredly on his mind.

He was in the same frame of mind when he returned to Dublin in early November to record a special television performance for the RTE cameras. Morrison had agreed not only to answer a few pre-approved questions, but to play a few favourites in an uncharacteristically intimate manner. For the first time since the break-up of Them, he consented to give a solo performance.

Though he recorded an unwelcome smattering of lesser songs from *Hard Nose*, out also came the likes of 'Madame George', 'And It Stoned Me' and 'Saint Dominic's Preview', songs from an ancient homeland. Unfortunately, none of these would feature in the actual RTE broadcast. However, a signpost had been planted, even if neither these songs nor those Morrison had written in the preceding weeks were given a public airing on *Talk about Pop*.★

Almost an album's worth of songs had been written in Ireland, though the record's contents would remain a mystery for some time yet. Asked by a reporter, shortly before his departure, if it felt good to be back in one's motherland, Morrison admitted that it had been a very productive period, and that he had written eight new songs in less than three weeks. And this was no exaggeration. Everything on *Veedon Fleece* save 'Bulbs', 'Country Fair' and 'Come Here, My Love' appears to date from this Irish 'vacation', as does 'Street Theory', a song he would attempt a number of times before letting it evolve into 'The Street Only Knew Your Name'.

For Morrison, writing such a homogeneous collection of songs in such a short period of time must have been an enormous relief. He had begun to feel that he had entered some kind of rut over the past few albums, something he later deemed inevitable:

★ The songs actually broadcast on the programme were 'Wild Children', 'Slim Slow Slider', 'Warm Love', 'Drumshanbo Hustle' and 'Autumn Song'.

Van Morrison: By the fourth or fifth album you're writing more songs but you write from the point of view that you are searching – but you're actually not. But in order to be able to write something you have to pretend you are. Otherwise there is nothing to write about. So you have to pretend that there is something you are searching for, or . . . an idea that you take somewhere. So it seems like you're searching, but in fact you're just telling little stories. [1987]

Veedon Fleece proved a welcome exception to the above 'rule'. It was the product of genuine inspiration, a return to the channelled form of writing evident on *Astral Weeks*, much of *Moondance* and slivers of *Saint Dominic's Preview*. Although, according to Stephen Pillster, Morrison has 'never taken particular pride in authorship, he thinks of himself more as a channel', he must have been relieved to find that channel still open when he sought to reconnect with his roots. The album he was set to record came out of an inner turmoil he had largely suppressed on *Hard Nose the Highway* as he returned to the eternal quest, even coining the memorable 'You Don't Pull No Punches, But You Don't Push the River' to describe the process.

Van Morrison: At that time there were so many strange things going on in my life . . . I got the carpet pulled out from under me by a lot of people in a short space of time, and that's when [my search] started. Everything was just pulled out from under me. It was over a couple of months in 1973 when just BANG!, and it was up for grabs. I had to start being responsible for *me*. [1985]

A number of the songs on *Veedon Fleece* depict someone uprooted by circumstance and unsure of the way ahead, notably the two songs that segue together on side one, 'Linden Arden Stole the Highlights' and 'Who Was That Masked Man?' Morrison described the former as being 'about an image of an Irish-American living in San Francisco – it's really a hard man type of thing', whilst the latter was 'a song about what it's like when you absolutely cannot trust anybody. Not as in some paranoia, but in reality.' Of course, only a closet paranoid could have written either song.

The autobiographical elements are unmistakable. This Linden Arden, who 'loved the morning sun, and whisky . . . [but] loved to go to church on Sunday' is as idealized a self-portrait as Dylan's Jack of Hearts, whilst the Masked Man provides a particularly vivid insight into the fearfulness of the lonely. Singing like a man who has let the booze do the talking for too long, he knows all too well 'the ghost [who] comes round at midnight . . . he [who] can keep you from the sun'. The fact that Morrison felt prompted to write such songs in Ireland suggests he had his own share of Celtic ghosts to exorcize.

For once, though, the songs on *Veedon Fleece* also spoke of the healing power of love, a lesson he had allowed himself to forget at the end of his marriage. 'Comfort You' and 'Come Here, My Love' also 'melt together, top to tail'. Here at last are songs that speak of what he can do for her, rather than concerned solely with *his* needs and wants. In the latter, as he sings of 'this melancholy feeling that just don't do no good', he seems mystified by its presence. He offers to fly away with his love, to spend a couple of days 'contemplating the fields and leaves and talking about nothing'. Though he overstretches himself, becoming 'enraptured by the sights and sounds in intrigue of nature's beauty', this is no 'Autumn Song'. Rather, it sounds a lot like a man learning how to love again.

The remaining songs composed on that little trip to Ireland – 'Fair Play', 'Streets of Arklow', 'Cul de Sac' and the discarded 'Street Theory' – directly address the island and its heritage. In 'Fair Play' and 'Streets of Arklow' he is taking in 'the architecture . . . with my mind' – in the first case prompting a form of emotional recall familiar to any *Astral Weeks* visitant; in the latter, simply detailing a perfect day 'in God's green land', with 'our heads . . . filled with poetry'.

Indeed, for the first time since *Astral Weeks*, Morrison was willing to see himself in self-consciously poetic terms. The album even has its share of literary references – previously absent, subsequently omnipresent – with Poe, Wilde and Thoreau all getting name-checks in 'Fair Play', and William Blake 'and the sisters of mercy' permeating 'You Don't Pull No Punches'. Discussing the latter, Morrison admitted that – aside from 'flashes of Ireland' – the song had 'other flashes on other kinds of people. I was also reading a couple of books at the time . . . [there's] a bit of Gestalt theory in it, too.' He had begun to uncover aspects of a heritage previously denied him.

Van Morrison: We didn't get Irish writers at school. All we got was Shakespeare, no Irish writers. There wasn't one book by any Irish writer in our school. So I was just writing these songs instinctively, and then I read . . . where people were making references, you know, saying this is sort of Yeatsian and I would go 'Really?' Because I didn't know, I never read him . . . I'm doing all this backwards. I discovered all these connections later on when I read books. [1991]

'Cul de Sac' and 'Street Theory' also suggested someone 'doing all this backwards', both being, in quite different ways, reflections on the old streets. 'Cul de Sac' addresses the pull the East Belfast of his youth continued to exert. A song he refused to interpret for Ritchie Yorke, it is a reminder to his friends, as they 'all go home, down the cobblestones', that he too would sometimes like to 'double back to a cul-de-sac'. 'Street Theory' evokes the mischievous child within, ringing doorbells and running away, before dutifully going to church on Sundays 'just like my mama did'. The original 1974 recording finds the singer getting 'a lump in my throat/when I find it so hard to go back home', lines absent from its 1980 incarnation. The past clearly retained its power over the present, no matter how much he filled his head with others' poetry.

On his return to the Bay area, Morrison began to assemble all these scraps of poetry into songs with some kind of internal logic, hoping to record them as promptly as his personal studio and the ability to acquire a set of musicians would allow. He had only recently told a reporter, 'If there's something to put down, you have to go in and take care of it when it's happening.' An album of songs now presented itself, pleading to be captured in the moment of fresh inspiration, and it would not be denied. Two of the musicians he had in mind had experience of those times when, in the words of Daoud Shaw, 'he would come into the studio and all these little scraps of paper would come out, this envelope, a paper bag . . . He's not just coming up with this stuff. He's working on it.'

Van Morrison: *Veedon Fleece* was a bunch of songs that I wrote and then I just recorded it about four weeks after I wrote it. When you make an album you write some songs; you might have four songs and maybe you write two more, suddenly you've got enough songs for an album . . . The way I work . . . is basically spontaneous, in the moment, in the non-moment. I really don't think about it. I just do it. And afterwards, I really don't think about it either. It isn't that complicated for me. You have a certain set of musicians, you block out a time period, and you just *go* for it. And it comes out the way it comes out. [1978]

If the rhythm section came direct from the Caledonia Soul Orchestra, only one other musician received the call. The sound Morrison was hearing in his head represented a 180-degree turn from the grandiose arrangements of earlier in the year. Bassist David Hayes, drummer Dauod Shaw and keyboardist James Trumbo didn't take too long to suss out how it was going to be. Shaw surely speaks for the others when he says it was 'like going back to *Astral Weeks*'. Even the recording methodology resembled that landmark release, the abstract nature of some songs being left to resolve itself in the studio moment. The recordings were sometimes so *ad hoc* that the drummer's wife, Jean Shaw, was required to be the session engineer.★

Dauod Shaw: During that time I kinda haunted the studio, and Van would come in and we'd just do tracks. My wife at that time engineered a lot of those tracks. I showed her the console: 'That's the "record" button, that's the most important thing. As soon as he walks in, hit that button.' . . . [*Veedon Fleece*] was very acoustic. Hand drums, drums with brushes. David Hayes was playing acoustic bass . . . that would be the vibe – come in, set up as fast as you could and hit the 'record' button. Sometimes we would have these performances that would just go on and on and on. 'You Don't Pull No Punches' is a pretty long track. [When] that happened, it was just acoustic guitar, bass, drums and piano, and that was the track, and it went the whole distance. It was like a nice sine wave. Jeff [Labes later] built the string arrangement around that, but from the parts that were already played.

And, as with *Astral Weeks*, most of the songs worked out first time around. It was clear that any upgrade in technology was not going to impinge on the man's methodology – the search for spontaneity in its assigned moment. As David Hayes recalls, 'It was one of those [sets of] sessions where Van just walked in and started playing . . . Every night for about a week he came in with two or three new tunes and we just started playing with him.' What they were cutting, raw or reborn as some of it was, would retain the same core even when sweetened up.

Dauod Shaw: Sometimes we'd come in and it wasn't happening. We'd try two or three takes and that was it: 'Wrap it, forget about it, let's come back later.' The vibe was the most important thing in the studio – that chemistry with those players – and you either got magic or nothing, but you're not gonna get a preconceived [performance]. Once he had laid down his basic track, we would never get him to punch a vocal. That would be totally impossible! Leakage be damned!

★ Sessions took place in October and/or November 1973. Jeff Labes's contributions were overdubbed on to the basic tracks.

The sessions themselves seem to have inspired a further song, 'Come Here, My Love', which was added to the eight 'Irish' songs and one left-over from *Hard Nose the Highway* that fitted easily into this pastoral vibe, 'Country Fair'. The latter was a song Morrison admitted at the time had the same kind of feeling as 'And It Stoned Me', save that 'And It Stoned Me' opened up a new avenue, whereas 'Country Fair' proved to be some kind of closure.

Again, once everything that Morrison felt like recording was in the can, he proved surprisingly willing to relinquish control of this rich vein of material, leaving it to his drummer and trusty engineer to mix the tapes.

Dauod Shaw: He had hooked up with Jim Stern. Jim was an engineer at Fantasy at the time, and was instrumental in setting up Caledonia. Then I learned the console, and mixed *Veedon Fleece* with Jim Stern . . . It appeared to be a nice creative atmosphere. It looked like it couldn't be any more perfect . . . But [after the recording sessions], Van would leave, and that would be it – 'You mix it.' . . . I can't remember him ever saying, 'Wow, this is a great record.' Ever. 'Cept maybe after a take at a session, just nodding, or saying 'Yeah' . . . Once he's done [it in the studio], it's like he can turn the key – 'That's over' – and then he can hand it over to whoever – the producer, the mixer, the arranger.

Of course, Morrison continued to reserve the right to intervene. Indeed, after espousing an aesthetic where 'it comes out the way it comes out', Morrison couldn't resist tampering with the end product. Initially, any changes were fully in keeping with the spirit of the album as Morrison turned to Jeff Labes to embellish some of the songs with strings and flute – a combination associated with a certain previous album . . . When Labes heard the basic tracks, he certainly felt 'there was a little breath of *Astral Weeks* in there', but responded to the Larry Fallon role assigned him with an equal flair for the understated.

Jeff Labes: I was living in New York in those days, and he had the [basic] tracks, and he needed me to do [the] arranging on it . . . The first thing he played me was 'Don't Push the River'. At that point it was about twelve minutes long, and it just seemed to go on for ever – so I suggested a cut. We got it down to about nine minutes, and then I wrote some arrangements for woodwinds, and then we put some strings on it too . . . When we started [working on] the album, I started writing for oboe and clarinet. I was trying new things, on instruments I hadn't written for before.

The results pushed upstream everything caught at Caledonia. Whilst he was delighted with Labes's textures, Morrison still couldn't help but feel that the album was guilty of too great a uniformity of mood, a criticism he alone had made of the finished *Astral Weeks*. He decided to tinker some more with the song-sequence.

At the beginning of 1974, Morrison had assembled a looser, more flexible version of the Caledonia Soul Orchestra. The rechristened Caledonia Soul Express had been playing around the States, mixing up the sets and pulling out some real surprises for the fans, including 'Mystic Eyes', 'It's All Over Now, Baby Blue' and 'Friday's Child', the latter two in semi-acoustic mode, part of a three-song set with acoustic instruments. This set within a set usually featured at least one song from *Astral Weeks*, 'Ballerina' and/or 'Astral Weeks', and the occasional 'Streets of Arklow', a solitary début from *Veedon Fleece*.

Morrison, it seems, had tired of the formality that came with the CSO. Three years later, he would insist that he 'was [simply] beginning to realize that there was nothing else to do within that particular context. We'd been doing practically the same show for five years . . . Instinctively, I knew when it was over.' Dauod Shaw, who stayed put behind the drum kit, recognized the symptoms.

Dauod Shaw: I think Van is into changing elements ever so slightly, and accepting change, but he's also perceptive enough when something clicks to say, 'This is fun. Let's do this.' He'll always leave himself open to that.

In the case of *Veedon Fleece*, the compulsion to change 'elements ever so slightly' blew this beautiful vision off course as Morrison made a belated decision to recut a couple of songs in New York. The way Labes remembers it, 'He wanted to redo "Bulbs" and "Cul de Sac", 'cause he didn't feel they had the right feeling . . . It was me, Van and a bunch of other guys that he'd never played with.' Where exactly Morrison came up with guitarist John Tropea, bassist Joe Macho and drummer Allen Schwarzberg, he alone knows. Why he chose not to use the band he was gigging with, preferably in some stripped-down guise, was another whim he kept to himself (he *had* already re-recorded 'Street Theory', as well as 'Twilight Zone' and 'Caldonia', with the Caledonia Soul Express).

In all likelihood it was a less than rapturous response from Warners to the album that prompted Morrison to push the boat out again. Certainly 'Bulbs', which had been recorded with different lyrics at the *Hard Nose* sessions, had little in common with the songs recorded in California. When questioned about the song by Yorke, Morrison said that it was definitely going to be the single, but that there was 'nothing [else] to say about it'. And the single it would be, backed by 'Cul de Sac', which was also now given a full rock treatment. With these two songs 'jarringly misplaced' at the start of side two, *Veedon Fleece* lost a little of its integrity. Only with 'Comfort You' did the album return to a more appropriate power level.

With its new running order and requisite overdubs in place before Morrison's return to Europe in the spring, Warners had their first Van Morrison studio album in a year. But it was not the album they wanted. Nor did they have a slot in their schedule for another Van Morrison studio album at this point. Instead, in March 1974, they issued the much-awaited double set of the now-defunct Caledonia Soul Orchestra, the legendary *It's Too Late to Stop Now*, to almost universal plaudits and highly respectable sales from the traditionally sluggish live-souvenir market. In the US, they even splashed out on a triple fold-out sleeve. The last thing they needed was *another* Morrison album in the stores, particularly one on which, in the words of Irish journalist Jack Lynch, 'Morrison's singing style cloaks the immediate understanding of many of the words and phrases by a smooth vocal slurring, [whilst] words constantly deliquesce, making the feel of the songs paramount and the decipherment a long-term process.'

Morrison's own feelings about *It's Too Late to Stop Now* were ambivalent. He had always aspired to make a live album that showed the breadth and range at his command. As he'd observed back in 1971, 'I do a lot of different styles . . . I can't get all my music on one album so I try to vary it as much as I can . . . Eventually, I'd just like to record live. It's a true form.' And yet it would be a long time before he would attempt to replicate the type of show captured on *It's Too Late to Stop Now*, perhaps because, as Phil Coulter suggests, 'In Van's book the way to react to that success was to dismantle it.' He was evidently uncomfortable with any fixed view of himself as a performer, feeling it imposed another burden he would now have to live down. Paul Jones, of Manfred Mann fame, tells a story of how Van appeared on his BBC radio show in the early eighties and when Jones, leading off with a track from *It's Too Late to*

Stop Now, called it one of the great releases of the last decade, Morrison responded, 'Well, [maybe] you can hear it. I can't.'

Much as he viewed the whole 'live double album' as little more than record-company product, Morrison was still very careful what songs he allowed on it. The selection seems to have been dictated, at least in part, by the publishing rights in question. Certainly the omission of two outstanding arrangements from *Astral Weeks*, 'The Way Young Lovers Do' and 'Sweet Thing', cannot have been made on musical grounds – nor can the all too obvious omission of 'Brown Eyed Girl', one of the highlights of the Rainbow TV broadcast.

When Morrison returned to Europe in March, hot on the live album's heels, he seemed wholly uninterested in promoting it. Instead journalists found him enthusing about an album Warners were already shunting down their schedule, enticingly describing *Veedon Fleece* to one journalist as having 'a lot of quiet music, sort of like *Astral Weeks*. Long, improvised songs with lots of acoustic guitar.' Morrison also let rip at Warners and their so-called release schedules: '*Veedon Fleece* was finished in the spring, yet it won't come out until the autumn. I wish I had more control over things like release dates . . . It takes so long to get them out sometimes that I really can't believe it.'

And yet the European shows that spring provided very little evidence of the album he was championing. According to Ritchie Yorke, who was able to tag along in Dublin, where Morrison was scheduled to play four shows over two nights at the end of March, the Belfast cowboy intended to make the first half of the show acoustic, playing 'Madame George', 'Astral Weeks' and 'Ballerina', as well as four songs from the forthcoming album – a gesture that would inevitably have drawn parallels between the respective collections.

However, Morrison contracted a bad case of the flu and the acoustic set was trimmed, and then dropped. Even in the electric sets, though, the *Veedon Fleece* songs remained on the shelf until the final night, at London's Hammersmith Odeon, when he pulled out 'Bulbs' and, as an audacious first encore, a ten-and-a-half-minute, one-off rendition of 'You Don't Pull No Punches'. Asked at the time about the contradictions at work in the live set, bassist David Hayes suggested that 'a lot of very good tunes, a lot of the new tunes, get thrown aside . . . [Though] the sessions were fantastic, we can't seem to get them happening on stage'.

No second opportunity would be afforded. If Morrison chose to sideline the *Veedon Fleece* songs that spring, they never returned to centre stage.* By the time the album was actually released, in October 1974, the only song on it to feature regularly in Morrison's live repertoire was 'Bulbs', a song that never truly belonged on the album. Greeted by a mixed bag of reviews, the album was depicted as almost an afterthought to the incandescent *It's Too Late to Stop Now*. Gary Herman, in his *Let It Rock* review, even accused Morrison of hiding behind his music:

I for one feel uneasy about communicators who won't communicate; who go beyond their sadness and doubt to allow that same sadness and doubt to become an excuse – just one more reason for failing to get through or for ceasing to progress . . . On too many tracks he falls behind the instruments – blotted out by a particularly nifty bass line, some shimmering piano or a pastoral flute.

If *NME*'s Nick Kent seemed an almost solitary advocate for the album, describing it as 'his most intriguing project since *Astral Weeks*', he still called it 'nigh impenetrable . . . at times, at others downright off-the-wall loony'. It would take most of his fellow critics some time to break through its well-nigh impenetrability, and a few more spins of the wheel before the more astute began to champion *Veedon Fleece* as Morrison's great lost masterpiece. In recent years, it has been called 'almost faultless . . . [with] little to jar or date'; 'a touchstone of deep mysteries and some kind of inner healing . . . a perfect B-side of a C-90 to *Astral Weeks*, [that] seems to me that album's equal'; and, the first side in particular, 'as coherent a set of songs, sounds and performances as any other sequence in Van Morrison's recorded work'. All true. Duly recognized in the fullness of time.

Veedon Fleece closed what could be designated the Warners era by delivering on much of the promise of *Astral Weeks*, albeit with attendant sales resulting from a return to the same non-commercial base as his Warners début. Unconcerned with trends and styles, focusing solely on the music, buoyed by a lyrical well of inspiration all too often suppressed, Morrison again displayed a welcome disregard for where his contemporaries might be heading.

---

* Only 'Streets of Arklow' from *Veedon Fleece* was featured in the acoustic set in Europe, as it had been in the US. In subsequent years, only 'Bulbs' has ever featured in live shows, making *Veedon Fleece* by far the most underplayed album in the man's canon, though a recently surfaced tape of an autumn 1974 show in Anaheim reveals a one-off 'Cul de Sac'.

He would take a certain delight in reminding various critics, a few years down the line, of their initial antipathy to the album. By then, he really was putting out albums with which these same critics found it hard to connect.

Van Morrison: You put albums out and people somehow get the wrong end of the stick and start reviewing the album . . . as being about *something* . . . When *Veedon Fleece* came out a lot of people fuckin' hated it! Five years later the same people love it all of a sudden. [1979]

The critics' sense of dislocation would not be theirs alone. It would take Morrison just as long to stumble upon the same deep well again.

18

1974–75: Naked to the World

In the past year, I've managed to please a lot of audiences; when it gets to that point, then it's time for me to be myself . . . It's hard for me to do all that show-business stuff. All these hundreds of people show up and want to be involved. I've just reached the point where I don't want to deal with those people.

—*Van Morrison, 1974*

If you don't like it, go fuck yourself.

—*Van Morrison to a member of the audience,*
Montreux Jazz Festival 30 June 1974

The Caledonia Soul Express remains one of Morrison's most schizo-phrenic set-ups as a live performer. On one level, it was merely a slimmed-down CSO, performing many of the same songs as those on the live double album, minus the big-band arrangements. But it was also prone to shifting into acoustic mode for a trip down memory lane; or vamping through a series of jazz instrumentals (much to the bafflement of many an audience); or seguing into R&B favourites like 'Kansas City', 'I Like It Like That' and 'The Night Time Is the Right Time'.

Dauod Shaw: We shoved an awful lot of stuff down those audiences' throats that they probably really didn't want to hear, but *we* were having a great time.

Crafted in its creator's image, the Caledonia Soul Express was an attempt to escape the confines of prearranged sets and predictable arrangements, yet playing to audiences expecting both. As David Hayes observed at the time, 'We make up the set-list just before we go on. After a couple of weeks, you start to get afraid of the tunes you haven't played in a week or two, so you drop them.'

And yet Morrison was not entirely disregarding his audiences. He seemed willing to 'reward' hipper audiences, say at San Francisco's Winterland or London's Hammersmith Odeon, with songs outside the official canon such as 'Family Affair' (later rechristened 'Try for Sleep'), 'Wonderful Remark' and 'Twilight Zone'; or those still awaiting release like 'Streets of Arklow', 'Bulbs' and 'You Don't Pull No Punches'. In Kansas City and Vancouver he stuck with more familiar favourites – whilst in Cambridge, Massachusetts, he tacitly acknowledged the part the town played in his history by performing three songs from *Astral Weeks* in the acoustic set.

The expectations of his audience would plague Morrison for the next twelve months, as he resisted every preconception, all the while railing at any consequences attendant upon each display of perversity – poor reviews, disaffected audiences, disappointing sales. In May 1974, the first mystifying clue to his confused state came with the release of a seven-inch 45 credited to Van Morrison and the Caledonia Soul Express. It perhaps should have been issued on a ten-inch 78. 'Caldonia (What Makes Your Big Head Hard?)', a Fleecie Moore composition from the jump era,★ was backed by the equally surreal 'What's Up, Crazy Pup?' If Warners were humouring him by releasing it at all, they certainly weren't about to promote it, and the single sank like shellac, despite both songs being given regular airings at the spring shows. The other song to post-date *Veedon Fleece* in composition, 'Twilight Zone', adopted the falsetto used on 'Who's That Masked Man?', but suggested none of the lyricism of its immediate predecessor, being largely an excuse to recite the entry for 'zone' from a rhyming dictionary: bone, known, phone – did I mention honeycomb, honey comb . . . ?

Morrison, to his credit, refused to be dissuaded from his new path, reaching for a greater musical freedom. When he indicated his intentions to his manager, Pillster gave him his honest opinion, thus ending their association. Morrison told Yorke that he 'just stopped doing what I

★ Fleecie Moore was the wife of Louis Jordan, in whose name he copyrighted a number of songs whilst in dispute with his music publishers. When she subsequently divorced him, he lost the songs for good.

wanted . . . He was working for me, but it ended up he wasn't working for me. So we just couldn't go any further' – a familiar enough incantation from an increasingly difficult artist.

The Caledonia Soul Express was also deemed surplus to requirements that spring, as Morrison cleared the decks of all prior associations. When he arrived at the Montreux Jazz Festival in June, though, he refused to admit that they had definitively parted company, telling one journalist, 'Right now I'm experimenting with other things . . . [but] I don't think anything is the be-all and end-all . . . The thing with me is that I am definitely not a programmed performer. I can only perform when I feel like I want to perform and it's coming out of me. It's hard for me to just push a button and start performing.'

In Montreux a familiar conflict arose between his own thirst for spontaneity and an audience's preference for being eased into any new musical progression. Talking at a point, less than a year later, when he had decided enough was enough, Morrison would reveal his concern that as soon as 'you are committed to a series of concerts you lose all spontaneity. It's not jazz any more. The reason I first got into music and the reason I was then doing it were conflicting. It was such a paradox.' Getting this across to fans and critics would never come harder than in 1974.

Van Morrison: What I'm trying to get at is that music to me is spontaneous, writing is spontaneous, and it's all based on not trying to do it, y'know? . . . That's my trip from beginning to end, whether it's writing a song or playing guitar, or a particular chord sequence, or blowing a horn, or whatever it is, it's based on improvisation and spontaneity. That's what I keep trying to get across in interviews, and it's very hard because the process is beyond words. [1978]

The first clue that Morrison was preparing to remove his musical safety net came when he phoned his loyal road manager, Ed Fletcher, to tell him about the first booking of the summer:

Ed Fletcher: Van called me up and said, 'Hey Ed, we're gonna go to Montreux.' I said, 'OK, I'll call the guys.' And he said, 'No, no, we're not gonna bring the band over there. We're just gonna go over and do this gig. Claude [Nobbs] says there're guys [there] we can play with.' And I'm going, 'Oh God! That could be rough, if they don't know your stuff . . .' 'Ah, he's given 'em some albums. [Anyway,] we'll have a couple of rehearsal days.'

The albums in question would have provided precious little aid to the hapless musicians, Morrison playing exactly one released song in his hour-long set at Montreux – and that was one absent from the set since 1971. Nor was there a band waiting for Morrison on landing – just drummer Dallas Taylor, of Crosby, Stills, Nash and Young fame, brought along at Bill Wyman's instigation; and British keyboardist Pete Wingfield. Wingfield had received a phone call from organizer Claude Nobbs, saying, 'Look, Morrison is coming over. He's got no manager, he's just sacked his band. He's just coming with his girlfriend and his roadie. Would you come?' Wingfield admits he wasn't too familiar with the records. 'It didn't matter . . . because Van didn't want to do any of his songs. He wanted to do all these Bobby Bland numbers.' The bass player didn't even have those few Morrison albums to learn the man's schtick.

Ed Fletcher: We see Claude Nobbs and I say, 'OK, so . . . where's the musicians?' There was one guy there – Pete Wingfield. There's a guy who plays bass who's supposed to be there, from a group called Back Door. Bill Wyman [then] brought Dallas Taylor by. But [still] no bass player. So I go out in this [hospitality] room. There's all these musicians . . . they'd bring over to back up the blues artists. Anyhow I go in this room and . . . I go, 'Are there any bass players?' Three guys raise their hands. Two white guys and a black guy. 'OK, where are you [guys] from?' [And Jerome Rimson says,] 'Detroit City.' 'You're from Detroit City? Come with me.' So we went and did the jazz festival. They did a couple of rehearsals. [But] it wasn't the most awe-inspiring set I ever heard. They were catcalling a bit, [and] some Frenchwoman shouted from the audience, 'Those are not the blues.'

All things considered, it was a remarkably tolerant audience to whom Morrison débuted his new sound. Even after the first four songs – all unreleased: one cover, 'I Like It Like That'; 'Twilight Zone'; 'Bulbs'; and a new tune, 'Foggy Mountain Top' – he continued to receive respectful applause. Morrison was still determined to push his luck, following an energetic 'Bulbs' with two ersatz-jazz instrumentals. Returning to the mike after a few muttered instructions, he continued to baffle all comers with another funky vamp, 'Naked in the Jungle', the lyrics of which detailed someone 'naked to the world/gotta keep 'em humble, or else you'll come unfurled'. When he finally unfurled 'Street Choir', the shock of recognition alone prompted a healthy smattering of cheers. However, it was a brief respite from confusion, the band conclud-ing with another instrumental.

When Morrison returned for an ill-deserved encore, after a good three minutes of insistent hand-clapping, a Gallic woman in the front row told him in no uncertain terms to leave the blues to black people. Ever the gentleman, Morrison responded by telling her to go fuck herself. He then attempted to justify his performance, informing her, 'There's a guy paying me to stand on this stage, and that's what I'm doing. If you don't like it, do you want to come up on stage and do it? Do *you* want to come up here and do it? The only blues you know are on your shoes.' Just to rub more aural salt into the poor woman's wounded pride, Morrison played out with the Lenny Welch standard, 'Since I Fell for You'.

As Ed Fletcher concisely observes, 'not the most awe-inspiring set'. Audacious, ambitious, but hardly appropriate. It wasn't very good jazz, and it was hardly the most accessible introduction to the work of George Ivan Morrison. The musicians themselves were as perplexed as the audience. Certainly Dallas Taylor wasn't too sure he wanted to take this any further, and made his feelings known. Meanwhile, Jerome Rimson was introducing road manager Ed Fletcher to a friend of his, drummer Peter Van Hooke, at a music fair the morning after the débâcle before. When Van Hooke gave an impromptu demo on a set of Sonor drums, Fletcher became convinced that he was the perfect replacement for the disenchanted Taylor. Morrison, though, would take further convincing.

Ed Fletcher: Van [had been] moved by the trio and wanted to play some gigs. We were suddenly doing these make-up dates [in Europe], and Dallas Taylor, [who] was trying to change some of his lifestyle, couldn't keep up with things. Not that I ever called the shots, [but] I told Van about Van Hooke. I said, 'Go see him.' He never went and saw him. Came the day [Van Hooke had to leave] – he was ready to get on the bus – and I [actually] put it on the line [with Van]: 'Trust me, this guy'll make a lot of difference. I just have this really strong feeling.' I couldn't understand why he wouldn't go and listen to him. And then, at the last minute, Van said, 'Go get him.' Sight unheard. And he did the [remaining] dates.

Van Hooke believes that Morrison *had* heard him play, with Eddie Vinson at the festival. He had certainly caught Morrison's own set. Despite having 'no idea who [Morrison] was', Van Hooke was impressed: 'The first thing he sang was a ballad. And I listened to the concert and I thought, "God! I could do this," [but] didn't think any more of it . . . I was off on holiday to Cyprus . . . [when] I got this note from Ed saying, "Don't take that plane!" The first time I met Van was probably on the plane. We went to Hamburg, and I think we did the first concert that night.'

If Morrison again had a rhythm section that played in tandem, his experience at Montreux had not dissuaded him from his chosen course. The German shows were equally disorienting, even if the ninety-minute sets incorporated half a dozen highlights from *It's Too Late to Stop Now* as a sop to any French ladies. He would need more than a few gratuitous sops to appease the audience at the final show of this mini-tour, three weeks after Montreux, and the real money-spinner on this little jaunt: co-headlining an open-air festival at Knebworth Park, in the heart of Herts.

Thankfully, as the tour progressed, Morrison's moods acquired some upward motion and he began to enjoy the experience of playing with such a flexible unit, one without preconceptions as to what they should play. He also enjoyed the personal rapport established with British musicians like Wingfield and Van Hooke (both of whom would become long-term associates) and, when he landed in London, he chose to stay at Peter Van Hooke's house rather than some impersonal hotel. Indeed, the Van Hooke household became Morrison's preferred base whenever he came to London, as he now did on a regular basis. The day before the Knebworth event, Van Hooke invited his musician friend John Altman round to meet Morrison. They immediately hit it off, each enthusing about the particular brand of anarchic British humour they shared. Altman accompanied the quartet to Knebworth, where the ribald mood persisted.

John Altman: Van had a caravan, but balanced on a log, and what we found was that if we stood at one end of it, it tipped, and then if we all ran at the same time to the other end it tipped the other way. So you have [co-headliners] the Allman Brothers all posing around, being 'rock stars' – and then you got this trailer going up and down, with [all] these people hooting with laughter.

Such informality spilled over to the stage, as a bespectacled Morrison in casual shirt and jeans led the band into an instrumental shuffle. However, this was not destined to be another Montreux, as Morrison astutely intertwined new songs with more recognizable tunes, slipping in a magnificent 'Listen to the Lion' and a syncopated 'Into the Mystic' amid largely unfamiliar fare in the first half of the set. After a powerful 'Since I Fell for You', Morrison began to give the crowd more of what they wanted, playing four consecutive *It's Too Late to Stop Now* faves – 'Help Me', 'I Believe to My Soul', 'I've Been Working' and 'Take Your Hands out of My Pocket' – before 'Naked in the Jungle' and 'Brown Eyed Girl' left the large crowd bellowing for more. The seventy-five-minute set was rapturously received, with even the new songs making inroads.

Morrison had spent his last couple of days in mainland Europe getting these very songs down on tape whilst they remained vibrant, having recently informed his current chronicler that he'd like to 'take a song on the road for a couple of months and live with it for a while – that would be the best time to record it'. In Hilversum, Holland, he set out to test that theory.

The results of the sessions in Holland were impressive even for a man known to cut songs in a hurry of inspiration. Three years later, after the material's non-appearance had imbued it with a certain mythical status, Morrison would suggest that the sessions were 'more or less [an excuse for] a blow and we ran the tape . . . Really, the whole thing was just getting out of the hotel because we had this gig in Amsterdam that was supposed to happen on a certain day and then went wrong. You go nuts if you're in a hotel all the time.'

At the time, though, Morrison was a far more willing proselytizer, portraying the results as his next but one album. He would inform *Sounds* journalist Rob Mackie in his unstable Knebworth trailer that '*Veedon Fleece* is supposed to be out now, and . . . the album I've just recorded . . . is called *Naked in the Jungle/Mechanical Bliss*. And then I might do a live one in the fall.' Quite how Warners felt about these plans went unmentioned, though they signally failed to release the results.

And still Morrison continued to talk about these songs as his forth-coming album, even previewing four of them during an impromptu appearance on Tom Donahue's KPFA radio show that autumn – 'Naked in the Jungle', 'Twilight Zone', 'Mechanical Bliss' and a tune named after a comedy radio show from his youth, 'Much Binding in the Marshes', one of a handful of instrumentals they'd recorded. Also captured at the snappily-named Wisseloord studios in Hilversum were Morrison's reworking of 'T for Texas', 'Foggy Mountain Top', and a song left over from the Jackie DeShannon sessions back in 1972,

'Flamingoes Fly', which Pete Wingfield later described as 'so off the wall, and I was so shaken by it, that I had to go for a walk around the block in the middle of the night. I just couldn't take it.'*

It was probably the instrumentals that most freaked out the folks back at Warners. The man had just delivered a 'difficult' new album and before they could even stop dragging their heels and deliver it to the shops, he already had another 'album' in the can, this one featuring his music-hall impersonation of an English toff ('Mechanical Bliss'), a couple of meandering instrumentals, and a pair of eight-minute songs that burbled on about watching flamingoes fly, and how honeycomb is not the twilight zone.

Morrison was fast becoming one of the more worrisome artists on the Warners roster – difficult to work with, unwilling to accommodate, but expecting total cooperation. Despite never delivering an album that captured the American public's imagination like Neil Young's *Harvest*, James Taylor's *Sweet Baby James* or Joni Mitchell's *Blue* – not even *Moondance* – he continued to think of himself as having similar corporate clout. Sure, any of the above could behave in a way to make even the very prima of donnas blush, but at least they all paid lip-service to the Warners mind-set. But not Morrison. Jeff Labes recalls one particular press party Warners laid on for Morrison's benefit:

Jeff Labes: We had the new album with us – *Hard Nose the Highway* – and Van reacted very badly to some reporters. They were there to ask him questions. He actually struck somebody, saying, 'That's none of your goddamn business!' He was definitely conflicted about that.

Such an explosive overreaction did nothing to retrieve ground lost in his commercial stock; such outbursts merely promoted the legend of Belfast's curmudgeonly cowboy, taking attention away from the music. Morrison's response to his diminishing hold on the American music media – prompted by Pillster – was to come up with the ultimate counterproductive press kit: a professionally-produced, seventy-two-page book entitled *Reliable Sources*.

According to its introductory page, '*Reliable Sources* is a compendium of facts, opinions and impressions of Van Morrison – singer, songwriter, performer. It contains everything you wanted to know about Van and

---

* The Dutch recording of 'Flamingoes Fly' appears on *The Philosopher's Stone*.

never asked. It is a resource, a reference, and should clarify myths and answer almost any question.' However, according to Morrison, its actual intent was, 'to show how ridiculous the journalists were, and the press in general. I don't know if I accomplished that . . . [but] I'm just concerned with getting to my audience. I care about what my audience thinks. But if people are going to tell my audience things that aren't true, I don't need that.'

Needless to say, *Reliable Sources* was as valuable a resource for those wishing to puncture the man's ego as for those willing to inflate it. The departure of Pillster only made Morrison appear more hostile to the media. When the time came to promote *Veedon Fleece*, he approved a full-page ad that comprised a shot of the album cover, a list of concert dates and a single quote, clearly designed to raise two fingers to the press:

Really the only thing that's important is that I play music for people to hear, either on album or at concerts. That's it, the music and the people. All the other stuff – the personal managers, the photographs and the publicity kits [*sic*] and the articles and the pressure merchants and the music magazines – so much of it is bullshit . . .'Cause in the end it all comes back to music.

Quite so. And yet the absence of any quotes from the reviews of *Veedon Fleece* smacked of sour grapes, especially towards *Rolling Stone*, which was guilty of giving the album cursory attention and precious little regard. In the sleeve notes he intended for *Philosopher's Stone*, Morrison recalled sitting in the back of a car, reading the *Rolling Stone* review, and thinking, 'It's time for me to get out of this right now. This is the right time.' At a twenty-three-year remove, he insisted that he had known *Veedon Fleece* was not going to sell, that the record company had known this too, and that the prospect of beckoning anonymity had filled him with a rare joy – none of which explains why, after the so-called *Veedon Fleece* tour that autumn, where he confined himself to playing 'Bulbs' from his latest waxing, he turned on his main supporter at Warners with a fury that permanently alienated the man previously most inclined to fight his corner:

Joe Smith: He was such a hostile, difficult guy. He really didn't get along with anybody, but he got along with me less bad than with others . . . Soon I became his only contact at the company. He was so self-destructive professionally. He would tour six, eight months after his record came out . . . The tour never helped the record, and the record never helped the tour. But finally, in 1975 [*sic*], Van made a record, and he was about to go on tour. We're now going to seize the opportunity and break him wide open. Van had certain demands. He wanted someone from the company to travel with him. He wanted Jon Landau . . . to do an interview with him. He wanted a bunch of other things. I said OK to everything . . . His first stop was Dallas. Everything went well . . . and now I go to England . . . I come back on a Thursday, the day before Christmas Eve . . . I'm jet-lagged and I haven't bought any Christmas gifts. I get a call from Van's agent, Peter Golden, and he says Van wants to meet with me. I say, 'Can't this wait until after the holidays?' . . . 'No. It's an emergency.' Van and Peter arrive with Van's lawyer, Bob Gordon, at 1.30. The building is closing down. Van comes in and sits in front of my desk . . . in a suit and tie, very dignified. He picks up a trade paper and begins going through a litany of things that didn't go right on the tour . . . I say, 'Time out. I've been away for a month. Everyone's gone home for Christmas. Can't this wait until after the holidays?' As I'm talking, Van stands up and screams at me, 'You fucking liar! You're just like everybody else. I didn't think you were a liar, but you're just like everybody else.' He's screaming, getting red in the face. So I scream, 'Stop yelling at me and sit down. I have Christmas shopping to do. I promise you, after the New Year I'll find out what went down.' Van stands up again, and he's screaming again. But now he takes the trade paper and slams it down on a set of Cross pens I have on my desk . . . [breaking] both pens. Normally I'm not a violent person, but I'm jet-lagged and aggravated and I blew [my top]. I grabbed Van by the tie and collar and I yanked his head down on to the desk. I picked up my broken pen set, and I started screaming, 'You broke my pen set!' . . . Out of the corner of my eye I see that Peter and Bob have gone slightly ashen. Van is a little pale, too. I pushed him. I screamed, 'Get out of here, all of you. I don't ever want to see you again.'

When Morrison shortly afterwards wrote a lyric about 'cut[ting] my nose to spite my face/made my own odds ten thousand to one' in 'I Have Finally Come to Realize', he would have no better example to hand. Relations with Warners would never be as good again. The deteriorating situation prompted at least one more bilious ditty, 'Not Working for You', in which he tells some abstract entity that he isn't prepared to be their boy any more, so they had better get used to 'one less nigger' minding the store.

Various conversations with Frank Zappa – himself about to become embroiled in an acrimonious dispute with Warners over a four-album conceptual work called *Läther* – convinced Morrison that he had found someone who 'says things about how it works, what you shouldn't let happen, and what . . . should happen'. Zappa's example may have only inspired a greater belligerence. Such an attitude did neither Zappa nor Morrison much good. Morrison, though, had already decided he had had enough and, after two years of sporadic but regular touring, he pulled the plug on such 'promotional' operations.

Van Morrison: I was completely at the end of my rope. I was doing gigs, I was uptight, I wasn't getting anything out of it . . . And I remember I was . . . sitting in my hotel room looking out the window, and I was thinking, 'This isn't worth it, man.' I'd done two American and two European tours in the 1973–74 period. These record-company people were always ear-bending with their line, 'He never works.' I blew that one out the window. So I was just kind of sitting, thinking that I had all those people, doing these gigs, and something wasn't right. I wasn't getting off, it wasn't what I had planned my life to be like. I wasn't going to let show business control my life. So I decided to take a break, get my shit together for me, and think about what I was doing . . . [But] it was a conscious decision. [1978]

On 30 December 1974 Morrison made his last planned appearance for a while, popping up at the Keystone in Berkeley at a benefit for Tex Coleman, an old friend of John Lee Hooker's, who had badly burned his hand in an accident. The evening, intended to help towards Coleman's medical expenses, featured sets by both Hooker and Elvin Bishop of Paul Butterfield Band fame, as well as an hour-long jam featuring Morrison fronting Bishop's band, working through familiar fare like 'Trouble in Mind', 'Bring It on Home', 'Help Me' and 'Baby Please Don't Go'. Morrison said afterwards that he had expected a more relaxing evening, and expressed disappointment that his name had been included in the publicity, as if the purpose of the concert was to give him an outlet for informal jamming and not to raise funds for someone a whole lot less fortunate than himself.

If gigging had begun to lose its appeal, the strictures of recording weren't far behind. The supposed freedom his own studio provided had become just another burden. As he told Jeff Labes at this time, '[It] looks like freedom but in the end it's much better to be pressured, 'cause then you really get right down to the business.' The recordings made in the early months of 1975 were unfocused, suggesting no obvious niche.

Originally, he may have harboured the hope that they could be integrated with the material from Hilversum – as he re-recorded 'Naked in the Jungle' for the *n*th time.

According to Morrison, he also sought 'to renegotiate my contract . . . after *Veedon Fleece* . . . It was a reaction to doing too much.' And yet, according to the man who would have to go through the 1975 tapes for the *Philosopher's Stone* set, engineer Walter Samuel, 'He was always in the studio, and [when] he made recordings that he then decided weren't good enough . . . he went on to do [them] again. So there were two albums' worth of material [from this period] that never saw the light of day.'

These 'two albums' retained the same core material, reworked in a more pressurized situation at Record Plant after initial sessions at Caledonia.★ Morrison apparently had very little in the way of finished songs when work began, hence presumably 'Naked in the Jungle' and Merle Travis's world-weary 'Sixteen Tons' (its line about selling one's soul to the company store constituting another dig at Warners). Three originals were also realized: of these, 'Joyous Sound' had already been aired at the autumn shows, while 'The Street Only Knew Your Name' took the specialness of one's street from 'Street Theory', and developed it into a lyrical longing for a time 'before fortune and fame/ No such thing as a star when you've played that game'. However, it was 'I Have Finally Come to Realize' that suggested someone who finally aspired to self-awareness, with just a trace of humility in the face of revelation: 'I saw that it was not up to me/I'm just one tiny, tiny grain of sand'.

This was one troubled man. As Morrison wrote in another song from this period ('Down to Earth'), it can be very painful to witness one's metaphorical death and (re)birth. He had come to feel that his immersion in the fame game had drowned his very soul. It was something he would only later articulate, 'Most artists go through an identity crisis about who they really are . . . When they finally realize that they're not what they thought they were, [they] have [already] built up that part of their identity to the point where it's overtaken everything else.' But in 1975 the inner struggle went on away from prying eyes. Even the songs that documented

---

★ The recordings lodged with Warners were made on both eight-track and sixteen-track machines. It is highly unlikely that the Record Plant would have been using eight-track as late as 1975, though Caledonia continued to do so.

the process would be held in check. Only when Morrison felt that he had come out the other side did it become something he would discuss.

Van Morrison: You go through periods and you get to one level, and you get to that level and you find that there's as much problems as the other level, and you go through the levels, and none of them are IT, you know? Nothing that you can do is IT . . . The whole point is, dig yourself . . . I went through some *identity* thing, some shit like that, what they call in psychology an identity crisis, but what it is, as a matter of fact, is called *growth*. [1977]

He was having a hard time learning to dig himself – though, as he wrote in one of the new songs, 'It Hurts When You Want It So Bad'. It was a pain he now dated all the way back to being an only child, and wanting a baby brother. In many ways, the songs he summoned up in the spring of 1975 stand as the most confessional songs in the man's canon – hence perhaps the reason why they would not be permitted to enter the public arena for another two decades.

A song called 'When I Deliver' even gave the game away about his 'craft'. This six-and-a-half-minute tirade depicted the blues as something that came through him, not from him. All he had to do was learn to sing it naturally. Morrison here attempts to convey some sense of that moment, usually late at night, when one is thinking about poetry and jazz, and it begins to come through as a series of images. 'When I Deliver' was primal therapy in song. It was never likely to be something Warners might dig themselves, as Morrison must have known.

In fact, when the sessions moved to the Record Plant in Sausalito later that spring, 'When I Deliver' made way for the likes of 'Down to Earth' and 'It Hurts When You Want It So Bad'. The Record Plant sessions seemed to signal the end for both Caledonia Studio, which ceased to be the centre of Morrison's recording activities, and the Hilversum 'album', which became permanently interred in the Warners vault. These new sessions attempted another medley of original and cover material, combining the sort of blues he had derived second-hand, like Lead Belly's 'Western Plains', the traditional 'John Henry' and Little Willie John's 'All Around the World', with Morrison's own form of late-night lyrics.

Van Morrison: The music I really like to get off on is the old rhythm & blues and rock & roll stuff . . . That's what I really dig. And I also dig to sing ballads as well. And I also dig writing my own songs. I was just trying to find a way of integrating the whole thing. [1977]

This attempt at 'integrating the whole thing' may have been part of a strategy to reinvigorate his audience in the wake of *Veedon Fleece*'s fleeting appearance in the charts. A year of testing his fan base had reaped few rewards. When he announced a series of shows at San Francisco's Great American Music Hall in March 1975, retaining the same musicians with whom he was recording, the response from his most loyal public was muted at best, especially after they read of Morrison's intentions in the *Chronicle*:

It'll be a pilot gig for other gigs to take off from. I'm getting into something different; out of old songs, more into an instrumental thing – freer-type improvisation on horn . . . [I'll be] singing songs I've recorded, new songs I've just written and instrumentals. It's a different trip. I just don't want people to come expecting me to be singing 'Domino' or something.

Nor did they – come, that is. Further shows at the same venue the following month were to be Morrison's last concert appearances for three and a half years, guest appearances and private gigs excepted. The fortunate few were rewarded with a fair number of surprises, including a twelve-minute 'Saint Dominic's Preview' that took in parts of 'You Can't Always Get What You Want' and 'Walk on the Wild Side'. Morrison also turned over those 'TB Sheets'. However, he had just reached a point where it all seemed, well, pointless. Even the old-time music that had previously sustained him failed to lift the burden.

There would be the occasional half-hearted, unannounced appearance at small clubs in Santa Barbara, Cotati or Santa Cruz that spring; even the odd call to his latest set of musicians at two or three in the morning, suggesting that they record something. But, as Morrison would admit with hindsight, 'I got burnt out on recording. When you're free to go in the studio anytime day or night, it's quite easy to overdo it – and that's precisely what happened to me . . . One day I found out that I just wasn't getting into it any longer.' The Record Plant album would never be completed. Two years on from those memorable Too Late to Stop Now performances, Morrison finally came to realize it was never too late to stop.

Van Morrison: There was a period where I didn't write . . . I didn't do anything. I didn't play guitar, I didn't even listen to music. I had overdosed . . . It was a period where I just completely overdosed. It was about '75 . . . I just had to stop. I had had enough. I was mentally exhausted, physically exhausted and I just needed to get away from music completely. [1981]

19

1975–77: Not Working for You

The commercial thing is fine, but you can never really pin it down. Artists suddenly get real hot and then . . . they just as quickly get cold . . . Honestly, I don't know what it all means except that you either do what you think is right – and stick with it – or you go along with current trends. But whatever you decide to do, you've got to be prepared for the consequences.

—*Van Morrison, 1977*

By the summer of 1975 Morrison's career had arrived at a commercial cul-de-sac. The fall-out, personally, for this troubled man continued to be an almost total absence of normality in his life. California and its 'lifestyle choices' had begun to pall some time back, but he refused to rip too savagely at these roots. With his young daughter ensconced in the Bay area for the duration, he was reluctant to forgo the kind of regular access proximity provided.

Now five, Shana was old enough to share some of her father's passions. She would later tell a local journalist that the legendary curmudgeon 'was a wonderful dad – we had a lot of wonderful experiences when I was growing up. He took me to really interesting places – cathedrals and gardens, and other places he loved in Ireland.' Shana provided Van with some much-needed stability in a rocky existence, as well as an audience for fatherly advice, both in person and in song. In 'I Have Finally Come to Realize' it seems self-evident that words of admonishment to this child 'not [to] do what I have done' are those of a father to his daughter.

Wonderful as the 'really interesting places' to which Morrison took his daughter may have been, he longed to take her on the kind of mystical journeys of the imagination he had ventured on as a working-class, East Belfast lad. Two songs from the *Hard Nose* era seemed to address her so, 'There There Child' and the ethereal 'Flamingoes Fly'; the former pictures the pair sailing over the white cliffs of Dover hand in hand, whilst the latter sings of taking 'that moonlight ride/When I hear you gently sigh, I wanna take you where flamingoes fly'.

Save for the time he managed to spend with his daughter, Morrison's sense of isolation was now exacerbated by a rapid curtailment of musical activities. Although after the divorce he had deliberately placed himself far from the beaten track, the joke was perhaps now on him.

Greil Marcus: He lived . . . between San Rafael and [Bulinis], and I remember driving by [one time] and there was this big sign. It said, 'Van Morrison's Self-Improvement Camp'. I have no idea if someone put it up there as a prank, or if he'd put it up [himself]; [nor whether] you went there to improve yourself or whether you went there to improve him, but it somehow struck me as very appropriate.

The disorienting cocktail of wealth and fame, combined with a career in seeming free-fall, seems to have led Morrison back to the booze. This time, though, he was determined to separate himself from his most persistent companion. Initially he turned to Alcoholics Anonymous but, after attending a few meetings, decided that his own personal notoriety ran too much interference between him and fellow drinkers in search of temperance. He later complained to a friend who knew his concern, 'Alcoholics Anonymous wasn't anonymous! I don't know whether it has ever been anonymous, but I think that's the biggest lie for me. Because people still related to me as what I did, not as an alcoholic. I had to say to people at meetings, "I don't give a fuck whether you've got the [last] album or not. I'm here because I think I've got a drink problem" . . . For me the attraction was the [supposed] anonymity.' The oppressions of fame continued to shut out most elements of that joyous sound.

Van Morrison: People would be sitting and talking about Van Morrison, and I'd wonder who they were talking about. I knew it wasn't me. So there was the other Van Morrison who was [supposed to be] me, and was the one I had to deal with . . . Being famous was extremely disappointing for me. When I became famous it was a complete drag. [1985]

Unfortunately, the void remained even when he tried to beat a path away from Fame's ornate door. His was still a hunger without a name, no matter what he read or to whom he spoke, and at this time he was prepared to turn to anyone who might be willing to show him a way to improve himself. According to a press statement issued the following year, he now tried 'a bunch of different things. For example, I attended special sessions conducted by a pupil of Ada Rolf, the Swedish tension expert, to release accumulated tension. I got into reading and studied various subjects including Jungian psychiatry, Celtic history and supernatural activity on an academic level.'

Studying subjects as arcane and problematic as Jungian psychiatry, Celtic history and the supernatural 'on an academic level' in little more than a year of inactivity would have been truly something. And yet such autodidacticism was indicative of a crucial shift in Morrison's psyche, one that would lead on to a genuinely remarkable burst of creativity between 1979 and 1982. Ada Rolf's unnamed pupil was one of many whom Morrison later described as 'people who gave me pointers. I wouldn't call them gurus. I would call them "spiritual friends".'

Van Morrison: The thing is, you grow up and you're not that kid . . . [who] wanted to be a rock & roll singer . . . any more. So you have different goals and ambitions. Sometimes you don't have any ambitions, sometimes you find that you really don't have that ambition . . . I realized when I became twenty-eight or twenty-nine that I'd lived out a certain thing, and that was the dream of the kid. The boy had his vision, but the man had a different one, and it's your option whether you want to change your vision of life. And it was time for me, as an adult, to have another dream. [1978]

The dreams now envisaged, though, were no more realistic. As Morrison put it to one journalist shortly after returning to earth, he hoped to do 'things I like to do . . . just living as if I were nobody, instead of somebody. I have to be nobody so I can live my life.' However much this desire lay in the realm of pipe dreams, it was compounded by a similar aspiration in his work – hence perhaps the non-appearance of songs as confessional as 'I Have Finally Come to Realize' and 'It Hurts When You Want It So Bad'. The fact that people actually treated his work seriously only seemed to cause him grief.

Van Morrison: I just got tired of that syndrome of putting out an album and then some reviewer claims that this song or that song has something to do with x, y or z . . . I have to accept the fact that I was putting out records that reviewers were going to get an image from. The media is going to stick a label on it. And the public is going to pick it up from that. [But] that's what I was getting sick of – the whole analysation [*sic*] thing. [1977]

A fear of letting go, which had begun to creep into Morrison's work after *Astral Weeks*, made the albums between *Moondance* and *Veedon Fleece* a detached experience for artist and audience alike. It had reached such a pitch by 1975 that Morrison was seeking to second-guess his audience, an exercise fatal to *anyone's* artistry. One of the songs that would appear on the 1978 album, *Wavelength*, 'Take It Where You Find It', Morrison described as something written 'on a plane from Los Angeles to San Francisco', presumably during those few months in the spring of 1977 when he had a place in Brentwood, LA.

Van Morrison: [I] carried it around with me for a long time . . . ['cause] I knew people were going to ask what it was about. And not really knowing or even caring what it was about[!], I tried changing it . . . But that line [about 'lost dreams and found dreams in America'] kept sticking . . . I couldn't get away from it.

Hardly a successful reinvention of working methods! No matter how surreal the idea may sound of an author objecting to *anyone* interpreting work presented for public consumption, it became part of a very real, and not so beautiful, obsession. Morrison clearly still felt twisted by all that he had put himself through to become the famous person he now sought to disown. The result was not that he conceived a disregard for all such preconceptions, continuing to plough the homespun furrows of *Veedon Fleece* until his audience caught up. Rather, he allowed himself to get wrapped up in knots worrying about whether lyrics he was now writing might be decoded, until one fine day he found that there were no lyrics left to decode.

Van Morrison: It became unreal. Even the way people were reacting at gigs . . . Before, it was coming through me inspirationally and I was writing it down and singing it – no big statement about anything. But *they* were projecting a whole other reality to it . . . I had to get away. I became too self-conscious about what I was doing, 'cause of the weight of what people were saying and writing. That's probably the reason why I didn't write. [1989]

Strange but true. Bypassing the passage from unconscious flights of imagination to a more conscious artistry, Morrison found himself in a self-conscious heap on the floor, quite unable to unravel these inspirational flights, or to rekindle the more craftsmanlike approach once reached for on *Street Choir* and *Tupelo Honey*. His attempts to second-guess his own art failed on all fronts, forcing him to revive the inspirational approach or abandon his art altogether. After the choice had been made, he began to insist that he was neither a conventional songsmith nor a crafter of words – he was a carpenter who thought more about the wood than those for whom he might be asked to create!

Van Morrison: Where I get the whole idea, the lyrics and the melody to the song – that's [truly] inspirational writing, which is very rare . . . [But] you can't think of anything when you're writing except that [very thing]. It's like if you're a carpenter, you can't build a shelf if you're thinking about who you're going to sell it to . . . I don't classify myself as a songwriter. I'm an inspirational writer . . . I write when I'm inspired. I wouldn't say it's [like I'm] a poet . . . because sometimes poets craft things academically . . . I'm just an inspirational writer. If I'm inspired, I write. If I'm not inspired, I can't write. [1981]

Only as the process itself began to elude him, in the summer of 1975, did it occur to Morrison that it was practice that had made art out of a necessary imperfection. As he subsequently put it, 'If I stop writing songs for a while, it's harder to write them. It's a matter of consistency.' One song he worked on that year would take until 1981 to flower into one of his finest illuminations, 'Tore Down A La Rimbaud'.★ He had been reading nineteenth-century French symbolist Arthur Rimbaud 'when I got the original idea . . . I wasn't writing anything at all and I really [could]n't understand why.'

Van Morrison: [It was] during the period . . . between *Veedon Fleece* and *Period of Transition* [that] I started 'Tore Down A La Rimbaud' – after I read that he stopped writing altogether when he was twenty-six, became an arms dealer or something. Anyway, he never wrote a line after that. Ironically, that sorta got me writing again. Took a long time to finish, though – eight years before I got the rest of the lines. That's the longest I've ever carried a song around. [1989]

★ 'Tore Down A La Rimbaud' would be recorded for *Beautiful Vision* in 1981, though it is a 1984 re-recording that appears on *A Sense of Wonder*.

References in the song to an earlier poet who failed to make that leap into a mature, conscious artistry, writing his last poetry in his early twenties, who 'showed me visions, showed me nightmares . . . showed me light out of the tunnel, when there was darkness all around', smack of a thirty-seven-year-old Morrison looking back on his own earlier self, slowly piecing together a route back to the world at large.

In the spring of 1976, as he began to see the end of the tunnel, Morrison took the unprecedented step of issuing a press statement explaining his absence, and insisting that he felt revitalized and ready to start work again. The statement read, in part:

As far as the past year is concerned, things simply came to a grinding halt. Everything just came to a standstill as far as being into the music and being into the trip. I simply stopped doing it for a while in order to get a new perspective on what it was all about. I wanted to change the way I was working; I wanted to get more of a solid business thing together. I wanted to open up new areas of creativity so I had to let go of everything for a while. I went through a lot of personal changes – there were a lot of things within myself that I had to sort out.

The impetus for issuing such a statement almost certainly stemmed from Morrison's new manager. It had been some time since Stephen Pillster had been deemed surplus to requirements. The lack of any external career guidance in the interim had done Morrison few favours, and he was already making enquiries when Bill Wyman suggested a familiar phone number. The pair had recently shared a studio, Morrison having arrived unannounced at the Record Plant in Sausalito during sessions for the Stones bassist's first solo album, *Stone Alone*, offering to play sax and sing some backing vocals. Morrison had even been prepared to duet with Wyman on a by-product of his own Record Plant sessions some months earlier, 'Joyous Sound', before a phone call from a 'representative' brought an abrupt end to their working association.

Bill Wyman: I went back to England and we mixed the album down. Then I got a call from his lawyers in New York saying I wasn't allowed to use anything that had a performance of Van on it . . . It was really embarrassing at the time . . . A strange thing really. He just became paranoid about the whole thing and wouldn't let me use anything . . . [ ] . . . Three months later, I bumped into

Van at some Clapton do at the Savoy, and he said, 'What happened to that album we did together? Has it come out?' And I looked at him and said, 'Van, your lawyer stopped me using you. I wiped you off almost everything.' And he [just] went, 'Oh.' [WL/RC]

Having established a relationship with Morrison, thanks to a mutual love of skiffle music and early blues, and having also learned the hard way always to *read* contracts drafted by fast-talking New York businessmen, Wyman was happy to offer some much-needed business advice. If Morrison was looking for a manager, Wyman felt he should speak to Harvey Goldsmith, the legendary British concert promoter, renowned for his from-the-hip opinions and astute grasp of the strengths and weaknesses of the various players.

Goldsmith wasn't interested in taking up the reins himself. As he later told Johnny Rogan, he was already aware that 'every single person that had ever been involved with him, be it record company, publishing, promoting, agency or whatever, [might have] had tremendous respect for him, but everyone also said that he was the most difficult person in the world to deal with'. Nevertheless, Goldsmith agreed to meet Morrison for lunch and share some personal insights.

Harvey Goldsmith: I went through a list of people that I felt would be suitable and he said, 'No, I've been through all that lot. I'm not interested in them. Why don't you do it?' I said, 'I don't manage. I'm too busy promoting.' And about a week later he phoned me up, he came to see me, we had lunch and he said, 'I really want you to manage me.' I said, 'I'm not going to give up promoting.' At that point he had disappeared – he had gone through the AA programme. I knew he wasn't easy, but we talked it through and I said, 'I'll help you out. If it doesn't work, I'll have tried.' And he said, 'Well, we'll have to do a contract,' and we spent most of the time talking about what would happen if it *didn't* work . . . He said he was going to come and live in England. I felt if he was restarting his life, then it sounded interesting . . . He was straightened out, he'd had his time in the wilderness and wanted to come back into music . . . He was completely professional about it.

Morrison may well have mistaken Goldsmith's initial disinterest for dispassionate detachment, a much-needed quality he intended to push to the very limit. His expressed intent to re-establish Britain as his home base was a major factor in Goldsmith eventually agreeing to manage him, something reiterated in his press statement that May:

I am moving back to Britain for a while, primarily because I want to get back to the roots, back to where I started off. And that's what's happening now with my music as well. I'm getting back to basics – basic rock & roll stuff. I've been trying out some different things – experimental projects at various times and places . . . [But] I want to combine a vacation with checking out a few things, jamming with a few different people and finding out what's going on back in Britain . . . I've been writing a lot of new material lately and I'm working towards releasing an album in September.

Before he could return to his musical roots, though, he needed a base from which he might work his magic. Goldsmith's experience of house-hunting for his new client suggested that every tall tale he had heard about the man fell short of capturing his true eccentricity.

Harvey Goldsmith: One day he sent me a postcard with a drawing on it, and he [wrote], 'Find me this house.' And I was driving along St Mary Abbot's Terrace in Kensington and I suddenly stopped dead and I said, 'I can't believe this! This is the house!' So I banged on the door, and this woman answered the door and I said, 'I'm terribly sorry to [disturb you] but is this house for rent?' She said, 'Actually, it is.' . . . Rented the house for six months, called up Van. I said, 'I've got your house.' Told him where it was. He said, 'Yeah, that's the house.' He got on a plane. Arrived at the airport. I went to pick him up – he was a bit moody at the time – drove him up to the house, and he opened the front door, walked around and said, 'I don't want to stay here. I'm going back to America.' I said. 'This is the house you want.' He just said, 'I'm out of here.' . . . He said the karma wasn't right . . . He got in the car, went back to the airport and flew straight back to America.

So much for returning to Britain full-time. Morrison's rootlessness duly led him to hole up in Los Angeles in the months preceding his 'comeback' album, *A Period of Transition*, even though he seemed equally miserable there. His good friend Jeff Labes, who had recently moved west, remembers hanging out at his house in Brentwood, wondering what his erstwhile boss was doing in such an artificial environment: 'It was a different space. It wasn't right for him. Mostly he complained

about how he couldn't get along with people in LA.' According to
Ritchie Yorke, again in touch with the man, he 'maintain[ed] a very low
profile, whipping around LA in a brown Toyota, studiously staying away
from the Hollywood rock scene, relaxing in the backyard by the pool
. . . romping around with his dog Tupelo'.

Thus Morrison continued to flit between London and southern and
northern California, where he retained his Self-Improvement Camp in
Lagunitas and where he made his long-awaited return to live performance
on the most star-studded bill this side of Woodstock, at the Band's
filmed farewell to gigging at San Francisco's Winterland Ballroom on
Thanksgiving Thursday, 25 November 1976, a.k.a. The Last Waltz. It
had been some time since Morrison had stalked a stage. He had been
offered the opportunity to shine during Rory Gallagher's set at the
Reading Festival in August, but nerves had got the better of him.

Donal Gallagher: [We were] at Reading, in the teeming rain, and Harvey
was there with Van in tow, and I was really hoping this would be a jam session
tonight . . . Rory was kind of looking around. He *did* indicate, 'Do you want
to come on?' but [Van] was too nervous.

As it was, he couldn't have picked a more high-pressure environment
in which to make his return to performing. With Neil Young shoving
so much white powder up his nose that they had to airbrush it out of the
subsequent film frame by frame, whilst everyone wondered aloud what
the fug Neil Diamond was doing there, and Bob Dylan started playing
his usual mind games with the film crew, Van began to feel increasingly
anxious at the thought of sharing a stage with his old Woodstock 'chums',
the Band.

Nor was Robbie Robertson the only one nonplussed when it came
time for Morrison to take to the stage and he emerged wearing what
looked at first glance like a ballerina's purple leotard. When Robertson
had seen Morrison for the run-through, he had been 'dressed like Sam
Spade . . . I just thought he was wearing a raincoat . . . So when it's the
concert, Van comes out on stage, and he's dressed in this little purple
outfit . . . I was like, "What happened to the Sam Spade thing?" . . . He
was just shaking his head.' Robertson was not to know how close
Morrison had come to pulling out altogether, consumed by the self-same
stage fright that had attacked Robertson the first time the Band had
played the Winterland back in 1969.

Harvey Goldsmith: We worked the running order, we had the rehearsals, and Van was involved in what music [to do]. And about half an hour before Van was due to go on, the show was going really well, and I said, 'Van, get yourself ready. You're on in [x minutes].' He looked out from the side and he said, 'I got to go back to the hotel.' 'Why?' 'I can't wear what I'm wearing.' I said, 'We haven't got time.' He said, 'I'm going back to the hotel.' I thought I'd better go with him. He shot back to the hotel, got changed and he put on this old, tight leather [outfit] that barely fit him, and was really grumpy about it, and suddenly he had this strange [mood]: 'Can't do it. Can't get on stage. Not in the mood [etc. etc.].' [Pure] stage fright . . . Got back to the gig. He [was still saying], 'I'm not going on.' He was standing on the side of the stage and suddenly they announced, 'Ladies and gentlemen, Van Morrison,' and he just stood there. I said, 'C'mon, Van,' and I literally kicked him out there – and he did two of the most blindin' songs. The whole place was just set alight.

'Tura Lura Lural (That's an Irish Lullaby)', which was apparently Robertson's suggestion, gave Morrison a chance to share his love of Irish melodies with Richard Manuel. 'Caravan' was a crowd-pleaser pure and simple, providing Morrison with the opportunity to match the intensity of Joni Mitchell beforehand and Dylan's set to come. When he was finally out there, he enjoyed the experience. A few months later he even talked about how 'If you're with a good band and everybody's from the old school, it's different. When you're in your element, you're in your element and things just come. You don't have to drag them out or force them out. They just happen.' Unfortunately the Band were otherwise engaged when Morrison returned to the studio that autumn.

The album he had said he was working on in his May statement was presumably one he envisaged coming from sessions with Joe Sample of the Crusaders that spring, after auditions at SIR (Studio Instrument Rentals) in Los Angeles assembled enough of a band to fulfil a need. Even though Eric Clapton – then at work on *No Reason to Cry* at the Band's studio in Malibu – apparently agreed to participate, the results were so uninspiring that not even a single cut features on the archival *Philosopher's Stone* (or its unreleased 1977 predecessor). When pressed as to the sessions' content in a 1978 interview, Morrison denied 'going in to make an album. And some of the things I did . . . with Joe Sample of the Crusaders weren't really that good. It's not a question of trying to hide the tapes. If it feels right, you put it out, and if it doesn't, you don't.' One man who did get to hear the tapes was John Altman, with whom

Morrison continued to enjoy a relationship akin to the one he'd had with Jon Gershen in Woodstock.

John Altman: He was fed up with the gigging, and fed up with the touring, and wasn't into writing that much. It was like the album [*A Period of Transition*] . . . was [an example of] throwing a bunch of people together and saying, 'Let's see how this appears to be.' I know he did a lot of recordings. He played me the stuff he did with Eric Clapton and the Crusaders, and it sounded good, but he wasn't comfortable with it. He didn't think it worked . . . I just think . . . he wasn't very happy with his recording situation. But he still enjoyed making music, and being involved and being around music.

Such was the dearth of usable new product that Warners began calling up session reels with a view to issuing an *Odds and Sods*-style collection from what resided in the vaults. It was something Morrison himself had talked about in the wake of *Veedon Fleece*, telling Yorke how he'd 'like to try and get some of that old stuff out sometime, but I just don't know where it's going to fit in'. He also told Tom Donahue that he planned to release an album called 'Highlights', which would include the 1971 Pacific High version of Dylan's 'Just Like a Woman'.

In fact, the fourteen-track album Warners compiled – presumably with Morrison's input – featured very little material that pre-dated *Hard Nose the Highway* – just 'I Shall Sing' from the *Moondance* sessions and a 1972 non-album B-side, 'You've Got the Power'. Instead, it concentrated on the Caledonia era, incorporating three songs from the scuppered *Hard Nose* 'double'; the 'Street Theory' omitted from *Veedon Fleece*; and a full seven songs from the Hilversum and Record Plant sessions in 1974–75. As to why the collection★ remained unreleased, it would appear that Morrison already realized it was better to move forward and not look back.

Van Morrison: I went through all these tapes a couple of years ago . . . but by

★ The fourteen-track collection, compiled under the generic heading Repackaging Project, includes just three recordings replicated on *The Philosopher's Stone* (as asterisked). The track listing of the scheduled collection was as follows: 'I Shall Sing'. 'Laughing in the Wind'★. 'Street Theory'. 'Foggy Mountain Top'★. 'There There Child'. 'It Hurts When You Want It So Bad'. 'Feedback out on Highway 101'. 'You've Got the Power'. 'Try for Sleep'★. 'Naked in the Jungle'. 'The Street Only Knew Your Name'. 'All Around the World'. 'Don't Change on Me'. 'Down to Earth'.

the time you go through everything . . . you realize it would be better just to do it fresh, rather than get hung up on old tapes. [1981]

Morrison presumably sensed that Warners were looking to turn up the heat just as he was hoping to chill out. As he would put it, 'I'd taken some time off and I was enjoying myself. [But] everyone I'd run into would say, "What are you doing? Doing an album?" . . . I mean, there wasn't any album in me at the time . . . I did some sessions that were not an album as such. They didn't rate. Everybody said, "You should put it out." Simply 'cause *they* were putting albums out.' At least the act of going through 'old' tapes served to remind Morrison of the existence of 'Flamingoes Fly' and 'Joyous Sound', two 'old' songs with which he retained a heavy connection.

To record new versions, though, he would need backing musicians. And though he had now returned to London, for the first time in a country mile he was genuinely unsure with whom he should be working. The extraordinary good fortune he had enjoyed with musicians in the previous decade had perhaps convinced him that such chemistry was his on demand. Relying on instincts that had served him well to date, he initially considered fellow Irish bluesman Rory Gallagher, but spontaneous synergy failed to happen. At which point he couldn't even bring himself to inform Rory that it wasn't going to work out.

Donal Gallagher: He called Rory . . . and Rory went down to the Manor [Studios, to record]. Rory postponed some gigs, and was very honoured to be asked. [He] went in, and Van put the tapes on. I think Dr John was there. And [then] Van seemingly disappeared. Rory waited till four in the morning and [then] packed up his gear. He felt very snubbed, and said he'd never have anything to do with [Van] again . . . The following day somebody said he'd gone off to the States. As far as Rory understood, he'd gone off to get something to eat.

If so, the place at which he wanted to dine was five thousand miles west – Morrison apparently hailed a cab and took off for Heathrow Airport, leaving a bemused retinue in his wake. A similar incident occurred with jazz veteran Chris Barber, a long-standing idol of Morrison's, who at least garnered a single-line explanation. According to Harvey Goldsmith, '[Van] was really, really excited about working with Chris Barber and his whole jazz [ensemble] and [then] after about

half an hour he came down and said, "This isn't working. Goodbye."
And he [just] went.'

A despairing Goldsmith, unaccustomed to Morrison's working
methods, asked him to spell out his methodology: 'We talked through
all the different things he wanted to do. He wanted to get back in the
studio, and he explained how he worked – "If I don't get it on the third
take, I don't do it." He [said he] wanted to do something funky. I think
I suggested Dr John.'

Mac Rebennack a.k.a. Dr John had that Louisiana funk deep down
in his soul. He had also been a surprise success at The Last Waltz, which
may have set Goldsmith and/or Morrison thinking. When the two
performers met, Goldsmith recalls, 'they got on really well together. Van
had a whole raft of songs that he had written down in his little book and
he wanted to get them out.' Dr John, though, was also thrown by the
insensitive way Morrison had of dispensing with musicians.

Dr John: I have memories of him auditioning a lot of guitar players – including
many of the premier players in England . . . There were players all over the
studio: I'd give one guy a downbeat, he'd hit one note, and Van would cut him
off – 'Next!' The whole Chris Barber band came there to play on a tune, and
they all got axed real fast. We never did find a steady player . . . He's probably
one of the few guys that I ever felt like punching out in the middle of a session
. . . He's a very hard guy to deal with, but his music is powerful. He's a mystical
cat.

If Dr John was never sure enough of his own footing to confront
Morrison, Goldsmith was. He can still recall 'a terrible fight one day in
his house. I said to him, "You can't dick people around. If you set
something up, you got musicians, crews depending on you. You're either
going to do it, or you're not. If you don't want to do it, that's fine, but
don't leave it to the last minute."' Though Morrison may not have
appreciated the lecture, it seems to have sunk in and he began to buckle
down to the idea of settling on a group of musicians, and then going in
and cutting an album. Initially, there had been talk of Mac and Van
working with veteran R&B producer Henry Glover, but Dr John felt
that 'it woulda been a whole other thing'. Rather than risk further friction
Dr John and Morrison decided to produce the sessions themselves. The
results reflected a number of tensions still at work.

Dr John: He knows he is difficult to work with, but he knows what he is looking for . . . [even if] it is hard to get it out of him [sometimes]. It's like I did that record . . . and I still don't know a lotta things I wanted to know when we were doing it . . . He never answers questions straight up.

Van Morrison: There was no real concept of the album at that point. I just decided to do an album with Mac Rebennack and use all the same players on it . . . That way it's like a clean album . . . We co-produced it together for openers . . . Normally I don't like working in the studio that much. I get keyed up about it, but Mac kind of slowed me down, which was really good for my head. [1977]

Where the 'whole raft of songs' went when the sessions began has never been explained. The fact is that just seven songs were recorded,★ and two of these had already been cut at the Record Plant back in 1975. And yet progress on the eagerly-awaited album proved slow and painful. Morrison seemed to be there under some kind of contractual duress, and it showed. Just one song aspired to break out of its surroundings, the atmospheric 'The Eternal Kansas City'. Dr John saw it as the key to the album.

Dr John: It was the song that Van got the whole album hooked up around. When I first met up with Van [to discuss] doing this project he played this song for me, which was a real deep thing for him to focus on. He used a real sparse instrumental backing on it, just hooking at different angles. Lyrically, the song is about a dream he focused in on, or a scene that he witnessed and put into a song. It's like about a 'trip' he took with Billie Holiday, Jimmy Witherspoon, Big Joe Turner and Pete Johnson.

Morrison later said that he wrote this particular song whilst staying at Steve Winwood's place in the Cotswolds. 'I went into this nearby small town and they had a little pond in the middle of the town with a sign saying "Birdland".† It was just a place for birds. And from that whole thing, I got Charlie Parker's Birdland and the whole trip in the dream.' His description suggests it was the first song in a while to 'come through from dreams, daydreams, night-dreams . . . experiences that are [actually]

★ According to the Warners files, there were no out-takes to *A Period of Transition* deposited with the label.
† The place in question is in Bourton-on-the-Water.

happening to you'. Of the other new songs, only 'Cold Wind in August' suggested a real experience, diffused or not through a broken dream.

Morrison seemed less than galvanized by the results. Even at the time of its release, in April 1977, he described his new album to Capital Radio DJ Nicky Horne as 'a piece of product . . . This is nothing special, that I cut some "stuff" in the last year.' Even the album title itself, *A Period of Transition*, suggested impermanence.

Van Morrison: If I tell you how it was got together, it won't sound good . . . After all these years of recording . . . I get absolutely unexcited about how a record was made. It's just making records – that's all. [1977]

The album's reviewers seemed to share Morrison's sense of disinterest, damning it in comparison to the overlooked *Veedon Fleece*. Michael Watts of *Melody Maker* chose to spend most of his review addressing a 'paradox concerning Morrison's new album, *A Period of Transition*, which centres upon the question implicit in its title: if it's intended to be a bridge between *Veedon Fleece* and some other, unknown shore, why does its content recall the music made between *Moondance* and *Hard Nose the Highway*, only a good deal inferior? . . . *A Period of Transition* merely keeps inviting questions. Like the blue-toned photographs of Morrison, reminiscent of old bubblegum cards, that occupy the back sleeve, the final impression it leaves is oddly self-conscious.' Even Nick Kent, previously a steadfast champion of Morrison, couldn't help but think that *A Period of Transition* was some kind of delayed reaction to the critical and commercial failure of *Veedon Fleece*:

Fleece . . . [which] made a strong impression, if only because Morrison was embracing new ideas and themes just when many of his contemporaries were snowed under in their old hand-me-down conceits . . . though reviewed agreeably in this country by the critics . . . was greeted with several slighting critiques in the States . . . Whether these reviews had anything to do with Morrison's strange twists of resolve over the subsequent two and a half years is anyone's guess, but those months did witness a whole gamut of projects started, completed, then suddenly shelved for reasons only decipherable in the head of their instigator and creator.

Kent was not alone in thinking that *A Period of Transition* sounded like one more project that should have been shelved. Perhaps Morrison was thinking about the imminent expiry of his Warners contract, and was trying to fast-track the process. Whatever his true motive, *A Period of Transition* was a disastrous choice with which to signal a return to the world of product. Inevitably, its singular title and short-changed feel were just two issues raised by the retinue of journalists to whom Morrison was obliged to expose himself in lieu of undertaking any real performing activity in the spring of 1977. Many of these journalists, from a new generation of wannabe scribes, were unimpressed by the man's credentials. The frustration that Morrison felt at their seeming incomprehension inevitably spilled over into the odd battle of words.

Paul Charles: If you're a pure artist – and I genuinely believe Van is – and you sit down with somebody who's a little spotty Herbert from whatever, and they don't really have the big picture, [it's a problem] . . . Where they're coming from is 'This is what we did with Bon Jovi and Rod Stewart.' He's got a totally different canvas, he paints totally different pictures, he uses different coloured paints than these people ever dream of. So if you're trying to force Van to sit down with somebody that hasn't got a bit of this perspective, it's an impossible thing. You can sit down and be polite, but life's too short. I've never seen him be rude to anybody, [but] I've seen him be upset – as in 'What's the point in doing this?'

Charles, who would become Morrison's *de facto* manager at the end of the decade, may have 'never seen him be rude to anybody', but the poor Warners publicist, Pete Johnson, who set up this series of confrontations with the press in the year of punk, assuredly did. Several of the journalists called to arms were at the forefront of punk's iconoclastic media presence, and were never going to be fazed by a gruff Morrison after sparring with Johnny Rotten. Perhaps the liveliest of these was Vivien Goldman, personal friend of Rotten's and occasional presence in the music press. Given Morrison's expressed preference for bright, assertive women, he should have been delighted to encounter Goldman. Apparently not, on the evidence of the resultant dialogue, which Goldman chose to reproduce verbatim:

Vivien Goldman: A lot of people feel they have a base somewhere. Know what I mean?
Van Morrison: Do they?
VG: Have you ever felt like that?
VM: Is that what you want to talk about?

VG: Well, it must be. Otherwise, why would I be asking?

VM: It doesn't really interest me. I don't know whether I can go anywhere with that topic.

VG: Well, what would you like to talk about?

VM: I'm just doing this promotion, see. I have this new album out. It's called [A] *Period of Transition*, and I'm doing some promo. That's why I'm here.

VG: Yes, but the point about asking that question is that if you felt like answering it − and fair enough if you don't − perhaps it would have given some slight insight into the man who created the music.

VM: Well, if you're looking for that, you'll never get it . . .

VG: What did you study [in the years away]?

VM: Can't tell you. It wouldn't be right for this paper. It would just throw the whole thing into a totally different context . . . People who are interested in pop music would not be interested . . . You're a journalist, you're making points, but I'm not making any points at all. I'm not getting anything over. I don't have anything to get over.

It seemed Morrison couldn't help but demean his own audience, informing the persevering Goldman, 'If I knew you or if I'd known you for five years and we were just sitting around talking, then I'd feel like maybe I could tell you about what I'm doing . . . [but] this kind of situation, the context in which this is being wrapped up and sold, is not the context to talk about music.' If an interview in a music paper was not an appropriate context in which to discuss his new album, no alternative sprang to mind.

The discomfort evinced by Morrison's answers in these interviews may have been quite real, but his way of expressing it only invited ridicule and sarcasm − hence *NME*'s rather witty banner headline, 'Portrait of a Moody Bugger', when it came Roy Carr's turn to lock horns. Perhaps, sensing a certain unexpected hostility from the press, Morrison began to assume a studied indifference. Maybe he knew all along that the album was fast becoming a commercial stiff. He certainly seemed uncomfortable sitting in a radio-station studio talking about the record, if the notorious Nicky Horne interview is any indication. Harvey Goldsmith went to great pains to set up the interview and 'prep' Horne, but all to no avail.

Harvey Goldsmith: The record got finished and we started to do some promotion . . . I got two weeks out of him to go and promote the thing, and we were going to do some live dates. We had this very interesting time up at Capital Radio with Nicky Horne. I remember going to see Nicky before this famous interview and I said, 'Nicky, there's certain things that Van doesn't want to talk about. Don't ask him about his private life, his wife or his girlfriends. He's here to talk about the album.' So we go in the studio, and of course after the third question [Nicky] suddenly launched into something about his previous wife, and Van looked at me, Mac looked at me, and Van and Mac started a diatribe about fishing, and then the pair of them just got up and walked out.

The interview as broadcast contains no such interaction, though Horne distinctly remembered 'Mac . . . standing there with a shillelagh in order to stand upright'. Nor were the questions remotely personal, and it sounds as if it was Horne who finally gave up on the pair, after Morrison simply refused to discuss the meaning of the title to a certain 1972 release.

The interview route had proved something of a bust. Perhaps it was time Morrison returned to doing what he had always done best – performing in front of a live audience. Of course he would need a band, the American sessionmen responsible for the album's sonic sludge being mercifully unavailable.★ Dr John, though, tagged along for the ride, whilst drummer Peter Van Hooke, the one musician from the 1974 quartet to have stayed in regular contact, was a given. Van Hooke in turn recommended bassist Mo Foster, who was duly introduced to Dr John (and, somewhat incongruously, guitarist Mick Ronson of Bowie/ Rolling Thunder Revue fame) at his first – and only – rehearsal.

Mo Foster: Pete [Van Hooke] brought [Van] round my flat near Portobello Road, and I'd heard that he liked the Goons, so we talked about the Goons. [Then] we had a rehearsal. We did so many songs that both he and Dr John knew, [but] I knew none of them really. I was frantically trying to copy Dr John's left hand. [It was a] high-speed learning curve . . . They knew all the[se] R&B songs, so one would start it and the other [would] join in straight away, and they'd assume everyone else knew them. [And] I've got the task of trying to find the tonal centre and the chord sequence while we're doing it . . . You'd maybe do the front and end of a song, and leave the rest to the gig. They'd

---

★ Elements of the album band were, however, used on a thirty-minute *In Concert* for the NBC TV series *The Midnight Special* in March 1977, on which Morrison débuted 'Heavy Connection', 'Cold Wind in August' and 'The Eternal Kansas City'.

condensed the rehearsals down to as many songs in the shortest possible time
. . . By the eightieth title in three hours, I've forgotten the first ten.

Peter Van Hooke confirms that 'all we played [in rehearsal] were blues
numbers that Van knew all the lyrics to. He has an encyclopaedic memory
. . . and then the gig came, [and] we played something completely
different.' The gig in question was an invitation-only shindig at a small
club on Jermyn Street called Maunkberry's. As it was a promotional gig
for *A Period of Transition*, even Morrison was expected to stick largely to
songs from his new album. However, he preferred to veer between an
occasional R&B song they may or may not have rehearsed and some
entirely new song such as 'Venice USA', which he clearly dug doing.
Only infrequently did he remind the select few as to the purpose of
proceedings.

When asked, in the earlier spate of interviews, about a return to
performing, Morrison spoke of a need to break a lot of that 'expectancy'
down: 'I know from experience that I go to see some artists expecting a
particular thing. If they don't come up with that then I'm disappointed,
but if I have no expectations they usually do something I haven't heard
before, and I'm turned on.' At Maunkberry's, Morrison did eventually
turn to his transitional material, but by then he had already lost a fair few
members of the press. Chas de Whalley, reviewing the show for *Sounds*,
depicted a man still having to force himself into that performer straitjacket:

For a [supposedly] warm and romantic singer, Van made no attempt whatsoever
to communicate with the crowd. Off mike, he faded into the wings, chain-
smoking all the while. On mike he barked and bayed with his eyes tight shut,
or else he stared wildly at a point above the audience's heads, stricken it seemed
by a strange and dispassionate terror.

Part of that 'dispassionate terror' undoubtedly stemmed from the
cameras filming the performance for later broadcast. The murky footage
was eventually beamed out on a regional half-hour TV show devoted
largely to the punk revolution, Tony Wilson's *So It Goes* – presumably
having been passed on by Michael Appleton at *The Old Grey Whistle
Test*, the Beeb's solitary concession to an intelligent televisual context for
rock music. Performing 'The Eternal Kansas City', Morrison preferred to
shut out the light, 'bay[ing] with his eyes tight shut'. When he found

himself back in Hilversum a week later, recording a similar set of songs for a Dutch TV special, he blocked out the studio lights in similar fashion. However, this time he witnessed the studio playback, and so caught sight of just how it came across.

Peter Van Hooke: There was always a quandary with Van, whether he was an entertainer or an artist. One moment he would think, I should be an entertainer here, and at another point [it was], I want to be an artist . . . That's the conundrum that Van has some [of the] time – when he [would] look at a show like the one at [Hilversum], and go, 'Christ! I had my fucking eyes closed. I should be an entertainer' . . . because he's looking at himself slightly removed [then]. But you can't always say that . . . There's always that dichotomy going on in his life. It's how he feels at that moment.

The Dutch TV show followed on from an hour-long set at Vara studios, recorded for European radio. This oft-bootlegged broadcast suggested that this set of musicians could yet evolve into an interesting advance on the 1974 band, even if bassist Foster found that he was still expected to play 'mostly songs I'd never heard before, [until finally] Van started giving me the chords with the [left] hand behind his back'. The Vara set re-emphasized the fact that Morrison wanted to work from a clean slate, as he skimmed over his entire pre-*Transition* canon. Only a recast 'Foggy Mountain Top' delved into his own past, Morrison surrendering the first half of the show to familiar R&B fare like Little Willie John's 'Fever', James Brown's 'I'll Go Crazy', a most un-Themlike 'Baby Please Don't Go', Willie Dixon's 'Hallelujah, I Love Her So' and an impassioned rendition of Blind Willie Johnson's 'Nobody's Fault but Mine'.

Only in the second half of the performance were songs from *A Period of Transition* squeezed into the format. Indeed the Hilversum experiment concluded with newly scrubbed renditions of the album's only two gems, 'The Eternal Kansas City' and 'Cold Wind in August'. This unexpectedly powerful finale suggested a possible purpose to the imminent European tour, above and beyond 'just do[ing] some singing and some sweating, you know, not worry[ing] about the words and what they mean'. However, a sleepless night convinced Morrison he should opt for the no-sweat option. When the other musicians awoke the following morning, they found that their bandleader had already moved to the outskirts of town after giving Goldsmith the early-morning news at his home in London:

Harvey Goldsmith: He would build up in his mind what he wanted – he would get really excited about it – and then, when it came to it, he'd just [go], 'No.' . . . There was a whole European tour booked. He just wasn't up for it. He . . . phoned up at one, two in the morning . . . and said, 'Not doing the tour,' and went back to America. He always went back to America!

Perhaps the one unguarded moment in that abortive Capital Radio interview was in response to Horne's enquiry about the possibility of gigs. After a two-minute discussion of the meaning of 'expect', Morrison admitted, 'I'm getting [it] together. I'm playing music. And if the vibes are right, we'll do some gigs. [But] I'm not expecting anything. If it happens, it happens.' Evidently the weight of expectation was still too great to bear. It would be over a year before he would begin searching for that vibe again.

20

1978–79: In Transition

In those three dormant years preceding [*A Period of Transition*] the likes of Graham Parker, Bruce Springsteen, Phil Lynott, Elvis Costello, Bob Seger and others have sprung into prominence, all bearing the mark of Morrison's influence . . . One could only have hoped that *Transition* would have at least spotlighted the man's pre-eminence in this quarter, to have borne proof once and for all that this is where all the *Heat Treatments* have stolen their thunder. Unfortunately, the album's failure in that area is one dilemma for which there are no answers. And the questions themselves look right now to be so uncomfortably close to the bone that I, for one, don't even want to ask them.

—*Nick Kent, NME,* 23 April 1977

I don't know why my record company isn't selling more records . . . People who are copying me are selling more records than I am. That part confuses me.

—*Van Morrison,* 1977

If *A Period of Transition* hardly convinced the loyal legions of these 'new Morrisons' that they should dump their 'copycats' and return to the old master, its failure to find a place in modern music only prompted Morrison's further withdrawal. When he announced to his manager Harvey Goldsmith, 'I don't want to work with this lot any more – I'm off,' Goldsmith took it as his cue to do the same, bequesting Morrison to a man who could be his belligerent equal:

Harvey Goldsmith: After a while the toll of me going backwards and for-wards to America was just too much . . . He really needed personal attention at the time . . . I went to see Van, and we had a bit of a set-to, and I said to him, 'I can't do this any more.' He was a bit upset about it and I said, 'Look, Bill Graham's there, he's got a structure, he can handle you. If you want to live in America, then you need someone there that's gonna spend the time looking after you.' I persuaded Bill to take Van on, and graciously ducked out.

Bill Graham was an obvious replacement, Morrison having played at most of Graham's venues from the Fillmores to Winterland, whilst Graham had organized some of the biggest tours in rock music. And, crucially, Graham was a Van fan – surely the only kind of person to whom such a job was worth the headaches!

And in the beginning there was a genuine mutual respect. Graham recognized Morrison as 'the only artist who never gave in to the supply and demand game, having had the choice . . . Throughout the years, whenever Van could have played a 10,000-seat hall he played a five. When he could have played a five, he did a 2,500-seater. He played clubs when he could have played bigger places. He spent more money to get the musicians he wanted . . . Every once in a while, he went out and painted in public – but never for the grandstands.'

Morrison, though, was starting to feel the pressure to perform at larger venues, admitting in 1979, 'I have to play the bigger joints, which puts the whole thing into a subject–object thing. A lot of people are coming to see SOMETHING . . . The best gig for me on the whole [*Wavelength*] tour was a small club in Colorado . . . Bang. It was happening. But that doesn't happen in a 30,000-seater [*sic*]. People there are too concerned about images and stars and subject–object relationships.'

Morrison, who was fully aware of a fundamental shift in popular music in his time away, needed to find his own way back into the modern musical maelstrom. For the New Wave crashing over his own musical genre he had very little time – even after he spent some of his precious downtime trying to figure out 'the point'.

Bill Graham: Once I went to his house and he was just waiting for me to say something. I said, 'Have you been listening to any new music lately?' He said, 'Yeah, I went out and got some new records last week. I came home and put them on the record player here. I put the needle here and I put the needle there and wherever I put the needle, it's shit. Shit here and shit there. Wherever I put the needle it's shit.' [RG]

However much he had influenced the more articulate of this new brigade of brigands, he still preferred searching for his own roots. Whilst in LA awaiting *Transition*'s reception he had told Yorke, 'You are who you are. It doesn't make any point to go out and buy the Top Forty albums to see what those acts are doing. There's no point in hearing what's going on. The only thing that's going on is what's been going for ever.' And yet his bitterness at the fact that those 'bearing the mark of Morrison's influence' were outselling him never lay too far below the surface, compounded by an awareness that he needed to prove himself again.

Shortly before the end of their professional association, he informed Goldsmith that he wanted to go into the studio again and do another album, but as Goldsmith notes, 'He just wasn't ready for it.' In fact it would take almost a year for his newly-formed musical ideas to warrant a return to the studio. And yet the first clue as to a possible way back into the music came at that promotional gig at Maunkberry's. The gig, in Mo Foster's words, 'turned into a jam session at the end, [with] Roger Chapman on vocals, Brian Auger on keys and one of Van's earlier keyboard players . . . it was like a crowded stage of people making a racket'. It proved to be the next prototype.

John Altman: I'd jam with Van at Pete's house but we never actually played together in public until 1977, Maunkberry's, Granada TV, where he did a little set with Dr John [and] Mick Ronson, and then we had a little break and then they expanded the band for a big jam session, which was myself, Roger Chapman, Bobby Tench, Brian Auger – it was an amazing line-up – and they filmed the whole thing . . . By then I was playing baritone sax. I was talking [to him] about a big band, and he said, 'Oh I'd love to have a big band.' . . . What I remember vividly about that night [at Maunkberry's] is how much he enjoyed the jam session in the second half, and that's probably the moment when he thought about [these musicians] as being a part of something that he did . . . To me, that was the defining time. That was when he re-energized himself. When you look at the band he finally put together . . . for *Wavelength*, it had the organ, the horn section, the backing singers. It germinated, for me, in that jam session . . . He was definitely looking for a route to move back into the mainstream . . . He wanted to get back with [his old friend] Herbie [Armstrong]. [The *Wavelength* band] was a mix of people he'd got to know lately and people he'd

known for a long time. It was always going to be something interesting because
of the scale of the band – two guitarists, keyboard player, fiddle player, two
backing singers – [which] meant that it would obviously be a lot more structured
than just having three people he might call and say, 'Get down here. We're
gonna do a gig.'

The band Morrison started to assemble in the spring of 1978 was a
return to many of the textures abandoned (too soon?) at the end of the
Too Late to Stop Now tour. After a period of indecision, he took, if not
the easy way out, certainly the commercial way back. As he had rhetorically suggested, shortly after completing *A Period of Transition*, 'What am
I going to do – move to Ireland and open a grocery store? I'm in the
music business. I'm not gonna sit up on a hill somewhere, writing songs
that are gonna sell ten or twenty albums.' The album he now made
reflected such sentiments, being an unashamed collection of upbeat pop
songs. The entertainer was again donning that ill-fitting suit. When the
results failed to enhance the man's reputation, out would come a familiar
mantra, repeated a number of times over the years:

Van Morrison: I felt pressured into doing something . . . The *Wavelength*
album was just doing an album for the sake of it. I didn't really feel up for it. I
just thought, 'Well, it must be time to do an album so get on with it.' [1984]

Probably closer to the truth was something said to *Musician*'s Bill
Flanagan, to whom he described the album as 'a diversion. It was just to
have a bit of fun and go back to how it felt to play rock & roll . . . It was
intended to be a bit less serious than my other projects.' Recorded mostly
at the Manor Studios in Oxfordshire – with post-production work at
the Band's Shangri-La Studio in Malibu, where accordion and organ
overdubs were provided by Garth Hudson – the album reunited
Morrison with two old friends from the Belfast days, Herbie Armstrong
and Peter Bardens. Peter Van Hooke was the one bridge still retained
from Morrison's mid-seventies sound as he grafted three guitarists, two
keyboard players, two bassists and a three-piece street-legal choir on to
the songs. The sound he was reaching for was certainly ostentatious
enough to draw comparisons with the CSO.

Unfortunately, the songs still failed to come. Though the finished
album clocks in at close to fifty minutes, this merely reflects a lack of
judicious editing. Songs were simply allowed to run out of steam, rather

than be curtailed by a fade or two (as Max Bell wrote in his *Sounds* review, ' "Venice [USA]" degenerates when Morrison allows the chorus to outstay their welcome [by] some two minutes'). Morrison contributed eight new songs from his notebook, supplemented by an old song written with Jackie DeShannon, 'Santa Fe', which worked surprisingly well. The new songs, though, were slight. Even the opener, 'Kingdom Hall', which sought to instil the same gospel fervour he'd heard as a child at the Kingdom Hall, fell short but faded long. In fact, the two most successful songs on *Wavelength* – 'Checkin' It Out' and 'Hungry for Your Love' – worked precisely because of their resolute lack of ambition in the subject-matter department, and their ability to stay the safer side of four minutes.

Yet another series of mixed reviews on the album's release in October 1978 failed to dissuade Morrison from championing the new songs. This time he elected to promote *Wavelength* in the States in the most direct, appropriate way possible – by pounding the boards. This was where Graham could earn his cut, and where a carefully pruned selection of *Wavelength* songs, blended with some familiar strains of yesteryear, could highlight the album's strong points – good ensemble playing, its upbeat nature, Morrison's powerful singing – while shuffling fillers to the bottom of the pack.

Instead, the opening show, at the Graham-owned Old Waldorf Theater in San Francisco on 5 October, set a pattern for the tour, with six of the ten cuts on *Wavelength* given an airing. Indicative of the way Morrison felt that his commercial standing had been eroded in the years away was the stultifying choice of old favourites, which smacked of throwing audiences a bag of bones – a murdered 'Moondance', 'Into the Mystic', 'Brown Eyed Girl', 'Help Me', 'Wild Night', 'Caravan', 'Gloria' and 'Cyprus Avenue' were all songs he had fiercely resisted playing in the years since *It's Too Late to Stop Now* set its own FM standard.

The reviews of opening night, though, were extremely positive. Joel Selvin in the *Chronicle* called the set 'a perfect blend of new and familiar material', though he also noted how Morrison's own performing persona was a manifestation of a tortured psyche, as he continued to 'sing with his eyes closed and his body held stock-still. He had little or nothing to say to the audience, and his terror of performing was obvious.' Though Morrison went to great pains to dismiss the relationship between his performing self and the man inside, such protestations merely served to affirm someone still thoroughly detached from his performance art:

Van Morrison: A performance, it's an act . . . You're not aware that you're in a certain city. It's more emotional for the audience, I think . . . You have to deal with this projected image that's got fuck all to do with you basically! Because what you're doing is just presenting a show and music . . . Have you ever watched an actor? He gets a script and he's got a part . . . and when he hits the stage he turns on a different thing. His mind changes, his concept changes, he's got to play a role for a certain amount of time. I do the same thing. Tonight I had to play a role for one hour. [1979]

Such detachment encapsulated the way it came across at many of the shows during the Stateside *Wavelength* tour. If, as Morrison claimed at the time, he was 'just try[ing] to get to the point where I'm putting across what I want to say', he was assuredly failing. As Sylvie Simmons wrote, in *Sounds*, of one of the November shows, at Royce Hall on the UCLA campus:

I'm convinced that Van Morrison doesn't do soundchecks, he just uses the first half of his show as a soundcheck instead . . . The man himself deserves more accolades than I can give, but his performance lately doesn't. On both nights [in LA] he gave up just when he was getting warm, and I've seen him enough times before to know that he can get so hot it burns. Maybe it's a good thing he's been walking out before the end of some of his shows. If he's not careful, he'll be racing the audience to the exit.

Despite Warners releasing a widely distributed promotional album from one of the better shows – at the Roxy in LA – and a show from New York's Bottom Line being syndicated to various radio stations, fans seemed to respond solely to the novelty of hearing the old songs recast, albeit in some peculiar guises (as in 'Cyprus Avenue' where Morrison pictures himself in a Fellini movie, as the schoolgirl stands in all her 'sanctified . . . vaginal Baptist revelation!'). Of the new songs only 'Checkin' It Out' really warranted its esteemed company, with its insidious riff and barked commands to 'Bring it up!' As the tour ran out of steam the shows got shorter, and Morrison's mood murkier.

After playing two sets on the night of 1 November at the intimate Bottom Line – presumably designed to ensure the right environment for an important radio broadcast – Morrison found himself the following night in the less intimate, more demanding confines of the New York Palladium. Forty minutes into the show – in the words of the unfortunate

Warners spokesman who was required to explain Morrison's behaviour – 'he just got freaked out. He was very tired and the show was not going particularly well . . . [And] he has always had a bit of an unstable character.' Morrison was furious with Warners for what he designated 'a direct ATTACK on my career', and demanded that the person(s) responsible be fired. Only some years later did he offer an explanation as to what strange state of mind prompted such a peremptory departure from the stage:

Van Morrison: I was completely exhausted. I just didn't have whatever it takes to perform. I was just . . . fed up. I felt about as much like performing as . . . going to the moon . . . The tour was too long . . . I compromised when I shouldn't have. A terrible thing to do *as an artist* [my italics] is to compromise when you know better . . . By the time I got to New York I'd already *done* it, and I was completely exhausted. [1984]

As the aftermath of this incident proved, the situation at Warners was such that Morrison could not be assured of the support of many people at the label. Referring to one of their premier acts as 'a bit of an unstable character' in a press release suggests that certain folk were quite happy to sabotage the man's 'comeback' – and good riddance! But then, as rock publicist Keith Altham duly notes, 'As a star you can behave as badly as you like, but don't do it with the people who are actually helping you. Don't do it to the record company who is providing you with the distribution for your records, don't do it with the management. If you start to do it with those people, then you've got nowhere to go.'

The support Morrison had once commanded at or near the top of his record company was a thing of the past. Joe Smith had bought himself a new pen set, and Mo Ostin, the president of the record division, had become weary of Morrison's continual demands some time before they had their final contretemps. As he later told the *LA Times*'s Robert Hilburn:

Mo Ostin: I loved his music, but I just couldn't [renew] the deal after looking at his sales, and [considering] the fact that you could have no input with the guy at all. He was as difficult as anyone I ever dealt with. He would explode on stage, in your office, having dinner at the house. I remember we almost came to blows because he kept insisting that I guarantee him a number-one single . . . I kept saying, 'Van, who can guarantee you a hit?'

The incident in which Morrison and Ostin 'almost came to blows' came when Harvey Goldsmith was trying to steer the ship – and was, if anything, more disturbing than the one that proscribed Joe Smith's goodwill. Ostin was a powerful figure, and was not used to artists who became physically threatening. Morrison, though, had become someone who at a certain point in a heated exchange could be genuinely out of control.

Harvey Goldsmith: He wanted to work, he was pleased with the album, and he started working [while] we were sorting out his deal with Warners in America, which wasn't going too well. We went over to Mo Ostin and he had a terrible fight with Mo . . . in his house. He threw an ashtray at him. [It was] just about the fact that he didn't feel he'd been treated right at Warners. He was very angry about the whole way Warners had or hadn't treated him in the past. And in a lot of instances he was right – they hadn't treated him that well. So that didn't help the Warners front, [and] it was an uphill struggle getting Warners back in the fold . . . He just got to the point where he just wanted to get out . . . They just couldn't get round his mood swings. And the one thing about record companies, the minute you get angry with them, they just turn off. I think that was really the end of it.

No matter how prepared Morrison was to promote his latest offering, he had in all likelihood already decided he wanted out of his deal with Warners. *Wavelength* certainly comes across as another contractual-obligation album. Seemingly resigned to an inevitable break with his record company, Morrison told one journalist whilst recording *Wave-length*, 'I don't get along with Warner Brothers very well . . . As a matter of fact, I don't get along with them at all . . . I've just been with them too long . . . It just doesn't feel like it felt.' What he was expressing was a not uncommon view – that the post-*Rumours* Warners was no longer the label that had championed the ruminations of a whole roster of talented singer-songwriters in the early seventies, no matter how solipsistic the results. The man who was to take over Morrison's business affairs from Bill Graham saw ample evidence of such a shift in emphasis.

Paul Charles: In those days, there was the Warner family. The Warner thing that he was part of . . . [was being] part of a family [for whom] the artist was the issue. The music that these special people created was the important thing. They followed the artist. What happened [with] the next generation of Warners

[was] the music-business executives became the important people, their bonuses became the issue: 'Well, Van, that last one only shipped three million and Sony shipped five million on Paul Simon and we have to find a way to learn lessons from what they did.' [Then] you've lost it.

For Morrison time had stood still, and it remained a question of not 'compromis[ing] on certain things. [But] I'm not a good business venture. I don't tour a lot, I don't play big halls, I don't sell a tremendous number of albums.' And yet, as long as he retained a certain critical kudos, and his demands were related to the reasonable, Warners were not about to give him the heave-ho. But by 1979 he had become increasingly convinced that there were a number of hidden agendas at Warners working to subvert his best interests.

Van Morrison: When I started, I had to play all sorts of games and jump through hoops to do certain things . . . I stopped playing that game over ten years ago with Warner Brothers because . . . I got to the point where I didn't have to play it any more, and I didn't want what that was going to get me. [1988]

Though Morrison would remain tied to Warners in the US for another four albums, *Wavelength* signalled the end of their worldwide distribution deal. In the months ahead, it became increasingly apparent that he was seeking to leap labels (as indeed he did, signing a long-term deal with PolyGram in the spring of 1979). If his relationship with his label had slumped to an all-time low, Morrison was finding it equally problematic working with his American manager. Two days after the Palladium walk-out, he was scheduled to appear on prime-time NBC comedy show *Saturday Night Live*, performing two songs from his new album. Bill Graham was there to ensure everything ran smoothly.

Bill Graham: I watched him during rehearsal and I said, 'Van, you're going to be in front of forty million people tonight.' 'So?' 'I watched you on the monitor. During the entire rehearsal, you sang with your eyes closed.' He turned to me, with his eyes closed, and said, 'Why don't you just do your fuckin' job and I'll do mine?'

Unbeknownst to Graham, Morrison had voiced just such a concern to Mo Foster at the playback of a Dutch TV appearance the previous year – 'Got my fucking eyes closed again! How can I be a performer

with my fucking eyes closed!' And yet on *this* occasion the comment
sparked a furious row. Peter Van Hooke, who witnessed both incidents,
saw 'a very exhausted' Morrison turn on Graham: 'And he is devastating
in an argument. He can tear you apart. It's quite frightening really, 'cause
it's so *lucid* – what he's saying – and it hits home. And he did one of these
with Graham: "It's your fault . . ."' But, as Van Hooke says, 'Eventually,
it all got patched up. And then we got a week off.' Then, just as the tour
was about to resume its winding way, Van Hooke came across a despairing
Graham hanging from the end of his tether.

Peter Van Hooke: I met Graham in Mill Valley one day and he says, 'I just
had this phone call from one of these Canadians, and we got this tour with Van
that finishes on . . . the 10th and they've got this show, with cameras, on the
11th, and it's for some mad money,' and I told Van this, and he turned round
and said, 'The tour finishes on the 10th.'

Graham simply could not understand such disregard for filthy lucre.
Though his management company would continue to work with their
troublesome charge for a while longer, it became an increasingly formal
arrangement, conducted by intermediaries, as Graham washed his hands
of the man *and* the artist.

As it happens, Morrison was again considering relocating to Britain,
making a complete break with the Graham organization inevitable.
However, the relocation process would be a long, drawn-out exercise,
as he attempted to retain a west-coast end to operations, all the while
tentatively exploring those British roots, both musical and personal. It
would be 1982 before the relocation could be termed permanent. The
first stage of the repatriation, though, came in February 1979, when his
touring band resumed operations in the British Isles. The eight-piece
band was now augmented by violin player Toni Marcus, and two sax
players, one of whom, John Altman, was finally given an opportunity to
arrange his friend's work – not that he was given a great deal of time to
show the originality of his ideas:

John Altman: [When] we started rehearsals, we were gigging the following
week. The Belfast and Dublin films – they were the second [and third] gigs.
We did one gig in Cork, reading music on the stage; the following night all the
music was gone.

Morrison intended to offset the considerable expense of a one-month tour of Irish and British theatres with an eleven-piece band by agreeing to have a documentary film made about his long-awaited return to Ireland – specifically Belfast, where he was scheduled to play two nights at Whitla Hall, his first shows in his home town since the Troubles resumed. As rehearsals began, at least one of the new recruits sensed that his new boss was surprisingly unenthused about the prospect of touring the UK for the first time in five years.

Pat Kyle: We spent a lot of time during [tour] rehearsals concentrating on getting the feel right. He's very particular about the way things happen . . . [But] I found him very distant [and] quite moody . . . He didn't mix with us a lot . . . [and] at the time he was a vegetarian, and totally teetotal.

Meanwhile, Warners needed to recruit a freelance publicist because Morrison would not work with anyone at the label (and vice versa), and so turned to Keith Altham, of *NME* fame.

Keith Altham: Moira Bellas [at Warners] got on the phone to me one day and said, 'Keith, would you consider doing Van Morrison's publicity?' I said, 'Ha ha ha.' . . . The legend was already self-perpetuating. She said, 'We've had problems.' I said [somewhat sarcastically], 'I am surprised.' Somebody in the press office had had the temerity to say that perhaps he wasn't the most co-operative person on God's earth . . . and Morrison had insisted that he be sacked, and that he would no longer have anything to do with the WEA press office, and Moira was obviously forced into the situation of having to look for an independent press officer . . . and I said, 'To be honest with you, Moira, I know how difficult he can be. If I'm gonna do it, how long's it gonna be for?' 'No more than three months.' So I said, 'I'll do a deal with you – I want the money up front, because if it doesn't work out I'm not suffering the consequences.' So she said, 'Fine.' I [thought,] 'Damn! Now I've got to do it.'

Altham would also find the artist slightly distant, and invariably ended up spending 'a lot of time with the musicians, sympathizing with them . . . [In] his performance he was a perfectionist – and good musicians rise to that particular challenge . . . What's difficult is all the stuff that goes on backstage, or during the soundcheck or whatever. He was quite solitary. Maybe the teetotal aspect made him more solitary. Most of the guys would go down the bar for a drink, and he wouldn't. So maybe he was just trying to keep himself together during that time, and not get sucked into the drink problem.' If so, the barrier erected between singer and musicians only mirrored the one that kept him detached from the wellspring of his art. The early shows were again a little stilted, prompting a review that was cruel to be cruel from *Melody Maker*'s Allan Jones, caught one more time in the stalls at Hammersmith Odeon:

The concert was certainly notable for the soporific effect it had on this spectator, at least. The same medium tempo was maintained throughout; the same structure applied to each song. Van would meander in, his voice gliding over the notes without embracing them with any kind of conviction (his performance was, at times, no more than a demonstration of his vocal dexterity) . . . The legend dies; a future in cabaret seems the only answer.

This review must have been particularly galling to Morrison, who had seemingly forgiven *Melody Maker* for running a cover story on the Palladium incident the previous November, giving their Chris Welch a surprisingly conversational interview in the run-up to the tour. However, the big-band aspect of Morrison's sound in the post-punk era just seemed to invite ridicule from most 'rock' critics, even if Altman proudly asserts, 'the actual quality of the music . . . was unmatched by anyone else [around]'. Indeed the old Morrison was slowly reasserting himself, even as he continued to mangle those familiar favourites.

John Altman: There was this thing that made everybody in the band cringe. He did a medley of his greatest hits, and he'd bow at the beginning of each one – I think he was sending it up.

Morrison turning over the main vocal on 'Moondance' to one of his backing singers – who shredded every nuance in a crescendo of crescendos – also suggested a wilful disposition reborn. That disposition, needless to say, was in full evidence when it came to dealing with the record company and the press – hence the presence of Keith Altham, an experienced publicist from the old school.

Keith Altham: I was dispatched to the Royal Garden Hotel for my first meeting with Van, and was confronted by him sitting on his own in the coffee area, where people were having their lunch, and he was sitting there vigorously flaxing his teeth, which he continued to do while he talked to me. He made it fairly clear to me that he was still as obstructive about the press as he'd been when I met him ten, fifteen years ago . . . 'My problem,' [he] mumbled mid-floss, sawing at [his] molars with a length of tooth flax, 'is that I do not consider the media have any right to any kind of insight into my private life. Now I have my *Wavelength* album to promote, and an Irish tour. I will talk music, and I will only talk music if the questions are intelligent and appropriate.' . . . I said, 'Well, fine. You do whatever you want to do. I'll give you what advice I can, and you can either take it or leave it.' I think he was a bit flummoxed by that.

Altham's first suggestion, after he had survived the ubiquitous confrontational interview, was a photo session, as he felt that the photos in the Warners files were out of date and inappropriate. Morrison, though, was still in testing mode and arrived two and a half hours late. Altham was fast discovering that 'he loves to test people with confrontation – but it [soon becomes] extremely wearisome, and a lot of people [just] say, "Forget it."' Altham was of the latter school.

Keith Altham: This is something that Morrison does all the time . . . getting people uptight, confrontation test: let's see how they react when I get there . . . When he [finally] got there, [the photographer] Brian Aris took him into the studio, and I think he was in there for about ten, fifteen minutes, then there was a crash of tripods and the words, 'I finished with this fucking posing years ago.' He emerged, with Brian Aris trailing behind him. And he said, 'I don't want to do this . . . This is not what I do.' And then he made the mistake of going a little bit too far with the confrontation and got the finger out – 'What I'm paying you for is to say no, no, no.' At that point I lost it a bit and said, 'In that case, get yourself a fucking parrot . . . You either accept my advice or you don't, but if you're not going to what is the point in my being here?' So he said, 'I'll think about that,' and exited stage left with his girlfriend . . . Then about three days later I got a call at home. He said, 'I been thinking about what you said, Keith. I think you know what you're talking about. What do you want me to do?'

Having passed the final test, Altham was allowed to do his job – which was to arrange interviews, organize press and generally ensure a profile worthy of his client's stature. Altham suggested they hold a series of interviews in Ireland while Morrison was on tour: one for the national press, one syndicated, and one for the music press. His suggestion for the music press, given that *Melody Maker* had already had their fifteen minutes, was *NME*'s Tony Stewart, a respected journalist and a closet fan. Stewart was flown over to Belfast, where Morrison was due to perform his home-coming concerts, and was promised the opportunity, either in Belfast or in Dublin, to ask some questions. Only on his arrival was Stewart made aware that there was also a film crew present to document the man's musical moods, and that he was down for a cameo role.

Keith Altham: [That night] he had a heckler in the audience [who] gave him a bad time. I thought, he's gonna be in a great mood when we get back to the hotel to do the [*NME*] interview. We get back to the hotel, he disappears to his room, which was his custom, to sit in a darkened room for about an hour – having had all the furniture, TV and everything else taken out of his room; incidentals were removed from his room that might disturb his equilibrium – and Van came downstairs. Meanwhile I'd spoken to Tony [Stewart] and Tony had said, 'Do you think he still wants to do the interview?' I said, 'What do you think?' He said, 'Well, look, if he's gonna be in a bad mood, forget it. I'll just do a review – I loved the concert – and we'll leave it at that.' If Tony Stewart had gone over and said, 'When are we gonna do the interview?' he would have ridden it out straight away, but because nobody pushed him, least of all me, he went the other way. He wanted to do it: 'No, no, I want to do it. I want to film it. I want it to be part of my documentary.' So I go back to Tony: 'Do you want the good news or the bad news? The good news is he's gonna do the interview, the bad news is he wants to film you doing the interview.' Tony [asked], 'Am I being set up?' . . . So we go up to his suite, set the tape up, three-man camera crew, and Tony starts with his first question: 'Well, Van, when you did *Veedon Fleece*, was that a particular time –?' 'I'm not answering personal questions.'

A familiar downward spiral ensued. Though the two-hour interview did run, and as a front-cover story, the piece Stewart wrote – accurate as it undoubtedly was – did Morrison few favours. Using the headline 'When Irish Eyes Are Scowling', Stewart detailed an interview conducted at Morrison's behest to illustrate why he doesn't like doing interviews. It culminated not with an irate Morrison pulling the plug, but with a frustrated journalist bellowing at Altham, 'He used *me* tonight to get over *his* point. And I was set up!'

However, it was *NME* photographer Pennie Smith who came up with the most damning comment in the published piece, after Stewart argued that he had stuck to his brief and 'asked about the songs'. She suggested another possibility – that 'he just hasn't anything to say that counts'. Mike Radford, the film director caught up in his own *cinéma vérité* moment, as part of an attempt to placate one pissed-off journalist, perhaps came closer to capturing the man: 'I just think Morrison is terrified, absolutely terrified of revealing too much about himself.'

Radford was to find out just how incisive was his assessment when attempting to put together his fabled documentary. Though he had filmed Morrison walking down Cyprus Avenue and through Belfast city centre, *Van Morrison in Ireland* featured no interview footage – not even the Stewart–Morrison confrontation – the informal footage being used merely as a visual counterpoint to the musical soundtrack of what became, in truth, simply another 'In Concert' film. Presumably it was Morrison who ensured that he remained unrevealed, preferring to simply document the point at which he rediscovered the will to perform. And some of the concert footage is riveting, in a way that live footage of the American *Wavelength* band failed to be.

John Altman: [In Dublin] there was a fight between somebody out of his head and a bouncer [who] jumped in to subdue him, and Van got a bit edgy about that, but those Belfast and Dublin gigs, (a) they were fantastic concerts, (b) he was in a great mood. It was very upbeat! But Van had started to feel that he was being manipulated into a filmmaker's vision of what he should be doing and how he should be, and he didn't want that. He wanted a film record of where he was, so I think the mood turned.

If the performances in *Van Morrison in Ireland* were evenly divided between Dublin and Belfast, there was no mistaking the location of the performance of 'Saint Dominic's Preview' as the reference to Belfast raised the ceiling. The two shows at Whitla Hall were a real test for Morrison. As the promoter Paul Charles, who booked these shows, recalls, 'People expected him to walk on water – the expectation was amazing! I'm sure to him it was [just] another opportunity for him to go on stage and sing his music. He came on stage, and he just dug in. He didn't play to that I'm-back-again [thing].'

Nevertheless, the air of expectancy pushed him to search out the performer within, and some of the songs burned with renewed energy. Notably, 'Checkin' It Out' and 'Tupelo Honey' suggested that new girlfriend, Brenda, was doing something right. A new verse inserted into the latter spoke of 'a rose pressed inside a Bible, that she reads on the balcony/She's sweet in slumber and I've got her number/from the beginning of the century'. This first reference to the good book in Morrison's work was to presage a swift change in direction later in the year.

Indicative of another change in direction was the positive bond Morrison quickly established with Irish tour promoter Paul Charles, whose perseverance had made the shows in Cork, Belfast and Dublin a reality. Charles had initially approached Harvey Goldsmith back in 1977 but, as we know, the planned European tour never happened. When the *Wavelength* shows began in America, Charles duly phoned Bill Graham's office in San Francisco, only to be told, 'Well, we've no plans, but Van's not just gonna go to Europe to play six shows in Ireland. We need to do England as well.' Charles volunteered to organize that too, and so a viable tour began to come together. As Charles says, 'I don't think there was anybody else from Ulster in the English music business at that point.' Charles had first seen the man perform at the legendary Cookstown riot back in 1964 and such common roots evidently endeared him to Morrison. Sure enough Morrison soon began to sound him out about booking some further shows in the summer.

Paul Charles: We drove from Cork back to Dublin, arrived back in the early hours of the morning. [I'm] just about to go to bed and I get a call from Van: 'D'you fancy a cup of tea or coffee?' – which is Van's [way]. [When I arrive] he says, 'Do you book acts all over the place? Do you do Europe and things?' I said, 'Yeah, yeah.' So he said, 'Well, maybe we should think of doing a tour of Europe.' That's really how [our association] started . . . He'd got a group of people together, he liked the band, the shows were great, being in Ireland was quite magical. He'd [also] been away for so long . . . [Eventually I became] his business manager. I was his agent. I also looked after his business arrangements. We were his base . . . [but] you don't manage Van. Van Morrison will always be the best manager for Van Morrison. 'Cause he sees through bullshit so quickly . . . It's never 'Well, let's see what happens. We'll work it out as we go along' . . . Everyone knows exactly where they stand.

Morrison's new-found faith in Charles further slackened America's hold on him. Its grip had been lessening with each passing year anyway, for an obvious enough reason. As he duly admitted, 'When my daughter Shana grew up, that's when I left [America]. When she became a teenager, I got out because there was no reason for me to be there any more.'

He also missed the familiarity of Britain, that uniquely Anglo-Saxon sense of irony and understatement, and a common delight in shared references. Magnificent a drummer as he was, Peter Van Hooke's continued presence on American tours and sessions was as much to help keep his boss sane as to supply the necessary rhythmic foundation.

Peter Van Hooke: We used to hang out a lot, just for fun. We'd have our own little British jokes that we had between us . . . There's a couple of reasons why we got on. One, he'd been steeped in America for a long time and we both liked some of the same things, and I was English and I think I reminded him a bit of some of his roots . . . We never talked music, ever. We discussed people like Tony Hancock.

As Morrison had told Ritchie Yorke back in the spring of 1977, when he first threatened to abandon the west coast, 'I've never become an American. I'm talking about the whole thing – psychologically, citizenship, the whole trip.' After all the time he'd spent writing about 'lost dreams and found dreams in America', he was still searching for a way to replenish the wells of inspiration, which had been running dry for almost half a decade.

If his actual environment had always been a factor in his art, Morrison had become increasingly aware that, no matter how much America offered in the way of opportunities, it was Britain and Ireland that lent his writing its strength of purpose. In the months that separated the end of the *Wavelength* US tour from its British leg, Morrison found himself searching for 'an environment where you can get all of it . . . a lot of peace and quiet at certain times, and a lot of activity at other times . . . where you can get all the dynamics happening . . . finding that balance that's conducive both to your art and [to] putting it together'. He came to realize that neither Ireland nor the States could fulfil both roles; hence his divided loyalties.

Van Morrison: Most of *Astral Weeks* and *Veedon Fleece* was written in Ireland and recorded here. The songs on the other records were done mostly in [America]. But nowadays I go between two places: the United States for recording, working and organizing, and Ireland – Belfast and the South – for inspiration and composing. [1978]

As of 1978 the evidence for this was a tad thin on the ground. The subject matter of *Transition* and *Wavelength* was almost quintessentially American, albeit from a dislocated point of view. However, come the winter of 1979, Morrison found himself immersed in another flood of songs, prompted by his trip to Ireland and England. Reinforcing the sense of *Veedon Fleece* revisited, on returning to the States he almost immediately set about assembling such studio musicians as were necessary to record the album that would finally restore him to the bright side of the road.

AGE SIX

Back into the Music

21

1979–80: Down by Avalon

The only two powers that trouble the deep are religion and love.

—*W. B. Yeats*

That's when I got back into it. That's why I called it *Into the Music.*

—*Van Morrison, 1984*

Into the Music was about the first album where I felt, 'I'm starting here.' . . . the *Wavelength* thing, I didn't really feel that was me.

—*Van Morrison, 1988*

Though clues aplenty of renewed commitment to his muse stray across the performances on *Van Morrison in Ireland*, it was only on the month-long British leg that directly followed these shows that Morrison relaxed enough to let the music flow. Having reversed the conventions of touring, which dictated building the arrangements before hitting London, Belfast and Dublin, Morrison found himself at the end of February with the three capitals done and dusted, yet with three weeks of shows left to get through. And the shows just got better. The band finally gelled, and John Altman was coming up with arrangement ideas they would just try, a methodology of which Morrison greatly approved.

John Altman: I don't think I ever worked with anyone who was more liberal-minded about what I did. I could have walked in and said, 'Oh, "Caravan" is now a waltz with reggae overtones,' and he'd say, 'Fine. Tell me when to come in.' . . . It was a trust thing . . . He gives his musicians freedom. If you suddenly picked up your clarinet during 'Goodnight Irene' that would be OK. At the same time, if you hit on something that might be wrong, he would simply say afterwards . . . 'I don't want it that way.'

Once Morrison began to chill musically – all the while staying hitched to his self-imposed wagon – the band could begin to relax into its appointed role. Peter Van Hooke, who had witnessed each and every musical shift since 1974, believes it all comes down to the man's musical 'instincts': 'If he's enjoying what's happening at the time, he's happy . . . The instincts of the moment are trying to get it right. "Lock it in." "Do this." "Soft." They weren't detailed comments. That would be it. And also he didn't care where they came from.'

Some of the band members who took liberties with this new licence incurred the animosity of the other musicians – but not Morrison. Saxophonist Pat Kyle remembers how violinist Toni Marcus, 'after two or three of the gigs . . . decided to do her own thing. And she was a great success. She would fling herself about, and Van seemed to like it, and the crowd liked it, but I thought it was very rude to actually abandon the arrangements.' Morrison shared no such qualms and as Kyle also remembers, 'on a couple of occasions [Van] decided to take a solo [himself] . . . so he got his alto out, and there were quite a lot of squeaks. [But] it was just something he fancied doing.'

The squeaks that emerged when Morrison fancied a honk fitted in surprisingly well with the creaky noises ushering from Marcus, placed in the Scarlet Rivera role. The other musicians, though, cruelly rechristened her Vile Din. John Altman describes how '[it] got to the point where I would go [through] a squeaking door and everyone would go, "Stop playing, Toni." . . . We couldn't work out what [Toni Marcus] was doing there . . . There was a tape Mick Glossop made, and he was soloing every track for balance, and we were sitting there with Van listening to this and he soloed the violin track and there was this horrendous screech, and Van said, "What the hell's that?" [But] he sort of had a smirk on his face about it.'

Morrison knew all along what he wanted and retained Marcus for the forthcoming sessions and a summer tour. On the other hand, when Altman, a more than competent player, turned up at rehearsals one day with a set of vibes, which he proceeded to play on a number of songs, 'the tour manager came up . . . and said, "Leave the vibes at home. Van doesn't like vibes."' Morrison's instincts were telling him that this particular mix worked – whereas recent combinations, perhaps with 'better' musicians, had not. As a lesson it struck home, Morrison retaining the method until the present day.

Jonn Savannah: [There were] some people who were appalling players but [had] something – I do think that he'll put wild cards in to shake the whole thing up, and upset people. He likes to upset someone, because it makes them play in a different way . . . There's several people he's had that I've thought, 'Why are they here?' . . . They didn't know their stuff – but they were all there for a reason.

Morrison was entirely aware of the tensions between the other musicians, but as he put it at the time, '[The musicians] have to be tuned into what I'm actually doing – more even than the music.' Some time later he told a writer that this particular band didn't want to work together, and he didn't know why, but 'musically they worked'. And *he* was starting to enjoy himself enough to allow himself some after-hours crooning.

John Altman: I remember we were rehearsing one day and we were doing 'Georgia on My Mind' and I got on the piano, and Van was singing his heart out . . . then we never did the song. But when we were in the hotel in Edinburgh, I sat at the piano in the bar and he just stood in the well of the piano and we did like half an hour of Hoagy Carmichael songs and these two American businessmen said, 'Gee, you sound good. Have you ever thought of doing this professionally?'

As they entered the final week of the tour, Marrison even turned up at a student party – after a gig in Edinburgh – and, the following day in Glasgow, as John Altman recounts, 'we all met up in Henderson's wine bar up there, and Van and Herbie were telling stories about their days in the showbands in Ireland, and they had the whole restaurant gathered round in a circle. It was fantastic!'

Morrison's mood, though, could still pivot on a knife-edge. When he got to that night's venue, the Glasgow Apollo, he walked to the front of the stage and said, 'Someone could get killed with that drop. How can you put people on a stage like this?' As Altman says, 'that obviously triggered off something [because when it came to the gig] I looked round to cut off "Moondance" and I couldn't see him. I could hear his voice, but he was hiding behind the bass amp.'

Pat Kyle: There was this huge twenty-foot drop. So he retired to the piano, which he was due to play [on] one or two numbers. But he did the whole concert from the piano. And since the lighting was set for a ballad it was all blues and pinks – the rest of the stage was in darkness . . . We did the whole concert in this one lighting set.

When the tour ended, two days later in Newcastle, Morrison stayed on in England, writing songs, soaking in its spires and searching for a way to translate the spirit of his recent performances on to record. It was a feeling he had voiced a couple of years earlier, when in a bind about just such a dilemma, 'The records are merely the songs. You've got bands on records, you've got three minutes . . . whereas, in performing, the song is not just a song, it's the song *plus something else*, which may last eight or ten minutes.' At last he had some songs that he could take to that other place, having remembered what it was he did: 'We do spontaneous, improvised music now – more poetic music.'

The sessions for *Into the Music*, held in the spring of 1979 at the familiar Record Plant in Sausalito, continued the quest for that 'spontaneous, improvised . . . poetic music'. They may well have begun with a blues jam, an instrumental called 'Sacramento', and a ramble through the blues standard 'I'm Ready',★ but the first song that occupied a linear line from *Veedon Fleece*, and the singer's wayward muse, was 'Troubadours', an evocative re-creation of the original travelling singers and their trade, singing 'songs of love and chivalry from the days of yore'. Morrison gives the tale modern relevance by asking the ladies fair to 'lift your window high – do you dig that sound?/It's the troubadours coming through town'. He was firmly establishing himself in the same tradition, even on a collection with precious few 'songs of love' and fewer chivalric deeds.

Having cut the basic take, Morrison felt that the song might benefit from some horns. Mark Isham, a trumpeter present at the sessions at the suggestion of bassist David Hayes, said he knew exactly the right person – and mentioned the magical words James Brown and the JBs.

Pee Wee Ellis: Mark told him that I lived down the street – that was Mill Valley, where Van also lived. He just knew I'd been one of the JBs, and that

---

★ This recording was originally scheduled for inclusion on *The Philosopher's Stone* but was pulled at the last minute, finally appearing as an incongruous 'bonus' track on the CD single of 'The Healing Game'.

was enough! . . . So he called me in and we listened to 'Troubadours' and Van said, 'Can you do anything with this?' I said, 'Yeah, sure.' We did one song and then within a couple of days the whole album was done. It was as straight ahead as that . . . When I heard the song 'Troubadours' I said to myself, 'This is some very important stuff here.' . . . He gave me the freedom to put the horn charts together. I liked that. [SG]

Pee Wee not only got to arrange charts on the remaining songs but was retained as a member of Morrison's band throughout all the days of experimentation that were to produce *Into the Music*, *Common One* and *Beautiful Vision*. The drummer on 'Troubadours', Kurt Wortman, was not so lucky. For although Peter Van Hooke – one of just four survivors from the winter tour invited to the sessions (Katie Kissoon, Herbie Armstrong and Toni Marcus being the others) – found himself initially excluded from the game, it was only until he reminded Morrison just what he was missing, on the one cover to make the finished album.

Peter Van Hooke: After he'd brought me all the way to San Francisco, I walked in [and] there was another drummer playing – which was typical Van, completely oblivious to my feelings – and the recordings got under way and this other drummer was playing . . . There was a thing called '[It's] All in the Game' – first time we ever played that really – and the original version was much longer; it [went] on for another six minutes in the middle – and this guy was playing, and I could see it wasn't working – good player but not really locked into the moment – and Van said, 'Let Van Hooke have a go.' I came in and . . . I'm one of these guys who can play first takes, and Van's exactly the same. He's in for that moment. That exploring moment is the most exciting time [for him] . . . On the *Into the Music* sessions it was done as a small ensemble, [with] brass added. John Allair also came in and added some Hammond. That was a brilliant band. If Van said, 'Brass,' Pee Wee would make up an arrangement on the [spot].

Needless to say, Van Hooke never left his stool again. 'It's All in the Game', incorporating Morrison's own 'You Make Me Feel So Free', would come to typify 'the song plus something else' ethos in concert, though on *Into the Music* it was squeezed into its 4.39 with no room to spare, as Morrison jammed on so much music that *Wavelength* by comparison came out an EP. The songs were coming easily again, both from the pen and in the studio, as the guitarist on these sessions Herbie

Armstrong had cause to observe: 'He knows what he wants in the studio. It's like he's got every instrument in his brain.'

Among the songs for which there was no room at the inn were two that Morrison later returned to – 'Spirit' and 'Quality Street'. Indeed 'Spirit' was, in many ways, the key to *Into the Music*, even though it found a firmer voice on that album's successor, *Common One*. In addressing both the pit of despair into which his absent muse had sent him, and the chasm in his soul that faithlessness had brought, the singer began to pray, 'Help me, angel'. The answer that comes through – whether from 'the One' or from just 'turn[ing] inside' – is simple and direct: 'Oh no. Never let the spirit die'.

'Spirit' 's siblings, 'Bright Side of the Road' and 'Full Force Gale', would open *Into the Music*, introducing an upbeat (by-)product of the renewed spirit inside. The joyous sound no longer sounded forced. As to the unmistakable Christian elements running through much of the album, Morrison would later suggest, 'It's something I've always carried. There was no conversion experience . . . I've been a Christian since I was born.' The conversion depicted in the album's opening couplet was 'from the dark end of the street/to the bright side of the road', not necessarily from the road leading down to death to the narrower path of righteousness.

Nevertheless, something had freed his spirit. It may have been partly the direct 'religious' influence of a physical muse – as it undoubtedly was with Dylan, that very winter, five thousand miles away. The references in contemporary songs are certainly there: 'We'll be lovers once again on the bright side of the road'; 'Angel on high, from heaven so high above/I thank God for sending me you'; and, most conclusively, in the spoken passage to 'Angeliou', one of the album's more celebrated songs, which addresses a true soul partner:

When you came up to me that day, and I listened to your story, it reminded me so much of myself. It wasn't what you said, but the way it felt [as if it were] about a search and a journey just like mine.

Seven years later Morrison would write one of his most memorable songs, 'In the Garden', about a similar experience. The light of God was likewise alluded to in the *magnum opus* that would dominate *Common One*. Experiencing the beauty of God's creation with this soul partner, presumably girlfriend Brenda, finally seems to have allowed Morrison to bathe in some of its reflected glory.

'Rolling Hills', one of the slighter songs on *Into the Music*, was written, according to Herbie Armstrong, 'about the Cotswold countryside, which he spent much of his time exploring by car. Sometimes he would take his guitar with him and walk through fields making up songs.' The song itself, an off-kilter jig, envisaged living 'among the rolling hills/With my wife and child . . .' Needless to say, Morrison had no such intention. In fact, his peripatetic lifestyle had again made him a man without a home, and for a short while he was obliged to rent a house in Stadhampton, Oxfordshire, on an *ad hoc* basis, simply to allow himself necessary access to those inspirational rolling hills.

Hilary Sanderson: He would call directly and ask if the house [in Stadhampton] was free. Sometimes when we weren't going to be away he would come and stay in the house during the daytime and then go back to [a] hotel [at night]. We'd go out to work and he'd move in. It was a point at which he was becoming interested in Christianity. He always had a girl with him – often a different girl. He was terribly shy at first and wouldn't communicate directly. He asked his girlfriend to do it, unless it was a practical matter of how something worked in the house.

The real triumph on *Into the Music*, though, again addresses his true 'home'. 'And the Healing Has Begun' was 'a celebration of recollection', as one writer put it. Right from its evocative opening, it conjures up a whole series of common reference-points: 'And we'll walk down the avenue again/And we'll sing all the songs from way back when . . .' At eight minutes – with a spoken bridge depicting a carefree time of music and passion – it is another epic attempt to bring that feeling into the present, to illuminate the here and now with the light of experience. In performance the song would invariably be a show-stopper as Morrison reached inside the words, searching for the undying spirit. But what makes the song, and indeed *Into the Music*, work is its self-awareness. Gone is the awkward self-consciousness of something like 'Take It Where You Find It', whose attempt to 'see it all now/through the eyes of a child' digs no deeper than a pot-hole in the road. It is replaced by a newly assured tone, born of a genuine awareness of what he was attempting.

Van Morrison: When I started writing songs, it was totally unconscious. I didn't start writing consciously, or shall we say observing it consciously, until I was twenty-eight years old. Before that everything I wrote was completely unconscious; I hadn't a clue what it was about. [1986]

Part of the process, probably the first part, was a determined study of childhood visions. He was looking, as he later expressed it, for 'somewhere to put my experiences, to find out what they were'. Told about William Blake's early visionary experiences, he found that Blake's own description of the experiences 'came close to describing what the feeling was'. He also read similar accounts of and by other poets, metaphysical and modern, undoubtedly encountering Yeats's *A Vision* early in his mystical studies.

Though nothing Morrison ever experienced seems to have resembled the detailed transmissions documented in *A Vision*, William Butler became one more talisman in the search. Despite later claims that his own 'lineage would be more [fellow Anglo-Irish poet and theosophist] AE . . . as opposed to Yeats', the latter became another name to conjure when it came time to draw the lineage of these poetic vessels in 1983's 'Rave On, John Donne'. Morrison would also in time incorporate beat poet Allen Ginsberg into what he called 'the Blakean lineage', after finding a book describing Ginsberg's 'own visionary experience, not on drugs, and it sounds like the same as mine . . . [at least] as far as the way poetry happens'.★ These historical examples helped to provide some sense of the direction in which he had been unknowingly heading.

Van Morrison: It's like I'm receiving some sort of inner direction. There's something inside of me that directs me to do this, and I don't know why myself. It directs me to do my work and my study, to study religion and to study various aspects of this in relation to [my] experiences. [ST]

As he continued to 'develop these things that come through the subconscious mind and put shapes on them [so] they become songs', his control over this development returned. He was also asking questions not only about other beneficiaries of the process but about the ultimate source of such lines of communication. Those he subjected to these questions were not only his nearest and dearest, but also his landlady, well-known rock writers . . . and so on. The process would occupy much of the ensuing decade.

★ Though Morrison would subsequently meet Ginsberg at a London tea-room, Ginsberg was unimpressed by the man and his discourteous ways.

Hilary Sanderson: He was always searching, inquisitive. I felt that he definitely wanted to go back to his Celtic roots. And he'd get into quite deep discussions about things like Stonehenge. Questions rather than answers. I remember I was always finding scraps of paper with writing on them.

Steve Turner: He asked me a lot of questions . . . Once I was having a meal with him, and he said to me — it was almost his first question — he said, 'What do you think about the blood of Jesus?' It's a strange question for a rock musician to ask.

All those references to weighing up given situations before moving ahead had led him to a simple truth, first suggested by 'Checkin' It Out''s bridge: 'All the obstacles along the way, sometimes they feel so tremendous/[But] there are guides and spirits all along the way, who will befriend us'. It had been a tortuous process to arrive at a clean slate, having found that he could 'only burn up with that passion/When there's absolutely nothing left to lose' ('You Make Me Feel So Free'). Something clearly prompted him to let go of the many layers of psychological armour he had built around himself. As he put it in the 1980 song 'Real Real Gone', 'I got hit by a bow and arrow/Got me down to the very marrow'. Derek Bell of the Chieftains believes that a potential suicide brought Morrison to the brink of self-awareness.

Derek Bell: A friend of his had threatened to commit suicide and for two years he'd done no work and just gone into his shell reading and studying theosophy, the Rosicrucians, Scientology . . . Van knew that I must be up to my neck in all this so we became friends.

That 'threatened suicide' probably went all the way. Morrison's old friend, writer Donall Corvin, who at one point had been mooted as the possible author of an authorized Morrison biography, had recently taken his life, having burned bridges and candles for too long. As a result, Morrison found himself asking uncomfortable questions of himself. He also allowed Derek Bell to bring him into an inner circle of friends with occult leanings, in the hope that answers he had previously sought from conventional religion might be found on these outer limits.

Derek Bell: In the days when I first met him, he was really looking for some sort of spiritual answer to things. At the time . . . he wanted to discuss mysticism and he wanted to know did I think there was anything he should be studying. I suggested various things, but it was very difficult because he had already read something like three thousand books on mysticism . . . Anything I mentioned was covered somewhere in those three thousand books.

Morrison, though, was delighted just to find someone in the same musical field with whom he could have a sensible conversation about philosophical matters. Having grown up in an environment disturbingly proud of its anti-intellectualism, and having moved at a relatively impressionable age to America's west coast, where every philosophy and spiritual preoccupation was prone to faddism, he had previously been denied any real outlet for those questions that came in the middle of the night, and the books he read refused to talk back. Another Irish musician, a close friend of Derek Bell's, Clive Culbertson, would complete what was to be a very tight triangle of would-be adepts for the bulk of the eighties. Culbertson too was amazed by the depth of knowledge Morrison had gleaned from his after-hours studies.

Clive Culbertson: I was sitting in [my home] outside Ballymoney, and the phone rings. It's [Van's personal manager] John Rogers. He goes, 'Clive, [are] you doing anything tonight?' 'No, why?' 'Van's over . . . in the Grimsport Hotel, and he wants somebody interesting to talk to. So I was telling him you're a Rosicrucian and a few other things. So do you want to come up?' 'Aye, when?' . . . That's how we met and we talked till four or five in the morning. It was great, 'cause generally when he spoke to people about [Madame Helena Petrovna] Blavatsky or Alice Bailey, [they] didn't know [them]. But I'd read a lot of it, and [what] with the fact that I do ritual magic and stuff, [it] meant that there were a lot of areas that he could cover with me that he couldn't cover with anybody [else]. [And] he is a walking library – I was amazed. There were times [when] you would say about a certain master doing such-and-such, [and he'd say,] 'Yeah man, that's 1883, that's whenever he was in so-and-so.' And he could quote [Alice] Bailey, and he could quote [Dion Forch], and he could tell you what book he read it in.

Though Blavatsky and Bailey would only begin to make their presence felt on Morrison albums from *Beautiful Vision* onwards, for almost a decade after the initial breakthrough that came shortly before *Into the Music*, the response of this autodidact to the holes in his thinking became increasingly intense. His scattershot approach to a vast subject was the classic response of the self-taught, as was the credulity he brought to the process. As he revealed at a time when the appeal of further study had begun to pall, 'I'm into all of it, orthodox or otherwise. I don't accept or reject any of it. I'm not searching for anything in particular. I'm just groping in the dark . . . for a bit more light.' His explanation for the impetus behind his search suggested a rejection of orthodoxy in all its guises:

Van Morrison: The reason that people pursue theosophy and related subjects is because they've come up with blank answers about the programmes they've been fed. It's just another, more open way of looking at things. That's why I got into it. I couldn't find any answers in the existing framework. I just drew a blank . . . So I started reading, broadening out the picture to give me a different take on it. [1989]

One of the most challenging thinkers Morrison encountered in those early months of 1979 was the composer Cyril Scott, whose book *Music: Its Secret Influence Through the Ages*, first published in 1933, set him seriously thinking about the actual 'effect' music had on the human spirit. In fact, it was a recording Derek Bell had made of some of Scott's music that had prompted Morrison to make contact with the Chieftain.

At around the same time, Morrison came across a double cassette of a 1978 lecture by spiritual teacher Elizabeth Clare Prophet, entitled *The Science of Rhythm for the Mastery of the Sacred Energies of Life*. David Tame, author of *The Secret Power of Music* (1984), remembers discussing the impact of Prophet with the man: 'Van [was] saying he agreed with 95 per cent of it . . . This lecture [gave] a very powerful message about the positive and negative effects of different forms of music. These sources reinforced Van's astonishment that we have this whole huge music industry, including rock, and yet so few people seem to be interested in its implications, or the effects it might be exerting upon [the] listener.'

Though many of the dictates dispensed by Scott and Prophet would not be felt until *Common One*, *Into the Music* was the first Morrison album to allude to the healing power of music – to that moment 'when you hear the music ringin' in your soul'. Likewise, using the word to 'explain' his music was something that occurred first in interviews promoting his 1979 album:

Van Morrison: I might write about a feeling, or about love. But to me, I think I'm writing about NOTHING. Except at times I write about the feeling of

LOVE . . . Music is like a healing thing, and we're all being healed. I'm being healed – that's what I know, [it's] what I feel. [1979]

Not every reviewer sensed the healing power of the music. But then not every reviewer was still paying attention. Certainly not *NME*'s Paul Rambali, who accused Morrison of 'floundering in his own backwash' since *Veedon Fleece*, before suggesting that his habit of writing 'songs just for the feel of them . . . can't lend conviction to his singing, and much of *Into the Music*, despite the earnest pose struck on the cover, suffers from a deficit of just that'. On the other hand, *Sounds*'s Dave McCullough recognized *Into the Music* as 'one of Morrison's most rounded, complete and ordered albums ever'.

Morrison knew he had struck a rich vein, and immediately (re)-assembled his European travelling band for a series of mainland shows. Essentially a slimmed-down version of the winter *Wavelength* combo – with one old hand replacing another – the eight-piece unit was given an entirely different brief from the winter shows.

John Altman: I think that what we were doing in the gigs was definitely making his mind work in those [new] directions, and when we did the summer tour of Europe, we were basically doing *Into the Music*. That's what it was. It was a slightly smaller band; Pete Wingfield had come in for Pete Bardens. Bobby Tench had gone. The other sax player had gone. It was a much more streamlined feeling – a looser feel. We still did some things from *Wavelength* but it was a lot freer. The *Wavelength* band was a showband . . . I had one solo, on 'Don't Look Back' – but when we were [doing] *Into the Music*, I was soloing on everything. I was having a ball. It was like, 'Let's take it on a stage.'

With Morrison usually playing seven songs from the new waxing, but just 'Kingdom Hall' and 'Wavelength' from its ten-month-old precursor, this was a truly revamped show. The nightly highlight was usually 'It's All in the Game' segued into 'You Know What They're Writing About', culminating in that pile-driving finale where he would ask to meet her, 'Down by the PYLONS!!'. But just because he had been reading Aleister Crowley didn't mean that everything was permissible. Certain musical directions were still out of bounds.

John Altman: We were playing at this festival in Oslo. We'd just done 'It's All in the Game' – a couple of nights [earlier] he'd suddenly gone into it on stage

— so we were doing it [again], and I started playing an alto solo, and Pete Wingfield really got into a Ray Charles-type groove and we were vamping between G7 and C7, and the crowd went mad. Anyway, the gig finished and we came off stage, and Pete was [saying], 'Great gig, Van. Great, great, great.' And Van just walked up and said, 'No sevenths.' What he was saying was 'The mood of the song is not where I want it to go.'★

Though the tour retained the ready camaraderie of the British leg, and Morrison remained generally upbeat about being back on the road, there were the inevitable judders. In particular, Altman recalls a show in Bergen in Norway where 'somebody yelled out, "You're number one," and he dropped the band right there and said, "You know, we don't have to do this. We don't *like* travelling around and sitting in airports and hotels, just to entertain [etc.]."' It turned out that he had thought the guy had shouted, 'Play the number one.' On such moments did his mood on stage hinge. But then the greater the musical highs, the more he felt the depths.

Peter Van Hooke: Van is a very instinctive guy. He plays for necessity. There's a part of him that needs to communicate in music, which he enjoys sometimes and other times he feels is a burden. So when it came to doing a concert [tour] . . . getting off on a gig was important. I was always ready for that moment where you could take it a stage further. It wasn't just playing the song as it comes up, it was really exploring it, [being] willing to really understand the platform, how to build it up and work as a team to get to a higher height with these songs . . . [But] like most artists, [he] doesn't know where it comes from.

Morrison continued to hanker after a way of containing such moments in permanent form — to transplant that platform to a studio and stretch on out. He felt like testing his own artistic nerve again, even though the sales of the renaissance album *Into the Music* failed to match those of its ephemeral predecessor. The thought processes now at work he would articulate only after the fact, when the results were there for all to hear and *feel*.

★ In a typical twelve-bar, a seventh often 'telegraphs' the end of a given sequence. It may be this aspect that is not to Morrison's taste.

Van Morrison: If I really did what I really felt I wanted to do, it might be sort of inaccessible because, for instance, when you make an album you end up with three-, four-, maybe five-minute songs, but when I actually play . . . just play with other musicians, things stretch out to much longer than that . . . and you have to edit a lot of things . . . you have to make it more accessible, shape it and edit it and reshape it to make it accessible for people to 'get it' in their working day . . . to make it more compact. [1981]

The feeling that commercial considerations served to constrain him was not a new preoccupation. Back in 1972 he had suggested that there was 'a lot of stuff. . . . I've never recorded that's totally far out. But I make albums primarily to sell them, and if I get too far out a lot of people can't relate to it.' *Common One* would be the first – and last – time he would make an album almost wholly composed of 'far-out stuff' and, though Johnny Rogan would later dismiss the results as 'a grandiloquent but failed attempt to retrace the steps that ended with *Veedon Fleece*', *Common One* did a lot more than retrace steps. Morrison mapped out a whole new direction. Indeed there was an almost unprecedented degree of preparation before the album sessions themselves, which occupied nine days in February 1980.

Mick Cox: In '79 I went out to the States with a friend of mine and I rang Van, who was in Sausalito, and [he] invited me up to his place. I stayed a couple of weeks and we mucked about playing bits and pieces, and working on the early stages of *Common One*. He was doing little club gigs like Inn of the Beginning – as Mechanical Bliss [Plus One] . . . At those shows at the Warfield and the Great American Music Hall [in January 1980] we started doing 'Haunts of Ancient Peace' as an instrumental . . . [And] during November and December '79 there were lots of rehearsals with this band, when we did 'Haunts' and 'Summertime in England' in 4/4 time . . . Van brought it right down at the end to nothing, so he's just saying, 'Can you feel the silence?' but he's still keeping the beat, and then Pee Wee takes his mouthpiece off and Mark Isham takes his mouthpiece off, and they're both making quiet percussive noises in time to the rhythm . . . I still think some of these performances at the rehearsals were far better than the final recordings. [SG]

'Haunts of Ancient Peace' and 'Summertime in England' proved to be the two central tracks Morrison brought to the *Common One* sessions. The former, he later claimed, was 'the title of a book I bought in a second-hand bookstall in Cornwall one time . . . That was the kind of thing I was doing . . . at that period.'* 'Summertime in England' came from, well, a hyperactive mind and a mountain of ideas crossbred into a jumble sale of a song. Coherent it ain't.

Van Morrison: ['Summertime in England'] was actually part of a poem I was writing, and the poem and the song sorta merged . . . I'd read several articles about this particular group of poets who were writing about this particular thing, which I couldn't find in the framework I was in. [1989]

This poem was apparently about a literary pilgrimage to the Lake District, where Wordsworth and Coleridge had worked on the poems that made up their joint literary landmark, *Lyrical Ballads*. Morrison subsequently informed Desmond Hogan that he originally planned 'to do that poem on its own', and after incorporating it into the greater whole even he did not 'know if it was connected'.

The version of 'Summertime' that the band was working on in December 1979 came without the spoken section in 3/4 time that begins on the studio recording with a beautiful church-organ fugue from John Allair. As the lyrics lurch between images of Wordsworth and Coleridge 'smokin' up in Kendal' and those that invoke Jesus wandering through the ancient kingdom of Albion (*sic*), Morrison addresses a third person, one unconversant with any of the history surrounding these two quite distinct pastoral images. When he asks his 'baby' whether she has ever heard of William Wordsworth or Samuel Coleridge, it sounds as though he is addressing the daughter he 'took . . . to really interesting places – cathedrals and gardens'. The offer to 'meet me in the long grass . . . with your red robe dangling all around your body', on the other hand, sounds a tad salacious to be directed at his daughter.

The red robe his companion is wearing serves in turn to remind the narrator of the robe in which Jesus was wrapped after the crucifixion, and which seems to have been transmuted into a tattered coat that had been 'wore down . . . through the ages'. And so we return to the Church of St John, imbued again by the physical presence of Christ. It has been claimed that this was a common English myth. It is no such thing. Though the myth of the Holy Grail, sought by medieval knights in

* The book in question, published in 1908, was written by Alfred Alexander and was part of a sequence of novels involving a character named Lamia.

haunts of ancient peace, tells of Joseph of Arimathaea bringing the cup with Jesus's blood to the vale of Avalon, only with William Blake does a poet ask the question 'And did those feet in ancient time/Walk upon England's mountains green?' It is to this that Morrison is alluding in 'Summertime in England'.

Though the song passes through several tiers of consciousness, it always returns to the temporal state – a day in the country with his daughter and/or sweetheart. In this sense 'Summertime' resembles 'Cyprus Avenue'. Like its eminent predecessor, it concludes with the singer back in the present, though not alone, as he asks his companion a key question, 'Can you *feel* the silence?' As with the *Astral Weeks* songs, 'Summertime in England' evolved in performance to allow different sections of poetic ramblings to cross its bridge. Eleven- and twelve-minute live performances became the norm, but the fifteen-minute symphony on the album would remain the benchmark until, a decade later, in the company of Georgie Fame, Morrison picked the lock again.

If this pair of songs, along with *Into the Music* reject 'Spirit', gave Morrison the core of a truly groundbreaking album, the other songs he brought to the sessions were of lesser mettle. The selection of musicians, though, was as good as it got. The presence of guitarists Mick Cox and Herbie Armstrong gave the sound further Belfast roots, whilst a rhythm section comprising Peter Van Hooke and David Hayes continued an association pre-dating Morrison's brief retirement. The newly-favoured Bay area trio of John Allair, Mark Isham and Pee Wee Ellis completed the *Common One* septet. Morrison also decided to enlist a (co-)producer. Henry Lewy of Joni Mitchell fame was the surprising choice. It was perhaps Lewy who suggested the quite extraordinary location for the ensuing sessions. The Super Bear Studios had a unique position, and a genuinely spooky vibe.

Mick Cox: We were all ensconced in a very, very intense, highly charged situation for those eleven days, but it did bring out that album. The studio was a very strange place. It was a monastery up in the French Alps, and it used to be a monastery-cum-safe house [for] the Knights Templar. They caught a whole bunch of them hiding out at this place and massacred the lot of them. It's obviously haunted . . . I [certainly] believe in ghosts after staying there. It was most atmospheric, in a slightly malevolent way . . . We're sitting round at breakfast and Herbie said to his wife, 'What were you doing walking round the bedroom last night?' She says, 'I wasn't walking round the bedroom.' He said, 'Yes you were. I woke up and saw you standing at the bottom of the bed.' Then the drummer comes down with his missus and says, 'Who were those people who came in the room last night?' and then Van comes down and says, 'There was all these heads floating around in my room last night.' So . . . [ ] . . . it was most atmospheric in a slightly unnerving way. [And] it burned down a few weeks after we left.

This eerie environment, in which Morrison planned to summon up haunts of ancient peace and the spirit of the Lord, one might have expected to fuel the man's creative fire. In fact, as Mick later confided to Clive Culbertson, '[Van] was a bit freaked by it: "Man, we're sitting there doing a take and this fucking guy walks through the wall. He walks through the studio, and he walks out the other wall. What the fuck's that about?" Apparently one of the guitar players got so freaked out he packed his stuff and left. He walked off the session . . . [Van]'s open to that, [and yet] he's scared of it.'

Nor did a mountain top seem an obvious recording venue for a man who less than a year earlier had been struck by a serious attack of vertigo from a twenty-foot stage, haunted or not. Indeed Peter Van Hooke remembers Morrison turning to him on their arrival and saying that he felt 'a bit strange'. The other musicians, though, rose to the challenges, some technological, some psychological.

Peter Van Hooke: We arrived at the studio and John Allair immediately took the piano apart. It was all in pieces on the floor . . . And we set up in this room, and it wasn't that great. I think the guy who engineered it [in the end] was the tape op, because Henry Lewy didn't have a clue [how to handle Morrison]. It was a bit of a disaster, that side of things . . . [But] Mark Isham was very much [into] recording modern kinds of sound. There was a feeling of exploring the music . . . That particular album, we just got into the mood of playing, and the tapes kept rolling. It felt like a natural route to go. If it went on, it went on. Everyone was an instinctive musician. If Van went somewhere, they'd go with him. I think there were a few little grooves that we'd worked on before that Van liked. [But] when it was finished, I wasn't sure what we'd done. Sonically, it wasn't a great-sounding record, 'cause technically they were having real problems . . . but I remember Mark Isham saying to me, 'You know what, that's a great record.'

Common One certainly had many of the components required for a great record, and when the band recorded the album's central work in just a couple of takes on day one, the prognosis looked good to excellent. 'Summertime in England' was an extraordinary coming-together of a bare-boned structure, the words to one or more songs, a poem or two and that feeling that one was 'exploring the music', all fully realized on 24-track tape.

Mick Cox: 'Summertime' . . . had never, ever been played with those 3/4 changes. The first part of it's in 4/4, then it moves into the 3/4 situation, waltz-time, and that situation, along with the speaking improvisation, was brand-new. He'd just been singing, 'Will you meet me in the countryside . . .' So the first day he did this improvisation, and we got about five minutes into the song and he went into the 3/4 for the first time, came out of it very quickly, and then went into the improvisation, and it was just so good that it blew the band away, and we all fell apart. The second take is the one that's on the album . . . [When] we listened to it, there was complete silence from all the guys in the studio and Van says, 'Does anybody think it's too long?' And of course nobody wants to answer, 'cause you've [just] done a seventeen-minute track, and you've got it right and [don't want to] do it again. So there's a long silence and I pipe up, 'Yeah, I think it's much too long. There's no such thing as a long summertime in England.'

Of course, 'Summertime in England' was not the only song Morrison brought to the session with just the framework in place. Cox recalls that 'everything was partly written beforehand, and we had rehearsed sections of all the other songs – [though] "Wild Honey" and "Spirit" were nearly finished, and so was "Satisfied".' Not every song made the necessary transition. 'Real Real Gone', which would have made a splendid single (and did – ten years later), was one song that guitarist Herbie Armstrong remembers 'Van started to play . . . really slow, sort of Sam Cooke type of thing, and then I brought it up [in] tempo with the rhythm guitar'. Though Armstrong gave the song life, it no longer fitted into the kind of therapeutic record Morrison had in mind. Nor did 'Street Theory', which Morrison resurrected, then rejected. Instead he set about recording an equally ambitious counterpoint to 'Summertime', intended for the opposite side of a jam-packed album. The fate of 'When the Heart Is Open', which would require another fifteen minutes of vinyl, was even more bound by happenstance.

Pee Wee Ellis: I was talking to Van the other day and he was saying that he thought we had something really special going on [with *Common One*] . . . I remember [with] that song, 'When the Heart Is Open', we were just taking a break from recording and sitting in this café and we just decided to go straight back into the studio and put the song down straight away. Somehow, by the time we got back we'd lost the drummer so we carried on without him! Van told them to turn on the tape recorder – and that was it – we hadn't worked it out beforehand or anything – we just played. He just stood there in the middle and we followed him. [SG]

Mick Cox: The five of us are standing there, and Van says, 'Off you go, Mick!' I say, 'What key is it in?' 'It's not in any key.' I say, 'Right, what's the tempo?' 'There's no tempo – I don't want normal stuff, I want something different.' . . . I have no idea what the tuning is to this day! We went through fifteen minutes of music without anybody going wrong – that's as you hear it, apart from [the] Mark Isham [horn] overdubs . . . at the beginning. [SG]

'When the Heart Is Open' is presumably what Morrison had in mind when he referred, a couple of years later, to just 'sitting down and singing on my own. [Doing] nothing in particular, but making noises . . . finding the primal depth . . . [and] sometimes there's a question, what do you do with this? See, I find when you're making albums and you have to make them for people, sometimes it's difficult to know what to do about that. Because . . . some of the things I'm into are not songs.'

The results on side two of *Common One* divide aficionados and critics to this day. Personally, I'd rather listen to quarter of an hour of dolphin noises. The sentiments may be laudable, but the execution is crass: 'you will change just like a flower slowly openin'' – gimme a break!; and the musicians' burblings barely warrant enough attention to qualify as elevator music. Now this really *was* a grandiloquent failure! Jack Lynch of *Hot Press*, on the other hand, found it to be 'a slow, gentle, sustained and repeating meditation which draws you into its hushed vortex'. Like quicksand, I presume.

Sadly, 'When the Heart Is Open' was not allowed the opportunity to be salvaged by the semi-miraculous arrangements of Jeff Labes. Both of *Common One*'s other two epics, 'Summertime in England' and 'Haunts of Ancient Peace', were swathed in orchestral effects by an increasingly ambitious arranger back in California, after the basic tracks were completed. 'Summertime in England', in particular, benefits from Labes's superb score.

Jeff Labes: He had done *Common One* and he wanted arrangements from me. We actually brought in singers from one of the gospel choirs from the east Bay. Turned out they couldn't really sing other people's songs that well. You know, gospel sounds awfully different from what we were looking for . . . [though] I think we did keep one thing for the album. Van was a lot of fun during that whole [process] . . . but what I always tried to do with string arrangements for him was to just try to mimic what he was singing, 'cause he was such a song instrument.

The omission of lighter fare like 'Real Real Gone' and 'Street Theory', coupled with a fifteen-minute musical mural as the album's closing track, turned what could have been another compelling argument for the restitution of the man's critical reputation into a gruelling display of artistic indulgence. For which the reviews were largely unforgiving. *Sounds*'s Dave McCullough, who had praised *Into the Music* to the heavens, concluded that '*Common One* is where Van Morrison leaves rock . . . where economy and self-measurement go to the dogs and a self-obsessive notion of pastoral harmony assumes unflattering, epic status . . . For the fan, as I am myself, it's not even possible to romanticize and say that Morrison has lost his way temporarily, so stern and so acute is his departure.' *NME* gave the album to Graham Lock, who called it 'colossally smug and cosmically dull; an interminable, vacuous and drearily egotistical stab at spirituality'.

The wisest, sharpest, wittiest review was by Lester Bangs, and came as the prologue to a review of the *Common One's* successor – almost the last example of Bangs's inspirational rock criticism before his premature death in June 1982:

When *Common One* was released in late 1980, I called up fellow rockcrit Greil Marcus and raved about it: 'This is it! The ultimate Van Morrison we've been waiting for all these years!' 'No,' he said, 'it's a facsimile of the ultimate Van Morrison album. Van acting the part of the "mystic poet" he thinks he's supposed to be: "Didja ever hear about William Blake?" [*sic*] Well, yes, Van, I did . . . so what?' . . . [And] in a way Greil was right: lines like 'James Joyce wrote stream-of-consciousness books' and 'Wordsworth and Coleridge were smokin' up in Kendal!' are pretty silly, especially repeated over and over. But it makes absolutely no difference (in fact, I like it) because the context is so gorgeous: rapturous quarter-hours that pass like vast moments . . . Van was making holy music even though he thought he was, and us rock critics had made our usual mistake of paying too much attention to the lyrics.

By the time Bangs argued for a reassessment – as 'Summertime in England' began to gain a degree of recognition as certainly the man's most ambitious work in a decade – Morrison had recoiled from *Common One*'s spirit of innovation, producing work that was easier to categorize and harder to love (or hate). His musical retreat coincided with some bitter words spat at all the forces that had conspired to prevent his vision from reaching its true audience:

Van Morrison: [With] the last album, *Common One*, I tried to get into [extending the songs] a bit . . . The thing is, with these record companies, they just don't level with you . . . And if I'm really going to do that . . . if I'm really going to do what I'm supposed to do, then I need support . . . That's something you have to think about when you're making a record, because when you're trying to do something different you've got a lot of people saying 'yeah yeah yeah' before you do it, and when you do it. But when it comes out – that's when you separate the sheep from the goats, because all the people who've been saying 'yeah yeah yeah yeah' have suddenly disappeared. [1982]

He would not attempt anything quite so ambitious again. Henceforth every radical idea would be tempered by some notion of commerciality. Morrison was bruised by the reaction to the album, which he insisted was never 'meant to be a commercial album. In fact, the original concept was even more esoteric than the final product as it was recorded. Because the idea behind it was nature – and it's not really a saleable commodity!!' Its enduring legacy was a decade of inspired attempts at re-creating 'Summertime in England' in concert. Its immediate bequest was a band ready to take that level of experimentation on the road and see what gives.

22

1981–83: The Days of Dominion

I take my involvement with music as a whole thing . . . Like, this album
coming out . . . it's taken me twenty-one years to make this album . . .
it's not just something that I've done six months ago and suddenly come
along and say, 'Hello I've got a record.' It's taken me twenty-one years
to get here . . . I just didn't get here from last year.

—*Van Morrison, 1981*

In the months separating the *Common One* sessions in February 1980
from its October release, few limits were placed on this band's potential.
In the summer, the core components, minus Morrison's two Belfast
buddies, were joined by two important contributors to the previous
body of work: pianist Jeff Labes, who after scoring 'Summertime' simply
found 'the energy of working together [again] so good', and guitarist
John Platania.

The results – recorded by Henry Lewy for a possible live album –
were some of the finest shows in living memory. The spirit of innovation
present at the sessions was harnessed at the Casino de Montreux, where
Morrison returned for the first time in six years to record this live album
and again present a wealth of songs new to these 'jazz' fans. The likes of
'Spirit', 'Satisfied', 'Summertime in England' and 'Haunts of Ancient
Peace' – now placed alongside the likes of 'And It Stoned Me', 'Ballerina'
and 'Listen to the Lion' – made sense of earlier connections and suggested
extensions to come. The audience could hardly fail to respond. 'Summertime in England', now in its appropriate state, was about to become the
centrepiece of every Morrison show, not just as a result of its positioning
and sheer length but because it provided the broadest example of a new

aesthetic intent: to deny any residue of rock, whilst taking Morrison's music where most contemporaries dared not fly.

Van Morrison: I was trying to show the dynamics in the music . . . These expressions of energy are in music. But if you just go out and you don't know what you're doing with it – you're just blasting this energy and you don't know what it is – then it becomes destructive . . . Rock & roll is a mind trip now. It's not music any more . . . It took me twenty years to get to that point, to get to the point where I'm actually consciously involved in what I'm doing . . . I definitely think that we need some new music, and I think the young kids are just crying out . . . for something new. That's why you're getting all this really destructive punk music – because they're saying, 'We can't take it any more. We'll do anything.' [1981]

If *Astral Weeks* had been an anti-rock statement, Morrison now entered on an anti-rock crusade, evangelized by the way that *Common One* was cruelly disregarded. At a concert at the Great American Music Hall in March 1981 he even had a go at *San Francisco Chronicle* critic Joel Selvin for labelling his music 'rock'. He informed the bemused audience that he had spent the past fifteen years developing a jazz–blues fusion, and that Selvin (and, by implication, all his kind) did not really understand the music he was making. In a series of statements made while promoting *Common One*'s two immediate successors, Morrison would spell it out:

Van Morrison: I'm not really interested in pop or rock music . . . I'm interested in doing *music* – and the pop field or rock field is out of the question. We're dealing with something that's much more subtle. [1983]

Van Morrison: Rock has become a meaningless word . . . I personally don't have anything to do with 'rock', in any shape or form. [1984]

Perhaps it would be more accurate to say that rock was having nothing to do with him. Indeed very few of the legion of singer-songwriters who had applied a few brain cells to the form back in the early seventies were at home in contemporary rock. With Dylan all but dismissed for finding religion, Neil Young making albums of beeping noises, Joni Mitchell making Mingus music, and Lou Reed and Richard Thompson 'between' record contracts, Morrison was keeping very good company in his own solitary way. It would be fair to say that he felt the loss.

Van Morrison: When I started there were more people like me, let me put it that way. When I started there were more people my age writing music or writing songs . . . and now . . . there's less people doing creative stuff. [1981]

He still remained an icon of modern music, just not a very relevant one. Even though he insisted he was 'not interested in the past . . . it's boring to me', for the media it was where he largely remained. Praise of past achievements merely made the man uncomfortable, as he proved when Paul Jones of Manfred Mann fame invited him on to his World Service show the following year to talk about his latest album, *Beautiful Vision*. When Jones proceeded to heap plaudits on *It's Too Late to Stop Now*, 'he just completely contradicted me, as if we were total strangers . . . [and] had never had a friendly conversation. I thought, this is the Van they've warned me about . . . but I think effusive praise in front of millions just embarrasses him. I think it makes him shy.'

If his own past failed to interest Morrison, his Irish heritage was gaining a grip on his songwriting. As he phrased it some years later, 'In the sixties, when I started my first bands, my influence was more R&B . . . [and] the "folk" element of the music I was [originally] into was sort of buried temporarily. But I suppose I've come back around again to that basic folk element I started with.' Though imagery from the folk lexicon had crept into a number of songs over the years, the first evidence of a renewed interest in his own musical roots came with 'Rolling Hills' on *Into the Music*. Morrison's revitalized concern for the folk music of his native country became, in his eyes at least, part of his anti-rock crusade, itself bound up with the healing potential of song.

Van Morrison: I don't think there's enough education about what music is, and where it's going, and the force behind it. There's a tremendous force behind it . . . I'm a traditionalist. I believe in tracing things back to the source and finding out what the real thing was . . . how it became what it is today . . . I also think it's important for people to get into the music of their own culture . . . I think it can be dangerous to not validate the music of where you're from . . . I think now that it's much more important to explore real things . . . [like] music as a healing force . . . that's what I'm interested in at the present time. [1982]

There was no mistaking the polemic at the heart of the opening song on *Beautiful Vision*. 'Celtic Ray' was among the first songs to issue from

Morrison's pen when he began writing for his next album in the early months of 1981. It was also the central song recorded at the first set of sessions in the spring of that year (from which only 'Scandinavia' would make the final album). In this original guise, with Mark Isham's synthesizer servicing the melody and not an Irish pipe in sight, the song seemed a continuation of that oblique search for the Veedon Fleece, the lyrics turning a personal desire 'to go home/[having] been away from the ray too long' into a grand calling to every emigrant soul: 'All over Ireland, Scotland, England and Wales/I can hear the mothers' voices calling, "Children, children, come home"'. As he later admitted, Morrison failed to retain the purity of the song, ditto a few other things written with a similar mood in mind. Some, like the unfinished 'Down the Road I Go', were not revisited when the sessions evolved into that something else.★

Van Morrison: Some of the material [on *Beautiful Vision*], when it started, was more traditional. Some of the songs – like 'Solid Ground' and 'Celtic Ray' – they started basically as folk-oriented stuff, and . . . ended up being integrated as folk/R&B. [1982]

When work resumed, again in California, songs of a different hue began to occupy tape, drawing, as 'Celtic Ray' did in its use of the word 'ray' to describe the pull of home, from a treatise on 'a world problem' entitled *Glamour*, which had been telepathically 'communicated' to Alice Bailey back in the forties by an unidentified Tibetan master. In *Glamour*, the Ray comes in seven factors: soul, personality, mind, emotional nature, physical vehicle, the energy of the sun sign, and the influence of the rising sun. Morrison was thoroughly taken with the ideas Bailey expressed in her book, and duly credited her on the sleeve of *Beautiful Vision* as the inspiration behind a number of the songs on the album, notably 'Dweller on the Threshold' and 'Aryan Mist'. Jack Lynch, in his excellent eight-part overview of Morrison's work, published in *Hot Press* in 1983, attached great importance to Bailey's message when it came to understanding the songs of this period:

★ Down the Road I Go' would, however, reappear as the title track of Morrison's 2002 collection.

The sleeve notes [to *Beautiful Vision*] point out that a couple of songs were inspired by the book *Glamour: A World Problem* (Lucis Press) by Alice Bailey. Written in the '40s, it is one of a series of books on the instructions of the Tibetan, an esoteric teacher of occult meditation, written by Bailey and intended for groups of initiates who strive to arrive at 'an intuitive knowledge and an intelligent understanding' of personal and world glamour to enable them to work at its dispelling. This is to be done by people decentralizing life from the personality, and acting purely as a channel for the energy of the soul. The present world race ('the Aryan') is seen as controlled by the accumulated misconceptions of maya (on the ethereal level of personality), glamour, on the emotional plane, and illusion, on the mental. 'The sum total of the forces of the lower nature as expressed in the personality prior to illumination' is the so-called Dweller on the Threshold . . . and the dweller on the threshold must be confronted by the Angel of Presence, the soul.

When the light of the Angel of Presence succeeds in enveloping the Dweller, the burning ground – the terrain that must be crossed three times before the Dweller can pass through 'the door' – has done its work and the Dweller's personality has become a purified shell. So, not exactly your obvious source of inspiration for your average rock artist. To Lynch, the lyrics to 'Aryan Mist', 'Dweller on the Threshold' and 'Across the Bridge Where Angels Dwell' 'reflect[ed] an eloquent and heartfelt identification with the concerns of the book'. To other critics they were merely symptomatic of a dearth of new ideas after a hectic period of self-education.

The absolute identification with Bailey's tenets, and the way that 'Dweller on the Threshold' operates as little more than a précis of her views, suggests a person subscribing to someone else's philosophical view hook, line and kitchen sink. Thankfully, Bailey's views were New Age enough to spare Morrison much of the sheer vilification that had greeted Dylan's equally credulous adoption of a fundamentalist Christian creed back in 1979. Morrison, like Dylan, made no bones about the debt he felt he owed, coming as close to discipleship as his contrary nature would allow.

Van Morrison: I've read *Glamour* four or five times, and I get different things out of it each time. [Alice Bailey]'s saying a lot of things. It's depth reading. You might read it on Wednesday and on Thursday you pick it up again and get an entirely different thing. I don't feel qualified to speak about what it's about – you really have to read it yourself . . . because there's so much in there. [1982]

Where the album made a lot more sense to the average listener, and made for a welcome return to previous preoccupations, was in the songs that addressed a more physically real muse, notably 'Vanlose Stairway' and 'She Gives Me Religion', perhaps Morrison's most captivating love-songs since the days of *Veedon Fleece*.

It was whilst playing a series of shows in Europe in the spring of 1981 that he had met a Danish lady involved in PR, Ulla Munch. Munch was to become the man's first long-time partner since his ex-wife, 'Vanlose Stairway' being the most overt testimony to Munch's impact on Morrison. Though he would subsequently suggest that there was 'absolutely nothing mystical about it whatsoever – it was just a block of flats'. 'Vanlose Stairway' was a powerful invocation of those songs of temporal distortion that had littered his early albums, as he turned this mundane set of stairs in an uninspiring block of flats into a 'stairway [that] reaches up to the moon/And it comes right back . . . to you'. As he asks his new love to 'Send me your Bible, child/Send me your *Gita*', he has returned to Madame Joy.

'She Gives Me Religion' finds Morrison treading more familiar terrain, as he walks 'down the mystic avenue . . . again'. Whether 'the angel of imagination/[who] opened up my gate [and] said, "Come right in/I saw you knocking with your heart"' is a past or present preoccupation (or both) he leaves the listener to disentangle. Both songs were realized at a third set of sessions, where Morrison finally abandoned two of the original impetuses behind his new collection – reflecting the strains of Irish folk music, and introducing some instrumentals.

Van Morrison: I don't really have a concept until there's maybe three or four songs . . . [But] I always try to keep a centre going that I can come back to. [1982]

The first set of sessions had employed those musicians with whom he played a memorable residency at the Great American Music Hall in March 1981. Jeff Labes remembers it being mostly 'early versions of songs that he later re-recorded, just trying various things'. Herbie Armstrong thinks it was more focused. He recalls them spending 'quite a while in San Francisco recording . . . [before he decided] to go in a different direction and . . . change things around a bit'. Attempted at these early sessions – aside from 'Scandinavia' – were two equally lengthy instrumentals, 'Daring Night' and 'All Saints' Day' (which would appear as a B-side the following year). Also intended for an album with a strong Irish theme was an early version of 'Cleaning Windows', in which the young Morrison was not only 'a working man in [his] prime', but also 'a dirty old man on the side'.

By the time Morrison resumed recording – the line-up now augmented by girl singers, Dire Straits guitarist Mark Knopfler and his old *Moondance* drummer Gary Malabar – he had completed the words to 'Cleaning Windows' to his satisfaction and was seeking to make it one of a number of songs recut in double-quick time. Malabar remembers the 'name' guitarist at these sessions 'being very disillusioned recording with Van, because Van moved so quick. He was so looking forward to doing stuff with Van. I think he wanted more time, and a nicer flow. It was like, "What just happened?" "Erm, guess what, you just recorded a tune and we're done."'

Whatever guitar tone Morrison had in mind at the *Beautiful Vision* sessions, neither Herbie Armstrong nor Mark Knopfler alighted upon it. Finally Jim Stern, who was again engineering these Record Plant sessions, suggested a guitarist friend, Chris Michie, who was given the usual baptism of fire.

Chris Michie: I got the call when I was doing a session in San Francisco. Van's producer Jim Stern said, 'Can you get to the Plant [in Sausalito] in twenty minutes?' I said, 'Yeah.' I walked into the studio with my gear as the band and Van were doing . . . basic tracks. I was set up and playing before the end of the song – 'She Gives Me Religion', I think . . . Fortunately I was in tune from the session I had done earlier that day. [Then] I came back later that week to finish up the basics and do the lead overdubs.

Those overdubs, which included some additional guitar on two cuts from the Knopfler session, meant that Mr Mellifluous's negligible contribution on 'Cleaning Windows' and 'Aryan Mist' would be rendered all but inaudible on the album. Michie, though, had made his mark and was quickly adopted as the new guitarist whilst continuing to be surprised by Morrison's studio methodology, which seemed to consist of stretching each tune to its limit, and then editing the results down into song-shape. The *Common One* experiment, where songs survived unexpurgated, was already shaping up to be an isolated exception. The new album had no track, save its closing instrumental, that broke the five-minute barrier – whatever the studio reels might reveal.

Chris Michie: We used a lot of tape on those sessions. We were recording on an old Studer multi-track that could handle reels that were much longer than usual. [But] there were a couple of times that the engineer would change reels in the middle of a song and we would edit the two versions together. I can't remember which songs we did that for, but I remember doing some very long versions that never made it to the final album.

Of the selections on *Beautiful Vision*, 'Vanlose Stairway' contains the most annoying fade, Morrison working himself into a frenzy just as the song begins to disappear. As released, in February 1982, *Beautiful Vision* was very much in the spirit of *Into the Music*. Like its 1979 kin, it was essentially an album of *songs*, even if Morrison signposted a movement towards the merely tuneful with its six-minute instrumental closer, 'Scandinavia'.

In concert, the songs were given more breathing-room. As with the album's two immediate predecessors, Morrison seemed to be champing at the bit for an opportunity to air the new material. Knowing the lugubrious pace at which modern record companies moved, he faced a six-month wait before the record was in the shops. No matter. In October 1981, he took the musicians who had completed the album along for a series of shows confined to the sunny climes of California, at which he aired three-quarters of the new album. By the time *Beautiful Vision* did appear in the shops, the songs with an enduring live identity had already been established. After successful residencies at the Palace of Fine Arts and the Great American Music Hall in San Francisco, it was decided to repeat the trick at the Dominion Theatre in the heart of London's West End, announcing the album's UK release in February 1982 in an appropriate fashion.

Paul Charles: The idea [behind the Dominion residencies] was [to go against the] 'come into town, do one show, get all the press down, get the radio and TV and record-company people' [mentality]. My logic was, 'Look, with Van it's not just a rock & roll tour. It's not just here's the hits, here's the new record, please buy it, whatever.' It was a *performance*. I nicked a few theatre ideas [where] you'd . . . base yourself in town and stretch out. From a band's point of view, you get to work [on things] . . . A certain number of people would come back every night, [knowing that] Van will not have a set-list that he adheres to religiously – he may have a few islands along the way that he'll [usually] go to but where he goes in the middle depends on how he's feeling, and how the band are playing. So I thought, 'Here's a way. Van is not having hit singles. Van doesn't do TV. How can we get attention to him by doing what he does?' Well, the best thing that he does is perform live. I think we did four the first time. We ended up doing eleven [in 1984]. We got a lot of coverage, we got a lot of attention, without him having to do something he didn't like – which he wouldn't do anyway.

It was an inspired approach that helped to rekindle Morrison's love of performing, as well as making him examine London audiences afresh. As he commented at the time of the 1984 Dominion residency, the experience was 'more like appearing in a play, going to the theatre and doing your job every day – which I prefer to touring because that's very fragmented and disorientating'. The success of the exercise led to it being repeated in Belfast and Dublin, at the Ulster Hall and Gaiety Theatre respectively; and then again in 1983, in London and Belfast, where he would record his first live album in a decade.

Meanwhile, Morrison and girlfriend Ulla were spending more and more of their downtime in London, and a semi-permanent base was becoming a necessity. The choice of Holland Park, sandwiched between the earthier realms of Notting Hill Gate and Shepherd's Bush, was initially made on a make-do basis. On one level it offered him the opportunity to continue his studies into various arcane religions and spiritual creeds.

Donal Gallagher: Like anybody, [he] wants a home, and wants it as normal and as natural as possible. [But in his position] you're never given the chance . . . He probably didn't want London as a base, but needed to have an address here, or a place to put his head overnight . . . He was searching at that time. It is hard to know what he was looking for. I heard lots of reasons, 'Oh, Holland Park, because it's near the Scientology [meeting room] in High Street Ken.' He went through that phase, which I think he was always a bit embarrassed about. It came up [one time]. Somebody said something about it in his company, and I sensed he didn't know how to [react]. I made some comment to the effect of 'Well, whatever path you take to the top of the mountain, you have to search and find your way,' and he went, 'Yeah, that's it.'

Morrison inevitably came in for a fair degree of stick in the press for his brief espousal of Scientology, after he unwisely name-checked L. Ron Hubbard, founder of the cult, on his 1983 album, *Inarticulate Speech of the Heart.* According to an 'auditor' with whom Steve Turner spoke, Morrison only ever 'finished what we call fourth grade, which is about three-quarters of the way to being clear'. The fact that passage through the curiouser and curiouser degrees of Scientology could begin only after the initiate was considered 'clear' suggests a flirtation akin to his mother's visits to a faith-healer. On the other hand, Morrison later informed a friend that he had in fact made a substantial financial commitment by the time he decided enough was enough.

Clive Culbertson: He was very disillusioned at the end of Dianetics. [He] thought that his loyalty deserved better treatment, and I think that did colour [his] subsequent mystical life . . . His quote to me was 'I gave those fuckers six figures. And they told me before I went into the next grade that I had to guarantee them *x* amount every year to get the secrets of the next degree,' and Van said to them, 'Tell me what the secrets are and I'll tell you whether it's worth a few million. Give me a clue. I don't know what I'm getting.' The guy said, 'Look, it's either done it for you up to this degree or it hasn't. If it's done it, you're in and you'll want it. If it hasn't done it, it's time for you to move on.' And Van goes, 'OK, time to move on.'

Talking in 1994 about his various experiences with cults and spiritual outlets, Morrison admitted that he had found various possibilities, 'but they don't necessarily give you satisfaction. It's usually the opposite.' Though he owned up to taking 'courses in Scientology over a period of eighteen months', he described himself as 'not a joiner − I don't join things'. The quest, rather than its resolution, preoccupied him. This very restlessness and a naturally suspicious streak led him to reject each and every path whilst still in the foothills. But then in his chosen profession he often struggled to find the necessary intellectual stimulation. When he found himself in a conversation with one rock journalist about Rudolf Steiner, he decided to allow the association to go further than ever before.

Mick Brown: The reason we started talking to each other was because of his interest in spiritual disciplines and spiritual teachers . . . I went to do an interview [for] *Inarticulate Speech of the Heart* and we started talking about people like Rudolf Steiner, who he seemed to be very interested in. He was living in a mews off Holland Park. So sometimes I'd go round and see him, and we'd step out and have a cup of coffee, go for a walk in Holland Park and chat, or go and have some lunch . . . [But] I never got the sense that he's someone who's ever really been happy with himself or happy with his place in life. Certainly the time that I knew him he was looking very hard for something.

A sense of isolation continued to pervade Morrison's work, something that as central an address as Holland Park did nothing to assuage. Indeed he never seemed to accept his fashionable West London address as his true postal code. When keyboardist Kenny Craddock was introduced into Morrison's musical circle in 1983, at the instigation of engineer Hugh Murphy, and he went down to see Van at his house in Holland Park, he found it incredibly sparse – 'I didn't [even] have a seat. The TV and video had [just] been delivered, and they were [still] standing on top of the box.' When he found Craddock to be a lover of literature, he was also invited to become an occasional lunch guest. Craddock was relieved to find the man refreshingly down to earth.

Kenny Craddock: At that particular time . . . he was very interested in the great poets. I didn't live too far from him, just across the park, so I would occasionally go across there and have lunch with him, and we would just chat about literature. The music thing rarely came up . . . There was never any star stuff around at all. That part of it was always very comfortable . . . I often used to pick him up and we'd go to rehearsal. He'd just drag out his guitar. At one place we rehearsed some guy said to him, 'I see you're having to carry your own guitar now,' and he said, 'Yeah, man, I light my own cigarettes . . . and wipe my own arse as well.'

Despite his reluctance to lay down firm roots, London was increasingly replacing San Francisco as Morrison's base of operations. Though sessions for *Beautiful Vision*'s successor, *Inarticulate Speech of the Heart*, began at a trio of studios in California, and then moved to Lombard Sound Studios in Dublin, they only reached resolution due to a series of marathon sessions at the Townhouse in West London.

For the first time in his recording career, Morrison planned a largely instrumental album. Having considered it on a number of occasions, he perhaps felt that his last album for Warners was the time to do it. Though it was a thread barely represented in the canon, instrumentals had occupied several album sessions, notably in 1970 when he recorded two songs – one of which would have filled an entire album side – under the title 'Caledonia Soul Music', and in 1974 when several instrumentals were recorded for the ultimately-abandoned *Naked in the Jungle/Mechanical Bliss* album. *Beautiful Vision* became one more album on which, by his own admission, he 'planned to do a lot more instrumental stuff . . . than actually got on it'. By 1982, though, it would appear that his head was simply not in a space where these tunes necessarily acquired lyrics.

Van Morrison: Sometimes when I'm playing something, I'm just sort of humming along with it, and that's got a different vibration than an actual song. So the instrumentals just come from trying to get that form of expression, which is not the same as writing a song. [1984]

The title of the new album, *Inarticulate Speech of the Heart*, offered its own clue to the content, though Morrison claimed he had merely adopted a Shavian saying that represented 'that idea of communicating with as little articulation as possible, at the same time being emotionally articulate'. The results could have been even more 'inarticulate'. A number of instrumentals, listed simply as 'Irish Instrumental No. 2',★ 'Irish Folk Instrumental No. 3' and 'F Sharp', were recorded at the sessions but discarded. Meanwhile the one literary lyric recorded, 'Mr Thomas', was conferred only B-side status – not that this jet-fuelled performance of a Robin Williamson song had an obvious slot on a soundtrack for suppertime.

Morrison, though, seemed to enjoy himself at the Townhouse sessions. Afforded the opportunity to play piano, guitar and sax, he thrived on the opportunity to be a musician. Drummer Van Hooke witnessed '[Morrison] dabble a bit with [the] piano, [and] come up with a few ideas. [Though] he's not a great pianist – he's not a great sax player either – it doesn't bother him because he's communicating what he wants to do.' Those final sessions at the Townhouse even contained a certain inarticulate inspiration.

Peter Van Hooke: There was an album we did in Shepherd's Bush, which was literally done in three days . . . There was a song . . . that was just a rant. It was long enough to have two tapes on it. It just went on and on and on, and at the end of it we just smiled. The room wasn't much bigger than [my living room]. I have a great memory [of] Van with his Fender-Rhodes, his sax round

★ Presumably 'Irish Instrumental No. 1' became 'Celtic Swing'.

his neck, his mike here, and there was Chris Michie, Mark [Isham] playing a little keyboards, David Hayes and me, and we were just really locked in on those sessions, and it was all nailed. The reason it worked was that [by then] we knew each other so instinctively. But no A&R people! . . . No one [ever] told him when to go into the studio.

One presumes that the 'rant . . . long enough to have two tapes on it' was 'Rave On, John Donne'.★ According to the bassist at these sessions, David Hayes, it did indeed fill 'two reels of twenty-four-track tape. There was a gap in the middle where the engineer frantically put the next tape on – it was some session, it was like being in a church.' Though the song in question was allocated a mere five minutes on *Inarticulate*, in concert it could stretch to double that (on the live album from the *Inarticulate* tour it sails past the nine-minute mark).

'Rave On, John Donne' was presumably intended to inhabit the same space as 'Summertime in England' in a more condensed form, grasping at a new-found conceit: establishing a chain of seers who paved the way. Unfortunately, the performance on the album had none of the compelling dynamics of its predecessor, and lines like 'Rave on down through the Holy Rosey Cross/Rave on down through theosophy, and the Golden Dawn/Rave on through the writing of *A Vision* . . . Rave on John Donne, rave on thy Holy fool' were neither emotionally articulate nor compellingly evocative. In concert, where word-sounds could be more persuasive, the song blossomed. Whether the full two-reel version of the studio take managed to find its dark dank depths, Morrison wasn't about to say. The days of fifteen-minute album cuts were past and gone.

His experience with *Common One* had again made him a trepidatious artist, unsure of his footing. And yet, making an album so firmly planted in the middle of the road was a form of commercial hara-kiri at least as perilous as the wild ambition of *Common One*. Morrison, though, was a willing advocate for his new album – at least in Britain, where his label did their best to promote a record on the ambient side of easy listening. The Dominion again offered shelter for a week of shows, as did the Grand Opera House in Belfast, where tapes rolled on a long-awaited successor to *It's Too Late to Stop Now* which detailed many of the routes

---

★ Van Hooke believes the song in question was 'Showbusiness', which later appeared on *The Philosopher's Stone*, though the released take hardly suggests a pruned epic.

from *Into the Music* to *Inarticulate*, but none from *Hard Nose the Highway* to there.

Live at the Grand Opera House Belfast was in fact a swan song for the band that had stood Morrison in such good stead since the days of the *Common One*, hence perhaps the choice of songs. If six cuts from *Beautiful Vision* and one from *Inarticulate* was a balance that perhaps reflected those albums' relative merits, the omission of 'Summertime in England' (which was instead given its own 12-inch single) rendered *Live at the Grand Opera House* incomplete as both a document and a musical representation of their days of wonder. The more attuned musicians sensed that the end was nigh. Though Hayes, Isham, Ellis and Van Hooke would get another reprise on a summer European tour, the Brits were moving in and the Yanks were moving on.

Peter Van Hooke: Van has to explore his own music, 'cause some of it's very similar, and if you start to play it the same way [or] you get too familiar with it, you don't start to explore it, and so you're not giving him anything different to focus on.

Morrison was turning his attention to the European markets, playing two full British tours in 1983 and beginning a series of summer blitzes of Scandinavia, Italy, Germany, France and the Low Countries. Save for half-yearly visits to the Bay area, which retained its personal appeal, the US market began to be viewed as hardly more important than that of Italy or Holland.

Possibly Warners simply refused to offer any further tour support, the only realistic way an American tour would be practical. Morrison no longer cared. The feeling was evidently mutual as, after fifteen years of grief, Warners ended the association. Morrison, though, couldn't help applying a spin all his own to his departure from the most nurturing label he would ever know.

When Warners issued a press release, saying that they had been in negotiations with Morrison only for him to announce a worldwide deal with PolyGram, Morrison struck back, claiming that Warners' lawyer Sy Waronker 'said we were negotiating but . . . we weren't negotiating. The fact of the matter is . . . Warner Brothers had the rights for the US up to a certain point – which was the *Inarticulate Speech* album. When they got that, they didn't have any rights.'

Van Morrison: I'm simply not playing their game. They can have their party and keep their party. If I can't be myself, retain my own dignity, then whether I have a wider audience doesn't matter . . . There was no intention on my part to stay with Warners . . . The record companies don't accept me, because I stimulate something in them. I press a button: fear, because I haven't laid down and said, 'I give up – manipulate me.' [1984]

An alliance with PolyGram made a lot more sense at this point, as did Morrison's association with the London-based Paul Charles, who began to push back a number of European frontiers for his ever-challenging artist. PolyGram duly found that they were no longer immune to some of the cumulative pressures Morrison could bring to bear. Since they now owned Decca Records, it lay in their power to ensure that Morrison belatedly gained a degree of control *and* revenue from the interminably anthologized Them catalogue.

Paul Charles: Them released two albums and I think I had at that point collected something like fourteen compilations, and Van wasn't getting a penny . . . But at that time that situation was addressed, and it was all brought into line. At that point he'd signed to Phonogram, and Phonogram were also owned by the people who owned Decca, and I said, 'You can't possibly pretend to have an artist that you respect, and at the same time another of your arms is taking advantage of him.' 'Well, that's the deal.' 'It might have been the deal then, but this is now. You've got to address this.' And it was addressed.

Morrison was gaining a degree of control of his early 'pop' recordings just as his current work was placing him outside the musical mainstream. The broad balance of styles achieved on the best of *Into the Music* and *Common One* had not been retained, and his California-based band soon passed its apex. To his credit, these were issues he realized and addressed. The result, after a long-playing false start, was perhaps his finest-ever collection of songs and an unexpected return to critical favour.

23

1984–86: Days of Blooming Wonder

I just find it hard to be a so-called pop star. It conflicts with creativity. You're expected to be at certain places at certain times and do certain things. Which is contrary to the muse. I mean, you just get it when you get it.

—*Van Morrison, 1984*

The dissolution of the post-*Common One* band, and the successive commercial failures of *Common One*, *Beautiful Vision* and *Inarticulate Speech of the Heart*, might have suggested that a respite from the treadmill was nigh. Morrison's feelings about the demands of touring had always been ambivalent, and his new record contract meant that he was released from the tyranny of an album a year – if a tyranny is what it was. In fact, after the burst of inspiration that had sustained him from 1979 to 1982, the songs seemed to have dried up again.

It would be almost two years before the next album, on which evidence of a real renewal would be thin on the ground. And yet, in this 'fallow' period, he would assemble one of his finest touring bands and undertake a series of European tours suggestive of a continuing work ethic (only to then return to the States when he felt he had enough to record *A Sense of Wonder*). Since he had placed himself outside the loop of modern music, touring remained perhaps the only way he could retain any kind of connection to his audience.

Morrison has certainly often expressed how much he hates the rigmarole of touring. As he pointedly remarked in the spring of 1982, 'I started touring when I was fifteen. I made my first record and became successful when I was eighteen. So I'd had a lot of touring under my belt even before I had any success. By then I'd already had enough.' Needless to say, 1982 was still one of his busiest years of touring activity. As John Allair has said, 'He has that hate/love thing with performing. He gets self-conscious, but he needs it. Has to get that adulation, even though he says he hates it.'

The essential problem was not – and never had been – the gigging. Rather it was the actual touring and its mind-numbing routine, which Morrison correctly portrayed as 'carrying a lot of bags around and taking a lot of flights, and waiting in airports . . . It's nothing to do with playing.' When one musician asked Van's personal manager, John Rogers, why he kept doing something he didn't seem to enjoy, Rogers explained the problem in these terms: 'He wakes up this morning, he hasn't gigged for three months and he goes, "A gig'd be great now, man. John, I want ten days. I'm in the vibe." But it takes three months to get ten days, so by the time they get it done, he doesn't want to do it any more. So he goes out, and huffs and puffs.' Whatever the original intent, the torpor of the experience rarely took long to seep into Morrison's soul.

Peter Van Hooke: There's a need to perform . . . and the only way to do it, [certainly] at that time, was to do a tour. So he would do this and then the first three or four gigs would be fantastic, 'cause everyone was getting off. Then it would go down [to], 'Why am I doing this?' . . . [But] he was trying to explore himself all the time and if people got it, fantastic, and if people didn't get it, fine. Van could do a fantastic gig with twelve people in the audience. If he got off, he was fine. He could then perform in front of six hundred thousand people, and if he didn't enjoy it, it wouldn't mean anything to him . . . Van performs for himself. It's selfish, but it's the real guy. He gives you his feelings at that time. And 'pop' doesn't communicate on that level.

The move from the Bay area had removed one big plus point – access to intimate venues for which a single phone call was all it took to put Morrison on that night's bill. The whole rigmarole of organizing a 'tour' was something with which he frankly didn't want to be bothered.

Arty McGlynn: He enjoys being on stage. But getting there, and the wasteland that he has to put up with [when he's] offstage, I don't think he enjoys that. The wasteland that he has to put up with during the day gets him so knotted up, that he gets fucked up by the time he gets on stage . . . [Yet] he's just like a kid . . . when it's good.

Of course, the man's low boredom threshold – this need for things to happen right here, right now – was precisely what made certain live experiences so riveting. Here was a man who revelled in removing safety nets – as when he was invited to play the Midem Festival in Cannes in January 1984, with the entire set being broadcast across Europe on *Rockpalast*. About to play in front of perhaps the largest audience of his career, Morrison recruited a new drummer, Terry Popple, and a bassist who had last gigged with him ten years earlier – albeit in similar circumstances – Jerome Rimson. Having tethered them to his most recent touring band, Morrison played the gig without a warm-up show or a reliable set-list.

Martin Drover: He was always into what he was doing – once he was out there. But that didn't involve . . . any stagecraft. In fact, he would buck against it. They asked Van if he would do [*Rockpalast* to] fifty million viewers. We'd done a tour [the previous September] and then we got together again to do this [*Rockpalast* gig] . . . and you're talking [about learning] maybe thirty-odd tunes. We're in the rehearsal studio, rehearsing for the tour, and it's a wing and a prayer trying to get all this together [in time]. So we actually said, 'Van, do us a favour, please stick to the set-list.' 'All right, all right.' Three tunes in, and he's away – he just left it. And a lot of Van's tunes start the same . . . Somehow we got through [it].

The experience of playing with his first Anglo-Irish band seemed to signal a welcome return to sets that reflected more than just his latest musical preoccupation. Since his return to performing in 1978, the lead singer had never truly reconciled himself to performing earlier work, no matter what the critical stance.

Van Morrison: You say what you've got to say and people want you to say it again. Part of the problem with performing is this expectancy that you're going to do stuff you did five years ago or ten years ago. You're not there any more. You're going backwards. Performing is like going into the past. It doesn't exist. You're moving on. [1983]

A change in direction attendant upon the Irish roots of saxophonist Richie Buckley and guitarist Arty McGlynn mingling with English drummer Terry Popple, keyboardist Kenny Craddock and trumpeter Martin Drover, saw the reintroduction of songs like 'Hard Nose the

Highway', 'Ballerina', 'Saint Dominic's Preview' and 'Cyprus Avenue' to the live set. Morrison was at last released from any obligation to promote the latest 'product', which was in fact a live album featuring no such golden oldies.

The transition was bound to be abrupt. For the European shows in the summer of 1983, Morrison had brought in Kenny Craddock and Arty McGlynn who, along with Van Hooke, constituted the British contingent. But this Anglo-American combination proved too combustible. McGlynn remembers being given 'a hard time . . . until one night in Berlin . . . I said to Pee Wee [Ellis], "Are you MDing the band? Explain the gig to us or we're going home. Are we playing out of context here, or what?" After that it was OK.' Much as Morrison enjoyed a little tension, he wanted that energy directed through him, and the American musicians had probably reached the point where they had become a little too settled in their roles.

Arty McGlynn: Van likes a floating situation. He doesn't like a static band. You don't feel safe inside the band at any one time. He's getting his energy off you 'cause you're not sure if you're gonna be here next week. That's how he works . . . It's a very high-tension situation to play with Van. When it's good, then it's as good as you ever feel if you're a musician . . . If it's not working, then he knows . . . somebody has to go.

By September 1983, when Morrison embarked on a second UK tour in six months, Kenny Craddock was the new musical director, having survived his earlier introduction to the man's working methods.

Kenny Craddock: The very first tour I did with him . . . we had one day's rehearsal, and all we actually did on the rehearsal was this new song, which was a William Butler Yeats thing called 'Crazy Jane on God'.★

Craddock's job, such as it was, involved 'watching him all night to guide the band – mainly the drummer – just to keep the dynamics [up]'. He found it 'quite handy that I did know the music', as Morrison continued to throw the band musical curve-balls, constantly testing, pushing, goading – personally *and* musically.

★ Needless to say, 'Crazy Jane on God' was never actually performed on the tour in question.

Thankfully, Craddock had a full tour to find his feet before being put in charge of 'dynamics'. Whilst some adjustment on Morrison's part was also required, after his experience of the supersmooth musical shifts his California crew had specialized in, his own musicality remained as untutored as ever and new musicians would continue to have to figure things out for themselves.

Arty McGlynn: He can't tell you what he wants, but he knows what he doesn't want. He makes you work . . . There's no charts, so you have to hook in right away. If you can't play on the hoof, then you can't play in the band. If you can't groove, if you can't comprehend what he's doing, his ups and downs, all those dynamics, then you're no good to him. If you're just a straight player, and don't know how to get offside and not play, then you can't play in the band. 'Cause it's all dynamics – it's getting out of the way as much as playing. It's all [hand] signals . . . And Van is the best bandleader I ever worked with, 'cause he knows what he wants and he knows where everything should be. He's like an old-time bandleader, like Joe Turner . . . He doesn't want anything to be the same every night. And it makes it exciting for the band as well, 'cause you're not sure when you're gonna get a call to play a solo. So you've got electricity in the band. And you can't get drunk before the gig, because . . . you have to be able to play, 'cause he'll call on you, he'll read you. He's very aware [of] what's going on . . . You think about what you're going to do every night . . . and you walk on stage with adrenalin pumping out of your system, and he instils that in people. He has a certain aura about him, of electricity and energy, that very few people have.

Whatever the new band brought to the stages of Europe, though, Morrison preferred the sonic stability of his last two vinyl offerings, and when he came to record his first album for PolyGram International *per se*, once again he summoned Pee Wee Ellis, Chris Michie, David Hayes and John Allair, along with engineer Jim Stern, to the Record Plant in Sausalito, to repeat a familiar exercise.

Whether Morrison had enough for an album was the question. The album he released suggests not. *A Sense of Wonder* comprises three covers, two instrumentals and just five Van Morrison songs. Of these, the stand-out track is album opener, 'Tore Down A La Rimbaud', a song begun back in 1975, and completed in time for *Beautiful Vision*, when its reference to 'show[ing] me light out of the tunnel' had a certain contemporary significance.

The promise offered by such an opening in 1985 was not one he was able to sustain to album's end. When he was forced to pull one of the more successful songs, 'Crazy Jane on God', at the last minute – after promotional copies had gone out – because of a disagreement with the estate of W. B. Yeats (whose poetry it was), the only replacement track to hand was a cover of Mose Allison's 'If You Only Knew', presumably recorded as a warm-up to one of the Record Plant sessions. Of the songs that drew on his mystical investigations, 'The Master's Eyes' seemed like an interesting expression of personal experience. Just not his.

Clive Culbertson: He said to me one day in the car, 'What sort of mystical experiences have you had?' So I said, 'Well, I had an experience of one of these Rosicrucian masters one night [appearing] in my room and he took me into his eyes and let me see, and I did the whole thing.' And [on] the next album he did 'The Master's Eyes'. And I said to him after, 'Van, where did that come from?' 'Ah, I don't know. Something somebody said.'

Even those songs inspired by what he had read seemed to have run dry. As he said at the time, 'For seven or eight years, I was reading a tremendous amount, like every day. And then it just stopped. I haven't found the next book yet.' Yet *A Sense of Wonder* was an album littered with literary references – even the portrait of Morrison on the cover seemed positively Gravesian. And still *A Sense of Wonder* makes for a strangely impersonal collection. It is certainly hard to agree with Brian Hinton's assessment in his book-length study of Morrison's art, *Celtic Crossroads*:

After three albums in which he tried to hide himself, become anonymous, drop himself from the lyrics, [*A Sense of Wonder*] is a wonderfully egotistical effort. It is as if Van's personality – and his poetic individuality – have emerged from Celtic mists into sharp sunlight.

The daring conceit of putting great poetry to music was Morrison's but the process itself proved beyond his own musical powers. It devolved to Mike Westbrook and William Mathieu to provide the music for 'Crazy Jane on God' and the remarkable 'Let the Slave', an adaptation of Blake's 'The Price of Experience'.

The only framework in which Morrison seemed able to paint his own visions was an all too familiar one. 'A Sense of Wonder' evokes that familiar streetscape but, masterful as its execution is, we had all been here before: 'Over Newtownards and Comber, Gransha and the Ballystockart Road/With Boffyflow and Spike . . . Wee Alfie at the Castle Picture House on the Castlereagh Road . . . Pastie suppers down at Davey's chipper'. Indeed. Reinforcing the sense of *déjà vu* was the reference to 'shining our light into the days of blooming wonder,' a line taken verbatim from a fifteen-year-old demo, 'Hey, Where Are You?'

Where 'A Sense of Wonder' did work was in the musical department, Morrison having temporarily abandoned his familiar crew to work with Irish folk combo Moving Hearts, who had been drafted in for a session in London to see what might transpire if they were given no advance preparation and zero chance to learn the tunes.

Donal Lunny: Van was quite abrupt. He very consciously tried to destabilize us, and it worked. He made us uncomfortable and removed any air of predictability from what was about to happen. From a music point of view, that's a brilliant thing to do. But he didn't stop to explain what he was doing. It just felt as if someone was putting the squeeze on us. It wasn't very pleasant!

How much Morrison intended to record with Moving Hearts remains unclear. Morrison may have originally intended *A Sense of Wonder* to realize the folky Irish element he had flirted with on the *Beautiful Vision* sessions back in 1981. According to Arty McGlynn, Morrison consciously planned to 'make some links with an Irish Celtic band. At that time the most obvious band to work with was Moving Hearts. But they blew it. They went off one day and [recorded] a jingle for RTE, and Van was waiting back at the inn.'

Certainly all three songs known to have been recorded with Moving Hearts – that seven-minute title track, the 'Boffyflow and Spike' instrumental, and Yeats's 'Crazy Jane on God' – contained indubitably Irish elements. Assuming that this was Morrison's intent, he again wandered from the point. Steve Turner later described 'every Morrison track [on *A Sense of Wonder* as] a digression that spoke of non-specific shiny lights and fiery visions', and many of the allusions in 'Ancient of Days', 'The Master's Eyes' and 'A New Kind of Man' suggest either a cursory knowledge of his Bible or an inability to transmute its language into song. If the lyrics were intended to be Blakean, the inclusion of Blake's own poetry in 'Let the Slave' showed who was the poet and who, on this showing, the poetaster.

Morrison perhaps gave away a certain residual uncertainty as to the strengths of his new album at the shows promoting its release in Britain in the autumn of 1984. The tour included five nights at the New Vic Theatre in Belfast, where 'Madame George' followed by 'Ballerina' at the main set's end became a show-stopper every night. However, Morrison unveiled very little from the new album – just its opener, title track and 'Boffyflow and Spike'. Given the way that every album since *Wavelength* had been milked to the max on its respective tour, this suggested a less than galvanized artist.

When some metaphorical arm-twisting led to Morrison agreeing to his first-ever Australian tour in the new year, he continued to keep most of the new songs at arm's length, adding only 'Ancient of Days' and the Ray Charles cover 'What Would I Do' to the set-list. If he was already intending to change direction, only his Irish buddy, Arty McGlynn, and bassist Jerome Rimson were privy to his plans in the weeks leading up to the Australian shows.

Arty McGlynn: This tour of Australia was looming, and about six weeks before the tour I get this call from Van: 'I want you over to rehearse an acoustic set.' I thought it was an acoustic set for the Australian tour. So we're over in Riverside [Studios in Hammersmith], this rehearsal room – myself, Jerome Rimson on acoustic bass and Van – and we do this acoustic set. So I says, 'What's this for?' He says, 'I want to do smaller gigs, Ronnie [Scott]'s, and maybe Dublin. Don't wanna do the big gigs any more. Just maybe do an acoustic thing, maybe get a fiddle player eventually. I just want us to "shape" these things.'

Commercial considerations, though, were inevitably brought to bear. While the Australian tour did eventually take place, the 'acoustic thing' did not. As Morrison turned on his own band, the man who had originally suggested an antipodean tour, and whose machinations made it happen, safely ducked the flying flak. Paul Charles had always known just how counterproductive it would be to say to Morrison, '"You should do this" or "You should be doing that." [Rather] it would be very organic: "You haven't done something for a while" . . . or he would have ideas himself . . . As an agent . . . you pass on requests, and you make your recommendation . . . [But] there'd been requests for Van to do Australia for years and years and years.' However, after all the Australian shows had been booked and the local reps geared up for the big push, Morrison informed Charles that he had changed his mind, placing his manager in an almost impossible situation.

Arty McGlynn: [So] Paul used all the band members as part of the package that he laid in front of Van . . . Paul was in a hard place at that time, and he used people that didn't use their head . . . I get this call from Paul Charles saying that Van's not doing the Australian tour – Paul didn't [seem to] understand that I'd been over rehearsing with Van for these small club gigs that Van wanted to do – 'He's not doing the tour, but you're entitled to a cancellation fee, which is half your fee for the whole tour.' I says, 'Fuck that! If he doesn't want to tour, he's not going to tour. That's it.' So I get on the phone to Richie Buckley and say, 'Listen, Richie, Van's not doing the tour. You're gonna be offered this half-fee thing. It's up to yourself.' So Richie says, 'I'm not gonna ask for half the fee either.' But the English guys, Jerome Rimson and Terry Popple and Kenny Craddock, [all] fell for it, and they all went for the half cancellation fee. So Paul Charles went back to Van and said, 'Listen, if you don't do this Australian tour, it's gonna cost you whatever, 'cause [of] the cancellation for the stadiums plus your band fees.' 'What!! Band fees? The band! Half-fee! Everybody?'

Charles thus successfully diverted Morrison's ire towards his hapless band, not necessarily calculating the long-term effects. The first person Morrison phoned after he had been read the economic riot act was his MD, Kenny Craddock.

Kenny Craddock: He didn't want to do the tour. He had a dodgy leg – the tour before that he was occasionally going on stage on crutches – and . . . I got various calls and I sent in a cancellation invoice, as per [Musicians] Union rules. But he [then] phoned me up, and we had a row on the phone . . . about the fact that I'd put a cancellation invoice in. I think his words were separating the [wolves] from the sheep.

The seven-date tour duly went ahead, though as promotional exercises go it lay somewhere between the 'bodyline' Test series and Gallipoli. Craddock recalls, 'Sydney, in particular, was a disaster. He was literally fulfilling his contract as to how long he was on stage, looking at his watch.' The editorials in the Australian papers wanted to know what they had done to offend the man, not knowing the real cause of his sustained sulk. McGlynn believes that Morrison didn't speak a word to a single English musician for the entire tour, leaving Ulla Munch to bear the brunt of the man's increasingly short fuse. On his return to England at the beginning of March, Morrison effectively fired the whole band,

McGlynn and Buckley excepted, determined to show that he wouldn't be held to ransom even if it meant dissolving one of his best touring bands.

Arty McGlynn: The rest of the band were fucked. They were gone. And Kenny Craddock was a big figure in that band, Hammond organ. That was a great band we had, and that just fucked that band up, and after that I didn't really enjoy it . . . The band had [had] respect for Van, and it was a wired-up respect. It was something that I never found in any other band after that. We worked our arses off for Van. OK, he had his moods. But dark concert or bright concert or mediocre concert, they all had a different essence to them, [and] the band followed him every place that he went.

If Morrison's unpardonable behaviour in Australia might have shocked some previous band members, it was only a slightly more extreme version of the persona he now presented most of the time he was on the road, plying his wares. It was as if the process had become more painful with each passing year and he couldn't decide who to blame. With the pressure cooker inside the man always set to explode, the band now preferred to steer clear of their unpredictable boss.

Martin Drover: He was almost a social cripple in terms of being able to enjoy himself and . . . trust people. I never did really get down to the bottom of it, because it meant doing an awful lot of talking to Van on a one-to-one basis, and that was a very difficult thing to initiate. Just occasionally he would warm. You'd be sat in some bar – he wouldn't drink in it, but he'd sit in there with you – and pontificate about all sorts of stuff, [going] way back. But that was rare . . . [Most of the time,] he was just an angry poet. [But with] some of the situations Van got himself into I'd find it hard to believe that he didn't know where he was going with it, and what he was doing. To me, it manifested itself as an anger he had inside him, and [although] he knew . . . he shouldn't be doing it, he used to dress [road managers] down unmercifully . . . [It] wasn't even a prima donna thing with Van, it was just a loss of control: 'I don't want to be here and I'm gonna make someone bloody pay for it' . . . And I put it down to the fact that he . . . wouldn't [have been] there in the first place had it not been for some pressure, making him tour or whatever. So it all gets [to a point] where he goes wallop, usually at the road manager . . . [But] he [only] gave me a ticking-off [once]. We were in NOMIS rehearsing, and some of the guys were in another studio with [some other singer], and we had a break. So I went over there and [didn't come] back until fifteen minutes after the rest of them, and he says, 'You interested in this job or not? You interested in this fucking job!? You want the fucking job!! You wanna stay here or you wanna fuck off!!!' [There's] no way you [can allow yourself to] get into any of this. You just let it go, 'cause you know it's just gonna get more hysterical. After you've been in the band a while and seen a few of them, [you know] that nothing will pacify him – only the lady from Scandinavia.

Ulla Munch does indeed seem to have been capable of instituting a quite remarkable transformation in this Molotov cocktail of a man, and has been credited by certain friends with keeping Morrison on the straight and narrow for most of the eighties. Not that this necessarily improved his moods or made him easier to live with – sometimes quite the opposite. She also displayed a tenacity rare in recent girlfriends, standing by him almost as long as Janet Planet. She would have her reward of sorts on the next album, perhaps Morrison's most romantic collection in fifteen years, as the warmer side of her curmudgeonly boyfriend reasserted itself in song.

Martin Drover: When [Ulla] was there – that was the only time he was a human being. He was really sweet. He'd get up in the morning and you'd know immediately. He was absolutely approachable. Most of the time, he wasn't. He was like a bear with a sore arse. But when his Scandinavian lady was around she had a very, very good influence on him, [he was] really quite happy. [But] it was a marathon task . . . [Then] there was the odd occasion when he would have half a bottle of wine and he'd blossom, he'd be approachable.

The bitterness, though, still blew through – and on *No Guru, No Method, No Teacher* it made its presence felt on two songs, 'A Town Called Paradise' and 'Thanks for the Information', both of which raised personal paranoia so high it threatened to obscure reality altogether. In the former, where Morrison set his sights on the 'copycats [who] ripped off my songs', his introduction to the song on its live début in May 1986 said it all, 'If I was a gunslinger, there'd be a lot of dead copycats out there.'

The idea that others ripped off his songs, his words, his melodies – as if *he* was the first guy ever to think of a riff like 'Gloria', or a jig like 'Rolling Hills', or to refer to Rimbaud in a song lyric – was something that clearly ate at him. When Bill Flanagan asked if he took such 'borrowings' as a compliment, he said he was flattered, 'but at the same time you feel sort of ripped off – not in the way one would think you would feel, but in the way that there's just people who *don't know*'. The following year, when the subject of Bruce Springsteen – unquestionably the biggest rock act in the world at the time – came up, it became apparent that Morrison resented the scale of Springsteen's success. It may even have been this that prompted 'A Town Called Paradise'.

Van Morrison: I was very influenced by Ray [Charles] and other people when I was starting out, but there came a point when I found my own voice. And then I found myself influencing lots of people, after I had originated something . . . For years people have been saying to me – you know, nudge, nudge – have you heard this guy Springsteen? You should really check him out! I just ignored it. Then four or five months ago I was in Amsterdam, and a friend of mine put on a video. Springsteen came on the video . . . and he's definitely ripped me off . . . I mean, he's even ripped my movements off as well . . . [and] I feel pissed off now that I know about it. [1985]

An overwhelming sense of injustice was a cross that Morrison had always carried, but had largely suppressed in song prior to 1986. Save for the magnificent bile of 'Drumshanbo Hustle' and the odd rant at his record company in 1975, evidence of a truly paranoid perspective was kept in check. However, just as his behaviour on tour became less and less stable, so a number of 'oh woe is me' songs began to infiltrate his albums. Even at his most beguiling, as on 'Ivory Tower', he could no longer resist a dig at those who don't know 'the price that I have to pay/ Just to do everything I have to do'. Why the burden should have become so insupportable at a time when his public profile was confined to think pieces in the Sunday papers and the odd review in the music press was something these songs failed to address. The bitterness of failure cannot be discounted. As his voice was left crying to be heard, the anti-rock rants to journalists in the mid to late eighties served to compound the chasm between him and his actual audience.

Van Morrison: The [current] rock & roll is not music, it's a lifestyle and you've got various things feeding that, simply because people are making a lot of money out of it. That's the beginning and end of it. Rock & roll makes money. The lifestyle attracts money. The media aspect makes a lot of money. This has absolutely nothing to do with music. My feeling has always been – ever since my lights went on – that the man in the street is being manipulated. [1988]

Having reached a financially comfortable middle age, Morrison still longed for some kind of recognition as yet denied him. After writing for his last couple of albums in a style that often pastiched former efforts, he began to consider publishing some of the poetry out of which his songs came, much as Patti Smith's *Babel* (1978) had revealed the poetic sources to many of her songs.

Mick Brown: I was working on the *Sunday Times* at that stage, so we were talking about trying to get some of his poetry published – I had the idea that some of his writing should be published in the *Sunday Times*, and of course nothing ever came of that. [What I got to see] was very much stream-of-consciousness stuff, some of which subsequently became songs on *No Guru, No Method, No Teacher* . . . I got the sense that he was not someone who sat down with the specific intention of writing four verses but would actually just write because it needed to be written. This stuff would sort of present itself, and would then be shoehorned into songs.

The lyrics on *No Guru, No Method, No Teacher* suggested not merely a rediscovery of the power of words, but a return to the more channelled writing of yesteryear. The most impressive example is the album's centre-piece, 'In the Garden', which cleverly draws its imagery from past songs to tell its tale and speak its message, reinforced by the album title and by a number of contemporary statements to the press.

Van Morrison: This finally states my position. I have never joined any organization, nor [do I] plan to. I am not affiliated to any guru, I don't subscribe to any method and, for those people who don't know what a guru is, I don't have a teacher either. [1986]

The album title originated with Krishnamurti, who had been co-cocooned since childhood by the Theosophical Society in the belief that he was the coming world teacher prophesied by its founder, Madame Blavatsky. When he reached adulthood, though, Krishnamurti rejected his assigned role, and when questioned as to his reasons replied, 'No guru, no method, no teacher.' Clive Culbertson, with whom Morrison discussed Krishnamurti, believes the meaning to be relatively unambiguous: 'God is the guru, God is the teacher, and there is no intermediary guru between you and God.' 'In the Garden' was one of Morrison's most channelled works in many a moon. After he had discussed its composition in a surprisingly self-conscious way for a special televised show at Coleraine University in April 1988, the TV producer chose to omit the answer from the broadcast.

Clive Culbertson: We did a TV show at Coleraine University, Derek, Van and myself . . . [And] Van has never admitted publicly where he gets a lot of his material. The guy was saying to him about 'In the Garden' – and you have to understand that the symbolism of the garden [is] a path-working in the Rosicrucian thing, where they take you to the garden and who you can meet in the garden – . . . and [Van] says, 'Oh yeah, I didn't write that. I was sitting in my flat one night and this voice said to me, "Write this down," and I pulled out the paper and I just wrote down what he told me, and that was the song "In the Garden".' And the guy goes, 'Really, Van. And what was it like playing in the Maritime in 1967?' And Derek Bell said to me afterwards, 'You can be sure they [will] cut that.' And they did.

'In the Garden' is one of several songs on *No Guru* containing allusions to Blake and the Bible, as well as harking back to the kind of glistening imagery employed on *Astral Weeks*. But this is no pastiche. The image of this creature consumed with rapture, entering a 'childlike vision [that] became so fine' until they 'felt the presence of the youth of Eternal summers', is entirely original. Likewise 'Tir Na Nog' (apparently a legendary Irish land of eternal youth), finds this pair of lovers 'standing in the garden wet with rain' before, at song's end, we are returned to 'Astral Weeks', as 'many many many times you kissed mine eyes/In Tir Na Nog'.

The grand themes of Morrison's canon here coalesced again into a sustainable whole. Whether he was depicting days when he 'used to gaze out/my classroom window and dream/and then go home and listen to Ray sing "I believe to my soul" after school'; or the warm feeling that 'filled me with religion' in her presence; or alluding to 'a world that seems like glamour . . . through your rose-coloured glasses'; this was an artist broaching a broad sweep of perennial preoccupations and carrying it off.

In 'One Irish Rover' Morrison even places himself in a one-to-one with Christ, a particular Christ that a last-minute change obscured: according to Chris Michie, back on lead guitar, 'When we first recorded "One Irish Rover" the lyrics were ". . . one Roman soldier . . ." I never asked him why the change was made. I feel that the importance of expression is [so] personal [it] shouldn't be discussed, it should just be experienced.' I feel no such qualms, and presume that the one Roman soldier with whom Morrison originally identified was the one who, in order to spare Christ further suffering, pierced his side on the cross. If so, that opening stanza, in which our now-Irish rover asks to be told 'the story/now that's it over/wrap it in glory, for one Irish rover', takes on powerful resonances.

Morrison, though, failed to see the absurdity of highlighting his own predicament in the face of such suffering, as 'One Irish Rover' moves into 'Ivory Tower', where a chorus about how tough 'it really must be/ To be me, to see like me, to feel like me' threatens the spiritually self-effacing mood he had previously maintained. Indeed the false humility of 'Thanks for the Information' and the smug superiority of 'Ivory Tower' sit uneasily at the end of a collection rich in insight and artistry. It was as if Morrison couldn't help but show himself to be the perennial dweller on the threshold. Such a lack of self-awareness was already blurring his restored vision and would begin to irrevocably colour his work come the nineties.

Steve Turner: What I find remarkable is that as an artist and writer he obviously does have perception and he's been into all these religions and psychologies. At the end of all that you should have some realistic estimation of what you're like. Some people might say, 'I've got a bad temper and I'm trying to overcome it,' or, 'I've got a bad temper but I don't give a shit.' But somebody like Van Morrison would say, 'I've not got a bad temper' – and probably shout it at you.

If, in the eighties, his attempts to overcome that darker side prompted as many 'yearning songs' as the search for philosophical insight, *No Guru, No Method, No Teacher* was his most rounded portrait to date, wrapped in some of the most gorgeous melodies the man could muster. Even the choice of musicians bridged the best from a decade and a half of shifting musical sands. Though the basic tracks were again compiled in Sausalito, under the watchful eye of Jim Stern, the only components retained from recent collections were guitarist Chris Michie and bassist David Hayes. Using a genuinely different kind of percussionist, Baba Trunde, Morrison again asked Jeff Labes to weave the thread that tied together *Moondance*, *Veedon Fleece* and *Common One*, with a series of string overdubs.

Chris Michie: We recorded the basics for *No Guru* at Studio D in Sausalito, California. It was a magical bunch of sessions with just five musicians: me, Jeff Labes, Baba Trunde, David Hayes and Van. That made it possible to really pay attention to the subtleties of our instruments. You can hear that especially on songs like 'In the Garden' and 'A Town Called Paradise'. We went to the Plant in Sausalito to do the early overdubs, like guitar solos, strings on 'Tir Na Nog', and back-up vocals. Then Van took the masters to Townhouse Studios in London.

Back in London, the sound was further smoothed by a series of subtle overdubs, with Richie Buckley, Martin Drover and Kate St John applying sax, trumpet and oboe. The lack of directions left veterans like Buckley and Drover unfazed, but not so the young, inexperienced St John.

Kate St John: There were no arrangements. Van just said, 'Go in and blow through it,' and there were no other instruments doing answering phrases. So I just twiddled through it, warming up, thinking we'd come back and analyse, do four or five takes and compile something; but Van said, 'That's great, let's do the next song.'

The result was a richly textured album which departed from the homogeneity of recent offerings. Equally understated vocally, but with lyrics that again read like final drafts, not random thoughts, the album finally gave fans an LP unafraid of comparison with those produced in Morrison's twenties. Not surprisingly, it garnered his best reviews of the eighties. Barry McIlheney, in *Melody Maker*, warned anyone 'who may have lost faith in the last few years, '[that] this magnificent return to form will come as a major shock to the system'. John Wilde in *Sounds* was even more effusive:

His most consummate record since *Wavelength*[!] and his most intriguingly involved since *Astral Weeks*, this is bursting to saturation point, Morrison at his most mystical, magical best. Like *Astral Weeks*, it comes with a full-fledged scenic atmosphere, his own childhood fragments taking on supercharged lust . . . Without flaws, it gently coaxes much gripping sublimity out of the softest of refrains, the lowest undercurrents of sound. At his most effective when understated, the crescendos here are never dampened by their subtle nature, and never fall short of blinding . . . The best record of this year so far.

Morrison thought so too, and on 17 May 1986 – with the album still six weeks away from the shops – he previewed three songs at Ireland's answer to Live Aid, Self Aid. And such was his faith in the material that he reunited the likes of Pee Wee Ellis, David Hayes, Jeff Labes, John Platania and Daoud Shaw for a month-long US tour in July, something that Platania describes as 'a conscious thing, bringing us together again'. The tour culminated in a show at the Greek Theatre in Berkeley, which was broadcast on a syndicate of American radio stations. Morrison and his hardcore musical sidemen were again stretching the songs in ever-new directions. 'In the Garden' also acquired the string arrangement that its album incarnation was denied, courtesy of Jaff Labes, giving every show that all-important crescendo.

Van Morrison: From about half-way through ['In the Garden'] until the end I take you through a definite meditation process . . . So when this happens in the song I say, 'And I turned to you and I said, "No guru, no method, no teacher, just you and me and nature, and the father and the son and the holy ghost."' You really have to do the whole line to know what it means . . . It's very difficult to do this . . . The bigger the audience . . . the harder it is to put across what you're doing. When you've got intimacy you've got more of a chance of taking people through this experientially. So this is really . . . what I'm doing in this song, 'In the Garden'. I used to do this quite a bit. For instance, when I did this in the sixties we'd get to a place where there's a meditative part, say at the end of 'Cyprus Avenue' . . . Maybe this wasn't explained to people properly. What actually happened was that when we got to this point, some people got that it was about meditation and they were willing to receive it, and other people thought this was a chance to say 'Right on' or something . . . It's very difficult to do this in a situation where it's [considered] rock & roll 'cause rock & roll isn't set up that way, it's set up to do the opposite. It's set up to stimulate . . . Well, this has got nothing to do with the meditation process, which is what I'm about, and what – ultimately – the songs and everything else is about . . . so at some point I'll have to make that split from rock & roll . . . What I'm talking about is trying to eliminate all the bullshit, because that's all in the way . . . Hopefully I would like this to maybe lead me to the next stage, which I think it will. I think something's happening . . . and maybe people can come and see me under different circumstances, in different sort[s] of places, that aren't rock & roll places. Hopefully that might happen, but I certainly don't want to do this album-tour bit any more. I'd like to make this the last time I do that. [1986]

But still Morrison threw himself into the rigmarole of touring, with a month-long tour of Europe following the US stint – though not with these musicians – which was in turn succeeded by a further set of shows in Ireland and London. At the same time, he continued his search for an environment where – as he put it back in 1979 – he could 'really explore that part of my music . . . It has to be very sensitive and quiet, or else it's really frustrating to try to do it . . . [and] I haven't found a channel yet to present it.' The relentless promotion of *No Guru* only confirmed a suspicion that such channels still remained closed. His cynicism occasionally would surface in a risible rendition of 'Send in the Clowns' at a concert's end.

Mick Brown: I think he genuinely had an almost evangelical desire to find some new way of working, some new way of relating to the audience outside the confines of being put in a Van Morrison box. He felt a contempt for the industry – about how industry is just about dealing product, and he's not product. And he was obviously reading very extensively at that time in that spiritual/ theosophical area, and a lot of those ideas were filtering into what he was trying to do. There was a sense that he was trying to use his music as a tool of spiritual/ psychological awakening, and [he was] exploring ways of doing that.

The return he was getting from nightly attempts to transcend the rock format refused to equate with the psychological demand made on him. If Morrison was searching for what Yeats called 'the [actual] purpose of rhythm . . . [which] is to prolong the moment of contemplation, the moment when we are both asleep and awake, which is the one moment of creation', his audience faced a long period of re-education, supplemented by a series of pronouncements both in the press and, most tellingly, on a promotional interview album Morrison made with Mick Brown, on which he talked at length about the intention behind his new music:

Van Morrison: When you write songs and record albums, you rely on a song's pattern, but that's not really what I do when I play live at all. In fact the whole thing is geared to the parts in between, the extensions of the songs, beginnings or endings, more than anything else. The songs are great for jumping off on, but they're really the background to what I do – the repetitions. That's what I'm really about. [1986]

Van Morrison: I can do what I want to do in ten minutes [on stage]. I can take the essence of everything I've ever done and everything I will do, and put that into ten minutes. I often think, why should I go out and play for an hour and a half when I can really do it in ten minutes – if it was a concentrated effort of doing the real thing . . . rather than basically camouflaging it for an hour and a half or two hours? [1988]

Such assertions suggested a man looking to break through to another art form. However, as a couple of songs on *No Guru* perhaps indicated, Morrison may not have been entirely prepared for the consequences. As on the occasion when he actually came face to face with the spirit world in that haunted monastery on a French mountain top, as soon as he began to play with musicians who intuitively sensed the presences he liked to sing about, his reaction became one of fear, and his response was to recoil.

Clive Culbertson: When he's in form, what he does live, that nobody else does live, [is] allow the presence to come in him . . . I've been to his gigs when he's going through motions and you know it and everybody in the audience knows it, and there's the nights when I can see the energy round him. Generally speaking, people know. Whenever he came off after a big one he was burnt out. And it wasn't that he put anything more into it. It was just this high-voltage energy that was coming through him. [When Derek and I were both there] there were three of us on stage who were mediating the power as it came in – that's all I ever felt my role was. [But] it seemed to be if it didn't catch him, it never seemed to go through any of the rest of the band – even though I could see [these energy forces] trying to get into him. If they couldn't get into him, they never bothered going into me. He was the transmitter. You could see them surrounding him. You knew something spiritual was happening . . . There were nights when you would see the luminous ones appear around him, and you could actually see the light coming down on him and those were the nights he hit it . . . [But] there were nights the light didn't go into him. Those were the nights that he didn't hit it. Sometimes if he caught it, he caught it for the gig. Sometimes it got more colourful [on certain songs], and I used to say when he came off, 'Van, there were these two [presences] when you were doing [such-and-such].' I did this for the first four, five gigs of the tour and I remember one night he came off and I said, 'Van, there was this guy [with] a robe . . .' 'Stop fucking doing this! I don't want to know this fucking stuff! Don't fucking tell me!'

Though there would be one last attempt to embrace the spiritual power of music, it would leave Morrison unhappy and uninspired. Shortly afterwards, he would begin his passage back to the mainstream, and 'In the Garden' would become — save on those very special nights when the transmitter was still working — just another song with which to explore the art of dynamics.

24

1987–88: The Secret Heart of Music

He said to me once, 'I'm thinking of going back to the window cleaning . . . I'm sick of this shit. At least you know where you're at – window cleaning.' And I got the feeling he really meant it, and yes he really did think it would be all right.

—*Roy Jones*

When I knew Van he had fantastic houses but there was no real lifestyle in them. You're talking about somebody who's looking for something all the time. He's a great reader. The problem is when music is so central to your life, you resent it. You fight against it. It's like this drug, 'You gotta do it! You gotta do it!' And he goes, 'I don't wanna do it. I want to clean windows. I don't want to think about this. I want to have another reason.' And Van has that dynamic. It's an obsession that he really would like to get away from . . . [but] there's nothing else really in his life as driving as music.

—*Peter Van Hooke*

The burning desire 'to find some new way of working' would not always manifest itself in a positive way. Morrison had allowed long sloughs of depression to stand between him and the obvious – music was his life. At the end of 1986, when he had again fried a number of nerve ends to get through half a year of continual touring, he again spoke about 'winding down . . . I'm not going to say this'll be my last tour. I'll just say hopefully I won't do it this way any more.' Having reasserted himself as a vital artistic force, with the vibrant *No Guru, No Method, No Teacher*, he continued to search for a form of self-effacement in his personal life. The sheer incompatibility of these two designs seemed to escape him.

Van Morrison: If it gets to the point where I don't have any of my own space left any more, then it'd have to mean [my] getting out of it . . . What I'd like to do is talk about [fame] . . . the total emptiness of all that . . . [and] get that across to people. [1986]

By the late eighties, Morrison's constant complaints about fame and fortune, in song and in interview, had become tiresome to both his audience and the media at large. First, it broke a cardinal rule of fame – don't bitch about your life to people who will never be famous themselves. Secondly, it began to leave a bad taste on albums that professed to address transcendence and glory. Not that he confined himself to public bitching – protestations to friends about 'escaping it all' also became increasingly frequent.

Clive Culbertson: He used to ring me up at four in the morning to discuss this. This was a regular discussion, 'I want out, man. I want out.' 'Van, just get out.' 'Ah, jeez, you don't understand. You don't know enough about this business.' I said, 'You set the lawyers to run the thing and get out, walk away from it.' 'I can't walk away. They'd be screwing me, taking my money.' 'Van, the people that are looking after your money are the same people that've been looking after your money for twenty-five years. You've had them checked and double-checked, triple-checked.' 'But how can I walk away? People want me out there.' 'Hold on, if people want you out there, and you want to go and do it, go and do it, but stop going on about it . . . When you're doing it, you don't want to be doing it. When you're not doing it, you do want to be doing it. So just make a decision. There're only two options.' 'You can't talk to me [like that]. Who the fuck do you think . . .' And he's woken me at four in the morning to discuss this . . . I said to him a few times, 'You can pay somebody to put a false beard on you. Let's not hang out where you usually hang out,' and he often talked about it: 'If I thought I could get away . . .' But he's nothing else to do. I kept talking to him: 'This is your dharma. This is what you are about.' I remember one of the mornings he rang me, must have been '83, '84, and . . . I said, 'Well, to be honest, this is what you have to do. This is the entire reason you're alive.' 'Ah, you're fucking dumping all this shit on me!' I said, 'Just get away. Take a couple of friends. There's loads of places you'll not be recognized.' But he never seemed to be able to do one or the other. When he was away, he wanted to be playing; when he was playing, he wanted to be away.

Morrison's response was in fact quite disproportionate to his 'fame' at this point. He remained a major celebrity largely in his own mind. By 1986, he had long passed the peak of his currency, and was on the highway to nowhere in particular. His albums still reached those attuned but, as Steve Turner duly observed, 'the search for meaning [which] now dominated his songwriting . . . rendered his new material almost inaccessible to anyone who was not a fellow seeker'.

Paul Charles's personal experience, when in his company in or around Holland Park, was that '99 per cent of the time . . . [Van] would go about his day, he would meet with his friends, he'd play music, he would go to the cinema, he would read books, and maybe for 1 per cent of the time someone would try and infringe [on that]'. Morrison, though, amplified such minor incursions on his time into a major hassle, until the escapist longing in his music – another long-term thread – began to express itself in a way that suggested someone genuinely looking for a life outside music. Indeed, he informed Desmond Hogan in 1987 that 'for the past twelve years or so I've only been in [the music business] part of the time'. It suggested other preoccupations had intervened more than they had.

One of the songs on Morrison's 1987 album, *Poetic Champions Compose*, suggests that he was looking for a way of fading away altogether. 'Alan Watts Blues' eulogizes the maverick writer Watts, a contemporary of Alice Bailey, who 'disappeared' after achieving a cultish kind of literary fame with books like *Cloud Hidden* and *The Spirit of Zen*. Here Morrison writes in the first person of someone who has grown 'tired of the ways of mice and men/And the empires all turning into rust again . . . That's why I'm cloud hidden, whereabouts unknown'. Clearly a part of him longed to go there too. And yet, when drummer Roy Jones found Morrison sitting outside at a 1989 session, 'being a bit philosophical', the conversation they had suggested a man still determined to have his say to the world at large: 'I was [saying], "We're not important, Van. None of us are more important than that ant in the scheme of things." He said, "Do you really believe that?" He didn't see it. He was incredulous that I didn't have a problem with that.' The ego at the centre of his musical ambition was still whispering to his heart.

Like many a so-called celebrity, Morrison had learned to value obscurity when it was no longer a realistic option. Again repeating common patterns, his response was to compartmentalize his life – as if his self-evidently autobiographical form of songwriting could be detached from the man behind the curtains. Assuming some all-embracing 'right to privacy' in the face of public interest in his very public work, he ensured that his private life was fiercely guarded by a series of buffers designed to separate him from the famous persona. Journalist Mick Brown was one regular lunchtime visitor to Holland Park who was deemed suspect, the relationship being conducted from the doorstep to the café and back again. Only once was he allowed across the threshold.

Mick Brown: What he would usually do was answer the door and sort of step outside the door and close it behind him. So that you didn't feel that you were terribly welcome. It must have been on one occasion, when he'd left his coat upstairs, that he had no alternative but to say, 'Come in. Have a cup of coffee.' . . . It looked like the furniture you find in a rented flat. Sofa, table and two chairs, lots of books of the kind we'd been talking about, Dylan records, Irish folk music, Lead Belly, John Lee Hooker, empty fridge. Occasionally I'd get calls at two o'clock in the morning and I'd get out of bed – 'Hi, it's Van. I was just thinking about what Steiner said about . . .' 'Van, it's two o'clock in the morning.' [But] when you went into his place that all became clear. This was the sort of place where somebody would be at two o'clock in the morning, playing some Irish folk music, reading about Alice Bailey, and just thinking, 'I'll just call up . . .' A completely enclosed universe.

Steve Turner, another rock journalist capable of wide-ranging conversation, never even got to the lounge. Those who had more success in their sorties across the threshold encountered a very isolated figure with little in the way of communication skills, and without even the creature comforts wealth usually brings. Martin Drover is one of those who remember 'his house in Holland Park [having] no furniture in the place. Magnificent house, [but] all there is is a nice sound system and a TV and some boxes and books. He's not a material person . . . nice settees don't interest him.' Roy Jones, another lunch guest, couldn't help but feel a degree of pity for his sometime boss.

Roy Jones: You couldn't sit down. There were books everywhere, about 'My Guru' and 'My Faith'. This was the desperate search for something . . . You'd often go meet him to go have coffee or lunch. If he fancied it, [and] as long as you paid for yourself . . . [But] he was really difficult to fathom.

These lunch guests usually found someone armed with a battery of questions, sometimes wishing to discuss some way of circumventing 'the fame game', as if this would somehow bring inner peace. In 1986 Morrison actually told one journalist that he was thinking about 'mak[ing] tapes and distribut[ing] them myself – be[ing] in more control of my own destiny and what I want to do without having to play everybody else's game'. Needless to say, it was simply one more pipe dream. For all the rhetoric about controlling his music, Morrison still desired a large, populist audience. At the same time, he began seriously to consider how he might add an educational dimension to the music-making. When Bill Flanagan, interviewing him for *Musician*, asked if he had ever thought of becoming a teacher, he admitted to thinking 'about it quite a bit . . . That's the kind of thing I'd like to do, actually.' Mick Brown presented him with an appropriate opportunity in the early months of 1987.

Mick Brown: He wanted to do something more than music, and he was talking about having a small group or organization that would put out a newsletter. Then he would wonder whether he should be giving lectures that included music. He wanted somehow to get involved in some kind of 'networking' activity . . . [ ] . . . I introduced him to the Wrekin Trust, which was a holistic/spiritual education trust set up by Sir George Trevelyan, and he was invited to a mystics' and scientists' conference, where he was supposed to talk about the mystical effects of music. [At least,] the original idea was that he was going to talk. [ST/CH]

Through Brown, Morrison was introduced to the Trust chairman Malcolm Lazarus, who was in the early stages of organizing a weekend conference on some of the more metaphysical aspects of music. Lazarus soon realized that 'he wanted to do something serious. I wouldn't have worked with him if he had not wanted to do something serious. He wanted to take the whole debate about what he perceives as the purpose of music on to a higher level.'

After some prevarication, Morrison finally agreed to perform at the conference, as well as involving himself in a group discussion about 'The Secret Heart of Music'. This was precisely what he had been mentioning in interviews at the time of *No Guru*: finding 'a format where the audience or the listener would have to hear, and they would have to be there for the reason of participating in a sort of meditation experience for that night, for that performance'. In the programme notes for the convention, Morrison's music was painted in decidedly esoteric terms:

His passion for the music and his bemusement with the contradictions inherent in being famous have led him to deeply question many of the underlying attitudes of our age. In particular, he has investigated the esoteric influences on music with a view to discovering more about its effect on the body–mind relationship. His own work is now increasingly intended as a means for inducing contemplation, and for healing and uplifting the soul . . . His struggle to reconcile the mythic, almost other-worldly vision of the Celts, and his own search for spiritual satisfaction, with the apparent hedonism of blues and soul music, has produced many inspired and visionary performances.

The conference, hosted by the Wrekin Trust, was scheduled for the weekend of 18–20 September 1987, at Loughborough University in the East Midlands. Morrison played an informal set on the Friday with Robin Williamson, Clive Culbertson and Derek Bell, all fellow searchers. Examples of Celtic folklore were recited between songs inspired by a number of appropriate mystical sources – including 'Tir Na Nog', 'And the Healing Has Begun', 'Celtic Ray' and 'In the Garden'. A Saturday set backed by the *Poetic Champions* band was given to both delegates and paying punters. Guitarist Mick Cox recalls that 'at the end of . . . the [set] Van brought the music down to near silence and told the audience to close their eyes and that he was going to make himself disappear. And he walked off to the wings while they had their eyes shut!'

Finally, on the Sunday, an open forum afforded a panel of musical 'experts', including Morrison, Derek Bell and Professor Joscelyn Godwin, author of *Music in America*, the opportunity to respond to written questions. Morrison remained guarded in his responses and, after the weekend ended, expressed disappointment at the numbers attending (approximately 270 delegates). Despite his previous rhetoric, he failed to embrace the format fully, retaining many of his own buffers in a situation intended to dissolve barriers.

Malcolm Lazarus: He was engaged in a sort of battle between not being able to grasp the intellectual dynamics and nevertheless wanting to, and between not being willing to grasp the experiential side and yet, at the same time, wanting to incorporate it into his music. I think that, like a lot of artists, he was afraid to do anything to the creative process . . . He [also] chose to book accommodation off campus, so he lost a lot of contact there.

Shortly after the conference Lazarus was forced to resign from the Trust, owing to ill-health, and the Trust itself was subsequently dissolved. By 1997 Morrison was telling the man who had introduced him to the Trust that he felt they were just using the name Van Morrison, that it was just one more hustle, and that everything he attempted to do to separate himself from the music business came down to the same thing – business. At the time, though, his new songs embraced the possibility of a new platform. The song that opened the weekend, 'The Mystery', expressed a sentiment he would prove unable to embrace: 'To carry on/ You've got to open up your heart to the sun . . . Let go into the mystery'. The sentiments came more easily than the necessary willpower. As he expressed it in a contemporary live performance of 'Northern Muse':

When the heart is open you will change. Just like a flower slowly opening. Give, give, give more, give better. When you're completely empty and you're completely drained, and you can't go on any more, you have to give, give again, give more, give better. When you're down, depressed, despondent, pissed off, fucked off, you have to give, give more, give again, give better. When the heart is open.

But only then. Only when Morrison was willing to lay himself open to the hurt. And for all his philosophical musings, he remained a deeply sceptical student. Nor was this the only example of such a contradiction denying him the chance of a life-affirming experience. Mick Brown, in *The Spiritual Tourist*, details an occasion when Morrison was introduced to a Sri Lankan swami. As Brown piercingly observes, 'Van's response to such [meetings] often seemed to fall into a pattern of interest, followed by an equally intense suspicion which could border on hostility.' This proved to be just such an instance. After Morrison was finally ushered into the swami's presence, he stayed for a few minutes and then emerged 'look[ing] pale and flustered, as if he had been shown his own worst nature. His palm was clenched tight . . . He pushed past me without a word . . . "What a fuckin' joker," he said at last.' Though Brown never managed to find out what had occurred, Clive Culbertson witnessed a similar reaction, and an even more hostile version of the man, when the two of them met a Rosicrucian master in the summer of 1988.

Clive Culbertson: We'd just come home from a European tour, and this German Rosicrucian guy had asked to see Van. So Van, John Rogers, Derek Bell and myself went up to the temple in London to meet this Rosicrucian master and his minder . . . But Van, [who] had just come off the tour, was like four bears each with three sore heads. So the guy is sitting, talking [about] the mysteries of the universe, and Van goes, 'I've heard this shit before, man. You fucking bring me all the way down here to listen to this crap.' So of course the guy goes straight back to the start again and says exactly the same thing again – 'cause this is the way they do [it] – and every time he gets to the [same point] Van [goes,] 'Man, this is fucking Rudolf Steiner. I've heard this shite. I don't want to hear this again,' [and] the man goes back to the start and starts again. So by the time he does it for the fourth time the steam is coming out of Van's ears! 'Right, I've heard enough of this shit. Everybody out. That's it. Fuck you!' The man goes, 'Fine.' So as Van's walking away, I said [to him], 'I wouldn't mind keeping in touch with this guy.' 'You wanna waste your fucking time, you waste your fucking time.'

Coming from a man who had just penned the line 'You've got to have some faith to carry on', such a response suggested the glamour was upon him, and the spiritual quest seemingly detailed in the albums from *Into the Music* to *Avalon Sunset* largely illusory. Derek Bell tersely expressed just such a sentiment to the Chieftains' official biographer, 'Van wanted teachings at the time but he didn't want to do any work. He was in a hurry. He wanted them now, and if you didn't have them you could fuck off.'

Others with whom Morrison discussed the more philosophical aspects of life are prepared to give him the benefit of the doubt. Jonn Savannah, who would replace Georgie Fame in the nineties bands, contrasts Morrison with 'someone like Alan Watts [who] would go down that route, get it completely and then live it for the rest of his life. Whereas . . . Van would think . . . that all makes perfect sense but after a little while, because of the nature of his personality . . . he wouldn't get that enlightenment. I [just] think that his life is so tortured, and always has been.'

On the other hand, Morrison could prove quite adept at presenting an open front when he was in fact being extremely guarded. Ed Fletcher, who remained his American tour manager throughout the first half of the eighties, is not sure he ever knew the real man: 'There were times when I was younger, and first met him, that I think [we] were close, and then I became presumptuous . . . [But] there were times when we'd really lock in, and have profound talks and connect . . . Most people have experiences or relationships to some degree with Van, but [as to who he is] for the broadest part [of the time], I think it's pure speculation.'

In conversation, as in life, Morrison could readily mask his true feelings – even if sparing other people's feelings was never a strong point, as the Chieftains' frontman was about to find out.

Paddy Moloney: He tends to shun intimacy. You could be talking to him for ages and feel that this conversation has to go on, but at one point he'll have to get away from it. He feels if you've said what you have to say, there's no point in coming back to that person the next day and saying the same thing all over again. And some people misinterpret that.

The strain of dealing with Morrison almost daily had certainly taken its toll on Paul Charles, who took his leave of the man, at least on a professional basis, at the end of the *No Guru* tour. Charles depicts his departure as a natural enough process – 'if you're managing somebody, you do give up a part of your life in terms of time [and] in terms of emotional investment, and I kind of reached that point in my life . . . whereby I wanted a bit of my life back again' – but it left Morrison without a certain kind of much-needed guidance.

The band Morrison had recruited for European *No Guru* duties included familiar elements – Arty McGlynn, Martin Drover, Jerome Rimson, Richie Buckley – but he also drafted in a new drummer and new keyboardist, Roy Jones and Neil Drinkwater, after catching them at that important testing-ground, a Christmas pantomime with Irish singer Dana in Oxford (according to Jones, Morrison came twice). After a dry run in June 1986, for the *Wogan* BBC TV chat show, at which Van sang a single song, the band reassembled in early September for a length-and-breadth tour of mainland Europe, Ireland and – seemingly as an afterthought – London. The rehearsals, which were intensive, though not perhaps extensive enough, gave some indication of the man's likely moods. Martin Drover particularly remembers Morrison turning on drummer Jones at the first rehearsal and saying, 'Look, I'm forty fucking years old. I don't need this shit!'

Roy Jones: It was good to have done two weeks' rehearsal but it was hardly worth it because whatever happened on stage, happened . . . Neil and I used to drive to the rehearsals, and he'd given us a really scrappy tape of a live recording, but only from the engineer's desk, so that was [the way of] learning the numbers before you got to the rehearsal studio . . . [But] the music isn't that challenging – [you're] just not allowed sevenths! And he'd turn around and glower if someone dropped one in . . . [But] there were [an] endless number of occasions on stage when [he] left the band looking at each other going, 'Any idea what's going [on]?' . . . I always remember the night he was doing 'Cleaning Windows' and he closed the band down, and then actually described, step by step, how to clean windows: 'You need a ladder, a bucket and a scram[!]. You take the bucket . . .' I even think he talked about getting in the corners. There he was telling these foreigners how to clean windows – difficult to keep a straight face! . . . [And yet] even though it would be different every night, you could read where it was gonna [go] . . . He kind of found a path, and he used it again the next time.

When Morrison occasionally strayed from that path, though, he expected the others to follow, and Jones was considered culpable when he failed to take account of one of the hand signals it had taken Van Hooke a decade to learn to anticipate. Half-way through the tour, Morrison unwisely decided to humiliate his drummer in public.

Martin Drover: I forget the tune but there's a slapdown; he says, 'Take it down' – knock, knock – and he'd go like that [*gives a hand signal*]. And now and again, very occasionally, Roy would miss it and there was no slapdown so Van would vamp and give a few looks! It only happened a couple of times but one of them was in Amsterdam and he stopped the band and he publicly dressed Roy down: 'We have a drummer that can't see a signal.' Nothing [more] transpired that night but the next morning somebody brought a paper to Roy and it was in the paper, [that] he'd had to tell [the drummer] off on stage. Roy went ballistic. We're in to do the next gig and there's a backstage bar. Roy's at the bar and ten minutes before the performance he sends for the road manager and says, 'Tell Van without an apology to me, in front of the band, I'm off home.' And Van came and apologized to him. I gave him a few points for that.

As Jones says, 'He didn't give me so many signals after that,' and the tour continued on its merry way – until the next blow-up. Jones was used to working with entertainer-types, and was amazed at the way Morrison 'would walk off the stage if something upset him. There was one night he saw a red light on a Walkman in the audience and he [went] offstage and screamed at security. [Another time] we were playing and all of a sudden he turned to storm off the stage, and of course he was still attached [to his guitar] and so he bounced back . . . took the guitar off, threw it on the floor and went off the stage. And we're vamping [for] quite a long time . . . Apparently he'd seen someone near the front of the audience making faces at him. There was a few occasions when things like that happened . . . There were nights when it was a very short set – one night it was forty minutes – and there would [also] be nights [when you'd get] the really drawn-out [songs] . . . but it never seemed to have any relationship to us.'

In spite of these ructions, the tour was a musical triumph. The band did all that could reasonably be expected of them, and the sets were a genuine cross-section of Morrison's strongest material, albeit with the emphasis on modernity. In Frankfurt, the lucky Germans got all 'the really drawn-out songs' in one forty-minute fix at the concert's end, beginning with a revamped 'And the Healing Has Begun' that segued into 'Gloria'. The trilogy of 'In the Garden', 'Summertime in England' and 'Rave On, John Donne' completed that night's deep dark delve into the mystery.

With the end of the *No Guru* tour, in November 1986, there were a couple of musicians who fully expected that to be that. One could certainly feel the silence as Morrison indulged himself in little except guest appearances with the Dave Gold Big Band, the Blues Band, Elvis Costello, the Danish Big Band and the Gil Evans Orchestra in six months of uncharacteristic inactivity. Come the spring, though, he fancied a 'blow' and summoned Neil Drinkwater, temporary new bassist Steve Pearce and that bolshy drummer, Roy Jones, to a small studio near Bath, the Wool Hall.

Roy Jones: There were odd gigs [we]'d still be doing, and then the album [*Poetic Champions*] happened. We went to Bath to do it, which was a very nice experience, but it was literally a track a day – perhaps [even] two. He had like a school exercise book with words in it, not always all the words, and he'd just play it through. He'd explain briefly what he wanted or ask what d'you think, and then you'd have a go at it. And that was just with the trio. And it was literally just play it through a couple of times and then a take. But it was mostly only one take, perhaps two takes, no more, and then repairs. But he didn't repair! . . . Quite often he'd get in his car and go into Bristol after the take, and we'd be left there to do the repairs on our own. He'd disappear.

According to Morrison, the initial sessions worked the idea of recording instrumentals out of his system: 'When I started [*Poetic Champions*] off, I thought I'd like to do a whole sort of jazz instrumental album. But when I did three numbers I thought, "No, I don't wanna do that," [and] changed my mind. So I started to bring in songs.' Martin Drover, who was brought in after they had done a few days' recording as a quartet, to play trumpet and flugelhorn, found that a number of the songs evolved out of these jazz instrumentals, as Morrison began to enjoy exploring multiple musical avenues.

Martin Drover: It was a jam, that album [*Poetic Champions*]. We went to Bath, we went to the Wool House [*sic*], and we sat there, looked at one another: 'What do you fancy, Van?' 'Sod it! [Let's] just have a play.' You don't usually do that – you['ve] usually got some dots in front of you. The first couple of days Van was just playing alto, we were just busking, playing over things . . . He's a frustrated jazz alto player . . . That's basically what he wanted to be. Van's alto playing always sounded like an amateur. But it's [usually] the case that people who are brilliant at something . . . would rather be doing something that they can't do very well . . . He played it loads in Bath on the album [sessions], and he was very happy . . . Stuff evolved out of that, and that's how that album was made. But he was fairly relaxed.

However, the most intriguing song attempted at the sessions would not make it on to the record. Morrison admitted to Jones that he had always wanted to do the song 'Jerusalem', but no one seemed too sure exactly how to play it. Eventually, Jones recalls, 'we went to a local church. There was no one in there, and I rifled about in the organ loft and there was a hymn-book and we borrowed it . . . But he couldn't get the time sorted out. He wanted to do it in 4[/4], but there are a couple of places where you [just] can't.' After a whole day of working on the nation's favourite hymn, Morrison returned to jazz instrumentals – three of which would make the album – and songs, now that he had something to say. The tapes were then taken up to the Townhouse in London, where Mick Cox overdubbed guitar on a couple of tracks and Morrison found an Irish Jeff Labes, Fiachra Tench, to score some strings.

Rarely had an album come together as easily. And yet *Poetic Champions Compose* was hardly a step sideways. One of his most seductive-sounding albums, it was everything that *Inarticulate Speech of the Heart* had attempted to be – yearning, beguiling, musically adventurous, even tender on occasions. 'Queen of the Slipstream' and 'I Forgot that Love Existed', the latter a superior template for 'Have I Told You Lately', were worthy additions to the canon of great Morrison love-songs; whilst 'Did Ye Get Healed?', 'The Mystery' and 'Alan Watts Blues' continued his metaphysical preoccupations, with *élan*. However, the most heartfelt performance on the album is a song that takes its refrain and title from a well-known traditional gospel song, 'Motherless Children', and turns it into Celtic Ray Part Two. When Morrison sings 'sometimes I feel like a motherless child' like this, one has little choice but to believe him.

And yet Morrison seemed curiously reluctant to champion the album in person or in concert. If, as Brian Hinton claims, 'his new contract with Polydor [in 1988] stipulated that marketing campaigns for future "product" be non-aggressive and not intrude on his privacy', the non-campaign for *Poetic Champions* provided something of a benchmark. Save for a brief tour of Ireland, he continued his relapse into silence as a travelling performer, devoting his energies to finding those alternatives he had talked about in the days when he granted the occasional interview to promote a release.

The set played at the 'Secret Heart of Music' weekend proved to be the solitary English performance of the *Poetic Champions* material performed by the band responsible. The weekend seems to have persuaded Morrison to work more with fellow searchers Derek Bell and Clive Culbertson, with whom he performed that first evening, and with whom he clearly felt comfortable, rather than with the musicians who had done him proud at the Wool Hall. At one point, according to Culbertson, 'he actually said to Derek and myself . . . "Right, guys, we're gonna get a villa in France, in the sun, and we'll bring in the gear, and we'll sit down and . . . we'll let the inspiration come in, and I'll pay you guys twenty grand a year each, I'll pay all your expenses, and all you got to do is be there for me for a year."' Though he continued to talk about this idea through the summer, by the time Culbertson had done a single tour with him, the 'offer' had lost a lot of its appeal.

Clive Culbertson: Because Van and I had been friends since '81 and I didn't actually work with him till '88, it was always very chummy – until I joined the band. Then I became an employee and the friendship thing went to the bin . . . We were doing the RDS in Dublin and he was in really bad form and he came on: 'Right, I'm bored with this set. We're gonna do such-and-such off *Into the Music*.' And I look blankly at him. If he'd even have told me the night before,

I'd have bought the album and learned the thing. He just starts and it's like, 'What *do* you fucking know? How can you be in this job and you don't know [such and such] . . . Maybe you're not the right man.' Just ate me in front of everybody. And this was early in the tour. Nothing had gone wrong [yet]. So Derek Bell, [who] was there, bounds off the stage after him and down the tunnel, into the [dressing] rooms, and says, 'Van, I don't think that was very nice, what you did to Clive. You shouldn't speak to him like that. That's the only friend you have up there.' And Van goes, 'Ah, but you see, psychology, Derek. You have to remember the rest of the band know he's my only friend up there. So if I fucking dump on him then they know what sort of a mood I'm in.' And I thought, 'Oh no.' And that was how it was [to be].

By the time this incident occurred, in September 1988, Morrison had already returned to the ritual of touring to promote product. In the months separating 'The Secret Heart of Music' from the release of his next (collaborative album) in May 1988, Morrison still continued attempting to find a route that might return him to rapture. He had indicated as much on *Poetic Champions*, which ends with the selfish plea 'Give Me My Rapture', followed by the question 'Did Ye Get Healed?', before sinking into the instrumental acquiescence of 'Allow Me'. As he said on one of two important TV appearances in these months, 'At the minute I'm pathless . . . I'm in limbo.' The search for a path, aligned to a new musical direction, led him the month after the conference to record a TV special with Derek Bell's own band, the Chieftains. It was a not entirely unexpected move. Morrison's frustration with the sheer predictability of modern popular music, which induced a variation on the usual anti-rock rant in a contemporary interview, also suggested a return to enduring forms:

Van Morrison: The problem is not rock, because if you break rock down you again have a spectrum . . . between various types of what you call rock . . . Rock was something that was introduced to break down a structure that was apathetic. I mean, the musical structure at that period . . . So this came along at a period to shake all that up – to break that up, because that wasn't going anywhere . . . [Well,] turn on the radio [now] and you get a certain station . . . Radio 1 or whatever it is – and they'll play the same music for two hours. They're all different singers with all the same rhythm tracks. Rhythm tracks are all the same: they've got the same click-machine drums; they've got the same synthesizers; they've got the same bass part. On every track . . . [ ] . . . That's

why a lot of serious musicians are either in the folk field or heading that way
. . . When I started there was rock & roll, there was skiffle, there was folk, there
was jazz, there was gospel . . . So now what you have is the whole thing turned
into rock. And rock, to me, it's not my scene. It just doesn't mean anything to
me, it's a word . . . To cut a long story short, the truth now lies in the traditional
forms of music. [1987]

As before, he took a return to his roots as his escape-route, but this
time those roots were more traditional than Lead Belly, more indigenous
than Lonnie Donegan. According to Morrison, his route back to Irish
tradition this time was a by-product of a meditation practice he had been
experimenting with at the time of *No Guru, No Method, No Teacher*: 'I
started meditating and doing sounds, and seeing what I could do with
my voice when I was meditating. That led me more into listening to
Irish folk music and Scottish folk music and the drone, the pipes and all
this sort of stuff.' Once Morrison began thinking about an Irish collection,
there were a number of directions in which he could go, and a number
of voices offering suggestions.

Arty McGlynn: What I wanted to do with Van at that time was bring him
into [Coolay], and get into soul Irish music. That's the album I wanted to make
with Van Morrison. I did [discuss it with him], but [then] he met Paddy
[Moloney] and they made an album that was successful. Well, I [put it] upon
him before the album was made that we should make a serious album of Irish
music – y'know, meet older singers and learn the songs and then rehearse.
That's the album that I saw Van making. But it went another way. At that stage
Van wanted to make an Irish-identity album. It was part of wanting to be Irish
in some way. So that's what he did.

Derek Bell's membership of the Chieftains was bound to become a
factor, and in September 1987, shortly after the 'Secret Heart' conference,
Paddy Moloney, the Chieftains' guiding force and chief self-publicist,
received one of those late-night phone calls from Morrison:

Paddy Moloney: We [had] joined him at the Edinburgh Festival for a couple
of songs in about 1980 [and] then we met again a few years later, and had a chat
over a few jars, [but] nothing came of that. Then I got this strange phone call
in about 1988 [*sic*] saying, '[*gruff mumble*], Paddy, Paddy, we gotta do an album
together!' There wasn't very much talk about it. Van's not really a great one for

discussions about music. He'll talk about everything else but music . . . [ ] . . . I think at that time Van was searching for his Irish roots . . . Musically we were going to meet each other half-way . . . It was a friendship and trust. Very important to him I think is trust. But I doubt it was the other way round.

Morrison's whole-hearted commitment to the project was not secured until late in October 1987 when, as a dry run for the sessions and an excuse for a TV show, if nothing else, Morrison joined the Chieftains at Balmoral Studios in Belfast for a BBC TV St Patrick's Day special. After the Chieftains had done their thing for the first half of the broadcast, a sweaty, self-conscious Morrison, dressed in a shamrock-green shirt, almost barrelled over two of the Chieftains getting to the drum kit, behind which he intended to stay whilst performing 'Raglan Road', and to which he returned after 'The Star of the County Down' and 'My Lagan Love', to wrap the show up with an impassioned 'Celtic Ray'. As Hinton suggests in *Celtic Crossroads*, 'his performance is mesmeric but bizarre, meatily beating at a drum kit with brushes, or strumming his guitar. He hums, fills his lungs and roars, moans like an old bluesman, and whispers: it's all too much for one violinist, who cannot prevent a grin breaking out.'

The alliance worked. All they now needed to do was decide which other songs they fancied recording. Moloney was determined to have some input and, after the obligatory toing and froing, 'I said, "Look, Van, I have a list of songs that we could do." And he said, "So have I." We met up and went for a walk around St Stephen's Green in Dublin . . . and eventually we settled on the songs we'd do. I went away and got what Van calls "the shapes" – the arrangements – together. Then I got a message on my answering machine saying, "Great shapes, Paddy."' The sessions, which were finally booked for the start of a new year, lasted barely a week. Morrison again played drums, whilst the Chieftains struggled to follow what Moloney later called 'these long cadenzas, very traditional west of Ireland keening, [with] long warbling endings'. Morrison, though, wasn't about to change his working methodology to accommodate his fellow folkies.

Kevin Conneff: There's no fiddling around . . . trying things out . . . If it went past take three he would lose interest. He'd say, 'You're wasting your time. Go on to something else.' . . . And I like that. OK, there may be a few skid marks . . . but what the hell.

If the songs broadcast by the Beeb in March 1988 were 'mesmeric', the six songs not débuted on the *As I Roved Out* TV special included a couple that verged on the kitsch form of folk music. Of the three attempts at rousing boisterousness, 'Star of the County Down' was a pleasantly lightweight opener, 'I'll Tell Me Ma' was nauseatingly chirpy whilst 'Marie's Wedding' was impossible to treat seriously (especially for those conversant with Billy Connolly's devastatingly funny skit on his first album). These songs were among those that seemed to be included as a nod to Morrison's mother, from whom his knowledge of Irish folk music largely stemmed.

Violet had always delighted in sharing this material with her kith and kin. Even Van's own daughter admitted that her 'grandmother taught me the first songs I ever learned, "Star of the County Down", "Danny Boy", "I'll Tell Me Ma". She would hold me on her knee and the whole afternoon just sing song after song.' Morrison, though, was also paying tribute to the influence of his father, whom he had to thank for his introduction to Irish tenor John McCormack, from whom Violet presumably learned 'Star of the County Down' – where else? – and from whom Morrison self-evidently acquired 'She Moved through the Fair'.

Van Morrison: My father loved John McCormack, and he had lots of John McCormack records. So it was always part of the picture. And I always liked those sort of songs anyway. So whether I did it with the Chieftains or not was neither here nor there. I always loved those songs. So that's where I came in on that. I was coming from the John McCormack angle . . . That stuff comes from that tradition of those Scottish and Irish type of singers that just sang with piano accompaniment. I always liked that music, so it was just a matter of getting the right songs. [2000]

The idea of an album of traditional songs with the plainer accompaniment preferred by McCormack probably crossed Morrison's mind. The Chieftains, though, remained a more attractive, nay, commercial option. In fact, Morrison would perform a version of 'Raglan Road' with just piano and bass on another TV special that April – along with 'Western Plains' and 'Foggy Mountain Top'! Between these songs Morrison found himself locked into a painfully stilted 'philosophical' discussion with two po-faced academics, which at least seems to have persuaded him to give a wide berth to such types in future. On these songs, recorded shortly before the release of *Irish Heartbeat*, the accompanists were Derek Bell and Clive Culbertson. And riveting as the performance on *As I Roved Out* had been, the 'Raglan Road' recorded at Coleraine University with Bell and Culbertson was far more in keeping with the spirit of the song, and its portrayal of a man ensnared by a beautiful revenant whom he had mistaken for 'a creature made of clay'.

Indeed the reaction from some to the release of *Irish Heartbeat*, in May 1988, fell little short of cries of 'Judas!' The *Belfast Telegraph* reviewer expressed the belief that, if Morrison sang his version of 'My Lagan Love' at a party in Belfast, people would leave early, whilst his interpretation of 'Raglan Road' would prompt 'trouble in the Dublin pubs'. In fact, the reviewer here highlighted two of the songs on the album that, along with a truly ghost-ridden 'She Moved through the Fair', Morrison successfully made his own. He was less at one with his material on 'My Match It Is Made' and 'Carrickfergus', both of which not so much bathed as drowned in that chirpy Chieftain sound. In fact Arty McGlynn believes he can hear evidence of Moloney's input on virtually every song.

Arty McGlynn: I think [Van] was sort of shafted on [it] – musically. 'Cause it was a very simple album . . . It's an album [of songs] that Van knew. But I don't think that he moved any further into Irish Celtic music. I think Van sang those songs that he was enticed to sing by the Chieftains.

Derek Bell, who had experienced every type of performance from Morrison, readily accepts that 'from the purist's folk point of view it's grotesque . . . I mean no purist is going to sing things like "She Moved through the Fair", repeating "our wedding day" three times. That's an element of soul music. The repetition and jazz-like style of words for the sake of emphasis . . . It has nothing to do with our tradition at all . . . and the folkies don't like it.' On the other hand, the rock critics – that reviled breed who hadn't 'got' Morrison's music in a long time – responded to *Irish Heartbeat* with unbridled enthusiasm. John Wilde, in *Melody Maker*, was especially effusive, not merely about the collaboration but about overlooked achievements from the man's recent work:

Irish Heartbeat is, predictably, a bloody considerable marvel. Not that Morrison ever lost the plot. The last three LPs represent to me arguably his most consistent sequence. Indeed I would burst a forest of veins in my neck to persuade the casual onlooker that *No Guru* penetrates as far as any Van Morrison record . . .

In this sense, *Irish Heartbeat* is a kind of sidestep. It is not without reflection. But, broadly, his collaboration with the Chieftains has awakened the roisterous spirit . . . The climb continues. Widespread. Van Morrison has found that the path to joy does not have to be such a difficult one.

When Wilde's fellow critics concurred – one calling the album 'some of the most haunting, rousing, downright friendly music of the year' – Morrison decided not to be churlish: 'It's a breakthrough, it's different – this is the consensus of every critic that's reviewed it. So I'm prepared to accept that. I don't need any more than that.' He would later claim that '*Irish Heartbeat* . . . had nothing to do with nostalgia. It was a militant act. It was to shake up the Irish recording industry.' This might be overstating the case, but influential it certainly was, and at long last the charts and the critics achieved a consensus of sorts. Of course, this didn't actually make Morrison any more willing to discuss the album with journalists.

Paddy Moloney: When [Liam Mackey from *Hot Press*] asked how this [one] song came about, Van started to get angry. 'Well, what are you after? It's obvious how the bloody thing happened. There's no point in asking.' Only Van was using slightly stronger language.

Possibly the most significant change attendant upon the success of *Irish Heartbeat* came from the man himself. As he returned to the UK Top Twenty – garnering a number of critical overviews that reminded a wary audience of the man's remarkably productive output throughout the eighties – Morrison, for better or worse, seems to have come to terms with the demands of the life he had chosen to lead, and separate from which he would be like a ship without a sail.

Arty McGlynn: I remember one time, at the end of the tour, we're travelling home and I'm sitting beside him on the plane and he says to me, 'So what are you doing when you get back home?' 'I'm off to America with this [little folk] band Patrick Street.' And he says, 'You're so fucking lucky, man. You can do that. I can't do that. If I went into that band, I'd fuck [it] up. On the second gig there'd be a queue of people at the door. I'd fuck up the band because I'm Van Morrison. I can't do what you do.' And it was absolutely true, what he said . . . Van fought for a while with trying to do small things – being the common man and play[ing] himself down – but it's too late for him. [It was about] a year after he said that to me that he realized, 'Fuck it! I have to be "Van". I can't be anybody else.' [So now] he wears his hat and he wears his black glasses. I think it's sort of sad.

AGE SEVEN
All in the Game

25

1989–91: These Are the Days

Booze, pot, too much sex, too much failure in one's private life, too
much attrition, too much recognition, too little recognition, frustration.
Nearly everything in the scheme of things works to dull a first-rate
talent. But the worst probably is cowardice – as one gets older, one
becomes aware of one's cowardice, the desire to be bold which once
was a joy gets heavy with caution and duty.

—*Norman Mailer*

B. P. Fallon: What about this ethereal thing called fame?
Van Morrison: It fucks up a lot of people and it's probably fucked me up too.
BPF: In what way?
VM: Because people relate to me as the person who's done 'Brown Eyed Girl'
    or *Astral Weeks*, and I'm not that person any more. Communication is a
    two-way street and if people are communicating with an image which is not
    [there] any more, how the hell can you communicate with them?
BPF: And did you ever think of abandoning ship and becoming a gardener or
    something?
VM: I tried.

The good press didn't stop with the release of *Irish Heartbeat*. When
Morrison agreed to a short British tour to promote the album, playing
an hour-long set with his own band, comprising *Poetic Champions* material
and the obvious favourites from recent years, before joining the Chieftains to perform the entire album live, the spate of positive critical reviews
continued into the daring night. *NME*'s Denis Campbell, in reviewing
both show and album, couldn't help but be caught up by the contagion:

Van Morrison's recent live shows with the Chieftains were a revelation, offering further proof . . . of the man's legendary unpredictability. They were joyous, passionate occasions, almost celebratory in mood; Van's best performances for many a long year . . . The album recaptures the exuberance and intensity of those now historic shows, thus preserving some of the most fervent performances of Morrison's career so far.

This British tour, which happened when the album was still Morrison's latest preoccupation, comprised just eight shows, three of them in London. By its very brevity it managed to maintain a relative truce between the egos battering at each other across the stage, the generally positive response to the album and the recently broadcast *As I Roved Out* special helping to carry everyone through. And Morrison seemed genuinely glad to be back on the boards, after eighteen months of near silence.

Paddy Moloney: When we did that tour Van came out of himself a bit . . . He only really gets that when he's on stage, and there's that music that comes out of improvising and interplay and reaching some kind of state. That's the only time he feels he can let loose. He's in a cage otherwise.

However, any suspicions from the supporting players that this might not last were well founded. Derek Bell remembers one particular undercurrent threatening this joint commercial renaissance: 'Paddy was a bit slow to sign some contract and Van was in a bit of a hurry to have it signed up. And, for a while, neither one of them would give way. Bad feeling continued to brew . . . They didn't talk for a while . . . But you couldn't be with a personality like Van and not run the risk of something like that happening.' One can only assume that the contract in question pertained to the percentages and credits accorded to the respective parties for their 'desecration' of Irish traditional song. The impasse might explain a delay in the album's release, which transpired only after the shows spread the word. Tensions finally spilled over, along with a couple of glasses of wine, after one of the London shows.

Clive Culbertson: The first night that it went really bad on the first leg of the tour, we were all sitting about and Van goes, 'Let's do something important here. Let's talk some shit. Where do you want to be with your life? What do you want to be doing in twenty years' time? Let's get deep here, man. We're living on top of each other.' So we go all the way round, and Paddy refuses to tell . . . [Van] wasn't baring his soul [himself], but he opened the cage a wee bit: 'Well, I want to look for the answer. I want to get free.' It wasn't from the soul, it was only from the head. But Paddy wouldn't give. So of course Van goes, 'Everybody else has told us. Where do you want to be spiritually?' 'I just want to be playing with the Chieftains.' 'Look, hold on here. Everybody else has bared their soul. Now I want you to bare your soul like we have.' So [finally] Van says, 'Fuck you!' and he flings the glass of wine at him. So Paddy gets up, flings a glass of wine [back].

Moloney later played down the exchange as 'a group of people sitting around in a hotel after a show, a certain type of conversation starts up, there's a bit of drink involved and before you know where you are there's glasses of wine being thrown'. And yet he admitted that he 'honestly thought that would have been the last of [us] working with Van – but I got a call about three or four months later, asking if we'd do a couple of shows with him'. Actually it was a six-week tour, and this time things really would go pear-shaped. The May incident, though, was quickly forgotten by Morrison, a man who seems capable of holding grudges that span the centuries whilst dismissing such altercations from his mind with nary a flicker of recognition.

Morrison's resentment towards Moloney does not seem to have been entirely subsumed. Shortly after the end of the (second) *Irish Heartbeat* tour he was to turn on Derek Bell when the latter refused to leave the Chieftains to join his band. According to Bell, Morrison accused him of being 'too much under Moloney's apron-strings. He told me that it was no good reading all these books about these masters and then not living the life. And of course for the sake of peace I had to agree with him . . . [He] said I just hadn't got the guts to break out, stand up on my own and do something . . . Then he says, "Look, where do you think I am? I've got to the top of the tree here. Where do you think you are? You're down here."' Unable to get his way, Morrison finally just stormed out, banging the door behind him, leaving Bell to walk the two miles back to his own house in Bangor.

Morrison was on the phone the next day 'as if nothing had happened', though one could hardly have blamed Bell if he had told him where he could go and what he could do with his opinions once he got there. When Morrison attempted the same rap with Clive Culbertson, after their friendship had already cooled, informing his erstwhile employee,

'You were at the top of your tree. It doesn't get any bigger than this, and look where you are now, you're fucking playing bars again. If you'd have done this for me . . .', Culbertson was obliged to spell it out: 'Van, you no longer pay my wages. I don't have to listen to this any more.' It was the last time they spoke. Having been bombarded with questions throughout the eighties, Culbertson had been forced to accept that, no matter how many questions he addressed, the man himself would never embrace change.

Clive Culbertson: The mystical thing has to be done once a day, ten minutes. But it has to be done, and no amount of reading will ever do . . . I really tried . . . I'd say, 'Van, there's a fifteen-minute meditation. Do that.' 'Where'd that come from?' It's a Rosicrucian thing.' 'Ah, I'm not fucking doing it. I don't want to get attached, man.' . . . I think he plays around it. I don't think he's in it, I don't think he does it, I don't think he's ever done it. That doesn't mean he doesn't *know* stuff . . . [But then] he talked to Paul Jones and Paul said, 'Van, here's the deal. God sent a son, he died for you, you can be saved, you can go to heaven, I will not discuss it further.' And Van said, 'But I want to discuss . . .' 'But Van, either he died for you or he didn't. If he didn't, we've nothing to talk about. If he did, then you're already free.' That's the Christian shape. And that drove him mad . . . [In the end] he still walked away as [unhealed] as when he came in.

Morrison's use of overtly Christian imagery, first evident on *Into the Music,* had become a perennial backdrop to his albums until on *No Guru, No Method, No Teacher* the Christ became that album's central motif, appearing in representational form in both its central songs, 'In the Garden' and 'One Irish Rover'. On *Poetic Champions,* 'I Forgot that Love Existed' even suggested that Morrison had accepted Christ into his heart – 'then I saw the light!' Amen. Save that the questions persisted. Indeed curiosity continued to curb his faith.

Paul Jones: He was invited by Cliff Richard to go to one of [his] supper parties. Now Cliff used to have these supper parties where basically he invites people in any branch of show business to go to this sort of club, the Art Centre Group, which is a meeting-place for Christians in entertainment. They just used to throw it open on these Sunday nights every couple of months. There would be food, and then there would be a discussion. I met Van at one of those evenings. I had already become a Christian. This would be some time in the late eighties

. . . Van was very interesting because he'd obviously thought deeply about all of it. So he could come back with another question, or come at it from another angle. He'd respond to anything that somebody said, [and] he'd thought [about it]. He knew what he was talking about. And at the end of the evening, somebody said, 'Could you give Van a lift home?' and Van was asking me questions about how I could be a Christian and sing the devil's music.

Jones recognized a man yearning to be surprised by joy, and they maintained sporadic contact in the months after the Art Centre Group meeting, culminating in a surprise appearance at a Blues Band concert at the Mean Fiddler in December 1986, at which Morrison performed 'Help Me' in his overcoat. However, in the end, Jones had to lay it on the line – in much the way Culbertson describes – leaving Morrison to move on, secure in his insecurities. Jones's take on the man has much in common with that of Morrison's friend from the mystic church:

Paul Jones: There's a line in an old blues that says, 'I'm like a Mississippi bullfrog sitting on a hollow stump/I got so many women I don't know which way to jump'. I've come to think that Van is like that with faith. Just when you think he's gonna commit himself to something, he buys a book about something else. He's voracious about acquiring knowledge and spiritual insight, but he doesn't seem able to make a commitment.

This inability to commit was troubling even Morrison. He addressed it – and Christ – in a song destined to become among his most misinterpreted, 'Have I Told You Lately'. For the first time since 'In the Garden' he makes Christ an inextricable part of a relationship. Emulating the Dylan of 'Precious Angel' and 'Covenant Woman', Morrison writes of 'a love that's divine' precisely because it includes The One. Whether it was Christ or 'she' who was able to 'fill my heart with gladness/take away my sadness/ease my troubles' he deliberately left unresolved, but the song clearly suggested that he needed someone. If the song was as much a testimony to Ulla's love as to Christ's, she would no more survive the vagaries of Morrison's yearning spirit than the Lord Himself. By the time the song was released, he was contacting another angel, after Munch heard the disturbing echo of a singer falling off a carefully-maintained wagon.

In the summer of 1988, though, everything seemed to be returning to that fabled higher ground. *Irish Heartbeat* was selling consistently,

Morrison's music was back in the news and his muse was back in Holland
Park. During this hard-won, fleeting moment of contentment and contemplation, Morrison wrote a set of songs that captured all the melodious
charm of *Poetic Champions Compose*, and added a soupçon of commerciality. Though the imagery was becoming a little well-worn, and the
catch-phrases from half a lifetime's reading occasionally tiresome, this
mattered little to those who only began paying attention again with *Irish
Heartbeat*.

Avalon Sunset, as Morrison was to christen the collection, released in
June 1989, would be shot through with contemplations about Christ.
Some, like 'When Will I Ever Learn to Live in God?', addressed the right
sort of questions but knew none of the answers. The more successful ones,
like 'Daring Night' and 'These Are the Days', merely basked in the
moment. Perhaps surprisingly, the overtly Christian element in no way
dissuaded potential punters. Perhaps the sound of the words was enough.

Certainly in 'Orangefield', another instalment in Morrison's perennial
paean to a 'lost love in Belfast', the words say very little but the mood is
persuasive. Back in touch with the spirit of yesteryear, he walks through
the old park remembering 'a gold autumn day/[when] you came my
way in Orangefield'. Evocative as a song like this aspires to be, Morrison
preferred to present it as just another song, even to those who knew him.
As Arty McGlynn observes, 'He doesn't explain things . . . to you. He
doesn't say, "Well, this song is about where I went to school." He won't
talk in those terms.'

If *Poetic Champions* seemed to have almost composed itself, *Avalon
Sunset* came together equally easily, though this time Morrison brought
the songs to the sessions. Indeed, so anxious was he to begin work on
them that when speaking to Clive Culbertson about some planned
rehearsals, he insisted that Culbertson come over immediately to help
him form some 'shapes'.

Clive Culbertson: He rang me up: 'So when you coming over?' 'I'm gonna
come over Monday morning.' 'No, no, no, no, ring the office, come over
Sunday. I've got a few ideas, man. You could come round here and run through
a few things with me.' 'What time d'you want me?' 'You need to be at my
door at three o'clock. Don't be a minute later.' So I cancelled a booking, arrived
in London . . . and arrive at his door three o'clock on the dot. So I'm knocking
for about ten minutes and I can hear there's people [inside], and I'm still
knocking away. Eventually the door opens – 'Yeah.' 'Van, you wanted me to

come over on Sunday.' 'Nah, doesn't suit. See you tomorrow. Bye.' Slammed the door in my face.

So much for inspiration! When rehearsals did begin, the following day, everything fell into place – despite the minimal preparation – and before they had even completed three days' rehearsing, Culbertson remembers Morrison saying, 'This is all really happening . . . We gotta record this. It's fresh. It's happening.' Using the most basic of bands – drummer Roy Jones, Culbertson on bass, Neil Drinkwater on keyboards and guitarist Arty McGlynn – Morrison found these songs prepared to stay long enough to have their spirit caught. McGlynn, though, was as taken aback as Culbertson by the pace of the passage from these 'rehearsals' to finished product.

Arty McGlynn: He had all these new songs, but he didn't say they were new songs. He just started singing [them]. We started rehearsing this stuff. We knock [around] a few ideas chord-wise and all these songs are shaping up. Good songs. 'Joey Boy', 'Orangefield' [etc.]. So I'm thinking, 'Is this a rehearsal or what?' We're there for two days, and we have like twelve tracks down. [Finally,] at the end of the second day, he says, 'These songs are good. Let's find a studio. We should knock these down.'

The sessions transferred to Eden Studios where, according to McGlynn, the album came together in just two days – 'we [still] don't know if it's an album, or maybe a demo [for an] album'. An abiding reliance on serendipity meant that some of the finished takes were a tad unpolished, but only Morrison would have left in that lovely moment in 'Daring Night' where he calls out the change of tempo – '1/4, 1/4' – to Roy Jones at the song's end. On the other hand, the man's musical curve-balls could still louse up a good take. 'Have I Told You Lately' seems to have been one song they had not previously rehearsed, making it problematic enough without Morrison's little idiosyncrasies.

Clive Culbertson: I'd never worked in that manner, where it was a case of walk[ing] in[to] the studio, and Van's in the corner with the acoustic and everybody's in headphones, and he's going [*sings unintelligibly, except for the odd word*]. And this is all you're getting. 'OK, let's go.' 'What!' 'You got that, didn't you?' By the time we got to the second or third song, I got the vibe. As soon as he starts [wailing], you get the pen and paper. And I'm really quick at charting stuff. So I got a couple of them – first take! And he's going, 'Yeah, it's great, man.' So then we got to 'Have I Told You Lately'. And nobody had warned me that if you make a mistake, you let it go. Just let it go, don't stop, fumble 'round it. So [*Van starts mumbling*], 'No one else above you . . .' Right, I've got it. 'OK, right, let it roll,' and we get to the middle bit and he changes it. And I've got my bit, 'cause he's done it twice already, and the whole band moves [sideways] in the studio, and he stops. 'Who was that? Who was that?' and Arty always made sure someone else was to blame: 'It was Clive.' 'Ah man, what're you doing? Look, here's what it is, [sings] "Love that is divine/Love that is mine . . ."' 'Sorry Van, I'll get it this time.' And of course he changed it again. The whole band goes [wobbly], but I'd already put the marker up. 'Look, I thought you'd got that. What're you fucking playing at?' I said, 'Van, I wrote it down. You just changed it.' And the third time he sang it to me, and I wrote it [out], we got it. But what I didn't realize was rule number one – to make a mistake really quietly, stop until you get the vibe and start [again]. Whereas when I fell apart, soon as the bass went, Roy [Jones] stopped. And [so], of course, it was my fault.

On 'Orangefield', one of the more delightful additions to the canon (if a little over-orchestrated on the album), Morrison and Culbertson sat together working out this one part, Morrison saying, 'You gotta follow Roy down. Whatever Roy plays, you play.' Culbertson again did what he was told, and the song was cut with a minimum of fuss, one of the last songs to come from Eden.

Clive Culbertson: I come in the [following] morning to the studio: 'Is everything OK?' 'Oh yeah. It's great.' OK, call the taxi, pack my gear, and I'm half-way to the airport and, 'Taxi number 47. You've got a Mr Culbertson going to Heathrow. Could you tell him that we need him back here in the studio immediately.' I get hauled into the studio. I say, 'What's the [problem]?' 'Look, you followed the drummer in "Orangefield".' 'Van, you told me to follow the drummer.' 'Nah, but you followed him *all the time.*'

With *Irish Heartbeat* still in the charts, Morrison was again jumping the gun product-wise, producing the successor to *Poetic Champions* almost a year before it could be released. Although post-production duties – the ubiquitous Katie Kissoon backing vocals and a set of slightly slushy strings again arranged by Fiachra Tench – took their time, *Avalon Sunset* was ready to roll when Polydor were not.

Instead Morrison was expected to continue promoting his last Mercury album. So it was he found himself back on the road with the Chieftains at summer's end. Proceedings began in Dublin on 9 September, took in a televised gig in Belfast, and were scheduled to conclude with two shows at the Royal Albert Hall at the end of October. Possibly the experience of playing in Ireland itself served as a nervous reminder of the north/south divide that separated Morrison's own band – who continued to play their own set – from Moloney's. Arty McGlynn thinks 'it was a mismatch . . . We're all from Northern Ireland, and Van is very Northern . . . [so] there was a culture of tension on [that] tour . . . It was the first time this had ever happened, these two extreme elements . . . There were huge frictions, no doubt about that.'

Kevin Conneff of the Chieftains alludes to certain unspecified 'instances on tour with Van. There were times where he would get into a mood, usually alcohol was involved, and I didn't want to be near him. He could be quite unpleasant . . . you could get this vibe around him that things were not quite right for him, so everybody around him had to suffer.' It seems Morrison had returned to his most reliable 'closer-offer' – with predictable results.

Part of what may have been eating at him was an imminent end to his relationship with Ulla Munch, prompted in part by his choice of beverage. This apparently led to the cancellation of scheduled Danish shows. However, this idea that 'everybody around him had to suffer' was a conceit not every musician was prepared to embrace. The Chieftains, as a band in their own right, felt no obligation to toe the line – unlike the unfortunates in Morrison's own band over whom the threat of dismissal hung like a storm that never broke. And still Morrison continued to test the limits of loyalty and friendship, finding boundaries in the only way he knew how – by crossing them. At least Derek Bell and Clive Culbertson had their mystical studies to keep them sane.

Clive Culbertson: We're in Germany and we've got a day off [so] we phoned [the Rosicrucian master we'd met in London]: 'Is there anything happening Rosicrucian-wise?' His minder says, 'If you've got a day off come down to the temple, and we'll give you a day of meditation.' So we said to Mick, the tour manager, 'Don't say we're going anywhere. [Van]'ll not see anybody till Stockholm.' And we went down, and they gave us all these musical meditations, to help you connect more with the soul of music. Next day, we flew back to Stockholm. Two days after that, we're in Finland [and Van] phoned my room:

'What colour's your wallpaper? What channel's MTV on?', all this sorta stuff. Twenty minutes of absolute rubbish . . . and then he [starts shouting], 'WHERE WERE YOU YESTERDAY?' I goes, 'Well, we went down to see the teacher guy that we met in London.' 'I don't remember you fucking asking me?' I said, 'You told the guy he was an asshole. You told him you didn't want to know anything about him.' 'You're on my fucking tour. I'm paying your fucking wages. I have every right to be there.' I said, 'Van, can I point out it was our day off? You don't pay us on our day off.' 'Right! OK [then].' And he slams the phone down. So the next day is the gig in Finland and John Rogers phones me in the room: 'Clive, I've got a problem here. These meditations you got from this master in Germany – Van wants them.' I says, 'John, I have a phone number here for him. All he has to do is lift a phone and say, "I wouldn't mind those." He doesn't sign anything, he doesn't commit to anything, he doesn't pay anything, but this is the way the Rose Croix thing works – [if] you want it, you have to ask for it. It has to be you.' He says, 'Van's not going to go for that.' . . . [So] Van wouldn't talk to me once he knew I'd gone to see the German Rosicrucian guy – wouldn't even be in the same room as me.

With everything going from bad to worst-case scenario, Morrison decided he had had enough of the Chieftains at the exact same time they reached their own limit when it came to hearing his 'forthright' opinions, colourfully phrased. The show that night in Helsinki would almost certainly have been the last Van Morrison and the Chieftains performance if a ten-day respite hadn't cooled temperatures, before two prestigious shows at the Albert Hall closed the book on *Irish Heartbeat*.

Clive Culbertson: So we go on stage that night and . . . it's the worst I'd ever seen him. And he'd been bad for three or four days. He was drinking a bit more. Early part of the tour he wasn't drinking at all . . . He was in awful form. Van kept talking to [the Chieftains]: 'You guys wouldn't be anything if it wasn't for me' – he told them this at a few gigs . . . The walk-on point is beside me and my amp. So he comes on [and] stands beside me – Paddy's just sitting in front of me – and [he says,] 'Tell you what you do. Lean over to Paddy Moloney and tell him he's not allowed to talk between songs.' I says, 'Van, I can't do that. I'm the bass player in the band.' 'You don't do it, you're fired. Now. Right now. On the spot.' And I realize it's just going downhill. So I lean over to Paddy. I says, 'Paddy, forgive me, I know I should tell him to [go] fuck himself, but he says would you do a wee bit less talking between the tracks, and let's get this over as quickly as possible. He wants to go home.' Paddy talks on.

Paddy just chats away. [We] do the song. And Paddy's [now] talking longer and longer – [ever] since he was told not to. So [Van] leans over to me and goes, 'Right, you fucking tell him now. If he doesn't stop talking between songs I'm going home. Now.' This is all on stage . . . So [Van] goes out to the front, and Paddy comes up with a whistle to sing ['I'll Tell Me Ma'], and every time Paddy goes near a microphone, Van stands in front of it. So he walks to the other side of the stage, and Van goes over there to stop him getting to that microphone. He does this for the whole song. So he gets to the end of the song and he just turns around: 'You fucking Chieftains. I'm fed up carrying you fuckers,' etc. The audience start throwing cans, bottles, once they see him shouting at the Chieftains. So he storms off, 'Fuck this. It's over.' But Sean Keane got there first. Sean squares up to him and goes, 'What did you say about us out there?' 'I said I'm fed up carrying you guys. If it wasn't for me . . .' It was gonna get serious – Sean would've broken his legs – [but] Mick the tour manager comes off, just walks in, grabs the two of them by the scruff of the neck: 'You're getting paid to play here. Get out and fucking play!' Van goes, 'You can't fucking talk to me like that!' He says, 'Do it or I'll fucking plant you.' 'WHAAAT!!' And [Mick] sent the boys on to do the encore.

Amazingly enough, the Chieftains and Morrison would work together again, though only in short, productive bursts, separated by years. Derek Bell was never as close again, especially after Morrison 'teamed up with Cliff Richard [and] went back to Hallelujah Christianity again . . . that doesn't hold very much appeal to me'. Bell had also seen the man's other side, noticeably in his appalling treatment of their friend Clive Culbertson. Needless to say, Morrison returned from the Chieftains tour to deliver an ultimatum to Culbertson, via John Rogers: either hand over the Rosicrucian meditations or be fired. Realizing just how skin-deep the mystical teachings had penetrated, Culbertson conveyed his feelings to Morrison via his answering machine: 'What sort of mystical person are you? You should know that tradition is only given from teacher to pupil, and if you don't know this then obviously you're not a true mystical person. You're a fucking asshole!'

With time off for bad behaviour, Morrison had another opportunity to start thinking things through. On the cusp of a new-found commerciality, he needed to decide whether he wanted to push himself through this kind of tour – to not only produce but also promote. He evidently decided he did as he changed the arrangement he had with PolyGram and secured his first marketing manager, with a view to pushing the already completed album as some kind of Grand Return, even though it came hard on the heels of three strong(er) albums.

Chris O'Donnell: I came in when *Avalon Sunset* was finished, 'cause he realized it was an exceptional album. He felt very good about it and, as he didn't have a manager, he wanted it to be represented properly within Polydor Records. He'd just changed from Phonogram to Polydor. He [had previously been] signed to Phonogram International, which was based in Holland . . . [so] he was treated as an international artist. Technically, he had to go through Holland to get an answer about a question he may have had from someone in the UK and he felt a hands-on relationship with a UK company would suit his purposes far better, and [they] would give him more attention. I was brought in to deal with the record company [which] . . . was [now] English-based. David Munns gave him a budget for advertising and promotion [the like of which] he hadn't seen before.

However, Morrison still continued to be suspicious of the industry at large. As he told one writer at around this time, '[My] role as producer put me in that situation where I was actually producing records and delivering the masters . . . That's put me more in the position where I'm doing what I want to do. But then when it comes to the point of selling what I've done, it puts me in [this] other position where I have to deal with a lot more people, what they think and what they believe . . . basically the music business.' Unwilling to deal with too many people, and uncooperative at the best of times, he had lost numerous supporters along the way. Chris O'Donnell's role was to act as one more buffer. Of course, this was only going to work if Morrison was willing to be advised. For once, it seems, he was.

Chris O'Donnell: One of the juxtapositions [*sic*] is that, if you've been in the business as long as he has, how many ways can you promote a record? What can you actually physically do that he hasn't already done? He used to recite this, chapter and verse. People'd say, 'He doesn't do interviews.' He had reams and reams of interviews that he'd done in [the] files. [As] he said, 'How many TVs do you want me to do? I've done every TV [show] since dot. I've done every radio programme; I've brought out live records. I've toured constantly. What more do they want me to do? It'd be interesting if they asked me a different question, or they had a different take on the subject matter, but the reality is I get asked the same questions and it's boring.' So he declined to do that. But he was very proactive in terms of making sure that his records sold. On *Avalon Sunset* we decided, 'OK, what do you do? You play live, and we want to promote this record.' Therefore we did a gig at Ronnie [Scott]'s, and everyone [in the media] got a piece of him as it were. I remember driving in to the office the next day and listening to people on the radio raving about the show . . . He did [promo videos]. He wasn't comfortable doing them because of the constant hanging around, but he did them. We were asked to go to America, and I showed him that we could do three nights in New York and do a deal with HBO where they had rights to broadcast a concert which would be seen across the entire length and breadth of America, and it would entail us only ever being away from home for four or five days maximum, [at] which he thought, 'That's cool. That's a new way of exploiting [my] music.' So he did [start to] embrace that idea of get[ting] to his audience in different ways.

The HBO special, filmed at the end of November 1989, represented Morrison's new band at its optimum point – neither burnt out from exhaustion, nor drowning in the deep end. As a commercial video release it also introduced to a whole new audience the man's latter-day repertoire, as well as the band with whom he would persevere for a further two years of relentless touring. The band that would take *Avalon Sunset* to the people, reinventing itself a number of times, was fronted by a friend from the olden days, Georgie Fame. It incorporated elements of Fame's own band, the Blue Flames, along with Neil Drinkwater, Richie Buckley and Irish drummer Dave Early, who was offered no more clues as to what to expect than his predecessor, Roy Jones. *Hot Press* journalist Jack Lynch later related the story of Early's baptism, which, more than test his mettle, tested his sense of humour:

The call came at short notice, rehearsals were rushed and he had little time to become *au fait* with The Man's way of directing the band with hand signals. Come the first gig, everything went well until Van started them on 'Summertime in England', a long-time highlight of the show and one where, if moved, he takes it WAY DOWN and plays with the dynamics of silence. Dave on his drum-riser is looking down on Van's back. The latter with a chopping move-ment signals the horns to drop out. Dave, with his eyes peeled, adjusts his stickwork. Another cryptic hand movement and now we're down to bass, Van's warbling and Dave, who has switched to brushes. The audience are rapt. There's the odd yelp and audible sigh. Another sign from Van: palm down as if gently bouncing a balloon. The bass has slowed to an intermittent pulse, Dave is now whispering with the brushes. Van has hitched his Zen caravan to THE MOMENT. Dave is bug-eyed, sweating. Van reaches his right hand behind his back to signal to him. The hand is upturned, claw-like and clenching open and closed. 'What the!' thinks Dave, 'if I take it down any more it won't be there at all.' SUDDENLY another handchop and the brass are back in and the band are in full flight down the final straight. Chatting with Van after the gig, Early mentions that he couldn't quite understand the 'clenched claw' signal. 'Oh that,' says Van, repeating the gesture, 'That means I have you by the balls!'

'Summertime in England' had long been Morrison's most elastic song, but by the end of the Fame–Morrison alliance fifteen-minute performances had become the norm. Other would-be classics were required to become just as adaptable to Morrison's many musical moods, as the sets expanded to incorporate a number of songs left in the shade in recent years. In fact, despite Morrison telling one reporter the previous year that 'a lot of stuff before *Into the Music* I can't relate to at all', the old songs began to reassert themselves. Indeed 'Moondance' – the song specifically cited in that interview as an example of something he had done 'so many times I don't want to sing it. It doesn't hold anything for me any more. Why should I sing it if I've drained it dry?' – was now played just about every night, perhaps because O'Donnell convinced his employer of its continuing potency.

Chris O'Donnell: I [had] pointed out to him that 'Moondance' at that particular time was a huge record in clubs. People were playing that as a sort of chill-out song. I went to see him at the Royal Albert Hall and found it incredibly boring because the reverence of being at the Albert Hall just wasn't doing it for me, and I suggested that we do Wembley, and he said, 'Well, no, the sound – it's a big barn.' And I said, 'No, no, it's all changed. The technology that we have nowadays is completely different. The kind of kids that want to come and see you [there] will dance.' He was sceptical about that, [but] we did play Wembley and sold it out, and he was just thrilled. Kids got up in the front rows and they danced to his music. Whereas up to then you had this demographic of people sitting there analysing every number.

This altered emphasis became a fundamental issue when PolyGram finally got Morrison to agree to release his first *Best of . . .* , in March 1990. The success of *Avalon Sunset* was creating its own constituency, having sat in the charts for three months after its release, and then reappeared at Christmas, when the belated single release of Morrison's duet with Cliff Richard, 'Whenever God Shines His Light', went Top Twenty. Now was the time to reinforce the man's importance with a broad sweep of single hits and perennial favourites. For once, he elected to do the commercial thing.

Chris O'Donnell: I remember having a conversation with him about [a *Best of* . . .]. At that point various people had tried to get that album – Phonogram in their turn, Warner Bros in their turn had tried to get that released, and he'd always turned them down. But with the success of [*Avalon Sunset*] there was a new mood about Van . . . The audience changed, because they were [being] introduced to his music through that album. I had a much younger set of people calling me up asking for tickets.

The result of a judiciously chosen twenty tracks for a cross-licensed *Best of* . . . that covered most bases from 'Baby Please Don't Go' to 'Have I Told You Lately' was one of the best-selling albums of the nineties, as Morrison crossed over into Chris De Burgh/Billy Joel territory, racking up over 600,000 sales in the UK, over six million sales worldwide, and spending a year and a half in the UK charts.

Just as it transformed his audience base, *The Best of Van Morrison* seemed to transform, at least temporarily, Morrison's own view of his canon. Back came songs he had all but forgotten. In one extraordinary show, at a festival in Stockholm in July 1990, the opening nine songs were 'Gloria', 'Brown Eyed Girl', 'Baby Please Don't Go', 'Domino', 'Here Comes the Night', 'Jackie Wilson Said', 'Warm Love', 'And It Stoned Me' and 'Sweet Thing'. Nor was this some cursory medley. Every one of the nine had its cup filled to the brim until, with 'Sweet Thing', he passed into that rare state where the emotion of the song overwhelmed every barrier his psyche might construct. The alliance with Fame, which O'Donnell had brokered, freed Morrison from the view that his past need be a burden, enabling a celebratory tone to carry over into the performances.

Chris O'Donnell: I used to watch him come off stage some nights with such elation. It really was a joy to watch somebody who, let's be frank, I don't think [had found] gigging necessarily great for [some] years and then he got in with a bunch of musicians, and it became good again. He started doing more gigs, because he enjoyed doing more gigs . . . I remember one gig in Holland where

Georgie followed him all the way through this kind of musical roundabout. He threw something in and Georgie knew exactly where he was gonna go next . . . He was doing 'Summertime in England' and he went into 'Jerusalem', and Georgie almost played the chord before Van sang it.

Even Morrison was prepared to own up to a change, telling one journalist, 'Since [my] hooking up with Georgie Fame there's been a whole new thing happening in performing.' He told another journalist that though he had 'played with other bands in other situations where I didn't want to work, because it was so mechanical and boring' – mentioning no names – 'now it's working . . . we are working all the time'. Indeed they were. In 1990 alone, they played over seventy shows, Morrison running Dylan and his Never Ending Tour a close second for the hardest-working man in rock.

Dylan's example, experienced first-hand in June 1989, when Morrison joined him on stage in Athens to perform 'Crazy Love' and 'And It Stoned Me' for a BBC TV documentary (which would take a further two years to complete★), may even have helped to convince Morrison that it was his duty to use his gifts, not squander them. As Dylan's Never Ending Tour and Morrison's never ending weekend tour criss-crossed the globe (and each other) over the ensuing decade, the pair would take turns to join each other on the odd ramshackle duet until 1998, when they would twice tour as co-headliners.

Morrison was even happy with PolyGram, admitting that 'things with the record company are going well for once . . . For the first time ever in my career, I actually have people working [my] records.' On a rare commercial high, Morrison took this band into the studio in the spring of 1990, to record a successor to *Avalon Sunset* while the *Best of . . .* was still riding high in the charts. Sticking essentially to the same musicians who had proved themselves in almost a year of continual gigging, he cut *Enlightenment* in two sets of sessions, at the Townhouse in London and, primarily, at the Wool Hall in Beckington, which he had recently acquired, establishing his first personal studio since Caledonia.

★ This *Arena* documentary, originally planned as a conventional documentary on Morrison, was finally broadcast in March 1991, but by then it comprised a series of live performances with very little commentary. Footage of Morrison and Dylan playing together on a hill overlooking the Acropolis would be included in the finished programme.

The resultant album, *Enlightenment*, gave him his highest UK chart position ever, reflecting a new vogue, but it is a thin piece of work and a worrying indication that the man had simply run out of new themes to address. The best song, and first single, 'Real Real Gone', was a re-recording of *Common One*'s lost pop ditty. Other songs, like 'Avalon of the Heart' and 'Youth of 1,000 Summers', seemed to take opening lines of earlier Morrison songs and spin out inferior tangents thereon. If 'Avalon of the Heart' was a particularly cliché-ridden excuse for a song, the likes of 'She's a Baby', 'Start All Over Again' and 'Memories' were not merely second-division but strictly second-hand.

Disconcertingly, the title track appeared to suggest that the man's failure to find 'enlightenment' – 'don't know what it is . . . it keeps changing to something different' – had returned him to the path of least resistance. But in 'So Quiet in Here' he suggested, 'a glass of wine with some friends/talking into the wee hours of the dawn . . . this must be, this must be, what it's all about' – a presumably conscious allusion to Dylan's 'Sign on the Window'. His solution, like Dylan's more bucolic one, was transitory at best, as 'See Me Through' found Morrison pleading to his Higher Power to 'see me through the days of wine and roses/see me through one day at a time'.

It seemed it was time to return to the AA programme from which he had borrowed the 'one day at a time' philosophy, perhaps fearing the fate of Jack Lemmon's alcoholic character in *Days of Wine and Roses*. In this sense the influence of his sidekick Fame was not entirely beneficent, as they became tight on stage and off. But then Fame doubtless realized that a loose Morrison was like-as-not an inspired Morrison. Thirty years earlier, Tom Kielbania remembers the young Morrison being in equal need of libation prior to performing:

Tom Kielbania: He had to have a glass of wine when I was with him, 'cause he had to loosen up. He was so friggin' uptight. He didn't want to sing. We always had to go chasin' for him. Most of the times we played [and] it was time to go on, [it was] 'Where's Van?' He'd be someplace, and we'd have to track him down. Almost like 'Well, gee, maybe if they don't find me I won't have to sing.' He was all right once he got on stage . . . [but] he used to like to turn his back all the time. He'd face us and smile, take a drink, then turn back round.

A decade after 'See Me Through', Linda Gail Lewis witnessed a similar relationship between his performing and his drinking: 'He drinks a lot before he goes on, unless he's on one of his [stints] where he's not drinking. I think he just feels better about everything when he's drinking . . . [But] when he's sober he's in a horrible mood and the shows are different – he's listening for every little thing.' If the eighties had proved a sustained exception – hence, presumably, Morrison's own characterization of the shows as 'mechanical and boring' – by 1990 he perceived 'every night [as] different. I'm not going to be the same as I was the last night. Whatever the reservoir is, of touching on those things, however that is, that night, that's what you pull out.' Or put another way, 'Sometimes it's an experience, and sometimes it's just a gig.'

Thanks to Fame, the balance was better and the standard more consistent. Fame kept the band on its toes on Morrison's behalf. Alan Skidmore, who would play sax with a later incarnation, describes how '[Georgie] used to rehearse the band . . . Holding the whole show together, that's what he did. He had a microphone, not the house microphone, that was just for the horns – so he could just speak to us without anyone else knowing. That's how it had to be because you never quite knew how Van was going to be.'

And when Fame wasn't there, Morrison missed him. In March 1990 Van agreed to film a one-off set for Channel Four, sharing the programme with a long-time idol, jazz pianist Mose Allison. Feeling the need for a more jazz-oriented sound, and willing to play dangerously, he recruited jazz drummer Mark Taylor, bassist Alec Dankworth and tenor saxophonist Alan Skidmore (a recommendation of Fame's).

Alan Skidmore: So there was the three of us so-called jazz guys, and to this day I've never really figured out why we were there . . . It was kind of weird. There was no music. Van expected us to know all his music – like, 'We'll play this, we'll play that.' I said, 'We'll play what?' It was like he expected his musicians to be *fans* . . . He would count something in. None of us knew what it was, how it went or what key it was in. I'm afraid I probably upset him by telling him he was very unprofessional. [Apparently] you don't do that . . . Eventually they called for a guy called Bernie Holland, because he had already done a few things with Van . . . [But] it was rather nervy. We're in the hotel, trying to work out what it was going to be . . . We did scrape together a concert but, to say the least, it was scrappy.

If Morrison was already thinking about pursuing a jazzier direction, he reserved the experiment for another time (at which point both

Skidmore and Dankworth would be recalled). The filming of the TV special in Bristol, though, was symptomatic of a shift in Morrison's base of operations and personal psyche. The previous year he had sold his house in Holland Park and moved to his own country retreat, in Little Somerford, Wiltshire. Meanwhile the purchase of the Wool Hall gave him a recording studio at which he could continue to cut his annual instalments for Polydor, along with any other little project that sprang to mind. The move made his fruitful association with O'Donnell less logical, and they now parted by mutual consent.

Chris O'Donnell: He wanted to buy a studio in Bath, and he wanted to be closer to that, 'cause it's a pain being inspired and then ringing up somewhere like the Townhouse and [them] say[ing], 'I'm sorry, it's booked out for the next month.' Then he started to make albums in [Peter Gabriel's] Real World, and he enjoyed that part of the world. And it also gave him an office . . . There were different people around him . . . and he was in Bath, and I was in London . . . whereas previous to that we had a very hands-on relationship.

The change of environment coincided with a monumental shock. Morrison's father George died suddenly of a heart attack, aged sixty-eight. Perhaps surprisingly, the traumatic event prompted no obvious tribute-in-song, at least not until 2000's 'Choppin' Wood', though a whole battery of lyrics about the Belfast of his youth now came from Morrison's pen. Meanwhile he continued touring, and imbibing. Indeed, the painful memories may have prompted a more determined attempt to close off and shut down.

The first concerts of 1991, three shows in the Netherlands at the end of March, certainly featured a looser-than-loose Morrison delivering some quite remarkable performances. The most hilarious was a unique performance of a new Morrison song, 'Carrying a Torch', which he had previously donated to Tom Jones, hence presumably why Fame took to singing 'It's Not Unusual' as background vocals until Morrison broke up and the song broke down. Nor was a version of 'Send in the Clowns' introduced as 'a number I learned from Shirley Bassey', with Fame applying some falsetto echo of George Ivan Bassey, too far behind in the hilarity stakes.

Somewhat more worthy was the five-song R&B medley with which Morrison opened the final show, an eighteen-and-a-half-minute 'Summertime in England' and an awe-inspiring 'In the Garden', the reception to which was appropriately reverent. However, the time had come for Fame to pursue his own blue flame and for Morrison to find a more abstemious way to tap into his performing craft. The lost weekend caravan was about to refuel, just in time for the introduction of another twenty hymns to the silence to another hapless set of musicians.

26

1991–96: Fire in His Belly

It's very hard to live up to the constant pressure of having to come up with work that you feel honest about, and is not just more titillation.

—*Van Morrison, 1984*

I think I'm better at what I'm doing. But I don't know if *it's* better.

—*Van Morrison, 1987*

On the face of it, the early to mid nineties marked a new high point in Morrison's thirty-year career as a professional musician: three Top Five albums, two of them doubles; full houses for shows that continued to test his audiences' willingness to embrace his performing aesthetic; and a very public romance with 'the sexiest woman in Ireland', sayeth the *Irish Independent*. The crack seemed good.

In fact, taking the fifty or so songs Morrison released in these years, one would be hard-pressed to distil them down to a single album worthy of *Poetic Champions Compose*, let alone *Veedon Fleece*. When these new songs eventually 'shanghaied' the shows, the results were a pale-ale shadow of the Fame years. Meanwhile, conducting a courtship in the full glare of the tabloid press only made our irascible singer ever more volatile.

If the consequences were personally explosive, the songs became merely sour, something for which his new paramour need take no blame. The decision to detail the crushing burden of being rich and famous devolved solely on Morrison himself, and document it he did, in song after song after bleedin' song. The album he released in October 1991,

Hymns to the Silence, his first double album of original songs, devotes almost the entire first volume to whingeing about 'Professional Jealousy'; how the singer is 'not feeling it any more'; the fact that he just wants an 'Ordinary Life'; and why he can't find 'Some Peace of Mind'.

This indulgent exercise culminated in 'Why Must I Always Explain?', a song that in four minutes seemed to offer a prima-facie case for clinical paranoia. In lyrics set to the perfectly serviceable melody that had worked its charm on 'Tupelo Honey', Morrison sings of baring his soul to the crowd, only for them to 'laugh out loud' – an irrational fear born of career-long stage fright. Those known colloquially as paying punters he then portrays as 'hypocrites and parasites and people that drain'. Thankfully the singer, a paragon of *noblesse oblige*, is on hand to tell them 'things they're too lazy to know'.

Morrison would later claim that the song was 'about these people who are non-producers, and who set themselves up as authorities on the people that are doing the work, like me . . . They become authorities, even though they know nothing about doing it.' However, it was clear that his definition of a non-producing critic was anyone who actually thought about his work. As Steve Turner has written, 'The irony of "Why Must I Always Explain?" was that the thrust of his songwriting had always been explanation, giving his public detailed information about his problems, hardships and spiritual adventures.'

Seven songs into another sprawling offering Morrison finally gets such feelings out of his system – at least for this album – and turns his attention to 'when the world made more sense'. Unfortunately, songs like 'Take Me Back' and 'Hymns to the Silence' itself, rather than transporting the listener through time, as earlier evocations did, read like a series of shopping lists from the id.

When Morrison attempts another of his spoken monologues, 'On Hyndford Street', about 'the days before rock 'n' roll', Hyndford Street, Abetta Parade, Orangefield, St Donard's Church, 'Sunday six bells, and in between the silence there was conversation', its meaning hinges entirely on foreknowledge. To his old childhood chum, Gil Irvine, 'When he says in the poem about "St Donard's Church, Sunday six bells, when you could feel the silence", you could really *feel* the silence. Belfast used to shut up shop completely at ten o'clock on a Sunday night. Everywhere was closed, the buses stopped running, so you had complete silence at that time of the night.' To the remainder of Morrison's long-term audience he had said it all, and more poetically, in a single couplet from 'Beside You'. Feeling the silence was no longer enough. As the man himself said, communication is a two-way street, and the fact is he was driving the wrong way.

It is tempting, in the light of his father's death, to interpret such a relentless procession of childhood memories as some subconscious reaction to grief. The half-baked descriptions of 'Hyndford Street and Hank Williams, Louis Armstrong, Sidney Bechet on Sunday afternoons in winter . . . and the tuning in of stations in Europe on the wireless' certainly suggest some things left unsaid. But the bulk of these songs concern themselves with the contrast between a time 'when everything made more sense in the world . . . when you walked in a green field, in a green meadow/Down an avenue of trees' – as described in 'Take Me Back' – and the grey present, when nobody understands, and no one takes the time to explain.

These lyrical lessons in the layout of fifties East Belfast are lovingly presented in the album's accompanying booklet, even those that, like the title track, read like a random selection from a concordance of previous Morrison lyrics – 'I wanna go out in the countryside/Oh, sit by the clear, cool, crystal water/Get my spirit, way back to the feeling/ Deep in my soul' – thus convincingly arguing for the removal of all lyric-sheets from rock albums. Even the songs that work on *Hymns to the Silence*, and there are precious few, hardly benefit from their words being set in type. 'Carrying a Torch', a natural successor to 'Have I Told You Lately' and a minor hit for Tom Jones, to whom Morrison had initially donated the song, works best when lines like 'you're the keeper of the flame/and you burn so bright' are left unanalysed. 'Sweet Thing' it ain't.

The only song that really benefits from a set of lyrics is Morrison's powerful performance of the traditional hymn 'Be Thou My Vision', simply because the words are in that pseudo-King James syntax, though a leisurely enjoyment of Morrison's vocal delivery is all the listener really needs. Sadly it remains the only actual hymn he has tackled on record, though at a unique performance in a small village church in Stogumber, Somerset, in January 1990, he concluded a deeply symbolic selection of his own songs with the traditional gospel hymn 'Down by the Riverside'. 'Jerusalem' also occasionally filched its way into 'Summertime in England'. The simple faith these songs address – to which Morrison repeatedly expressed a desire to return – remained more than this complicated man could bring himself to embrace.

Instead, he felt compelled to return to the treadmill he'd described

with such scorn in the album's opening selections. In August 1991 he
unveiled a new band that incorporated two striking multi-instrumentalists,
Teena Lyle and Kate St John, who between them added vibes, congas, the
recorder, the oboe, cor anglais and a fashionable line in corsets, as well as
the more traditional backing vocals, sax and percussion. They would survive the many incarnations of this band, as fronted by guitarist Ronnie
Johnson. Original drummer Paul Robinson and keyboardist John Miller,
though, failed their finals and were soon replaced by a recalled Dave
Early and a baptismal Jonn Savannah,★ who was given a brief of sorts by
Johnson. He quickly learned to fend for himself.

Jonn Savannah: I was given a lot of preamble by Ronnie Johnson about what
this gig entailed, what it was about – 'This is what you're gonna be up against:
it's tough, it's hard, you'll be expected to know stuff, [but] don't ever be scared
of playing whatever you feel is right. He doesn't want to see people wimping
out.' Most of it prepared me for the band psychosis . . . unbelievable shit that
was going on – but I was prepared for this ogre to not speak to me, ignore me,
shout at me, and I was on edge. And there's no rehearsals, no preparation
physically, apart from 'Here's a couple of cassettes of a gig, learn what you can,
and we'll see you at the soundcheck in Birmingham.' I turn up and . . . I'd
been working on some Ray Charles [tracks], and Van walks on stage [at the
soundcheck] and we launch into a couple of blues numbers – he was very into
the blues at that time – it sounded great, the band was rocking, three tunes.
'OK, that's it' – walks straight over to me: 'So you been working with Brother
Ray?' He was particularly personable . . . [But] he's interested in one thing –
doing what he does. He's continually looking for what *it* is. When we were
playing sometimes, he'd say, 'That's it! What you're doing right now!' [What]
he's . . . saying [is], 'This is what I'm trying to attain. Right now we are at the
position that I perceive to be the correct point, but tomorrow that won't be it.'
He's changing, he's always looking for the correct set-up for the music that he's
doing, and when he's there – that's his enlightenment . . . He pushed me to do
things that I normally would never have been pushed to do. He won't accept
'I can't do it.' 'If you can't do it, why are you here?' . . . Sometimes he will give
quite distinct directions, [but] it tends to be 'That's not it.' All he wants is for it
to be blinding, in the way that he wants it, which might be nothing like anyone
[else] thinks.

★ Jonn Savannah changed his name from Don Snow after joining the band, but I have
retained his chosen pseudonym for consistency's sake.

The set-lists once again became abstract templates of possible street theories in the year of shows that followed on from Morrison's double album of diatribes. Geoff Dunn would replace Dave Early behind the kit before the year was out – Paul Robinson having been replaced after expressing an unflattering view of one of Morrison's performances. Dunn remembers participating in a number of 'workshop thing[s] . . . with the rhythm section. For a little period, there was [also] like a one-day-a-week thing, where we'd all get together and go through another list of songs. A lot of it was just kind of finding out what sounded good with that particular unit, and what didn't. A lot of it didn't ever get used.'

If the kind of R&B medleys in which Fame and Morrison had specialized became a thing of the past, the occasional 'Crawling King Snake', 'Good Morning Little Schoolgirl' or 'Route 66' signalled a good night ahead. Likewise, the number of songs from *Enlightenment* and *Hymns to the Silence* with which he would open a show – anything from four to eight – usually indicated the likely odds of his being in a mood to strip-mine his past catalogue for the real gems.

On such a night the fortunate few might get a fifteen-minute medley of 'My Lagan Love', 'The Star of the County Down' and 'Raglan Road', on which Morrison would intersperse breathless harmonica betwixt bursts of traditional poetry. Or an 'In the Garden' that veered into 'Since I Fell for You' before settling on 'Daring Night'. Or even a 'Did Ye Get Healed' that resolved itself as 'It's All in the Game'. Some of the songs that failed on record also came to life in concert – 'So Quiet in Here' usually intermingled with a remake of 'That's Where It's At', whilst an infectious 'Youth of 1,000 Summers' and a ruminating 'Why Must I Always Explain?' generally held up their end in a set that jazzed it up, rhythmed some blues before returning to the garden.

Richie Buckley: I've often been sent over the moon by . . . the way his energy comes up . . . Then again, he feeds off us that way, too, which is why it's so good playing with Van, because we really are a band playing together, not just a bunch of people backing a solo singer . . . At times he'll even draw you out centre stage and stand back and let you do your solo and he, himself, is really getting off on the music.

For much of the time Morrison played the genial father figure, especially after a good show when the celebratory mood and a few well-earned drinks afforded him temporary release. But at all times it was understood that nerves were there to be tested, limits established only to be breached. The scheduled breaks between the shows, which in the UK usually occupied weekends but overseas tended to be booked in week-long blocks, were a necessary panacea to release some of that stored-up tension.

Jonn Savannah: There was this feeling [at the end of each tour], I don't believe it was as extreme as it was. And then you go and do it [again] and . . . it was. It was the most extreme band I've ever worked with. I've never seen such drinking, from people in the band – Van, whoever. Frightening. Just total Bacchanalia . . . [But] with Van, he's either on or off. He doesn't do things unless they're extreme.

With his own studio again to hand, Morrison might also summon his core band to the Wool Hall at minimal notice, to try out some new song he had been working on between gigs. The resurgence in his commercial standing, and the new deal he had cut with Polydor, gave his label very little input when it came to the content and indeed length of the albums he delivered. All they were obliged to do was find a slot in their release schedule – in the case of *Hymns to the Silence*'s successor, *Too Long in Exile*, June 1993.

With the CD format containing the capacity to take up to an hour and a quarter of music, the onus to prune and shape material down to forty minutes had all but evaporated in a laser flash. Morrison was not alone among his contemporaries in abusing this new-found freedom. As *Hymns to the Silence* proved, only the limitations of vinyl had been keeping Morrison, a most reluctant sequencer of albums and hoarder of out-takes, fully focused. *Too Long in Exile*, at seventy-seven and a half minutes a single CD but another double album, was a product of the same *carte blanche* approach to recorded material as had produced *Hard Nose the Highway* and *Hymns to the Silence*. Recorded with the basic unit of Jonn Savannah, Ronnie Johnson, Nicky Scott, plus either Geoff Dunn or Paul Robinson on drums, the material became so thinned out that any substance disappeared between the cracks.

Jonn Savannah: One thing we did: tapes roll, he started to play a blues thing. I didn't even know they [were] taking it, but he's singing, band's all playing, trying to figure out what to play. At the end of it he said, 'That's it. Great. Done. That's the take that goes on the record.' And Geoff [Dunn] was like,

'But I didn't even know what I was doing.' He said, 'No, it was great.' I was just playing simple stuff on the Hammond, thinking I'd figure out something better later on: 'No. No overdubs. That's it.' . . . He's not adverse [sic] to that [overdub] process, but it is easier for him to redo the whole thing – like they used to make records . . . The whole of life might be agonized over, but the process of getting something on tape [is like], 'Sounds good. You can all play.'

Drummer Geoff Dunn seems to think that they cut some fifteen songs on the first day he found himself at the Wool Hall: 'It was [like], "Come down the studio, we're doing the album." I was probably only down there for a couple of days . . . You're all together, you're performing it. There may be a few horn overdubs, but usually Van's vocal at the time is *the vocal* . . . Most of the time . . . the first time we heard [a song] it was in the studio. Everyone would be set up and he would sing it, and we would just follow along with him . . . On certain ones, we thought we were running through [them], and it was actually being taken and ended up on the album. A couple of the blues things on *Too Long in Exile* were like that – he just started playing and everyone kinda joined in.'

Dunn would play on two-thirds of *Too Long in Exile*, including a number of covers such as 'Lonely Avenue', 'Good Morning Little Schoolgirl' and 'I'll Take Care of You' that they had been rehearsing and playing as the band began to take on a stronger R&B guise. The album also included a two-song jam with John Lee Hooker, recorded in California, though neither 'Gloria' nor 'Wasted Years' comes close to capturing the ominous undertow of their previous duet, 'I Cover the Waterfront', on Hooker's 1991 album, *Mr Lucky*. However, the most unexpected throwback was the album's penultimate offering, 'Before the World Was Made'. Its lyrics taken from another Yeats poem, it dates from the period when Morrison was intrigued by the possibility of putting poets of the ages to music. As with 'Crazy Jane on God', the actual music and arrangement were not his own.

Kenny Craddock: I read a lot of Yeats myself. I [also] wrote a few tunes to different Yeats things, one of which was 'Before the World Was Made', and I played it for Van at his house in Holland Park. There was no recording of it, or anything like that, I just played it a couple of times. I was down there with Arty McGlynn, just having like a little acoustic rehearsal . . . It must have been a year, year and a half later, we're playing somewhere in Europe, and he said, 'I haven't forgotten about that song. I'll definitely do something with it one of these days.'

The disparity of styles on the finished album confused the critics but, yet again, punters took the plunge. Even the lame attempt at a remake of 'Gloria' generated some airplay as a single. Morrison, though, was back-pedalling artistically and it showed. He would later speak of the album as an attempt at blues exploration at a time when he felt that 'the blues has become something else, it's become another vehicle . . . I don't think it's what it started out as, it's become chipped away . . . there are very few people now that are penetrating the depth of it.' This notion also seems to have prompted the Rhythm & Blues & Soul Revue, a self-conscious emulation of a redundant genre, assembled by Morrison in the wake of *Too Long in Exile*'s lukewarm reception but healthy sales.

The Revue was Morrison's way of updating the showband aesthetic. Though the band comprised essentially the same musicians with whom he had been playing for a year or more, two largely unknown male singers were drafted in to share vocal duties and sing the songs Morrison didn't feel like singing. In one more gesture of contempt for his paying punters, Morrison turned over the likes of 'Tupelo Honey' and 'Sweet Thing' to a man who used his eunuchoid voice to cut the balls off anything he was allowed to sing. The only thing that was smoking when Brian Kennedy stepped up to the mike was that jacket of his!

The response at the warm-up show which unveiled the Revue should have persuaded Morrison not to enter these murky waters. Ever since he had constituted the Fame–Morrison band in May 1989, he had been using the privately-owned King's Hotel, in Newport, South Wales, as a place to 'blood' new bands, rework the set and generally warm up for blocks of shows. The hotel, owned by an old friend of Morrison's, Gordon 'Mac' McIlroy, often booked blues and rockabilly artists, so Morrison's presence was not unknown. It finally gave him a Welsh equivalent of the fabled Lion's Share.

When, in August 1991, the Georgie Fame ensemble had been superseded by a more malleable set of musicians, their début came at the King's, where they returned on a regular basis until Morrison felt they had acquired the necessary musical chops. So it came as no great surprise when local adverts ran for two Van Morrison shows in the first week of October 1993. Save for a couple of festival gigs, it had been a quiet summer, and he presumably felt it was time to start promoting his latest offering in earnest. Sure enough, four of the first six songs at the 6 October show were lifted from his latest shiny silver disc.

Two songs later, the band finally broke into a familiar intro, 'Crazy Love', to hoots of approval from a suitably tanked-up crowd, only for some young whippersnapper to step up to the mike, and the whoops to fade. The next song, 'That's Where It's At', found Morrison back at the main mike. But not for long. 'Into the Mystic' was again hijacked by the False Falsetto. And so the show went on, Morrison singing the old R&B standards he fancied doing, tossing off the odd latter-day original and leaving songs like 'Have I Told You Lately' and 'Tupelo Honey' to a man who, when asked by Morrison if he knew 'Gloria', replied, 'Not really, but if you tell me what the words are, I'll go for it.' Not surprisingly, the crowd eventually began to turn, bellowing requests for any song they thought they might get the guy named on the ticket to sing. After one particularly persistent punter shouted for 'Brown Eyed Girl' one too many times, Morrison brought a tepid 'Vanlose Stairway' to a halt in order to set her straight:

This is not rock. This is not pop. This is called soul music. So in spite of all the motherfuckin' bastards that say something different, this is what it is. 'Brown Eyed Girl' is like lunchtime, and this is like dinnertime and beyond. 'Brown Eyed Girl' never was, never is; 'Brown Eyed Girl' is a fiction of somebody's imagination [that] I had to do to [*unintelligible*] from the fucking French people[!] [*returns to the song for a single line before . . .*] Talkin' 'bout soul! The main thing you don't understand with me is I'm a soul singer. I'm a motherfuckin' soul singer [*riffs on the word 'motherfucker'*]. I'm in China. I sing soul songs. I sing blues. Fuck the pop charts! . . . I don't want to play 'Brown Eyed Girl'. 'Cause I don't have to. Thank God I don't have to. If I had to, I'd commit suicide. I don't have to play 'Brown Eyed Girl' no more. I'm a soul singer and fuck the assholes!

It had been a long time since this belligerent drunk had shown his face on a public stage. Concentrating on consuming more beverages, he again turned the stage over to Brian Kennedy, to trammel through 'Into the Mystic' again before applying his unique dimmer to 'Celtic Ray'. But Morrison still felt he had not really had his say and, when he finally regained the mike for 'A Town Called Paradise', took to venting his spleen one more time. As requests he had no intention of fulfilling continued to rain forth, he began audibly to count them out:

Number three. Number four. That's old stuff! This room is full of dinosaurs. We're talking about now! No dinosaurs since last fucking year. We don't play that bullshit. What! We don't sing those numbers any more. Ah, c'mon, you don't expect me . . . [*the requests keep coming*] I'm not gonna play here any more . . . I don't do those fucking songs any more, don't you know that? I DON'T DO THOSE FUCKING SONGS ANY MORE!! No fucking way! I do the new fucking albums, last year and this year. That's what I do. We don't do those songs, we just do the current things. The old fucking things are patchwork [*shout of 'Get on with it, you old bastard!'*]. If you wanna come and see me next year in Newport, we're not gonna do those songs. We don't do those songs. Not even for Mac! I don't dig those songs. I've done them before – they're boring songs and I don't fucking do them. I'm talking about rhythm & blues. Now. N-O-W.

Never a man to be dissuaded by an adverse reaction, Morrison duly added another singer of no real distinction to his Revue, James Hunter a.k.a. Howlin' Wilf. As the shows expanded to take in ever more numerous guests, and ever less Van, he returned to San Francisco in December to record his third official live album at a residency at the Masonic Auditorium. The resultant double CD, *A Night in San Francisco*, features not only Hunter and Kennedy but noteworthy luminaries like Georgie Fame, John Lee Hooker, Junior Wells and Jimmy Witherspoon – as well as Morrison's own daughter, Shana, who sang 'Beautiful Vision' on his behalf. With just about every song either a medley of snatched refrains or turned over to a lesser vocalist, and with a total running time of 140 minutes, *A Night in San Francisco* is one long dark night of soul.★

The inclusion of so many of Morrison's idols was a worthy gesture, but they were soon gone – unlike Kennedy and Hunter. The release of *A Night in San Francisco* in April 1994 meant that the prospect of another studio album, and a much-needed change in format, also receded into the night. Having signalled his determination to persevere with the current show, Morrison allowed more songs to be ensnared by the Kennedy coloratura. 'Sweet Thing' and 'Queen of the Slipstream' became victims on the British leg that winter, whilst Kennedy also tangled with Shana Morrison over 'Beautiful Vision'. Just when it seemed that this maddening onstage democracy could go no further, Morrison

---

★ *A Night in San Francisco* actually derives from two shows: one at the Masonic Auditorium in San Francisco, the other at the Mystic Theater, Petaluma, six days earlier.

began to bring on his Irish girlfriend at the end of shows. The lady proceeded to read Yeats and other Irish poetry.

Shoving others, willing or not, into the limelight was a curiously self-effacing act, even for a man who generally recoiled from his own notoriety. Perhaps it was meant as a reaction to 'people [who] keep superimposing the profession I'm in on top of me . . . and just keeping that layer off me is a tremendous load of work'. In fact, though he continued to present himself, in the words of Gerald Dawe, 'as a vastly experienced and uncompromising critic of the contemporary world and the fate within it of genuine artistic endeavour', he was now prepared to expose himself to the kind of tabloid tittle-tattle that he had never previously warranted or wanted.

It was almost as if his fascination with fame had finally got the better of him. That fascination was certainly real, as David Tame, the author of *The Secret Power of Music* (1984), a book Morrison once cited, found out when they met: 'He had a virtual lecture he could give on the strange phenomenon of fame – not just his own, but the thing in general, and the history of fame and fandom.'

In the eighties, Morrison's response to the demands made had been an aversion to social interaction that had all but turned him into a social cripple. Martin Drover, who survived a number of tours in the eighties, witnessed someone who 'didn't want to be recognized, didn't want to be singled out, didn't want to be interviewed . . . I put that down to the fact that he lost the powers of communication with people – plus [there was] this almost resentment for having to do what he was doing, i.e. performing.' And yet a certain recognition was something he never entirely renounced, and on occasions almost demanded.

Clive Culbertson: We were doing Manchester [one time], and we drove up to the gig and he goes, 'Oh look, they're waiting on me. I can't take it, I can't take it. Oh man, they never leave me alone. I wish somebody would take it off me.' 'Van, do you want me to stop them getting to you?' 'Would you do that for me?' 'If you don't want to talk to them, I'll make sure you don't have to talk to them.' So there's five or six people. I said, 'Look, Van, I'll get between you and them, I'll tell them you're in a hurry for a soundcheck.' So we get out of the taxi and I go, 'Sorry, Mr Morrison's in a hurry here, OK Van . . .' and he's standing signing autographs. And we went in and I said, 'I thought you said . . .' 'Ah, I recognized a few faces there.' I hadn't got it yet. So we did the soundcheck, we come back round the hotel and they're standing outside, and

he does the same thing: 'Oh man, I don't wanna sign no fucking autographs!'
'[Well,] just come round the back of me, skip into the hotel.' 'OK, right, no
problem.' We get out. I go, 'Mr Morrison's in a hurry. Got a meeting.' Van's
standing in the rain for fifteen minutes signing autographs . . . He likes it in
doses.

The phenomenology of fame was something to which Morrison
seemed increasingly drawn. Back in 1985, he had described how he had
'gone through this process early on – the mill, what have you . . . and
it's not something I think is desirable . . . But all I can do is talk about it
. . . whether that's going to influence people or not.' By 1994 he was
back at the mill, but as a man who could better articulate his disquiet in
an epistle, rather than in his lyrics. Initially, he sought to respond to an
article in an Irish newspaper that commented on Morrison's recent
reported involvement with ex-Miss Ireland beauty, Michelle Rocca:

For long-time Morrison watchers, the singer's relationship with Rocca is a
bizarre occurrence, a dalliance with the social circle he has spent his life avoiding.
She's the sexiest woman in Ireland, according to the *Sunday Independent*, 'famous
for being famous'. As such, she attracts an attention which has embraced him
as well. With his 49th birthday just four months away, Van Morrison is in
danger of becoming a man about town, a regular fixture in the gossip columns,
a celebrity.

Morrison was quick to refute the charges. The following issue of the
Sunday Independent carried a letter from the man's own pen, firing a
number of volleys at the media that fed on what he later called, in song,
'the fame game':

Sir – There has been a lot in the papers lately in relation to myself being
referred to as a 'rock star'. I'd just like to set the record straight if I may. To
call me a rock star is absurd as anyone who has listened to my music will
observe. For the benefit of the unenlightened it is not my nature to be a rock
star. What I am is a singer and songwriter who does blues, soul, jazz, etc., etc.,
etc. . . .
  In fact, I have never claimed, in any shape or form, to be the above and if
anyone would care to do a bit of groundwork they would very easily discover
what I have been saying for the last thirty years, that I am not that, and do not
believe in it and never have.

On the one hand I am flattered by the sudden attention of the rock-star mythology, but on the other hand I do not need or want the attention, having spend [sic] most of my life living the role of an anti-hero and getting on with my job, so I tip my hat to the gods and goddesses of the media and say thanks but no thanks.

Van Morrison, Chiswick, London

The media weren't about to go away, but then he must have already known that. The following year, in a newspaper article, 'How Not to Get Screwed', he included as points four and six:

4. Test the lifestyle. Find out if your personality fits show business, because if it doesn't, don't bother in the first place.
6. Decide whether you want to be a gifted amateur or a dedicated pro . . . Serious musicians usually know what they want up front – i.e. to just keep playing and getting better, not having to be a star or living up to the expectations of others.

No mere dalliance, the alliance with Rocca was already of two years' standing. The pair had met at a charity dinner party at Desmond Guinness's house in the summer of 1992, though the striking thirty-year-old former Miss Ireland apparently mistook the singer-songwriter for crooner Val Doonican. Rocca later admitted that she 'thought he was a bit obnoxious in the beginning'. However, Morrison seems to have become smitten by the leggy lass, determinedly pursuing Rocca whilst insisting to all comers that they were just good friends. Rocca played along, calling Morrison 'a very good friend. I've tried to teach him a little bit. But how can you teach a guru?' The sheer physical contrast was striking enough for Rocca to insist, 'I'm more interested in intelligence than looks. Sure, Van's no oil painting, but he's beautiful in other ways.' Not exactly the usual way of describing one's beau.

The lid only really came off in January 1994, when the Irish *Sunday World* ran a story alleging, 'Friends say Morrison is to wed beauty queen Michelle'. Needless to say, the 'story' boiled down to a single unnamed 'close friend' suggesting that 'there is a gleam in Van's eye that no one has seen for some time', and that 'these days [the relationship] seems to have developed into something more than a friendship'. When another 'close friend' countered by saying that the pair were merely 'very fond' of each other, and describing Rocca as someone who just 'help[ed] him out in various situations as regards secretarial work or whatever', the bounds of credulity were being stretched to the limit. By now, the media interest had a momentum all its own and the publicity-magnet Rocca was beginning to enjoy a return to the limelight.* She even provided her own copy on their relationship for the Irish media-hounds:

Michelle Rocca: Since meeting someone as solid and decent and intelligent as Van I find all that [press] coverage a bit difficult . . . [But] he's always resented the press, he doesn't need publicity, [and] he's very centred . . . The more I get to know him, the more of a genius I feel he actually is. In the beginning it was a genuine friendship . . . [But] it's not like Marilyn Monroe and Arthur Miller. People are saying that I'm his muse. A muse to me is a house[!] but I do feel I've a lot to bring him . . . All this talk of marriage and when are you getting the ring isn't important.

Along with such unsecretarial copy, the various shots of the pair out on the town suggested their philosophical discussions had yet to light on Plato. The simple fact that Morrison was prepared to be photographed in the arms of Rocca indicated the extent to which, in the words of one Irish journalist, 'Van is quite besotted by Rocca. There is no other explanation for why he would open himself to such gossip, innuendo, speculation and begrudgery otherwise.' Rocca also seemed to have overhauled the man's wardrobe, dispensing with the ubiquitous denim. But the ultimate confirmation of their increasing closeness came with the June 1995 release of *Days Like This*, the first Morrison album in twenty-four years to feature a female companion on the cover, in this case a both overdressed and underdressed Rocca being pulled along by a hyperactive greyhound.

And yet there are few real love-songs on the album, and what there are come from the songsmith's catalogue of hand-me-down lines. Though the album opens and closes with songs suggestive of a new love, neither comes close to the love-songs of yore. If 'Perfect Fit', a song rhyming 'piss' with 'amiss', falls some way short of Charles Aznavour territory, 'In the Afternoon' definitely qualifies as too much information with its (hopefully non-autobiographical) chat-up verses, designed to persuade her 'to make love in the afternoon'. Morrison mishandles the

---

* Aside from being a former Miss Ireland, Miss Rocca had also been compère at the Eurovision Song Contest when Ireland played host.

one great love-song to be found on the album, Eddy Arnold's magnificent torch-ballad, 'You Don't Know Me', duetting with his off-key daughter in an uncharacteristically hesitant way. Like most untutored vocalists, Morrison was never the greatest duet-singer, and his daughter here sounds lost at C.

The closest Morrison comes to his muse is on 'Ancient Highway', where the images are largely appropriated but the delivery comes from some delphic storage unit, as he spends nine minutes of white-hot inspiration 'praying to my higher self/Don't let me down'. Drummer Geoff Dunn recalls 'Ancient Highway' being 'quite spontaneous. That was fantastic . . . It was just poetry really, and we got into this groove thing behind him and it just kind of evolved. A lot of the time it would just come, roll off the tongue. On those particular occasions you thought, "This is kind of special." And he was quite excited about those sort[s] of things, when it happened.' Morrison also presumably realized it was something he'd never be able to replicate, and 'Ancient Highway' – save for snatches added to 'In the Afternoon' – never made it to the live set.

Of the remaining songs, 'No Religion' seems to close the book on Morrison's spiritual quest as he muses upon the thought, 'Wouldn't it be great just to be born and nobody told you that there was such a thing called religion?'; whilst 'Raincheck' is apparently about 'having the ability to be objective about [something] and to step back and say, well, I can either accept a thing or reject a thing; or I can think about it, or come back to it later on'. If this really is its subject matter, it fails to convey its intent, however much the song meant to Morrison. However, along with the title track and 'In the Afternoon', it was to become one of a trio of *Days Like This* ditties to survive over half a decade of perpetual gigging.

On the album each of these songs is infected by what David Cavanagh described at the outset of his *Mojo* review as Brian Kennedy's 'intensely irritating habit of repeating whatever Van's just sung, in a higher-pitched voice. This becomes rather unbearable.' Tom Moon was less generous in *Rolling Stone*, accusing Kennedy's 'mindless echo' of reducing 'even the [more] profound lyrics . . . to a gibberish-filled ping-pong match'. And on an album of workaday catch-phrases – 'this could be the perfect fit'; 'they're playing Russian roulette with your mind'; 'my name is Raincheck'; 'my mama told me there'd be days like this' – profundity was at a premium.

Morrison was again diluting his talent over another hour's worth of

music. Tom Moon was being generous when he described the album as
'one campy indulgence, one masterpiece: that's the general pattern . . .
moments of genius followed by lavish displays of questionable taste,
sometimes within the same song'. And still Morrison bucked the trend.
His new audience, rather than tiring of the repetitive imagery, endless
bleating and annoying vocal echoes, would make *Days Like This* his most
successful non-compilation album ever. Go figure.

This was despite the fact that *Days Like This* was not an album he
unduly promoted in the immediate aftermath of its release. Less than a
month later, Morrison changed tack, embarking on a jazz tour that
promoted an album not even on the schedules. Even he, it seems, was
tiring of his Revue and its self-evident limitations. Michelle Rocca's
poetry party piece was also consigned to the past, though she continued
to make her presence felt at the shows. One musician recalls how, on
those occasions when she did appear, 'We used to say, "Uh-oh.
Michelle's about. Look out." . . . There were some wonderful shout-ups
at the side of the stage. Sometimes we used to be in hysterics. She'd walk
on to the stage and start combing his hair and putting his jacket straight
in front of thousands of people. There'd be times when he would not be
playing, for a chorus or something, and he'd wander off the stage and
there'd be the most almighty 'barney' going on in the wings, then he'd
stagger back on to the stage and have another drink. From that point of
view, there was a slight element of circus . . . There's no doubt he was
besotted by her. He worshipped the ground she walked on, [even if]
she walked all over him from time to time. [But] I think they set each
other off.'

By the summer of 1995, Rocca must have known she was playing
with fire and was going to get burned. An article in an Irish paper some
months earlier had reported an incident at the Chocolate Bar in Dublin,
where Morrison and Rocca were at a small gathering for Bono's wife's
birthday and tempers became frayed. Michelle departed the club in a
hurry with Morrison apparently being restrained by Bono's minders.
There was also a certain notorious incident in August 1994, which was
widely reported in the British tabloids. According to an eyewitness, after
a night of drinking in a hotel bar with Van fan and movie heart-throb
Richard Gere, Morrison turned on him, accusing him 'of moving in on
his girlfriend. Harsh words were exchanged and there was a scuffle.'
Having previously been allowed to play with his idol on stage at the
Brighton Dome, Gere checked out of the hotel early in the morning,

leaving Morrison to deliver one of the most perfunctory performances of a long career the following night.

Morrison and Rocca, though, continued to be seen out together, amid relentless speculation in the Irish press that they might be about to get married. There were even reports of the notoriously careful Morrison purchasing a £60,000 engagement ring. Inevitably, another 'close friend' was quoted as saying that 'they are a genuinely nice couple, and outside all the media speculation they seem really happy with each other . . . She has brought him out of his shell to an incredible degree, and she is older herself now so she should be able to deal with things.' The truth, one suspects, is that there was a right royal battle raging between two diametrically opposing lifestyles, one fun-loving, out-going and gregarious, the other introverted, occasionally belligerent, and home-loving.

The outcome remained in doubt up until the following June when, at a party at Marina Guinness's, Morrison began to act up and Rocca was heard to exclaim, 'At least try to behave yourself in public. There are other people to consider.' A week later Morrison received a particularly hurtful form of retribution. On the front page of the 7 June 1996 issue of the Northern Ireland edition of the *Daily Mirror* was the banner headline 'VAN'S FIANCEE CHEATS WITH RACING ROMEO'. The article went on to reveal that Rocca had been 'sharing nights of passion at a luxury hotel in Dublin' with horse-racing boss Angus Gold. Rocca was quoted, somewhat implausibly, as saying that she and Gold had spent two nights together 'but we didn't have sex. We're friends and we were just talking.' She then dared the journalist to print the story – which he did. In the following day's *Mirror*, Morrison gave his own response: 'I've been betrayed. It's over and that's that. We will not be getting back together. I am disgusted by the behaviour of all the parties involved. Michelle and I are finished.'

It was a very public 'end' to a relationship largely conducted in, and by, the media. However, the Irish papers were not done with Mr Morrison: the following Sunday the *Mirror* ran another story, on the 'SEX SHAME OF VAN THE 3-IN-A-BED MAN'. There seemed very little to the story: Morrison had met a couple of divorcées in a hotel bar, had a few drinks and suggested a threesome (not, apparently, for the first time). Persuading the ladies, named Sheila and Rose, to book a room, he then retired upstairs with them for two hours of lovemaking. According to 'thrill-seeker' Sheila, 'There was no kinky stuff. It was straight sex.' Aside from the blurry photo of Sheila that accompanied the article, and which suggested a certain lack of discrimination on the part of a man his ex-fiancée described as 'no oil painting' himself, it was hard to see what Morrison had to be ashamed about. But ashamed he was, as he revealed to a *Mirror* reporter backstage at Wembley Arena, where he was due to open a brief arena tour with 'Brother Ray':

I just felt lonely and rejected and wanted something to hold on to. I am so ashamed. I was devastated about the break-up of my engagement to Michelle – who I loved – and I just went over the top. I have let my fans and myself down but there's no excuse. I met the girls at a dinner party after drinking earlier in the day. We all got drunk and went to a hotel. It all happened so fast and things got out of hand. Everything got on top of me. I have been under enormous pressure after the revelations of Michelle's affair. I was feeling totally devastated about what she had done. I went to a friend's house for dinner to try to escape from this nightmare and it was there that what she had done suddenly hit me like a bolt from the blue. I didn't know who to turn to. I feel bad about what I did. It's not the sort of thing I would normally do but I could not cope with Michelle's betrayal. I just wanted to go off with the first woman I met. We all make mistakes. This was one of mine. But I have been to hell and back. Nobody knows the torment I have been through.

This was not merely uncharacteristic, this was character-changing. Morrison was visibly showing his distress at the show that night, speaking of his heartbreak to an astonished audience. Here was a man who had spent his life trying to hide the pain was caught in the headlines and there was nothing he could do about it, except learn to live with it. If he had proved incapable of writing a truly convincing love song about his relationship with Rocca, he managed to write a genuinely heartfelt song about the hurt he was now feeling. It would be three years before 'Reminds Me of You' was released. Should there be a version recorded at this point it remains unreleased, but even the version on 1999's *Back on Top* suggests a man who – whilst finding it very, very hard to forgive his fiancée – can think of no other way he can make it through: 'My head says no, but my soul demands it/['Cause] everything I do reminds me of you'.

Linda Gail Lewis: When we first talked about songwriting, he said, 'Oh no, I never write about anything I feel. I just make up songs like someone writing a book' . . . But then when we were in Bournemouth . . . he admitted his heart was broken when he wrote 'Reminds Me of You' . . . He said he had it a long time before he put it on *Back on Top*.

Though he would learn to overlook Rocca's indiscretion, the light had gone out of the relationship and eventually a darkness would come that drew from a deep well of resentment he could never fully displace.

27

1996–99: The Van Morrison Masterclass

People told me [things] and I didn't listen . . . that you need something else as well. You have to have something else. You can't just rely on [music]. Anything, another job, another hobby, another interest, another angle.

—*Van Morrison, 1985*

There are other things I want to do, other things I want to say outside of this framework. I don't know what they are but I didn't really plan to do this for this long . . . I have other needs and other requirements . . . I do need to play a certain amount of music. I do need to write. But I definitely don't need to be a star.

—*Van Morrison, 1990*

Unwilling to jump off the treadmill, Morrison's solution, come the spring of 1995, was to instigate a series of side-projects that echoed his real loves and gave him an outlet his own work appeared to deny him. Though the projects in question were largely a personal indulgence, they reflected the way that Morrison liked to see himself. As far back as 1973, he had described himself as 'like a jazz artist, where the jazz artist goes in and cuts an album and they put it out. That's where I want to get to: he walks in the studio, he blows, and then he comes out!' Whether this really betrayed the mark of a jazz artist was a moot point.

Morrison's engineer at his studio, the Wool Hall, was Walter Samuel, who after two years of working under Mick Glossop, was fully briefed as to the man's working methods: 'The tape just keeps rolling. Basically, as soon as he walks into the studio, the machine goes into "record" and keeps running until he walks out again. There are no beginnings and ends to the takes. He doesn't say, "Right, start the take now"; he rehearses the chorus and then suddenly goes into the song . . . Van's method of recording hasn't changed over all these years. If anything, he's working more live [now] than he was in the eighties.' Occasionally, the result would be something like 'Ancient Highway'. Usually it was something that needed a little more fixing. Fixing, though, was rarely allowed.

Van Morrison: I don't like to overdub anything if I don't have to, so the feeling I'm looking for is the spontaneity . . . at all times . . . I just don't like the whole mechanical thing of overdubbing. I just like that . . . instant thing of singing a song, and having it all played at the same time. For me, that's what the buzz is. [1996]

Morrison's ability to control the mood of a session transformed him into something more than a producer: '[I'm] a magician. I make things happen . . . Whatever is working in that particular space at that particular time, I use, I take advantage of. It's got nothing to do with parts, with who plays what. Either you come in that day and make something happen or you don't.' However, not only had the technology moved on, but the serendipitous space he had inhabited at numerous sessions in earlier times was no longer always available, especially when surrounding himself with incompatible musical elements.

His muse had a short fuse, especially when he decided to take the cut-it-and-quit aesthetic too far. That mighty wailer Pee Wee Ellis, who now returned to the fold, found that his old boss had dispensed with refining basic tracks altogether. He recalled one particular song they recorded in 1996: 'The solo on "Sometimes We Cry" was [entirely] spontaneous. We recorded the whole thing live, straight through. What happened is that I tried to get in the mood of the song. While the song is going on you absorb it, and when it's time to do the solo you take it from there . . . Whatever comes up now, that's the business. It's about the performance and [so] it's not fair to polish it and make it perfect . . . that's kind of cheating.'

Nor did Morrison any longer seem to cut songs with an end product in mind. Something would spring to mind. Brian Kennedy describes one set of 1994 sessions 'that we did in Dublin . . . which were, in true Van style, three albums at once . . . I think it was a four-day session and we recorded about seventeen songs . . . and out of those came the track for the Chieftains' *Long Black Veil*★ . . . [material] for a movie called *Moon-dance* . . . [And] then we did things like "Raincheck" and "I'll Never Be Free" [for *Days Like This*].' Such an approach lent itself to side-projects, though not to a sequenced set of original songs with an integrity all its own – hence *Days Like This*, the kind of finished product a workaholic with a short attention span might produce in such circumstances. As Morrison stated at the time, 'I'm never not working,' a credo that reflected the inspirational example of mentors like John Lee Hooker, James Brown and Ray Charles. Keyboardist Jonn Savannah notes that 'for [Van], the real true genius[es] had the same ethic that he has now: "You get up and do it."'

Starting in the spring of 1995, Morrison again began to edge away from the mainstream. At the beginning of May he rehearsed and recorded his first jazz album since *Astral Weeks* in a couple of days, using the legendary Ronnie Scott's in London. Perhaps he felt he was fulfilling a commitment made back in 1977, when he had suggested that 'it's part of the gig for musicians like myself to make people aware where certain things have their roots, and that things don't just materialize from out of nowhere. It opens up musical cultures that they might not realize exist.' The album *How Long Has This Been Going On?* – which had to wait until December 1995 to be released – was doubtless what Morrison had in mind when he suggested, a couple of years later, 'Progress means going further in what I love, in what touches me.'

In fact the idea of making such an album had occupied a number of discussions between Georgie Fame and Morrison over the years as Morrison continued to flirt with the jazz credentials he'd irrevocably established by *Astral Weeks*. (At some point in the eighties, Morrison had actually flown Richard Davis over to Ireland 'to dub some bass on to something he'd already done . . . He said he wanted me to present the feeling I did on *Astral Weeks*. [So] I went and listened to the album to see what I had done.' On the other hand, if Fame can be believed, *How Long . . . ?* – released on Verve – was little more than a whim: 'He just said one day that he wanted to do this record, so we cobbled together the tunes . . . I got the band together, and we ran through some ideas one quiet afternoon at the Bull's Head. That went very well, so Van said, "Let's do it."'

★ The track in question was a re-recording of 'Have I Told You Lately'.

Actually Morrison had made a habit since the mid eighties of popping up from time to time as a guest of the Danish Radio Big Band, with whom he would attempt jazzier takes on his own songs. Both Fame and he had also joined the Dallas Jazz Orchestra at the 1989 Montreux Jazz Festival, performing baroque renditions of 'A New Kind of Man', 'Listen to the Lion' and 'Vanlose Stairway'.

How Long . . . ?, needless to say, had more in common with these Big Band performances than with the intimate intensity of *Astral Weeks*, combining jazz arrangements of originals such as 'I Will Be There', 'Moondance', 'All Saints' Day' and 'Heathrow Shuffle' with songs by the likes of King Pleasure, Louis Jordan, the Gershwins, Mose Allison and Johnny Mercer. Somehow it convinced Morrison that this was the way to go, and within weeks of the recording he had arranged a special show at the Royal Festival Hall, where he planned to perform this material to the audience absent from Ronnie Scott's.

Alan Skidmore: They recorded the album at Ronnie Scott's club, not in the evening with people but in the afternoon when the club was empty. I don't know why they didn't do the recording . . . with an audience. The band never actually played 'at the club' . . . [After the album] Georgie asked me to join the band. The first [gig] was a big one at the Royal Festival Hall. The place was absolutely packed, but in order for that gig to come off properly Georgie asked me if I would rewrite [some of] the [arrangements]. I spent several weeks rewriting, listening to tapes, then came the gig. After[wards], there was a little reception backstage and Van came to me and said, 'D'ya remember we did a gig in Bristol once and you said to me I was [unprofessional].' . . . He['d] obviously harboured it for five years . . . I said, 'That's right. I did. And I meant it.'

As one of those musicians who stood up to his bandleader, Skidmore may have incurred Morrison's enmity, but his arrangement ideas were essential as Morrison proceeded to book a set of shows that schizo-phrenically sought to promote both the lightweight pop of *Days Like This* and the lounge jazz of the Ronnie Scott's album. Seeing this as the way ahead, Morrison informed one journalist that 'if I keep going in that [jazz] direction, I think I can be much more myself, and do what I want to do . . . instead of trying to fit into a sort of mould that I've been in for a long time'.

While audiences were less convinced by the likes of 'Sack of Woe' and 'My Mind Is on Vacation' than by new Morrison songs such as

'Melancholia' and 'Perfect Fit', the band were more convincing on the likes of 'It's All in the Game' and 'Stormy Monday' than 'In the Garden' or 'Have I Told You Lately', with which Morrison insisted on ending most shows on the autumn jazz tour. As with the Soul & Blues Revue, any failure to gel was not acknowledged, let alone addressed. Morrison was enjoying himself, back on the bottom again, confusing fans and critics alike, and that was what mattered.

Alan Skidmore: The two or three or four horns used to be on the right-hand side of the stage, and Van was practically centre stage, and very often he would sing the first part of the tune and then in a very haphazard way he would point at one of the horns to play a solo, 'You. Play. Now.' [But] with the sunglasses and the hat, we never knew which one he was pointing at . . . The man is a legendary blues singer, and he fancied his chances of running a jazz group . . . [save that] he isn't a jazz musician. He's a rhythm & blues singer; he's a great lyricist, but in no way is he a jazz musician . . . With the quality of musicians he had in his band, I would have thought that would have been a great inspiration to him – to be surrounded by such good musicians – but to me he never felt very comfortable. When he was playing his hits, then he was comfortable. But when it was [the jazz material] he never [looked] that comfortable . . . I think the man is a very good musician for what he does, [but] he should definitely leave jazz out. He shouldn't go anywhere near it. He [occasionally] hung a saxophone round his neck and played it. 'Put this in tune,' he said to me. 'Why's this saxophone not working?' And I played it, and it was working perfectly. [I'd] give it back to him and it would start squeaking.

Despite the opportunity it presented, the autumn UK jazz tour passed without the performance of a single *Astral Weeks* song. The presence of all the necessary components did not seem to have set Morrison thinking that way. However, when he was invited to perform a show on 7 December as part of the UK Year of Literature and Writing, at Brangwyn Hall in Swansea, the opportunity finally prompted a re-examination, and during the musical section of the show – which followed a surreal discussion of his literary roots with Irish academic Gerald Dawe – out came 'Ballerina', 'Slim Slow Slider' and 'Madame George'.

A week later, in Waterford, this trio of songs was augmented by a rare 'Listen to the Lion', and as 'Madame George' wandered down its maze-like streets it even came upon parts of 'Who Drove the Red Sports Car?' and 'TB Sheets'. Two days later, Morrison concluded the year's touring with a one-off show at the Point in Dublin, which was recorded for an FM broadcast. Unbeknownst to the boys in the band, Morrison was planning to reconfigure the sound, and only tenor saxophonist Leo Green was destined to feature in future plans.

As swansongs go, though, the show at the Point was a fine farewell. If Morrison had summoned up 'Madame George' and 'Ballerina' at previous shows in Dublin, this was the first 'Slim Slow Slider' in living memory. Why *Astral Weeks* was back on his mind was unclear. Perhaps it was something as straightforward as playing the album for the first time in a number of years. He suggested as much in conversation a year or so later: 'I heard *Astral Weeks* recently. It made me just sit up . . . and think, "Right, OK. I was really on to something different. There was a lot of stuff going on here that was definitely off-the-wall and out there." And it was good.' At some point, according to guitarist Jay Berliner, 'they were [even] talking about doing a reunion concert, bringing the band together and performing in Belfast, doing the tunes from *Astral Weeks* with the original band'. Sadly, Connie Kay's premature demise scuppered that idea for good.

Having the textures offered by double-bass, grand piano and trumpet again at his disposal − and used effectively at the Point − it seemed odd that Morrison should turn away from his latest jazz fusion at a time when they had ironed out many of the musical creases. Maybe he was concerned lest he should irrevocably distance himself from the mainstream he professed to disavow. Perhaps, as Skidmore posits, 'he [just] got cold feet with regards to taking this [sound] to America'.

However, *How Long . . . ?* would not be an isolated side-project. Before the end of 1996, there would be a second Verve release,* using many of the same musicians but, unlike those on *How Long . . . ?*, the songs on *Tell Me Something* were largely overlooked by Morrison's ongoing revue. The album was another old idea of Fame and/or Morrison, a 'tribute' album to jazz songwriter Mose Allison − perhaps best known in rock circles for 'Young Man Blues' − with vocal duties divided between Fame and Morrison. Aside from the opening 'One of These Days', clearly a favourite of Morrison's, the album only really hit

---

* Morrison had begun to use the Verve imprint for his sideline releases, even though the real Verve label had long ceased to exist, presumably feeling it imbued these releases with some attendant kudos.

its stride on two of the cuts, 'I Don't Want Much' and 'Perfect Moment', where Allison himself lent a hand.

Asked about the thinking behind these side-projects at the time, Morrison admitted, 'I've always found a problem with commercial releases, synchronicity-wise, [in terms of] what I'm doing live at the time . . . I just find . . . the commercial release situation too restrictive, so the Verve thing is the getaway from that [situation], do something different, do something more spontaneous and . . . maybe do material that I wouldn't ordinarily do . . . I want to do more of that . . . I wanna break down these barriers.' Those barriers lost a chip of paint, but nothing more. Neither album charted, and the record company put no real resources behind them. PolyGram simply patiently awaited the next original instalment in the Morrison saga.

For Morrison there seemed no obvious way of integrating these strands into the live format he had chosen for himself. Though he gave the *How Long . . . ?* songs a fair portion of the spring and summer 1996 sets, no segue from 'Symphony Sid' to 'Slim Slow Slider' was ever going to be smooth. That struggle for a format within which he could move forward *or sideways* was essentially fought out in the cramped confines of a little nightclub in the theatre district of New York.

New York's Supper Club had recently been graced with remarkable performances by the likes of Bob Dylan, Elvis Costello and Pete Town-shend, and Morrison was presumably looking for some of the same magic. It was the first time he'd played a New York club since the late sixties. As it is, the four shows at the end of April 1996 had a number of moments when Morrison brought the audiences to the very gates of paradise, only to down another shot of whoknowswhat and start rapping to the crowd. Back in 1990, Morrison had talked about how 'in a club you can let go a bit more and do different things . . . I just look at it now as two different things – the concerts being more of a structured show and the clubs being more just playing.' Though the Supper Club shows were real marathons, there was not enough playing. On the first night, the show lasted ten minutes short of four hours but for much of the time the stage was turned over to Georgie Fame and Jimmy Witherspoon. Morrison also interspersed the songs he sang himself with a solo audition for the Comedy Club:

(i) And now a word from our sponsor . . . [*plays 'Moondance'*].

(ii) Where's Ronnie? Let's strangle the motherfucker that got me to do this gig!

(iii) Listen, let me tell you what genius is. King Pleasure, hey wait a minute. Fuck all this bullshit. King Pleasure was a genius . . . I only know 1–4–5. That's what I do . . . I'm limited. I'm limited in my location here.

(iv) If anybody's got anything to say . . . this is the time to say it. Ya got a bitch? Ya got a grief? Now's the time . . . this is the soul-cleansing part of the fucking programme . . . Ya wanna believe in something? . . . Might be Jesus . . . might be Buddha . . . might be your Aunt Fanny . . . If anybody's got anything to say I think they should say it now . . . otherwise we're gonna close this down . . . Nobody gonna come clean – OK, so we're gonna go through this again. 'Cause nobody's gonna come clean, we're gonna pretend.

If Morrison was willing to toss away the title track from his most successful American album, requests for equally hoary chestnuts on subsequent nights only drew the man's ire, forcefully expressed:

'Into the Mystic'? Fuck you! That's ancient history. We don't do that any more, listen. That's only lip service . . . All right, let me explain myself here, come on let's get down . . . How many people actually know what we're doing here tonight? . . . Let me explain something, I haven't done those songs. No man, wait. I haven't done them . . . when I did them I didn't do them. 'Moondance' was put in as lip service . . . Yeah, afraid so. This is the real me. 'Into the Mystic', that's ancient history. A lot of water under the bridge . . . I haven't done that shit [forever] . . . when I played it in the first place I didn't like it. Why do you expect me to do it now? . . . If you're expecting that . . . you've got the wrong me . . . How many people are here to see the former artist known as Van Morrison? Well, I got news for you – you're in the wrong room. If you want to hear 'Brown Eyed Girl' – you're not going to hear that. You're not going to hear 'Into the Mystic'. You're not going to hear 'Gloria'. You're not gonna hear 'Crazy Love'. You're not gonna hear 'Domino' . . . See the promoter!

Four days after retreating from the Supper Club, nursing a hangover from hell, Morrison found himself playing the annual Beale Street Music Festival in Memphis. Opening with 'Moondance', he encored with 'Have I Told You Lately' and 'Tupelo Honey', and generally gave the fun-loving festival-goers what they wanted to hear. Evidently something the man had said back in 1974 still held true:

Van Morrison: Sometimes it doesn't bother me in the least doing all that old stuff, and other times it *does* bother me . . . It all depends on how it feels. [1974]

Indeed, as that remarkable show at the Point the previous December proved, Morrison remained connected to much of this earlier material on a profound level, and when he was in the right space he could inhabit the moment again. On the thirtieth anniversary of the release of *Astral Weeks*, Tom Adair wrote a long piece about this seminal album in the *Scotsman*, which concluded with the statement, 'Over the years in live performances, when you hear him reprise those songs, something less astral is guaranteed.' If Mr Adair is trying to say that none of the live performances recreates the mood of the album, he may well have a point – albeit a self-evident one.

But Morrison has a habit of performing these talisman songs only when he can remember their meaning. Thus he self-consciously prefaced a 1998 performance of 'Ballerina' in Spain by saying: 'I'd like to try something from *Astral Weeks*. I don't know if any of you can remember that. I'm not even sure I can remember it myself at this point!' As soon as he starts it, though, it all comes flooding back. The subsequent performance is suitably astral. And yet Morrison felt no obligation to reach for the same feeling the following night.

On a certain level, it is *only* Morrison's refusal to pander to the greatest-hits-lovin' portion of his audience that has enabled him to retain a connection with his songs which many contemporaries long ago lost with theirs. Of course, he continues to reserve the right to decide when such a connection can best be made, sometimes allowing the mood to take him spontaneously, at other times crafting a whole new arrangement.

Jonn Savannah: If he decides to do anything, he will do it. If he decides not to do something, then heaven or earth will not move him – and that has got to be admired. He doesn't care [what the fans want]. They're there for him, he's not there for them. He's not doing this to please people. He's doing it because he feels he has to . . . [But] he will never throw something in that'll make him look daft, or make him look unrehearsed, so he's very clever at gauging the state that the band's in – he's not going to have too many car crashes on stage if he can avoid it. If he's running in a new band, he won't suddenly put in a Louis Prima tune that half of them won't know. Songs like 'Madame George', that have a very complex structure because you have to count bars, he wouldn't just chuck at someone.

Despite temporarily abandoning performing as-yet-unreleased songs, perhaps fearful that he might supersede the studio take before offering it for public consumption, in 1996 Morrison introduced his next title track, 'The Healing Game', part of an album completed that summer but held over till March 1997.* According to Morrison, the song addressed the spirit with which he continued to connect in performance:

Van Morrison: The live thing is more where I'm at now. Maybe I've always been there and not known it. Maybe that's what this *Healing Game* thing is about . . . What I'm doing is putting forth the music and it's very intense, there's no let-up and everybody's on their toes all the time, from the minute they walk on stage till they come off. [1997]

'The Healing Game' placed our singer 'back on the corner again/back where I belong/where I've always been'. This corner, first name-checked on a 1969 demo, was evidently that special place – geographically and psychologically – where he could just be himself.

Gil Irvine: To me [he] never wanted to be a star, he wanted to make music. He doesn't want to handle the trappings of stardom. When he goes out for a meal, he doesn't like to be hounded for an autograph . . . [But] he would keep in touch with myself and Sammy Woodburn . . . He would phone me up and say, 'Gil, get so-and-so and so-and-so. See if you can find them, and we'll go for a meal.' He still appreciates where he came from. There's no airs and graces, it's just, 'Let's talk about [the] old times.'

The presence of a number of *Astral Weeks* songs in the set were not the only signposts back to a Belfast 'before everything got fucked up', which was how Morrison characterized the subject matter of 'The Healing Game' on one occasion. 'Saint Dominic's Preview' was another song that was a little too measured in tone and tune to be merely something 'we have to do . . . so I can do what I want to do'.

Having all but disappeared from the set in the eighties, the return of 'Saint Dominic' at the end of 1995 came at a time when the people of Northern Ireland were again praying for lasting peace. Then, in early April 1996, Morrison turned up at the Temple Bar Music Centre in Dublin to record an entirely new arrangement of the song, with Mary Black on backing vocals, Nollaig Casey on fiddle and Donal Lunny on

---

* Fans were allowed a further sneak preview on John Lee Hooker's album *Don't Look Back*, co-produced by Morrison and featuring a number of his vocal contributions.

bazouki, all for a Gaelic TV show called *Sult*. Sung with a passion rare, the 1996 'Saint Dominic's Preview' reminded everyone watching that the time had come to restate these sentiments.

A need for the healing power of forgiveness was not confined to those for whom the Irish question still required an answer. Morrison also sought to heal more recent wounds, being seen again in the company of Michelle Rocca in New York and New Orleans that spring. He had also written a couple of songs that appeared to address their reconstructed relationship: one, 'Fire in the Belly', simply suggested that absence made the heart grow horny, whilst the other, 'Sometimes We Cry', indicated that he had learnt some tough lessons along the way.

If Morrison had hopes that the relationship could now be conducted without the tabloids' intervention, they were dashed by a November 1996 edition of the *Irish Mirror*. Beneath a front-page headline 'VAN NAMES THE BIG DAY', the *Mirror* claimed that Morrison and Rocca had made plans to marry the following March.

The only big day that the winter of 1997 brought the pair was the very public outcome of a bitter feud waged between Rocca and her former lover Cathal Ryan. Whilst Rocca pursued Ryan to the High Court for an alleged assault dating back to March 1992, Morrison dutifully sat in the public gallery watching proceedings. Where Rocca found the substantial costs to mount such a case, which ended in a nominal victory but with the substantial costs being met by both sides, remained a closely guarded secret. However, for Morrison, who was known to use the threat of court action as a tactic to silence disquieting voices – as he did in September 1997, when the *Belfast Evening Telegraph* erroneously suggested that 'the personal relationship between Mr Van Morrison and Ms Michelle Rocca was over' – it was a reminder of the unpredictability of court cases.

Promoting the release of *The Healing Game*, a matter of weeks later, represented a far more worthy channelling of his energies. It had been two years since the last album of original songs, and early word-of-mouth on the album hinted at a dramatic return to form for this once prolific songwriter. As it is, although the ten-track collection was perhaps Morrison's best-sounding album in a decade, and the influence of Pee Wee Ellis as arranger and MD was certainly evident, the songs were again not there to be had. Particularly burdensome were 'This Weight' and 'The Waiting Game', nth instalments in the Morrison saga of personal suffering. The album sold significantly less than either *Days Like This* or

Too Long in Exile, suggesting that even newer fans were recognizing repeated patterns and giving the latest collection a miss.

And yet, on the evidence of both the title-track CD single and the album's memorable opening song, *The Healing Game* warranted some of the positive whispers that preceded its release. 'Rough God Goes Riding' signalled a return to the religious and spiritual preoccupations that had driven Morrison's work throughout the eighties, the image of the Rough God being derived from Robin Williamson's 'Mr Thomas' – recorded by Morrison for *Inarticulate* – in which 'the rough God goes riding with his shears', a reference to the avenging Messiah who shall return to wreak final judgement on Man.

With Morrison, needless to say, the Rough God became a personal settler of accounts, repaying those who had crossed him before the more mundane matter of saving humanity got in the way. 'Rough God Goes Riding' is a sucker-punch of a song, deceptively engaging, disturbing in content but, as Hepworth wrote at the time, 'with all the shades of delight and wonder of his younger music now dispersed in a peevish fog of injured innocence'. Of course, universal retribution could come from either the Christ or the Antichrist and, if contemporary comments hold weight, he was not about to subscribe to salvation by faith or works.

Van Morrison: That [song is] basically more the Old Testament version, but only twenty-first-century. There are other forces at work on the planet than what we probably know, but it's just stripping away the illusion – there aren't really any heroes. You're born, you live and you die, you know. [1997]

Though this was a theme upon which he would later elaborate on *Back On Top*'s 'Precious Time': 'It doesn't matter to which God you pray/precious time is slipping away', as early as 1994 he was telling certain people, 'I don't believe in myths any more.'

Jonn Savannah: The ultimate thing he's ended up with is his own creed, which after a long evening [of my] discussing it with him ended up very nihilistic. He doesn't believe in anything. He was just saying, 'It's all bleak, you're born, you live, you die.' That would be five, six years back.

Savannah was one of the few musicians to whom Morrison confided his bleak view. But then the yearning spirit of the eighties was long gone. For Mick Brown, who came across his old coffee-time partner in 1997, their reacquaintance resulted in 'a rather odd, disjointed conversation. I said to him, "Are you still interested in Alice Bailey? Remember we used to have those fantastic conversations about [that] stuff." And he said, "I haven't got anybody to talk about that stuff any more. Musicians don't know about that." [But then] he was always rather contemptuous of his sidemen . . . or [felt] rather divorced from them in terms of his interests.' By the year 2000 Linda Gail Lewis witnessed someone whom 'no one debates with. It's not allowed. Every person that Van's got around him is a yes-person . . . Michelle argues with him sometimes . . . but if she sees he's getting mad, then she'll drop it.'

Bailey's work made a surprising reappearance on *The Healing Game*, in a song called 'The Burning Ground' – the place between the threshold and the door where those burdened meet the Angel, the site of the final purification. A potentially important song about a man still caught half-way between heaven and hell, the album version suffers from a rather nondescript tune and a truly embarrassing spoken bridge about dumping the jute.

Morrison's skewed world-view would take an even more disturbing turn on *Back On Top*, his 1999 claim upon an album-buying constituency. Another record that seemed to be all things to all critics, panned and praised in equal measure, it contained a single flawless jewel, 'High Summer', which Gavin Martin in *Uncut* recognized as 'the most fascinating manifestation of Lucifer in modern blues lore'. 'High Summer' also suggested that Morrison had reached that place where – having rejected the faith he had known as a child and flirted with as an adult – he was open again to the arcane. This time, though, his fascination lighted upon the prince of the power of the air.

On the one occasion it was introduced in concert, Morrison described 'High Summer' as 'a song about what made Christianity famous'. And yet it is to his own constructed mythology that he turns at the song's outset, referencing 'Cyprus Avenue' in the first line and 'Who Drove the Red Sports Car?' in the second: 'By the mansion on the hillside/ Red sports car comes driving down the road . . .' Having admitted, at the time of *The Healing Game*, that 'there [are] songs I've written . . . that go back to other things I've done before', he was again juggling a number of 'common threads'.

Only when the chorus comes around, though, does Morrison's intent become clear: 'And they shut him out of paradise/Called him Lucifer and frowned/She took pride in what God made him/Even before the angels shot him down to the ground'. Identifying with a Promethean Lucifer, Morrison depicted himself as someone to whom heaven had been/would be denied. The fact that 'she' was able to take pride in her man despite the misdeeds which 'shut him out of paradise' seemed to be the only thing that kept him going. What prompted him to go down such a scary path was unclear, but in conversations with his next singing partner it became plain that his apostasy was real.

Linda Gail Lewis: He's experimenting with this Church of Satan thing . . . He asked me to do a ritual with him and I said, 'Honey, I grew up in the Pentecostal Church. I've seen people with demons in them, and I wouldn't go anywhere near anything like that. I'd be scared to death.' We did have a long conversation about it . . . I don't like the sentiment of ['High Summer']. I didn't like to even play piano and sing on it. He decided that there's no such thing as God or Jesus – that there's only one spirit, and it's Satan. But that's a contradiction 'cause then he writes in the song about how he was cast out of heaven.

The almost Faustian aspect of 'High Summer' gave clear evidence that the visions still came, even if he remained increasingly fearful of welcoming them in. Indeed it seemed that he was now looking for a way to turn off those voices. Perhaps he had decided to take the advice that New York singer-songwriter Lou Reed had proffered back in 1996, and to which Morrison referred at those notorious Supper Club shows:

I said, 'Lou, all this stuff is going on . . . all these noises, voices in my head all the time.' So he gave me . . . the real rap . . . He says, 'You know what? When you hear the voice, ya just say that's not me . . . Just step back and say, "That's not really me . . . That's somebody else!"'

The voices took the hint and ceased to come. Morrison was now struck down by the worst case of writer's block he had suffered in twenty-five years.

28

1998–2001: At the Dark End of the Street

Since basing himself in the UK in 1980 with *Common One*, [Morrison] has made eleven albums . . . which have, whatever their other characteristics, exhibited a lack of ambition unparalleled among his contemporaries . . . There ought to be something endearing about a musician this unmoved by the gales of grunge or tides of trance. But the sad fact is that the last five Van Morrison records have lain back on the slab and pretty much defied anyone to get excited about them.

—*David Hepworth, reviewing* **The Healing Game** *in* **Mojo**.

Somewhere in the mid-eighties the poet/philosopher accolades seem to have seeped into his skull and he began churning out same-sounding albums on an almost annual basis. Musically, they were largely sub-Mantovani mush, while the lyrics resembled the work of chimpanzees cutting up extracts from Yeats, Hopkins, Blake and Donne, then pasting the resulting mess to the side of a bus shelter.

—*George Byrne, reviewing* **Back on Top** *in the* **Irish Independent**.

The critical tide turned with *The Healing Game*, prompting a suitably petulant artist to ask rhetorically, '[Since] my most recent stuff is much, much better . . . why [do] people keep going back to . . . the really old stuff?' Morrison answered the question himself the following June when he issued a two-CD, thirty-track collection that had more genuinely great Morrison music per CD than any of the last half a dozen releases. However, the collection served only to reinforce the critics' suspicions, for it was an archival set of previously unreleased recordings spanning the years 1970 to 1988.

The Philosopher's Stone Volume One had originally been scheduled for release in July 1996. When it was finally released two years late(r), it had been marginally reconfigured,★ and had lost the song-commentary that Morrison had originally planned to include, but was otherwise intact. In those original notes, Morrison spoke of how he hoped that this would be the start of an ongoing series illustrating the evolution of his music (hence *Volume One*), and of how he would have preferred to include different takes of the same songs, back to back, but practicalities had taken over. That said, the four alternative versions of previously released songs were among the most revealing recordings on the set: 'Wonderful Remark', 'The Street Only Knew Your Name', 'Joyous Sound' and 'Real Real Gone' were all in fact earlier incarnations. As to why some of these songs should have mouldered in vaults all these years whilst 'Almost Independence Day', 'Autumn Song' and 'Heavy Connection' had not, Morrison seemed to be as nonplussed as the rest of us.

Van Morrison: It's hard to work out why you didn't put something out at the time. Usually it felt like it didn't fit . . . When I was with Warner Brothers they were very minimalist. [1997]

What was truly perplexing about the collection's belated release was the lack of fanfare and its surprisingly muted presentation – something noted by Scott E. Thomas in the Morrison 'zine *Wavelength*: 'Everything about *The Philosopher's Stone*, from its format to its packaging to its song selection, seems designed to divorce the tracks from their historical milieu . . . When we open the package, there are no essays, no interviews, no archival photos – just lyrics (often incorrectly transcribed) and credits which include the year of the session.' The credits also contain their fair share of errors, with much of the first disc misdated.

In the era of lavish boxed sets, such an uninformative artefact was almost bound to pass unnoticed. Subsequent volumes have singularly failed to appear, even though Morrison has begun to use the bonus tracks on his CD singles to reveal a few more hidden crevices of his art. 'Tell Me about Your Love', a *Hard Nose* out-take composed even earlier, was a bonus track on the 'Back on Top' single, whilst 'The Healing Game'

★ Three songs were deleted from the original version – 'When I Deliver', 'I'm Ready' and 'John Brown's Body' – to be replaced by 'The Street Only Knew Your Name', 'Western Plain' and 'Joyous Sound'.

CD single revealed another superior album out-take, the intoxicating 'Celtic Spring'.

What caught most fans by surprise was Morrison's willingness to reconnect with these 'old' songs in concert, and to promote what was an archival release with performances of these lost songs that were more vital than those reserved for the last album. Perhaps it was simply a question of trying these songs on again, to figure out if they still fit. As he informed an audience during a performance of 'And the Healing Has Begun' the following year, 'Some of this stuff works, and some of it doesn't – as you've probably noticed. I've written over 250 songs and sometimes I do songs from way back when that used to work then, so we'll try it again and see what happens.' So whilst the likes of 'Drumshanbo Hustle' and 'Western Plains' were débuted and dropped that June, 'Mr Thomas', 'Naked in the Jungle', 'Crazy Jane on God' and an edgy 'I Have Finally Come to Realize' saw out the summer at what was soon to become an annual double-header at the International Festival of Literature at Ross-on-Wye.

These shows, and the twin gigs held at Hay-on-Wye in May, again afforded Morrison an environment where the audience would not 'assume it's going to be a commercial show . . . [which] it very rarely is. It's predominantly an introverted musical experience, more esoteric than people expect.' This was certainly the case at the 1998 shows, where Morrison pulled a number of surprises on the band, including Hoagy Carmichael's 'Georgia on My Mind' and Sam Cooke's 'A Change Is Gonna Come'. But then, as drummer Geoff Dunn soon realized, 'sometimes Van preferred me to not even know some of the stuff, and to just react to what he was doing . . . He wants your first musical instinct. He wants you to be creating something different for him [from] night to night.' With the likes of Dunn, Pee Wee Ellis, MD Johnny Scott and keyboardist Jonn Savannah having paid more than their fair share of dues with the man, such unpredictability became the only way to retain the possibility of 'enchantment'.

Van Morrison: The odd time something happens and you go into some kind of enchantment [on stage]. But you have to work very hard to get that. Most of the time you're just playing and singing the songs, and there's no guarantee that you are going to get anywhere . . . I think I'm at that stage that I'm doing it simply 'cause that's what one does . . . You're just back to square one, you're just standing up there singing. [2000]

Needless to say, Morrison still occasionally found a way to let off steam at his musicians' expense. After a joint European tour with Dylan had been cancelled the previous summer owing to Dylan's hospitalization in May with histoplasmosis, the idea was mooted again for the summer of 1998. As the tour came hard on the heels of a triple-header with both Dylan *and* Joni Mitchell in the States, the format for the performances was well defined, with Dylan and Morrison alternating as headliner until the final night of the tour, at Wembley Arena, where Dylan was scheduled to open. Unbeknownst to Morrison, though, the front ten rows of the front block had been allocated to subscribers of a Dylan fanzine, and when his set ended many of them, rather than experience what Morrison had to offer, simply left. As a result, when Morrison came on stage he found himself playing to a largely empty front block. Visibly unamused, he was soon looking for someone to steam into, and guitarist Johnny Scott drew the short straw:

Jonn Savannah: I've seen him [really] berate people . . . The one that really fried me, and that I think illustrates Van's lack of interest in ponce and ceremony, [was] at Wembley Arena . . . We're piling through something and he went over to Johnny Scott and said, 'Play funky,' and Johnny is not a funky player, so he plays something which is definitely not funky, and Johnny's whole family's sitting in the audience, and Van's looking at him, on-mike. 'That's not funky. That's not it. You don't have it.' I don't think it was a question of making this person feel small, but then he turns over to me and says, 'OK, you play funky.' [Well,] I [was] as funky as I could fucking be. 'Now that's funky!' This was all on-mike. And Johnny was mortified.

The set soon built up its own head of steam, culminating in a version of Dylan's 'Just Like a Woman' that put the lukewarm set his mentor had just offered to shame. Indeed, the way that Morrison rose to the artistic challenge of this joint tour with consistently inventive set-lists – a genuine balance of the familiar and the esoteric – pushed the more aware fans attending (largely for Dylan) to consider seriously who was more in touch with his performing self. Those for whom this was too close to the bone took their leave at Wembley. Those who stayed witnessed perhaps Morrison's most sympathetic band of the nineties pulling out every stop. Once again, when the man was released from an obligation to promote product, the sets took on a life of their own. Even the introduction of the *Back on Top* material in February 1999 failed to disturb this band's equilibrium. For this reason alone, it could never last. After aspiring to create the most professional, malleable, musical band he could find, Morrison decided to scrub it all and start again.

Jonn Savannah: He polarizes, with everything in life. It's all on, full-on religion, all or nothing. He's very black-and-white in things that he does. So I guess if he's had what some people would consider the best band he could possibly have, what's the point in doing that again?

The first clue that he was seeking to explore some roots again came in November 1998, when he played two nights at the Whitla Hall in Belfast in the company of Lonnie Donegan and Chris Barber. Billed on the concert tickets as the Skiffle Sessions, the shows were divided into two sets, the first of which was a forty-five-minute résumé of that fleeting fifties genre, with Lonnie Donegan providing the context on a handful of songs before Morrison lost himself on 'The Outskirts of Town', knowing he was 'Alabamy Bound', but still feeling 'Dead or Alive'. As an impromptu expression of former dependency it was a generous gesture. When the skiffle set became Morrison's next-but-one CD, it became fixed in time and failed to stand up. Colin Irwin, in *Folk Roots*, expressed serious reservations about the released artefact:

Songs like 'Worried Man', 'Don't You Rock Me Daddy-O', 'Midnight Special' and 'I Wanna Go Home' may indeed have been the staple diet of the skiffle boom (which was all done and dusted inside a year) but Van comes in bursting with his soul and jazz baggage and his hotshot band, drags in Dr John for good measure, with the result that we get the most expensive, polished skiffle band in history. Which kinda defeats the object of it really. You keep looking around wondering when Paddy Moloney's coming in . . . Those hapless skiffle bands of the '50s are easily forgiven their cheerfully shallow treatment of American blues. They and we knew no better, and they served a vital function in popularizing a music that had little voice in Britain before. But it's a different world now and there's no excuse for not unearthing the original blues and American folk artists who did this stuff for real.

In fact, Morrison was simply fulfilling an earlier wish. As far back as 1977 he had talked to Dr John about recording an album of blues and skiffle music '[be]cause I started off in a skiffle group and there must be millions of other musicians who also began their careers playing that kind of music, and I feel that there's still something to be gotten out of it'. He had certainly gone to great pains to court Donegan, going to see him perform at the King's Hotel and inviting him to dinner the next day. As Donegan recalls, 'He was talking about the old days and Lead Belly and Woody Guthrie, and he was obviously deeply into it . . . I met him a second time at the Ivor Novello Awards . . . It was a fabulous knees-up and we all had a few bevvies . . . Then he tackled me again about making an album. We [even] recorded a couple of tracks in a little barn-type studio in Reading.'* Thanks to Morrison's prodding, Donegan was able to issue his first studio album in nearly twenty years, but Morrison still felt he had not fully repaid a debt he readily acknowledged:

Van Morrison: [I] couldn't believe my luck when Donegan came out and was doing it. I was just a kid and just sort of bandwagoned that one. For everyone who was into music, skiffle was *it* at that period. His influence was massive. He kind of got the ball rolling for me. He made it possible for me to have a group. [2000]

It is unlikely that Morrison's new record label felt it quite such an honour to be allowed to issue *The Skiffle Sessions*, which appeared in the shops in January 2000, ten months after *Back On Top* had briefly entered the Top Ten. Morrison had finally taken his leave of PolyGram, after a twenty-five-year association, and had signed to Virgin on an album-by-album basis (legend has it that certain folk at PolyGram threw a party at the news of his departure, such was their sense of loss). Virgin, though, must have been very happy with the sales of *Back On Top*, particularly in the US, where Morrison was again selling units in notable numbers. What they weren't to know was that his next two albums would entirely reflect their difficult new artist's musical roots.

The Skiffle Sessions was treated by many fans as another non-essential release, despite some genuinely lucid sleeve notes from Morrison and a press drive ably supported by a garrulous Donegan. Morrison's own ideas for promotion extended to an occasional 'Muleskinner Blues' or 'Alabamy Bound' in concert, and inviting Donegan on stage at shows in Las Vegas and York for an appropriate musical interlude.

Meanwhile Morrison refrained from giving Virgin any real indication

---

* The two songs, 'Muleskinner Blues' and 'Alabamy Bound', would appear on Donegan's solo album *Muleskinner Blues* in January 1999.

of when or if he might have another set of his own songs to slot into their schedule. The shows that lasted through the early months of 1999 gave only a couple of clues: one promising – the beautifully understated 'Fast Train', which he performed at a handful of shows; the other not – 'Talk Is Cheap' displaying a command of the language, and a mind-set, no finer than the target he was seeking to lampoon, the tabloid press. What he wasn't about to admit was that his pen had simply run dry.

Linda Gail Lewis: Van was just looking for projects to do because he had writer's block. He had three songs – 'Two Way Pedro', 'Fast Train' and 'Sit Down Baby' – and he feels like he's got to have an album every year. He wouldn't just wait until he could write some songs. So he will do something with somebody else when he has writer's block. But rather than just admit that he has writer's block, he pretends to be interested in this [or that] artist or, like, 'I'm going back to my roots.' That's all bullshit. He's not going back to anything. He's only working with Lonnie Donegan, or the Rimshots, or me, because he thinks he has to have an album.

Morrison's ever-dependable touring band had seen the tide turn a number of times, but simply kept playing as if their lives depended on it whilst their boss decided what to do and when to do it. Despite reaching the stage where he was 'doing it simply 'cause that's what one does . . . standing up there singing', Morrison still seemed to enjoy an uncanny empathy with certain audiences. At the first British show of the new millennium, at the Oxford Apollo in early February 2000, he informed the paying punters, 'For those of you who prefer the early stuff, we will be playing some, but not much.' Almost immediately, out came 'Moondance', followed by 'Baby Please Don't Go' (on which ex-Pirates guitarist Mick Green was left to play rhythm) and 'Here Comes the Night'.

The night's highlight, though, was an 'It's All in the Game' that included the rant about how 'by the time solicitors get involved, it doesn't matter whose fault it is'. He might have been advised to remind himself of this truism the following year when he had a team of lawyers attempting to bury his next singing partner under a mountain of legal threats.

At this point, though, Morrison was still considering whether to release an album recorded the previous summer with a local pick-up band called the Rimshots. Another album of covers, this time from the country canon, here was another project he had been talking about since the early seventies. Though he had recorded a number of country covers for *Tupelo Honey* and *Saint Dominic's Preview*, he had rarely introduced any distinctly country material in concert in the nineties – that is, until May 1999 when he had pulled out Hank Williams's 'My Bucket's Got a Hole in It' at his annual booking at the Hay-on-Wye literary festival.

Immersing himself in the music of this childhood idol again, Morrison went and cut the likes of 'Your Cheatin' Heart' and 'You Win Again' with the Rimshots, before reprising the latter – along with 'Jambalaya' – at sessions held in the second week of April 2000, with the sister of Jerry Lee Lewis, Linda Gail Lewis, and a band of Welsh musicians with whom she had recently been playing, the Red Hot Pokers. If the Morrison–Lewis alliance began as another off-the-cuff experiment, it was one that Morrison quickly decided worked.

Linda Gail Lewis: I didn't think anything would come of that [first session]. When I got there and Walter told me he was gonna cut everything live on the floor, I said, 'Well, this is gonna be really fucked up.' But I was just having fun . . . We cut most of the songs [for the album] in one day – we did like eight songs in three hours. But we didn't have enough songs, and [so] we went back in . . . When we went in for the next recording session, Van was in a bad mood. He was fighting with somebody on the phone, but when we cut 'Baby, You Got What It Takes' his mood changed. We had great chemistry. I made him laugh and stuff . . . [But] he likes to cut everything live . . . I was supposed to be playing the piano, reading the lyrics, watching Van and singing – all in one live take. Everybody's feeding off each other and you've got all this energy and chemistry . . . Even the harmonica solos he did live, and he's cueing the band at the same time.

The April sessions must have gone well because by the time Linda returned to the UK at the end of May, for gigs of her own, Morrison was already trying to figure out how to turn the songs they'd cut into an album. Having finally accepted that staring at the tape wouldn't do it, he cut half a dozen more songs with Linda and the band. As a result, versions of 'Singing the Blues', 'Be Bop A Lula', 'John Henry' and a Morrison original, 'Sit Down, Baby', from the April sessions were discarded, leaving just one original, 'No Way Pedro', to force itself on to an album of rockabilly, country and gutbucket blues. Morrison, though, still felt something was missing and – after débuting his new sound at a show in

Poole, Dorset, in early July – returned with Linda and the Red Hot Pokers to the Wool Hall to record John Lee Hooker's 'Boogie Chillun'. As Linda recalls, 'Van decided he wanted it on the album, 'cause we did it live and he thought it was good.' At the same session they also ran down Ray Charles's 'Sticks and Stones', which apparently came out well but didn't seem to fit. Prior to Poole, Linda remained unsure what Morrison intended to do with the tapes.

Linda Gail Lewis: [One day] he invites me to come over to his office near his home in Bath for tea. He said, 'We've got to do a live gig and see if this will work. I can't release the album if we can't work live together.' We're about five songs into our set at this place in Dorset when he announces that we have an album coming out. I found out when everybody else did.

After a nervy show in Poole, the next show for Linda and the Red Hot Pokers was another two weeks away. However, Morrison had not entirely discarded his own band, who were booked to play two shows at Crathes Castle in Scotland, the second of which – the penultimate gig of this band – caught him in a surprisingly cooperative mood as he delivered 'Domino', 'Jackie Wilson Said', 'Brown Eyed Girl', 'Baby Please Don't Go', 'Moondance', 'Gloria' and a mid-tempo rendition of his first-ever single, 'Don't Start Crying Now'. Following his reinvention of himself as the consummate crowd-pleaser, it was time for the more perverse artist inside to reassert himself. Five days later Morrison booked himself into an intimate all-standing venue in Cardiff, the Coal Exchange, which over the past three years had become his replacement for the King's Hotel.

In its own way, the first Red Hot Pokers Coal Exchange show offered greater highs and deeper depths than any Van Morrison performance in living memory, setting the template for his most controversial year of touring in twenty-five years. Standing at the very lip of the tiny stage, without the shades that had been *de rigueur* for a decade, Morrison looked as nervous as his band when he joined Linda and the boys on 'Jambalaya', down into 'You Win Again', before pulling away with 'Old Black Joe'. All well and good – until, that is, he attempted to lead his new pub band through a 'Vanlose Stairway' that turned into a Trans Euro train-wreck.

So the pattern was set – rambunctious rockabilly confidently dispatched, Morrison's own music mutilated or massacred. 'Have I Told You Lately' by its end was a charred ember. On the other hand, when

Linda and Van swooped and soared through a couple of Webb Pierce heartache hits, 'There Stands the Glass' and 'More and More', the appeal of the alliance was apparent. Likewise, an encore of 'Whole Lot of Shakin' Goin' On' and 'Boogie Chillun' suited the band just fine. But Morrison refused to accept his new band's limitations, continuing to jam square pegs in concentric holes.

John Altman: [Sometimes] Van gets hold of somebody who's fantastic for what they do, and really digs them, and then suddenly decides to try and change them into something else which they can't do – and then gets angry with them.

Though the Red Hot Pokers were very much presented as part of the Linda Gail Lewis package, they were no such thing. Linda insists, 'they weren't really my band. I'd played with them one time [but guitarist] Ned [Edwards]'s best friend is "Mac" McIlroy, and Mac got 'em to play with me at the King's Hotel. Mac pushed that whole thing because he wanted to get his friend a job, basically.' In Morrison's mind, perhaps the Pokers were the showband he never led – they certainly dressed like it. However, in September, he was reminded that they were no such thing, the Monarchs re-forming for one night as part of a subsequently abandoned Morrison documentary.

Billy McAllen: He usually stays down at the Crawfordsburn Inn. They just had this room and cameras set up, but after a while . . . we just sat down and started to talk about old songs and old numbers we used to do and got the guitars out . . . We brought [out] a few acoustic guitars and we just messed about doing some of the old skiffle stuff, some of the stuff we used to do in the old Monarchs. The second part of the film that we would be in was gonna be an eight-, nine-piece band with Van, and we were gonna have to rehearse for two days and we would be putting on a show with all the local guys . . . [But] wee Van was in really good form that night, he really enjoyed it. I disappeared about half-past twelve but Roy told me that they sat there [until] half-past five in the morning, George Jones, Van and Roy [Kane].

Meanwhile, the Red Hot Pokers were coming in for some grief in the press, as fans and critics alike reacted angrily to being used as human guinea-pigs in a series of rehearsals to paying punters. The lack of warning at early shows, which were billed as simply 'Van Morrison' or the equally vague 'Plus Guests', made for a number of uncomfortable evenings. At

Torquay in early August, even Morrison seemed on the verge of admitting defeat as he cut short another hopeless 'Vanlose Stairway' with a
peremptory chop of the hand. Come September, and the release of *You
Win Again*, even the 'quality' dailies were on his back, as illustrated by
Dave Simpson's review of a show for the *Guardian*:

'It's not the Van Morrison we know and love,' sighs a veteran of many
campaigns, heading off towards the bar. Like Bob Dylan's long-suffering fans,
Morrison-watchers have begun to resemble the folk who gather at Loch Ness
waiting for a glimpse of something mysterious and mythical: in this case, the
Celtic rock colossus who gave us the band Them and classic solo albums such as
Astral Weeks and *Moondance*. After years spent crafting his distinctive sound, Van
the Man seems to have put it on hold as he reaffirms his roots. First there was *The
Skiffle Sessions — Live in Belfast* album (thanks Van, but really) and now he is further
exploring the music he listened to as a boy: rock & roll and country. Having
contributed so much to pop culture, perhaps Van has to return to zero to plan his
next move, or just remain interested. But the faithful are not impressed.

After a less than esoteric double-header at Ross-on-Wye at the end
of August, Morrison brought back Leo Green on tenor sax, to bolster
the band and help with the arrangements. Though the shows began to
improve, Morrison still couldn't resist tossing his pub band an occasional
'And the Healing Has Begun', 'Irish Heartbeat' or 'Wonderful Remark'
to pour water on drowning men. And yet, when on 3 October 2000
Morrison finally began work on *Back On Top*'s true successor, it was the
Red Hot Pokers who joined him at the Wool Hall to record three songs
he had written in a matter of days.

Following a show in Glasgow at the end of September, Morrison
admitted to Linda that he had been suffering from writer's block for
some time. Both 'Fast Train' and 'Talk Is Cheap' were already old songs,
and he felt at a loss. However, feelings he had not expressed in a long
time finally released him from this limbo, sparking the rather beautiful
'Meet Me in the Indian Summer'. Written in the present tense, this was
a seduction in song addressed to a woman he needs to have and hold 'to
keep from going wrong'. Wrapped in a beguilingly sensual melody, it
exuded a sincerity lacking in recent so-called love songs.

'Meet Me in the Indian Summer' was recorded along with 'Hey Mr
DJ' and 'The Beauty of the Days Gone By' at the 3 October 2000 session.
Though it was another two days before Morrison asked Linda to add the

piano fills that made the songs complete, she attended the original session at Morrison's request. Indeed she has fond memories of that whole time period: 'We were having an Indian summer in England that October, and it was beautiful.'

By the time they returned to the Wool Hall in the third week of October to redo all three songs, Morrison had more material he wanted to record. 'Choppin' Wood' was a song shot through with real affection, applying a real precision in depicting the life of forbearance his dear departed dad endured. Such was the ease with which the songs were coming again that before they had finished the weekend session, he had another one penned and ready to record.

Linda Gail Lewis: We came back in [to the studio] again and he wanted to cut 'Choppin' Wood' and . . . [to do] 'Meet Me in the Indian Summer' and 'The Beauty of the Days Gone By' over again . . . We were just supposed to go in and do that one day, [but] then we had to stay another day and then another day. . . . He had left early the night before [last] to go to a gig with 'Mac' in Cardiff . . . and while he was in the car he wrote 'For a While', while he was in a traffic jam. So we thought we were through. We're sitting up in the control room with [the engineer] Walter [Samuel], and Walter said, 'Where's Van?', so Walter turned the monitor on – 'cause the studio's downstairs and the control room is upstairs – and there was Van out in the studio with his guitar. And then [the technician] comes running and says, 'Van wants everybody back down in the studio right now.' So we got down there and Van said, 'I got this song.' . . . He didn't even run it [down] for us, we just cut it. He just started singing and playing, and we started with him.

'For a While' would ultimately be consigned to the canon of lost songs, despite being recorded on at least one more occasion by Morrison. On the face of it, the subject matter seemed disconcertingly autobiographical. A ditty of the 'so long, good luck and goodbye' variety, it spoke of a stop-start relationship that had never entirely maintained an even keel. In conversation with Linda Gail Lewis at the time, Morrison suggested that his girlfriend, Michelle Rocca, had taken the song personally, something he perhaps feared that certain critics might too.

Linda Gail Lewis: It was a couple of days later, when we were talking about songwriting, that he told me about Michelle being mad at him [about 'For a While'] . . . I talked to him a lot about songwriting. I said to him, 'Isn't it great

[that] you were able to write 'For a While' just the other night?' . . . He said, 'Well, you know when you live with these women, every time you write a song, they think you're writing it about them.'

After another year of tabloid speculation about when the pair might be getting married, Rocca was no closer to getting her ring, and perhaps the strain was telling on them both. At a show that spring in Llandudno, Morrison had performed a particularly intense 'It's All in the Game', embellishing his usual command to 'meet me down the river' with a suggestion that 'somebody's going in there, but it's not me'. When he came to the 'you know what they're talking about' coda, further doubts crept in: 'On second thoughts, maybe you don't know. Finally, it's clicked. You really don't know. What a relief!' – The Rocca–Morrison relationship certainly seemed a strangely impersonal one to Linda Gail Lewis, from the outside looking in:

Linda Gail Lewis: He never show[ed] her any kind of affection, that I've ever seen. When I started working with him in the studio, they were having a horrible fight then. She said she was leaving him and stuff, and he said good riddance . . . He['d] be talking about this late at night when we're sitting there drinking. That's when he wrote that song, 'Sit Down, Baby' [which was recorded at the *You Win Again* sessions].

Refusing to match Morrison drink for drink, Rocca was often made to feel as if she was excluded from some exclusive club. Linda Gail Lewis recalls how in Las Vegas at the turn of the year 'they finally had to close [the bar], so Van just ignores Michelle and turns round to me and says, "Well, you can just come to my room and we'll have a drink there."' Morrison's feelings about the purgatory of teetotaldom were perhaps most concisely expressed in an additional verse he duly improvised to the Louis Armstrong standard, 'When You're Smiling', at a handful of shows in 2001: 'When you're drinking, the whole world smiles with you . . . when you're sober, you bring on the rain/ Start drinking, get happy, my friend.' And yet Morrison's bouts of binge drinking were now subdivided by periods of abstinence, even though drink generally served to mask his spiteful side, save for a single occasion.

Linda Gail Lewis: He quit drinking right after Spain . . . He's not really a different person [when he drinks], [just] braver, more open. Van can be a nasty drunk at times, but not usually. He's a happy drunk, but I have seen him be a nasty drunk once.

That nasty drunk, though, was *really* nasty – the Jekyll-like Morrison few saw but no one forgot. It was the night of 17 December 2000, after a show in Basle that had been filmed by Swiss TV for later broadcast. Everyone was in a good mood, the evening having passed without incident. The shows had settled into a comfortable groove by now, Morrison meeting the Red Hot Pokers half-way. The Basle show actually featured rollicking good versions of 'Naked in the Jungle', 'The Outskirts of Town' and 'Have I Told You Lately', whilst Linda's opening performance of 'Dark End of the Street' came close to scaling the peak set by Linda Thompson's rendition back in 1975. This was the only time during their working relationship that Linda saw Morrison's dark side emerge, but it was a full-scale preview of what was to come.

Linda Gail Lewis: All I remember is, whatever we were talking about, I said, 'Van, it's been wonderful . . . but I can just walk away.' And he looked back at me and said, 'Oh really. Just like the song – walk away, Renée.' I said, 'Yeah, just like the song. I can do that. I can just walk away.' . . . And that's when he lost it: 'I'm gonna fix you! I'll get you! You'll never work again! I'll take everything away from you that I've ever given you!' Just really vicious. And it just crushed me. Because I'd never seen that side of him. And that's when he said, 'Don't fuck with me. I'm not a nice guy, Linda Gail. I am *not* a nice guy.' He wanted to make sure he got that point across to me . . . Until that moment I didn't know that he could ever be mean . . . So I just cried, tears just started rolling down my cheek, and I hated myself for that. And then Van was really cruel about it. He said, 'Have you got a problem with your hormones? Is that why you're crying?' Then he said, 'Get me a drink.' . . . And I thought, 'Well this is all gonna go bye-bye if I don't straighten my ass up real quick.'

The incident clearly continued to bother Morrison, and three days later, after perhaps the best Red Hot Pokers show to date, in Swindon, Wiltshire, he cleared the dressing room save for 'Mac' and Linda, and turned to her and said, 'Can you tell me what happened in Switzerland?'

Linda Gail Lewis: He was still concerned about the fight that we had. And I said, 'Van, to be honest with you, I was so drunk I don't know.' And he looked at me for just a second, didn't say anything, and then he threw his head back and just died laughing, and then he looked back at me and he said, 'No other woman in the world would admit that.'

Morrison and Linda Gail Lewis again ended up talking into the night, over another drip-feed of hotel booze. Morrison admitted that he was unhappy at the thought that he would be spending Christmas apart from his mother, with whom he had recently fallen out. According to Linda, 'He said she was arguing with him about something and it happened more than once, so he stopped speaking to her . . . She tries to call him, [but] he won't take her calls.' Linda Gail Lewis herself was returning to Nashville for Christmas, to spend it with her husband and family, but she sensed that Morrison felt he had nothing much to look forward to himself.

Ten days later the pair were reunited in Las Vegas, an appropriate place to see in the new millennium and kick off the American leg of the *You Win Again* tour. And initially the ebullient spirit of the autumn shows seemed to spill across the pond. Robert Hilburn's *LA Times* review of a show at the grandiloquent Wiltern Theater on 6 January adopted a tone of incredulity as he wrote, 'There were moments so unlikely during Van Morrison's concert at the Wiltern on Saturday that I was sure I was going to wake up with a start any minute. Get this: the notoriously eccentric and sometimes grouchy performer was having as much fun as the audience.' Little did Hilburn realize that he had witnessed the apotheosis of this unlikely association.

By the time the singers and their band had reached the windy city of Chicago three days later, everything had changed and Morrison was in Australia '84 mode. For reasons that Morrison alone knows and has never felt the need to explain, he no longer wanted Ms Gail Lewis within a country mile of him. One reviewer writing about the second show in Chicago for the fanzine *Wavelength* couldn't help but comment upon 'the shortness of the show . . . [as] for the second night in a row, Van did his just a job routine . . . He totally ignored Linda Gail Lewis, the band and the audience . . . showed no emotion . . . [and generally] looked like a man waiting for a bus . . . [Indeed] in the days that followed, there was a fair amount of controversy on the airwaves over Van's attitude.' The tour quickly began to derail visibly as he spent large portions of the shows with his back to a bemused Linda. If she was perplexed, so were the audiences.

Linda Gail Lewis: He was just in a horrible mood all the time . . . I think he expected me to stay there while he turned his back on me.

On their return to the UK Morrison decided to go back into the studio, a peculiar gesture given that he had already recorded an entire album of originals with some familiar faces during the first week of November 2000, after which he again brought in Linda to overdub her vocals and piano on every track but one. Though the results achieved with the Red Hot Pokers had evidently proved too tepid for his liking, he would never quite capture the spirit of their 'Indian Summer'.

Linda Gail Lewis: Van doesn't want to admit that he was wrong. 'Cause he decided that [the Red Hot Pokers] could play anything – [but] you can't make a silk purse out of a sow's ear. They can play rock & roll, that's what they play. That's what I play! . . . I suggested to him that he get his old band back . . . [and] he got David Hayes on bass, Bobby Irwin on drums. It was a secret for a while. He didn't want the band to know that he wasn't gonna use their recordings. Then he called me in and said, 'I cut all this again, and you got to do your piano tracks again.' . . . [On 'Indian Summer'] we tried overdubbing me [again] but it never sounded right. He had this thing that he didn't want another piano player on there. He even did a song ['Mama Don't Allow'] to feature me on piano.

The album Linda Gail's overdubs completed, provisionally entitled *Choppin' Wood*, might well have been greeted as a real return to form. At fifty minutes and a mere ten songs, it was an exercise in economy compared with a number of Morrison's nineties albums. Inviting the listener in with the catchy accessibility of 'Down the Road' (recorded originally for *Beautiful Vision*), 'Choppin' Wood' and 'Hey Mr DJ', it contained a charred centre that suggested 'High Summer' was merely an overture to some ongoing Faustian pact. 'Princess of the Darkness', 'Just Like Greta' (as in just like Garbo, he wants to be alone) and 'For a While' suggested that he was again staring into the darkness. At least he seemed to be prepared to give the listener a glimpse of life inside the goldfish bowl. With salvation seemingly hightailing into the distance on a discarded fast train, 'Meet Me in the Indian Summer' was a much-needed panacea that redeemed both album and artist, offering not only a truly touching end to the album but, in its Morrison–Lewis guise, a potential radio hit.

Morrison, though, was now seemingly prepared to jeopardize his own art to prove a point, as he began work on a largely reconfigured collection. Abandoning the sequence he had arrived at that autumn, he not only began to record a whole new series of songs without the input of Linda Gail Lewis, but rerecorded (her parts on) those songs where she had been so audibly in evidence. Persona non grata or what!

Linda Gail Lewis: He wrote some songs, and he wouldn't let me hear them. One of the last times I was at the Wool Hall, he was putting down new songs with the Pokers, just demoing them . . . It was . . . right before I gave my notice . . . He told Ned, 'Don't let Linda Gail come in here whilst we're recording these songs.' . . . [He] really hurt my feelings.

Sessions in the winter 2001 reworked the likes of 'Meet Me in the Indian Summer', 'Down the Road', 'Hey Mr DJ', and 'The Beauty of the Days Gone By', as well as introducing one of Morrison's most world-weary dirges, 'Man Has To Struggle', one of a number of songs now demoed without Linda. An attempt to requisition the vibe of 'That Lucky Ol' Sun' – a popular classic Morrison finally introduced into his own repertoire in the autumn of 2001 – 'Man Has To Struggle' had everything with which Ray Charles imbued that hymn, save its sense of ultimate salvation. As to who it is that 'by his nature [i]s never satisfied', who has to 'suppress his own desires . . . [and] keep them at bay', the subtext suggested for Man read Van. Quite what it was that he was afraid of, he was not about to say, and for Linda Gail Lewis any inclination to peer inside his empty mansion, stacked high with unopened boxes, had all but dissipated.

Sensing that the end was nigh, Linda chose to jump before she was pushed. Due to play Newcastle on 16 March, and with the following weekend off, she gave her notice. Morrison's reaction was as unpredictable as the man himself: 'During the week he had [his road manager] John Craig call me and start trying to butter me up, so I guess they were going to ask me to stay . . . he was like, "Well, you know Van wants you to be happy. He wants to know if you like where you are on the bandstand. He's gonna hire this organ player, but they're gonna put him in the back." I said, "That isn't necessary 'cause I'm going anyway." It was only maybe three, four days later that John Craig called me up [to] fire me, and I said, "You know what, just give him a message from me: if he wants to fire me, he ought to have the balls to call me himself."'

Linda Gail Lewis: So he called me up and cussed me out. He was screaming. Not yelling but screaming. I was afraid he would have a heart attack. I was saying everything I could to try calm him down but nothing worked. He called me . . . a bitch, a fucking cunt. I couldn't believe he was saying those things to me after he'd been so sweet . . . I'd seen him blow up [before], but he was screaming so loud I could hardly understand him . . . I said, 'Darling, I don't think you can fire me, 'cause I already quit,' and he said, '[Well,] I can keep you from getting any more money. I'm gonna fix it [so that] you won't get another dime from me' . . . And he did follow through with that . . . On [the following] Monday he had David Conroy ringing my bell to pick up the electric piano [he bought me], the tapes, the mobile phone that cost £39.

And yet somehow the portrait Linda paints of the Morrison she came to know manages to retain a tone of genuine pity mingling with the sorrow, anger and frustration – even after all the unpleasantness that has been allowed to follow on from her departure.

Linda Gail Lewis: I guess there's a real sensitive person in there somewhere . . . that's why it was so horrible when it just changed, without an explanation . . . When I tried to go nicely, then he exploded, which is so weird. When you start turning your back on somebody and you don't want them to be [there] any more, why would you get mad at them [for] going?

The *Choppin' Wood* ten-track platter was removed from the menu as Morrison discarded everything, fully realized or not, that had been taped in the year with Lewis. Somewhat surprisingly, he resurrected a pair of songs recorded in the months before Linda Gail Lewis crossed over from the dark end of the street (though he left behind something as good as 'At the Crossroads'). Winter 2000 recordings of the magnificent 'Fast Train', as well as the risible 'Talk Is Cheap', added filling to the American sandwich of an album Morrison finally completed to his satisfaction at the end of 2001. After numerous delays, he delivered to PolyGram – to whom he had returned in the interim – a fifteen-track meal and a half, sixty-seven minutes in all.

But *Down The Road* was no more than one more collection of Van Morrison songs, assembled in some kind of nominal order, neither chronological nor intuitive, and without any of the sense of pacing that its previous ten-track incarnation had retained. And without recourse to its former self, the majority of reviews were as unremitting as the album itself. Paul Du Noyer, in the music monthly *Mojo*, found the essence of that critical consensus: 'It's not only in comparison with Van's acknowledged masterworks – *Astral Weeks, Moondance* [&c.] – that *Down the Road* suffers. Even his less celebrated albums, from *A Sense of Wonder* to *Hymns to the Silence*, were always suffused with a spirit to nourish the soul. But it's hard to hear the fluttering of angels' wings on this record.'

Omitting those new songs bedevilled by the darkness removed a number of spectres, but the new songs/recordings – including a surprisingly lacklustre recording of that regular showstopper on recent tours, 'Georgia On My Mind' – were not merely similar as at times indistinguishable, movements in a maudlin suite of melancholia. If something was preying on his mind, it again showed up in his songs in a mean-spirited, self-absorbed way.

As Morrison pressed rewind, discarding songs that cast doubt on relationships past and present, the album suffered. Meanwhile Linda Gail Lewis seemed destined to become one more victim of Morrison's insistence on defining his history on his terms alone, being not only written out of Morrison's recording canon (*You Win Again* having been deleted barely a year after its release) but out of any contribution to the work that followed their initial collaboration.

Indeed, when it came to Morrison's attention that Ms Lewis had been interviewed for this very book, a letter from his Belfast solicitors was sent to a number of the larger British book distributors, asserting that the (as yet unfinished, sight unseen) biography contained 'a number of false allegations of an extremely serious defamatory nature' that was alleged to emanate from Ms Lewis.

When at least four newspapers published comments by Lewis about her time with Morrison, they found themselves on the receiving end of writs for libel. For Morrison, these legal actions involving Ms Lewis seem to have become another of his not-so-beautiful obsessions, clearly preying on his mind on a daily basis, distracting him from the calling that has made him a wealthy man. The shows have suffered, as has his art. None of the new songs recently débuted in concert – six of which appear on the man's latest collection, *Down the Road*, at the expense of the likes of 'For a While', 'Princess of Darkness' and 'Just Like Greta' – suggest a rampant muse riding roughshod over these legal distractions.

The reviewers of *Down the Road* have in most instances reflected a general despair at the lack of direction in the man's art, suggestive of a similar rootlessness in a life increasingly bereft of contentment. It seems that the melancholia that has haunted the man from the days before rock & roll has eaten away the will to rise above it all, which once inspired so many of his best songs. As it stands, the intellectual blindness that has resulted from this condition seems to have left George Ivan Morrison with little left to say in song, and nothing more life-affirming than, 'Don't fuck with me, I'm not a nice guy,' outside of them.

Epilogue:

It ain't why, why, why – it just is

We all move through the world surrounded by an atmosphere that is unique to us and by which we may be recognized as clearly as by our faces. Some of us, however, have thicker atmospheres than others, and a few of us have an atmosphere of such opacity that it hides us entirely from view – we seem to be nothing but our atmosphere.

—*Janet Malcolm,* **The Silent Woman**

His music may flow, but his ideas remain safely tucked away behind an invisible wall of self-defence. After all this time of listening to his records and memorizing every word – after all those long years of adulation – I didn't even like the guy.

—*Danny Holloway, 1972*

If Morrison's desire to communicate what *he* has to say is what has driven him to create, he has been less willing to receive transmissions, erecting 'an invisible wall of self-defence' when just a child. Later, as this social misfit struggled to be understood, he devised a language in song that could somehow convey what he was feeling. Here was a man whose social skills short-circuited some time back, forced to function in a world that operated along entirely unfamiliar lines.

Graham Blackburn: In general he lived in his own world. Wherever we would go, he would pay enough attention to know what was happening and go there, but he'd [for example] get out of a car and never shut the door.

Though Morrison has grown into a more articulate, functional figure, he is rarely comfortable in company, save when there is wine on the table and a gig behind him, when his willingness to converse still operates along internal lines. If a topic meets with his approval, and the company is suitably sympathetic, then he may peek above the parapet. As Donal Gallagher, brother of Rory, says, 'He's not inarticulate, it [just] takes him a while to open up.' Hence, presumably, why he so rarely opens up in interviews – and views those who seek to make him with genuine mistrust. He seemingly resents *anyone* who attempts to impose an agenda on conversation.

Gil Irvine: A lot of people still mistake his shyness for arrogance or rudeness. Anybody who knows Van Morrison [will agree that] you can talk to Van Morrison for hours about what he wants to talk about, but don't try to pigeon-hole him or [take] him into a line of debate that he doesn't want to go.

It is impossible to say at this remove how much of this inability to interact socially is a consequence of an ill-fitting fame and how much is down to those Morrison–Stitt genes. Even Gil Irvine, who has probably known the man longer than anyone save his direct family, cannot be definite about how much fame has affected him. His picture of the young George Ivan, though, does not seem greatly removed from an adult who, in the words of Chieftain Paddy Moloney, 'tends to shun intimacy . . . you feel that this conversation has to go on, but at one point he'll have to get away from it'. Though the natural response might be to view such a person as ill-mannered, many who know him well insist that he is just wired up differently.

John Altman: I was at his birthday party a couple of years ago and I finished a sentence and he turned round and walked away. Now I could go, 'Oh, that's offensive,' but he'd finished the conversation.

As a constant subtext to writing this book, I frequently mused about Morrison's level of awareness when his behaviour might be perceived as appalling, offensive or just plain mystifying. After all, when he 'threw a paddy' or generally misbehaved in a way only a rock star could, who would tell him that his behaviour was unacceptable? And how long would they last if they did? The adolescence that fame arrested was precisely the milieu in which Morrison began to feel he could act out with a certain impunity. As a single anecdote by Clive Culbertson suggests, it may simply not occur to him that there are consequences to every action, even for rock stars.

Clive Culbertson: [Back in 1988] he'd been in great form for the dates in Scotland, and a couple of dates in the north of England . . . It's been great. He hasn't been drinking, and we're standing waiting to go on stage [in Harrogate], and he walks down in the middle of us and he wheels on Dave Early: 'That thing you did in the middle of [such-and-such]. Don't you fucking do that tonight!' Then he shouted at me for something, then he shouted at Artie. [Finally he said,] 'You guys don't fucking get it together, I'll get a fucking new band.' Then we went on and did the show. And as we come off at the end of the night he stands and says to me, 'Band was a bit flat tonight. What happened?' I said, 'You chewed everybody out.' 'Ah, no, no, man. That's me getting a bit of steam off. That shouldn't affect anybody.'

At much the same time, in a rare moment of self-awareness, Morrison expressed what everyone else had been saying all along: 'For a long time . . . I didn't realize how important it is to actually explain what you're doing, so that it will be approached in the right way.' Any such explanations have always come hard to him. But then, according to Morrison the poetic champion, he is just 'trying to clear [my]self of these layers of experience, like peeling an onion, getting all that "stuff" off and being [my]self'. Having embraced such a surreal existence at such a tender age – coming from such a parochial background – he has led a life from which the most normal experiences have often been absent.

Jon Gershen: When I was in California [in 1972], he was doing a gig at a theatre . . . We drove into town and we went into a pancake house for a late lunch, and people were like pointing and saying, 'Look.' I'm thinking, 'My God! Has it gotten to that point?' He knew it was happening. Whatever his posture, I think he really likes that. And he was saying, 'I'm really bored. This whole thing sucks. I have to get up and play. Who needs it? Is this all there is?' The usual stuff. So I said, 'Let's do something.' I saw across the street a pool hall, [and] said, 'Let's play pool.' He didn't know the first thing about it. And he was like, 'This is *it*. This is what it's about.' And after the concert he kept talking about it: 'That was the most fun I've had in [so] long.' Because it was an authentic moment, it had no agenda. It also had that little delinquent quality.

Gershen here witnessed one of the constants in a long career – Morrison's claims that he never wanted this success to happen, the cry of every person who failed to see fame as a two-way street. The portrait of a man hopelessly caught by forces beyond his control is one that has become well established in recent years, and has given rise to an entire catalogue of lesser songs of the 'This Weight' variety. He seems genuinely unaware that few feel sorry for him in his predicament.

Van Morrison: When I was fifteen, I became a professional musician. I got involved with people and did certain things which led me to start making records and touring. And leaving Belfast and going to London and America, one thing led to another and I got caught up in the life that I'm living now . . . I was very young and I followed something. [1993]

Certainly the scars left by his tenacious ascent up the slippery slope are very real. Phil May of the Pretty Things recently related a conversation between the two of them in which Morrison said, '"You've gotta be the motherfucker of all motherfuckers." I say, "It's not in my nature, Van." He says, "No man. Be like me. Fuck 'em!"' His experiences with the Solomons, Bert Berns and, to a lesser extent, Bob Schwaid seem to have made him permanently distrustful. And yet, as his manager through the eighties, Paul Charles, testifies, 'When I started working with Van I was knocked out by how professional he was, and how his whole attitude to going about his business was so together . . . Van knows the music business, he knows the industry. Nobody takes Van . . . Van's been doing great deals on his own behalf for quite a few years now. Yes he's had managers, yes he's had advisers, but Van is the instigator. He learned the hard way, but he learned effectively.'

Perhaps so, but it clearly continues to eat away at him that Phil Solomon partially owns 'Gloria', that Ilene Berns should benefit from the continual airplay of 'Brown Eyed Girl', and that Warners still own the two albums he would most like to have for himself – *Astral Weeks* and *Moondance*. Even now, when the subject comes up, he is prone to blowing a fuse, though as journalist Mick Brown observes, a certain 'vulnerability doesn't lie too far below the surface. This carapace of outward hostility is what the world sees and what most people get, but I always felt there was a real kind of sweetness there.' Brown remembers one occasion when he and Morrison were 'having lunch with somebody [else] from the *Sunday Times* and he just started talking about going on

Top of the Pops with Them, and rather than it being a bitter diatribe about being used and abused, he was hilarious.' Two sides of the same coin.

Jonn Savannah: Part of it is healthy paranoia, and part of it is very unhealthy paranoia. He is a paranoid person. He is concerned that people are against him. He'll hang out with them, have a drink with them – but underneath that . . . if he can ever see an underlying agenda there . . . he has a very large scepticism: 'What's this person's angle?' He tests people all the time.

In Morrison's chosen business a degree of paranoia is undoubtedly necessary. His casual approach to making ends meet cost him dear in his twenties, and though he ultimately extricated himself from all the sharks and cut-throats, it took him a while to acquire the necessary toughness to twist the mind-benders back upon themselves. Jon Gershen suspects it may have been something he first acquired in 1969–70: 'There's the whole thing of what happens when you're exposed to the Albert Grossman/Dylan approach to dealing with people. I don't know whether Van began to learn about that when he moved to Woodstock . . . [but] it may be that he started to learn about those kinds of head-games from the masters,' i.e. the Band.

When, in 1989, Morrison spoke of how, 'if you don't have your act together, then you're not [typecast as] "difficult" – you're just ordinary Joe Blow, you'll take anything, there's no discernment about what you do', he was perhaps thinking about his earlier self. As he admitted to Desmond Hogan a couple of years earlier, 'If you're just dealing, say, on the creative level and not bothered about how things operate when you're dealing with hard-core facts of the business world, then you're sort of walking into walls.' It took Morrison a long time to stop doing this, and when he finally did, he found that any faith he had in human nature had all but vanished. He also began to treat those who worked for him, or with him, in an entirely different way from those who preferred life away from the fast train.

Mick Brown: I think the core problem with Van is that he always thinks, in the final analysis, that people are taking advantage of him on whatever kind of level. I think there is a fundamental kind of ontological distrust of his fellow man. Certainly my acquaintanceship with Van came to end at the point at which there was [any kind] of professional association. For as long as we were just going out and having cups of coffee, it was great . . . I was always very careful, when I knew him, not to be the journalist. The relationship was that we would meet and we would talk about different philosophical teachings, or music. It wasn't towards a work-in-progress . . . But the minute there became a professional dimension to it – and it was at his instigation, [*he* wanted] to do a TV programme – that's when it stopped.

Brown's experience was no isolated instance. Morrison's friendship with Jon Gershen was just one where they remained friends *because* neither played with the other on a professional basis. And yet, even here, Morrison couldn't resist asking Gershen to play guitar in a band he was putting together to promote *Street Choir*. It was Gershen who when 'it became clear to me it was not gelling . . . said to Van at one point, "I have to tell you this isn't for me." And that blew his mind. It was like no one would do that.' Clive Culbertson was another friend who was offered the option of becoming an employee, but at the expense of their friendship. But then gestures of friendship seem to make the man uncomfortable, as if they might somehow come back to haunt him.

Peter Van Hooke: He was very generous financially. He would give us good money for the tour, and all of a sudden a cheque would come and it'd be a tour bonus, maybe for the same amount again. Never mentioned it. [But] he'd never come up and say thanks . . . You never knew where you were with Van.

When his trusty road manager, Ed Fletcher, got himself mired in a serious substance-abuse problem in the mid-eighties, it was Morrison who 'stood by me and helped me out . . . I had to go to him and talk to him, [and] I went into treatment in '85 for drugs and alcohol. And Van . . . was there [for me], helped me financially, and visited me when I probably frightened quite a few people.' That shows a generosity of spirit that belies the man's reputation. And yet he has been quite adept at letting people into and steering people out of his life.

Peter Van Hooke: We were very close, and I'm not really sure what happened. Things just moved away. I had become very friendly with Herbie [Armstrong] . . . They brought back this other drummer to play. I think Van had thought, 'He's had his moment,' and he was probably right. After that, I didn't really get the call . . . With Van, it was always like, if you weren't in the band, you weren't asked to do the next gig . . . There was never any kind of retainer.

Morrison's relationship with Van Hooke had been one of the closest involving a musician with whom he worked, and yet when the professional relationship ended, so apparently did the friendship. Only that 'essential core of aloneness [that] could never be broken into', to which Janet Planet alluded in her notes to the *Street Choir* album, seems to endure, along with a compulsion to produce. And the two are inextricably entwined, as he admitted to an American reporter back in 1986: 'I'm compelled to do this. I don't really know why myself. I've been trying to understand it for twenty years. [Of course] it's a job, work, for one thing. [But] I just feel that I'm driven to do this.' Everything, it seems, stems from a burning desire to communicate, in a man for whom any act of communication is an enormous strain.

Jonn Savannah: He must have that work as a form of catharsis, [from] the amount that he writes, the amount that he gigs, the length of the gigs. It's got to be an essential element in his life. It is part and parcel of his existence. If he is not doing something in that area, he would explode . . . [And] he doesn't seem to have any particular interests in life apart from music-related things – apart from sitting and talking [about] shit and having a drink.

Music and 'talking [about] shit' remain Morrison's two primary channels for his communication skills, off kilter as they might be. But then, to introduce one of Nietzsche's pithy little sayings, 'Communication is possible only between equals.' Hence Morrison's continual attempts to get on the same wavelength as his archetypal audience. Sadly this audience exists only in his head. His relationship with his *actual* audience is ambivalent at best, even though his need to communicate through his art remains undeniably real. As publicist Victoria Clarke once put it to Morrison, if he doesn't care what people really think – as he told her twice he did not – how come he gets so upset when he reads things he doesn't like? For he certainly still gets upset.

Linda Gail Lewis: He still reads the reviews. He got upset about a guy that's a postman in London who writes a little-bitty column for *Fireball Mail*, [which] has a circulation of 890 worldwide. He wrote something bad about Van, and Van got really upset about that. He went on and on and on about that! . . . Van gets really upset when anybody writes anything about him, unless it's just something glowing. If it has any kind of criticism in it, or if it has anything about his personal life, he hates it . . . [But] he's always trying to prove something, with every performance, with every album . . . He really just wants to do his own [thing] all the time. He wants to be able to do any song in the world, and the audience to love and understand every song he does. I couldn't believe he had [stage fright]. After all these years, that's sad. How could he be that afraid? [But] he doesn't want people to know how he really feels . . . He wants to perform so bad, he's got to do it. He really has this great desire for everybody to appreciate what he does . . . He's a control freak, but he's controlled by his audience.

Perhaps the only documented time he let his guard down and gave the game away was in conversation with Ritchie Yorke in 1974, when he admitted that 'some people might think that I don't give a shit about the audience but the opposite is true. I think I care too much about what the audience thinks.' While he continually tests his audiences, he often rewards the more receptive ones. The challenge comes when he has to gauge the mood of the less receptive ones.

Certainly, second-guessing his audience when it comes to albums has done Morrison's art few favours. John Levesque, writing a reappraisal of *Veedon Fleece* in fanzine *Wavelength*, hit the ol' nail on the bonce when he wrote, '[Van] has produced his best work when he has abandoned all conscious considerations of the audience's expectations. Van's three finest albums share a benign disregard for the needs of the listener, and offer the listener the greatest rewards for precisely that reason. On *Astral Weeks*, *Veedon Fleece* and *No Guru, No Method, No Teacher*, Van is performing from a heightened sense of consciousness to which he aspires in much of his other work.' Though Levesque omits the more sublime parts of *Common One*, the sentiment holds good.

And yet Morrison's perception of those fans who *are* wholly committed is that they should be. Linda Gail Lewis informed the *Mail on Sunday* about one occasion when she 'was with him backstage when he asked his tour manager whether there was any way of stopping the fans from coming to every concert because they "unnerved" him'. The man seeks to deny the relevance of the 'star system', insisting that 'when I started and we played dances, you would finish a couple of songs and just walk through the audience. [There was] no stuff about being a star.' He certainly retains a real self-consciousness regarding his appearance, particularly as his frame has become bulkier and his hair has headed south. Perhaps he simply cannot equate this persona with his own fixed perception of what a star should be.

Jon Gershen: He was a total Elvis freak . . . it was like, 'This is it! This is the way it's done.' He had so much admiration for Elvis. There was such a conflict in this guy. He was immensely talented, but he felt short-changed in so many ways. [He liked] the idea that this guy could get up and command thousands of people, and have them screaming. He had an image in his mind of what the performer is about, what they're supposed to do, and every time he would compare himself to that, it didn't fit. Because he knew intuitively that he didn't have that [charisma]. He compensated for that with this whole routine of 'Ah, screw the audience.' I really think it was a psychological defence.

If there continues to be a side of Morrison that can play the entertainer, he also can't resist sending up that aspect of performance art. Thus a show that may include the primal fears of 'Madame George' can end with Morrison leading his band through 'When You're Smiling' or a risible 'Send in the Clowns'. The mood swings that are in the music, and can take a show from the kinetic intensity of a fifteen-minute 'Summertime in England' to the formless free-for-all of 'See Me Through' or – should his concentration be disturbed – take the music from a rare illumination straight back to vaudeville, clearly reside in the man. Barry Egan recently depicted him as just such a series of contradictions:

He can be rude and bad-tempered but the sway he holds over others is due not to his temper but to a sweetness that emanates from him unexpectedly, like perfume from a thorny rose. Once you get past the protective barriers – difficult admittedly – he will not stop talking. In a flurry of seemingly random ideas he'll eulogize Chet Baker, Nietzsche or Steiner . . . before ending up talking about the origins of religion, the Pope, UFOs and how he believes that when he dies, that's the end. Nothing but ashes. This was one night in the Berkeley Court after a concert. On another long night, this time in Galway, I sat mesmerized as he and Georgie Fame sat up through the night, drinking and talking about old jazz greats. The strange thing was that moments later it could be like you weren't talking to the same person. He had a way of making you feel like you were using him, just by being at the same table as him in a restaurant . . . Such apparent contradictions are the essence of Morrison.

However, the ability to discourse randomly on a number of discon-nected subjects does not a good person make, and Egan's tolerance of boorish behaviour may, like others', be coloured by an admiration for the man's art. In a later piece, he sought to suggest that, having 'been out with [Van] socially dozens of times . . . [I found that] like most people, he can be a wonderful, charming character one night and a curmudgeonly old bastard the next'. Egan may wish to imply that he surrounds himself with individuals who turn into 'a curmudgeonly old bastard' at the drop of a hat, but most of us do not. Morrison's moods remain the stuff of legends.

The fact that Morrison can alternate so easily, and the switch can come at any point, is genuinely disturbing. Or should be. He may not clinically qualify as a split personality, but there is a deep divide coursing straight through the middle of the man's soul. How the division manifests itself depends on the beholder. Clive Culbertson, who got to see Morrison as both employer and friend, describes him as 'either the most wonderful person or the most awful person, sometimes all in the one [night]'. Harvey Goldsmith concurs: 'You have to accept him for what he is. When he's on a good day, he's unbelievable, and when he's on a bad day he's just beyond awful.' Mick Cox depicts the man as 'a magician – there's no doubt about it – but . . . [also] an ordinary working-class Belfast yobo'. Linda Gail Lewis calls him 'a romantic – which is sad because he's so mean. It's sad when somebody can be that lovely, and then turn around and be [so] horrible.' A mass of contradictions.

In the end, the man is one walking dichotomy, and his art has always been a product of the disturbances in his psyche that these contradictions foster. Hence the heights he can hit, and the depths he can plummet. Though Morrison might prefer to think of himself as an Irish Blake, it is to William Wordsworth that he should perhaps look for a more apposite comparison. Like his eminent poet predecessor, his work defines both great and grim, and for similar reasons. Or as the Victorian poet J. K. Stephen, in parodying Wordsworth, put it:

> *Two voices are there: one is of the deep;*
> *It learns the storm cloud's thunderous melody,*
> *Now roars, now murmurs with the changing sea,*
> *Now bird-like pipes, now closes soft in sleep:*
> *And one is of an old half-witted sheep*
> *Which bleats articulate monotony*
> *And indicates that two and one are three,*
> *That grass is green, lakes damp, and mountains steep.*

Dramatis Personae

JOHN ALLAIR: California keyboardist who was a regular on albums and American tours from 1981 to 1986.

KEITH ALTHAM: An *NME* reporter when he first encountered Morrison as a member of Them in 1965, Altham went on to become one of the best-known publicists in the business, before working with Morrison again on the *Wavelength* tour in 1979.

JOHN ALTMAN: First met Morrison in 1974 at the behest of Peter Van Hooke. They stayed in contact throughout the seventies, culminating in Altman being chosen as musical director for two tours in 1979, before achieving acclaim as an arranger in his own right.

HERBIE ARMSTRONG: An old friend of Morrison's, who first crossed paths when they joined the Manhattan Showband together in the winter of 1964. Though Armstrong never joined Them, preferring to front his own band, the Wheels, he would feature prominently on a number of Morrison projects between *Wavelength* and *Beautiful Vision*.

JIM ARMSTRONG: Guitarist in the latterday Them, Armstrong has continued to work as a musician in the post-Van Them and, subsequently, in the Belfast Blues Band.

BROOKS ARTHUR: A legendary recording engineer whose home in the late sixties was Century Sound, Arthur was to engineer Morrison's various recordings with Berns, as well as *Astral Weeks*.

HARRY BAIRD: A member of Ulster showband the Regents.

RUBY BARD: A London agent who signed the International Monarchs and was responsible for arranging their trip to Germany.

PETER BARDENS: Keyboardist in a 1965 incarnation of Them, Bardens went on to work with Morrison on *Wavelength* and the subsequent American tour.

STEPHEN BARNCARD: Engineer on sessions for *Tupelo Honey*.

DEREK BELL: Pianist in the Chieftains and a devotee of the esoteric, Bell has known Morrison since 1979.

ERIC BELL: Guitarist in the post-Them combo Them Again, he would subsequently co-found Thin Lizzy.

JAY BERLINER: Renowned jazz guitarist whose contribution to *Astral Weeks* continues to provide inspiration.

ILENE BERNS: Widow of producer and record company mogul Bert Berns.

GRAHAM BLACKBURN: Played sax and flute for Morrison between *Astral Weeks* and *Moondance*.

ETHEL BLAKELY: A neighbour on Hyndford Street.

HERMAN BROOD: A Dutch musician who caught Morrison at the 1967 shows with Cuby and the Blizzards.

MICK BROWN: A journalist and writer, whose books include *The Spiritual Tourist*, he was befriended by Morrison after a 1983 press interview.

RICHIE BUCKLEY: A stalwart of Morrison's mid-nineties touring band.

PAUL CHARLES: First saw Them at the infamous Cookstown show, he would manage Morrison's business affairs in the years 1979 to 1988.

JIMMY CONLAN: One of the Three Js, who promoted Them at the Maritime.

KEVIN CONNEFF: A member of Irish folk combo, the Chieftains.

DONALL CORVIN: An Irish journalist known to most musicians in the sixties, Corvin was at one time touted as a possible Morrison biographer. He committed suicide in the late seventies.

PHIL COULTER: A musician and songwriter who, as an employee of Phil Solomon, worked with Morrison and Them on a number of sessions. They subsequently became fast friends.

MICK COX: Guitarist who first worked with Morrison in a 1967 combo, he later contributed to *Common One* and *Poetic Champions Compose*.

KENNY CRADDOCK: Was musical director and keyboardist in Morrison's mid-eighties European touring band. Died in a road accident in 2002.

STUART CROMIE: Worked with Peter Lloyd of Lloyd Sound, the Belfast demo studio where Them were first recorded.

CLIVE CULBERTSON: Introduced to Morrison via John Rogers in the early eighties, Culbertson remained friends with Morrison until 1988 when, after a year of playing bass in various line-ups, they parted ways.

RICHARD DAVIS: The legendary jazz bassist, and musical director on *Astral Weeks*.

ROD DEMICK: A neighbour in East Belfast.

JOHN DENSMORE: Drummer in the Doors, who shared a residency with Them at the Whisky in 1966.

PETER DOCHERTY: Road manager for Them.

DR JOHN: Renowned New Orleans jazz pianist who worked with Morrison on the 1977 album, *A Period of Transition*.

LONNIE DONEGAN: The king of skiffle, Donegan first recorded with Morrison in 1990. In 1998 they made the live *Skiffle Sessions* album together.

MARTIN DROVER: Versatile trumpeter who toured with Morrison through the mid to late eighties, working on *No Guru, No Method, No Teacher* and *Poetic Champions Compose*.

BILL DUNN: Played guitar in Morrison's early skiffle combo Midnight Special, before becoming a pastor.

GEOFF DUNN: Drummer in the mid-nineties touring bands, Dunn also plays on *Too Long in Exile*, *Days Like This* and *The Healing Game*.

PEE WEE ELLIS: Sax player in James Brown's JBs before working with Morrison on *Into the Music* in 1979; touring with Morrison and recording every album between 1979 and 1985; before returning to the fold in the mid-nineties to 'front' Morrison's touring band and work on *Days Like This*, *The Healing Game* and *Back on Top*.

B. P. FALLON: Irish photographer and writer.

GEORGIE FAME: A renowned solo artist in his own right, Fame first met Morrison at the Flamingo Club in 1963. They subsequently teamed up in 1989, touring in unison until 1991. Reunited with Van on a number of occasions over the last decade, Fame also proved a major sponsor of the *How Long Has This Been Going On?* and *Tell Me Something* albums, as well as contributing to most albums since *Avalon Sunset*.

ED FLETCHER: Morrison's American road manager from the early seventies to the mid-eighties.

MO FOSTER: Bassist in the short-lived quartet assembled to promote *A Period of Transition*.

LINDA GAIL LEWIS: Sister of Jerry Lee Lewis, and a solo artist in her own right, she first met Morrison at a convention in Wales in 1993. She was subsequently brought in to record an album of country-style duets, released in 2000 as *You Win Again*. A subsequent album she recorded with Morrison remains unreleased, though they toured together for nine months before a very public falling-out. Lewis continues to gig and record.

DONAL GALLAGHER: Brother of Rory Gallagher and executor of his estate.

RORY GALLAGHER: Legendary Irish blues guitarist who maintained a sporadic friendship with Morrison in the mid-eighties, after their first meeting in 1973. Gallagher died in June 1995 of complications resulting from a liver transplant.

JON GERSHEN: A member of Woodstock combo the Montgomeries, Gershen and his brother David remained close friends with Morrison throughout the period in Woodstock. The brothers subsequently recorded two albums with Jim Rooney as Borderline.

VIVIEN GOLDMAN: Punk journalist who interviewed Morrison for *Sounds* in 1977.

HARVEY GOLDSMITH: Concert promoter who briefly ventured into personal management, at Morrison's behest, in 1976, working with Morrison through *A Period of Transition*.

BILL GRAHAM: Infamous American concert promoter who took over managing Morrison from Harvey Goldsmith in 1977. Their association lasted into 1979. Died in a helicopter crash in 1991.

DAVEY HAMMOND: English teacher at Orangefield School for Boys as well as a folksinger of note.

BILLY HARRISON: Co-founder, guitarist and frontman of the Gamblers, who later evolved into Them. Harrison would leave Them in the summer of 1965 in acrimonious circumstances.

DAVID HAYES: Californian bassist, and perhaps Morrison's longest-standing musical collaborator, who first worked with him at the *Hard Nose the Highway* sessions and most recently worked on sessions for the *Down the Road* album in 2000 and 2001.

ALAN HENDERSON: Bassist in Them.

NICKY HORNE: Capital Radio DJ who interviewed Morrison in 1977.

'BOOTS' HOUSTON: Horn-player on the *Tupelo Honey* sessions.

GIL IRVINE: Childhood friend of Morrison's, with whom he founded his first skiffle band, the Sputniks.

GEORGE JONES: The frontman of the Monarchs.

PAUL JONES: Vocalist in Manfred Mann and the Blues Band, Jones has also become a radio personality and has interviewed Morrison on two occasions for the radio. He remains a willing proselytizer of his Christian beliefs, to Morrison *et al.*

ROY JONES: Drummer in Morrison's late-eighties touring bands, and on the *Poetic Champions Compose* and *Avalon Sunset* sessions.

ROY KANE: Drummer in the Monarchs.

CONNIE KAY: Drummer on the *Astral Weeks* sessions, who also subsequently worked on *Tupelo Honey*.

BRIAN KENNEDY: Maddeningly omnipresent backing vocalist at Morrison shows from 1994 to 1997 and on *Days Like This*, *The Healing Game* and *Back On Top*.

TOM KIELBANIA: Bassist in assorted Morrison combos in 1968–9.

PAT KYLE: Horn player in the 1979 touring band.

JEFF LABES: Keyboardist and arranger, Labes first worked with Morrison on *Moondance* and most recently on *No Guru, No Method, No Teacher*. In between he was responsible for arrangements for the Caledonia Soul Orchestra and for such important albums as *Veedon Fleece* and *Common One*.

ELLIOTT LANDY: Woodstock photographer who took the cover for the *Moondance* album.

MALCOLM LAZARUS: The organizer of the Secret Heart of Music conference in 1987, and a key member of the Wrekin Trust.

GEORGE LEE: Warners executive who brokered the deal that brought Morrison to the label (and its publishing company) in 1968.

SOLLY LIPSITZ: Owner of the Atlantic Record shop in Belfast, to which Morrison and his father regularly came in the fifties to buy their records.

MARTIN LLOYD: Brother of Peter Lloyd, see below.

PETER LLOYD: Owner of Lloyd Sound, the only recording studio in Belfast in the mid-sixties, to which Them came to record their first demo.

DONAL LUNNY: Member of Irish folk combo Moving Hearts.

GARY MALABAR: East coast drummer recruited for Morrison's studio band prior to *Moondance*. Relocating to the west coast, Malabar subsequently worked on the early seventies trilogy of Warners albums, fleetingly returning after his stint in the Steve Miller Band to work on 1982's *Beautiful Vision*.

GREIL MARCUS: Esteemed rock critic and writer whose *Rolling Stone* review of *Astral Weeks* first championed the album.

MARY MARTIN: Having worked for Dylan's manager Al Grossman in the sixties, Martin became Morrison's personal manager in 1970–71 before moving into A&R.

PHIL MAY: Frontman for British r&b combo the Pretty Things and an old friend of Morrison's.

BILLY MCALLEN: Guitarist in the Monarchs.

JACKIE MCAULEY: Keyboardist in various incarnations of Them.

HENRY MCCULLOUGH: Renowned Irish guitarist who first encountered Morrison in Dublin in 1966.

GEORGE MCDOWELL: An early employer of the teenage tearaway.

ARTY MCGLYNN: Guitarist who first worked with Morrison on *Inarticulate Speech of the Heart* and whose common roots helped establish a long-standing friendship. After touring with Morrison for much of the eighties, McGlynn last worked for the man on *Days Like This*.

GERRY MCKERVEY: One of the Three Js.

LEWIS MERENSTEIN: Producer of *Astral Weeks* and co-producer of *Moondance*, Merenstein has continued to work in the music industry as a jazz and pop producer as well as branching out into film soundtracks.

CHRIS MICHIE: American guitarist who worked with Morrison on the albums and many of the tours between 1981 and 1986.

RONNIE MILLINGS: Drummer in the original Them.

PADDY MOLONEY: Frontman for the Chieftains.

RONNIE MONTROSE: Guitarist on *Tupelo Honey*, Montrose went on to form his own band of the same name, which subsequently devolved into the Sammy Hagar Band.

SHANA MORRISON: Daughter of Janet and Van Morrison, and a singer in her own right, her latest album features two of her father's songs.

VIOLET MORRISON: Mother of George Ivan Morrison.

CHRIS O'DONNELL: Ex-manager of Thin Lizzy, and the man Morrison recruited to help market his records in the late eighties and early nineties.

ANDREW LOOG OLDHAM: Famed manager and producer of the Rolling Stones.

MO OSTIN: President of Warner Records for much of the period Morrison was on the label, and an early supporter of the artist.

JIMMY PAGE: Session guitarist on 'Baby Please Don't Go', who subsequently eked out a living with some band called Led Zeppelin.

JOHN PAYNE: Flautist and saxophonist in Morrison's 1968 three-piece, he subsequently got to play on the bulk of *Astral Weeks*.

STEPHEN PILLSTER: Manager to Morrison during the Caledonia Soul Orchestra era.

JANET PLANET: Née Janet Rigsbee, met Morrison in California in 1966. They married in 1968, and were divorced in 1973. In the interim, she would inspire many of Morrison's greatest songs, a debt Morrison has not always willingly owned up to.

JOHN PLATANIA: Woodstock guitarist who first worked with Morrison in the summer of 1969; Platania subsequently worked on *Moondance*, *Street Choir*, *Hard Nose the Highway* and toured with a number of Morrison bands, culminating in the Caledonia Soul Orchestra. Briefly returned to favour on *No Guru, No Method, No Teacher* and the US tour that directly followed its release.

MIKE RADFORD: Director of the *Van Morrison in Ireland* film documentary.

ROBBIE ROBERTSON: Guitarist-songwriter in the Band, Robertson first met Morrison in Woodstock; later organizing the *Last Waltz* concert in 1976;

and enjoining Morrison to contribute to the *King of Comedy* soundtrack album in 1982.

MICHELLE ROCCA: A former Miss Ireland, Rocca became Morrison's girl-friend in 1993–94. She is still 'on the scene' as I write, though they remain unmarried despite constant rumours of such an event.

CHRIS RYDER: Belfast pop journalist in the sixties.

KATE ST JOHN: A multi-instrumentalist who first worked with Morrison on *No Guru, No Method, No Teacher* before becoming a key component of the man's touring band in the late eighties/early nineties. Her last recordings with Morrison to date were on *Days Like This* as she has pursued her own solo career.

WALTER SAMUEL: Engineer at Morrison's Wool Hall Studios.

HILARY SANDERSON: Morrison's temporary landlady when visiting the Cots-wolds in the early eighties.

JONN SAVANNAH: Versatile keyboardist who was a regular in the mid-nineties touring bands, Savannah also worked on *Too Long in Exile* and *Days Like This*.

ELLIOTT SCHEINER: Engineer on *Moondance* and the initial *Street Choir* sessions.

BOB SCHWAID: Morrison's manager in the aftermath of Bang, Schwaid was subsequently replaced by Mary Martin.

TOMMY SCOTT: Producer of Them.

LEMMY SEGFIELD: London musician in the sixties, who later achieved notori-ety as the frontman of Motorhead.

DAUOD SHAW: First met Morrison in Woodstock in 1970, Shaw subsequently played drums in a number of bands up to 1974 as well as working on *Street Choir*, *Veedon Fleece* and various mid-seventies sessions. Shaw subsequently branched out into production, setting up his own studio in Philadelphia.

ALAN SKIDMORE: Jazz saxophonist and a member of the Blue Flames, Skid-more first worked with Morrison in 1990 on a one-off TV special, before touring in 1995 on the back of *How Long Has This Been Going On?*

JOE SMITH: Warners executive who played a large part in bringing Morrison to the label. Developed a good working relationship with Morrison until 1974, when they fell out over the 'non-promotion' of *Veedon Fleece*.

PENNIE SMITH: Well-known rock photographer.

WARREN SMITH, JNR: Percussionist on *Astral Weeks*.

MERVYN SOLOMON: Brother of Phil Solomon, and self-styled Belfast entrepre-neur who has taken credit for discovering Them.

PHIL SOLOMON: Manager of Them.

GEORDIE SPROULE: Belfast buddy of Morrison's, they played together briefly in 1964 in the Manhattan Showband.

TONY STEWART: *NME* journalist whose interview with Morrison in 1979 has passed into rocklore.

SHEL TALMY: Producer of the Kinks and the Who in the mid-sixties.

DAVID TAME: Author of *The Secret Power of Music*, a subject he discussed with Morrison in the eighties at a time when they shared the same interest.

TED TEMPLEMAN: Co-producer of *Tupelo Honey* and *Saint Dominic's Preview*.

STEVE TURNER: Esteemed writer and journalist, whose essay in *Too Late to Stop Now* remains a benchmark for Morrison biographers, Turner had enjoyed the occasional cup of coffee with Morrison in the mid to late eighties, which he drew on in his *Hungry for Heaven*.

PETE VAN HOOKE: Drummer in Morrison's tour bands from 1974 to 1983 and, as such, one of his longest-standing collaborators. Morrison also frequently stayed at the Van Hookes' when visiting London in this period.

JERRY WEXLER: Legendary Atlantic Records producer.

JOHN WILSON: Drummer in the latterday Them, and subsequently in Rory Gallagher's Taste.

PETE WINGFIELD: A member of the band that débuted at Montreux in 1974, before recording an album in Holland that would remain unreleased, Wingfield also toured the States with him in the autumn of 1974, and played on 1979's *Into the Music*.

ANTON WITKAMP: A&R guy at Phillips Records, who brought Morrison to Holland in the spring of 1967.

PETER WOLF: Frontman for the J. Geils Band, Wolf befriended Morrison in Boston in 1968. They have remained close ever since.

ERIC WRIXON: Keyboardist in the original Them.

BILL WYMAN: Rolling Stones bassist, with whom Morrison worked on his first solo album, *Stone Alone*, in 1975–6.

A Van Morrison Sessionography 1964–2001

This is an attempt to detail the various studio sessions of George Ivan Morrison, leaving aside those where he is clearly a guest artist, and to indicate which of the various official CDs, LPs, 45s etc. the recordings are available on. The sessionography does not in any way purport to be definitive, and where some piece of information is little more than an informed guess it is accompanied by its very own question-mark. Many, though by no means all, of the various outtakes indicated have appeared on bootleg CDs. The majority can be found on the first two volumes of *Gets His Chance to Wail* and the three-CD collection, *Genuine Philosopher's Stone*, all of which have been released by Scorpio and/or one of its hybrids. My especial thanks in the compilation of this sessionography go to 'Phast Phreddie' Patterson, Owen McFadden, Art Siegel, Simon Gee, Linda Gail Lewis and Jay Berliner.

Them

?11 June 1964 – Lloyd Sound Studio, Cromac Square, Belfast.
Producer: Peter Lloyd.
One, Two Brown Eyes. Stormy Monday. Don't Start Crying Now. Gloria. Hootchie Cootchie Man★.
★ – lead vocal Billy Harrison, Morrison harmonica.

5 July 1964 – Decca Studios, West Hampstead, London.
Producer: Dick Rowe.
{THE STORY OF THEM} One, Two Brown Eyes. Philosophy. Gloria. Don't Start Crying Now.
Outtakes: Groovin'. You Can't Judge a Book by Its Cover. Turn on Your Lovelight.

October 1964 – Decca Studios, West Hampstead, London.
Producer: Bert Berns.
{THE STORY OF THEM} Baby Please Don't Go. Here Comes the Night.
All for Myself.

November 1964 – Decca Studios, West Hampstead, London.
Producer: Bert Berns.
{THE STORY OF THEM} (It Won't Hurt) Half as Much. I Gave My Love
a Diamond I. Go on Home Baby. My Little Baby.
{THE STORY OF THEM mk 1} I Gave My Love a Diamond II.★
{14} Little Girl.

Winter 1965 – Regent Sound Studio, Denmark Street, London.
Producer: Tommy Scott.
{THE STORY OF THEM} One More Time. Little Girl. Mystic Eyes.
Don't Look Back. If You and I Could Be as Two. I Like It Like That. I'm
Gonna Dress in Black. Route 66. Just a Little Bit. How Long Baby. The Story
of Them. Baby What You Want Me to Do.

Summer 1965 – ?Regent Sound Studio, Denmark Street, London.
Producer: Tommy Scott.
{THE STORY OF THEM} I Can Only Give You Everything. Could You
Would You. My Lonely Sad Eyes. Bring 'Em on in.

October 1965 – Regent Sound Studio, Denmark Street, London.
Producer: Tommy Scott.
{THE STORY OF THEM} Something You Got. Call My Name. I Put a
Spell on You. I Got a Woman. Out of Sight. Bad or Good. Hello Josephine.
Don't You Know. Hey Girl. Times Getting Tougher than Tough. Stormy
Monday.

November 1965 – ?Decca Studios, London.
Producer: Tommy Scott.
{THE STORY OF THEM} Bring 'Em on in. Turn on Your Lovelight. It's
All Over Now Baby Blue.

Winter 1966 – ?Regent Sound Studio, Denmark Street, London.
Producer: Tommy Scott.

★ The first U.K. issue of THE STORY OF THEM 2-CD set mistakenly included
an alternative take of 'I Gave My Love a Diamond', which was subsequently corrected.

{THE STORY OF THEM} Richard Cory. Friday's Child.
{THEM FEATURING VAN MORRISON} Mighty Like a Rose.*

Winter 1966 – ?Decca Studios, London.
Producer: Tommy Scott.
{THE STORY OF THEM} Richard Cory.

Van Morrison solo (except where indicated)

March 1967 – ?Bert Berns's Office, New York.
Producer: Bert Berns.
{BANG MASTERS} I Love You (The Smile You Smile).

28 March 1967 – A&R Recording Studios, 48th Street, New York.
Producer: Bert Berns.
{BANG MASTERS} Ro Ro Rosey [take 4]. Brown Eyed Girl [take 6].
Brown Eyed Girl [take 22]. Midnight Special [take 9]. Goodbye Baby [take 13]
{BLOWIN' YOUR MIND†} Ro Ro Rosey [take 1]. Goodbye Baby [take
11]. Midnight Special [take 7].

29 March 1967 – A&R Recording Studios, 48th Street, New York.
Producer: Bert Berns.
{BANG MASTERS} TB Sheets [take 4]. Spanish Rose [take 14]. Who Drove
the Red Sports Car? [take 8]. He Ain't Gonna Give You None [take 4].
{BLOWIN' YOUR MIND} He Ain't Gonna Give You None [take 8].
{BLOWIN' YOUR MIND†} Spanish Rose [take 12]. Who Drove the Red
Sports Car? [take 2].

September 1967 – A&R Recording Studios, 48th Street, New York.
Producer: Bert Berns.
{BANG MASTERS} Send Your Mind. The Smile You Smile. It's All Right.
Chick A Boom.

---

* The only official CD source for 'Mighty Like a Rose' remains a now-deleted
German-only 2-CD set entitled THEM FEATURING VAN MORRISON. It
does, however, appear on THE GENUINE PHILOSOPHER'S STONE bottleg
set, and on the THEM – ROCK ROOTS vinyl album.
† The items on the asterisked version of BLOWIN' YOUR MIND are those alternative takes added to the expanded Sony CD reissue. They do not appear on the original
vinyl release, nor on the first CD remaster.

November 1967 – Century Sound Studios, New York.
Producer: Bert Berns.
{BANG MASTERS} The Back Room. Madame George.

11 December 1967 – Century Sound Studios, New York.
Producer: Bert Berns.
{BANG MASTERS} Beside You. Joe Harper Saturday Morning.

25 September 1968 – Century Sound Studios, New York.
Producer: Lewis Merenstein.
{ASTRAL WEEKS} Cyprus Avenue. Madame George. Beside You. Astral Weeks.

1 October 1968 – Century Sound Studios, New York.
Producer: Lewis Merenstein.
{ASTRAL WEEKS} The Way Young Lovers Do.
Outtakes: Train (aka On a Rainy Afternoon). I've Been Working. ?Madame George.

15 October 1968 – Century Sound Studios, New York.
Producer: Lewis Merenstein.
{ASTRAL WEEKS} Sweet Thing. Ballerina. Slim Slow Slider.
Outtakes: Royalty. Going Around with Jesse James.

Autumn 1968 – Warners Publishing Studio, New York.
Producer: Lewis Merenstein.
Thunderbolt Boogie. Bayou Girl I. Bayou Girl II. The Way Young Lovers Do. Ballerina. Domino I. Domino II. Domino III. When the Evening Sun Goes Down. Wild Night. Mona Mona I. Mona Mona II. I Need Your Kind of Loving I. I Need Your Kind of Loving II.

26–27 December 1968 – Century Sound Studios, New York.
Producer: Lewis Merenstein.
The Sky is Full of Pipers.

Winter 1969 – Warners Publishing Studio, New York.
Producer: Lewis Merenstein.
Bayou Girl I. Magic Night. Domino I. Domino II. When the Evening Sun Goes Down. Wild Night I. Mocking Bird. Domino III. Domino IV. Domino V. Hey Where Are You?. If I Had a Rainbow. I Can't Get Straight. At the Station. Lorna I. Lorna II. Train (On a Rainy Afternoon). Wild Night II. Lorna

III. Wild Night III. Domino VI. When the Evening Sun Goes Down II. (Sit Down) Funny Face. Come Running. Bayou Girl II.

10 March 1969 – Warners–Seven Arts, New York.
Producer: Lewis Merenstein.
Domino.

Spring 1969 – Warners Publishing Studio, New York.
Producer: Lewis Merenstein.
Domino. When the Evening Sun Goes Down. (Sit Down) Funny Face. Come Running. Bayou Girl. Lorna. If You Rock Me. Rock & Roll Band. If I Had A Rainbow. At the Station. I Can't Get Straight. Come Running. Hey Where Are You?. On a Rainy Afternoon. Bit By Bit. If I Ever Needed Someone I. If I Ever Needed Someone II.

Summer 1969 – Warners Publishing Studio, New York.
Producer: Lewis Merenstein.
Caravan. Everyone. Brand New Day. Come Running. These Dreams of You. And It Stoned Me. Set My Soul On Fire I. Set My Soul On Fire II. Nobody Really Knows.

30 July 1969 – Mastertone Studio, 42nd Street, New York.
Producer: Lewis Merenstein.
Everyone. Caravan.

August 1969 – Mastertone Studio, 42nd Street, New York.
Producer: Lewis Merenstein.
{MOONDANCE} Moondance.

?August 1969 – Century Sound Studios, New York.
Engineer: Brooks Arthur.
{PHILOSOPHER'S STONE} Really Don't Know.
Outtakes: My Main Man's in Georgia. Tell Me about Your Love. Wonderful Remark.

September–November 1969 – A&R Recording Studios, 46th Street, New York.
Engineer: Elliott Scheiner.
{MOONDANCE} Caravan. Come Running. Everyone. Crazy Love. Into the Mystic. And It Stoned Me. Brand New Day. These Dreams of You. Glad Tidings.

Outtakes: I've Been Working. Nobody Really Knows. I Shall Sing. Listen to The Lion.

Spring 1970 – ?A&R Recording Studios, 46th Street, New York.
Engineer: Elliott Scheiner.
{STREET CHOIR} I've Been Working. Crazy Face. If I Ever Needed Someone. Give Me a Kiss. Domino. Gypsy Queen.
Outtakes: Funny Face. Woodstock Special. Caledonia Soul Music I. Down in the Maverick. Caledonia Soul Music II.

Summer 1970 – ?A&R Recording Studios, 46th Street, New York.
Engineer: Dauod Shaw.
{STREET CHOIR} I'll Be Your Lover Too. Blue Money. Virgo Clowns. Sweet Jannie. Street Choir. Call Me Up in Dreamland.
Outtake: Shuffle[!].

Spring 1971 – Wally Heider Studio, San Francisco.
Producer: Ted Templeman.
{TUPELO HONEY} Wild Night. Moonshine Whisky. I Wanna Roo You. Straight to Your Heart (Like a Cannonball).
{K16120} When the Evening Sun Goes Down.

Late spring/early summer 1971 – Columbia Studios, San Francisco.
Producer: Ted Templeman.
{TUPELO HONEY} Tupelo Honey. When the Evening Sun Goes Down. Old Old Woodstock. Starting A New Life. You Are My Woman.
{PHILOSOPHER'S STONE} Ordinary People.
{SAINT DOMINIC'S PREVIEW} Listen To The Lion.

Late winter/spring 1972 – Wally Heider & Pacific High Studios, San Francisco; the Church, San Anselmo.
Producers: Van Morrison & Ted Templeman.
{SAINT DOMINIC'S PREVIEW} Redwood Tree. Almost Independence Day. Gypsy. Jackie Wilson Said. Saint Dominic's Preview. I Will Be There.
{K16210} You've Got the Power.
{PHILOSOPHER'S STONE} Wonderful Remark.
Outtakes: Wild Side of Life. Down by the Riverside. Boogie Chillun. Drown in My Own Tears. Hunnel Funnel. I Came out of the Blue. Don't Let Up. Let It Be Me. Give It to Me.

21–25 August 1972 – Caledonia Studio, Fairfax, California.
Engineer: Neil Schwartz.

{HARD NOSE THE HIGHWAY} Being Green. Purple Heather. Wild Children. Snow in San Anselmo. The Great Deception.
{PHILOSOPHER'S STONE} Madame Joy. Laughing in the Wind. There There Child.
Outtakes: Take This Hammer. Goodnight Irene. Beyond Words. Streamline Cannonball. Hey Good Lookin'. Bulbs. Feedback out on Highway 101. Spare Me a Little. Bring It on Home. ?Dead or Alive. ?Hard Nose the Highway.

October 1972 – Caledonia Studio, Fairfax, California.
Engineers: Neil Schwartz & Jim Stern.
{HARD NOSE THE HIGHWAY} Warm Love. Hard Nose the Highway. Autumn Song.

November 1972–Winter 1973 – Caledonia Studio, Fairfax, California.
Engineer: Jim Stern.
{PHILOSOPHER'S STONE} Don't Worry about Tomorrow. Lover's Prayer. Contemplation Rose. Not Supposed To Break Down. Try for Sleep. Drumshanbo Hustle.
{'BACK ON TOP' POBDX15} Tell Me about Your Love.
Outtakes: When I Begin to Realize. Sit There. Country Fair. Talking Harp.

?11 April 1973 – Caledonia Studio, Fairfax, California. w/Jackie DeShannon.
Engineer: Jim Stern.
{ATLANTIC 45-2919} Sweet Sixteen.
Outtakes: Flamingoes Fly. Santa Fe. Wonder of You.

November 1973 – Caledonia Studio, Fairfax, California.
Engineers: Jim Stern, Dauod & Jean Shaw.
{VEEDON FLEECE} Streets of Arklow. Fair Play. You Don't Pull No Punches, but You Don't Push the River. Who Was that Masked Man?. Linden Arden Stole the Highlights. Comfort You. Country Fair. Come Here My Love.
Outtakes: Street Theory. Cul De Sac.

March 1974 – Mercury Studios, New York.
Engineer: Elvin Campbell.
{VEEDON FLEECE} Bulbs. Cul De Sac.

9 April 1974 – Intertone Studios, Heemsteede, Netherlands.
Engineer: Pierre Geoffroy Chateau.

{K16392} Caldonia.*
Outtakes: Street Theory. Twilight Zone.

Mid-July 1974 – Wisseloord Studios, Hilversum, Netherlands.
Engineer: unknown.
{PHILOSOPHER'S STONE} Twilight Zone. Foggy Mountain Top.
Flamingoes Fly.
{K16986} Mechanical Bliss.
Outtakes: Much Binding in the Marsh. Heathrow Shuffle. Naked in the Jungle.
Boffy Flow. Cool for Kats.

Winter 1975 – Record Plant, Sausalito, and/or Caledonia Studio, Fairfax,
California.
Engineer: ?Jim Stern.
{PHILOSOPHER'S STONE} Naked in the Jungle.
And the Street Only Knew Your Name. I Have Finally Come to Realize.
When I Deliver. Joyous Sound. Sixteen Tons. You Move Me. Reminiscing.
Not Workin' for You.

Spring 1975 – Caledonia Studio, Fairfax, California.
Engineer: ?Jim Stern.
{PHILOSOPHER'S STONE} And the Street Only Knew Your Name. I
Have Finally Come to Realize. Joyous Sound.
Outtakes: All Around the World. Don't Change On Me. We're Gonna Make
It. Down to Earth. It Hurts When You Want It So Bad. You Move Me.

Spring 1975 – Caledonia Studio, Fairfax, California.
Engineer: ?Jim Stern.
{PHILOSOPHER'S STONE} Western Plains. John Henry.
Outtake: I Go Ape/Shakin' All Over.

Autumn 1976/early winter 1977 – Los Angeles.
Engineer: Gary Ladinsky.
{A PERIOD OF TRANSITION} Heavy Connection. It Fills You Up.
Cold Winds in August. Flamingoes Fly. Joyous Sound. You Gotta Make it
through the World. The Eternal Kansas City.

Spring 1978 – Shangri-La Studios, Malibu, California.
Engineer: Mick Glossop.

---

* 'What's Up Crazy Pup?', the B-side of 'Caldonia', is also attributed the same recording
date though – lest my ears deceive me – methinks it sounds like a live recording.

{WAVELENGTH} Kingdom Hall. Checkin' It Out. Natalia. Venice USA. Lifetimes. Wavelength. Santa Fe/Beautiful Obsession. Hungry for Your Love. Take It Where You Find It.

?1978 – Advision Studios, London. w/Frank Zappa.
Engineer: Mick Glossop.
Dead Girls in London.

Spring 1979 – Record Plant, Sausalito, California.
Engineer: Mick Glossop.
{INTO THE MUSIC} It's All in the Game. And the Healing Has Begun. Stepping Out Queen. Bright Side of the Road I. Angeliou. Troubadours. Rolling Hills. You Make Me Feel So Free. Full Force Gale. You Know What They're Writing About.
{PHILOSOPHER'S STONE} Stepping Out Queen II. Bright Side of the Road II.
{'BACK ON TOP' POPD15} John Brown's Body. I'm Ready.
{'BACK ON TOP' POBDX15} Sax Instrumental I.
Outtakes: Spirit. Blues Jam. Sacramento. Sweet Sixteen. Are You Ready? Quality Street.

11–19 February 1980 – Super Bear Studios, France.
Producer: Henry Lewy.
{COMMON ONE} Satisfied. Wild Honey. When the Heart Is Open. Haunts of Ancient Peace. Summertime in England. Spirit.
{PHILOSOPHER'S STONE} Street Theory. Real Real Gone.

?May 1981 – Record Plant, Sausalito, California.
Engineer: Jim Stern.
{BEAUTIFUL VISION} Scandinavia.
{MERX132} All Saints' Day.
Outtakes: Daring Night I. Daring Night II. Cleaning Windows I. Cleaning Windows II. Down the Road I Go. Celtic Ray. All Saints' Day.

27 July 1981 – Record Plant, Sausalito, California.
Engineer: Jim Stern.
{BEAUTIFUL VISION} Cleaning Windows. Aryan Mist.

Summer 1981 – Record Plant, Sausalito, California.
Engineer: Jim Stern.
{BEAUTIFUL VISION} She Gives Me Religion. Northern Muse (Solid

Ground). Celtic Ray. Across the Bridge where Angels Dwell. Beautiful Vision. Dweller on the Threshold. Vanlose Stairway.
Outtakes: Real Real Gone. Tore Down A La Rimbaud. Still a Man's World. Lovin' You.

Winter/Spring 1982 – Harbour Sound, Sausalito, California.
Engineer: Tom Anderson.
{INARTICULATE SPEECH OF THE HEART} Inarticulate Speech of the Heart I.
Inarticulate Speech of the Heart II.

Winter/Spring 1982 – Record Plant, Sausalito, California.
Engineer: Jim Stern.
{INARTICULATE SPEECH OF THE HEART} September Night.
{THE BEST OF VAN MORRISON} Wonderful Remark.
Outtake: F. Sharp.

Winter/Spring 1982 – Tres Virgos, San Rafael, California.
Engineer: Jim Stern.
{INARTICULATE SPEECH OF THE HEART} Cry for Home.
{MER 141} For Mr Thomas I.
{PHILOSOPHER'S STONE} For Mr Thomas II.
Outtake: A Man Called Time.

1982 – Townhouse, London.
Engineer: Mick Glossop.
{INARTICULATE SPEECH OF THE HEART} Higher Than The World. Rave On John Donne. Irish Heartbeat. Connswater. River of Time. The Street Only Knew Your Name. Celtic Swing.
{PHILOSOPHER'S STONE} Showbusiness.
Outtakes: Irish Instrumental II. Irish Folk Instrumental III. Make Me a Pallet on the Floor.

1983 – Record Plant, Sausalito.
Engineer: Jim Stern.
{A SENSE OF WONDER} Tore Down A La Rimbaud. Ancient of Days. Evening Meditation. The Master's Eyes. What Would I Do? If You Only Knew. Let the Slave. A New Kind of Man.
?Outtake: Before the World Was Made.

1983 –?Townhouse, London, w/Moving Hearts.
Engineer: Mick Glossop.

{A SENSE OF WONDER} A Sense of Wonder. Boffy Flow and Spike.
{PHILOSOPHER'S STONE} Crazy Jane on God.

1985 – Studio D, Sausalito & Record Plant, Sausalito.
Engineer: Jim Stern.
{NO GURU, NO METHOD, NO TEACHER} Got to Go Back. Oh
the Warm Feeling. Foreign Window. A Town Called Paradise. In the Garden.
Tir Na Nog. Here Comes the Knight. Thanks for the Information. One Irish
Rover. Ivory Tower.

Summer 1987 – Wool Hall Studios, Beckington.
Engineer: Mick Glossop.
{POETIC CHAMPIONS COMPOSE} Spanish Steps. The Mystery.
Queen of the Slipstream. I Forgot that Love Existed. Sometimes I Feel Like a
Motherless Child. Celtic Excavation. Someone Like You. Alan Watts Blues.
Give Me My Rapture. Did Ye Get Healed? Allow Me.
{PHILOSOPHER'S STONE} Song of Being a Child.
Outtake: Jerusalem.

September 1987 – Windmill Lane Studios, Dublin, w/ the Chieftains.
Engineer: Brian Masterson.
{IRISH HEARTBEAT} Star of the County Down. Raglan Road. My Lagan
Love. Celtic Ray.

December 1987/January 1988 – Windmill Lane Studios, Dublin, w/ the Chieftains.
Engineer: Brian Masterson.
{IRISH HEARTBEAT} Irish Heartbeat. My Match Is Made. She Moved
through the Fair. I'll Tell Me Ma. Carrickfergus. Marie's Wedding.

Spring 1988 – Homestead, Co. Antrim, w/ the Chieftains [+ Clive Culbertson
(bass); Dave Early (drums)].
Engineer: Chris Lawson.
{PHILOSOPHER'S STONE} High Spirits.

Summer 1988 – Eden Studios, London.
Engineer: Mick Glossop.
{AVALON SUNSET} Contacting My Angel. I'd Love to Write Another
Song. Have I Told You Lately? Coney Island. I'm Tired Joey Boy. When Will
I Ever Learn to Live in God. Orangefield. Daring Night. These Are the Days.

Autumn 1988/winter 1989 – ?Townhouse Studios, London.
Engineer: Mick Glossop.
{AVALON SUNSET} Whenever God Shines His Light.

1989 – Wool Hall Studios, Beckington; Townhouse, London; The Kirk, Rode.
Engineer: Mick Glossop.
{ENLIGHTENMENT} Real Real Gone. Enlightenment. So Quiet in Here. Avalon of the Heart. See Me Through. Youth of 1,000 Summers. In the Days before Rock & Roll. Start All Over Again. She's My Baby. Memories.

1990 – Wool Hall Studios, Beckington; Townhouse, London; Westside Studios, London[★ – w/the Chieftains].
Engineer: Mick Glossop.
{HYMNS TO THE SILENCE} Professional Jealousy. I'm Not Feeling It Any More. Ordinary Life. Some Peace of Mind. So Complicated. I Can't Stop Loving You★. Why Must I Always Explain?. Village Idiot. See Me Through II (Just a Closer Walk with Thee). By His Grace. All Saints' Day. Hymns to the Silence. On Hyndford Street. Be Thou My Vision★. Carrying a Torch. Green Mansions. Pagan Streams. Quality Street. It Must Be You. I Need Your Kind of Loving.

1990 – Pavilion Studios, London.
Engineers: Martin Hayles & Mick Glossop.
{HYMNS TO THE SILENCE} Take Me Back.

1991 – Wool Hall Studios, Beckington.
Engineer: Mick Glossop.
{TOO LONG IN EXILE} Ball & Chain. Till We Get the Healing Done. Close Enough for Jazz.

1992 – The Plant Recording Studios, Sausalito.
Engineer: Mick Glossop.
{TOO LONG IN EXILE} Gloria. Wasted Years.

1992 – Wool Hall Studios, Beckington.
Engineers: Mick Glossop & Richard Manwaring.
{TOO LONG IN EXILE} Too Long in Exile. Bigtime Operators. Lonely Avenue. In the Forest. Good Morning Little Schoolgirl. Lonesome Road. Moody's Mood for Love. Before the World Was Made. I'll Take Care of You/ Tell Me What You Want.

1994 – Windmill Lane Studios, Dublin.
Engineer: Brian Masterson.
{DAYS LIKE THIS} Raincheck. You Don't Know Me. I'll Never Be Free. {THE LONG BLACK VEIL – THE CHIEFTAINS} Have I Told You Lately?

1993–94 – Wool Hall Studios, Beckington; Real World, Bath.
Engineers: Mick Glossop & Walter Samuel.
{DAYS LIKE THIS} Perfect Fit. Russian Roulette. No Religion. Underlying Depression. Songwriter. Days Like This. Melancholia. Ancient Highway. In the Afternoon.
{'DAYS LIKE THIS' VANCD12} I Don't Want to Go On Without You. That Old Black Magic. Yo.

Winter 1996 – Wool Hall Studios, Beckington, w/ Georgie Fame & Mose Allison.
Engineers: Richard Manwaring & Tristan Powell.
{TELL ME SOMETHING} One of These Days. You Can Count On Me (to Do My Part). Benediction. Tell Me Something. I Don't Want Much. News Nightclub. Perfect Moment.

May 1996 – Wool Hall Studios, Beckington, w/Carl Perkins.
Engineer: Walter Samuel.
{GOOD ROCKIN' TONIGHT: THE LEGACY OF SUN RECORDS} Sitting on Top of the World.
Outtakes: Matchbox. All By Myself. Boppin' the Blues. My Angel.

1996 – Wool Hall Studios, Beckington.
Engineer: Walter Samuel.
{THE SONGS OF JIMMIE RODGERS} Muleskinner Blues.

1996 – Windmill Lane Studios, Dublin.
Engineer: Walter Samuel.
{THE HEALING GAME} Rough God Goes Riding. Fire in the Belly. This Weight. Waiting Game. Burning Ground. It Once Was My Life. Sometimes We Cry. If You Love Me. The Healing Game.
{'THE HEALING GAME' CD} Full Force Gale 96. Look What the Good People Done.

1996 – Westland Studios, Dublin.
Engineer: Enda Walsh.
{THE HEALING GAME} Piper at the Gates of Dawn.
{'THE HEALING GAME' CD} Celtic Spring.
{'ROUGH GOD GOES RIDING' CD} At the End of the Day. The Healing Game (alternative take).

1997 – Windmill Lane Studios, Dublin, w/the Chieftains.
Engineer: Brian Masterson.
{LONG JOURNEY HOME} Shenandoah.

1998 – Wool Hall Studios, Beckington.
Engineer: Walter Samuel.
{BACK ON TOP} Goin' Down Geneva. Philosopher's Stone. In the Midnight. Back on Top. When the Leaves Come Falling Down. High Summer. Reminds Me of You. New Biography. Precious Time. Golden Autumn Day.

Summer 1999 – ?Wool Hall Studios, Beckington, w/the Rimshots.
Engineer: Walter Samuel.
More and More. There Stands the Glass. Your Cheatin' Heart.*

Winter–spring 2000 – Wool Hall Studios, Beckington.
Engineer: Walter Samuel.
{DOWN THE ROAD} Fast Train. Talk is Cheap.
Outtake: At the Crossroads.

11–13 April 2000 – Wool Hall Studios, Beckington, w/Linda Gail Lewis & the Red Hot Pokers.
Engineer: Walter Samuel.
{YOU WIN AGAIN} Let's Talk about Us. You Win Again. Jambalaya. Crazy Arms. Old Black Joe. No Way Pedro. Real Gone Lover.
{'LET'S TALK ABOUT US' CD} Singing the Blues.
Outtakes: Be Bop A Lula. John Henry. Sit Down Baby. Not Working For You.

Early June 2000 – Wool Hall Studios, Beckington, w/Linda Gail Lewis & the Red Hot Pokers.
Engineer: Walter Samuel.
{YOU WIN AGAIN} A Shot of Rhythm & Blues. Why Don't You Love Me? Cadillac. Baby (You Got What It Takes).
Outtake: Sticks & Stones.

Mid-July 2000 – Wool Hall Studios, Beckington, w/Linda Gail Lewis & the Red Hot Pokers.
Engineer: Walter Samuel.
{YOU WIN AGAIN} Boogie Chillun. Think Twice Before You Go.

3 October 2000 – Wool Hall Studios, Beckington, w/Linda Gail Lewis & the Red Hot Pokers.
Engineer: Walter Samuel.

---

* Apparently an entire album of songs was recorded with the Rimshots, though the remaining songs are not known.

Meet Me in the Indian Summer. The Beauty of the Days Gone By. Hey Mr DJ.

21–23 October 2000 – Wool Hall Studios, Beckington, w/Linda Gail Lewis & the Red Hot Pokers.
Engineer: Walter Samuel.
{DOWN THE ROAD} Choppin' Wood.★
Outtakes: Meet Me in the Indian Summer. The Beauty of the Days Gone By. Hey Mr DJ. For a While.

Early November 2000 – Wool Hall Studios, Beckington, w/Linda Gail Lewis.
Engineer: Walter Samuel.
{DOWN THE ROAD} Down the Road. The Beauty of the Days Gone By. Hey Mr DJ.†
Outtakes: Down the Road II. Princess of the Darkness. Just Like Greta. For a While. Mama Don't Allow. Meet Me in the Indian Summer.‡ All Work & No Play.

Winter 2001 – Wool Hall Studios, Beckington.
Engineer: Walter Samuel.
{DOWN THE ROAD} What Makes the Irish Heart Beat. Man Has to Struggle.

[?3 or 4 to] 6 September 2001 – Wool Hall Studios, Beckington.
Engineer: Walter Samuel.
{DOWN THE ROAD} Meet Me in the Indian Summer. Steal My Heart Away. All Work & No Play. Whatever Happened To P.J. Proby. Georgia on my Mind. Only a Dream. Evening Shadows.

★ Linda Gail Lewis's contribution to this song has been removed from the mix prior to its release.
† Though the released versions of these songs appear to use basic tracks that were recorded at the November 2000 sessions, Linda Gail Lewis's backing vocals and piano have been removed and a series of overdubs, including vocal overdubs, added.
‡ According to the latest information, the November 2000 version of 'Meet Me in the Indian Summer' is due to become the second single 'from' DOWN THE ROAD, presumably also in remixed form.

Notes and Bibliography

In keeping with previous practice, I have preferred to utilize quotes given by my primary subject from the various interviews he has given over the years rather than surrender the element of control necessary to secure an in-person interview. My call. Mr Morrison, like Mr Dylan, is one of those figures in rock music accused of rarely giving interviews but who turns out to be comfortably into three figures when it comes to published and broadcast examples available to your humble researcher. Not every interview I traced provided a cooperative Morrison. Indeed, some of the best interviews feature a decidedly uncooperative individual. The ones, though, that have directly helped me in my endeavours, providing Morrison's own point of view in his own words, are as follows:

Unknown interviewer, *Belfast Evening Telegraph*, October 1965

Carol Deck, *KRLA Beat*, April 1966

Richard Robinson, *Go*, 4/8/67

Carol Deck, *Beat*, 2/12/67

Greil Marcus, *Rolling Stone*, 1/3/67

Happy Traum, *Rolling Stone*, 9/7/70

David Reitman & Jackie Solomon, *Sounds*, 12/12/70

Dan Goldberg, *Jazz & Pop*, December 1970

Rick McGrath, *Georgia Straight*, 15/4/71

John Grissim, Jnr, *Rolling Stone*, 22/6/72

Shay Healy, *Record Mirror*, 1/7/72

Danny Holloway, *New Musical Express*, 17/8/72

John Tobler, *Zigzag* #36

Steve Peacock, *Sounds*, 28/7/73

Richard Williams, *Melody Maker*, 28/7/73

Roy Carr, *New Musical Express*, 4/8/73

Cameron Crowe, *Rolling Stone*, 30/8/73

Cameron Crowe, *Creem*, October 1973

Ritchie Yorke, *New Musical Express*, 23/2/74*

Ritchie Yorke, *New Musical Express*, 6/4/74*

Ritchie Yorke, *New Musical Express*, 27/7/74*

Unknown source, *Veedon Fleece* press ad, November 1974

Donall Corvin, *Hot Press*, 1977

Cameron Crowe, *Rolling Stone*, 19/5/77

Ritchie Yorke, *Stagelife*, July & August 1977 edns.

Ritchie Yorke, unknown source, 1977

Vivien Goldman, *Sounds*, 25/6/77

Ian Birch, *Melody Maker*, 25/6/77

Roy Carr, *New Musical Express*, 25/6/77

Nicky Horne, Capital Radio, June 1977

Unknown interviewer, *Nuggets* #8 (summer 1977)

Davitt Sigerson, *Sounds*, 1/7/78

Jonathan Cott, *Rolling Stone*, 30/11/78

Chris Welch, *Melody Maker*, 3/2/79

Tony Stewart, *New Musical Express*, 10/3/79

Paul Vincent, KMEL Radio Station, November 1981 (transcript in *Wavelength* #7)

Michael Goldberg, *Rolling Stone*, 18/2/82

Dermot Stokes, *Hot Press*, April 1982

John Tobler, Radio Oxford, 5/3/83

Dermot Stokes, *Hot Press*, 1983

Geoff Brown, *Time Out*, 3/5/84

David Thomas, *The Times*, 4/6/84

Fred Schruers, *Rolling Stone*, 22/11/84

Stephen Davis, *New Age*, 17/5/85

Anthony de Curtis, *Record*, October 1985

Steve Turner, *Hungry for Heaven*, 1985

Bill Flanagan, *Written in My Soul*, 1986

R. D. Laing, *Laing: Creative Destroyer*, 1987

Desmond Hogan, *The Edge of the City: A Scrapbook 1976–1991*

Unknown interviewer, *Washington Post*, July 1986

Steve Morse, *Boston Globe*, 7/7/86

Anthony Denselow, *Observer*, 3/8/86

Mick Brown, PolyGram, *No Guru* promotional album, 1986

Bill Morrison, PolyGram, *Poetic Champions* promotional album, 1987

Chris Salewicz, *Q* #4 (January 1987)

Gavin Martin, *New Musical Express*, 15/10/88

Bill Graham, *Hot Press*, 6/11/88

Sean O'Hagan, *New Musical Express*, 3/6/89

Paul Du Noyer, *Q* #35 (August 1989)

David Jensen, *Which CD*, August 1990

Sean O'Hagan, *Select*, October 1990

Paul Jones, Radio Two, 22/3/90 (transcript in *Wavelength* #2)

* These interviews provide the bulk of original material included in Ritchie Yorke's 1975 book, *Into the Music*.

David Wild, *Rolling Stone*, 9/8/90

Victoria Clarke, *Irish Post*, 5/10/91

Sean O'Hagan, *The Times*, 9/3/91

Paul Lewis, *Now Dig This*, December 1991

Victoria Clarke, *Q* # 83 (August 1993)

Michelle Rocca, *Irish Independent*, 8/5/94

Scott & Susan Duncan, *Blueprint* #69 (December 1994)

Michelle Rocca, PolyGram, *Days Like This* Promotional CD, 1995

John Fordham – PolyGram, *How Long* Promotional CD 1995 (transcript in *Wavelength* #7)

B. P. Fallon, *Irish Independent*, 9/6/96

B. P. Fallon, *Guardian*, 15/6/96

Clive Davis, *Down Beat*, May 1996

Edna Gundersen, *USA Today*, 12/6/97

Hugo Cassavetti, *Telerama*, 2/4/97

Mick Brown, interview conducted for *Philosopher's Stone* notes (unpublished)

Jeff Gordiner, *Entertainment Weekly*, 7/3/97

Paul Du Noyer, *Q* # 127 (April 1997)

Unknown interviewer, PolyGram *Healing Game* Promotional CD, 1997

John Kelly, *Irish Times*, 11/4/98

Ivan Martin, *Sunday World*, 2/1/2000

Niall Stokes, *Hot Press*, 15/3/2000

The following interview(er)s have proved especially useful. They are included with the kind permission of the interviewer, save for Michael Walsh, whose whereabouts, like Alan Watts's, is unknown. Their initials are in brackets at the end of the appropriate quote in the main text; where there is more than one interviewer within these quotes, [ ] indicates where the break occurs.

ST = Steve Turner: *Too Late to Stop Now*

TH = Trevor Hodgett – interviews with various members of Them in *Wavelength* #s 2, 3, 5, 7, 13, 21

JS = Joel Selvin – an unpublished interview with Janet Planet

NC = N. C. Junker-Poulsen – an unpublished interview with John Payne

MW = Michael Walsh – interview with John Platania in *Into the Music* #2

RG = Robert Greenfield – excerpts from interviews with Bill Graham, published in *Bill Graham Presents* and the January 1997 edition of *Musician*

SG = Simon Gee – interviews with Mick Cox and Pee Wee Ellis in *Wavelength* #s 11, 12, 20, 22

TP = Thomas C. Palmer – interview with John Payne in *Wavelength* #23

OM = interviews conducted by Owen McFadden for 1 September 1991 radio special on the Maritime Hotel

There have been surprisingly few tomes specifically on Morrison and his art. The ones that I have referred to are, in alphabetical order, as follows:

Brooks, Ken, *In Search of Van Morrison* (Agenda Books, 1999)
Collis, John, *Van Morrison: Inarticulate Speech of the Heart* (Little, Brown, 1996)
DeWitt, Howard A., *Van Morrison: The Mystic's Music* (Horizon Books, 1983)
Hinton, Brian, *Celtic Crossroads: The Art of Van Morrison* (Sanctuary, 1997: second edition, 2000)
Kelly, Pat, *More than a Song to Sing* (Rowan Press, 1993)
Rogan, Johnny, *Van Morrison: A Portrait of the Artist* (Proteus Books, 1984)
Turner, Steve, *Too Late to Stop Now* (Bloomsbury, 1993)
Yorke, Ritchie, *Van Morrison: Into the Music* (Charisma/Futura, 1975)

Books with a Morrison content that have also been helpful include the following:

Brown, Mick, *The Spiritual Tourist* (Bloomsbury, 1998)
Dawe, Gerald, *The Rest Is History* (Abbey Press, 1998)
Densmore, John, *Riders on the Storm* (Bloomsbury, 1991)
Filene, Benjamin, *Romancing the Folk: Public Memory and American Roots Music* (Chapel Hill, 2000)
Flanagan, Bill, *Written in My Soul* (Contemporary Books, 1986)
Glatt, John, *The Chieftains: The Authorized Biography* (Century, 1997)
Graham, Bill, & Greenfield, Robert, *Bill Graham Presents* (Doubleday, 1992)
Hennessey, Thomas, *A History of Northern Ireland 1920–1996* (Gill & MacMillan, 1997)
Landy, Elliott, *Woodstock Vision* (Continuum, 1994)
Marcus, Greil (ed.), *Stranded: Rock and Roll for a Desert Island* (Alfred A. Knopf, 1979)
Oldham, Andrew Loog, *Stoned* (Secker & Warburg, 1999)
Power, Vincent, *Send 'Em Home Sweatin': The Showband Story* (Mercier Press, 2000)
Sarlin, Bob, *Turn It Up (I Can't Hear the Words)* (Simon & Schuster, 1973)
Smith, Joe, *Off the Record* (Warner Books, 1988)
Turner, Steve, *Hungry for Heaven: Rock 'n' roll and the Search for Redemption* (Virgin Books, 1988)
Wexler, Jerry, & Ritz, David, *Rhythm and the Blues: A Life in American Music* (Alfred A. Knopf, 1993)

Chapter notes

Preface: The Art of New Biography
Quotes by Harvey Goldsmith, Keith Altham, Jonn Savannah and Clive Culbert-son come from interviews conducted for this book by the author. The comment by Steve Turner derives from his own introduction to *Too Late to Stop Now*; Jim Miller, from his *Rolling Stone* review of *Veedon Fleece* in the 2/1/75 edition; and Janet Planet, from an interview by Lauren Wakefield, published in issue 18 of *Wavelength*.

1 On Hyndford Street
Quotes by Roy Kane, Gil Irvine and George Jones come from interviews conducted for this book by the author. Gerald Dawe's comment comes from *The Rest Is History*. Quotes by Steve Turner, Ethel Blakely and Rod Demick derive from *Too Late to Stop Now*. Violet Morrison's own words come from an article in *Sunday World*, 13/8/95. Also quoted: Alexander Gilchrist, *A Life of Blake*; Bob Dylan, from his January 1978 *Playboy* interview; and Patti Smith, from an interview with Lynn Goldsmith in *Hit Parader*, April 1975.

2 His Father's Footsteps
Quotes by Billy McAllen, Gil Irvine and Linda Gail Lewis come from interviews conducted for this book by the author. Davey Hammond's comment comes from *Too Late to Stop Now*; Solly Lipsitz's comes from a feature in the *Irish Times* in May 1998; and Mick Cox's from a talk given at a Van Morrison convention in Manchester in September 1998. Also quoted, with reference to Lead Belly, is *Romancing the Folk* by Benjamin Filene.

3 Riding on the Side
Quotes by Gil Irvine, Arty McGlynn, Billy McAllen, Roy Kane, Billy Harrison and George Jones come from interviews conducted for this book by the author. The comment by Bill Dunn comes from a Belfast newspaper article in December 1990; Phil Coulter's and Father Brian D'Ary's, from *Send 'Em Home Sweatin'* by Vincent Power; Herbie Armstrong's and George McDowell's, from *Too Late to Stop Now*; and Harry Baird's, from John Collis's biography. Brian Hogg's quote comes from his article in *Strange Things Are Happening #4*.

4 Leaving Ireland
Quotes by George Jones, Billy McAllen, Roy Kane and Geordie Sproule come

from interviews conducted for this book by the author. Ruby Bard's comment comes from Johnny Rogan's 1984 biography and Herbie Armstrong's, from *Too Late to Stop Now*.

5 Good Times
Quotes by Billy Harrison, George Jones, Geordie Sproule, Eric Wrixon, Ronnie Millings, Gerry McKervey, Jimmy Conlon, Eric Bell, Arty McGlynn, Peter Lloyd and Gil Irvine come from interviews conducted for this book by the author. Ancillary quotes derive from Trevor Hodgett's series of interviews with members of Them in *Wavelength*, as does Alan Henderson's comment; Gerald Dawe's, from *The Rest Is History*; and Violet Morrison's from Howard De Witt's book.

6 Gotta Walk Away
Quotes by Eric Wrixon, Stuart Cromie, Peter Lloyd, Martin Lloyd, Gerry McKervey, Billy Harrison, Ronnie Millings, Jimmy Conlon, Mervyn Solomon and Phil Solomon come from interviews conducted for this book by the author. Quotes from Eric Wrixon obtained by Steve Turner and Trevor Hodgett are indicated accordingly, as are quotes from Mervyn Solomon that derive from a 1991 Radio Ulster broadcast on the Maritime Hotel. Gerald Dawe's comment comes from *The Rest Is History*; Andrew Loog Oldham's from his autobiography, *Stoned*.

7 Angry Young Them
Quotes by Peter Lloyd, Stuart Cromie, Eric Wrixon, Mervyn Solomon, Martin Lloyd, Billy Harrison, Phil Solomon, Ronnie Millings, Keith Altham, Greil Marcus, Gerry McKervey and Paul Charles come from interviews conducted for this book by the author. Jimmy Page's comment comes from *Zigzag* 27; Phil Coulter's from an article by Myles Palmer in *Let It Rock*, January 1973; Peter Bardens's, from an interview in *Trouser Press*; Pete Docherty's, from a contemporary report in the Ulster press; Tommy Scott's, from Johnny Rogan's 1984 biography; Chris Ryder's, from an article in the *Belfast Evening Herald* in late 1965; Brian Hogg's, from *Strange Things Are Happening* #4; and Shel Talmy and Andrew Loog Oldham's, from Oldham autobiography, *Stoned*. One quote from Eric Wrixon derives in part from Trevor Hodgett's interview and is indicated accordingly ([as CH/TH]).

8 Getting Twisted
Quotes by Billy Harrison, John Wilson, Jim Armstrong, Phil Solomon, Clive

Culbertson and Eric Wrixon come from interviews conducted for this book by the author. Mervyn Solomon's comment comes from *Too Late to Stop Now*; Jackie McAuley's from Trevor Hodgett's interviews, as does one from John Wilson and one from Jim Armstrong, duly noted; Peter Bardens's quote comes from Pete Frame's *Rock Family Tree*; Phil Coulter and Tommy Scott's, from Johnny Rogan's biography; Chris Murray's, from an article in *Wavelength* #4; John Densmore's, from *Riders on the Storm*; Danny Holloway's, from an interview/article in *NME*, 17/8/72; Janet Planet's from an interview with Louis Sahagun in the *L A Times*, 17/11/98; Charlie Gillett's, from a 1971 issue of *Fusion*; Brian Hinton's, from *Celtic Crossroads: The Art of Van Morrison*; and Brian Hogg's from *Strange Things Are Happening* #4.

9 Can't Stop Now

Quotes by Eric Bell, Jim Armstrong, Geordie Sproule, Billy McAllen, Linda Gail Lewis, Tom Kielbania and Henry McCullough come from interviews conducted for this book by the author. Phil Coulter's comment comes from an interview in *Hot Press* in April 2000; Donall Corvin's, from Ritchie Yorke's *Into the Music*; Lemmy Kiminster's, from an article by Gavin Martin, *NME*, 28/5/83; B. P. Fallon's, from an article in the *Irish Independent*, 9/6/96; Rory Gallagher's, from the 1991 Radio Ulster special on the Maritime Hotel; Jerry Wexler's, from his autobiography; Anton Witkamp's, from his sleeve notes to the Dutch-only *Friday's Child* EP: Janet Planet's, from her sleeve notes to the *Street Choir* album and from a previously unpublished interview by Joel Selvin; Herman Brood's, from an interview by Diana De Roo in *Wavelength* #15; Lester Bangs's, from his article on *Astral Weeks* in *Stranded*, ed. Greil Marcus; and Brian Hogg's, from *Strange Things Are Happening* #4.

10 He Ain't Give You None

Quotes by Jon Gershen and Jeff Labes come from interviews conducted for this book by the author. Janet Planet's comments derive from an interview by Joel Selvin; Bill Flanagan's, from his sleeve notes to the *Bang Masters* CD; Brian Hogg's, from *Strange Things Are Happening* #4; Brooks Arthur's and Ilene Berns's, from *Too Late to Stop Now*; Greil Marcus's, from *Rolling Stone*, 1/3/69; Mick Cox's, from his talk at the Morrison convention in Manchester in September 1998, and from an interview by Simon Gee published in *Wavelength* #20; Michael Ochs's, from his sleeve notes to the *T B Sheets* album; and Johnny Rogan's, from his 1983 biography.

11 The Drumshanbo Hustle

Quotes by Tom Kielbania, George Lee, Lewis Merenstein and Jon Gershen come from interviews conducted for this book by the author. Ilene Berns's comment derives from *Too Late to Stop Now*; Janet Planet's, from an interview by Joel Selvin; Peter Wolf 's, from an interview in *Rolling Stone*, 12/11/98; Eric Kraft's, from the 1974 press-kit *Reliable Sources*; Bob Sarlin's, from *Turn It Up*; John Payne's, from interviews conducted by Thomas C. Palmer and N. C. Junker-Poulsen, respectively; Mick Cox's, from an interview by Simon Gee in *Wavelength* #20/22; Joe Smith's, from correspondence with the author and an interview given to Steve Morse of the *Boston Globe* in 1989.

12 Venturing into the Slipstream

Quotes by Roy Kane, Lewis Merenstein, John Payne, Tom Kielbania, Graham Blackburn, Richard Davis, Jay Berliner, Warren Smith, Jnr, and Jon Gershen come from interviews conducted for this book by the author. Elvis Costello's quote comes from a *Mojo* feature; Greil Marcus's, from his review of *Astral Weeks* in *Rolling Stone*, 1/3/69; Gerald Dawe's, from *The Rest is History*; Lester Bangs's, from his article on *Astral Weeks* in *Stranded*, ed. Greil Marcus; Albert B. Lord's, from *The Singer of Tales* (Harvard University Press, 1960); Connie Kay's, from *Rolling Stone*, 27/8/87; John Collis's, from *Inarticulate Speech of the Heart*; Bob Sarlin's, from *Turn It Up*; Ken Emerson's and Rick McGrath's from their reviews of *Astral Weeks*, as reprinted in *Reliable Sources*.

13 Entering the Mainstream

Quotes by Lewis Merenstein, Graham Blackburn, Greil Marcus, Tom Kielbania, George Lee, Jon Gershen, Jeff Labes, Gary Malabar and John Altman come from interviews conducted for this book by the author. The quote from Daniel Goldberg comes from a review in *Billboard*, 13/9/69; John Payne's, from an interview by Thomas C. Palmer in *Wavelength* #23; Elliott Landy's, from the original edition of *Woodstock Vision* (text translated from original German in *Wavelength* #3); Janet Planet's, from an interview by Louis Sahagun in the *LA Times*, 17/11/98, as well as an interview by Joel Selvin; John Platania's, from an interview by Michael Walsh in *Into the Music* #2; a quote from a live review by Greil Marcus comes from the *San Francisco Express-Times*, 25/2/69; Ken Brooks's, from *In Search of Van Morrison*; and Lester Bangs's, from his review of *Moondance* in *Rolling Stone*, 19/3/70.

14 The Sweet-Tempered Innocent and the Prickly Bear

Quotes by Jon Gershen, Lewis Merenstein, Gary Malabar, Jeff Labes, Graham

Blackburn and Dauod Shaw come from interviews conducted for this book by the author. The quote at the chapter's outset from Jon Gershen derives from an interview given to a Japanese journalist. John Platania's comments come from *Too Late to Stop Now*; Janet Planet's, from a posting to the Van-Info website on 2/4/99, her sleeve notes to the *Street Choir* album, an interview by Lauren Wakefield for *Wavelength* #18, and an interview by Louis Sahagun for the *LA Times*, 17/11/98; Elliott Landy's, from the original edition of *Woodstock Vision*; Joe Smith's, from *The Rolling Stone Interviews*, vol. 2 (1973); Bob Sarlin's, from *Turn It Up*; Elliott Scheiner's, from *Sound on Sound*, February 1996; and Mary Martin's, from *Rolling Stone*, 12/11/70.

15 Listening to the Lion

Quotes by Stephen Barncard, Gary Malabar, Jon Gershen, Ed Fletcher, Dauod Shaw and Tom Kielbania come from interviews conducted for this book by the author. The comments from Ronnie Montrose were obtained from his own website, ronnieland.com; those from Boots Houston, Stephen Pillster and John Platania, from *Too Late to Stop Now*; Ted Templeman, from Johnny Rogan's 1984 biography; Greil Marcus, from a review in *Creem* 1972; Ritchie Yorke, from *Into the Music*; Jon Landau, from his review of *Tupelo Honey* in *Rolling Stone* 25/11/71; Charlie Gillett, from his review of the same in *Fusion* 1971; and Dave Marsh, from his review of 'Saint Dominic's Preview' in 1972.

16 Hard Times and Fine Lines

Quotes by Gary Malabar, Jeff Labes, Ed Fletcher, Lewis Merenstein, Dauod Shaw and Paul Charles come from interviews conducted for this book by the author. John Platania's comments come from an interview by Michael Walsh for *Into the Music* #2, and from *Too Late to Stop Now*; Steve Turner's quote also comes from *Too Late to Stop Now*; and Brian Hogg's, from *Strange Things Are Happening* #4.

17 A Commercial Cul-de-Sac

Quotes by Dauod Shaw, Jeff Labes and Paul Jones come from interviews conducted for this book by the author. The comments by David Hayes come from an interview by Truls Meland, conducted in 1974, that was finally published in *Wavelength* #14; Stephen Pillster's, from *Too Late to Stop Now*; Phil Coulter's, from Johnny Rogan's biography; Jack Lynch's, from his series of articles in *Hot Press* on the Van Morrison story, 4/3–10/6/83; Gary Herman's, from his *Let It Rock* review of *Veedon Fleece*, December 1974; and Nick Kent's, from his review of same in *NME*, 12/10/74.

18 Naked to the World

Quotes by Dauod Shaw, Ed Fletcher, Peter Van Hooke, John Altman and Jeff Labes come from interviews conducted for this book by the author. The comments by David Hayes come from an interview by Truls Meland, conducted in 1974, that was finally published in *Wavelength* #14; Pete Wingfield's, from an interview in *Melody Maker*, 10/8/75; Joe Smith's, from his *Off the Record*; and Walter Samuel's, from an interview by Tim Goodyer in the February 1999 edition of *Studio Sound*.

19 Not Working for You

Quotes by Greil Marcus, Harvey Goldsmith, Jeff Labes, Donal Gallagher, John Altman, Paul Charles, Mo Foster and Peter Van Hooke come from interviews conducted for this book by the author. Shana Morrison's comment comes from an interview by Jane Ganahi, *San Francisco Chronicle*, 23/5/97; Bill Wyman's, from *Wavelength* #16 and an interview by Pete Doggett in the November 1998 *Record Collector*; Ritchie Yorke's, from an article in *Stagelife*, July 1977; Robbie Robertson's, from a VH-1 *Behind the Music* special on *The Last Waltz*, 1999; Dr John's, from an interview by Barney Hoskyns in the September 1995 *Mojo*, and an interview by Alan Bangs on *Rockpalast*, WDRTV, 9/7/99; Nicky Horne's, from Johnny Rogan's biography; Nick Kent's and Michael Watts's, from their 23/4/77 reviews of *A Period of Transition* in *NME* and *Melody Maker*, respectively; and Chas De Whalley's, from his *Melody Maker* review of the Maunkberry gig in June 1977.

20 In Transition

Quotes by Harvey Goldsmith, Mo Foster, John Altman, Keith Altham, Paul Charles, Peter Van Hooke and Pat Kyle come from interviews conducted for this book by the author. Nick Kent's quote comes from his review of *A Period of Transition*, *NME*, 23/4/77; Bill Graham's, from a feature by Robert Greenfield in *Musician*, January 1994; Joel Selvin's, from a review in the *San Francisco Chronicle*, 7/10/78; Sylvie Simmons's, from a review in *Sounds*, 16/12/78; Mo Ostin's, from an interview by Robert Hilburn in the *LA Times*, 6/6/96; Allan Jones's, from a review in *Melody Maker*, 10/3/79; and those by Tony Stewart, Pennie Smith and Mike Radford, from Stewart's *NME* feature, 10/3/79.

21 Down by Avalon

Quotes by John Altman, Peter Van Hooke, Pat Kyle, Jonn Savannah and Clive Culbertson come from interviews conducted for this book by the author. The comments by Pee Wee Ellis come from an interview by Simon Gee in *Wavelength* #11/12; Steve Turner's and Herbie Armstrong's, from *Too Late to Stop Now*; Hilary Sanderson's, from John Collis's *Inarticulate Speech of the Heart*; Derek Bell's, from *The Chieftains* by John Glatt; David Tame's, from an article in *Wavelength* #1; Johnny Rogan's, from his biography; Mick Cox's, from an interview by Simon Gee in *Wavelength* #20/22, and his speech at the Van Morrison convention in Manchester in September 1998; Jack Lynch's, from his series of articles in *Hot Press* on the Van Morrison story, 4/3–10/6/83; Paul Rambali's, from his review of *Into the Music* in *NME*, 25/8/79; Graham Lock's, from his review of *Common One* in *NME*, 13/9/80; Dave McCullough's, from his reviews in *Sounds* of *Into the Music* and *Common One*, 25/8/79 and 13/9/80; and Lester Bangs's, from his review of *Beautiful Vision* in *Village Voice*, 23/3/82.

22 The Days of Dominion

Quotes by Paul Jones, Gary Malabar, Paul Charles, Donal Gallagher, Clive Culbertson, Mick Brown, Kenny Craddock and Peter Van Hooke come from interviews conducted for this book by the author. Chris Michie's comments come from an interview by Nathan Wirth in *Wavelength* #13; Jack Lynch's, from his series of articles in *Hot Press* on the Van Morrison story, 4/3–10/6/83; David Hayes's, from an interview by Truls Meland, *Wavelength* #14; and Herbie Armstrong's and an unidentified auditor's, from *Too Late to Stop Now*.

23 Days of Blooming Wonder

Quotes by Clive Culbertson, Peter Van Hooke, Arty McGlynn, Martin Drover, Kenny Craddock, Paul Charles and Mick Brown come from interviews conducted for this book by the author. John Allair's comments come from an interview by Joel Selvin, *San Francisco Chronicle*, 30/4/95; Kate St John's, from *Wavelength* #6; Brian Hinton's, from *Celtic Crossroads*; Steve Turner's, from *Too Late to Stop Now*; Chris Michie's, from an interview by Nathan Wirth in *Wavelength* #13; Donal Lunny's, from a May 1996 issue of *Hot Press*; John Platania's, from an interview by Michael Walsh in *Into the Music* #2; Barry McIlheney's, from his review of *No Guru, No Method, No Teacher* in *Melody Maker*, 26/7/86; John Wilde's, from his *Sounds* review of same, 26/7/86.

24 The Secret Heart of Music

Quotes by Roy Jones, Peter Van Hooke, Clive Culbertson, Paul Charles, Mick Brown, Martin Drover, Jonn Savannah, Ed Fletcher and Arty McGlynn come from interviews conducted for this book by the author. The comment by Steve Turner derives from *Too Late to Stop Now*; Malcolm Lazarus's, from an interview in *Wavelength* #10; Mick Cox's, from an interview by Simon Gee in *Wavelength* #22; Derek Bell's and Kevin Conneff's, from *The Chieftains* by John Glatt, as is a quote from Paddy Moloney, along with further quotes from interviews in *Hot Press* and *Q*; John Wilde's, from his review in *Sounds*, 18/6/88; and Shana Morrison's, from an interview by Jane Ganahi, *San Francisco Chronicle*, 23/5/97.

25 These are the Days

Quotes by Clive Culbertson, Paul Jones, Arty McGlynn, Chris O'Donnell, Tom Kielbania, Linda Gail Lewis and Alan Skidmore come from interviews conducted for this book by the author. Comments by Paddy Moloney and Kevin Conneff derive from *The Chieftains* by John Glatt. Further quotes from Moloney and Derek Bell derive from interviews in *Q* and *Hot Press*; Denis Campbell's comes from an *NME* review, 18/6/88; and Jack Lynch's from an obituary for Dave Early, original source unknown, reprinted in *Wavelength* #13.

26 Fire in His Belly

Quotes by Gil Irvine, Jonn Savannah, Geoff Dunn, Kenny Craddock, Martin Drover, Clive Culbertson and Linda Gail Lewis come from interviews conducted for this book by the author. Steve Turner's comment comes from *Too Late to Stop Now*; Gerald Dawe's, from *The Rest Is History*; David Tame's, from an article in *Wavelength* #1; Ritchie Buckley's, from an interview by Joe Jackson, *Hot Press*, 19/8/98; Michelle Rocca's, from interviews in *RTE Guide*, 8/4/94 and the *Sun*, 19/12/94; Diarmuid Doyle's, from the *Sunday Tribune*, 1/5/94; Sheila's comment comes from the *Sunday Mirror*, 18/6/96; Tom Moon's, from *Rolling Stone*, July 1995; and David Cavanagh's, from *Mojo*, July 1995.

27 The Van Morrison Masterclass

Quotes by Jonn Savannah, Richard Davis, Alan Skidmore, Jay Berliner, Gil Irvine, Linda Gail Lewis and Mick Brown come from interviews conducted for this book by the author. Walter Samuel's quote comes from an interview by Tim Goodyer in *Studio Sound*, February 1999; Pee Wee Ellis's and Brian Kennedy's, from interviews by Simon Gee in *Wavelength* #12; Georgie Fame's, from an undated source; Tom Adair's, from an article in the *Scotsman*, 21/11/98; Gavin Martin's, from *Uncut*, June 1999; and David Hepworth's, from *Mojo*, March 1997.

28 At the Dark End of the Street

Quotes by Geoff Dunn, Jonn Savannah, Linda Gail Lewis, John Altman and Billy McAllen come from interviews conducted for this book by the author.

George Byrne's comment comes from a review of *Back On Top* in an undated Irish paper; David Hepworth's, from his review in the March 1997 *Mojo* of *The Healing Game*; Scott E. Thomas's, from his review of *The Philosopher's Stone* in *Wavelength* #17; Colin Irwin's, from *Folk Roots*, March 2000; Lonnie Donegan's, from an interview by Nigel Williamson on the Music365 website, 19/1/2000; and Dave Simpson's, from the *Guardian*, 9/2000.

Epilogue

Quotes by Graham Blackburn, Donal Gallagher, John Altman, Clive Culbertson, Jon Gershen, Paul Charles, Mick Brown, Ed Fletcher, Peter Van Hooke, Jonn Savannah, Linda Gail Lewis and Harvey Goldsmith come from interviews conducted for this book by the author. The quote by Janet Malcolm comes from *The Silent Woman* (Picador, 1994); Danny Holloway's, from a feature in *NME*, 17/8/72; Paddy Moloney's, from *Q*; Phil May's, from an interview by Paul Du Noyer in the January 1997 edition of *Q*; John Leveresque's, from an article in *Wavelength* #2; Barry Egan's, from an article in the *Sunday Independent* 30/1/2000; and Mick Cox's, from an interview by Simon Gee in *Wavelength* #20/22.

Acknowledgements

My first and greatest thanks, for her unfailing endeavours as my research assistant, go to Miranda Ward, who on my behalf cold-called well over a hundred souls with Morrison associations and prevailed upon as many as she could to talk on the record. Though the quotient of the merely discourteous (and indeed the outright rude) was undoubtedly higher than for most subjects, with a soupçon of paranoia and fear dissuading a depressingly large number of grown men and women, it would be fair to say that without her perseverance the list of interviewees would be far less impressive than it is.

Those willing to put their names into the ring, and their thoughts on to tape, also have my heartfelt thanks and I wish I could thank you all personally for your input. So thanks again, one and all: Keith Altham; John Altman; Jim Armstrong; Stephen Barncard; Derek Bell; Eric Bell; Jay Berliner; Graham Blackburn; Mick Brown; Paul Charles; Jimmy Conlan; Kenny Craddock; Stuart Cromie; Clive Culbertson; Richard Davis; Martin Drover; Geoff Dunn; Ed Fletcher; Mo Foster; Linda Gail Lewis; Donal Gallagher; Jon Gershen; Harvey Goldsmith; Billy Harrison; Gil Irvine; George Jones; Paul Jones; Roy Jones; Roy Kane; Tom Kielbania; Pat Kyle; Jeff Labes; George Lee; Martin Lloyd; Peter Lloyd; Billy McAllen; Henry McCullough; Arty McGlynn; Gerry McKervey; Gary Malabar; Greil Marcus; Lewis Merenstein; Ronnie Millings; Chris O'Donnell; Jonn Savannah; Dauod Shaw; Alan Skidmore; Joe Smith; Warren Smith, Jnr; Mervyn Solomon; Phil Solomon; Geordie Sproule; Pete Van Hooke; John Wilson and Eric Wrixon.

I would also like to thank the following writers who have been there before me but have been wholly supportive of my endeavours: Colin Harper, Brian Hinton, Steve Turner, Mick Brown and especially that legend in his own lunchtime, the *San Francisco Chronicle*'s very own Joel Selvin, who shared relevant material from a biography of Bert Berns he had once planned to write, including his own unpublished interview with Janet Minto Morrison, which filled in so many gaps in that part of the story whilst Greg Sowders at Warners suggested names.

Members of the Van Morrison collecting fraternity proved unfailingly generous with their time and resources, and especial thanks go out to Art Siegel, Thomas Palmer, N.C. Junker Poulsen and Nick Carruthers. The editor of the Morrison fanzine, *Wavelength*, Simon Gee, and his ebullient wife, Viv, were constantly supportive, and generously laid open a vast archive to this not-so-humble writer.

My unbounded thanks as ever go to my editor Tony Lacey who kept the faith at every hurdle, and to Penny Phillips for her fastidious copy-editing.

Finally, I would like to thank my friends Manny and Philippa, Paul and Naomi, Scott and Susie, Joel Bernstein and Susie Decapite, for providing me with a welcome and a bed on my various travels to research and write this book. Thanks to y'all, and may the results warrant your generosities and faith,

Clinton Heylin, January 2001

The magnificent, if undercapitalized, Morrison fanzine, *Wavelength*, edited by the indefatigable Mr Gee, remains an essential forum for information and insight. It can be found at:

WAVELENGTH, PO BOX 80, WINSFORD, CHESHIRE, CW7 4ES, ENGLAND

website: www.wavelengthltd.co.uk

Index